MONSTERS

BARRY WINDSOR-SMITH

MONSTERS

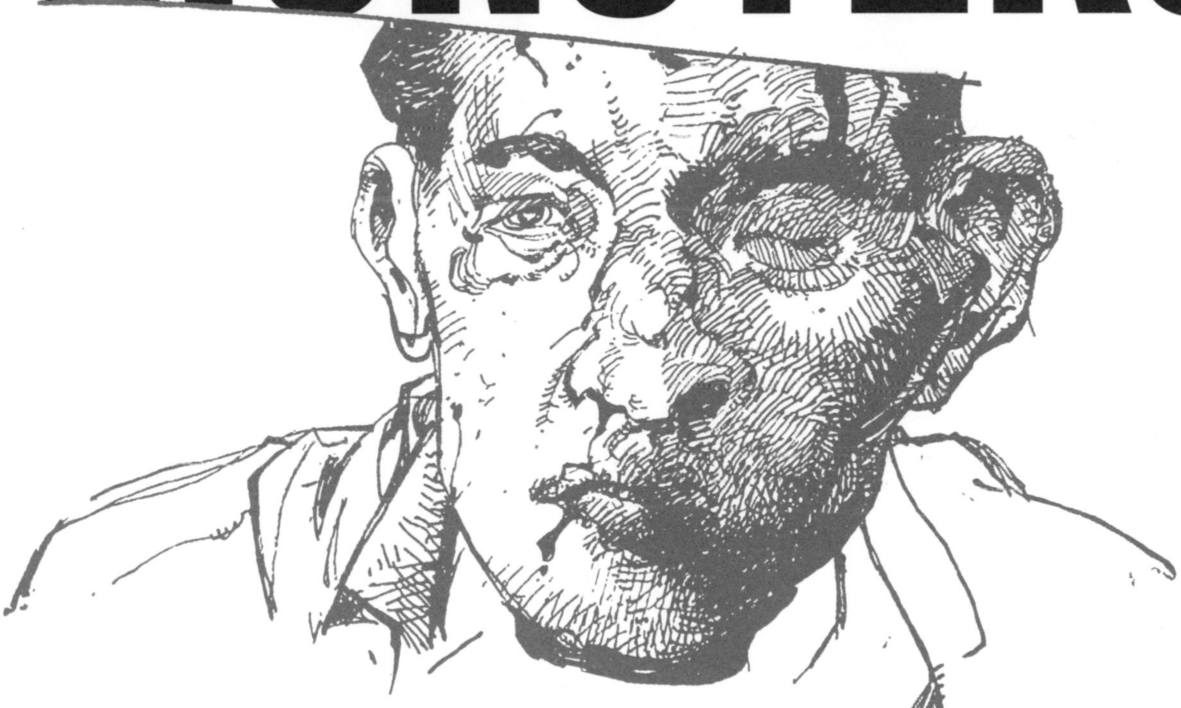

FANTAGRAPHICS

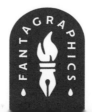

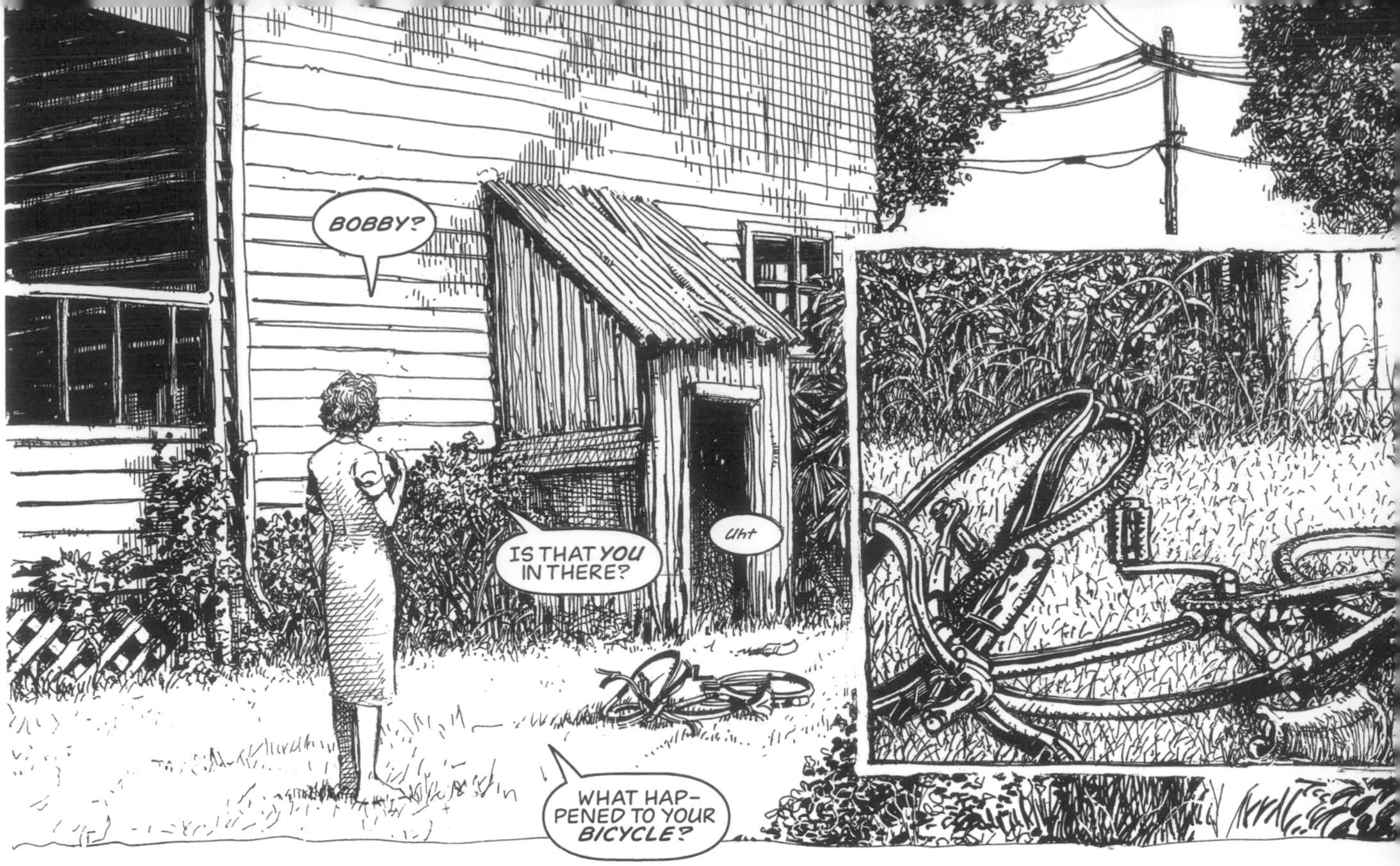
BOBBY?
IS THAT YOU IN THERE?
Uht
WHAT HAP-PENED TO YOUR BICYCLE?

1949 The Bailey home, Providence Township, Ohio Saturday, June 11

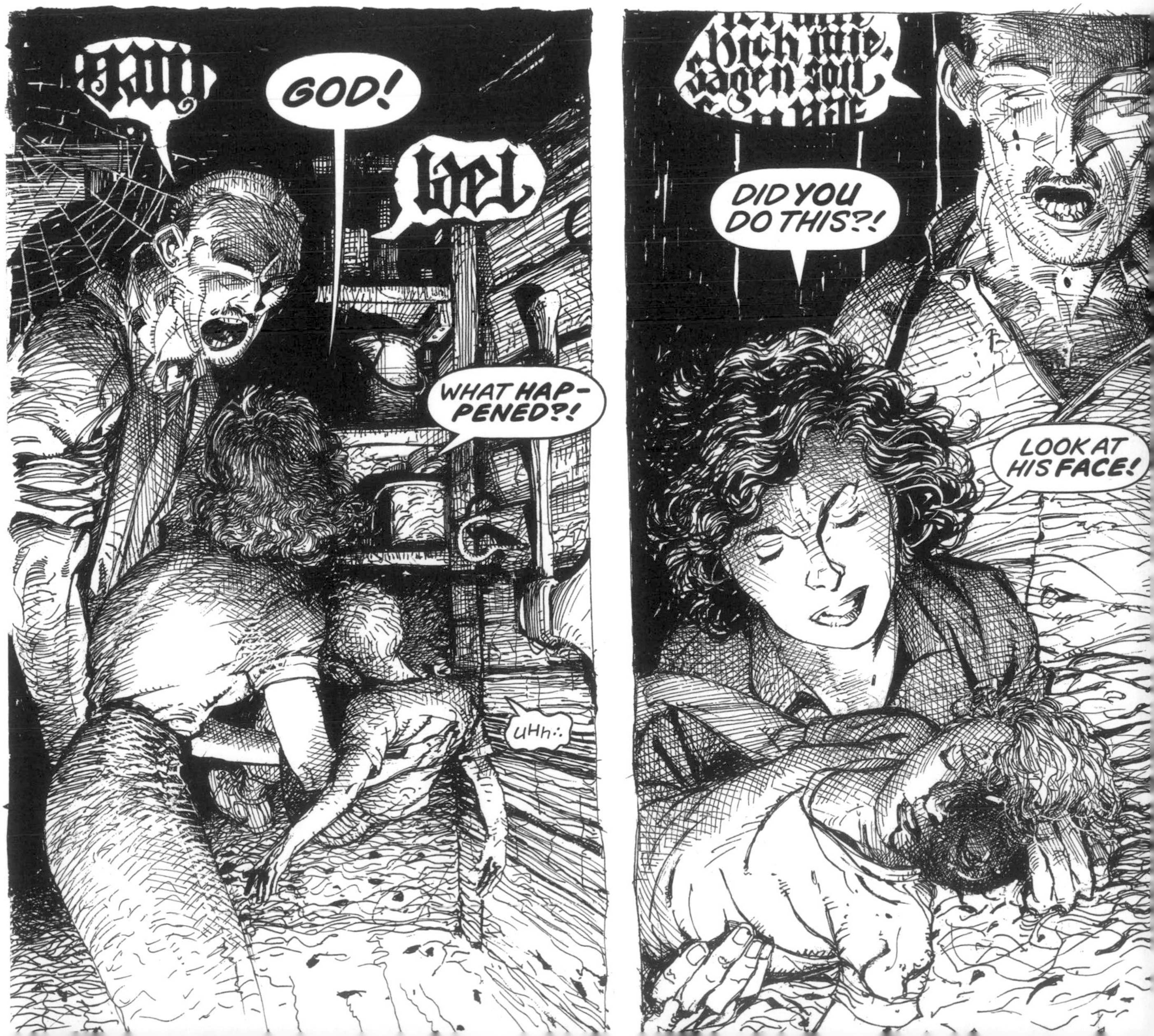
GOD!
WHAT HAP-PENED?!
UHh..
DID YOU DO THIS?!
LOOK AT HIS FACE!

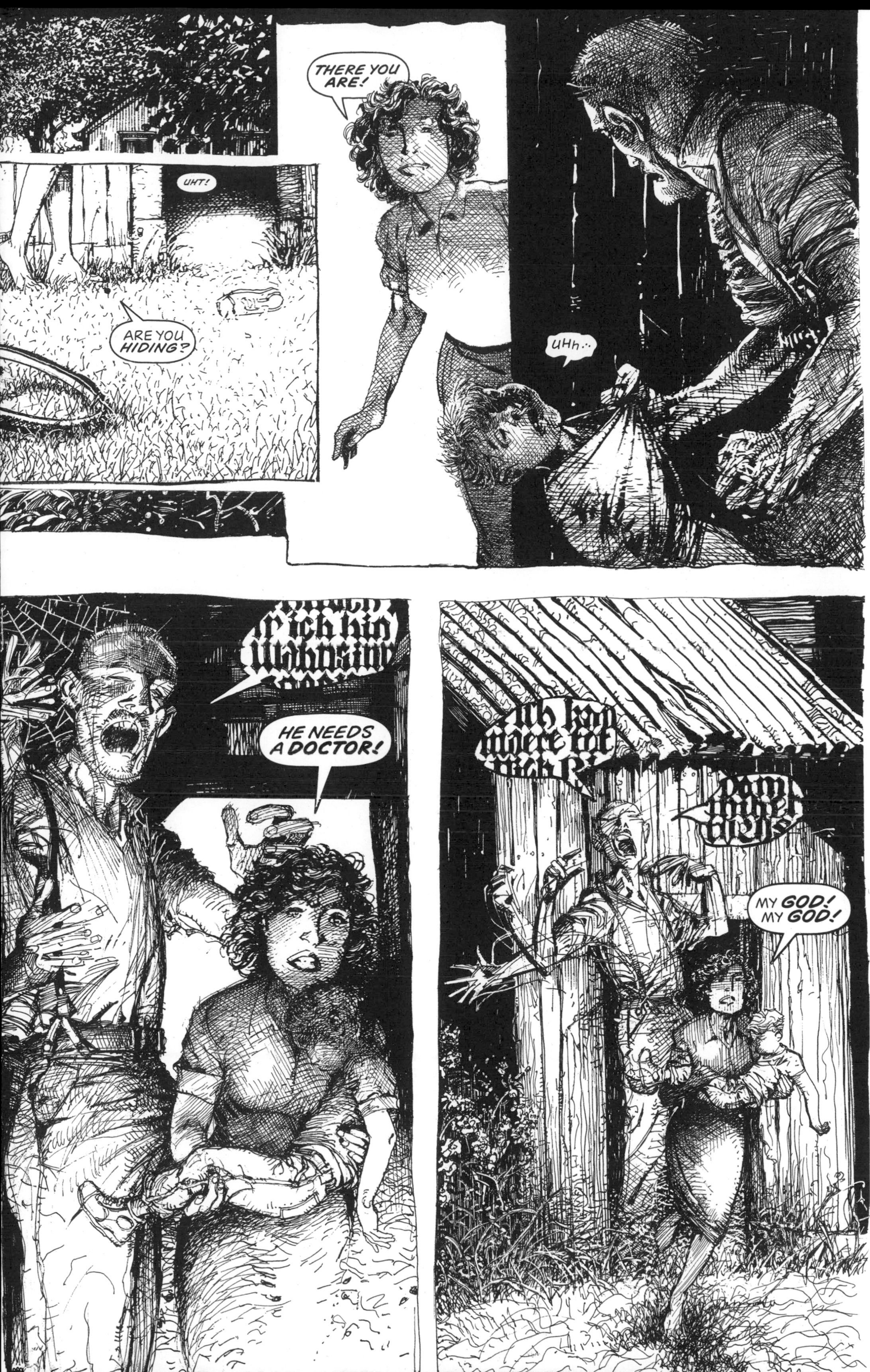
THERE YOU ARE!
UHT!
ARE YOU HIDING?
UHh...
HE NEEDS A DOCTOR!
MY GOD! MY GOD!

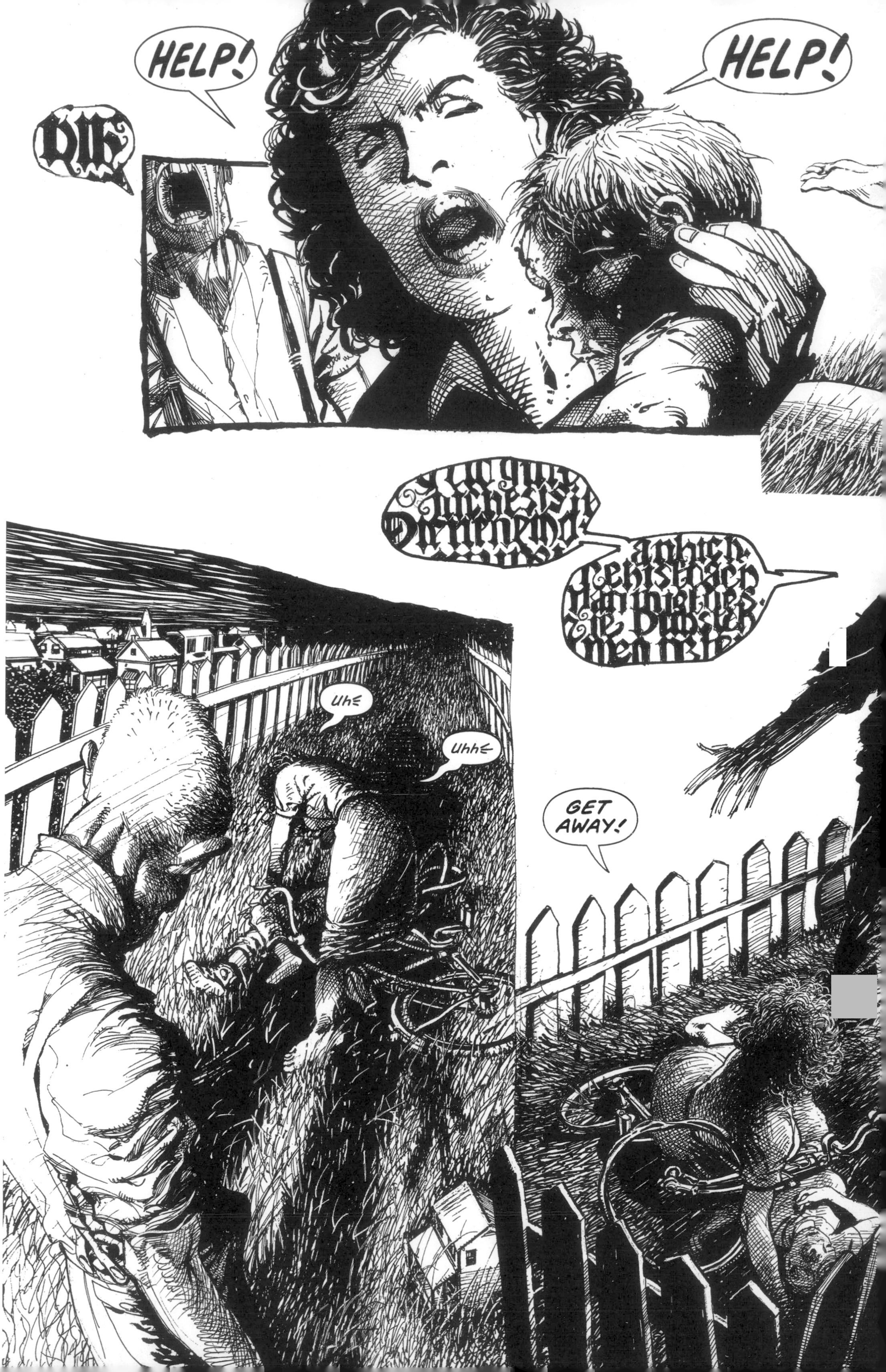
HELP!
HELP!
Uh
Uhh
GET AWAY!

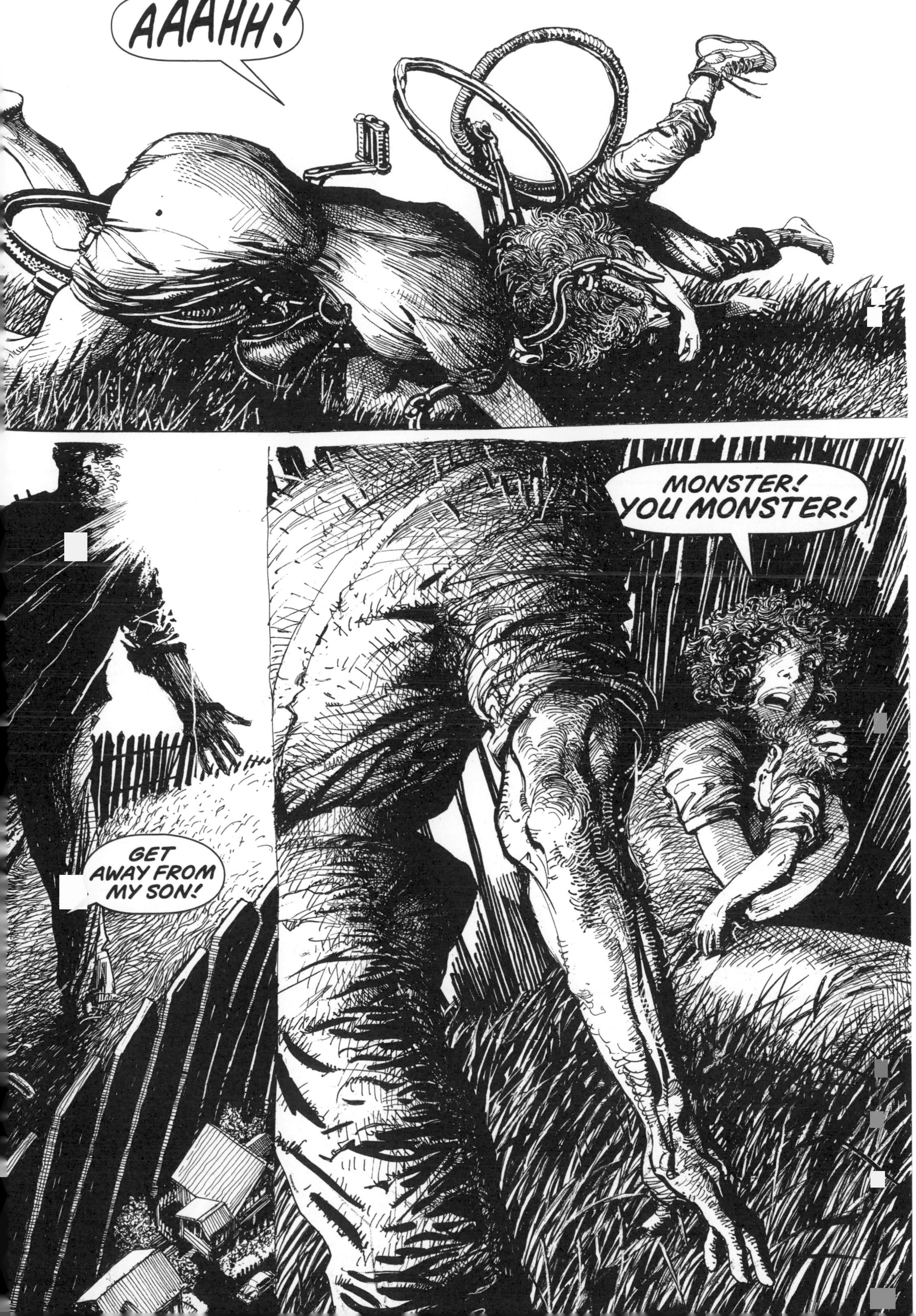
AAAHH!
MONSTER! YOU MONSTER!
GET AWAY FROM MY SON!

1964 Fourteen years later, Los Angeles, California Wednesday, April 22

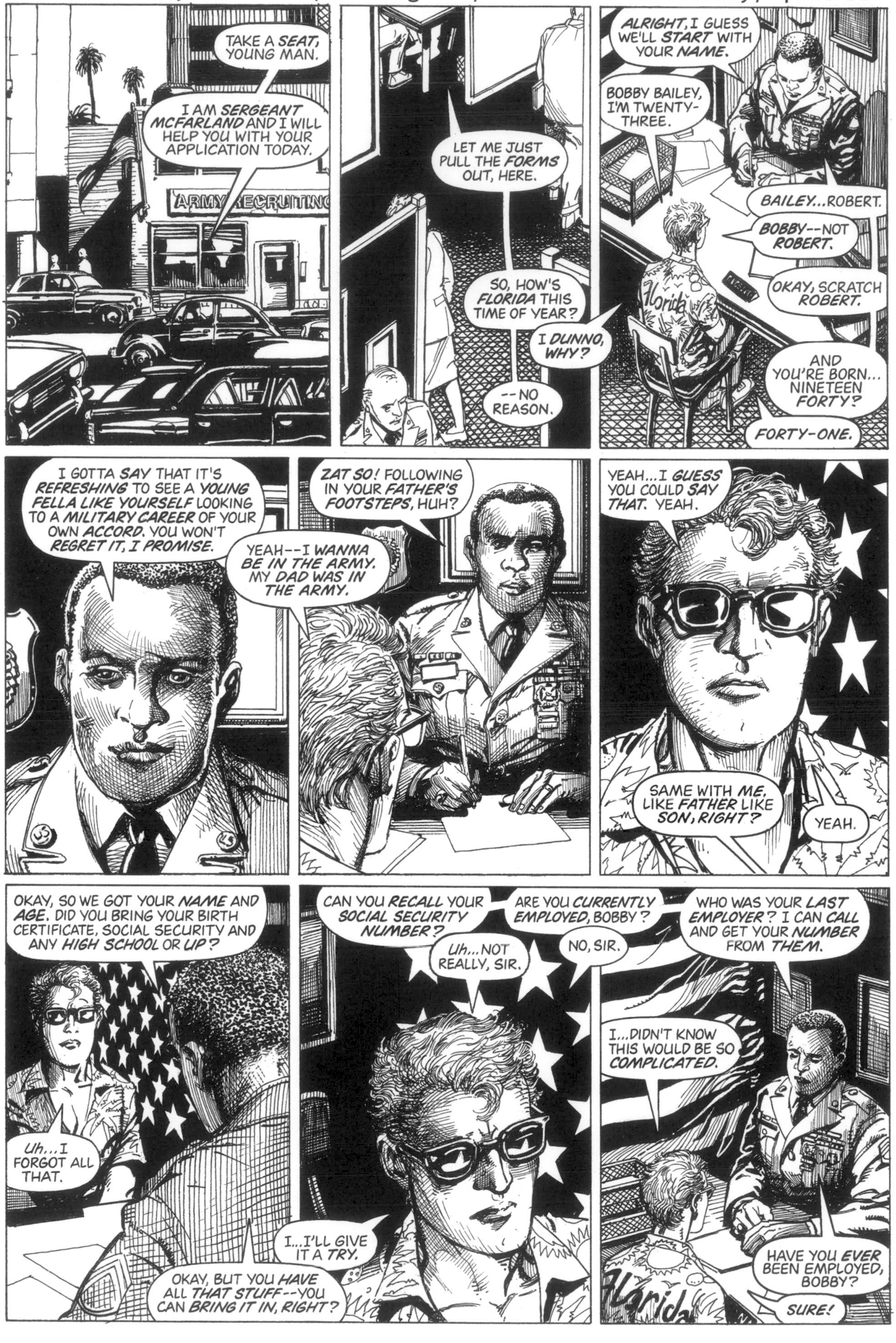
TAKE A SEAT, YOUNG MAN.
I AM SERGEANT MCFARLAND AND I WILL HELP YOU WITH YOUR APPLICATION TODAY.
ARMY RECRUITING
LET ME JUST PULL THE FORMS OUT, HERE.
SO, HOW'S FLORIDA THIS TIME OF YEAR?
I DUNNO, WHY?
--NO REASON.
ALRIGHT, I GUESS WE'LL START WITH YOUR NAME.
BOBBY BAILEY, I'M TWENTY-THREE.
BAILEY...ROBERT.
BOBBY--NOT ROBERT.
OKAY, SCRATCH ROBERT.
AND YOU'RE BORN... NINETEEN FORTY?
FORTY-ONE.
I GOTTA SAY THAT IT'S REFRESHING TO SEE A YOUNG FELLA LIKE YOURSELF LOOKING TO A MILITARY CAREER OF YOUR OWN ACCORD. YOU WON'T REGRET IT, I PROMISE.
YEAH--I WANNA BE IN THE ARMY. MY DAD WAS IN THE ARMY.
ZAT SO! FOLLOWING IN YOUR FATHER'S FOOTSTEPS, HUH?
YEAH...I GUESS YOU COULD SAY THAT. YEAH.
SAME WITH ME. LIKE FATHER LIKE SON, RIGHT?
YEAH.
OKAY, SO WE GOT YOUR NAME AND AGE. DID YOU BRING YOUR BIRTH CERTIFICATE, SOCIAL SECURITY AND ANY HIGH SCHOOL OR UP?
Uh...I FORGOT ALL THAT.
OKAY, BUT YOU HAVE ALL THAT STUFF--YOU CAN BRING IT IN, RIGHT?
I...I'LL GIVE IT A TRY.
CAN YOU RECALL YOUR SOCIAL SECURITY NUMBER?
Uh...NOT REALLY, SIR.
ARE YOU CURRENTLY EMPLOYED, BOBBY?
NO, SIR.
WHO WAS YOUR LAST EMPLOYER? I CAN CALL AND GET YOUR NUMBER FROM THEM.
I...DIDN'T KNOW THIS WOULD BE SO COMPLICATED.
HAVE YOU EVER BEEN EMPLOYED, BOBBY?
SURE!

WHERE WAS *THAT*, THEN?

Uh...

Aah...

FUH-FUH FLA-FLA *FLORIDA?*

WHAT WAS THE *NATURE* OF THE *WORK?*

Uhm...Uh, I CAN'T *THINK*--I CAN'T *REMEMBER.*

LONG TIME AGO, WAS IT?

YEAH, WAY, WAY *BACK!*

BOBBY, GIMME A *BREAK,* YOU'RE ONLY *TWENTY-THREE.*

I JUST WANT TO JOIN THE *ARMY,* SIR, ISN'T THAT *ENOUGH?*

MAYBE... MAYBE *NOT.*

BUT YOU'RE GONNA HAFTA START *TALKING STRAIGHT* WITH ME, SON--YOU *READY* TO *DO THAT?*

I...I'M NOT SURE.

WHERE DO YOU *LIVE* CURRENTLY?

I... UH...

THE WORST THING YOU CAN DO IS *LIE...* OR SAY YOU *FORGOT.*

I...I

YOU'RE *HOMELESS,* AREN'T YOU?

YOU CAN *LEVEL* WITH ME, BOBBY

YES.

YES, *WHAT?*

I HAVE NO *HOME,* SIR.

NOW WE'RE *GETTING SOMEWHERE.* YOU'RE BEGINNING TO *TRUST* ME, AREN'TCHA?

Uh huh.

YOUR *FATHER*--IS HE STILL IN THE *SERVICE?* WHAT *RANK?*

MY F-FF--FATHER IS *DEAD,* SIR.

TOOK IT IN THE *BIG ONE?*

N...NO, HE'S JUST ...*DEAD,* SIR.

SORRY.

YOUR *MOTHER?* OTHER *RELATIVES?*

Roth C.
PROMETHEUS Pjt
(Classified EO)
able subjects

TRE-7708
Hang Up,
Wait For
Call Back.

DO NOT
REFILE

White Male
under

MY M-MOTHER IS *DEAD,* TOO.

WIFE? KIDS?

NO.

THEN I GOT JUST *ONE MORE* QUESTION...

YES, SIR.

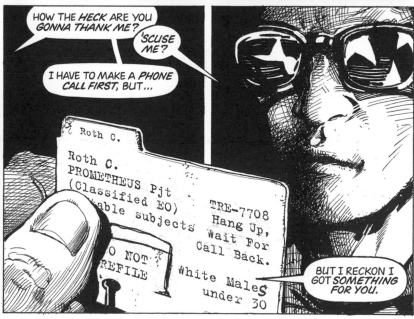

HOW THE *HECK* ARE YOU GONNA *THANK* ME?

'SCUSE ME?

I HAVE TO MAKE A *PHONE CALL* FIRST, BUT...

Roth C.

Roth C.
PROMETHEUS Pjt
(Classified EO)
able subjects

TRE-7708
Hang Up,
Wait For
Call Back.

O NOT
REFILE

White Males
under 30

BUT I RECKON I GOT *SOMETHING* FOR YOU.

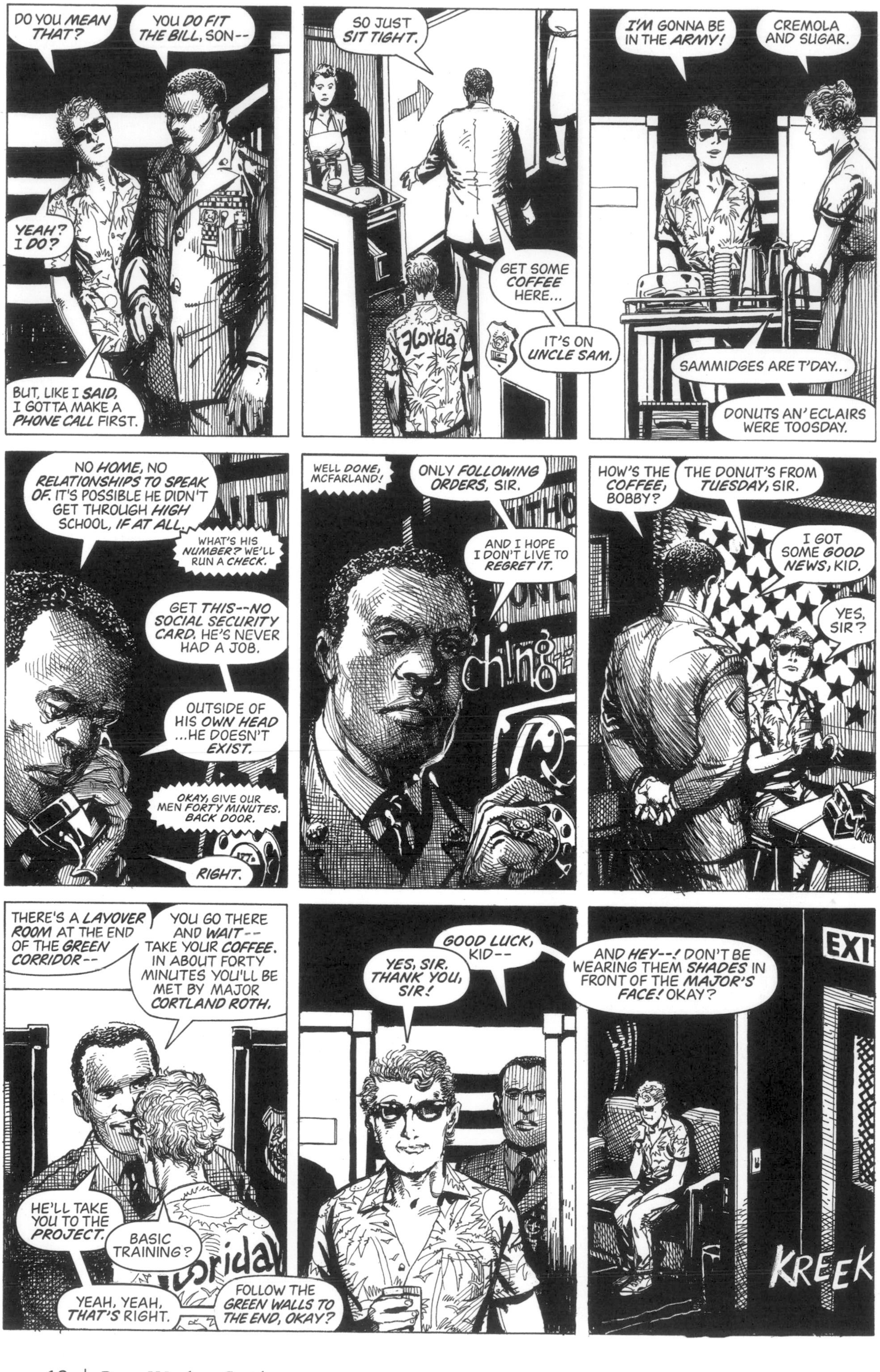

DO YOU MEAN THAT?
YOU DO FIT THE BILL, SON--
YEAH? I DO?
BUT, LIKE I SAID, I GOTTA MAKE A PHONE CALL FIRST.
SO JUST SIT TIGHT.
GET SOME COFFEE HERE...
IT'S ON UNCLE SAM.
FLORIDA
I'M GONNA BE IN THE ARMY!
CREMOLA AND SUGAR.
SAMMIDGES ARE T'DAY...
DONUTS AN' ECLAIRS WERE TOOSDAY.
NO HOME, NO RELATIONSHIPS TO SPEAK OF. IT'S POSSIBLE HE DIDN'T GET THROUGH HIGH SCHOOL, IF AT ALL...
WHAT'S HIS NUMBER? WE'LL RUN A CHECK.
GET THIS--NO SOCIAL SECURITY CARD. HE'S NEVER HAD A JOB.
OUTSIDE OF HIS OWN HEAD ...HE DOESN'T EXIST.
OKAY, GIVE OUR MEN FORTY MINUTES. BACK DOOR.
RIGHT.
WELL DONE, MCFARLAND!
ONLY FOLLOWING ORDERS, SIR.
AND I HOPE I DON'T LIVE TO REGRET IT.
ching-
HOW'S THE COFFEE, BOBBY?
THE DONUT'S FROM TUESDAY, SIR.
I GOT SOME GOOD NEWS, KID.
YES, SIR?
THERE'S A LAYOVER ROOM AT THE END OF THE GREEN CORRIDOR--
YOU GO THERE AND WAIT-- TAKE YOUR COFFEE. IN ABOUT FORTY MINUTES YOU'LL BE MET BY MAJOR CORTLAND ROTH.
HE'LL TAKE YOU TO THE PROJECT.
BASIC TRAINING?
YEAH, YEAH, THAT'S RIGHT.
FOLLOW THE GREEN WALLS TO THE END, OKAY?
GOOD LUCK, KID--
YES, SIR. THANK YOU, SIR!
AND HEY--! DON'T BE WEARING THEM SHADES IN FRONT OF THE MAJOR'S FACE! OKAY?
EXIT
KREEK

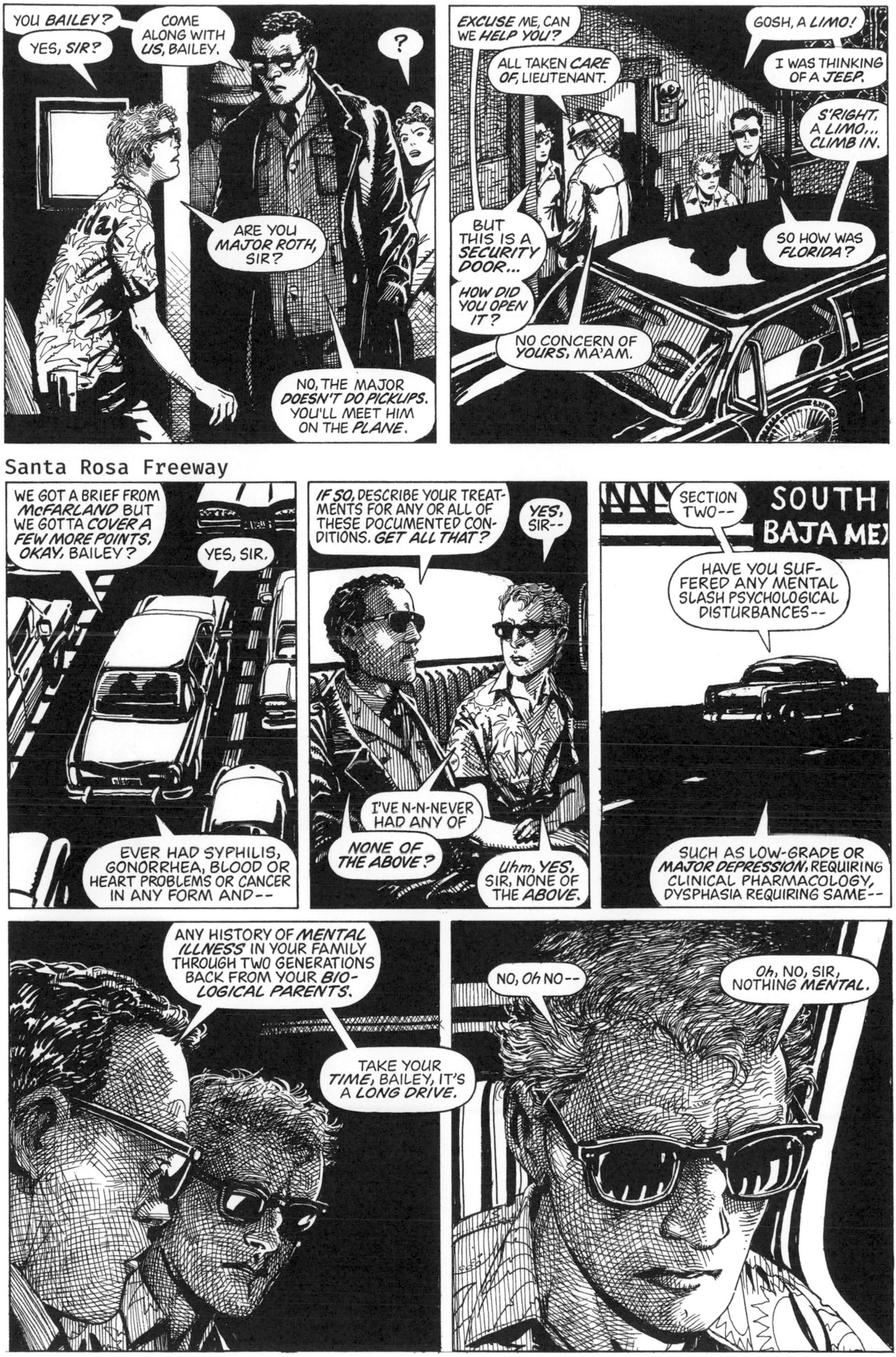
YOU BAILEY?
YES, SIR?
COME ALONG WITH US, BAILEY.
?
ARE YOU MAJOR ROTH, SIR?
NO, THE MAJOR DOESN'T DO PICKUPS. YOU'LL MEET HIM ON THE PLANE.
EXCUSE ME, CAN WE HELP YOU?
ALL TAKEN CARE OF, LIEUTENANT.
BUT THIS IS A SECURITY DOOR...
HOW DID YOU OPEN IT?
NO CONCERN OF YOURS, MA'AM.
GOSH, A LIMO!
I WAS THINKING OF A JEEP.
S'RIGHT. A LIMO... CLIMB IN.
SO HOW WAS FLORIDA?
Santa Rosa Freeway
WE GOT A BRIEF FROM McFARLAND BUT WE GOTTA COVER A FEW MORE POINTS. OKAY, BAILEY?
YES, SIR.
EVER HAD SYPHILIS, GONORRHEA, BLOOD OR HEART PROBLEMS OR CANCER IN ANY FORM AND--
IF SO, DESCRIBE YOUR TREATMENTS FOR ANY OR ALL OF THESE DOCUMENTED CONDITIONS. GET ALL THAT?
YES, SIR--
I'VE N-N-NEVER HAD ANY OF
NONE OF THE ABOVE?
Uhm, YES, SIR, NONE OF THE ABOVE.
SOUTH
BAJA MEX
SECTION TWO--
HAVE YOU SUFFERED ANY MENTAL SLASH PSYCHOLOGICAL DISTURBANCES--
SUCH AS LOW-GRADE OR MAJOR DEPRESSION, REQUIRING CLINICAL PHARMACOLOGY, DYSPHASIA REQUIRING SAME--
ANY HISTORY OF MENTAL ILLNESS IN YOUR FAMILY THROUGH TWO GENERATIONS BACK FROM YOUR BIOLOGICAL PARENTS.
TAKE YOUR TIME, BAILEY, IT'S A LONG DRIVE.
NO, Oh NO--
Oh, NO, SIR, NOTHING MENTAL.

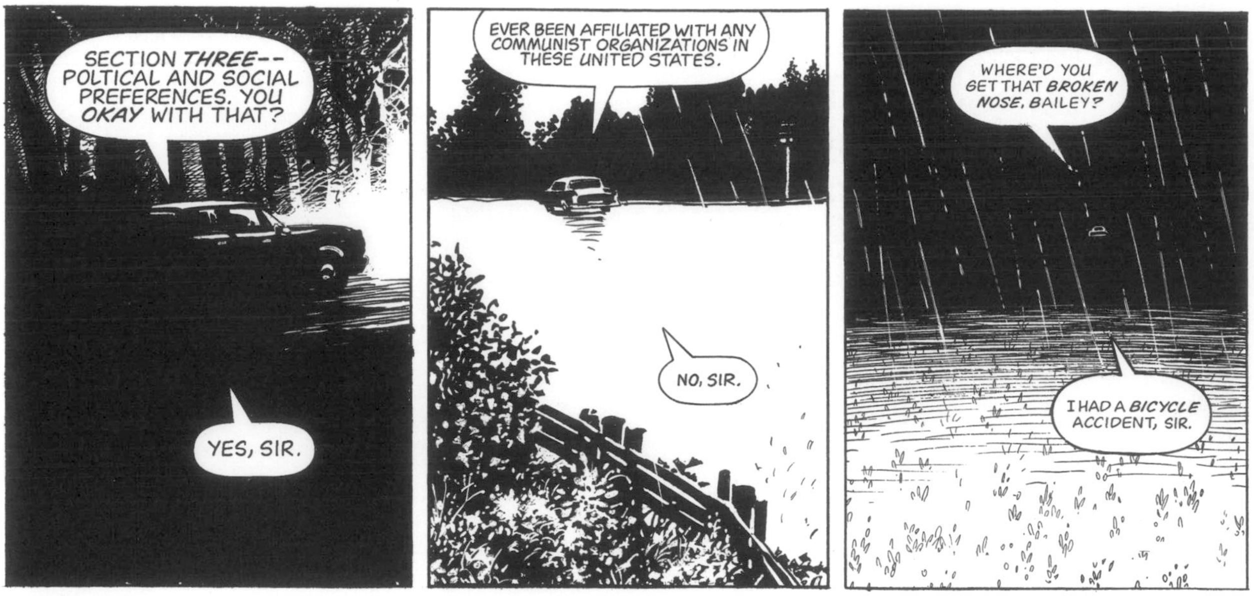
SECTION THREE-- POLTICAL AND SOCIAL PREFERENCES. YOU OKAY WITH THAT?
YES, SIR.
EVER BEEN AFFILIATED WITH ANY COMMUNIST ORGANIZATIONS IN THESE UNITED STATES.
NO, SIR.
WHERE'D YOU GET THAT BROKEN NOSE, BAILEY?
I HAD A BICYCLE ACCIDENT, SIR.

Corona Flats Air Force Base

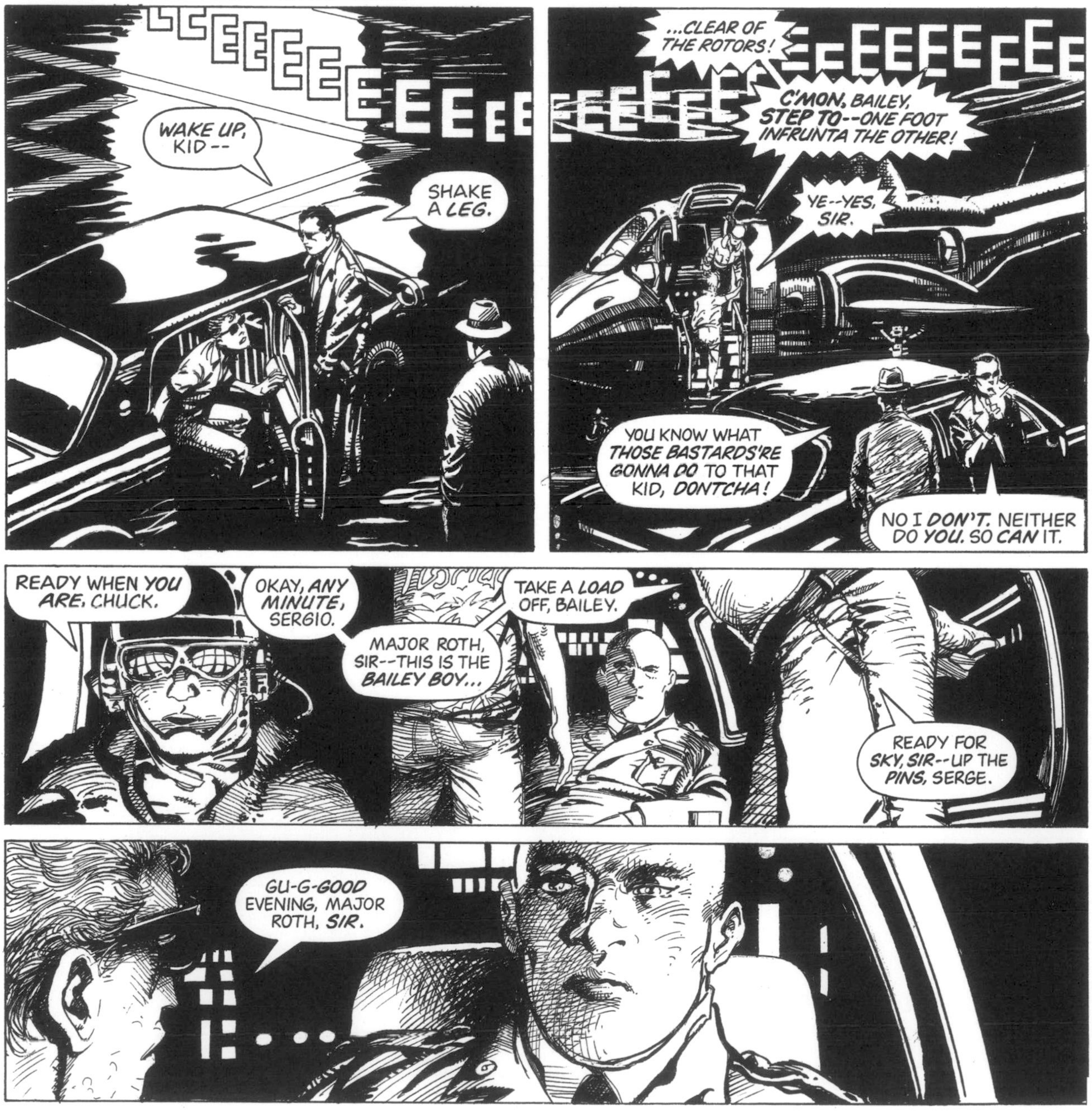
WAKE UP, KID--
SHAKE A LEG.
...CLEAR OF THE ROTORS!
C'MON, BAILEY, STEP TO--ONE FOOT INFRUNTA THE OTHER!
YE--YES, SIR.
YOU KNOW WHAT THOSE BASTARDS'RE GONNA DO TO THAT KID, DONTCHA!
NO I DON'T. NEITHER DO YOU. SO CAN IT.
READY WHEN YOU ARE, CHUCK.
OKAY, ANY MINUTE, SERGIO.
MAJOR ROTH, SIR--THIS IS THE BAILEY BOY...
TAKE A LOAD OFF, BAILEY.
READY FOR SKY, SIR--UP THE PINS, SERGE.
GU-G-GOOD EVENING, MAJOR ROTH, SIR.

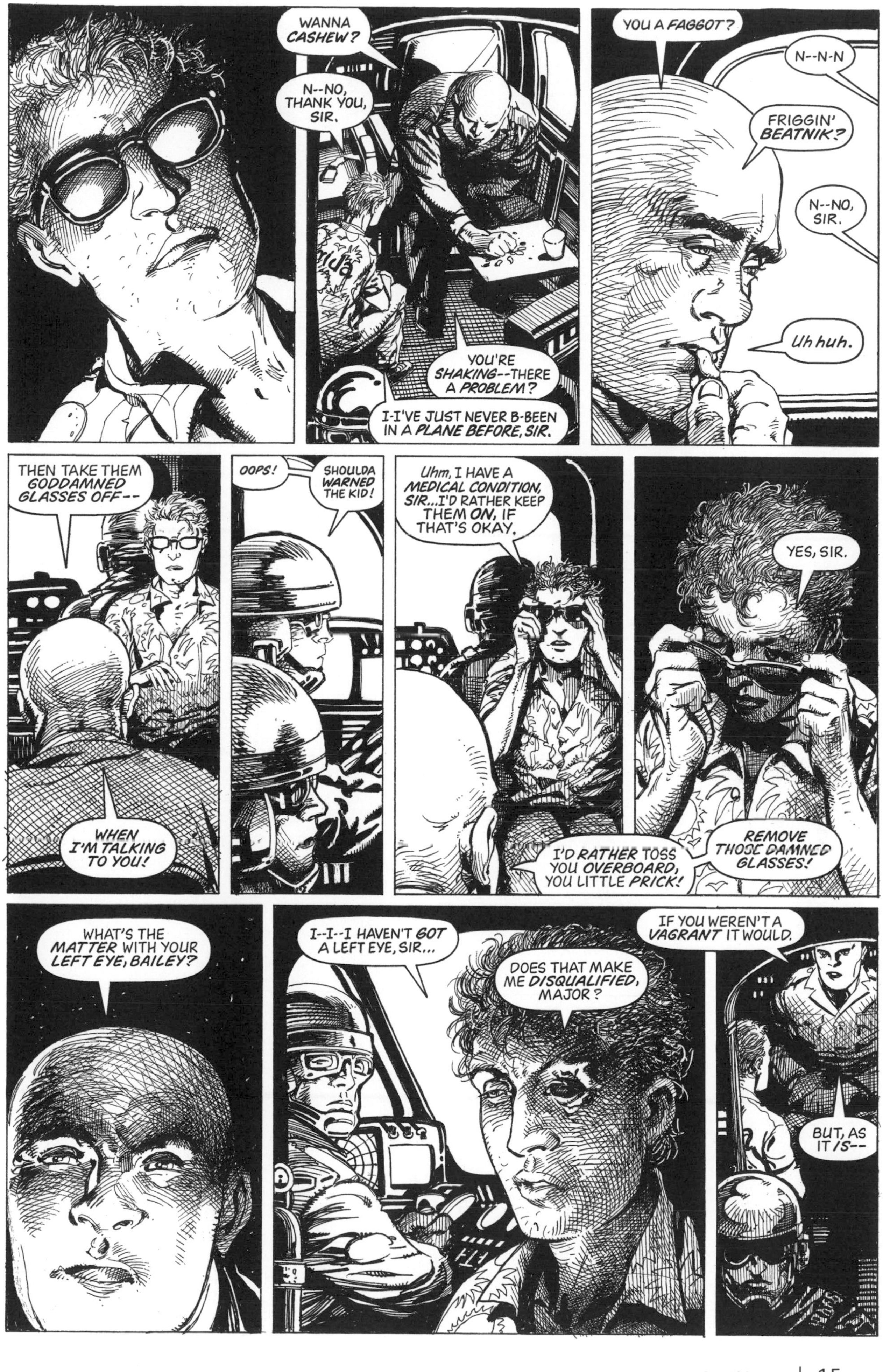
WANNA CASHEW?
N--NO, THANK YOU, SIR.
YOU'RE SHAKING--THERE A PROBLEM?
I-I'VE JUST NEVER B-BEEN IN A PLANE BEFORE, SIR.
YOU A FAGGOT?
N--N-N
FRIGGIN' BEATNIK?
N--NO, SIR.
Uh huh.
THEN TAKE THEM GODDAMNED GLASSES OFF--
WHEN I'M TALKING TO YOU!
OOPS!
SHOULDA WARNED THE KID!
Uhm, I HAVE A MEDICAL CONDITION, SIR...I'D RATHER KEEP THEM ON, IF THAT'S OKAY.
I'D RATHER TOSS YOU OVERBOARD, YOU LITTLE PRICK!
YES, SIR.
REMOVE THOSE DAMNED GLASSES!
WHAT'S THE MATTER WITH YOUR LEFT EYE, BAILEY?
I--I--I HAVEN'T GOT A LEFT EYE, SIR...
DOES THAT MAKE ME DISQUALIFIED, MAJOR?
IF YOU WEREN'T A VAGRANT IT WOULD.
BUT, AS IT IS--

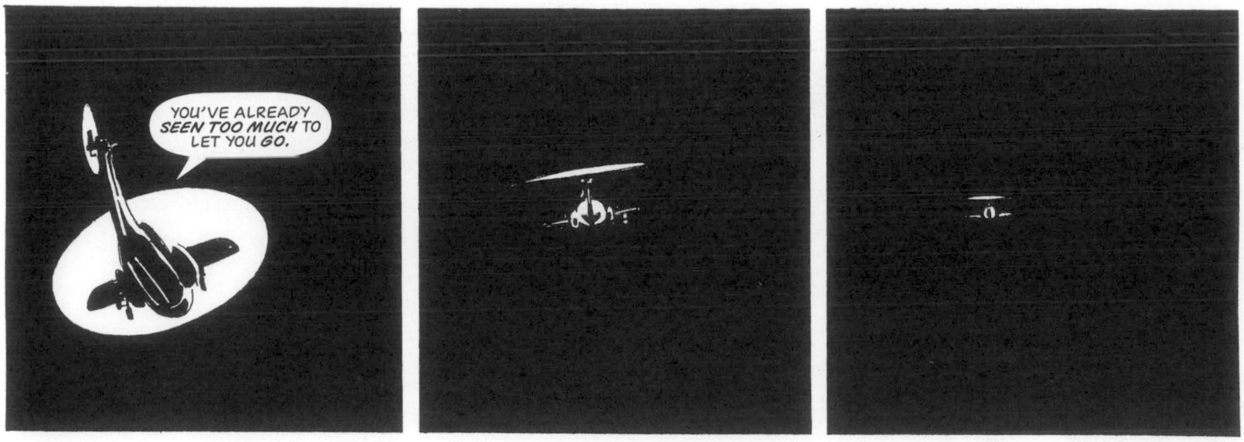
YOU'VE ALREADY SEEN TOO MUCH TO LET YOU GO.

The McFarland home, Los Angeles, CA Thursday, April 23

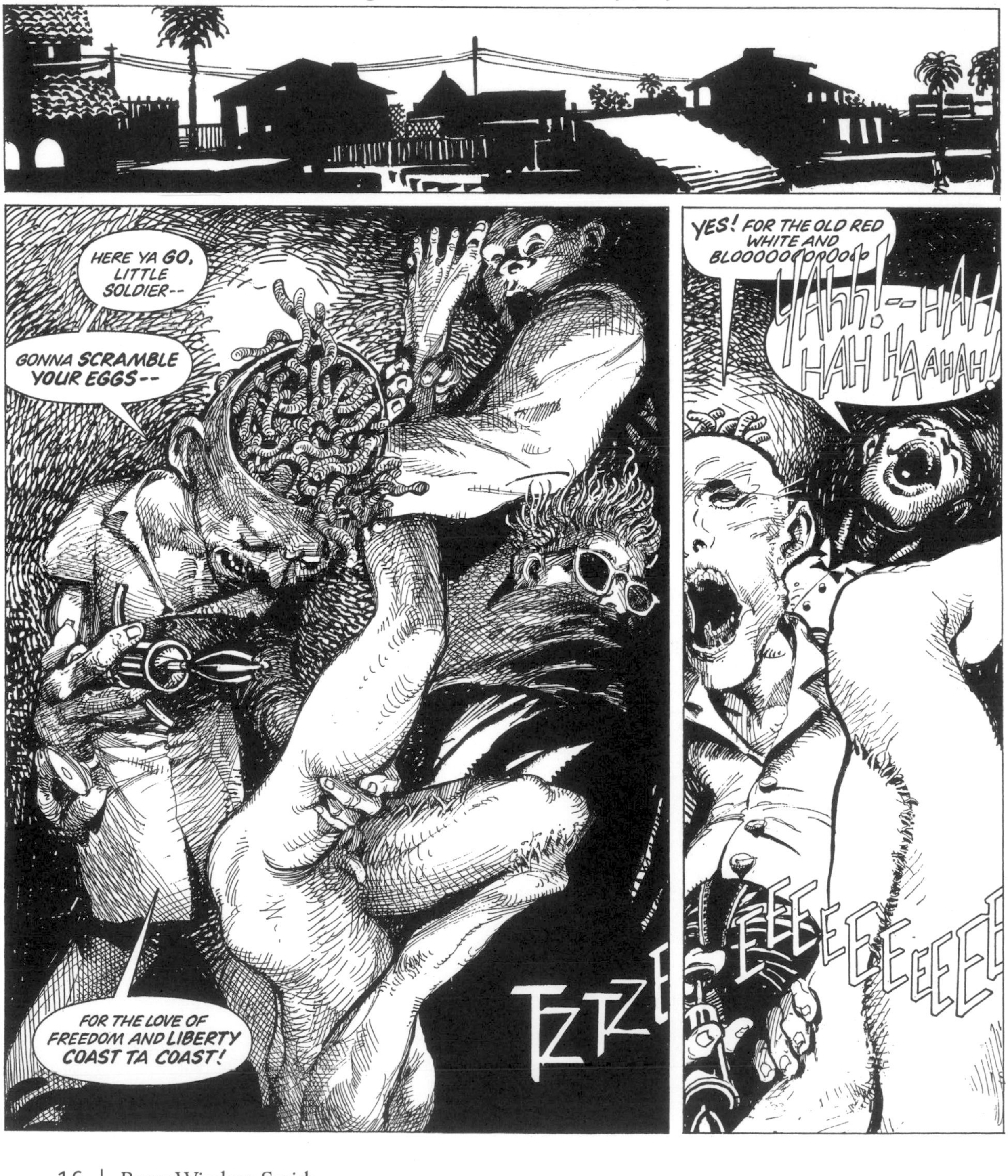
HERE YA GO, LITTLE SOLDIER--
GONNA SCRAMBLE YOUR EGGS--
FOR THE LOVE OF FREEDOM AND LIBERTY COAST TA COAST!
TZTZEEEEEEEEE
YES! FOR THE OLD RED WHITE AND BLOOOOOO
YAHH!--HAH! HAH HAAHAH!

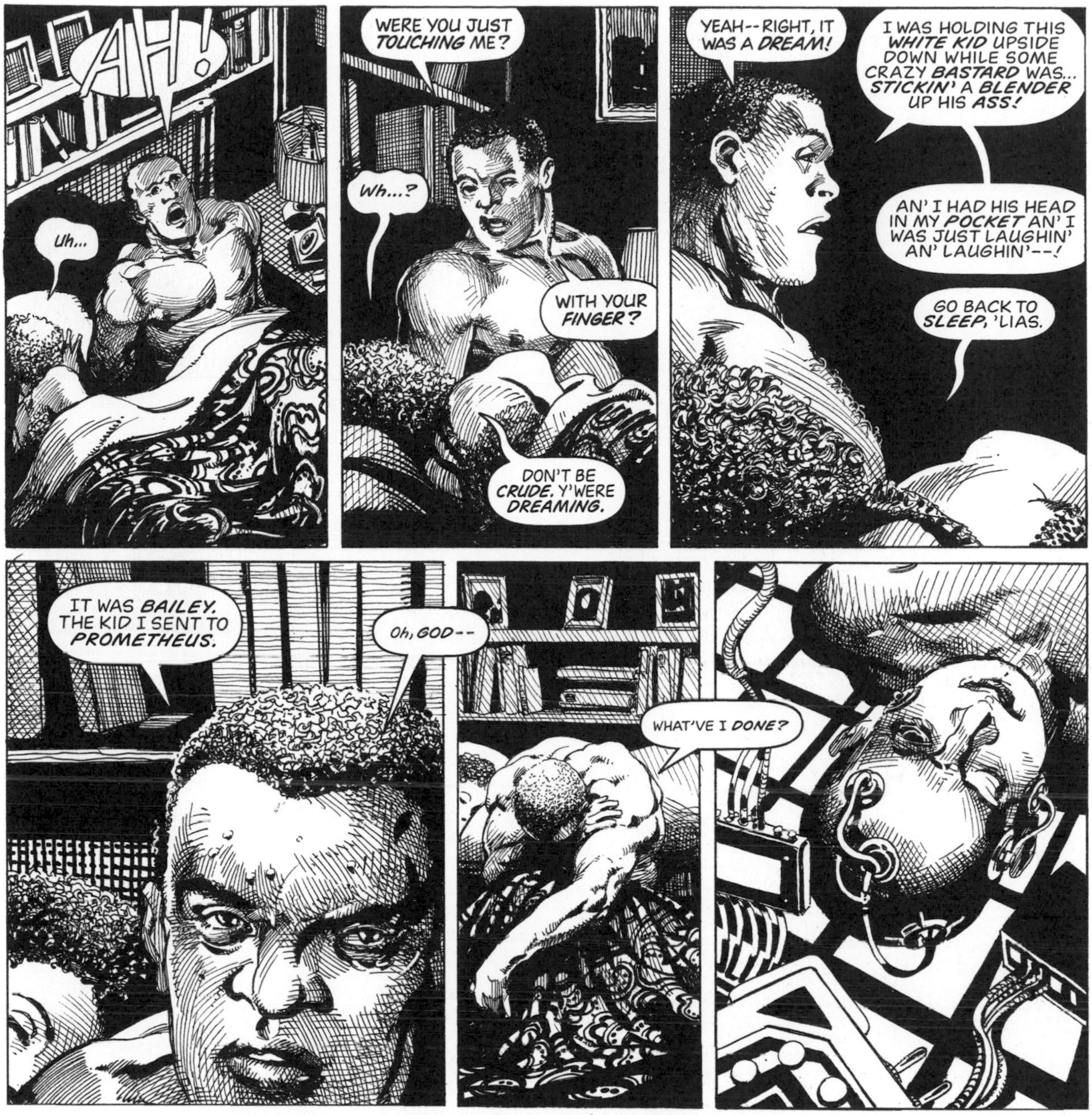

AH!
Uh...
WERE YOU JUST TOUCHING ME?
Wh...?
WITH YOUR FINGER?
DON'T BE CRUDE. Y'WERE DREAMING.
YEAH--RIGHT, IT WAS A DREAM!
I WAS HOLDING THIS WHITE KID UPSIDE DOWN WHILE SOME CRAZY BASTARD WAS... STICKIN' A BLENDER UP HIS ASS!
AN' I HAD HIS HEAD IN MY POCKET AN' I WAS JUST LAUGHIN' AN' LAUGHIN'--!
GO BACK TO SLEEP, 'LIAS.
IT WAS BAILEY. THE KID I SENT TO PROMETHEUS.
Oh, GOD--
WHAT'VE I DONE?

Fort Sherman (Prometheus HQ), Baja, CA Sunday, April 26

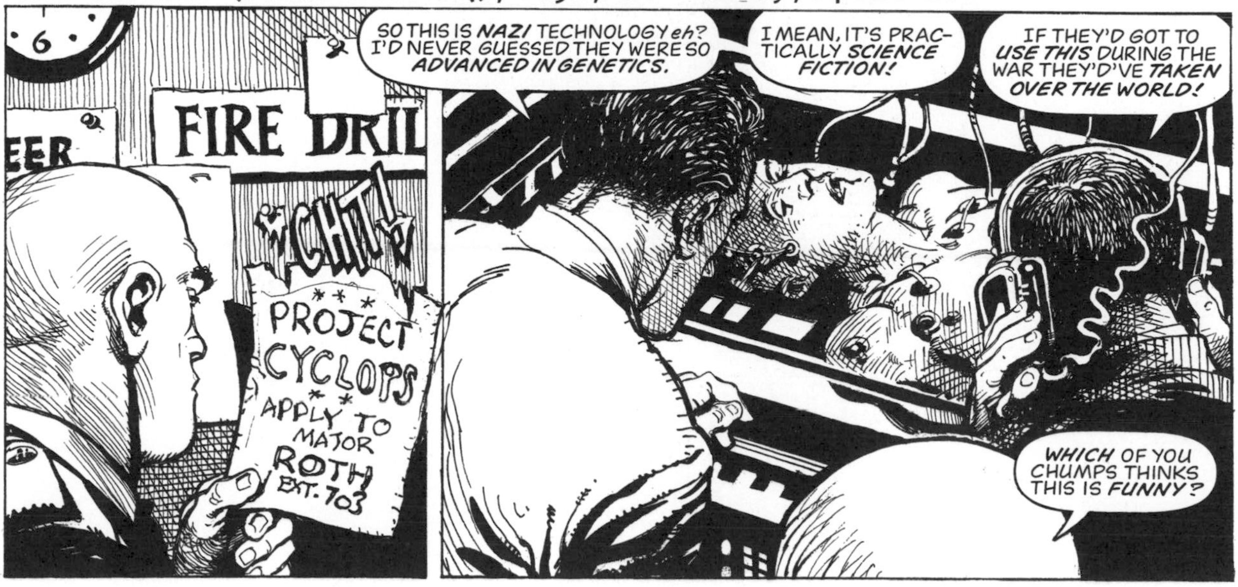

6
FIRE DRIL
EER
CHT!
PROJECT CYCLOPS
APPLY TO MAJOR ROTH EXT. 703
SO THIS IS NAZI TECHNOLOGY eh? I'D NEVER GUESSED THEY WERE SO ADVANCED IN GENETICS.
I MEAN, IT'S PRACTICALLY SCIENCE FICTION!
IF THEY'D GOT TO USE THIS DURING THE WAR THEY'D'VE TAKEN OVER THE WORLD!
WHICH OF YOU CHUMPS THINKS THIS IS FUNNY?

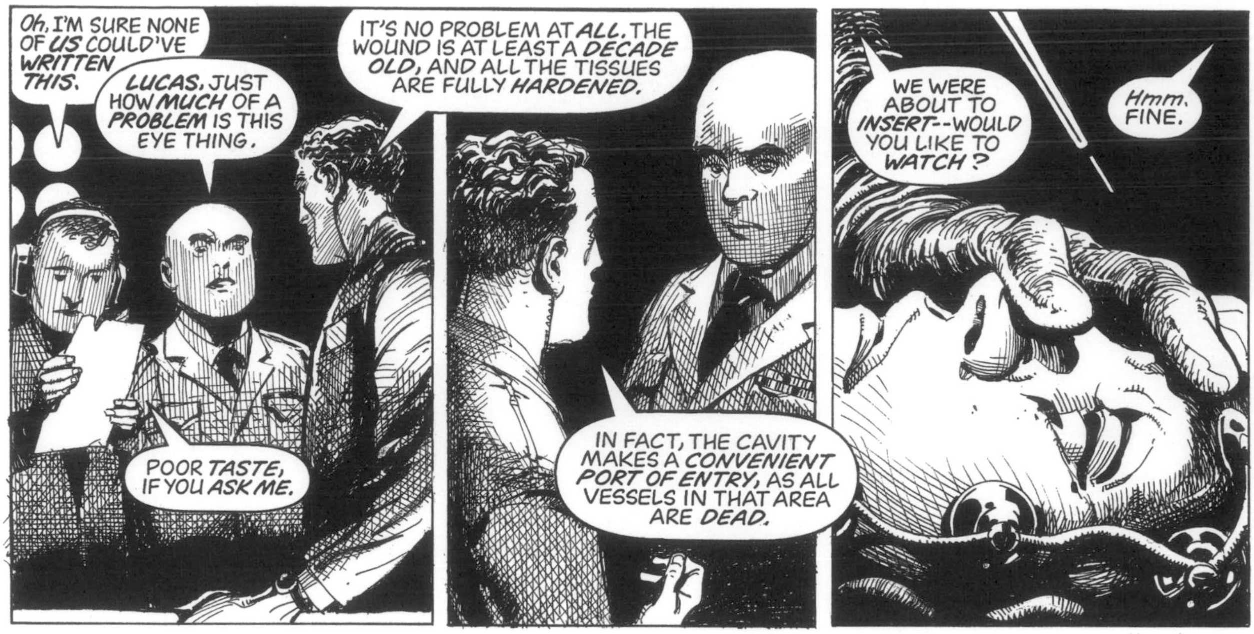
Oh, I'M SURE NONE OF US COULD'VE WRITTEN THIS.
LUCAS, JUST HOW MUCH OF A PROBLEM IS THIS EYE THING.
POOR TASTE, IF YOU ASK ME.
IT'S NO PROBLEM AT ALL. THE WOUND IS AT LEAST A DECADE OLD, AND ALL THE TISSUES ARE FULLY HARDENED.
IN FACT, THE CAVITY MAKES A CONVENIENT PORT OF ENTRY, AS ALL VESSELS IN THAT AREA ARE DEAD.
WE WERE ABOUT TO INSERT--WOULD YOU LIKE TO WATCH?
Hmm. FINE.

Bradley Army Medical Center, Toro, CA Saturday, May 2

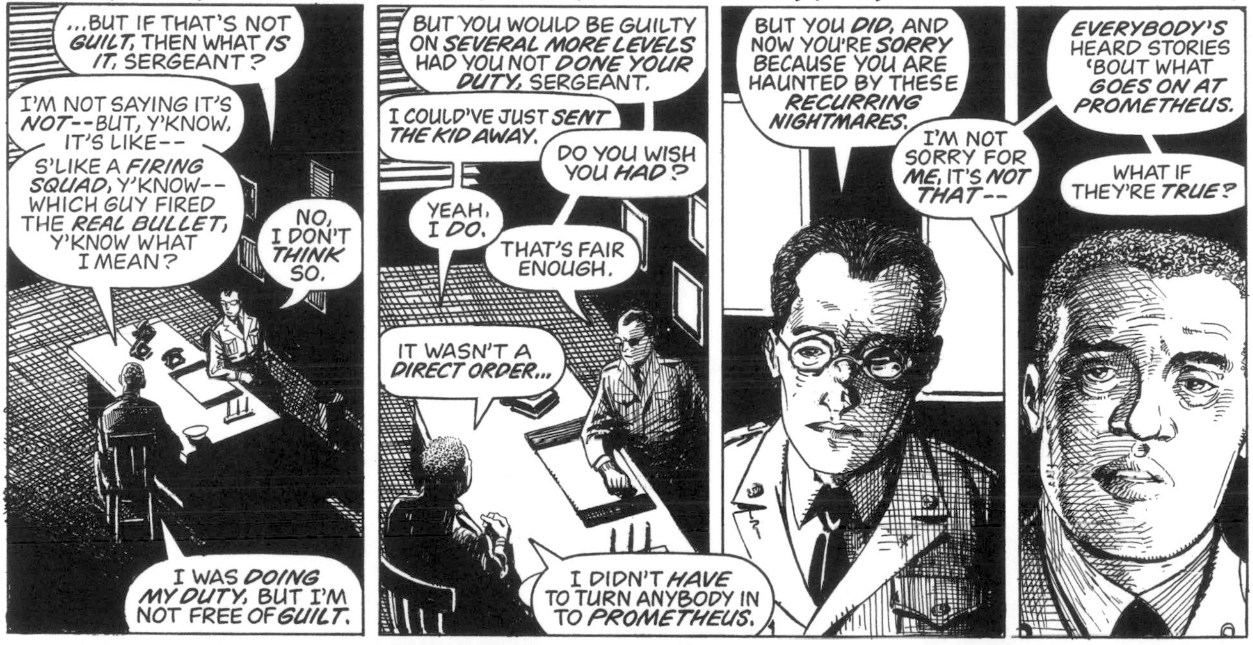
...BUT IF THAT'S NOT GUILT, THEN WHAT IS IT, SERGEANT?
I'M NOT SAYING IT'S NOT--BUT, Y'KNOW, IT'S LIKE--
S'LIKE A FIRING SQUAD, Y'KNOW--WHICH GUY FIRED THE REAL BULLET, Y'KNOW WHAT I MEAN?
NO, I DON'T THINK SO.
I WAS DOING MY DUTY, BUT I'M NOT FREE OF GUILT.
BUT YOU WOULD BE GUILTY ON SEVERAL MORE LEVELS HAD YOU NOT DONE YOUR DUTY, SERGEANT.
I COULD'VE JUST SENT THE KID AWAY.
DO YOU WISH YOU HAD?
YEAH, I DO.
THAT'S FAIR ENOUGH.
IT WASN'T A DIRECT ORDER...
I DIDN'T HAVE TO TURN ANYBODY IN TO PROMETHEUS.
BUT YOU DID, AND NOW YOU'RE SORRY BECAUSE YOU ARE HAUNTED BY THESE RECURRING NIGHTMARES.
I'M NOT SORRY FOR ME, IT'S NOT THAT--
EVERYBODY'S HEARD STORIES 'BOUT WHAT GOES ON AT PROMETHEUS.
WHAT IF THEY'RE TRUE?

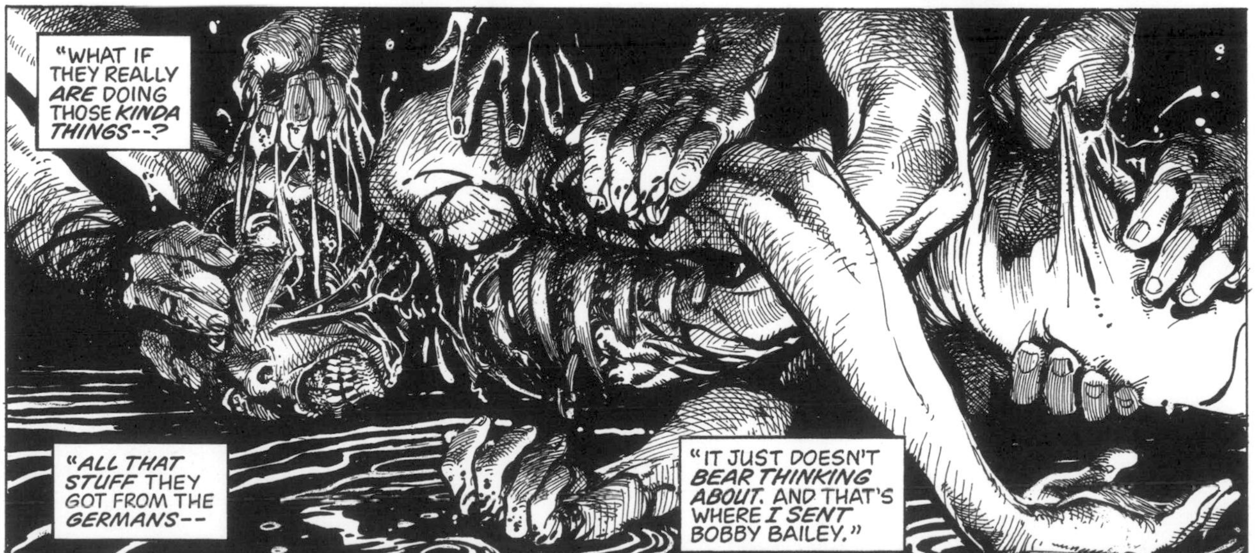
"WHAT IF THEY REALLY ARE DOING THOSE KINDA THINGS--?
"ALL THAT STUFF THEY GOT FROM THE GERMANS--
"IT JUST DOESN'T BEAR THINKING ABOUT. AND THAT'S WHERE I SENT BOBBY BAILEY."

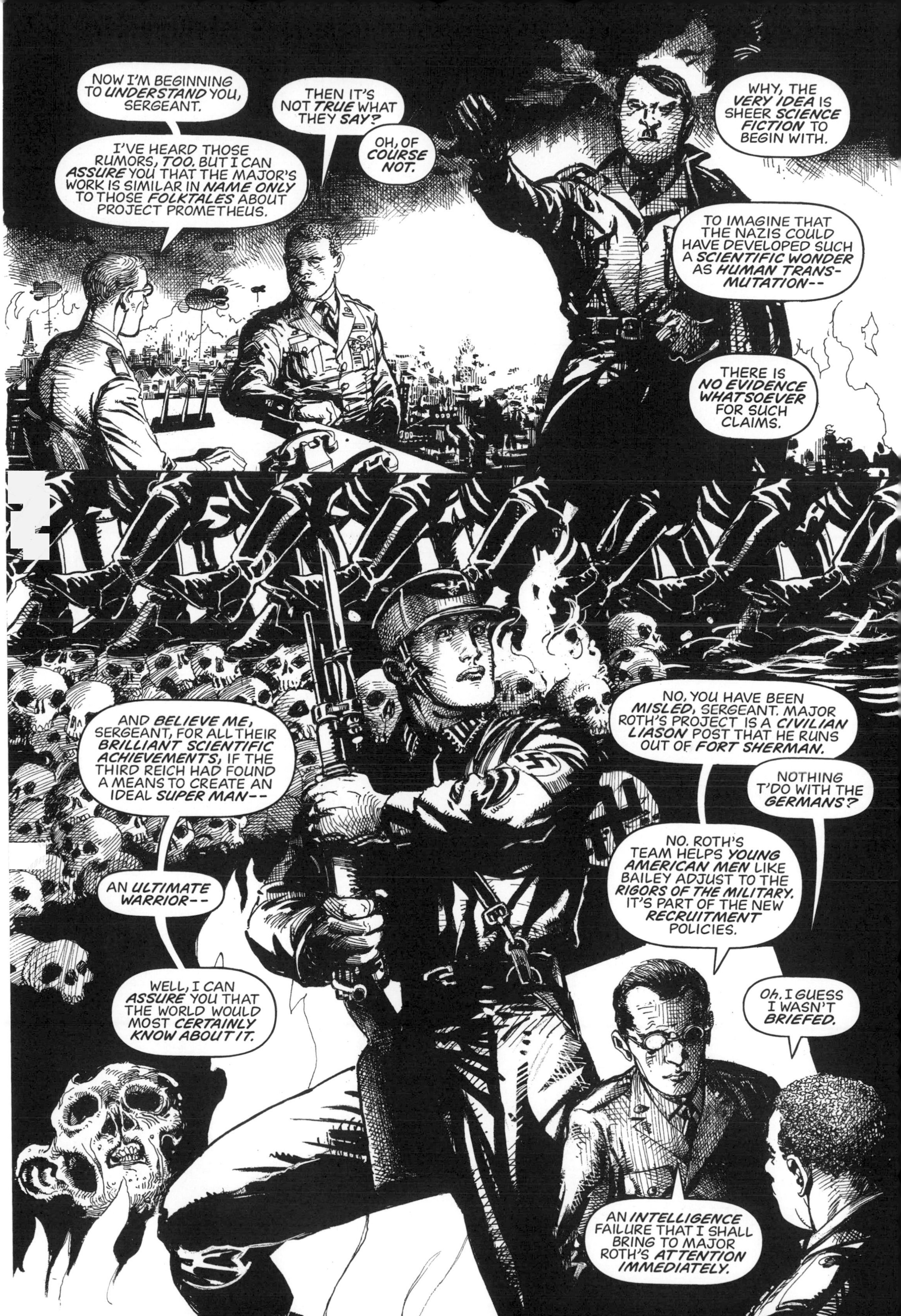
NOW I'M BEGINNING TO UNDERSTAND YOU, SERGEANT.
I'VE HEARD THOSE RUMORS, TOO. BUT I CAN ASSURE YOU THAT THE MAJOR'S WORK IS SIMILAR IN NAME ONLY TO THOSE FOLKTALES ABOUT PROJECT PROMETHEUS.
THEN IT'S NOT TRUE WHAT THEY SAY?
OH, OF COURSE NOT.
WHY, THE VERY IDEA IS SHEER SCIENCE FICTION TO BEGIN WITH.
TO IMAGINE THAT THE NAZIS COULD HAVE DEVELOPED SUCH A SCIENTIFIC WONDER AS HUMAN TRANS-MUTATION--
THERE IS NO EVIDENCE WHATSOEVER FOR SUCH CLAIMS.
AND BELIEVE ME, SERGEANT, FOR ALL THEIR BRILLIANT SCIENTIFIC ACHIEVEMENTS, IF THE THIRD REICH HAD FOUND A MEANS TO CREATE AN IDEAL SUPER MAN--
AN ULTIMATE WARRIOR--
WELL, I CAN ASSURE YOU THAT THE WORLD WOULD MOST CERTAINLY KNOW ABOUT IT.
NO, YOU HAVE BEEN MISLED, SERGEANT. MAJOR ROTH'S PROJECT IS A CIVILIAN LIASON POST THAT HE RUNS OUT OF FORT SHERMAN.
NOTHING T'DO WITH THE GERMANS?
NO. ROTH'S TEAM HELPS YOUNG AMERICAN MEN LIKE BAILEY ADJUST TO THE RIGORS OF THE MILITARY. IT'S PART OF THE NEW RECRUITMENT POLICIES.
Oh, I GUESS I WASN'T BRIEFED.
AN INTELLIGENCE FAILURE THAT I SHALL BRING TO MAJOR ROTH'S ATTENTION IMMEDIATELY.

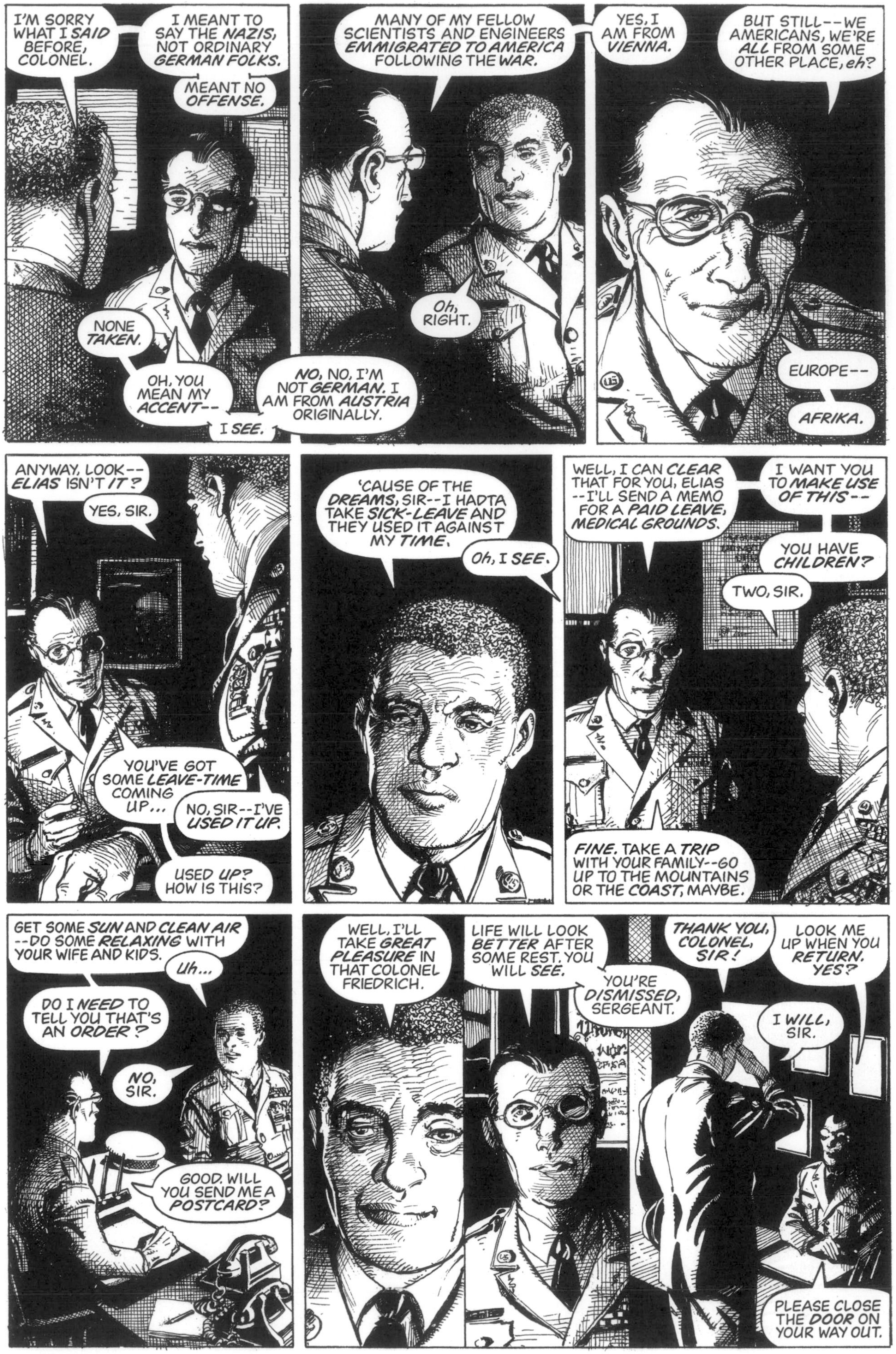

I'M SORRY WHAT I SAID BEFORE, COLONEL.
I MEANT TO SAY THE NAZIS, NOT ORDINARY GERMAN FOLKS.
MEANT NO OFFENSE.
NONE TAKEN.
OH, YOU MEAN MY ACCENT--
I SEE.
NO, NO, I'M NOT GERMAN. I AM FROM AUSTRIA ORIGINALLY.
MANY OF MY FELLOW SCIENTISTS AND ENGINEERS EMMIGRATED TO AMERICA FOLLOWING THE WAR.
YES, I AM FROM VIENNA.
Oh, RIGHT.
BUT STILL--WE AMERICANS, WE'RE ALL FROM SOME OTHER PLACE, eh?
EUROPE--
AFRIKA.
ANYWAY, LOOK--ELIAS ISN'T IT?
YES, SIR.
YOU'VE GOT SOME LEAVE-TIME COMING UP...
NO, SIR--I'VE USED IT UP.
USED UP? HOW IS THIS?
'CAUSE OF THE DREAMS, SIR--I HADTA TAKE SICK-LEAVE AND THEY USED IT AGAINST MY TIME.
Oh, I SEE.
WELL, I CAN CLEAR THAT FOR YOU, ELIAS--I'LL SEND A MEMO FOR A PAID LEAVE, MEDICAL GROUNDS.
I WANT YOU TO MAKE USE OF THIS--
YOU HAVE CHILDREN?
TWO, SIR.
FINE. TAKE A TRIP WITH YOUR FAMILY--GO UP TO THE MOUNTAINS OR THE COAST, MAYBE.
GET SOME SUN AND CLEAN AIR--DO SOME RELAXING WITH YOUR WIFE AND KIDS.
Uh...
DO I NEED TO TELL YOU THAT'S AN ORDER?
NO, SIR.
GOOD. WILL YOU SEND ME A POSTCARD?
WELL, I'LL TAKE GREAT PLEASURE IN THAT COLONEL FRIEDRICH.
LIFE WILL LOOK BETTER AFTER SOME REST. YOU WILL SEE.
YOU'RE DISMISSED, SERGEANT.
THANK YOU, COLONEL, SIR!
LOOK ME UP WHEN YOU RETURN. YES?
I WILL, SIR.
PLEASE CLOSE THE DOOR ON YOUR WAY OUT.

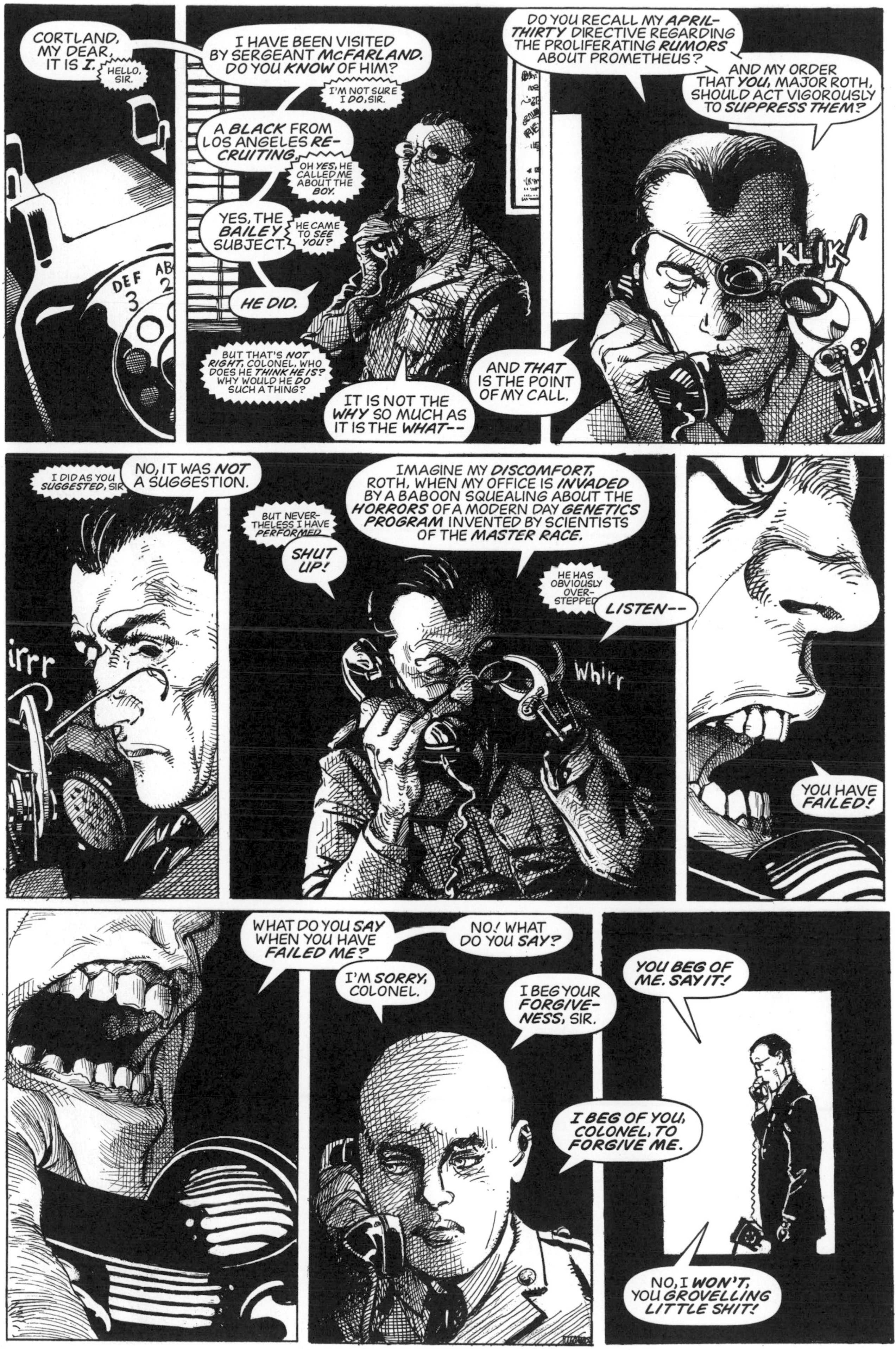
CORTLAND, MY DEAR, IT IS I.
HELLO, SIR.
I HAVE BEEN VISITED BY SERGEANT MCFARLAND. DO YOU KNOW OF HIM?
I'M NOT SURE I DO, SIR.
A BLACK FROM LOS ANGELES RE-CRUITING.
OH YES, HE CALLED ME ABOUT THE BOY.
YES, THE BAILEY SUBJECT.
HE CAME TO SEE YOU?
HE DID.
BUT THAT'S NOT RIGHT, COLONEL. WHO DOES HE THINK HE IS? WHY WOULD HE DO SUCH A THING?
IT IS NOT THE WHY SO MUCH AS IT IS THE WHAT--
AND THAT IS THE POINT OF MY CALL.
DO YOU RECALL MY APRIL-THIRTY DIRECTIVE REGARDING THE PROLIFERATING RUMORS ABOUT PROMETHEUS?
AND MY ORDER THAT YOU, MAJOR ROTH, SHOULD ACT VIGOROUSLY TO SUPPRESS THEM?
KLIK
I DID AS YOU SUGGESTED, SIR.
NO, IT WAS NOT A SUGGESTION.
irrr
IMAGINE MY DISCOMFORT, ROTH, WHEN MY OFFICE IS INVADED BY A BABOON SQUEALING ABOUT THE HORRORS OF A MODERN DAY GENETICS PROGRAM INVENTED BY SCIENTISTS OF THE MASTER RACE.
BUT NEVER-THELESS I HAVE PERFORMED
SHUT UP!
HE HAS OBVIOUSLY OVER-STEPPED
LISTEN--
Whirr
YOU HAVE FAILED!
WHAT DO YOU SAY WHEN YOU HAVE FAILED ME?
I'M SORRY, COLONEL.
NO! WHAT DO YOU SAY?
I BEG YOUR FORGIVE-NESS, SIR.
YOU BEG OF ME. SAY IT!
I BEG OF YOU, COLONEL, TO FORGIVE ME.
NO, I WON'T, YOU GROVELLING LITTLE SHIT!

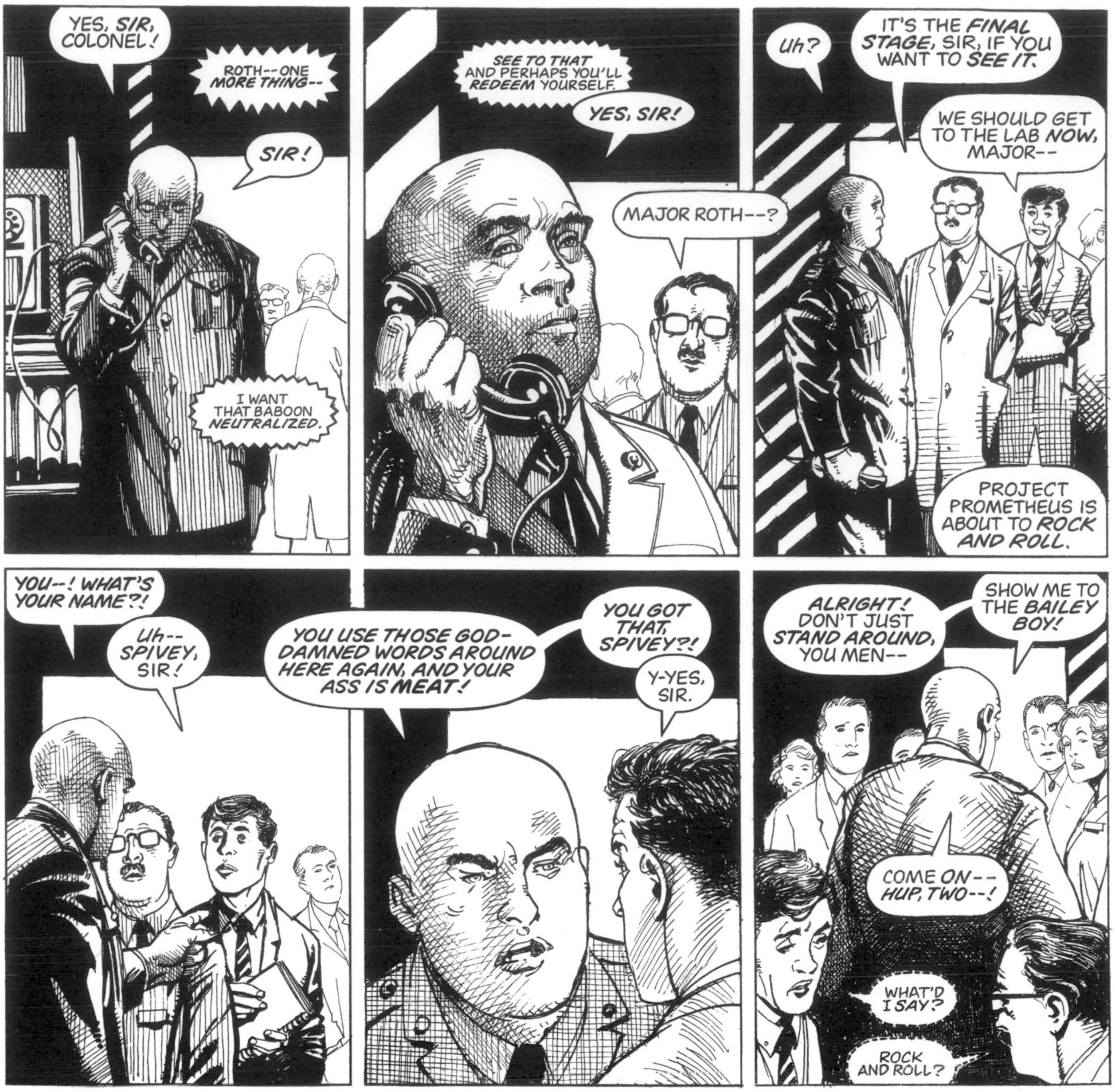
YES, SIR, COLONEL!
ROTH--ONE MORE THING--
SIR!
I WANT THAT BABOON NEUTRALIZED.
SEE TO THAT AND PERHAPS YOU'LL REDEEM YOURSELF.
YES, SIR!
MAJOR ROTH--?
Uh?
IT'S THE FINAL STAGE, SIR, IF YOU WANT TO SEE IT.
WE SHOULD GET TO THE LAB NOW, MAJOR--
PROJECT PROMETHEUS IS ABOUT TO ROCK AND ROLL.
YOU--! WHAT'S YOUR NAME?!
Uh-- SPIVEY, SIR!
YOU USE THOSE GOD-DAMNED WORDS AROUND HERE AGAIN, AND YOUR ASS IS MEAT!
YOU GOT THAT, SPIVEY?!
Y-YES, SIR.
ALRIGHT! DON'T JUST STAND AROUND, YOU MEN--
SHOW ME TO THE BAILEY BOY!
COME ON-- HUP, TWO--!
WHAT'D I SAY?
ROCK AND ROLL?

Los Angeles Sunday, May 10

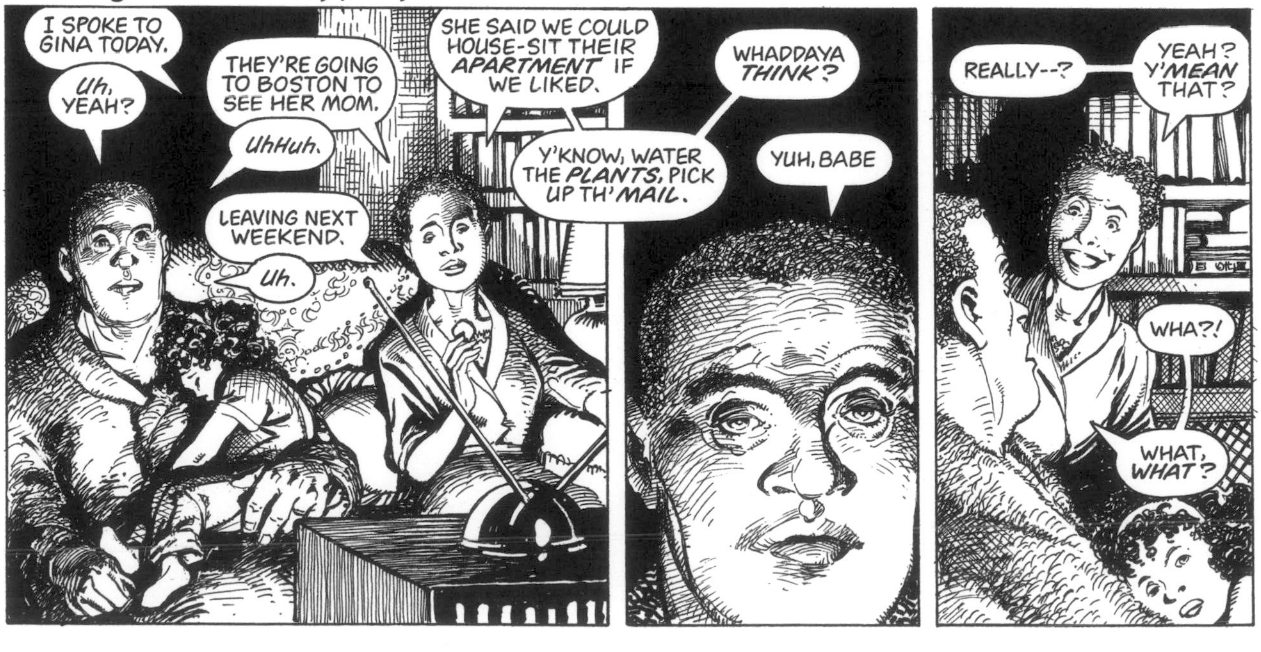
I SPOKE TO GINA TODAY.
Uh, YEAH?
THEY'RE GOING TO BOSTON TO SEE HER MOM.
UhHuh.
LEAVING NEXT WEEKEND.
Uh.
SHE SAID WE COULD HOUSE-SIT THEIR APARTMENT IF WE LIKED.
Y'KNOW, WATER THE PLANTS, PICK UP TH' MAIL.
WHADDAYA THINK?
YUH, BABE
REALLY--?
YEAH? Y'MEAN THAT?
WHA?!
WHAT, WHAT?

WERE YOU *LISTENING* TO ME?

SURE!

WHAT I *SAY*?

---

i'm hungry.

BOSTON, YOU'RE GOING TO *BOSTON.*

WHAT WOULD I BE DOING *GOING TO BOSTON*?

BEATS *ME.* HOW LONG Y'*STAYIN'*?

'LIAS--*GINA'S* GOING TO BOSTON.

OKAY, FINE.

SO--?

AND THEY *OFFERED US* THEIR *PLACE* FOR A COUPLE OF WEEKS--

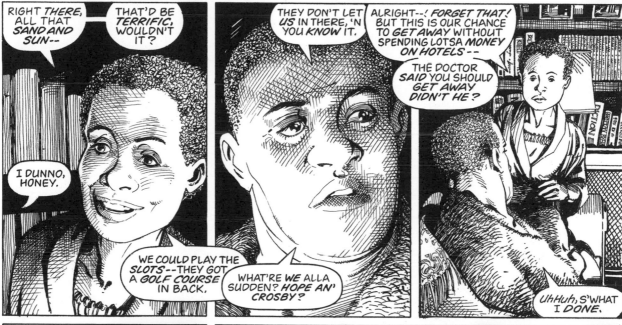
RIGHT *THERE,* ALL THAT *SAND AND SUN*--

THAT'D BE *TERRIFIC,* WOULDN'T IT?

I DUNNO, HONEY.

WE COULD PLAY THE *SLOTS*--THEY GOT A *GOLF COURSE* IN BACK.

THEY DON'T LET *US* IN THERE, 'N YOU *KNOW* IT.

WHAT'RE WE ALLA SUDDEN? *HOPE AN' CROSBY*?

ALRIGHT--! *FORGET THAT!* BUT THIS IS OUR CHANCE TO *GET AWAY* WITHOUT SPENDING LOTSA *MONEY* ON HOTELS--

THE DOCTOR SAID YOU SHOULD *GET AWAY* DIDN'T HE?

UhHuh, S'WHAT I *DONE.*

BUT, HONEY, ALL *YOU'VE DONE* IS SIT AROUND TH' *HOUSE* FOR A MONTH--

I'M JUST *WAITIN* ON THAT *CALL,* HON--

IT'S NOT DOING YOU *ANY GOOD,* BABY.

WHEN I GET TH' *CALL* --MAYBE WE CAN GO TO GINA'S, OKAY?

'LIAS--

THIS ISN'T *GOOD* --

WHY D'YOU THINK THAT *KID* IS GOING TO *CALL YOU BACK*--?

IT WAS *WEEKS* AGO--

IF HE WAS GOING TO CALL *BACK,* HE'D'VE *DONE IT* BY NOW, CAN'T YOU *SEE THAT*?

Uh...I TRIED THE PROJECT ON *WEDNESDAY,* TOO--

Y'CALLED *AGAIN*--?

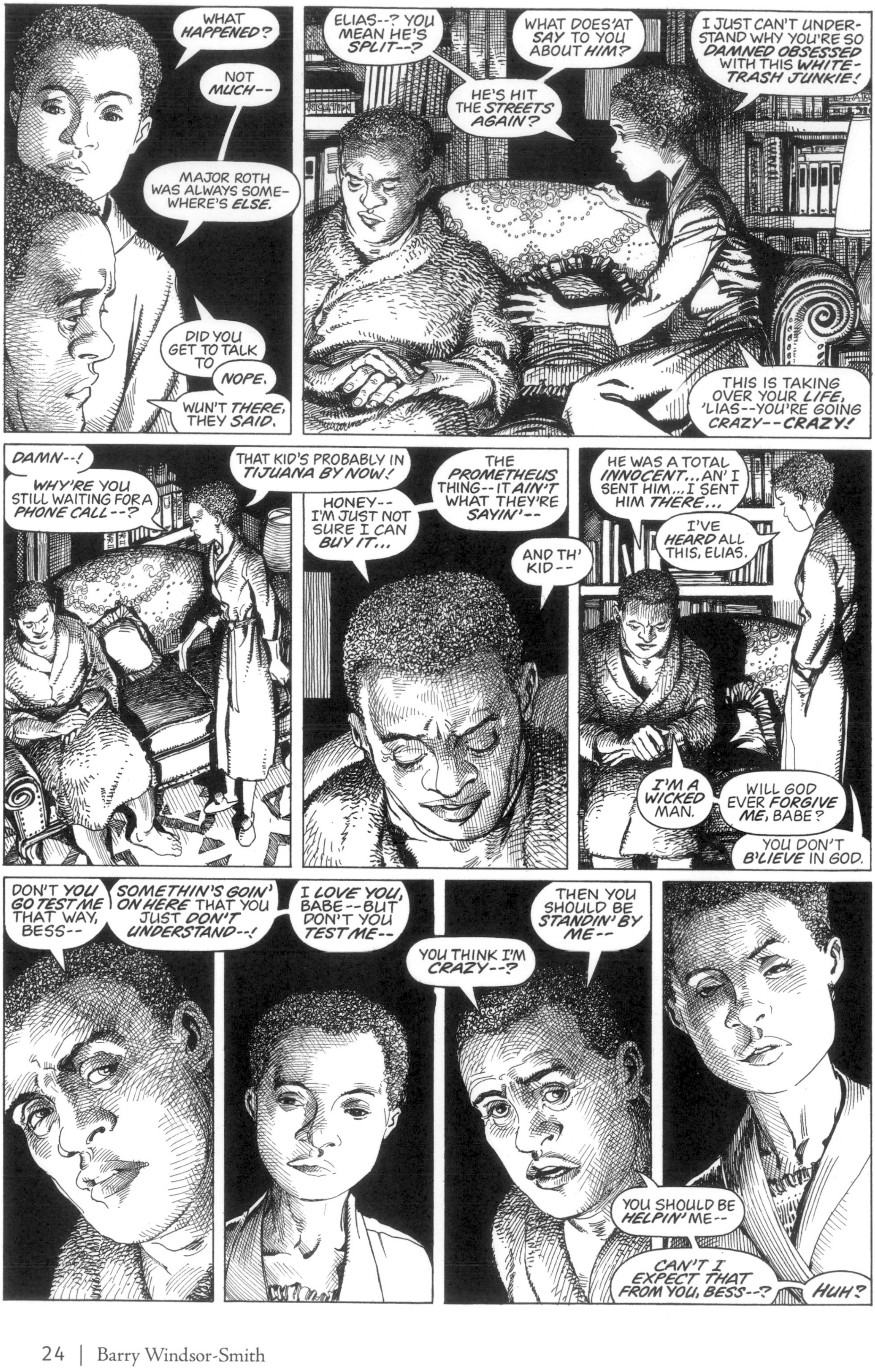

WHAT HAPPENED?
NOT MUCH--
MAJOR ROTH WAS ALWAYS SOME-WHERE'S ELSE.
DID YOU GET TO TALK TO
NOPE.
WUN'T THERE, THEY SAID.
ELIAS--? YOU MEAN HE'S SPLIT--?
HE'S HIT THE STREETS AGAIN?
WHAT DOES'AT SAY TO YOU ABOUT HIM?
I JUST CAN'T UNDER-STAND WHY YOU'RE SO DAMNED OBSESSED WITH THIS WHITE-TRASH JUNKIE!
THIS IS TAKING OVER YOUR LIFE, 'LIAS--YOU'RE GOING CRAZY--CRAZY!
DAMN--!
WHY'RE YOU STILL WAITING FOR A PHONE CALL--?
THAT KID'S PROBABLY IN TIJUANA BY NOW!
HONEY-- I'M JUST NOT SURE I CAN BUY IT...
THE PROMETHEUS THING--IT AIN'T WHAT THEY'RE SAYIN'--
AND TH' KID--
HE WAS A TOTAL INNOCENT...AN' I SENT HIM...I SENT HIM THERE...
I'VE HEARD ALL THIS, ELIAS.
I'M A WICKED MAN.
WILL GOD EVER FORGIVE ME, BABE?
YOU DON'T B'LIEVE IN GOD.
DON'T YOU GO TEST ME THAT WAY, BESS--
SOMETHIN'S GOIN' ON HERE THAT YOU JUST DON'T UNDERSTAND--!
I LOVE YOU, BABE--BUT DON'T YOU TEST ME--
YOU THINK I'M CRAZY--?
THEN YOU SHOULD BE STANDIN' BY ME--
YOU SHOULD BE HELPIN' ME--
CAN'T I EXPECT THAT FROM YOU, BESS--?
HUH?

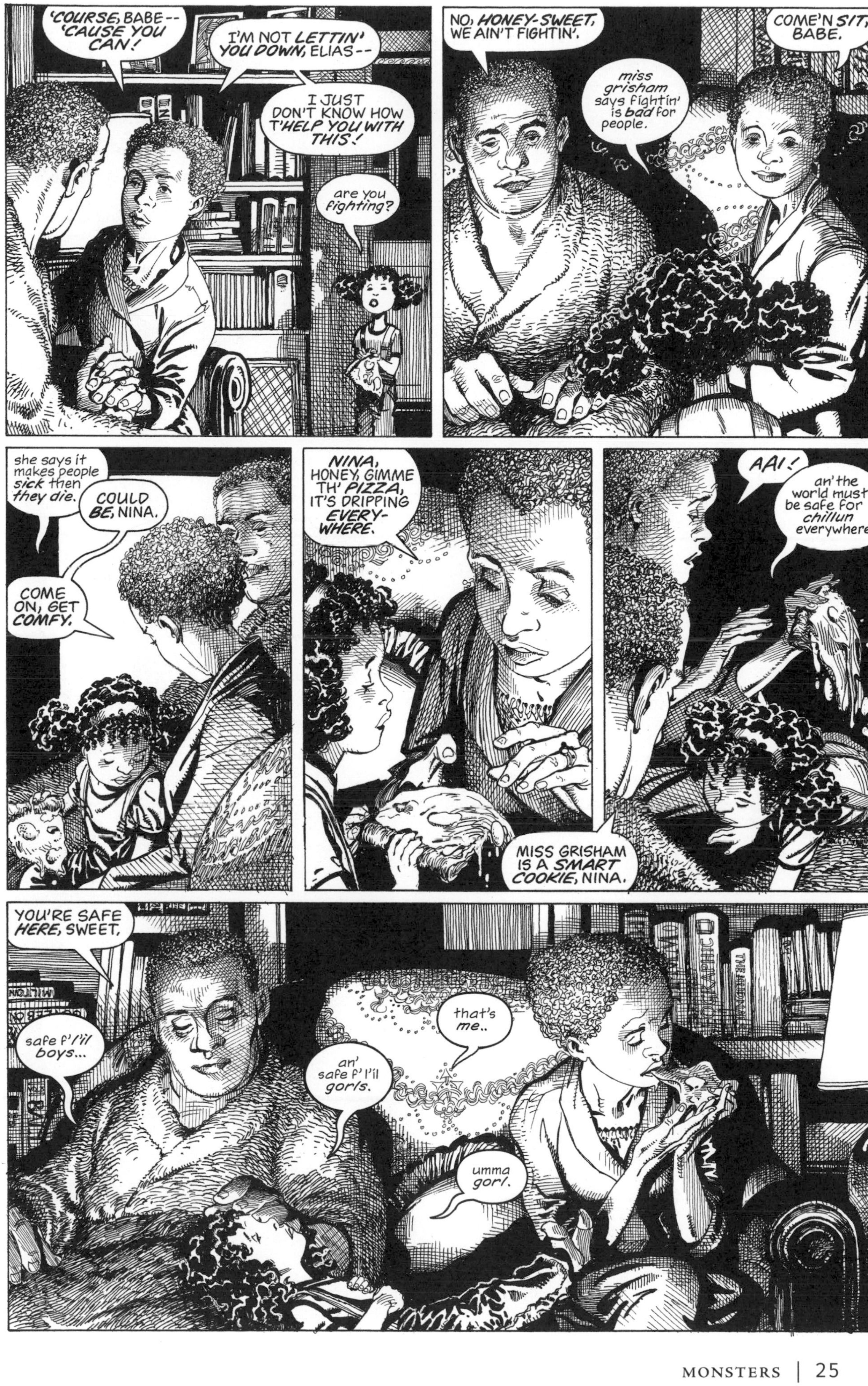
'COURSE, BABE-- 'CAUSE YOU CAN!
I'M NOT LETTIN' YOU DOWN, ELIAS--
I JUST DON'T KNOW HOW T'HELP YOU WITH THIS!
are you fighting?
NO, HONEY-SWEET, WE AIN'T FIGHTIN'.
miss grisham says fightin' is bad for people.
COME'N SIT, BABE.
she says it makes people sick then they die.
COULD BE, NINA.
COME ON, GET COMFY.
NINA, HONEY, GIMME TH' PIZZA, IT'S DRIPPING EVERY-WHERE.
MISS GRISHAM IS A SMART COOKIE, NINA.
AAI!
an' the world must be safe for chillun everywhere.
YOU'RE SAFE HERE, SWEET,
safe f' l'il boys...
an' safe f' l'il gorls.
that's me..
umma gorl.

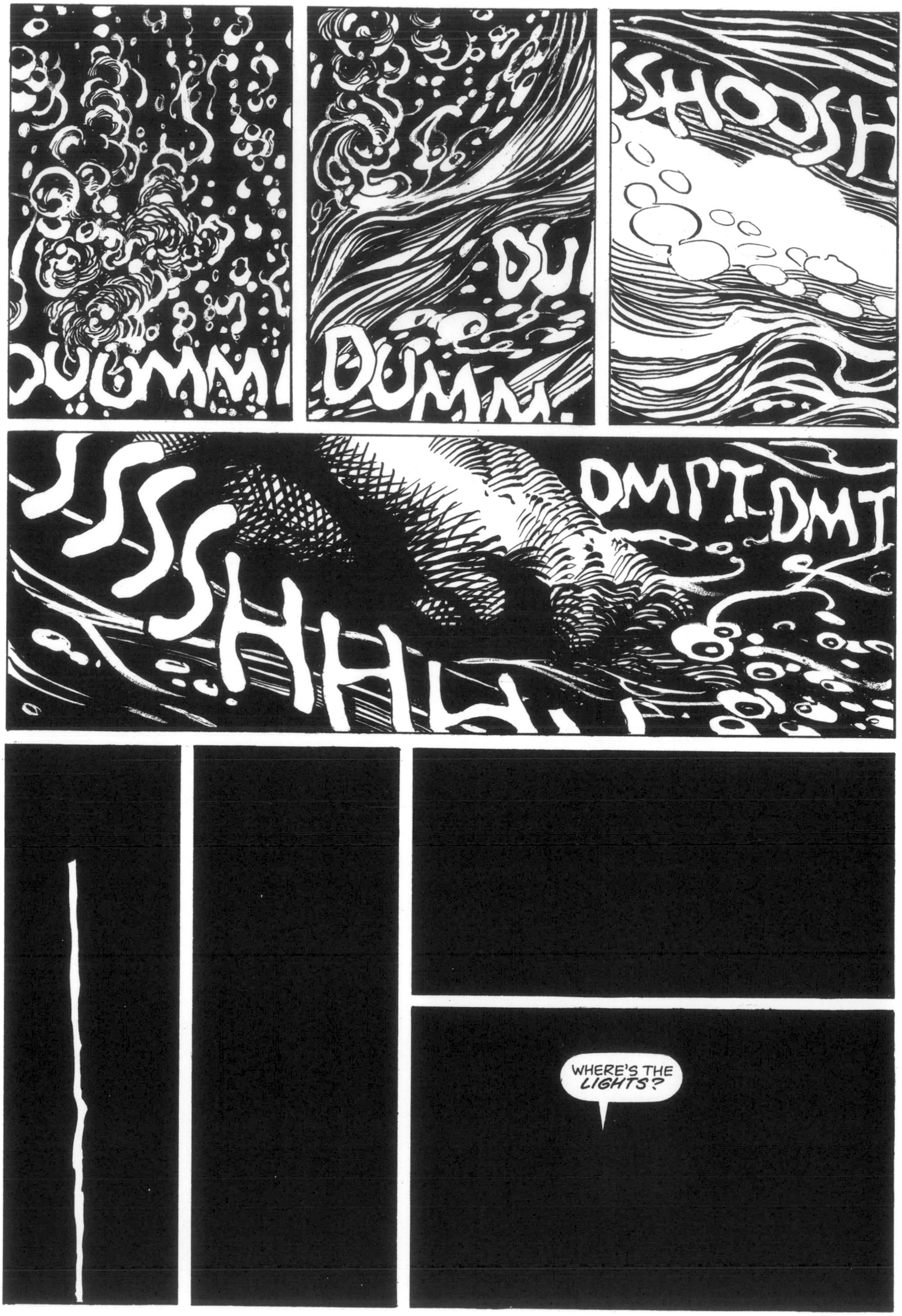
DUMM
DU
DUMM
SHOOSH
SSSHHH
DMPT DMT
WHERE'S THE *LIGHTS?*

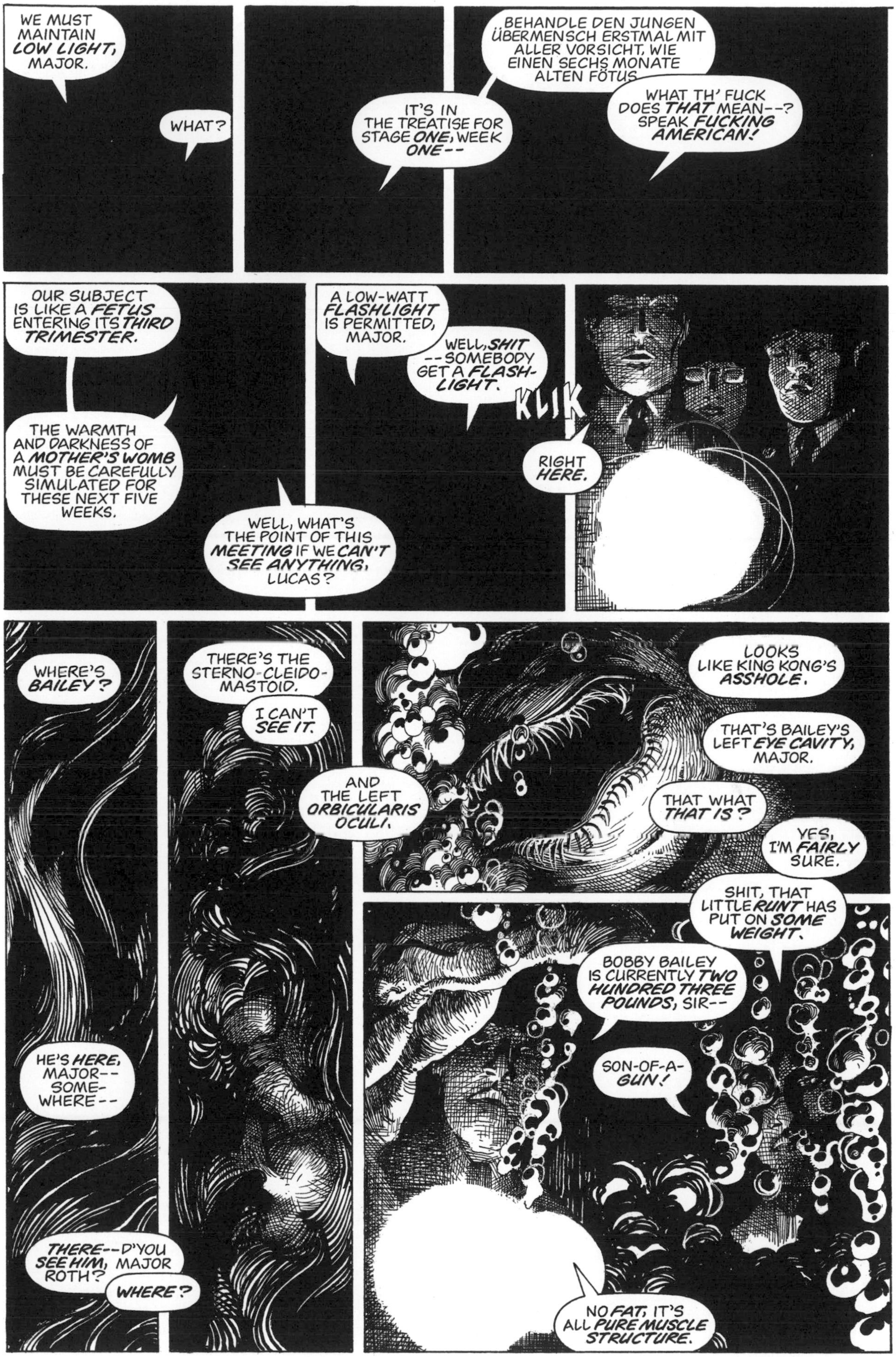
WE MUST MAINTAIN LOW LIGHT, MAJOR.
WHAT?
IT'S IN THE TREATISE FOR STAGE ONE, WEEK ONE--
BEHANDLE DEN JUNGEN ÜBERMENSCH ERSTMAL MIT ALLER VORSICHT, WIE EINEN SECHS MONATE ALTEN FÖTUS
WHAT TH' FUCK DOES THAT MEAN--? SPEAK FUCKING AMERICAN!
OUR SUBJECT IS LIKE A FETUS ENTERING ITS THIRD TRIMESTER.
THE WARMTH AND DARKNESS OF A MOTHER'S WOMB MUST BE CAREFULLY SIMULATED FOR THESE NEXT FIVE WEEKS.
A LOW-WATT FLASHLIGHT IS PERMITTED, MAJOR.
WELL, SHIT --SOMEBODY GET A FLASHLIGHT.
WELL, WHAT'S THE POINT OF THIS MEETING IF WE CAN'T SEE ANYTHING, LUCAS?
KLIK
RIGHT HERE.
WHERE'S BAILEY?
HE'S HERE, MAJOR--SOMEWHERE--
THERE--D'YOU SEE HIM, MAJOR ROTH?
WHERE?
THERE'S THE STERNO-CLEIDO-MASTOID.
I CAN'T SEE IT.
AND THE LEFT ORBICULARIS OCULI.
LOOKS LIKE KING KONG'S ASSHOLE.
THAT'S BAILEY'S LEFT EYE CAVITY, MAJOR.
THAT WHAT THAT IS?
YES, I'M FAIRLY SURE.
SHIT, THAT LITTLE RUNT HAS PUT ON SOME WEIGHT.
BOBBY BAILEY IS CURRENTLY TWO HUNDRED THREE POUNDS, SIR--
SON-OF-A-GUN!
NO FAT, IT'S ALL PURE MUSCLE STRUCTURE.

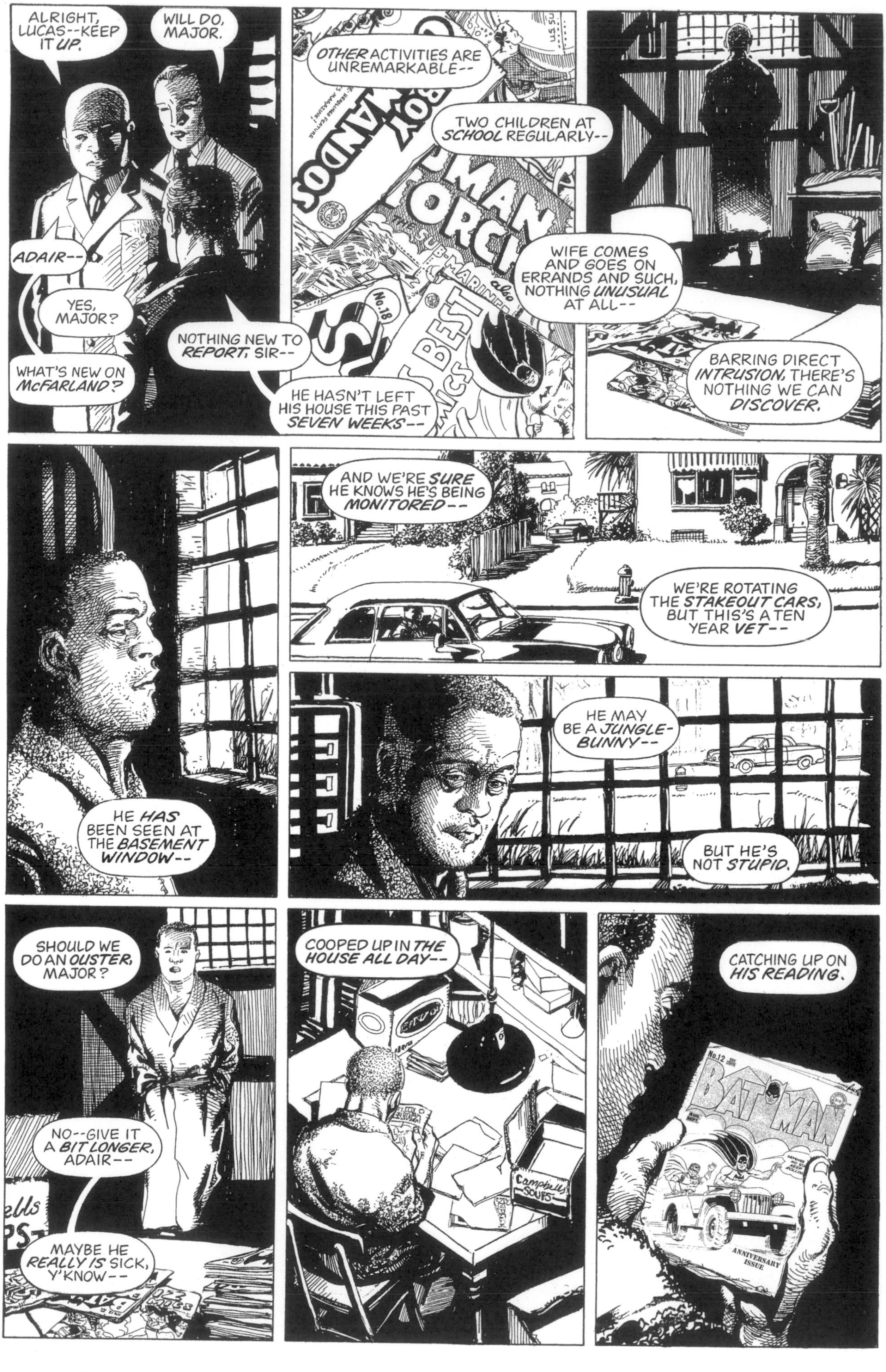

ALRIGHT, LUCAS--KEEP IT UP.
WILL DO, MAJOR.
ADAIR--
YES, MAJOR?
WHAT'S NEW ON McFARLAND?
NOTHING NEW TO REPORT, SIR--
HE HASN'T LEFT HIS HOUSE THIS PAST SEVEN WEEKS--
OTHER ACTIVITIES ARE UNREMARKABLE--
TWO CHILDREN AT SCHOOL REGULARLY--
WIFE COMES AND GOES ON ERRANDS AND SUCH, NOTHING UNUSUAL AT ALL--
BARRING DIRECT INTRUSION, THERE'S NOTHING WE CAN DISCOVER.
HE HAS BEEN SEEN AT THE BASEMENT WINDOW--
AND WE'RE SURE HE KNOWS HE'S BEING MONITORED--
WE'RE ROTATING THE STAKEOUT CARS, BUT THIS'S A TEN YEAR VET--
HE MAY BE A JUNGLE-BUNNY--
BUT HE'S NOT STUPID.
SHOULD WE DO AN OUSTER, MAJOR?
NO--GIVE IT A BIT LONGER, ADAIR--
MAYBE HE REALLY IS SICK, Y'KNOW--
COOPED UP IN THE HOUSE ALL DAY--
CATCHING UP ON HIS READING.
BATMAN
ANNIVERSARY ISSUE

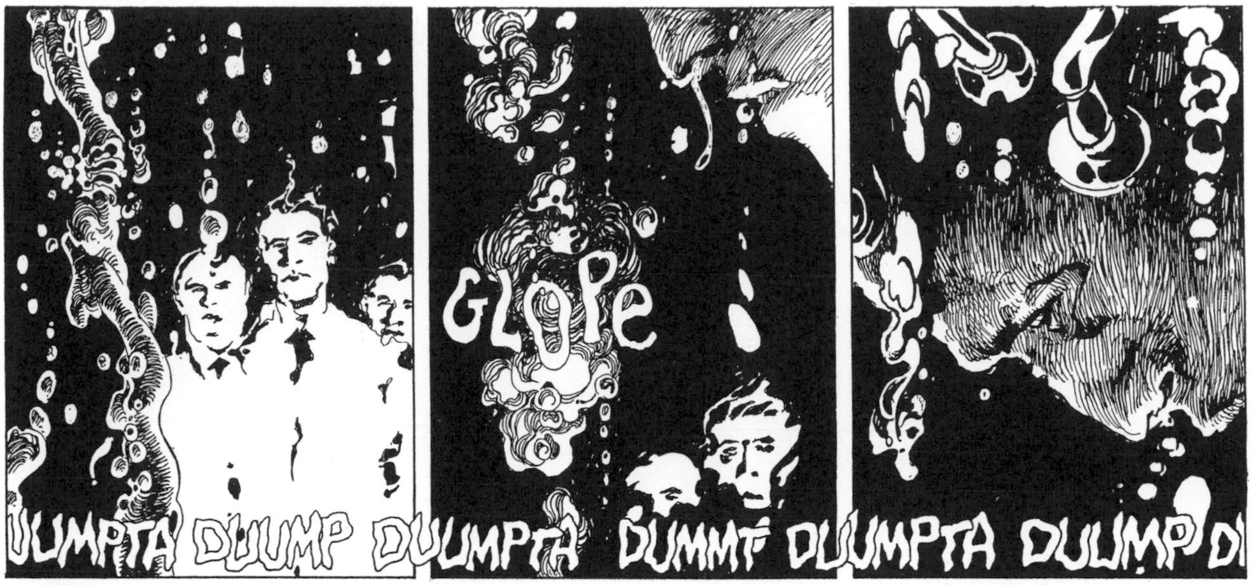
UUMPTA DUUMP DUUMPTA
GLOPE
DUMMT DUUMPTA DUUMP DI

Los Angeles Wednesday, July 1

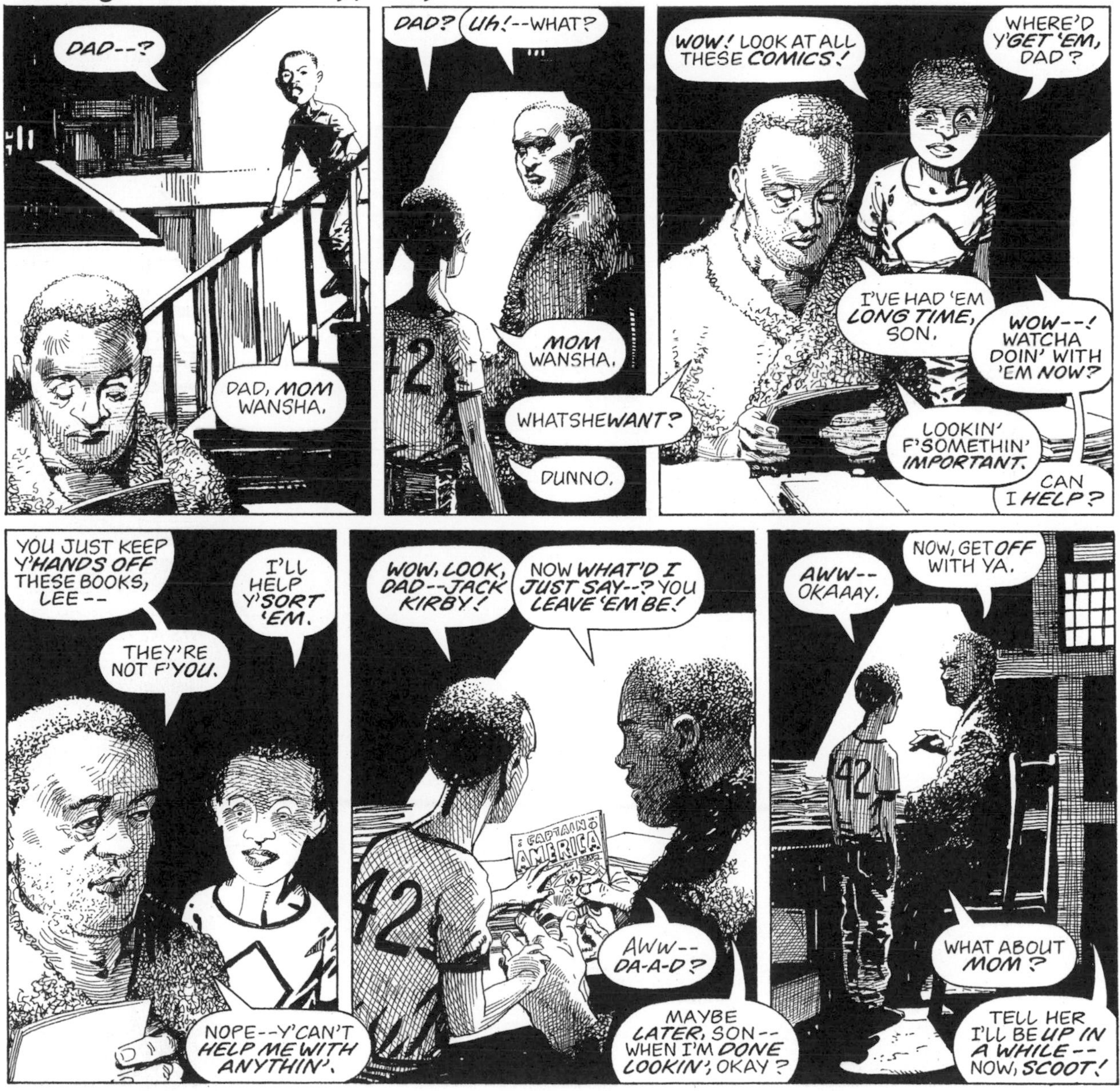
DAD--?
DAD, MOM WANSHA.
DAD?
UH!--WHAT?
MOM WANSHA.
WHATSHEWANT?
DUNNO.
WOW! LOOK AT ALL THESE COMICS!
WHERE'D Y'GET 'EM, DAD?
I'VE HAD 'EM LONG TIME, SON.
WOW--! WATCHA DOIN' WITH 'EM NOW?
LOOKIN' F'SOMETHIN' IMPORTANT.
CAN I HELP?
YOU JUST KEEP Y'HANDS OFF THESE BOOKS, LEE--
THEY'RE NOT F'YOU.
I'LL HELP Y'SORT 'EM.
NOPE--Y'CAN'T HELP ME WITH ANYTHIN'.
WOW, LOOK, DAD--JACK KIRBY!
NOW WHAT'D I JUST SAY--? YOU LEAVE 'EM BE!
CAPTAIN AMERICA
AWW-- DA-A-D?
MAYBE LATER, SON-- WHEN I'M DONE LOOKIN', OKAY?
AWW-- OKAAAY.
NOW, GET OFF WITH YA.
WHAT ABOUT MOM?
TELL HER I'LL BE UP IN A WHILE-- NOW, SCOOT!

Los Angeles Thursday, July 2

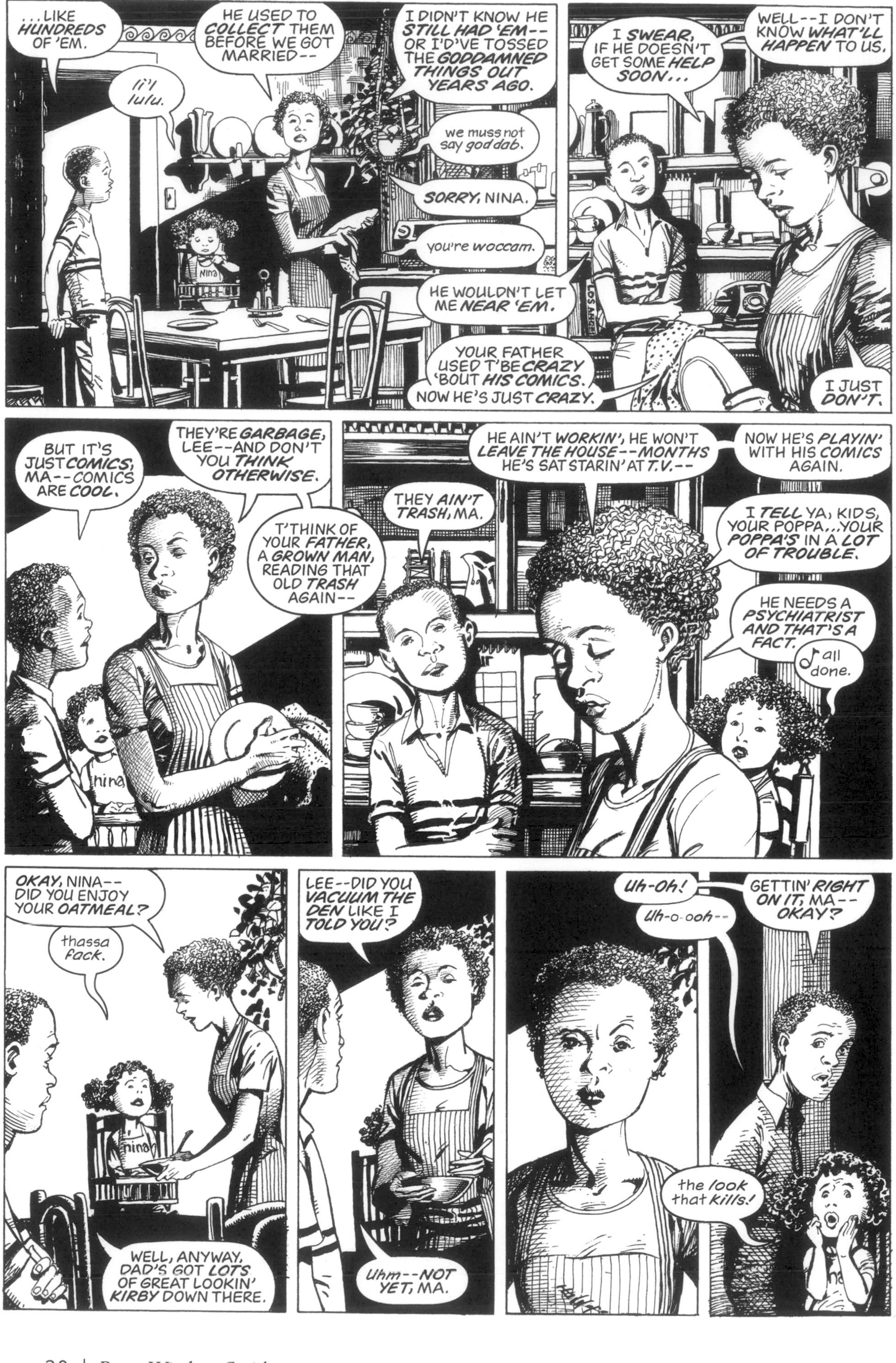

...LIKE HUNDREDS OF 'EM.
li'l lulu.
HE USED TO COLLECT THEM BEFORE WE GOT MARRIED--
I DIDN'T KNOW HE STILL HAD 'EM--OR I'D'VE TOSSED THE GODDAMNED THINGS OUT YEARS AGO.
we muss not say god dab.
SORRY, NINA.
you're woccam.
HE WOULDN'T LET ME NEAR 'EM.
YOUR FATHER USED T'BE CRAZY 'BOUT HIS COMICS. NOW HE'S JUST CRAZY.
I SWEAR, IF HE DOESN'T GET SOME HELP SOON...
WELL--I DON'T KNOW WHAT'LL HAPPEN TO US.
I JUST DON'T.
BUT IT'S JUST COMICS, MA--COMICS ARE COOL.
THEY'RE GARBAGE, LEE--AND DON'T YOU THINK OTHERWISE.
T'THINK OF YOUR FATHER, A GROWN MAN, READING THAT OLD TRASH AGAIN--
THEY AIN'T TRASH, MA.
HE AIN'T WORKIN', HE WON'T LEAVE THE HOUSE--MONTHS HE'S SAT STARIN' AT T.V.--
NOW HE'S PLAYIN' WITH HIS COMICS AGAIN.
I TELL YA, KIDS, YOUR POPPA...YOUR POPPA'S IN A LOT OF TROUBLE.
HE NEEDS A PSYCHIATRIST AND THAT'S A FACT.
all done.
OKAY, NINA--DID YOU ENJOY YOUR OATMEAL?
thassa fack.
WELL, ANYWAY, DAD'S GOT LOTS OF GREAT LOOKIN' KIRBY DOWN THERE.
LEE--DID YOU VACUUM THE DEN LIKE I TOLD YOU?
Uhm--NOT YET, MA.
Uh-Oh!
Uh-o-ooh--
GETTIN' RIGHT ON IT, MA--OKAY?
the look that kills!

Los Angeles Thursday, July 16

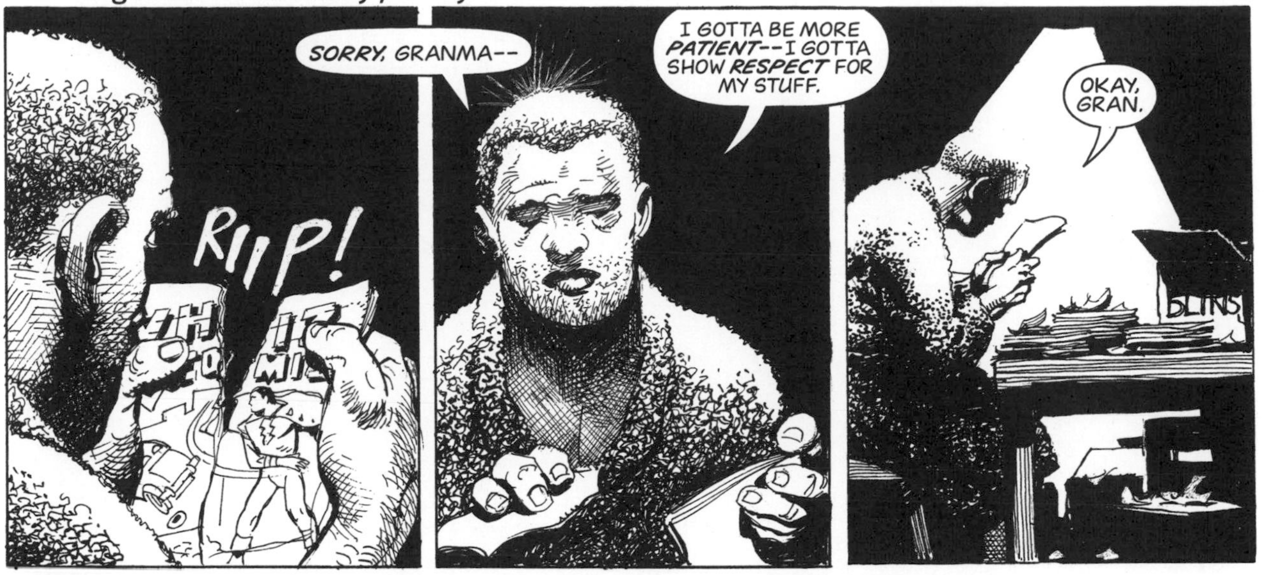
RIIP!
SORRY, GRANMA--
I GOTTA BE MORE PATIENT--I GOTTA SHOW RESPECT FOR MY STUFF.
OKAY, GRAN.

Fort Sherman Monday, August 3

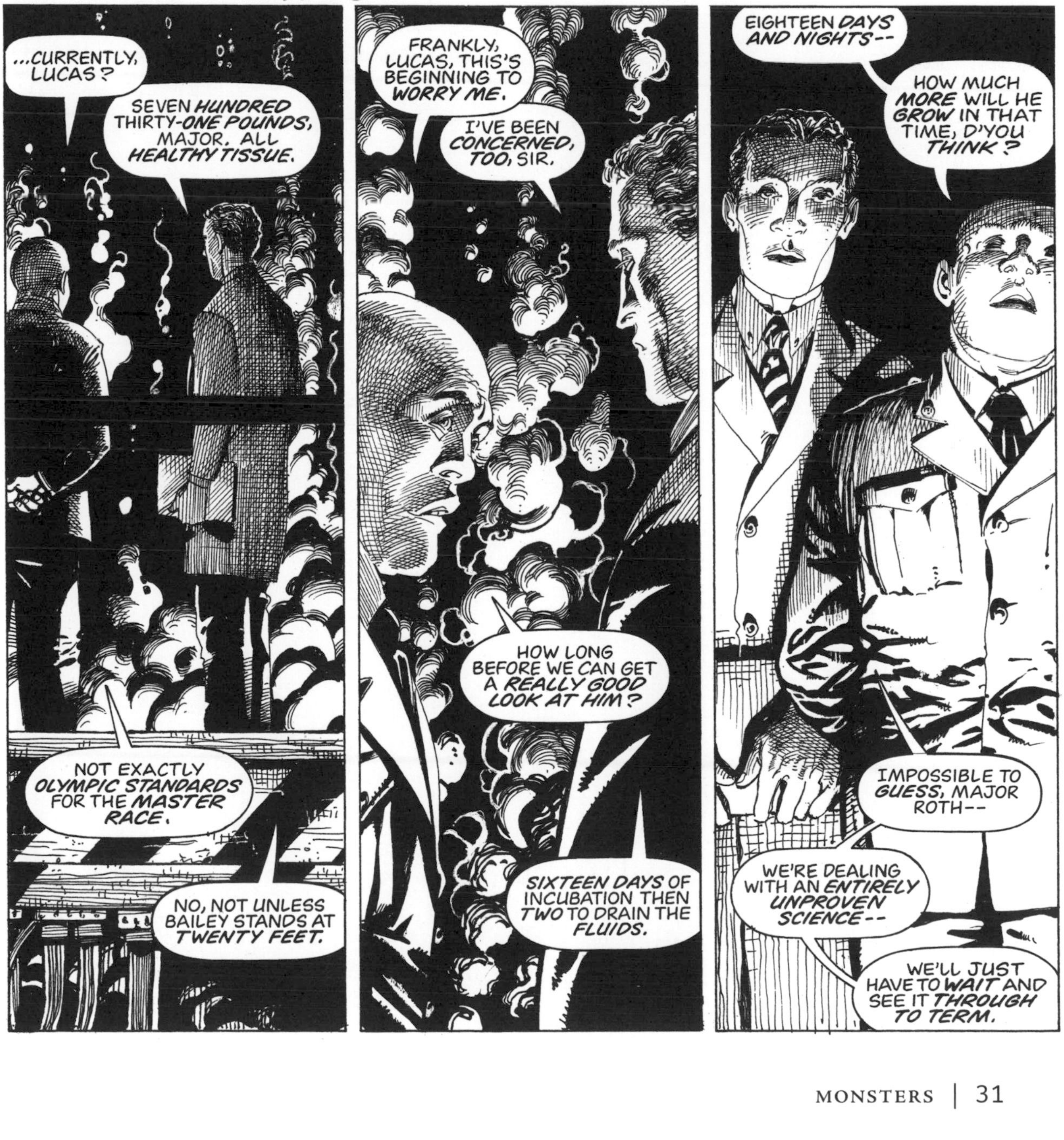
...CURRENTLY, LUCAS?
SEVEN HUNDRED THIRTY-ONE POUNDS, MAJOR. ALL HEALTHY TISSUE.
NOT EXACTLY OLYMPIC STANDARDS FOR THE MASTER RACE.
NO, NOT UNLESS BAILEY STANDS AT TWENTY FEET.
FRANKLY, LUCAS, THIS'S BEGINNING TO WORRY ME.
I'VE BEEN CONCERNED, TOO, SIR.
HOW LONG BEFORE WE CAN GET A REALLY GOOD LOOK AT HIM?
SIXTEEN DAYS OF INCUBATION THEN TWO TO DRAIN THE FLUIDS.
EIGHTEEN DAYS AND NIGHTS--
HOW MUCH MORE WILL HE GROW IN THAT TIME, D'YOU THINK?
IMPOSSIBLE TO GUESS, MAJOR ROTH--
WE'RE DEALING WITH AN ENTIRELY UNPROVEN SCIENCE--
WE'LL JUST HAVE TO WAIT AND SEE IT THROUGH TO TERM.

Los Angeles Friday, August 7

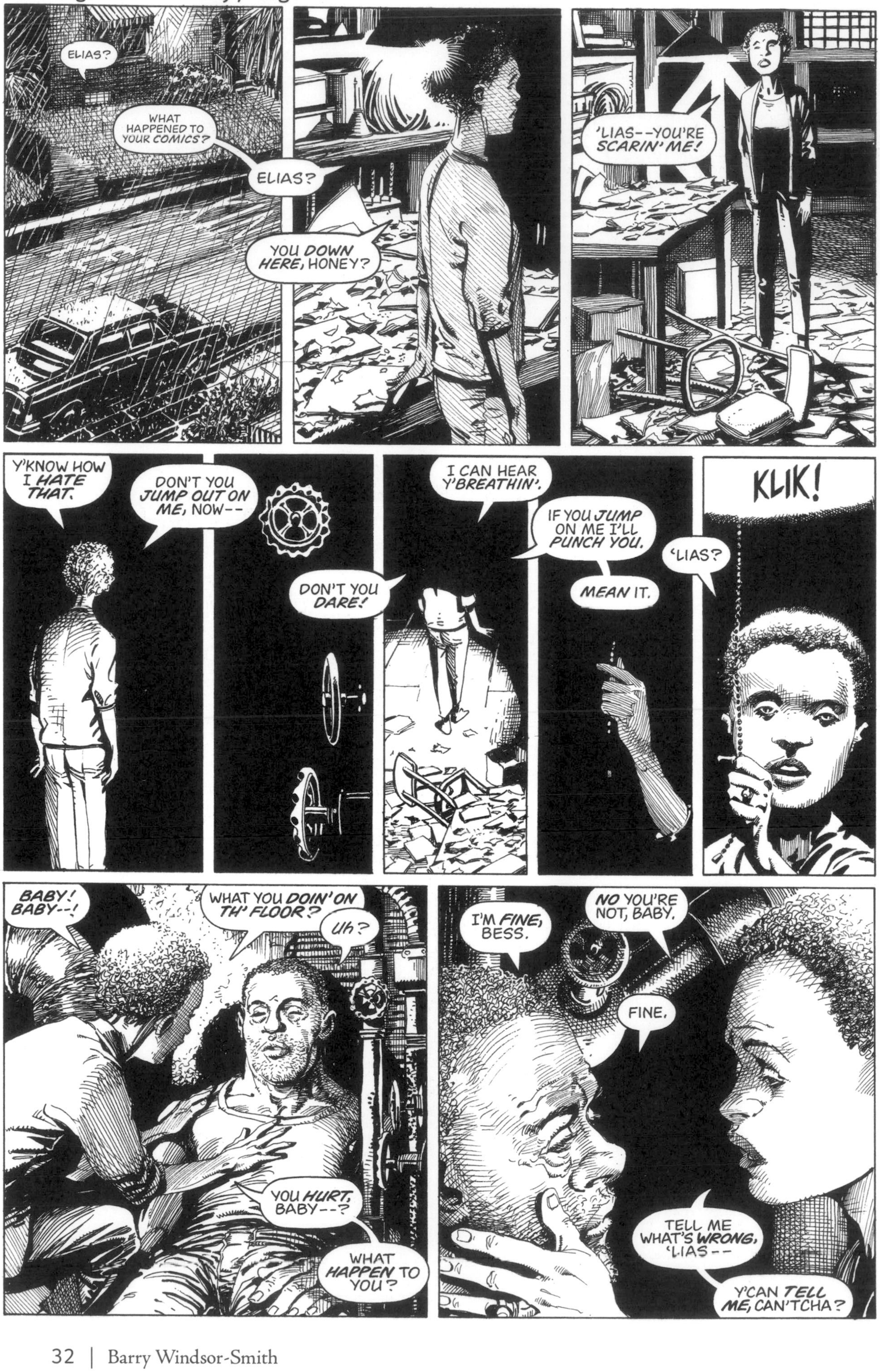

ELIAS?
WHAT HAPPENED TO YOUR COMICS?
ELIAS?
YOU DOWN HERE, HONEY?
'LIAS--YOU'RE SCARIN' ME!
Y'KNOW HOW I HATE THAT.
DON'T YOU JUMP OUT ON ME, NOW--
DON'T YOU DARE!
I CAN HEAR Y'BREATHIN'.
IF YOU JUMP ON ME I'LL PUNCH YOU.
MEAN IT.
KLIK!
'LIAS?
BABY! BABY--!
WHAT YOU DOIN' ON TH' FLOOR?
Uh?
YOU HURT, BABY--?
WHAT HAPPEN TO YOU?
I'M FINE, BESS.
NO YOU'RE NOT, BABY.
FINE.
TELL ME WHAT'S WRONG, 'LIAS--
Y'CAN TELL ME, CAN'TCHA?

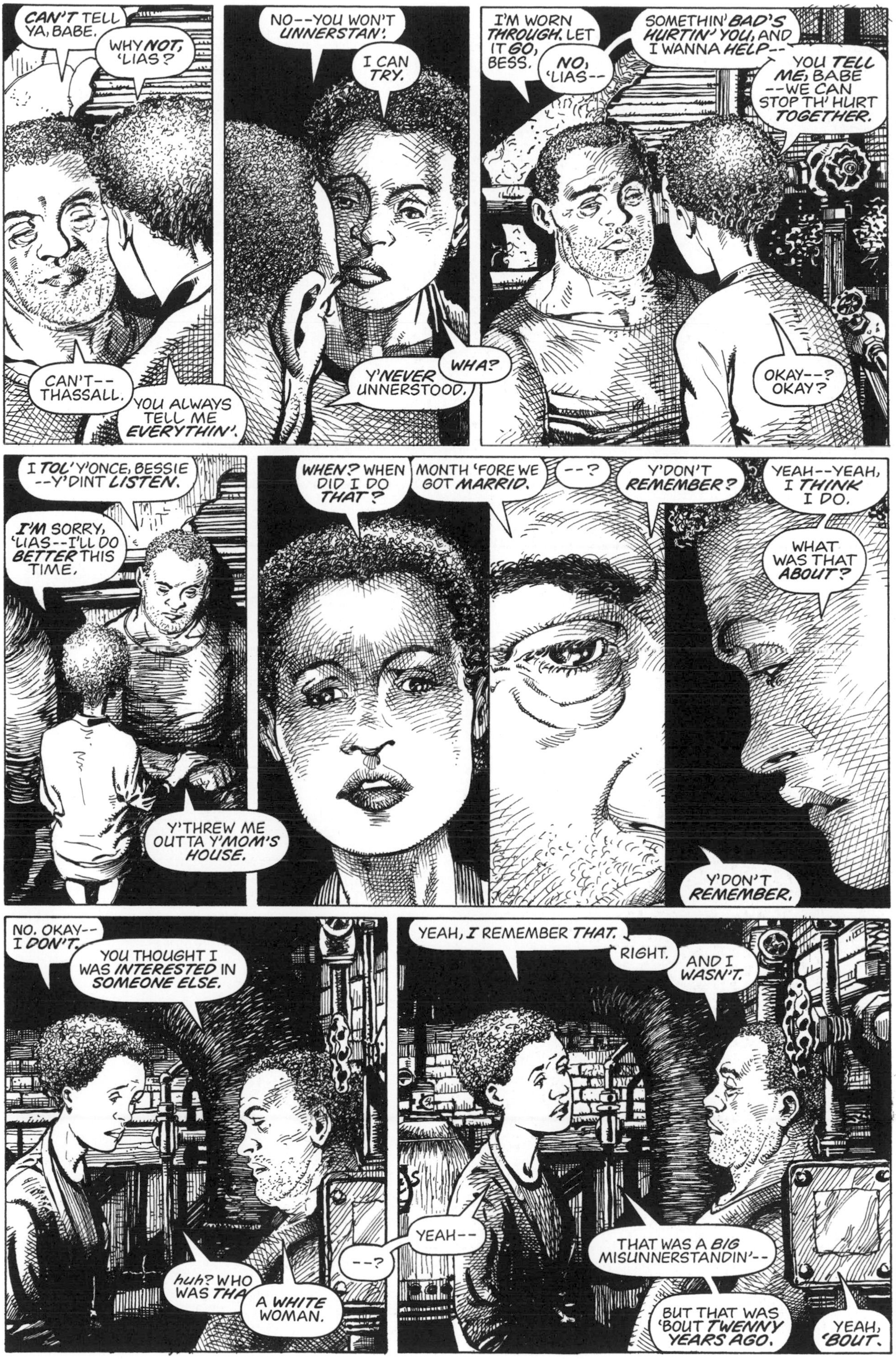
CAN'T TELL YA, BABE.
WHY NOT, 'LIAS?
CAN'T-- THASSALL.
YOU ALWAYS TELL ME EVERYTHIN'.
NO--YOU WON'T UNNERSTAN'.
I CAN TRY.
WHA?
Y'NEVER UNNERSTOOD.
I'M WORN THROUGH. LET IT GO, BESS.
NO, 'LIAS--
SOMETHIN' BAD'S HURTIN' YOU, AND I WANNA HELP--
YOU TELL ME, BABE --WE CAN STOP TH' HURT TOGETHER.
OKAY--? OKAY?
I TOL' Y'ONCE, BESSIE --Y'DINT LISTEN.
I'M SORRY, 'LIAS--I'LL DO BETTER THIS TIME.
Y'THREW ME OUTTA Y'MOM'S HOUSE.
WHEN? WHEN DID I DO THAT?
MONTH 'FORE WE GOT MARRID.
--?
Y'DON'T REMEMBER?
YEAH--YEAH, I THINK I DO.
WHAT WAS THAT ABOUT?
Y'DON'T REMEMBER.
NO. OKAY-- I DON'T.
YOU THOUGHT I WAS INTERESTED IN SOMEONE ELSE.
huh? WHO WAS THA
A WHITE WOMAN.
YEAH--
--?
YEAH, I REMEMBER THAT.
RIGHT.
AND I WASN'T.
THAT WAS A BIG MISUNNERSTANDIN'--
BUT THAT WAS 'BOUT TWENNY YEARS AGO.
YEAH, 'BOUT.

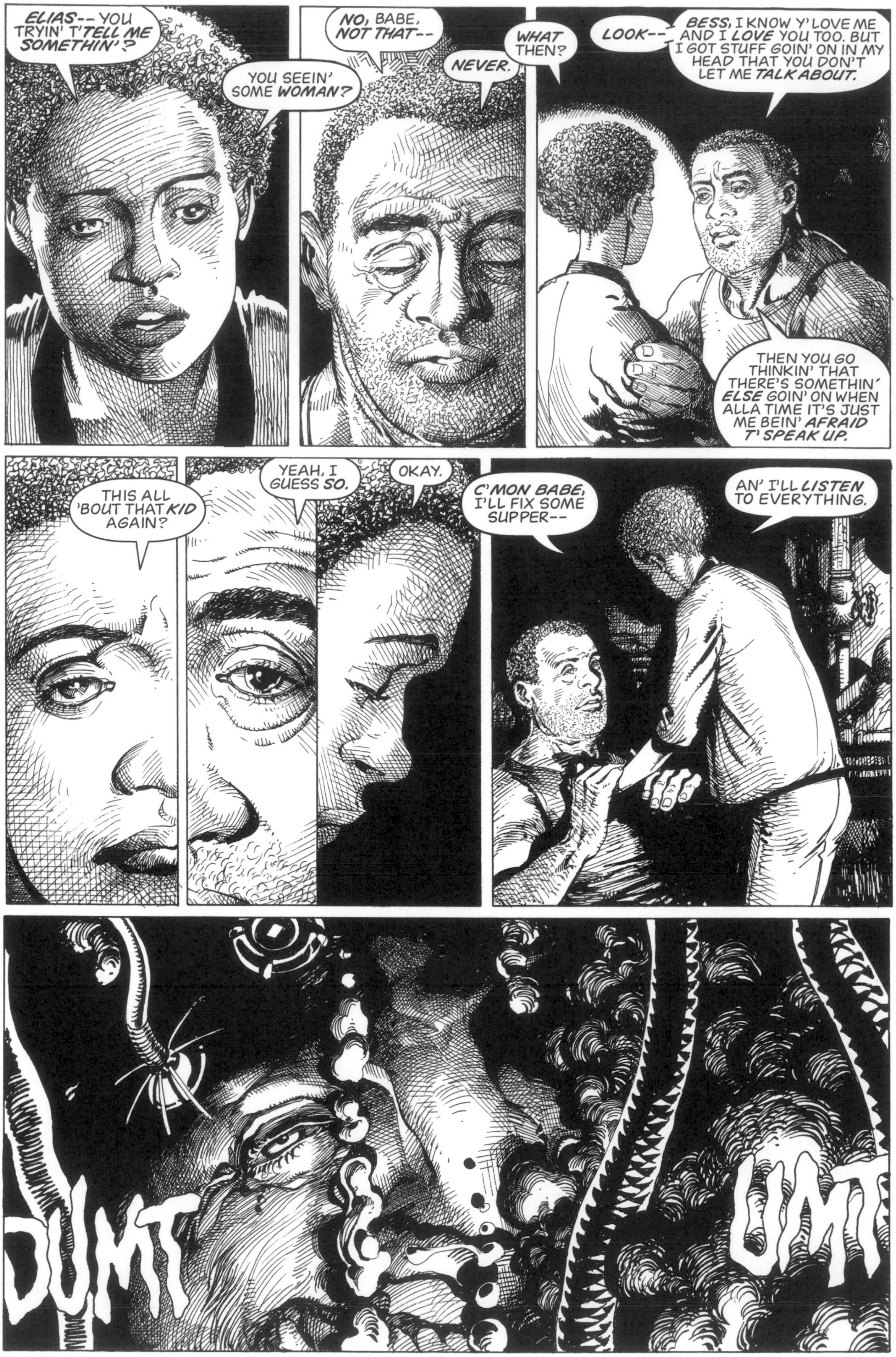
ELIAS-- YOU TRYIN' T'TELL ME SOMETHIN'?
YOU SEEIN' SOME WOMAN?
NO, BABE, NOT THAT--
NEVER.
WHAT THEN?
LOOK--
BESS, I KNOW Y' LOVE ME AND I LOVE YOU TOO. BUT I GOT STUFF GOIN' ON IN MY HEAD THAT YOU DON'T LET ME TALK ABOUT.
THEN YOU GO THINKIN' THAT THERE'S SOMETHIN' ELSE GOIN' ON WHEN ALLA TIME IT'S JUST ME BEIN' AFRAID T' SPEAK UP.
THIS ALL 'BOUT THAT KID AGAIN?
YEAH, I GUESS SO.
OKAY.
C'MON BABE, I'LL FIX SOME SUPPER--
AN' I'LL LISTEN TO EVERYTHING.
DUMT
UMT

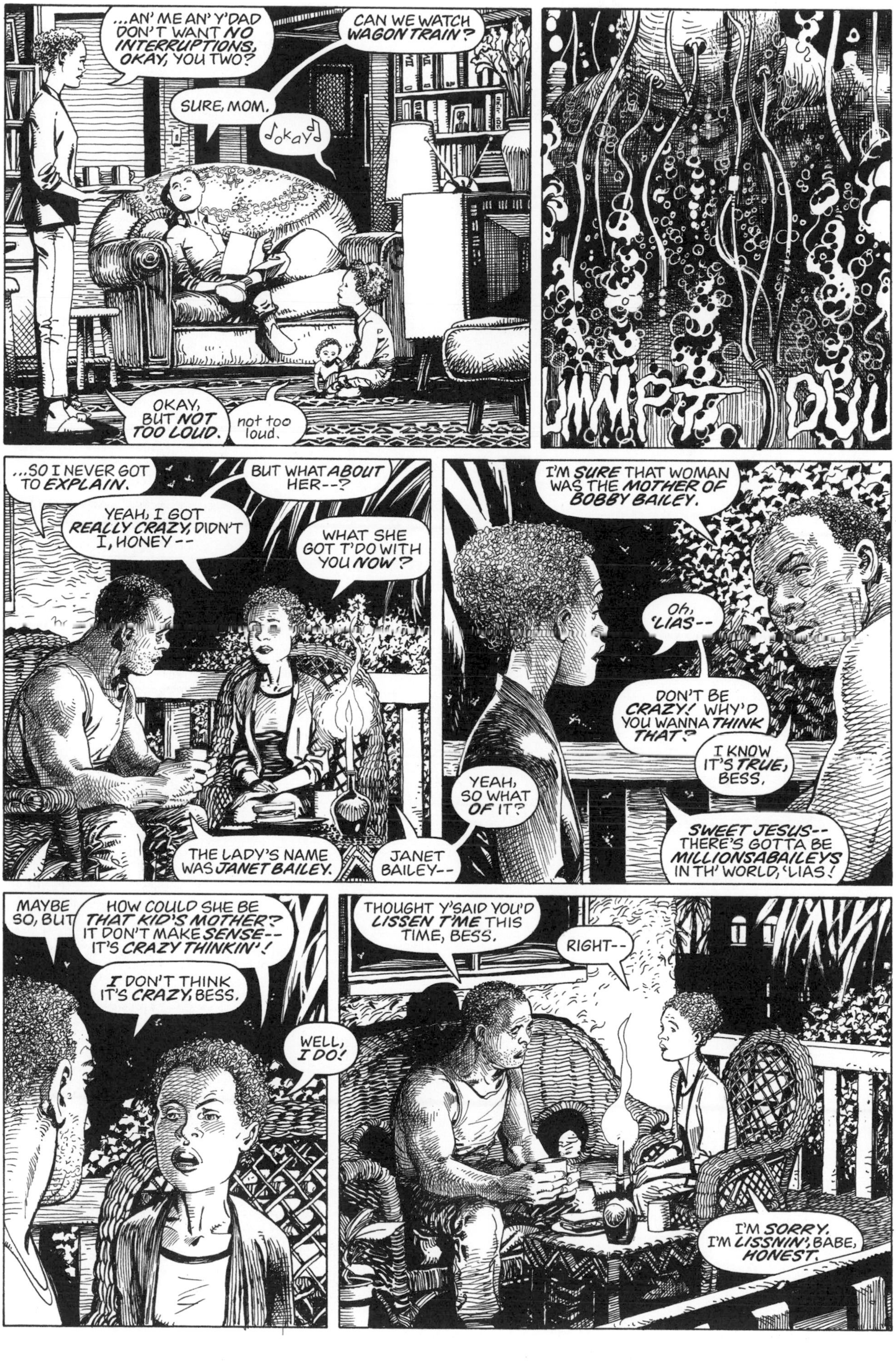
...AN' ME AN' Y'DAD DON'T WANT NO INTERRUPTIONS, OKAY, YOU TWO?
CAN WE WATCH WAGON TRAIN?
SURE, MOM.
okay
OKAY, BUT NOT TOO LOUD.
not too loud.
UMMPT. DUU
...SO I NEVER GOT TO EXPLAIN.
BUT WHAT ABOUT HER--?
YEAH, I GOT REALLY CRAZY, DIDN'T I, HONEY--
WHAT SHE GOT T'DO WITH YOU NOW?
THE LADY'S NAME WAS JANET BAILEY.
JANET BAILEY--
YEAH, SO WHAT OF IT?
I'M SURE THAT WOMAN WAS THE MOTHER OF BOBBY BAILEY.
OH, 'LIAS--
DON'T BE CRAZY! WHY'D YOU WANNA THINK THAT?
I KNOW IT'S TRUE, BESS.
SWEET JESUS--THERE'S GOTTA BE MILLIONSABAILEYS IN TH' WORLD, 'LIAS!
MAYBE SO, BUT
HOW COULD SHE BE THAT KID'S MOTHER? IT DON'T MAKE SENSE--IT'S CRAZY THINKIN'!
I DON'T THINK IT'S CRAZY, BESS.
WELL, I DO!
THOUGHT Y'SAID YOU'D LISSEN T'ME THIS TIME, BESS.
RIGHT--
I'M SORRY. I'M LISSNIN', BABE, HONEST.

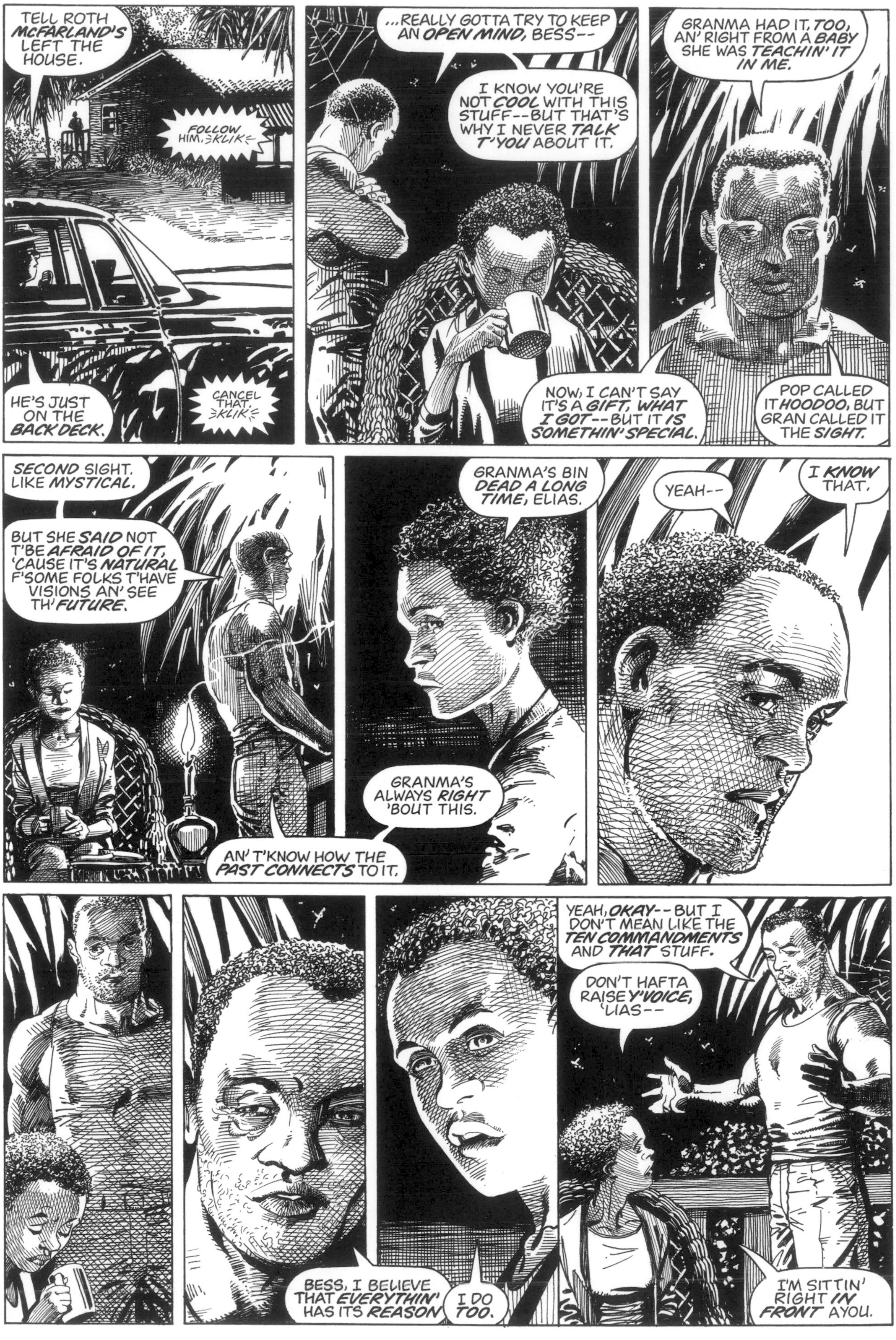
TELL ROTH MCFARLAND'S LEFT THE HOUSE.
FOLLOW HIM. ≷KLIK≶
HE'S JUST ON THE BACK DECK.
CANCEL THAT. ≷KLIK≶
...REALLY GOTTA TRY TO KEEP AN OPEN MIND, BESS--
I KNOW YOU'RE NOT COOL WITH THIS STUFF--BUT THAT'S WHY I NEVER TALK T'YOU ABOUT IT.
NOW, I CAN'T SAY IT'S A GIFT, WHAT I GOT--BUT IT IS SOMETHIN' SPECIAL.
GRANMA HAD IT, TOO, AN' RIGHT FROM A BABY SHE WAS TEACHIN' IT IN ME.
POP CALLED IT HOODOO, BUT GRAN CALLED IT THE SIGHT.
SECOND SIGHT. LIKE MYSTICAL.
BUT SHE SAID NOT T'BE AFRAID OF IT, 'CAUSE IT'S NATURAL F'SOME FOLKS T'HAVE VISIONS AN' SEE TH' FUTURE.
AN' T'KNOW HOW THE PAST CONNECTS TO IT.
GRANMA'S BIN DEAD A LONG TIME, ELIAS.
GRANMA'S ALWAYS RIGHT 'BOUT THIS.
YEAH--
I KNOW THAT.
BESS, I BELIEVE THAT EVERYTHIN' HAS ITS REASON
I DO TOO.
YEAH, OKAY--BUT I DON'T MEAN LIKE THE TEN COMMANDMENTS AND THAT STUFF.
DON'T HAFTA RAISE Y'VOICE, 'LIAS--
I'M SITTIN' RIGHT IN FRONT AYOU.

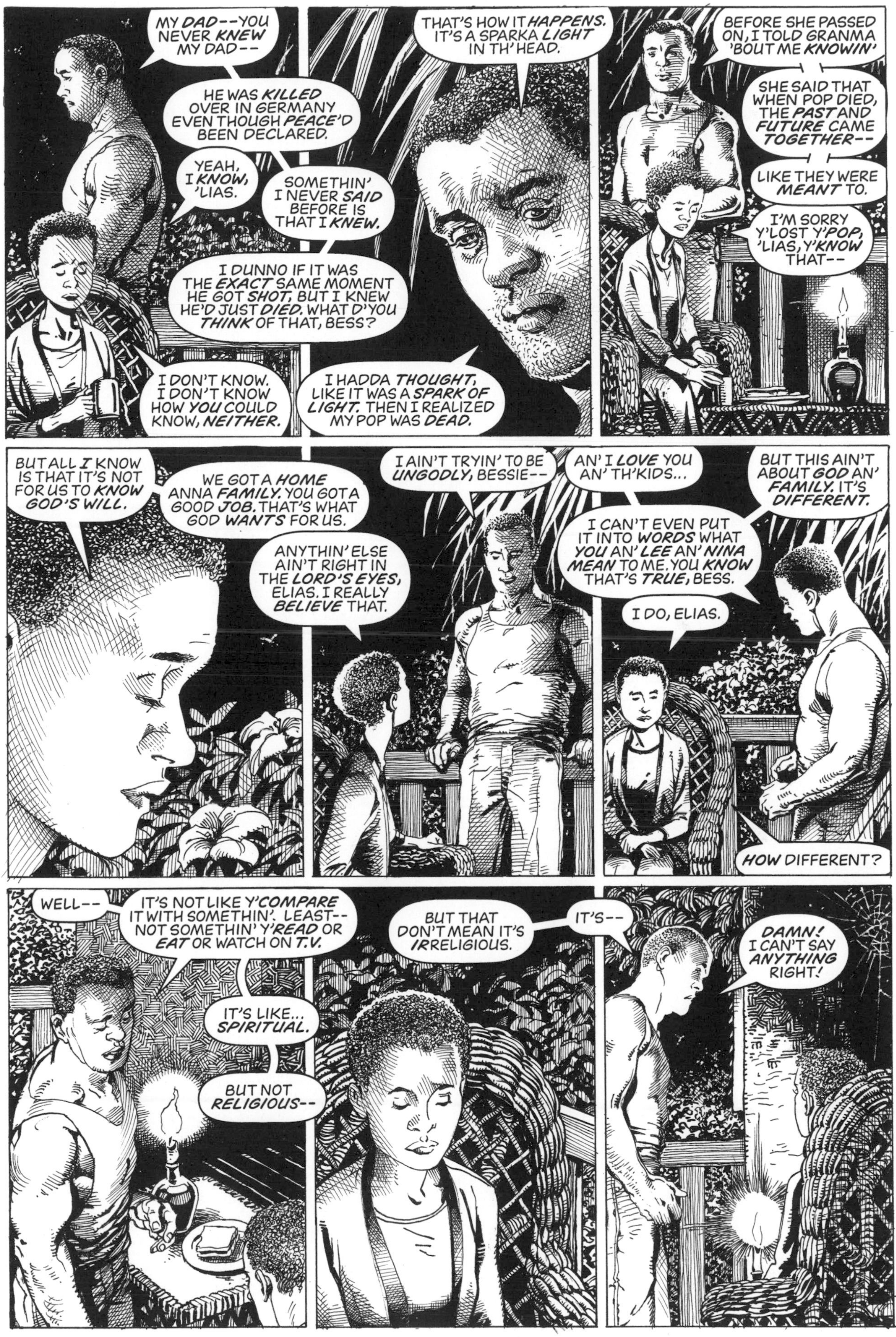
MY DAD--YOU NEVER KNEW MY DAD--
HE WAS KILLED OVER IN GERMANY EVEN THOUGH PEACE'D BEEN DECLARED.
YEAH, I KNOW, 'LIAS.
SOMETHIN' I NEVER SAID BEFORE IS THAT I KNEW.
I DUNNO IF IT WAS THE EXACT SAME MOMENT HE GOT SHOT, BUT I KNEW HE'D JUST DIED. WHAT D'YOU THINK OF THAT, BESS?
I DON'T KNOW. I DON'T KNOW HOW YOU COULD KNOW, NEITHER.
THAT'S HOW IT HAPPENS. IT'S A SPARKA LIGHT IN TH' HEAD.
I HADDA THOUGHT, LIKE IT WAS A SPARK OF LIGHT. THEN I REALIZED MY POP WAS DEAD.
BEFORE SHE PASSED ON, I TOLD GRANMA 'BOUT ME KNOWIN'
SHE SAID THAT WHEN POP DIED, THE PAST AND FUTURE CAME TOGETHER--
LIKE THEY WERE MEANT TO.
I'M SORRY Y'LOST Y'POP, 'LIAS, Y'KNOW THAT--
BUT ALL I KNOW IS THAT IT'S NOT FOR US TO KNOW GOD'S WILL.
WE GOT A HOME ANNA FAMILY. YOU GOT A GOOD JOB. THAT'S WHAT GOD WANTS FOR US.
ANYTHIN' ELSE AIN'T RIGHT IN THE LORD'S EYES, ELIAS. I REALLY BELIEVE THAT.
I AIN'T TRYIN' TO BE UNGODLY, BESSIE--
AN' I LOVE YOU AN' TH'KIDS...
I CAN'T EVEN PUT IT INTO WORDS WHAT YOU AN' LEE AN' NINA MEAN TO ME. YOU KNOW THAT'S TRUE, BESS.
BUT THIS AIN'T ABOUT GOD AN' FAMILY. IT'S DIFFERENT.
I DO, ELIAS.
HOW DIFFERENT?
WELL--
IT'S NOT LIKE Y'COMPARE IT WITH SOMETHIN'. LEAST-- NOT SOMETHIN' Y'READ OR EAT OR WATCH ON T.V.
IT'S LIKE... SPIRITUAL.
BUT NOT RELIGIOUS--
BUT THAT DON'T MEAN IT'S IRRELIGIOUS.
IT'S--
DAMN! I CAN'T SAY ANYTHING RIGHT!

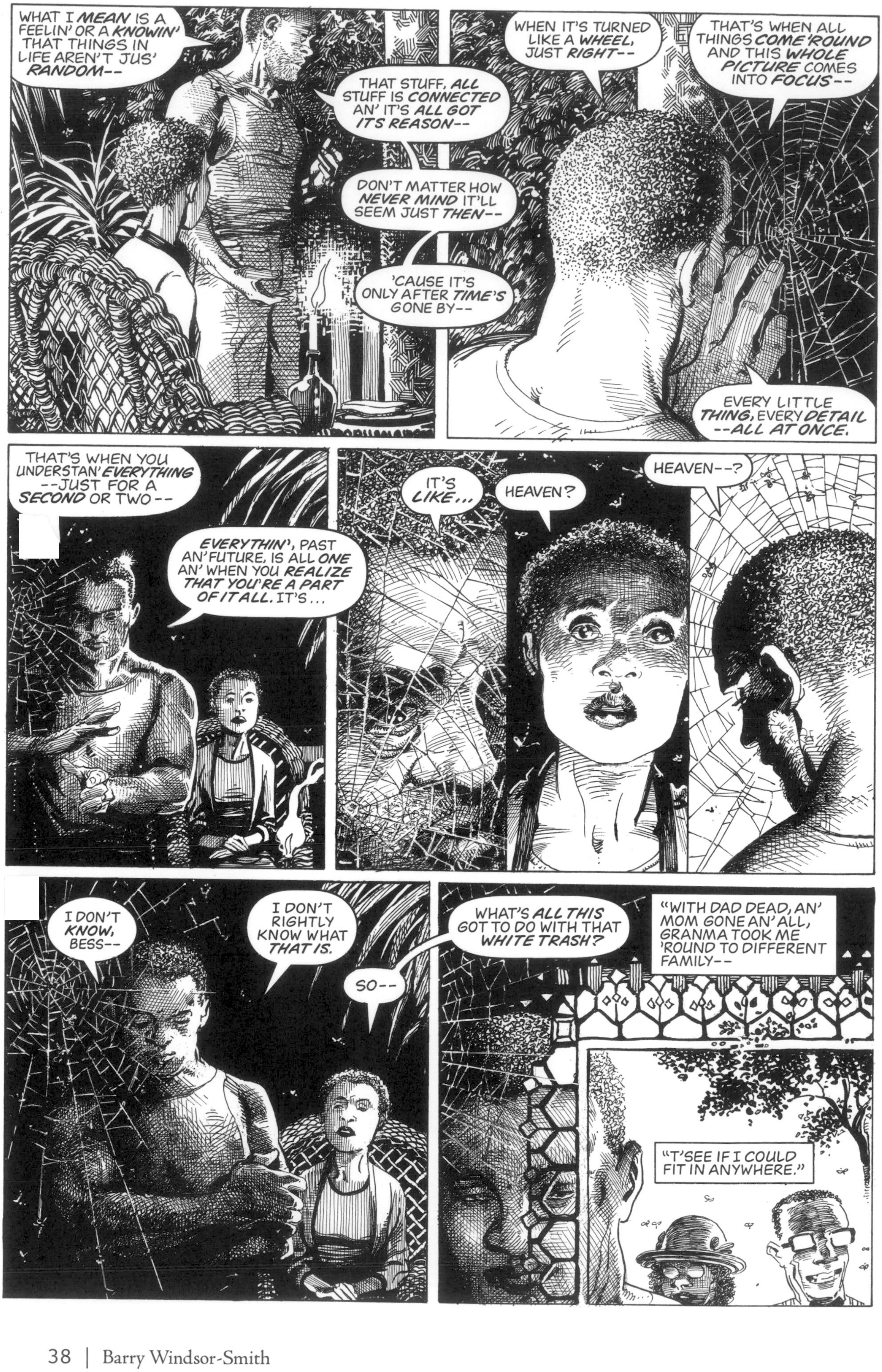
WHAT I MEAN IS A FEELIN' OR A KNOWIN' THAT THINGS IN LIFE AREN'T JUS' RANDOM--
THAT STUFF, ALL STUFF IS CONNECTED AN' IT'S ALL GOT ITS REASON--
DON'T MATTER HOW NEVER MIND IT'LL SEEM JUST THEN--
'CAUSE IT'S ONLY AFTER TIME'S GONE BY--
WHEN IT'S TURNED LIKE A WHEEL, JUST RIGHT--
THAT'S WHEN ALL THINGS COME 'ROUND AND THIS WHOLE PICTURE COMES INTO FOCUS--
EVERY LITTLE THING, EVERY DETAIL --ALL AT ONCE.
THAT'S WHEN YOU UNDERSTAN' EVERYTHING --JUST FOR A SECOND OR TWO--
EVERYTHIN', PAST AN' FUTURE, IS ALL ONE AN' WHEN YOU REALIZE THAT YOU'RE A PART OF IT ALL. IT'S...
IT'S LIKE...
HEAVEN?
HEAVEN--?
I DON'T KNOW, BESS--
I DON'T RIGHTLY KNOW WHAT THAT IS.
SO--
WHAT'S ALL THIS GOT TO DO WITH THAT WHITE TRASH?
"WITH DAD DEAD, AN' MOM GONE AN' ALL, GRANMA TOOK ME 'ROUND TO DIFFERENT FAMILY--
"T'SEE IF I COULD FIT IN ANYWHERE."

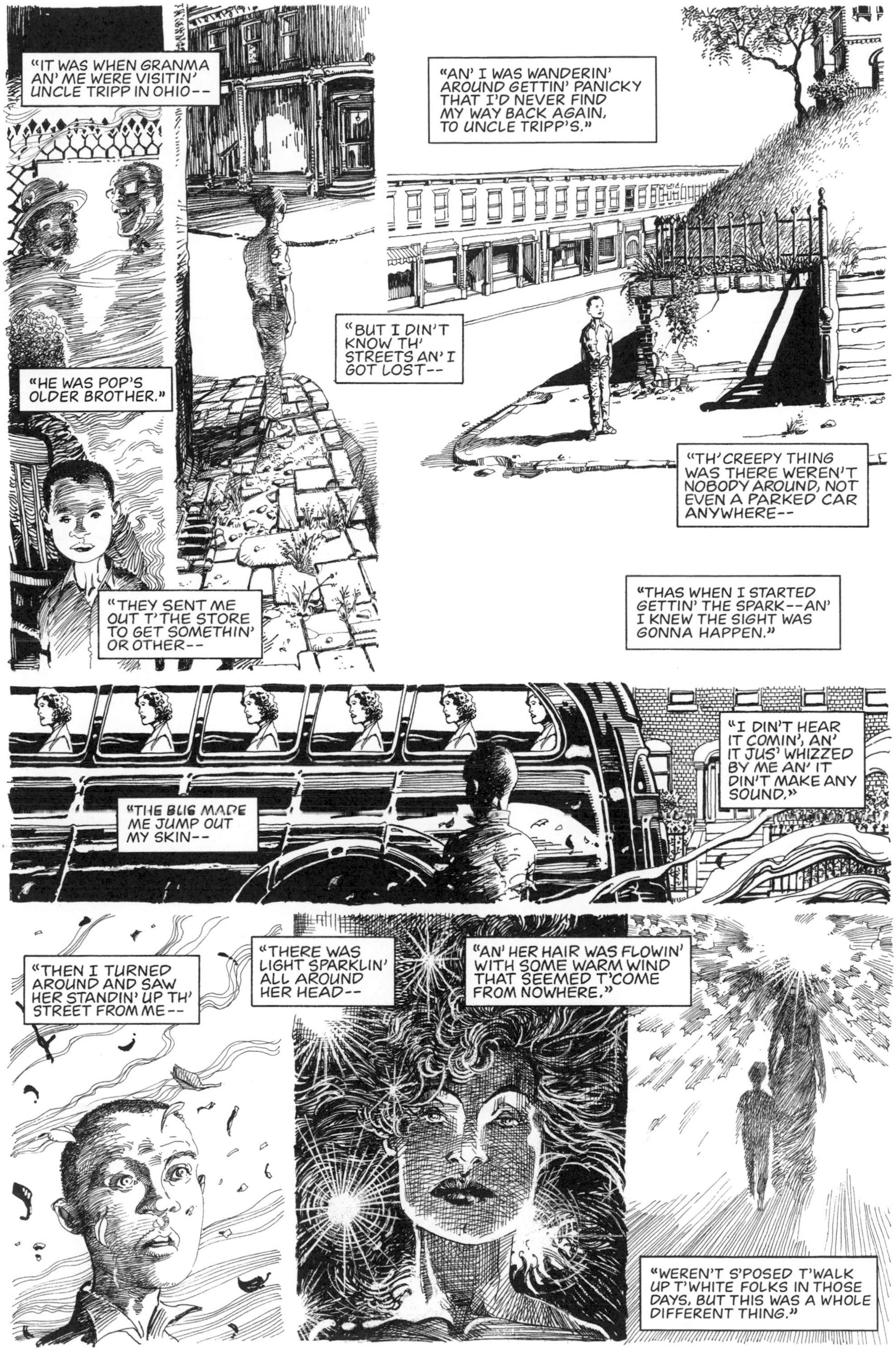
"IT WAS WHEN GRANMA AN' ME WERE VISITIN' UNCLE TRIPP IN OHIO--
"HE WAS POP'S OLDER BROTHER."
"THEY SENT ME OUT T' THE STORE TO GET SOMETHIN' OR OTHER--
"BUT I DIN'T KNOW TH' STREETS AN' I GOT LOST--
"AN' I WAS WANDERIN' AROUND GETTIN' PANICKY THAT I'D NEVER FIND MY WAY BACK AGAIN, TO UNCLE TRIPP'S."
"TH' CREEPY THING WAS THERE WEREN'T NOBODY AROUND, NOT EVEN A PARKED CAR ANYWHERE--
"THAS WHEN I STARTED GETTIN' THE SPARK--AN' I KNEW THE SIGHT WAS GONNA HAPPEN."
"THE BUS MADE ME JUMP OUT MY SKIN--
"I DIN'T HEAR IT COMIN', AN' IT JUS' WHIZZED BY ME AN' IT DIN'T MAKE ANY SOUND."
"THEN I TURNED AROUND AND SAW HER STANDIN' UP TH' STREET FROM ME--
"THERE WAS LIGHT SPARKLIN' ALL AROUND HER HEAD--
"AN' HER HAIR WAS FLOWIN' WITH SOME WARM WIND THAT SEEMED T'COME FROM NOWHERE."
"WEREN'T S'POSED T'WALK UP T'WHITE FOLKS IN THOSE DAYS, BUT THIS WAS A WHOLE DIFFERENT THING."

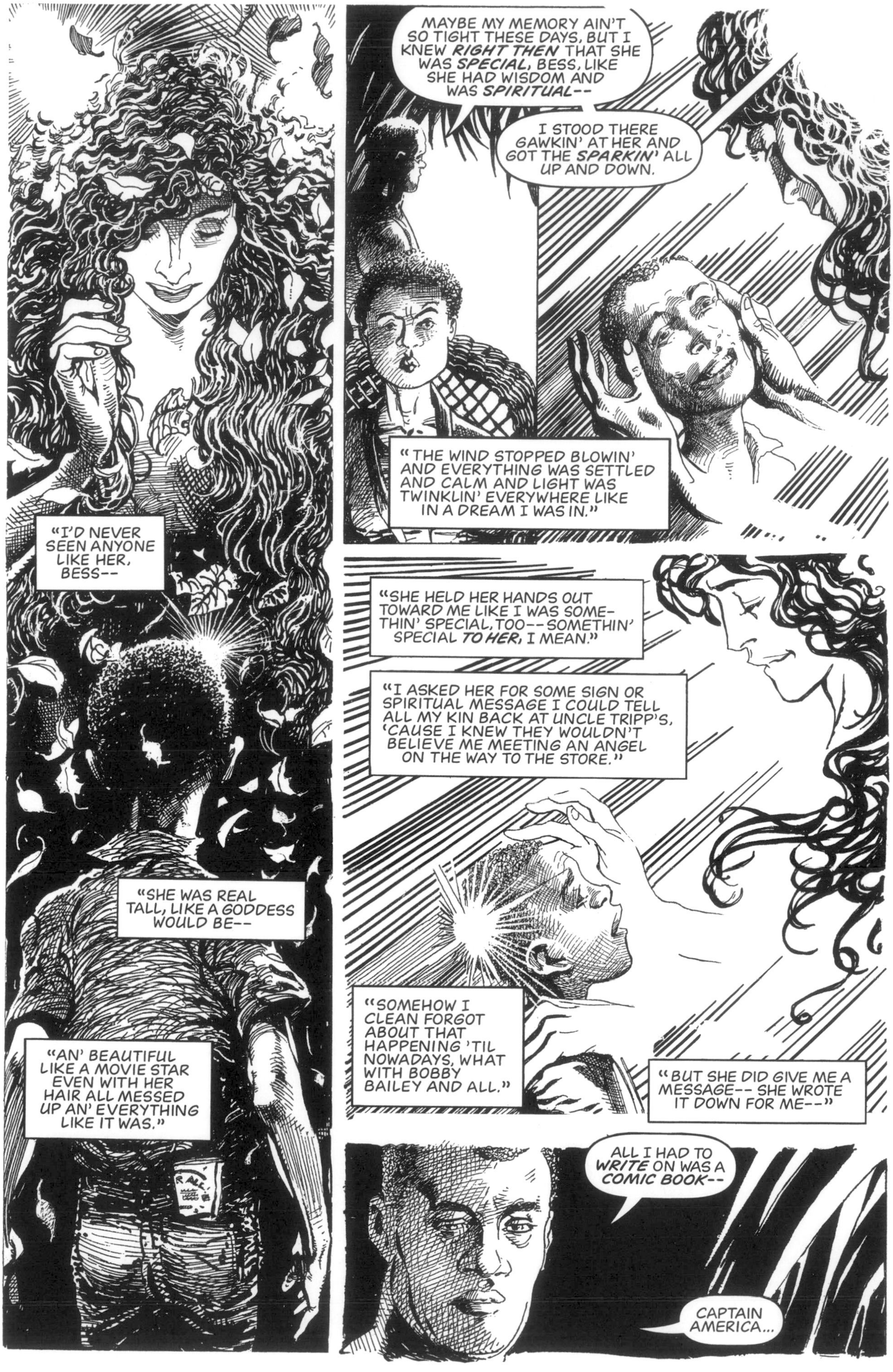
"I'D NEVER SEEN ANYONE LIKE HER, BESS--
"SHE WAS REAL TALL, LIKE A GODDESS WOULD BE--
"AN' BEAUTIFUL LIKE A MOVIE STAR EVEN WITH HER HAIR ALL MESSED UP AN' EVERYTHING LIKE IT WAS."
MAYBE MY MEMORY AIN'T SO TIGHT THESE DAYS, BUT I KNEW RIGHT THEN THAT SHE WAS SPECIAL, BESS, LIKE SHE HAD WISDOM AND WAS SPIRITUAL--
I STOOD THERE GAWKIN' AT HER AND GOT THE SPARKIN' ALL UP AND DOWN.
"THE WIND STOPPED BLOWIN' AND EVERYTHING WAS SETTLED AND CALM AND LIGHT WAS TWINKLIN' EVERYWHERE LIKE IN A DREAM I WAS IN."
"SHE HELD HER HANDS OUT TOWARD ME LIKE I WAS SOMETHIN' SPECIAL, TOO--SOMETHIN' SPECIAL TO HER, I MEAN."
"I ASKED HER FOR SOME SIGN OR SPIRITUAL MESSAGE I COULD TELL ALL MY KIN BACK AT UNCLE TRIPP'S, 'CAUSE I KNEW THEY WOULDN'T BELIEVE ME MEETING AN ANGEL ON THE WAY TO THE STORE."
"SOMEHOW I CLEAN FORGOT ABOUT THAT HAPPENING 'TIL NOWADAYS, WHAT WITH BOBBY BAILEY AND ALL."
"BUT SHE DID GIVE ME A MESSAGE-- SHE WROTE IT DOWN FOR ME--"
ALL I HAD TO WRITE ON WAS A COMIC BOOK--
CAPTAIN AMERICA...

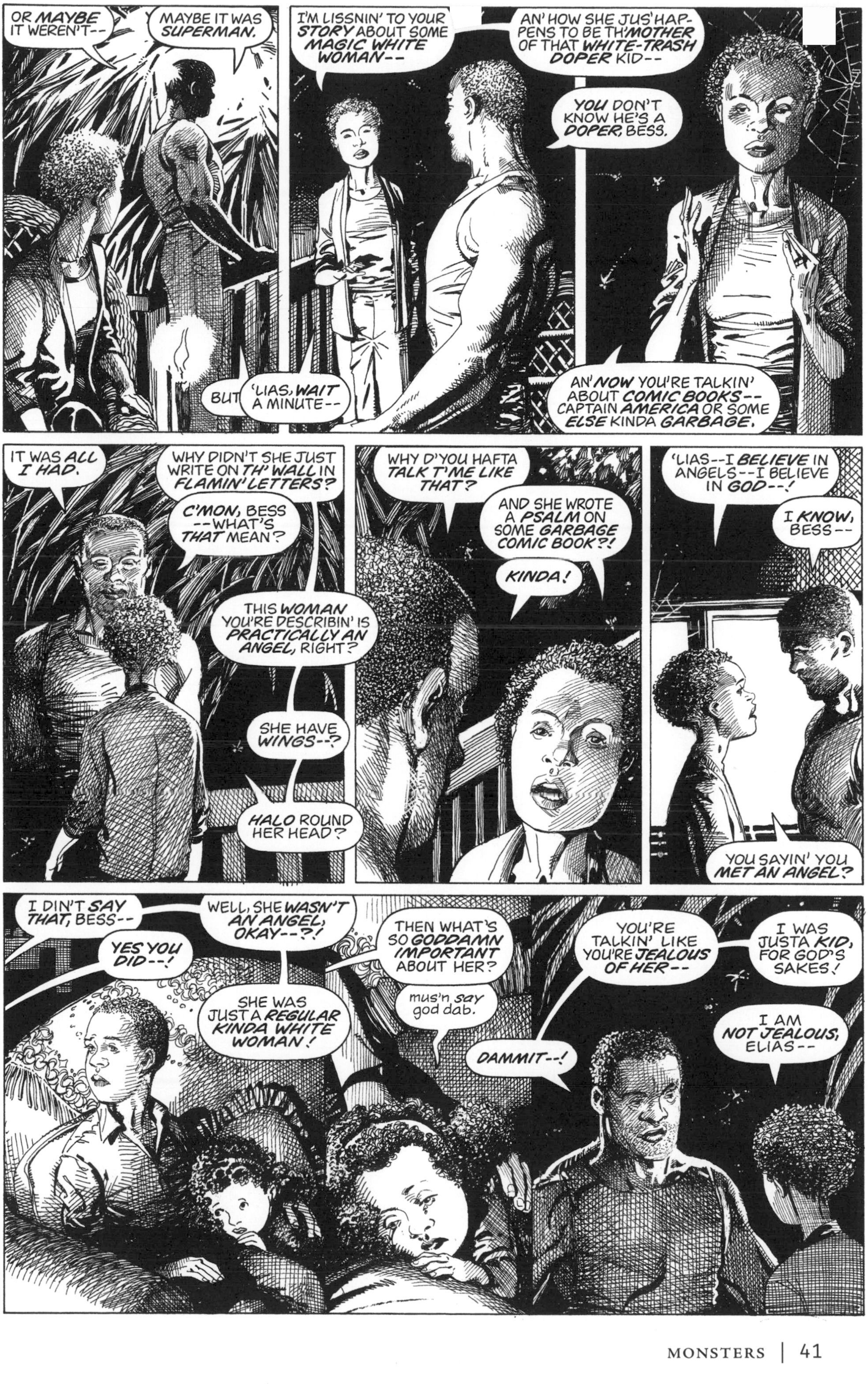
OR MAYBE IT WEREN'T--
MAYBE IT WAS SUPERMAN.
BUT
'LIAS, WAIT A MINUTE--
I'M LISSNIN' TO YOUR STORY ABOUT SOME MAGIC WHITE WOMAN--
AN' HOW SHE JUS' HAPPENS TO BE TH' MOTHER OF THAT WHITE-TRASH DOPER KID--
YOU DON'T KNOW HE'S A DOPER, BESS.
AN' NOW YOU'RE TALKIN' ABOUT COMIC BOOKS-- CAPTAIN AMERICA OR SOME ELSE KINDA GARBAGE.
IT WAS ALL I HAD.
WHY DIDN'T SHE JUST WRITE ON TH' WALL IN FLAMIN' LETTERS?
C'MON, BESS --WHAT'S THAT MEAN?
THIS WOMAN YOU'RE DESCRIBIN' IS PRACTICALLY AN ANGEL, RIGHT?
SHE HAVE WINGS--?
HALO ROUND HER HEAD?
WHY D'YOU HAFTA TALK T'ME LIKE THAT?
AND SHE WROTE A PSALM ON SOME GARBAGE COMIC BOOK?!
KINDA!
'LIAS--I BELIEVE IN ANGELS--I BELIEVE IN GOD--!
I KNOW, BESS--
YOU SAYIN' YOU MET AN ANGEL?
I DIN'T SAY THAT, BESS--
YES YOU DID--!
WELL, SHE WASN'T AN ANGEL, OKAY--?!
SHE WAS JUST A REGULAR KINDA WHITE WOMAN!
THEN WHAT'S SO GODDAMN IMPORTANT ABOUT HER?
mus'n say god dab.
YOU'RE TALKIN' LIKE YOU'RE JEALOUS OF HER--
DAMMIT--!
I WAS JUSTA KID, FOR GOD'S SAKES!
I AM NOT JEALOUS, ELIAS--

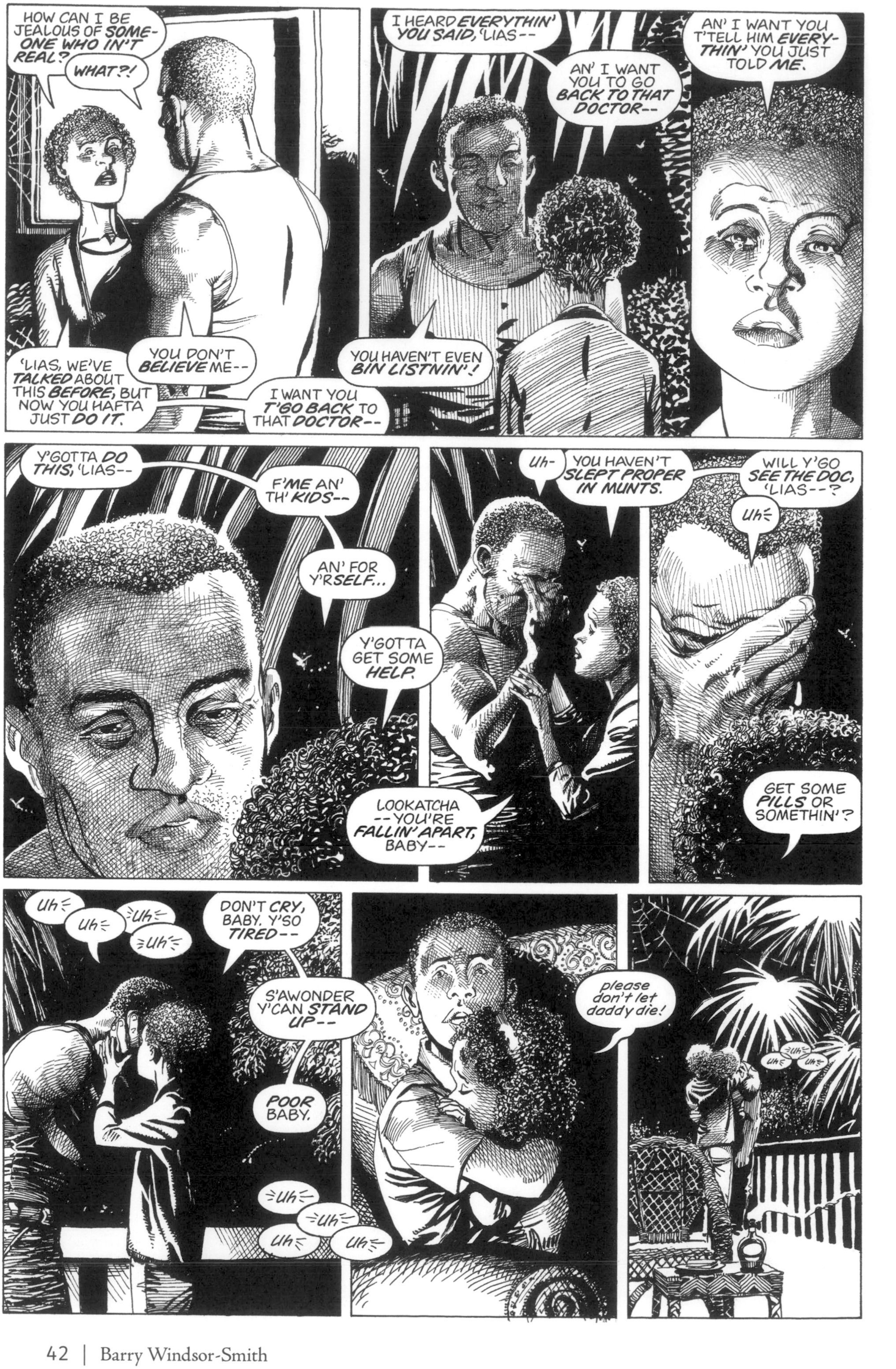
HOW CAN I BE JEALOUS OF SOME-ONE WHO IN'T REAL?
WHAT?!
'LIAS, WE'VE TALKED ABOUT THIS BEFORE, BUT NOW YOU HAFTA JUST DO IT.
YOU DON'T BELIEVE ME--
I WANT YOU T'GO BACK TO THAT DOCTOR--
I HEARD EVERYTHIN' YOU SAID, 'LIAS--
AN' I WANT YOU TO GO BACK TO THAT DOCTOR--
YOU HAVEN'T EVEN BIN LISTNIN'!
AN' I WANT YOU T'TELL HIM EVERY-THIN' YOU JUST TOLD ME.
Y'GOTTA DO THIS, 'LIAS--
F'ME AN' TH' KIDS--
AN' FOR Y'RSELF...
Y'GOTTA GET SOME HELP.
Uh-
YOU HAVEN'T SLEPT PROPER IN MUNTS.
LOOKATCHA --YOU'RE FALLIN' APART, BABY--
WILL Y'GO SEE THE DOC, 'LIAS--?
Uh
GET SOME PILLS OR SOMETHIN'?
Uh
Uh
Uh
Uh
DON'T CRY, BABY. Y'SO TIRED--
S'AWONDER Y'CAN STAND UP--
POOR BABY.
Uh
Uh
Uh
Uh
please don't let daddy die!
Uh
Uh
Uh

Fort Sherman Tuesday, August 18

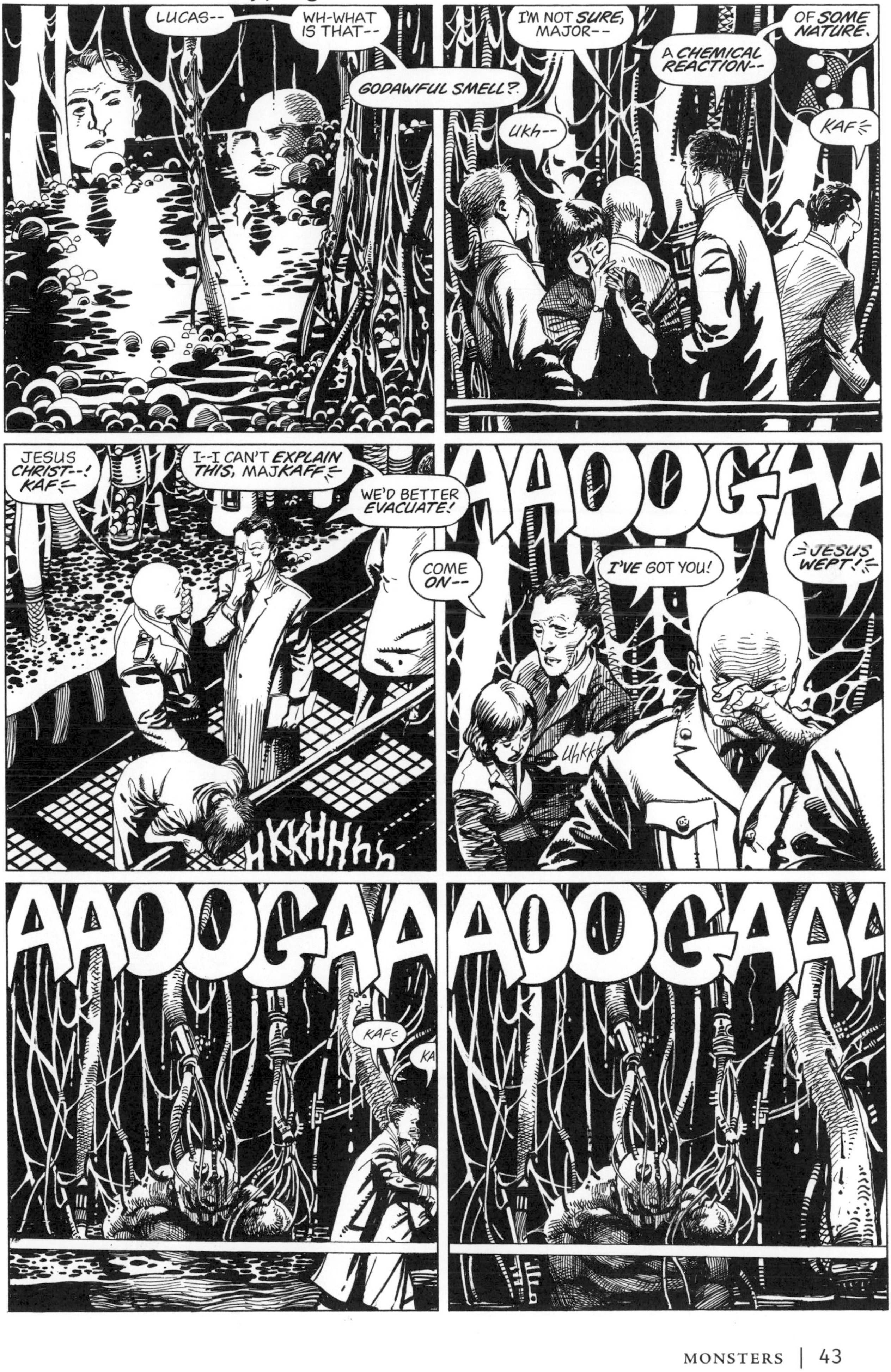
LUCAS--
WH-WHAT IS THAT--
GODAWFUL SMELL?
I'M NOT SURE, MAJOR--
A CHEMICAL REACTION--
OF SOME NATURE.
Ukh--
KAF
JESUS CHRIST--! KAF
I--I CAN'T EXPLAIN THIS, MAJKAFF
WE'D BETTER EVACUATE!
HKKHHhh
AAOOGHA
COME ON--
I'VE GOT YOU!
JESUS WEPT!
Uhkkk
AAOOGAA
KAF
KA
AOOGAAA

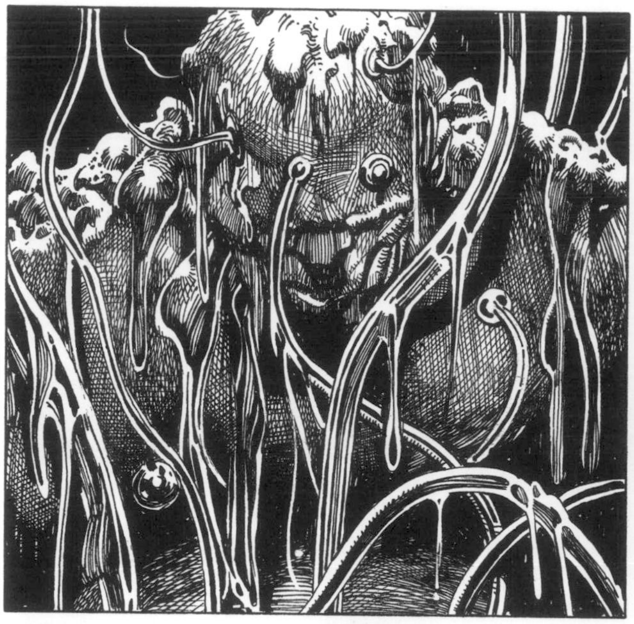

Los Angeles Tuesday, August 25

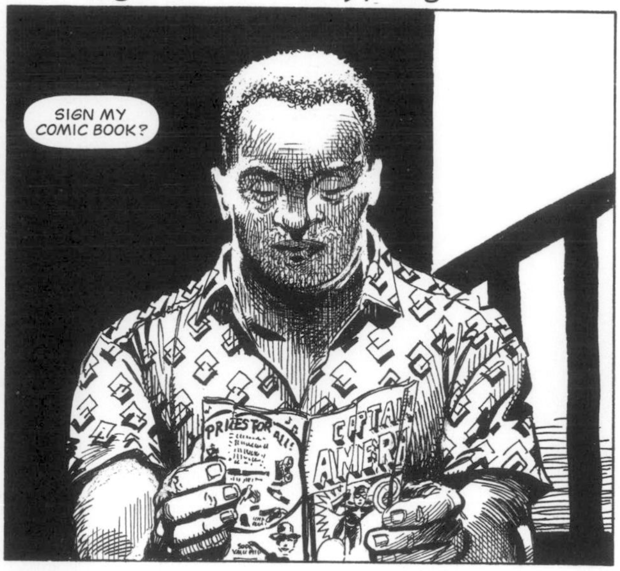
SIGN MY COMIC BOOK?
CAPTAIN AMERICA

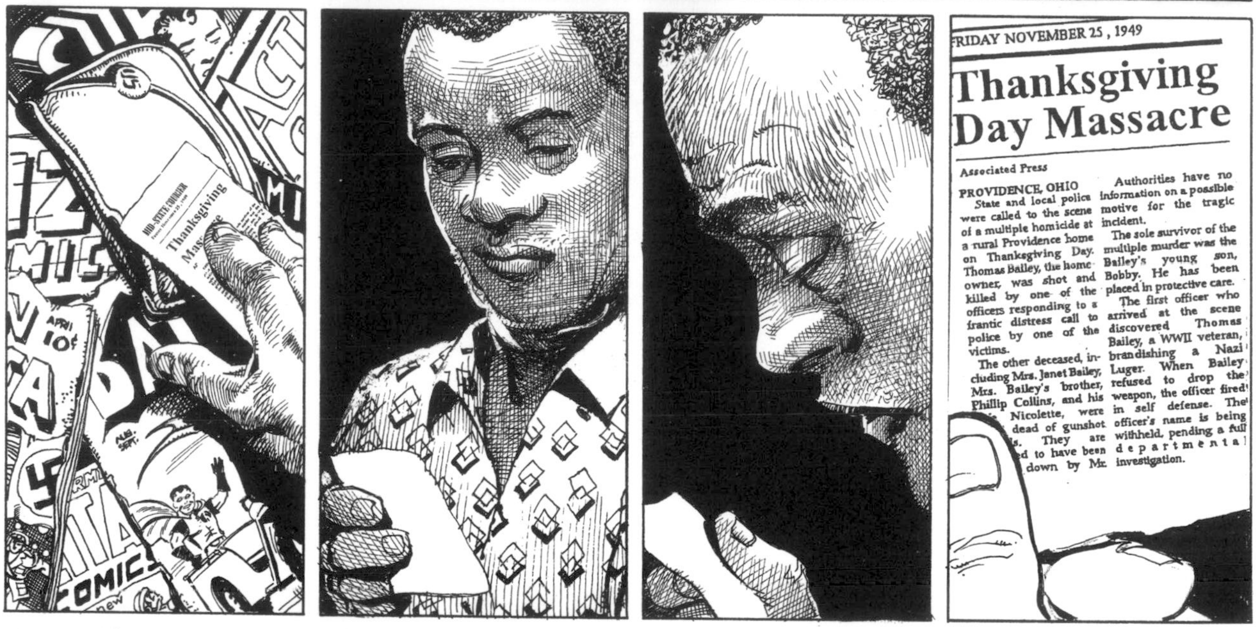
Thanksgiving
FRIDAY NOVEMBER 25, 1949
Thanksgiving Day Massacre
Associated Press
PROVIDENCE, OHIO
State and local police were called to the scene of a multiple homicide at a rural Providence home on Thanksgiving Day. Thomas Bailey, the home-owner, was shot and killed by one of the officers responding to a frantic distress call to police by one of the victims.
The other deceased, including Mrs. Janet Bailey, Mrs. Bailey's brother, Phillip Collins, and his
Nicolette, were
dead of gunshot
s. They are
d to have been
down by Mr.
Authorities have no information on a possible motive for the tragic incident.
The sole survivor of the multiple murder was the Bailey's young son, Bobby. He has been placed in protective care.
The first officer who arrived at the scene discovered Thomas Bailey, a WWII veteran, brandishing a Nazi Luger. When Bailey refused to drop the weapon, the officer fired in self defense. The officer's name is being withheld, pending a full departmental investigation.

Fort Sherman Saturday, September 19

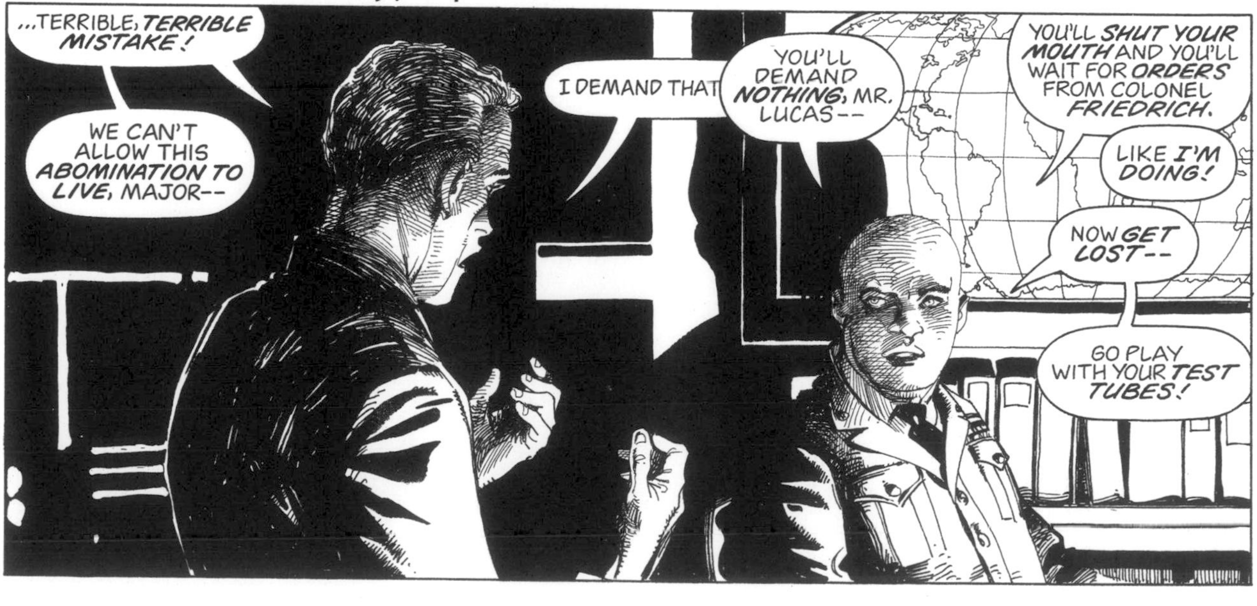
...TERRIBLE, TERRIBLE MISTAKE!
WE CAN'T ALLOW THIS ABOMINATION TO LIVE, MAJOR--
I DEMAND THAT
YOU'LL DEMAND NOTHING, MR. LUCAS--
YOU'LL SHUT YOUR MOUTH AND YOU'LL WAIT FOR ORDERS FROM COLONEL FRIEDRICH.
LIKE I'M DOING!
NOW GET LOST--
GO PLAY WITH YOUR TEST TUBES!

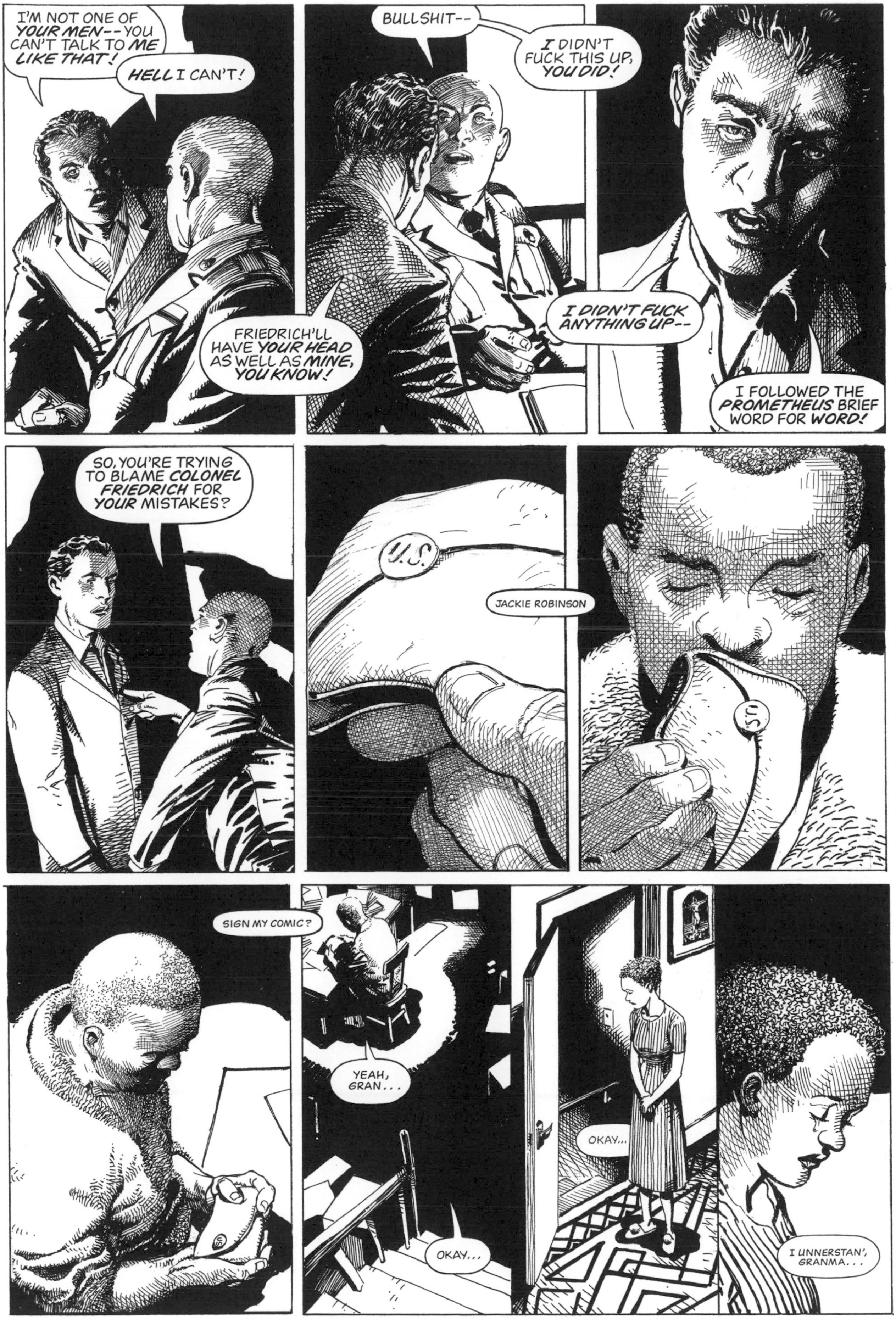
I'M NOT ONE OF YOUR MEN--YOU CAN'T TALK TO ME LIKE THAT!
HELL I CAN'T!
FRIEDRICH'LL HAVE YOUR HEAD AS WELL AS MINE, YOU KNOW!
BULLSHIT--
I DIDN'T FUCK THIS UP, YOU DID!
I DIDN'T FUCK ANYTHING UP--
I FOLLOWED THE PROMETHEUS BRIEF WORD FOR WORD!
SO, YOU'RE TRYING TO BLAME COLONEL FRIEDRICH FOR YOUR MISTAKES?
JACKIE ROBINSON
SIGN MY COMIC?
YEAH, GRAN...
OKAY...
OKAY...
I UNNERSTAN', GRANMA...

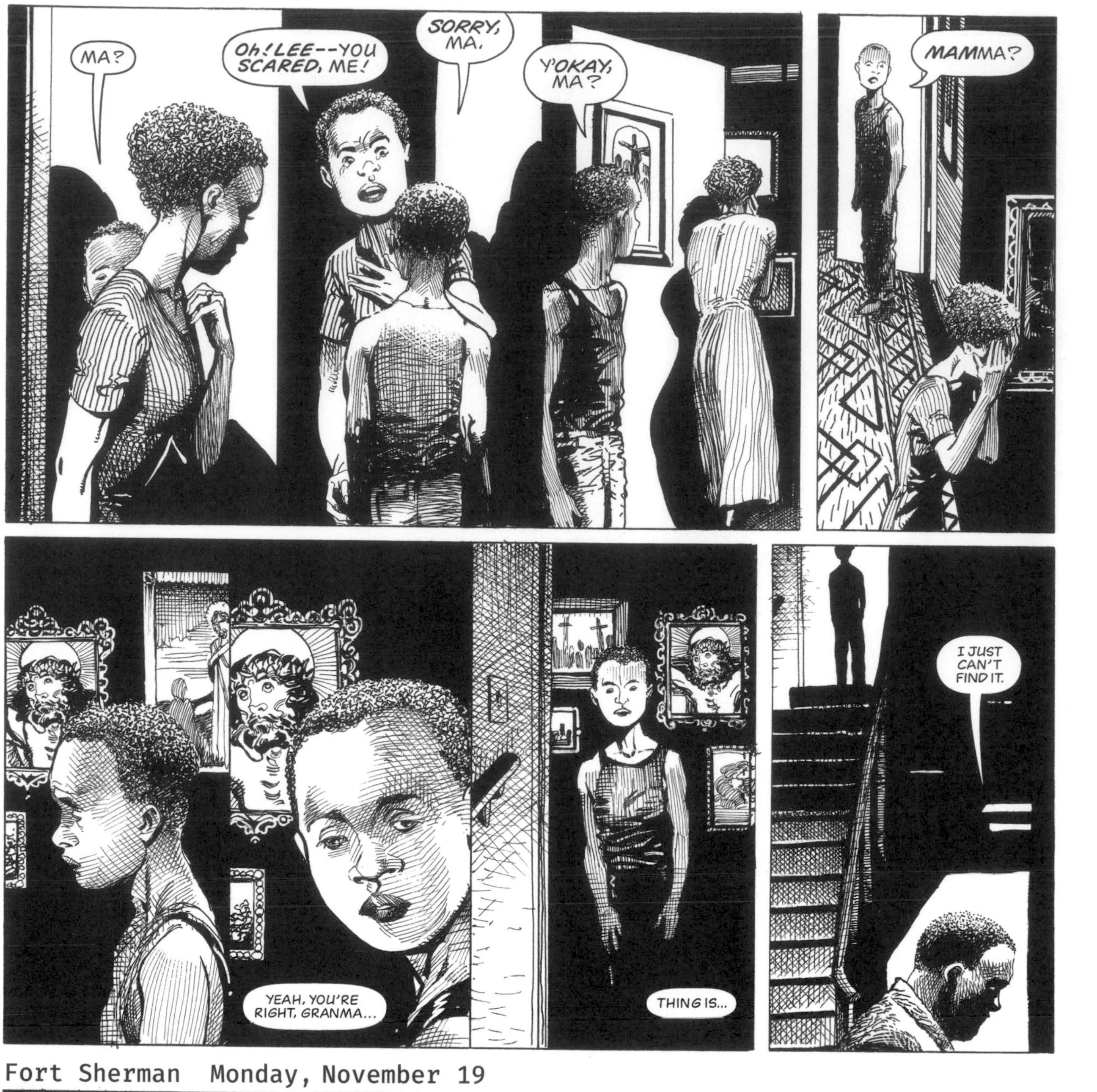
MA?
Oh! LEE--YOU SCARED ME!
SORRY, MA.
Y'OKAY, MA?
MAMMA?
YEAH, YOU'RE RIGHT, GRANMA...
THING IS...
I JUST CAN'T FIND IT.

Fort Sherman Monday, November 19

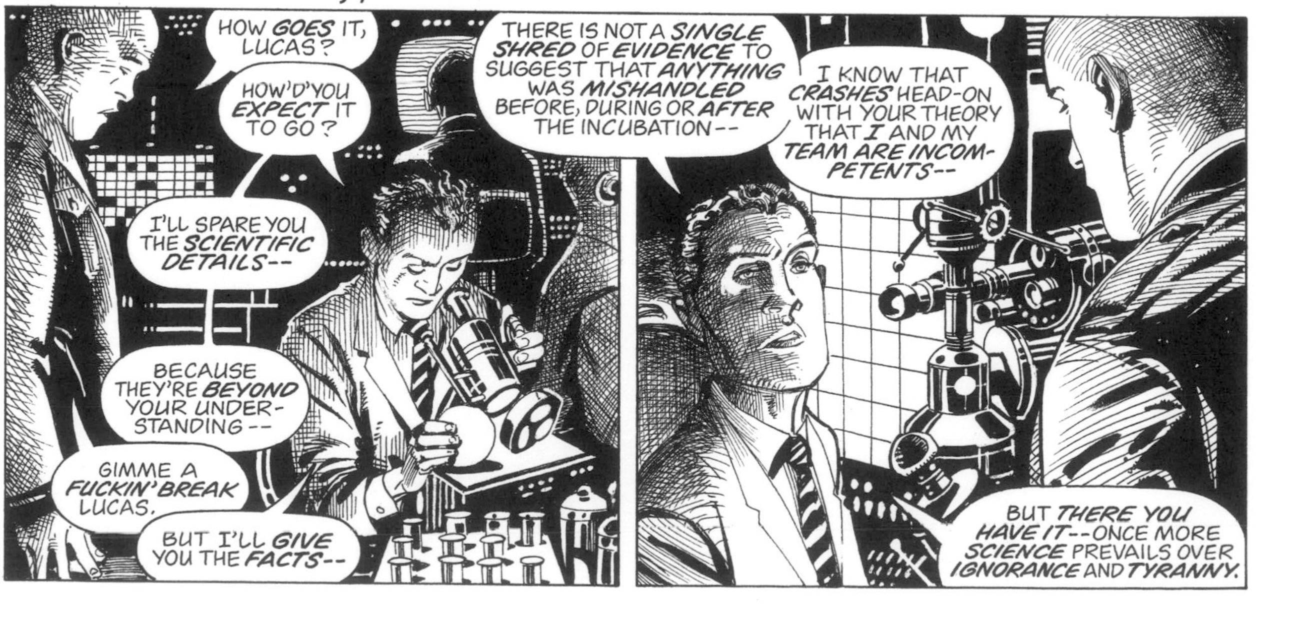
HOW GOES IT, LUCAS?
HOW'D'YOU EXPECT IT TO GO?
I'LL SPARE YOU THE SCIENTIFIC DETAILS--
BECAUSE THEY'RE BEYOND YOUR UNDER-STANDING--
GIMME A FUCKIN' BREAK LUCAS.
BUT I'LL GIVE YOU THE FACTS--
THERE IS NOT A SINGLE SHRED OF EVIDENCE TO SUGGEST THAT ANYTHING WAS MISHANDLED BEFORE, DURING OR AFTER THE INCUBATION--
I KNOW THAT CRASHES HEAD-ON WITH YOUR THEORY THAT I AND MY TEAM ARE INCOM-PETENTS--
BUT THERE YOU HAVE IT--ONCE MORE SCIENCE PREVAILS OVER IGNORANCE AND TYRANNY.

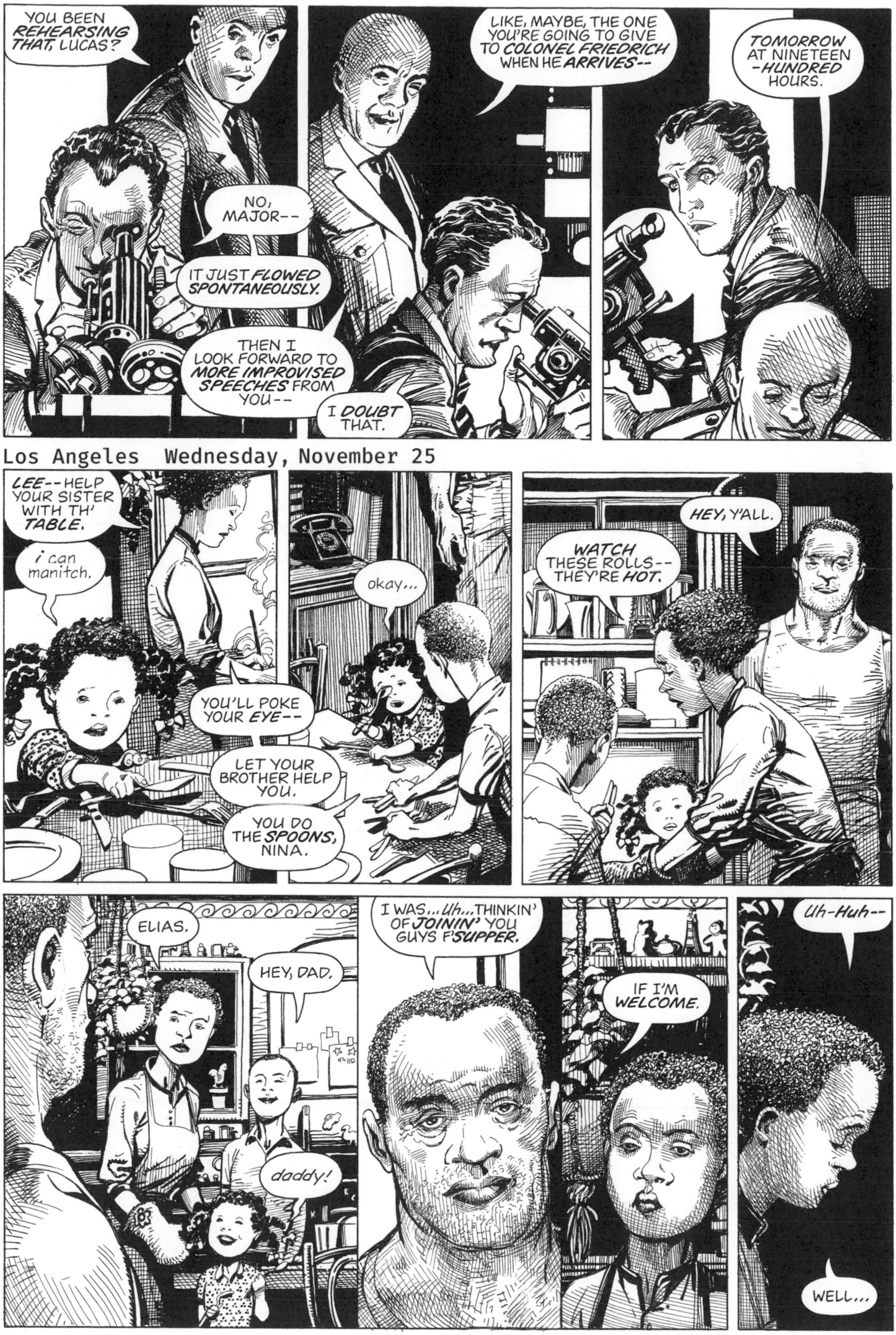
YOU BEEN *REHEARSING THAT,* LUCAS?
NO, MAJOR--
IT JUST *FLOWED SPONTANEOUSLY.*
THEN I LOOK FORWARD TO *MORE IMPROVISED SPEECHES* FROM YOU--
I *DOUBT* THAT.
LIKE, MAYBE, THE ONE YOU'RE GOING TO GIVE TO *COLONEL FRIEDRICH* WHEN HE *ARRIVES*--
TOMORROW AT NINETEEN-*HUNDRED* HOURS.
Los Angeles Wednesday, November 25
LEE--HELP YOUR SISTER WITH TH' *TABLE.*
i can manitch.
okay...
YOU'LL POKE YOUR *EYE*--
LET YOUR BROTHER HELP YOU.
YOU DO THE *SPOONS,* NINA.
HEY, Y'ALL.
WATCH THESE ROLLS--THEY'RE *HOT.*
ELIAS.
HEY, DAD.
daddy!
I WAS... *Uh*... THINKIN' OF *JOININ'* YOU GUYS F'*SUPPER.*
IF I'M *WELCOME.*
Uh-Huh--
WELL...

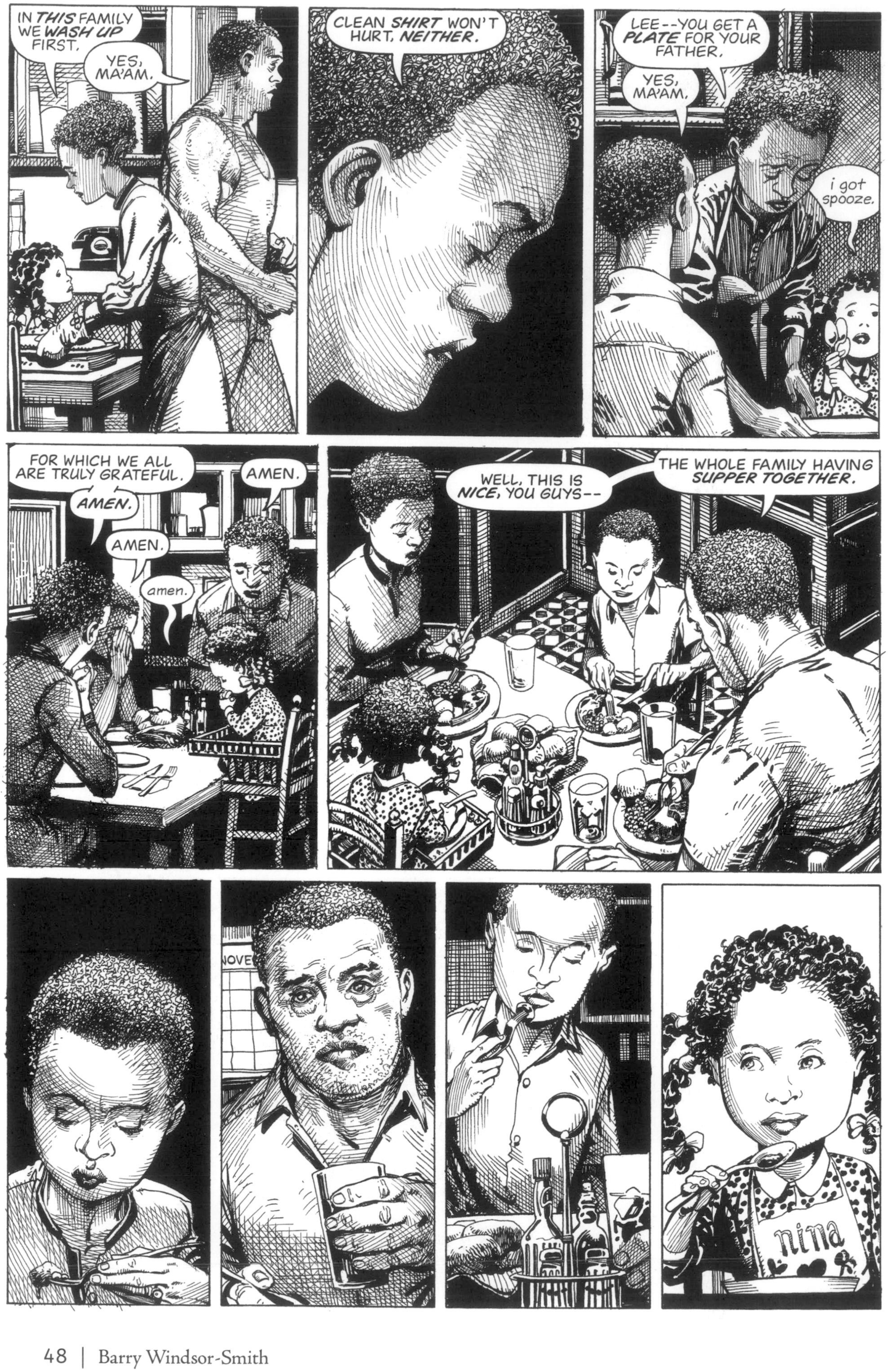
IN THIS FAMILY WE WASH UP FIRST.
YES, MA'AM.
CLEAN SHIRT WON'T HURT, NEITHER.
LEE--YOU GET A PLATE FOR YOUR FATHER.
YES, MA'AM.
i got spooze.
FOR WHICH WE ALL ARE TRULY GRATEFUL.
AMEN.
AMEN.
AMEN.
amen.
WELL, THIS IS NICE, YOU GUYS--
THE WHOLE FAMILY HAVING SUPPER TOGETHER.
NOVE
nina

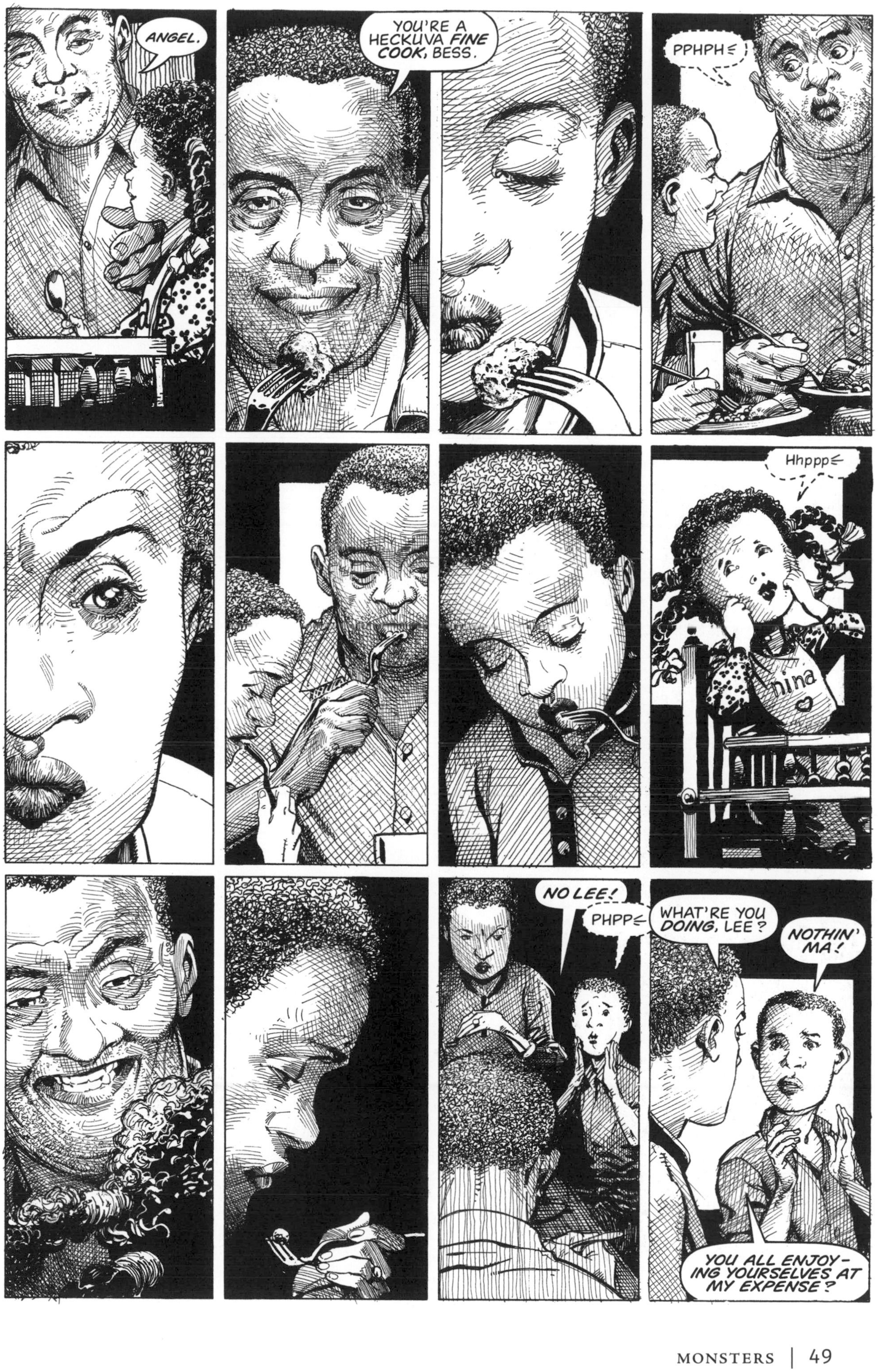
ANGEL.
YOU'RE A HECKUVA FINE COOK, BESS.
PPHPH
Hhppp
NO LEE!
PHPP
WHAT'RE YOU DOING, LEE?
NOTHIN' MA!
YOU ALL ENJOY-ING YOURSELVES AT MY EXPENSE?

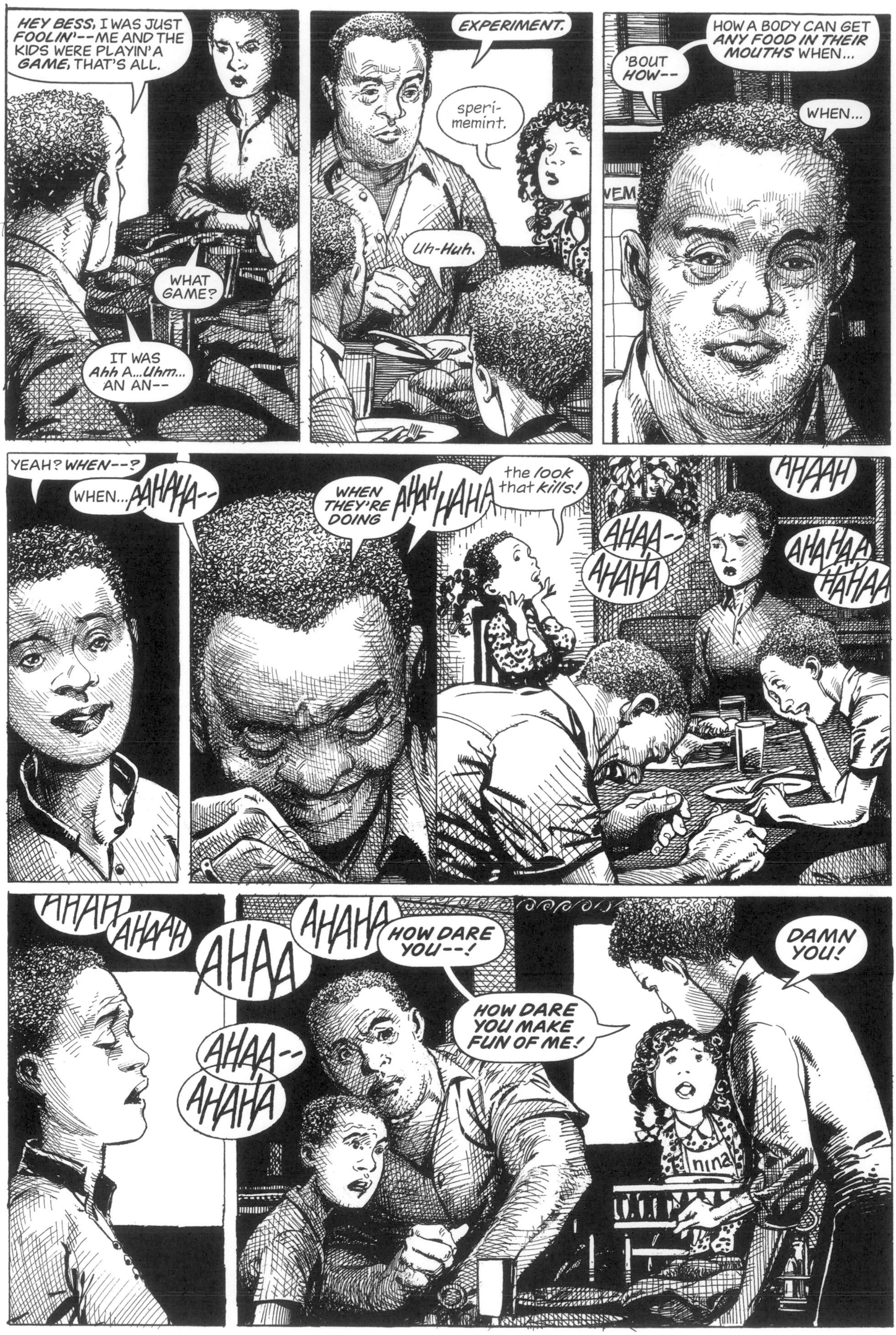
HEY BESS, I WAS JUST FOOLIN'--ME AND THE KIDS WERE PLAYIN' A GAME, THAT'S ALL.
WHAT GAME?
IT WAS Ahh A...Uhm... AN AN--
EXPERIMENT.
speri-memint.
Uh-Huh.
'BOUT HOW--
HOW A BODY CAN GET ANY FOOD IN THEIR MOUTHS WHEN...
WHEN...
YEAH? WHEN--?
WHEN... AAHAHA--
WHEN THEY'RE DOING
AHAH HAHA
the look that kills!
AHAAH
AHAA--
AHAHA
AHAHAA
HAHAA
AHAH
AHAAH
AHAA
AHAHA
HOW DARE YOU--!
HOW DARE YOU MAKE FUN OF ME!
DAMN YOU!
AHAA--
AHAHA
nina

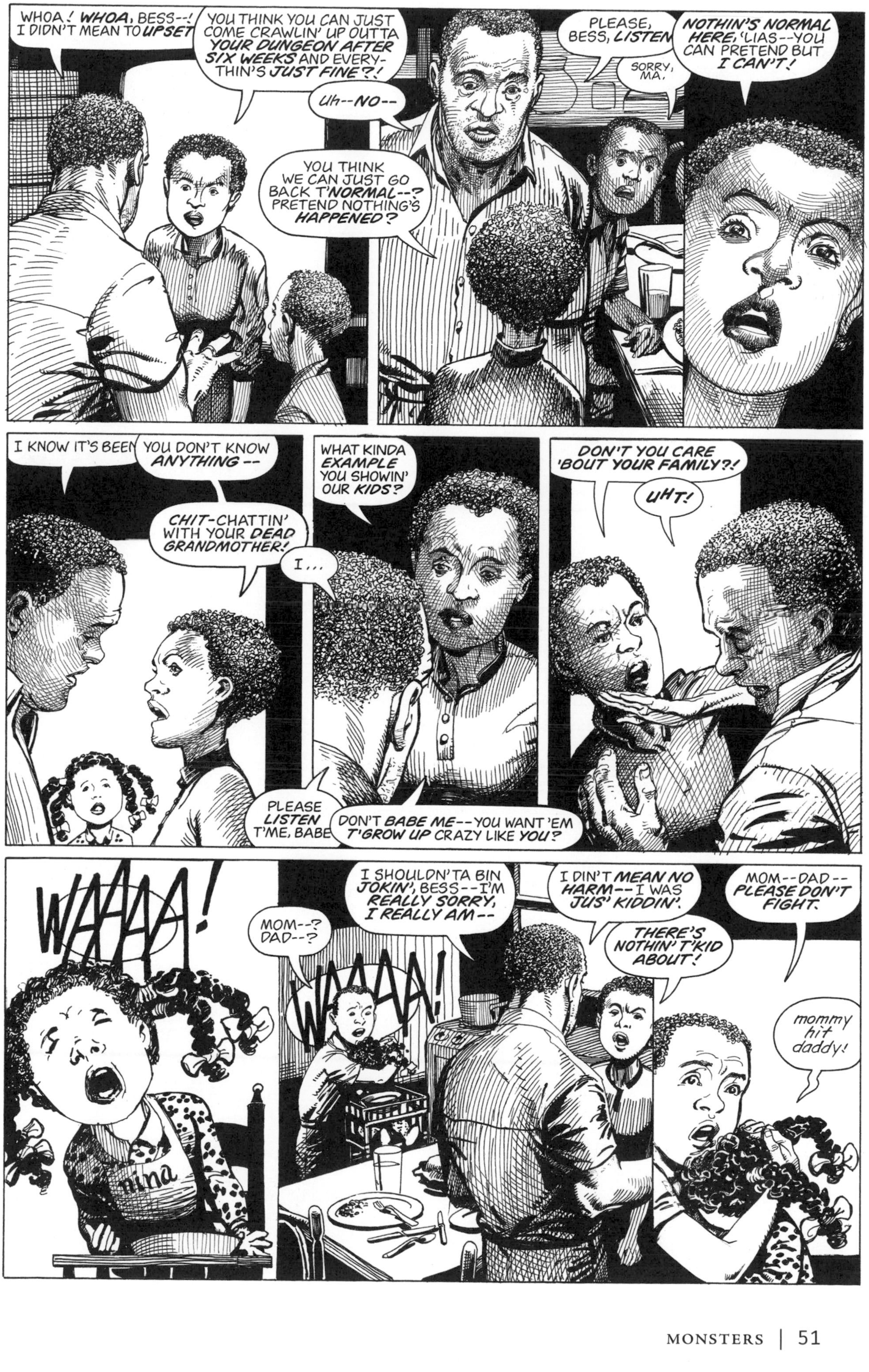
WHOA! WHOA, BESS--! I DIDN'T MEAN TO UPSET
YOU THINK YOU CAN JUST COME CRAWLIN' UP OUTTA YOUR DUNGEON AFTER SIX WEEKS AND EVERYTHIN'S JUST FINE?!
Uh--NO--
YOU THINK WE CAN JUST GO BACK T'NORMAL--? PRETEND NOTHING'S HAPPENED?
PLEASE, BESS, LISTEN
SORRY, MA.
NOTHIN'S NORMAL HERE, 'LIAS--YOU CAN PRETEND BUT I CAN'T!
I KNOW IT'S BEEN
YOU DON'T KNOW ANYTHING--
CHIT-CHATTIN' WITH YOUR DEAD GRANDMOTHER!
WHAT KINDA EXAMPLE YOU SHOWIN' OUR KIDS?
I...
PLEASE LISTEN T'ME, BABE
DON'T BABE ME--YOU WANT 'EM T'GROW UP CRAZY LIKE YOU?
DON'T YOU CARE 'BOUT YOUR FAMILY?!
UHT!
WAAAA!
nina
MOM--? DAD--?
I SHOULDN'TA BIN JOKIN', BESS--I'M REALLY SORRY, I REALLY AM--
WAAAA!
I DIN'T MEAN NO HARM--I WAS JUS' KIDDIN'.
THERE'S NOTHIN' T'KID ABOUT!
MOM--DAD--PLEASE DON'T FIGHT.
mommy hit daddy!

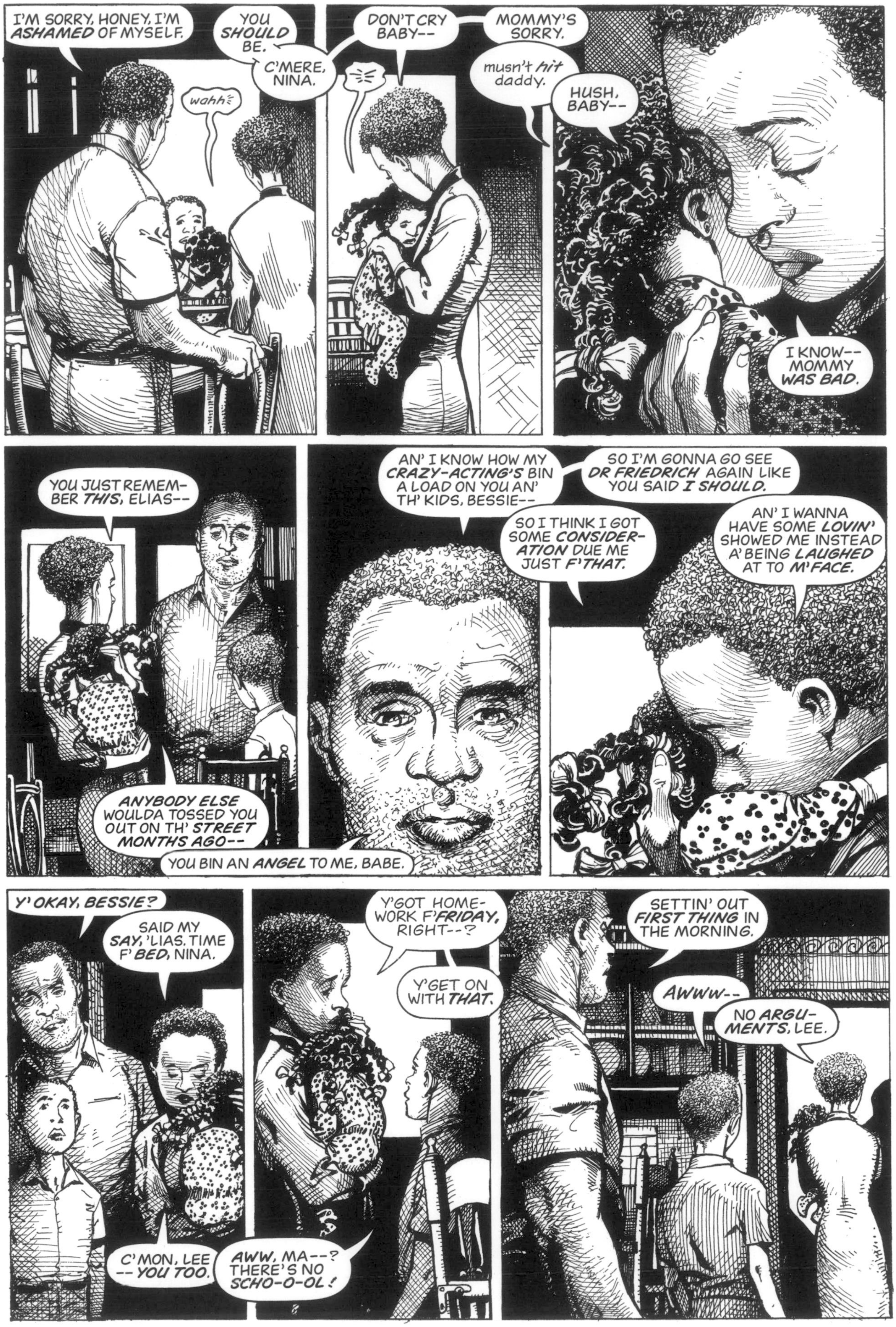
I'M SORRY, HONEY, I'M ASHAMED OF MYSELF.
YOU SHOULD BE.
C'MERE, NINA.
wahh
DON'T CRY BABY--
MOMMY'S SORRY.
musn't hit daddy.
HUSH, BABY--
I KNOW-- MOMMY WAS BAD.
YOU JUST REMEMBER THIS, ELIAS--
ANYBODY ELSE WOULDA TOSSED YOU OUT ON TH' STREET MONTHS AGO--
YOU BIN AN ANGEL TO ME, BABE.
AN' I KNOW HOW MY CRAZY-ACTING'S BIN A LOAD ON YOU AN' TH' KIDS, BESSIE--
SO I'M GONNA GO SEE DR FRIEDRICH AGAIN LIKE YOU SAID I SHOULD.
SO I THINK I GOT SOME CONSIDERATION DUE ME JUST F'THAT.
AN' I WANNA HAVE SOME LOVIN' SHOWED ME INSTEAD A' BEING LAUGHED AT TO M'FACE.
Y' OKAY, BESSIE?
SAID MY SAY, 'LIAS. TIME F' BED, NINA.
C'MON, LEE -- YOU TOO.
AWW, MA--? THERE'S NO SCHO-O-OL!
Y'GOT HOMEWORK F'FRIDAY, RIGHT--?
Y'GET ON WITH THAT.
SETTIN' OUT FIRST THING IN THE MORNING.
AWWW--
NO ARGUMENTS, LEE.

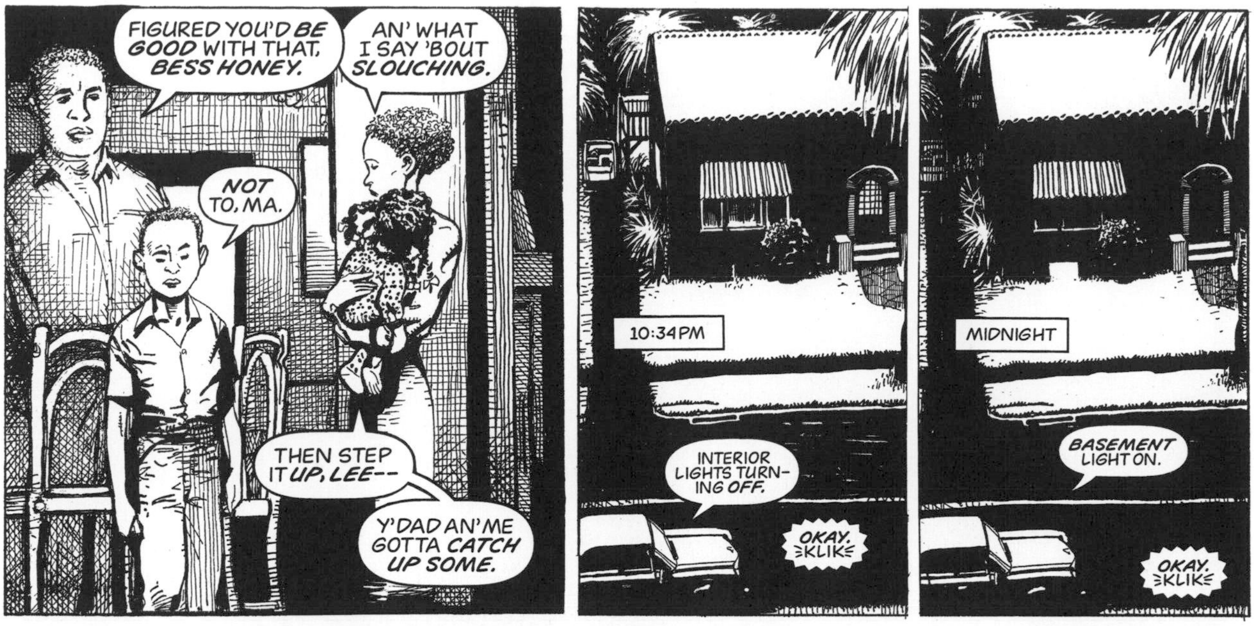
FIGURED YOU'D BE GOOD WITH THAT, BESS HONEY.
AN' WHAT I SAY 'BOUT SLOUCHING.
NOT TO, MA.
THEN STEP IT UP, LEE--
Y'DAD AN' ME GOTTA CATCH UP SOME.
10:34PM
INTERIOR LIGHTS TURNING OFF.
OKAY. KLIK
MIDNIGHT
BASEMENT LIGHT ON.
OKAY. KLIK

Fort Sherman Thursday, November 26

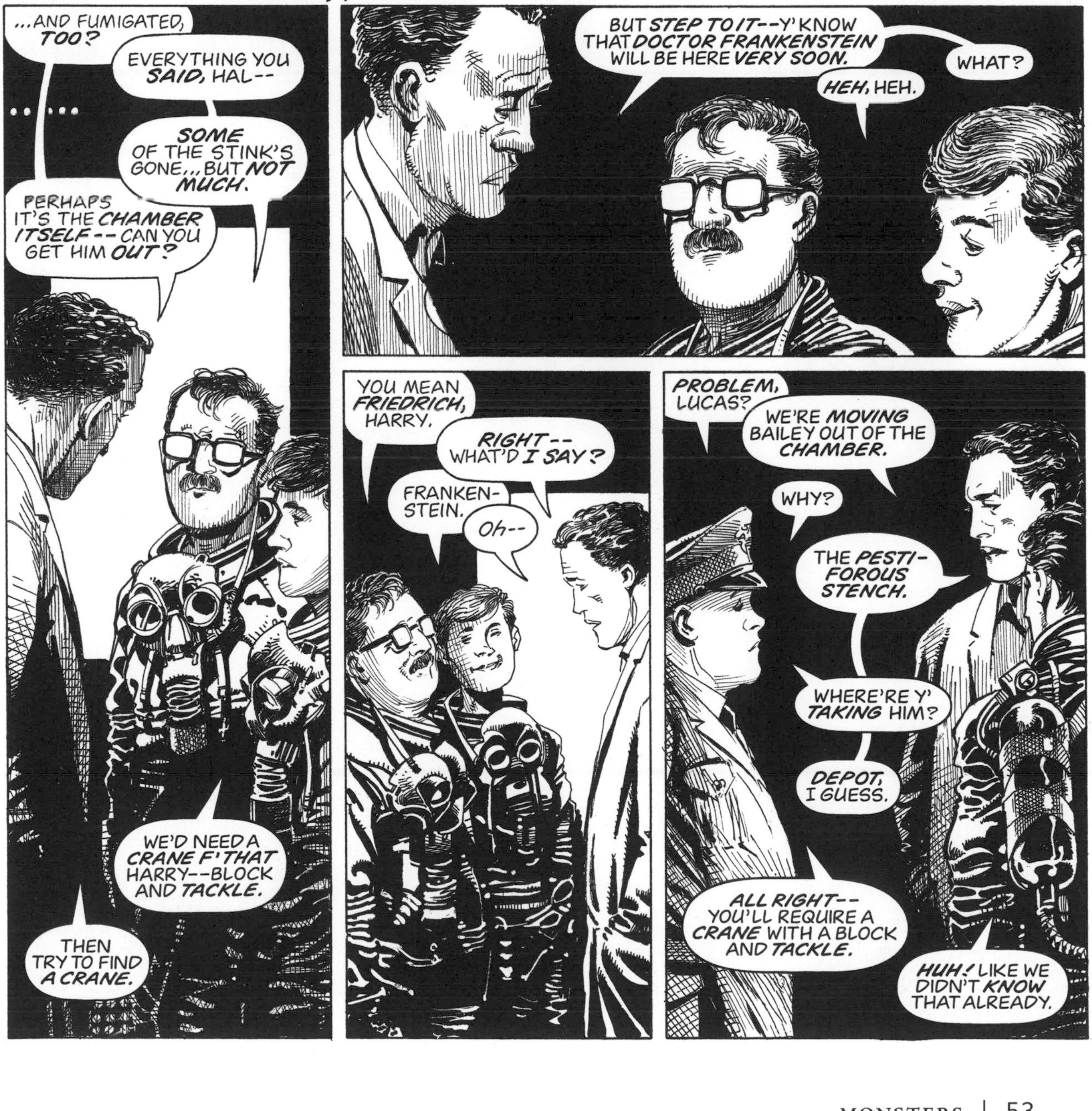
...AND FUMIGATED, TOO?
EVERYTHING YOU SAID, HAL--
......
SOME OF THE STINK'S GONE... BUT NOT MUCH.
PERHAPS IT'S THE CHAMBER ITSELF--CAN YOU GET HIM OUT?
WE'D NEED A CRANE F' THAT HARRY--BLOCK AND TACKLE.
THEN TRY TO FIND A CRANE.
BUT STEP TO IT--Y' KNOW THAT DOCTOR FRANKENSTEIN WILL BE HERE VERY SOON.
WHAT?
HEH, HEH.
YOU MEAN FRIEDRICH, HARRY.
RIGHT-- WHAT'D I SAY?
FRANKEN-STEIN.
Oh--
PROBLEM, LUCAS?
WE'RE MOVING BAILEY OUT OF THE CHAMBER.
WHY?
THE PESTI-FOROUS STENCH.
WHERE'RE Y' TAKING HIM?
DEPOT, I GUESS.
ALL RIGHT-- YOU'LL REQUIRE A CRANE WITH A BLOCK AND TACKLE.
HUH! LIKE WE DIDN'T KNOW THAT ALREADY.

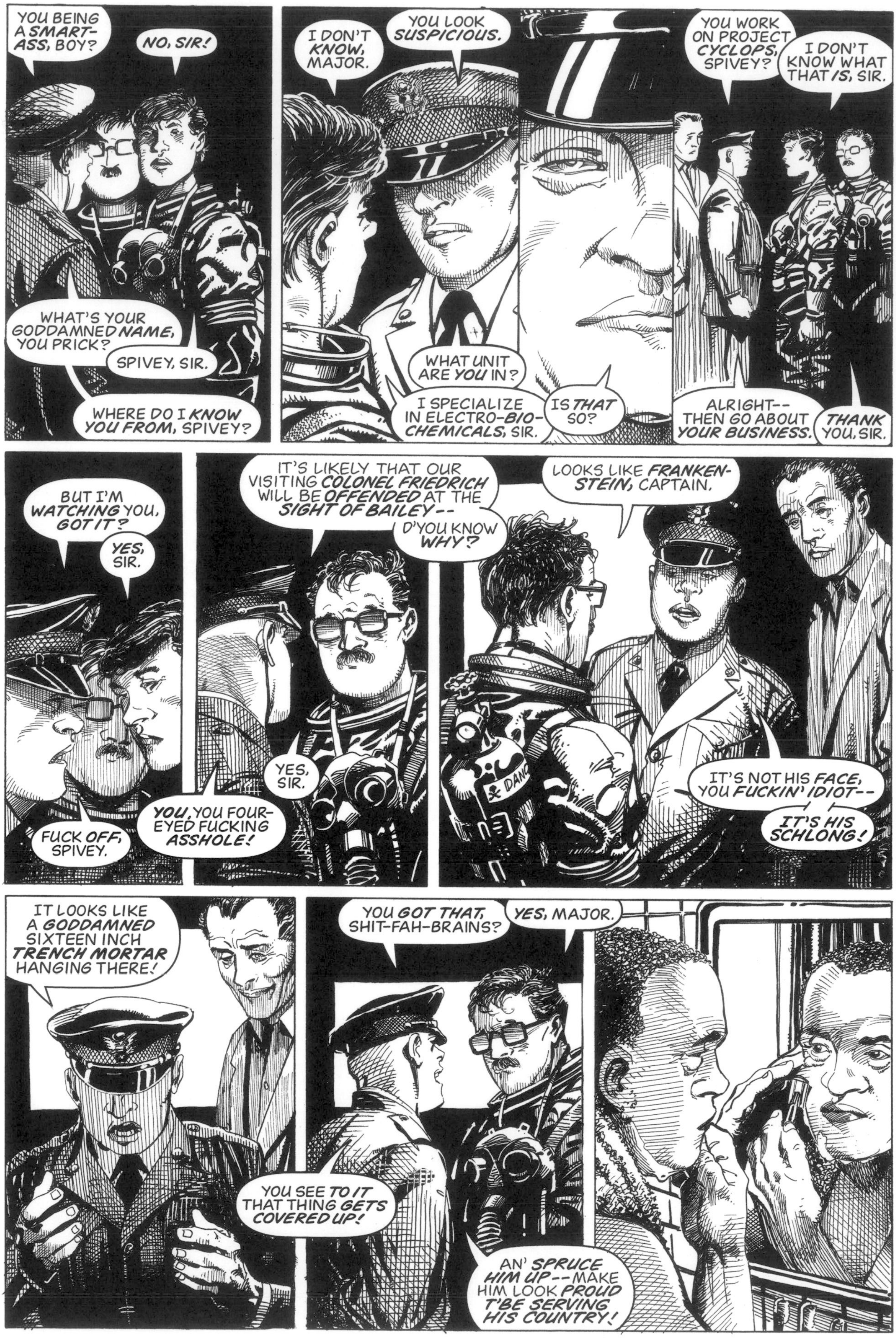
YOU BEING A SMART-ASS, BOY?
NO, SIR!
WHAT'S YOUR GODDAMNED NAME, YOU PRICK?
SPIVEY, SIR.
WHERE DO I KNOW YOU FROM, SPIVEY?
I DON'T KNOW, MAJOR.
YOU LOOK SUSPICIOUS.
WHAT UNIT ARE YOU IN?
I SPECIALIZE IN ELECTRO-BIO-CHEMICALS, SIR.
IS THAT SO?
YOU WORK ON PROJECT CYCLOPS, SPIVEY?
I DON'T KNOW WHAT THAT IS, SIR.
ALRIGHT-- THEN GO ABOUT YOUR BUSINESS.
THANK YOU, SIR.
BUT I'M WATCHING YOU, GOT IT?
YES, SIR.
FUCK OFF, SPIVEY.
YOU, YOU FOUR-EYED FUCKING ASSHOLE!
IT'S LIKELY THAT OUR VISITING COLONEL FRIEDRICH WILL BE OFFENDED AT THE SIGHT OF BAILEY--
D'YOU KNOW WHY?
YES, SIR.
LOOKS LIKE FRANKEN-STEIN, CAPTAIN.
IT'S NOT HIS FACE, YOU FUCKIN' IDIOT--
IT'S HIS SCHLONG!
IT LOOKS LIKE A GODDAMNED SIXTEEN INCH TRENCH MORTAR HANGING THERE!
YOU GOT THAT, SHIT-FAH-BRAINS?
YES, MAJOR.
YOU SEE TO IT THAT THING GETS COVERED UP!
AN' SPRUCE HIM UP--MAKE HIM LOOK PROUD T'BE SERVING HIS COUNTRY!

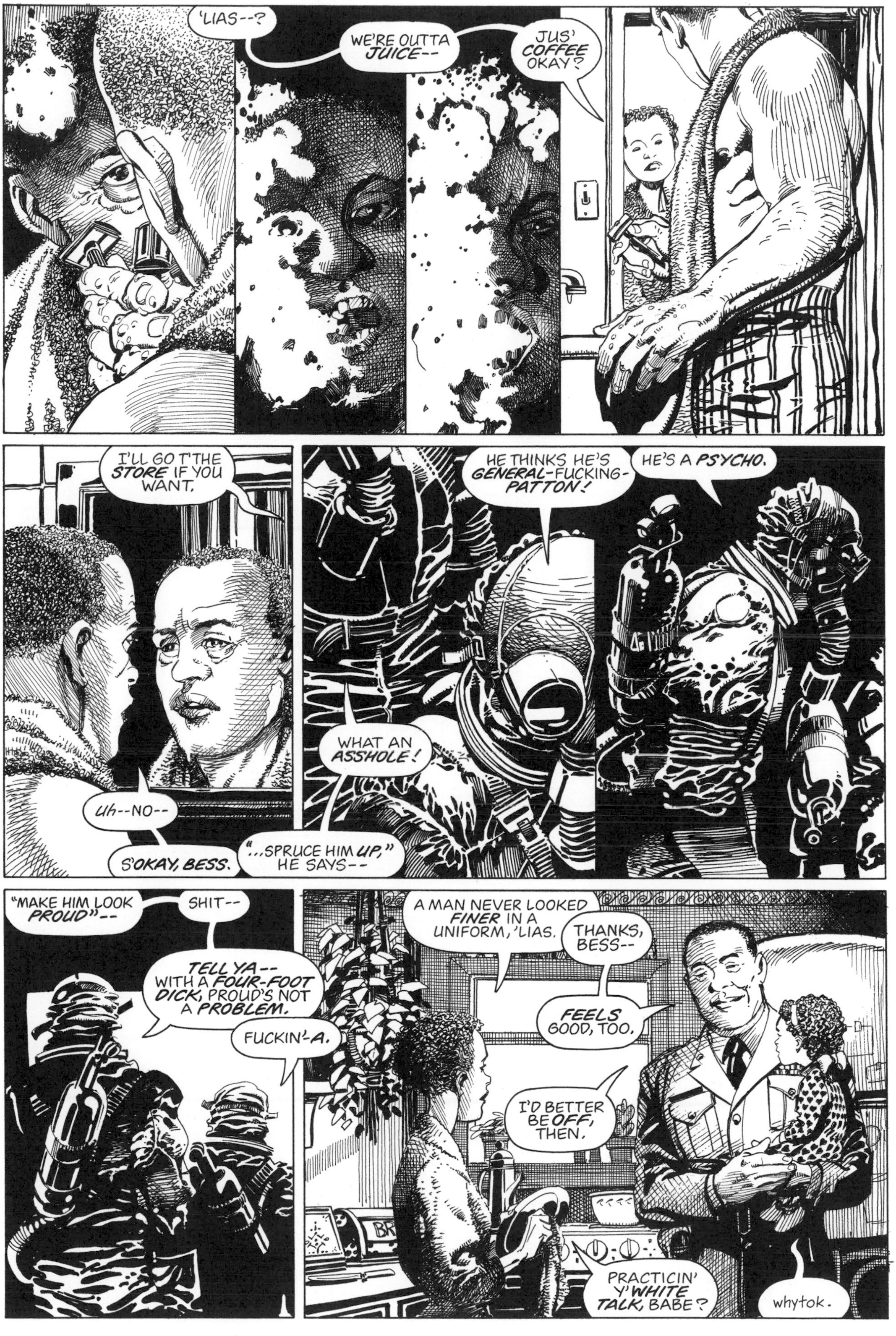
'LIAS--?
WE'RE OUTTA JUICE--
JUS' COFFEE OKAY?
I'LL GO T'THE STORE IF YOU WANT.
HE THINKS HE'S GENERAL-FUCKING-PATTON!
HE'S A PSYCHO.
WHAT AN ASSHOLE!
Uh--NO--
S'OKAY, BESS.
"...SPRUCE HIM UP," HE SAYS--
"MAKE HIM LOOK PROUD"--
SHIT--
TELL YA-- WITH A FOUR-FOOT DICK, PROUD'S NOT A PROBLEM.
FUCKIN'-A.
A MAN NEVER LOOKED FINER IN A UNIFORM, 'LIAS.
THANKS, BESS--
FEELS GOOD, TOO.
I'D BETTER BE OFF, THEN.
PRACTICIN' Y' WHITE TALK, BABE?
whytok.

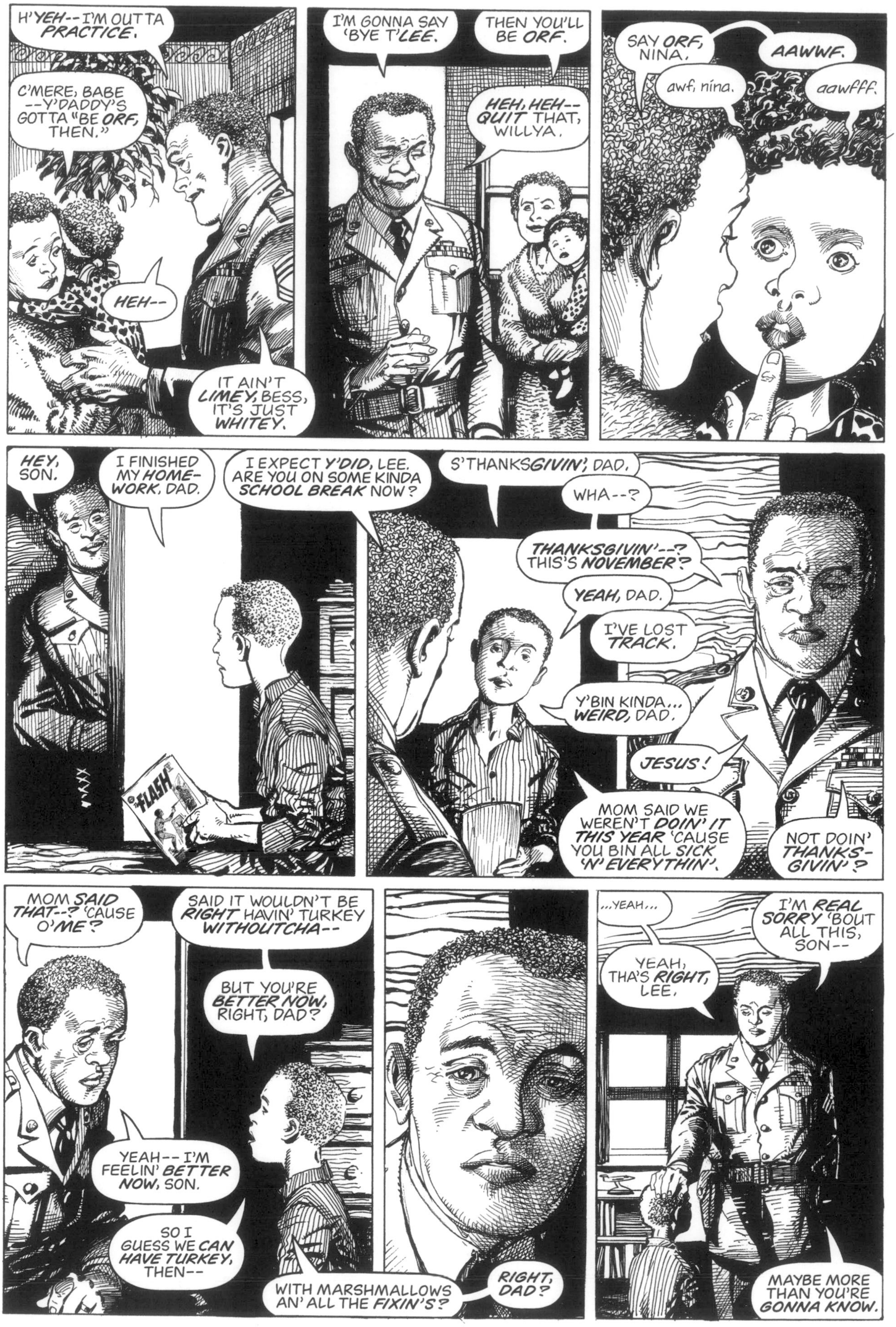
H'YEH--I'M OUTTA PRACTICE.
C'MERE, BABE --Y'DADDY'S GOTTA "BE ORF, THEN."
HEH--
IT AIN'T LIMEY, BESS, IT'S JUST WHITEY.
I'M GONNA SAY 'BYE T'LEE.
THEN YOU'LL BE ORF.
HEH, HEH-- QUIT THAT, WILLYA.
SAY ORF, NINA.
awf, nina.
AAWWF.
aawfff.
HEY, SON.
I FINISHED MY HOME-WORK, DAD.
I EXPECT Y'DID, LEE. ARE YOU ON SOME KINDA SCHOOL BREAK NOW?
FLASH
S'THANKSGIVIN', DAD.
WHA--?
THANKSGIVIN'--? THIS'S NOVEMBER?
YEAH, DAD.
I'VE LOST TRACK.
Y'BIN KINDA... WEIRD, DAD.
JESUS!
MOM SAID WE WEREN'T DOIN' IT THIS YEAR 'CAUSE YOU BIN ALL SICK 'N' EVERYTHIN'.
NOT DOIN' THANKS-GIVIN'?
MOM SAID THAT--? 'CAUSE O'ME?
SAID IT WOULDN'T BE RIGHT HAVIN' TURKEY WITHOUTCHA--
BUT YOU'RE BETTER NOW, RIGHT, DAD?
YEAH-- I'M FEELIN' BETTER NOW, SON.
SO I GUESS WE CAN HAVE TURKEY, THEN--
WITH MARSHMALLOWS AN' ALL THE FIXIN'S?
RIGHT, DAD?
...YEAH...
YEAH, THA'S RIGHT, LEE.
I'M REAL SORRY 'BOUT ALL THIS, SON--
MAYBE MORE THAN YOU'RE GONNA KNOW.

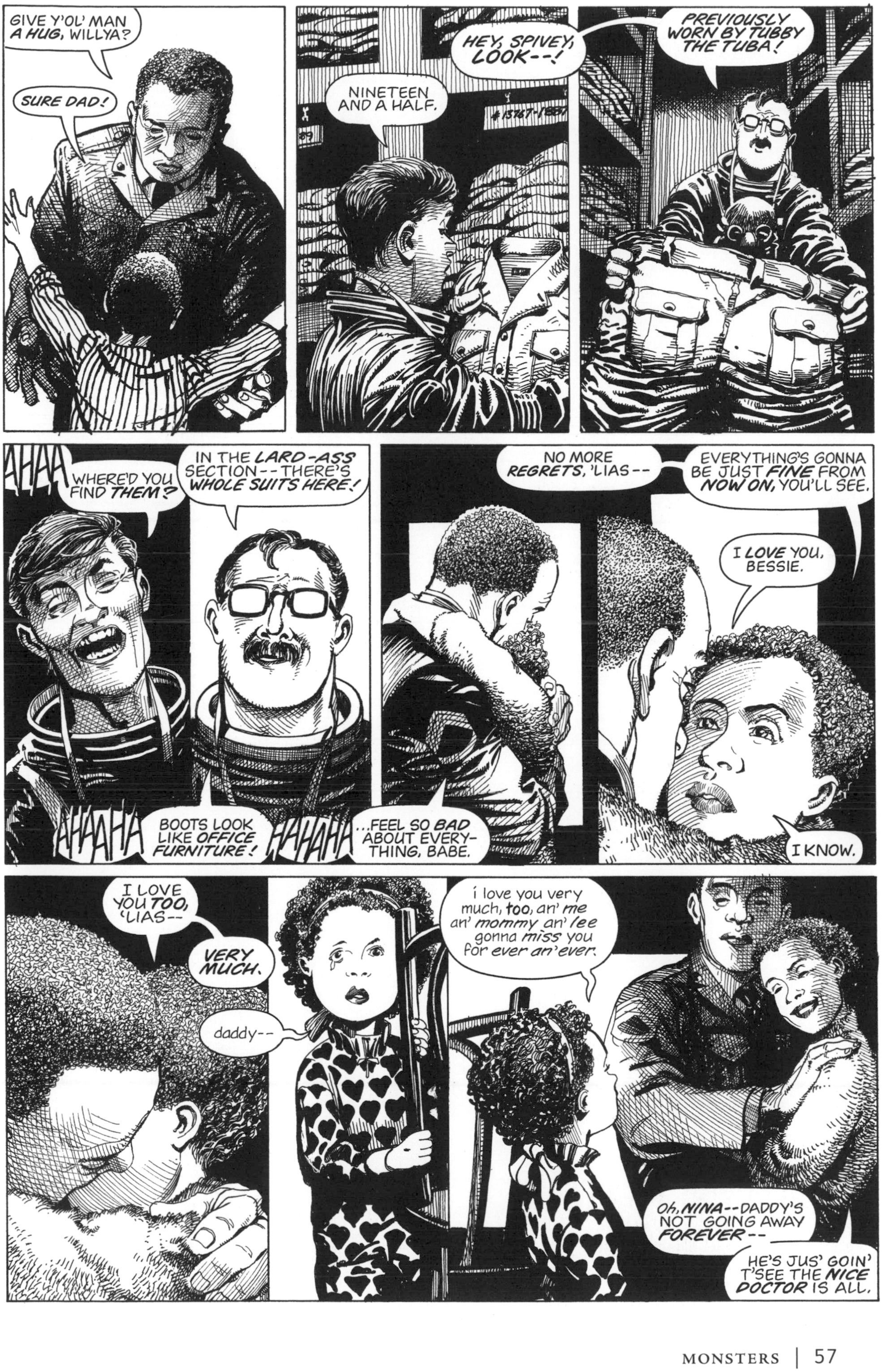

GIVE Y'OL' MAN A HUG, WILLYA?
SURE DAD!
NINETEEN AND A HALF.
HEY, SPIVEY, LOOK--!
PREVIOUSLY WORN BY TUBBY THE TUBA!
AHAA
WHERE'D YOU FIND THEM?
IN THE LARD-ASS SECTION--THERE'S WHOLE SUITS HERE!
AHAHAHA
BOOTS LOOK LIKE OFFICE FURNITURE!
HAHAHA
NO MORE REGRETS, 'LIAS--
...FEEL SO BAD ABOUT EVERYTHING, BABE.
EVERYTHING'S GONNA BE JUST FINE FROM NOW ON, YOU'LL SEE.
I LOVE YOU, BESSIE.
I KNOW.
I LOVE YOU TOO, 'LIAS--
VERY MUCH.
daddy--
i love you very much, too, an' me an' mommy an' lee gonna miss you for ever an' ever.
Oh, NINA--DADDY'S NOT GOING AWAY FOREVER--
HE'S JUS' GOIN' T'SEE THE NICE DOCTOR IS ALL.

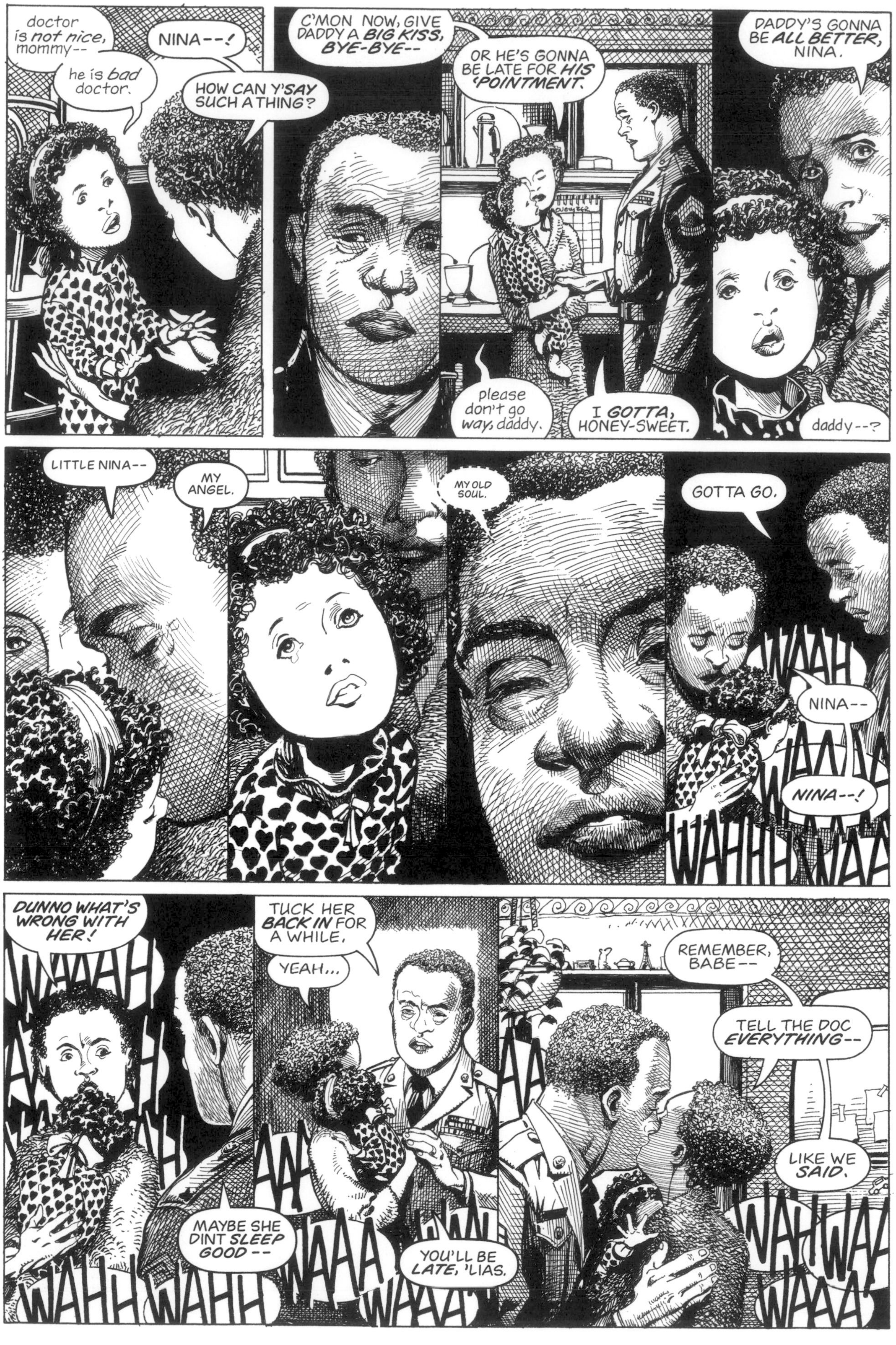

doctor is not nice, mommy--
he is bad doctor.
NINA--!
HOW CAN Y'SAY SUCH A THING?
C'MON NOW, GIVE DADDY A BIG KISS, BYE-BYE--
OR HE'S GONNA BE LATE FOR HIS 'POINTMENT.
please don't go way, daddy.
I GOTTA, HONEY-SWEET.
DADDY'S GONNA BE ALL BETTER, NINA.
daddy--?
LITTLE NINA--
MY ANGEL.
MY OLD SOUL.
GOTTA GO.
WAAH
NINA--
NINA--!
WAHH
DUNNO WHAT'S WRONG WITH HER!
MAYBE SHE DINT SLEEP GOOD--
TUCK HER BACK IN FOR A WHILE.
YEAH...
YOU'LL BE LATE, 'LIAS.
REMEMBER, BABE--
TELL THE DOC EVERYTHING--
LIKE WE SAID.

HUSH, BABY--
WAAHH
daddy daddy daaddy
MOM--?
DAD SAID WE COULD HAVE TURKEY T'DAY--
MA?
HELP ME WITH YOUR SISTER, LEE--
Home SWEET Home
GET THE BLANKET--
WHAT'S WRONG, MA?
SHE'S JUST CRANKY.
MA--?
DAD SAID WE COULD DO THANKSGIVIN' NOW.
OKAY, LEE, I'LL GO TO TH' MARKET.
CAN I COME WITH?
YOU STAY HERE--
LOOK AFTER NINA.
To my WIFE AND my CHILDREN
GONNA GET CRANBERRY JELLY, MA?
SURE.
AN' MARSH-MALLOWS?
OKAY.
SAUSAGE STUFFIN'?
YOU SIT WITH NINA, NOW.
OKAY, MA.

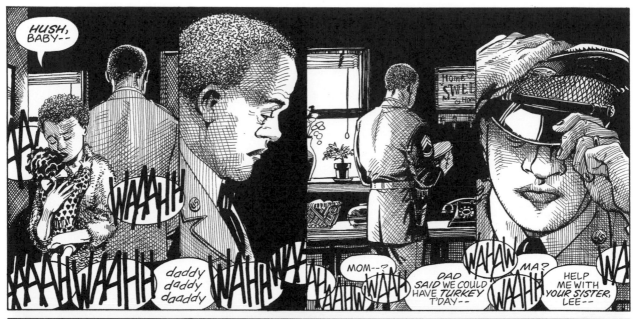

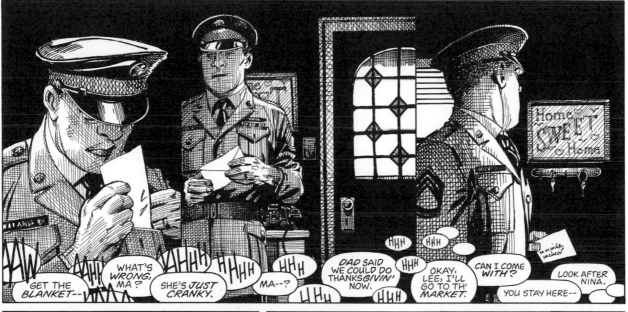

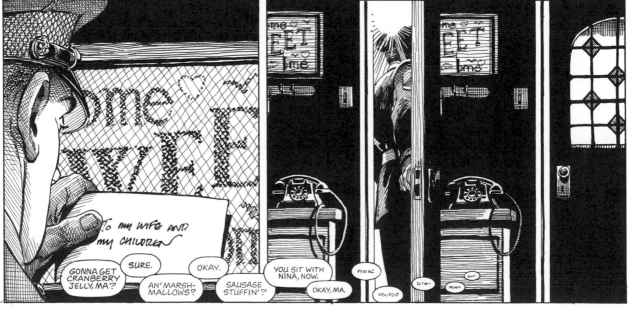

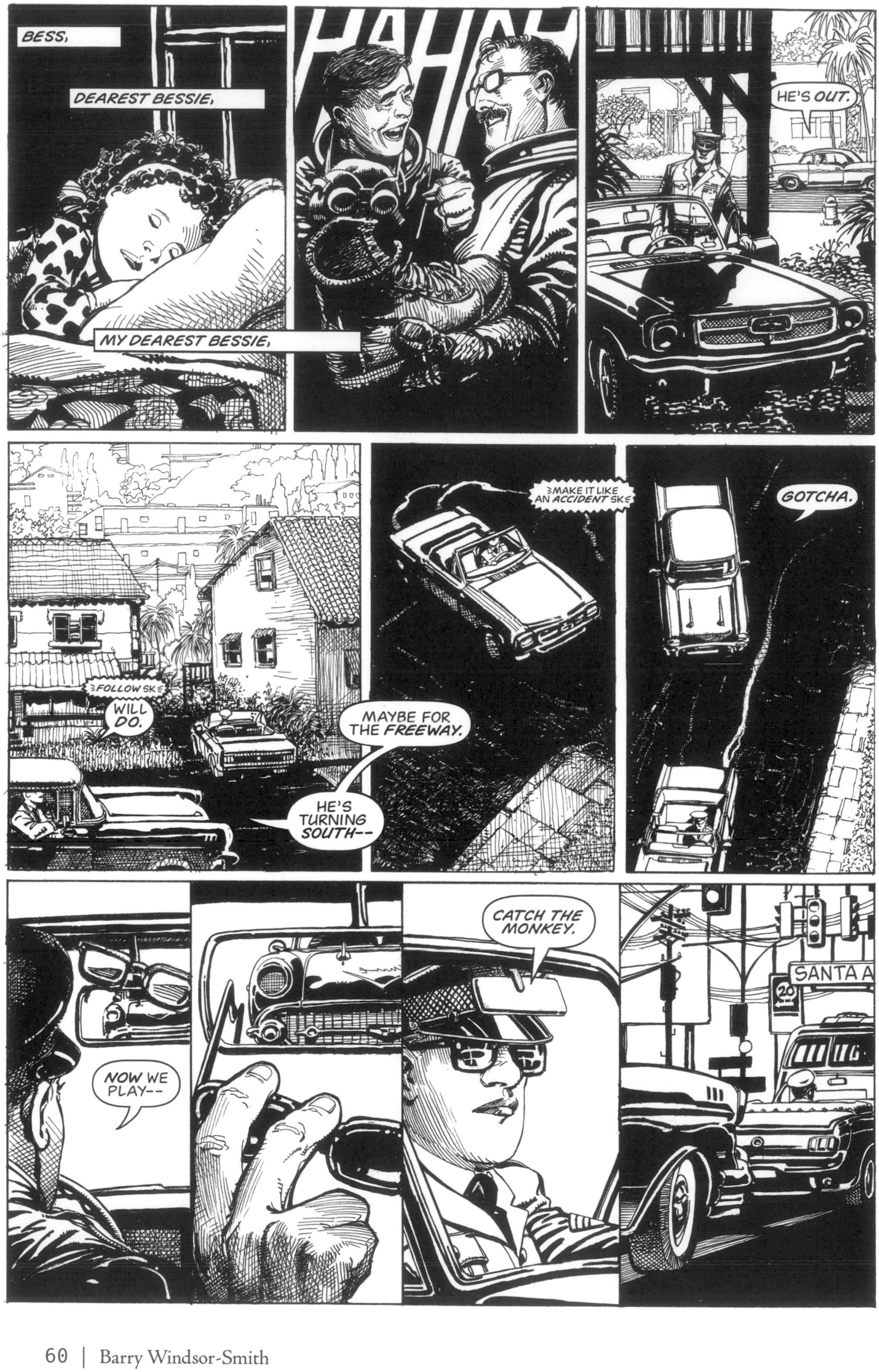
BESS,
DEAREST BESSIE,
MY DEAREST BESSIE,
HE'S OUT.
FOLLOW SK
WILL DO.
MAYBE FOR THE FREEWAY.
HE'S TURNING SOUTH--
MAKE IT LIKE AN ACCIDENT SK
GOTCHA.
NOW WE PLAY--
CATCH THE MONKEY.
SANTA A

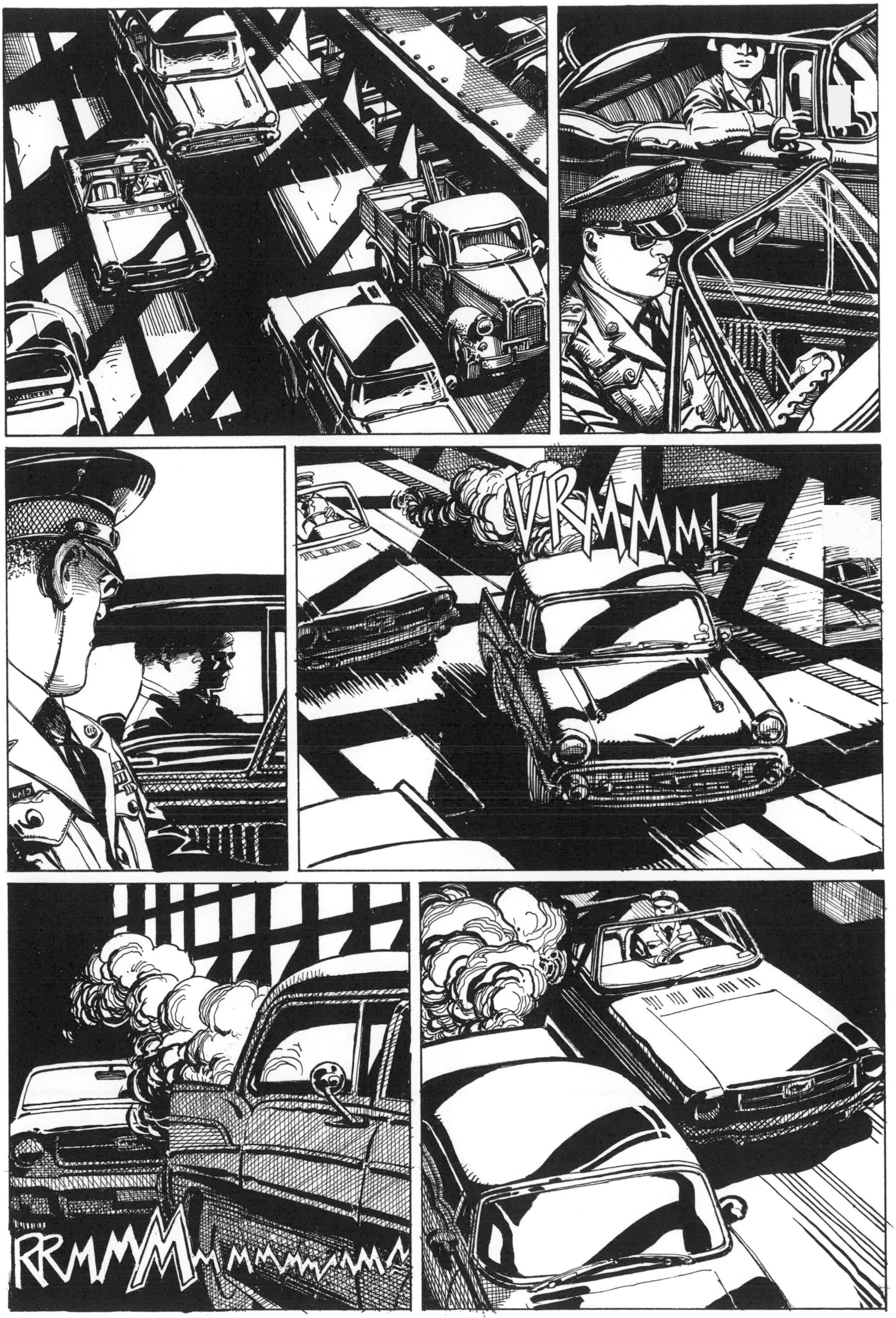
VRMMMM!
RRMMMMMMMMMMM

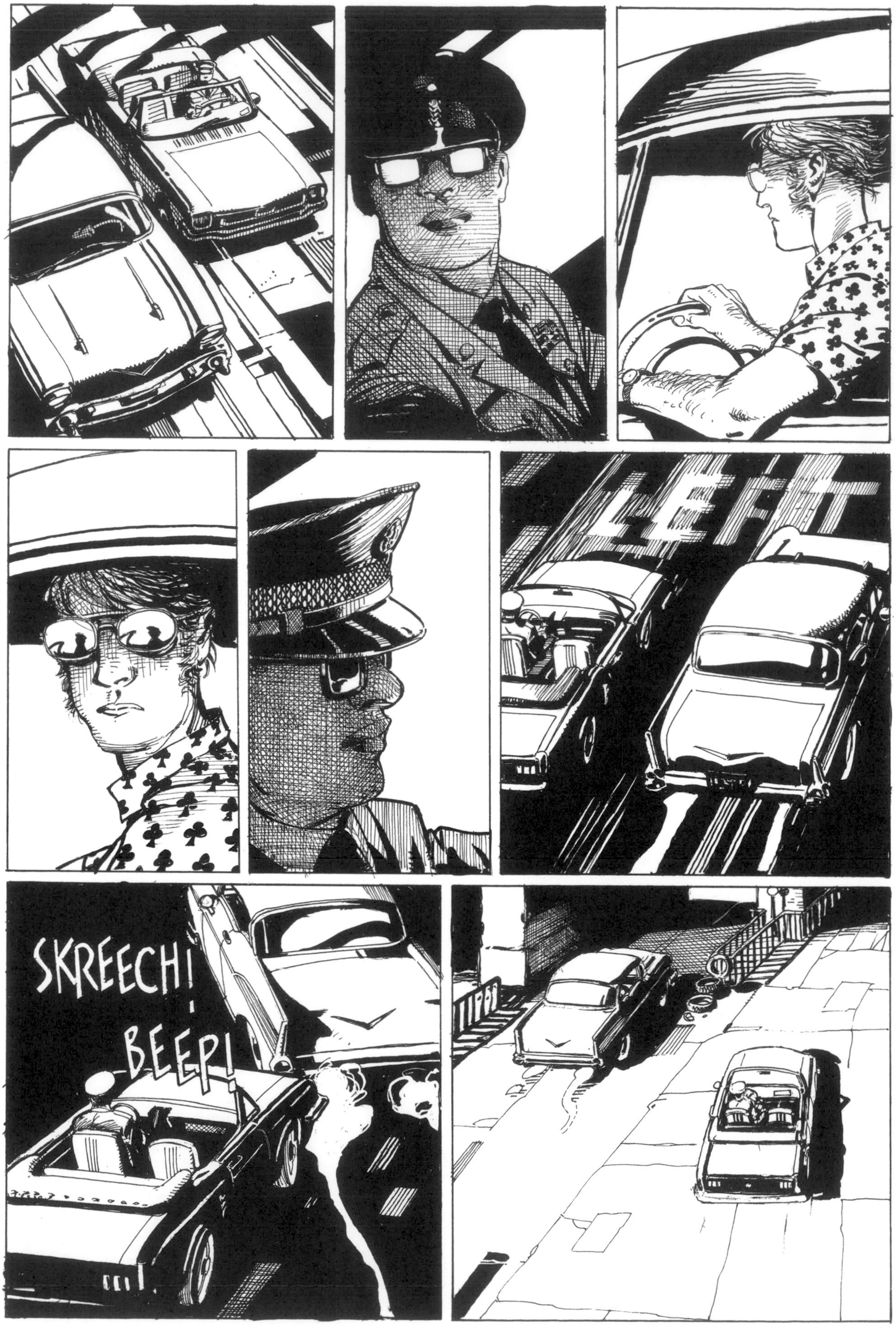
SKREECH!
BEEP!

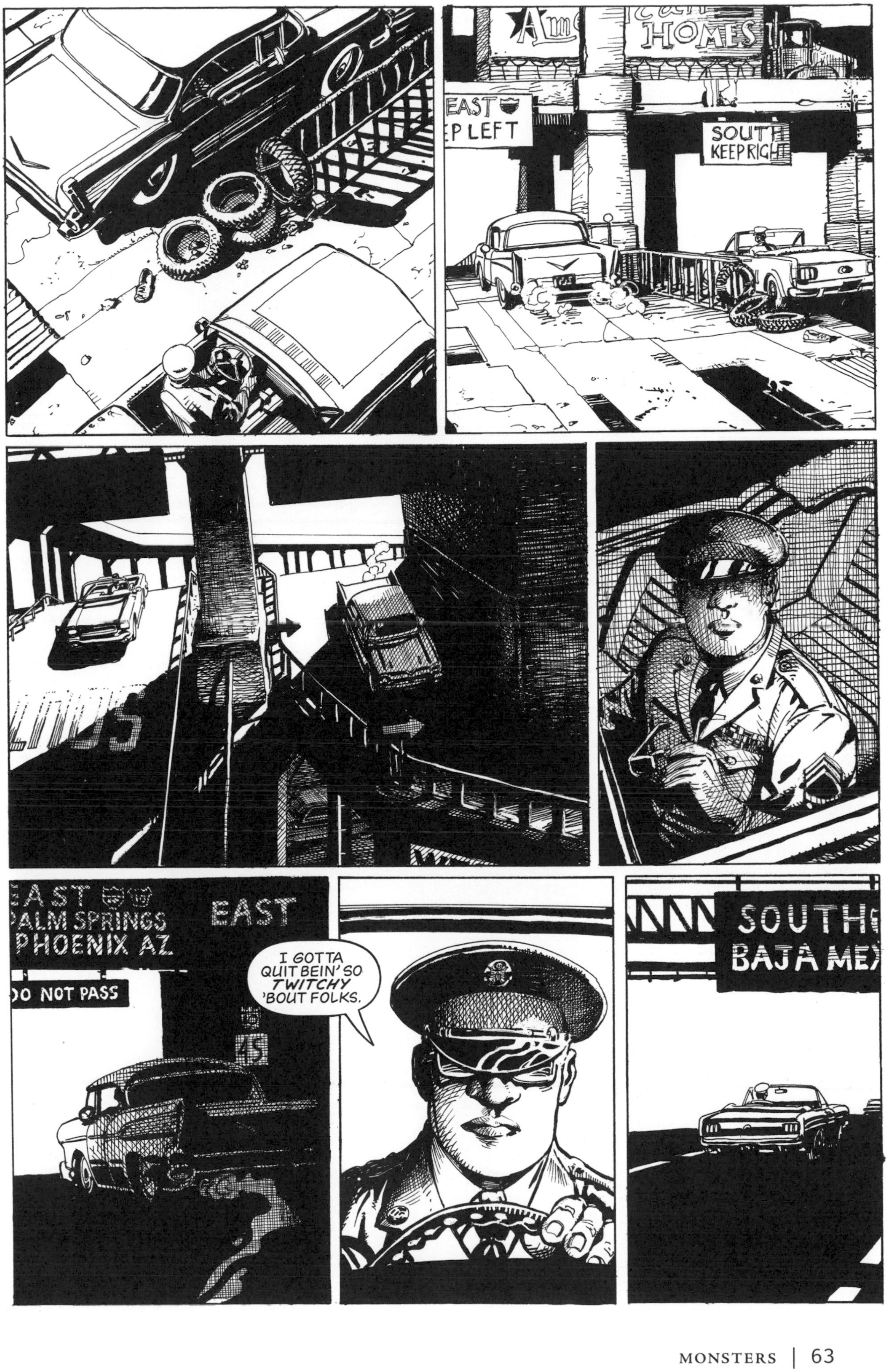
HOMES
EAST
EP LEFT
SOUTH
KEEPRIGH
EAST
ALM SPRINGS
PHOENIX AZ
EAST
DO NOT PASS
45
I GOTTA QUIT BEIN' SO *TWITCHY* 'BOUT FOLKS.
SOUTH
BAJA MEX

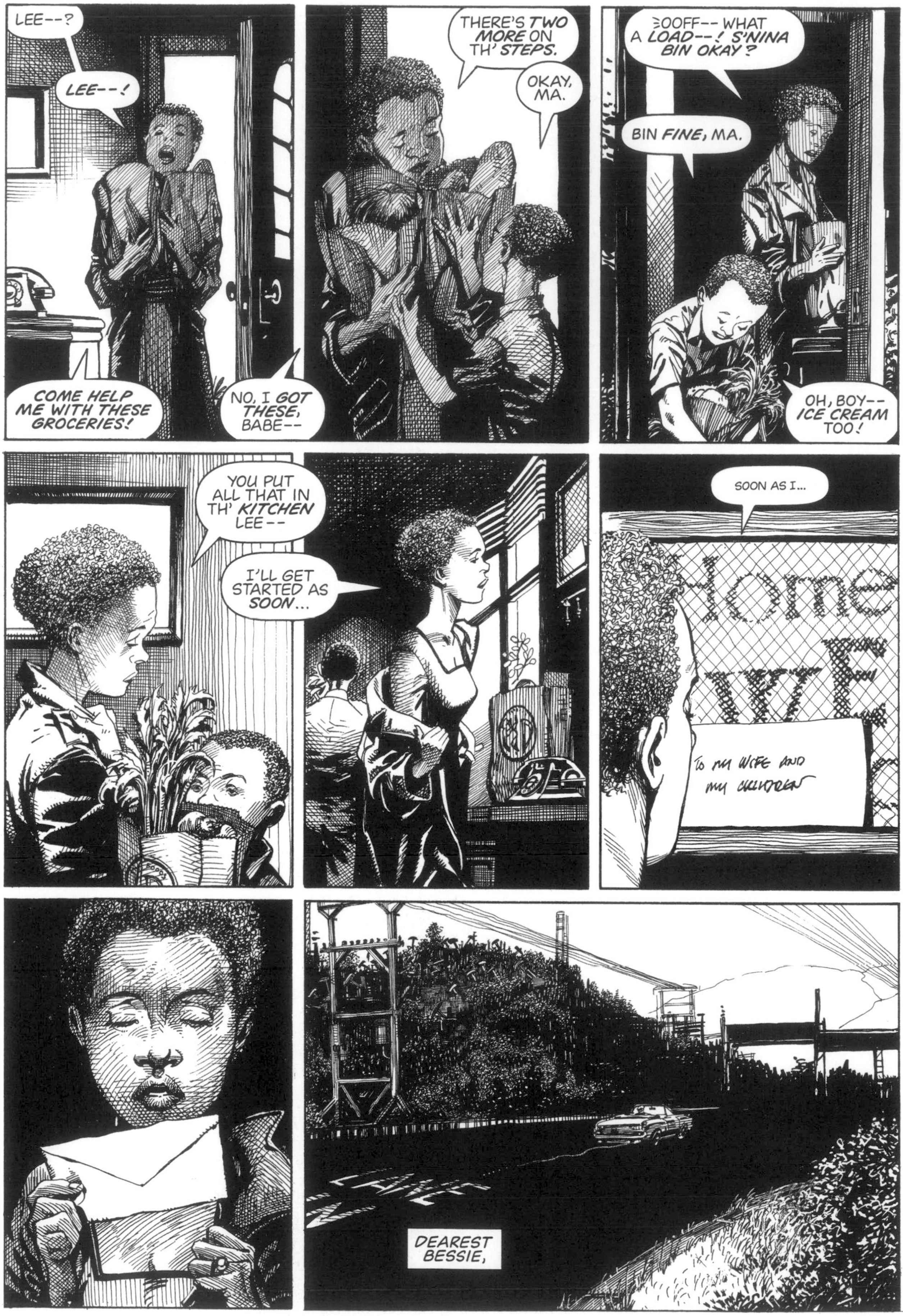

LEE--?
LEE--!
COME HELP ME WITH THESE GROCERIES!
NO, I GOT THESE, BABE--
THERE'S TWO MORE ON TH' STEPS.
OKAY, MA.
OOFF-- WHAT A LOAD--! S'NINA BIN OKAY?
BIN FINE, MA.
OH, BOY-- ICE CREAM TOO!
YOU PUT ALL THAT IN TH' KITCHEN LEE--
I'LL GET STARTED AS SOON...
SOON AS I...
Home
TO MY WIFE AND MY CHILDREN
DEAREST BESSIE,

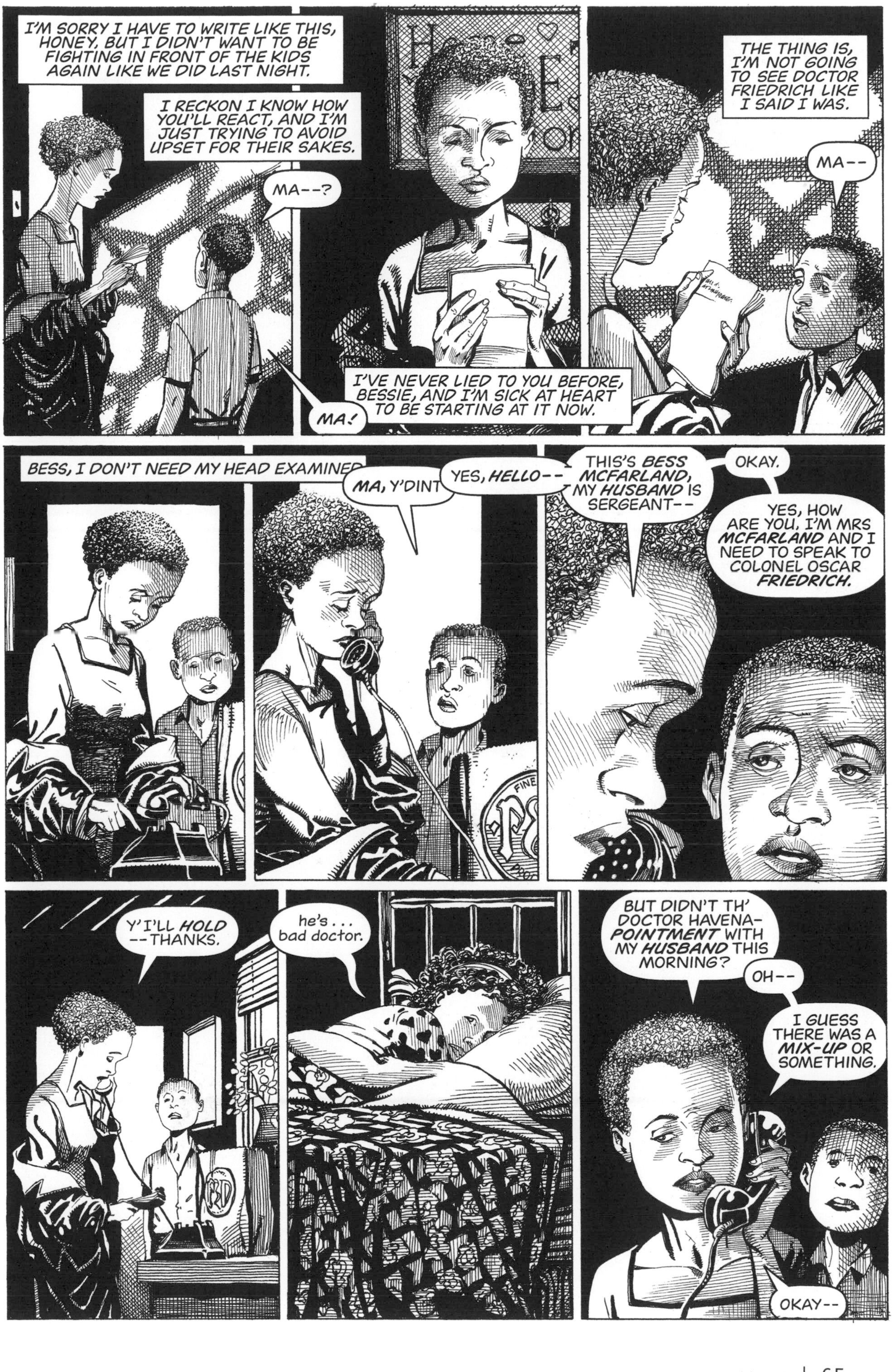
I'M SORRY I HAVE TO WRITE LIKE THIS, HONEY, BUT I DIDN'T WANT TO BE FIGHTING IN FRONT OF THE KIDS AGAIN LIKE WE DID LAST NIGHT.
I RECKON I KNOW HOW YOU'LL REACT, AND I'M JUST TRYING TO AVOID UPSET FOR THEIR SAKES.
MA--?
MA!
I'VE NEVER LIED TO YOU BEFORE, BESSIE, AND I'M SICK AT HEART TO BE STARTING AT IT NOW.
THE THING IS, I'M NOT GOING TO SEE DOCTOR FRIEDRICH LIKE I SAID I WAS.
MA--
BESS, I DON'T NEED MY HEAD EXAMINED
MA, Y'DINT
YES, HELLO--
THIS'S BESS MCFARLAND, MY HUSBAND IS SERGEANT--
OKAY.
YES, HOW ARE YOU. I'M MRS MCFARLAND AND I NEED TO SPEAK TO COLONEL OSCAR FRIEDRICH.
Y'I'LL HOLD --THANKS.
he's . . . bad doctor.
BUT DIDN'T TH' DOCTOR HAVENA-POINTMENT WITH MY HUSBAND THIS MORNING?
OH--
I GUESS THERE WAS A MIX-UP OR SOMETHING.
OKAY--

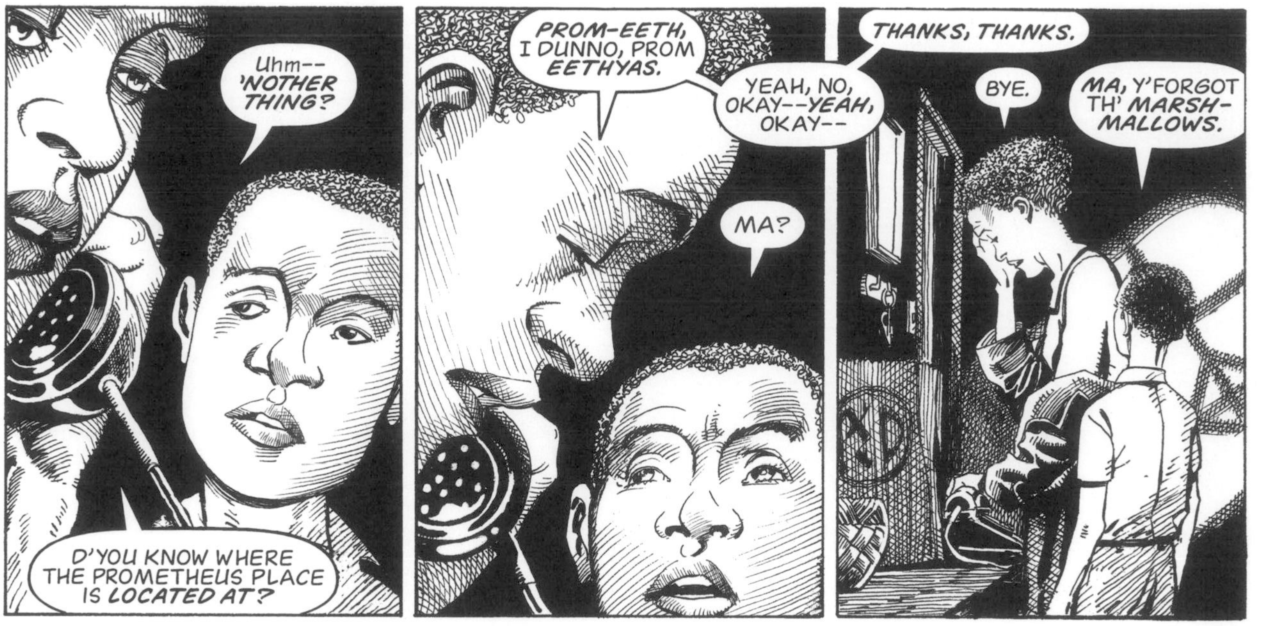
Uhm--
'NOTHER THING?
D'YOU KNOW WHERE THE PROMETHEUS PLACE IS LOCATED AT?
PROM-EETH, I DUNNO, PROM EETHYAS.
YEAH, NO, OKAY--YEAH, OKAY--
MA?
THANKS, THANKS.
BYE.
MA, Y'FORGOT TH' MARSH-MALLOWS.

Fort Sherman Thursday, November 26, 1:23 PM

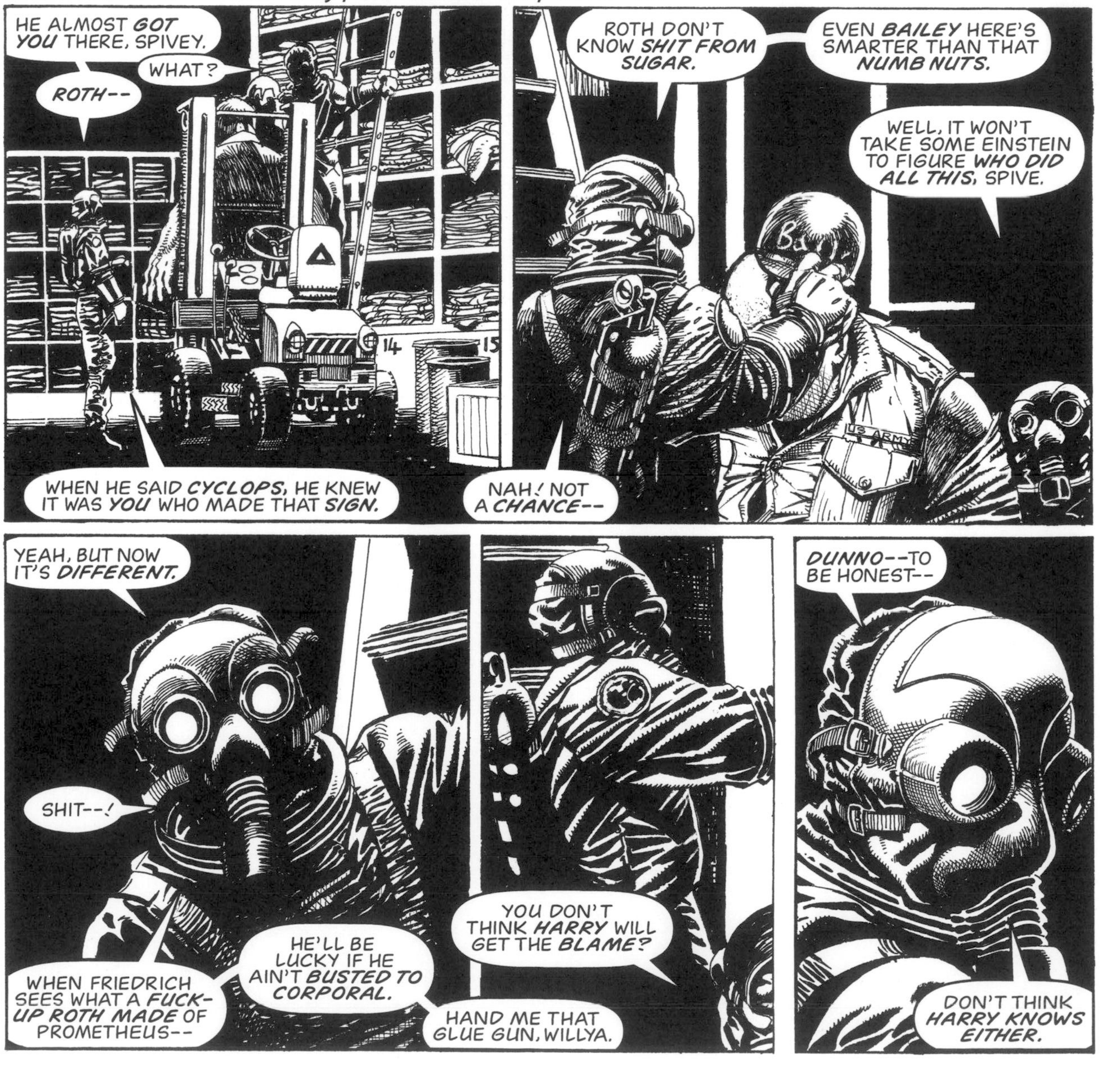
HE ALMOST GOT YOU THERE, SPIVEY.
WHAT?
ROTH--
WHEN HE SAID CYCLOPS, HE KNEW IT WAS YOU WHO MADE THAT SIGN.
ROTH DON'T KNOW SHIT FROM SUGAR.
EVEN BAILEY HERE'S SMARTER THAN THAT NUMB NUTS.
WELL, IT WON'T TAKE SOME EINSTEIN TO FIGURE WHO DID ALL THIS, SPIVE.
NAH! NOT A CHANCE--
YEAH, BUT NOW IT'S DIFFERENT.
SHIT--!
WHEN FRIEDRICH SEES WHAT A FUCK-UP ROTH MADE OF PROMETHEUS--
HE'LL BE LUCKY IF HE AIN'T BUSTED TO CORPORAL.
YOU DON'T THINK HARRY WILL GET THE BLAME?
HAND ME THAT GLUE GUN, WILLYA.
DUNNO--TO BE HONEST--
DON'T THINK HARRY KNOWS EITHER.

THERE Y'GO-- ALL *SPRUCED UP*--

SPIT 'N' POLISHED!

ROTH'LL *SHIT SIDEWAYS 'TIL SUNDAY* WHEN HE SEES *THIS*.

D'Y'THINK *HARRY'LL* BE PISSED, *TOO?*

HARRY--?

YEAH. I WANNA *SEE* THAT!

NAH--!

HARRY *LOVES* A *GOOD JOKE* AS MUCH AS *ANYBODY!*

Y'GONNA GO BACK TO THE *STORE*, MA?

LEE, PLEASE GO TO YOUR *ROOM*.

HUH? HOW COME?

'CAUSE I SAID *SO!* NOW DO AS YOU'RE *TOLD!*

BUT--

DON'T BUT ME!

GEE.

...HOW MUCH I LOVE YOU, AND THAT I KNOW YOU LOVE ME TOO.

SO IT'S REALLY DIFFICULT TO BE SAYING THESE THINGS TO YOU.

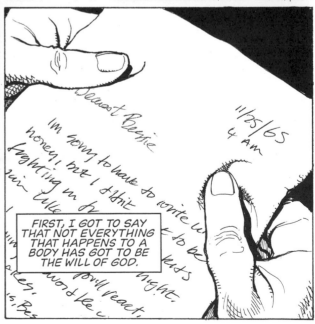

FIRST, I GOT TO SAY THAT NOT EVERYTHING THAT HAPPENS TO A BODY HAS GOT TO BE THE WILL OF GOD.

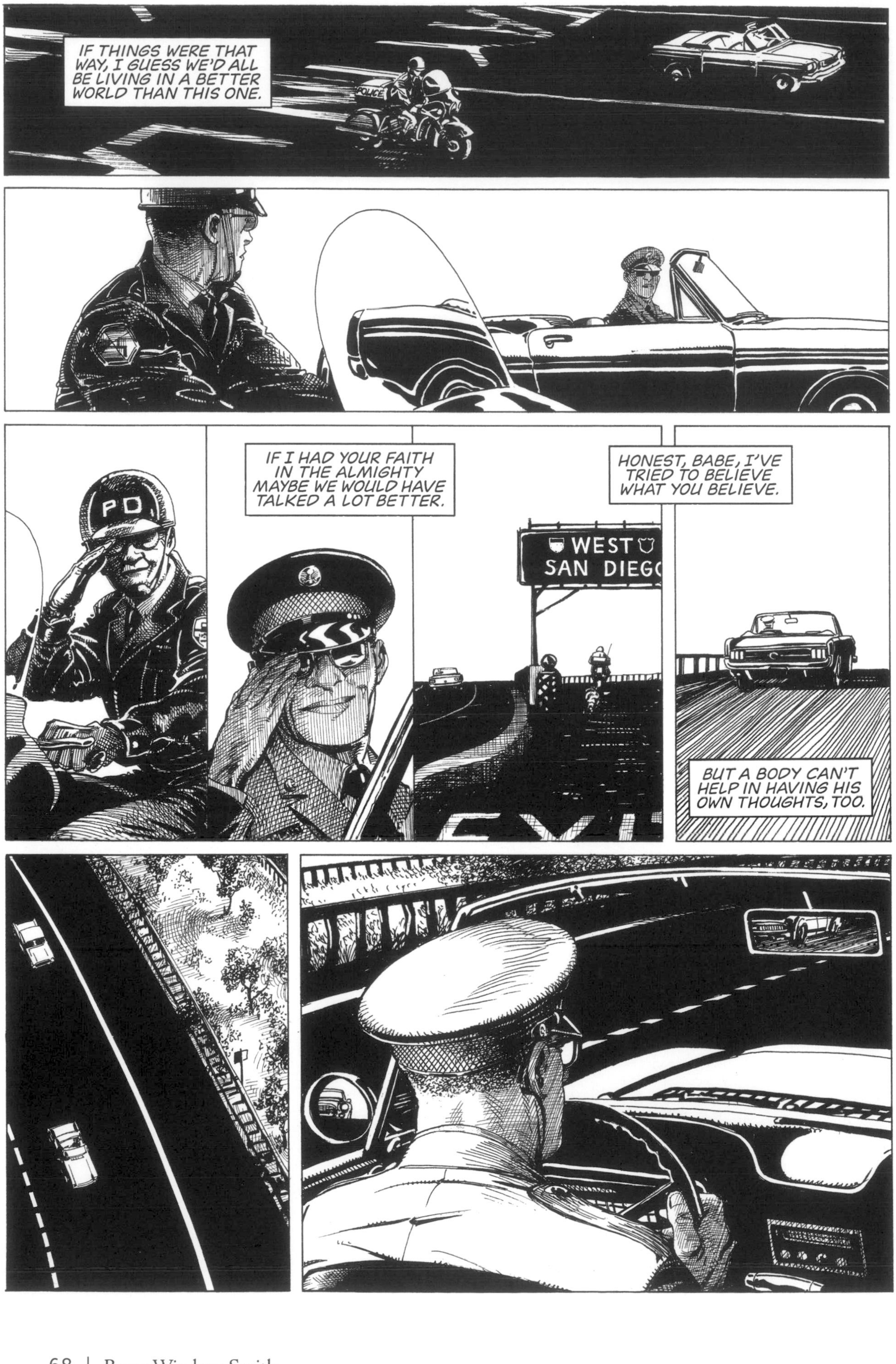
IF THINGS WERE THAT WAY, I GUESS WE'D ALL BE LIVING IN A BETTER WORLD THAN THIS ONE.
POLICE
PD
IF I HAD YOUR FAITH IN THE ALMIGHTY MAYBE WE WOULD HAVE TALKED A LOT BETTER.
WEST
SAN DIEGO
HONEST, BABE, I'VE TRIED TO BELIEVE WHAT YOU BELIEVE.
BUT A BODY CAN'T HELP IN HAVING HIS OWN THOUGHTS, TOO.

SKIH!
SKITCH
SKEEECH!
CHTUMP
KATSH!

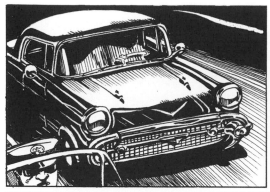

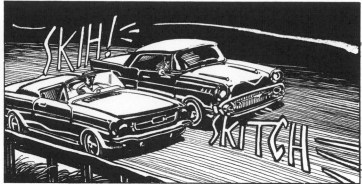

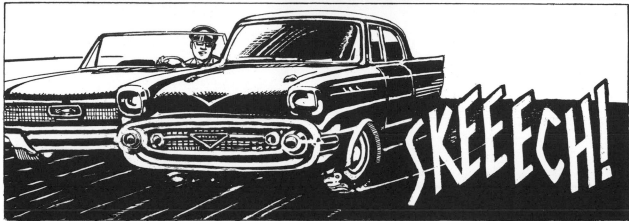

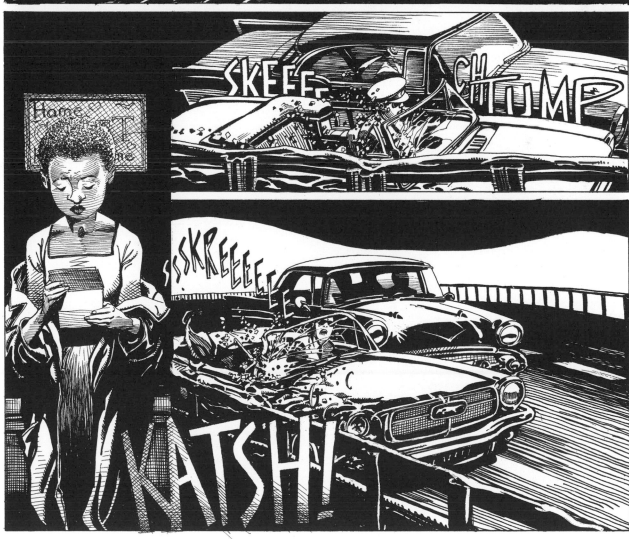

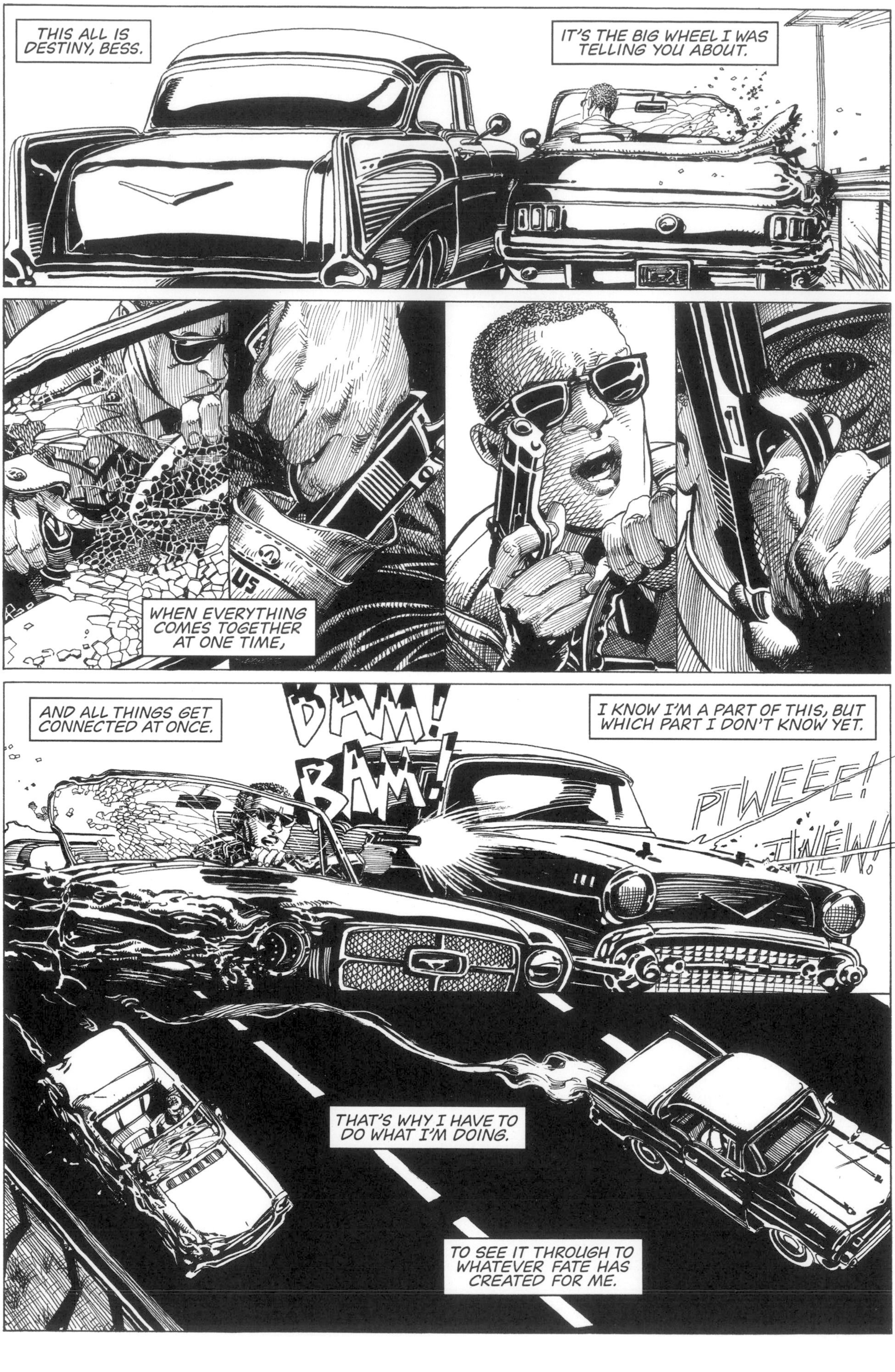
THIS ALL IS DESTINY, BESS.
IT'S THE BIG WHEEL I WAS TELLING YOU ABOUT.
WHEN EVERYTHING COMES TOGETHER AT ONE TIME,
AND ALL THINGS GET CONNECTED AT ONCE.
BAM!
BAM!
I KNOW I'M A PART OF THIS, BUT WHICH PART I DON'T KNOW YET.
PTWEEE!
TWEW!
THAT'S WHY I HAVE TO DO WHAT I'M DOING.
TO SEE IT THROUGH TO WHATEVER FATE HAS CREATED FOR ME.

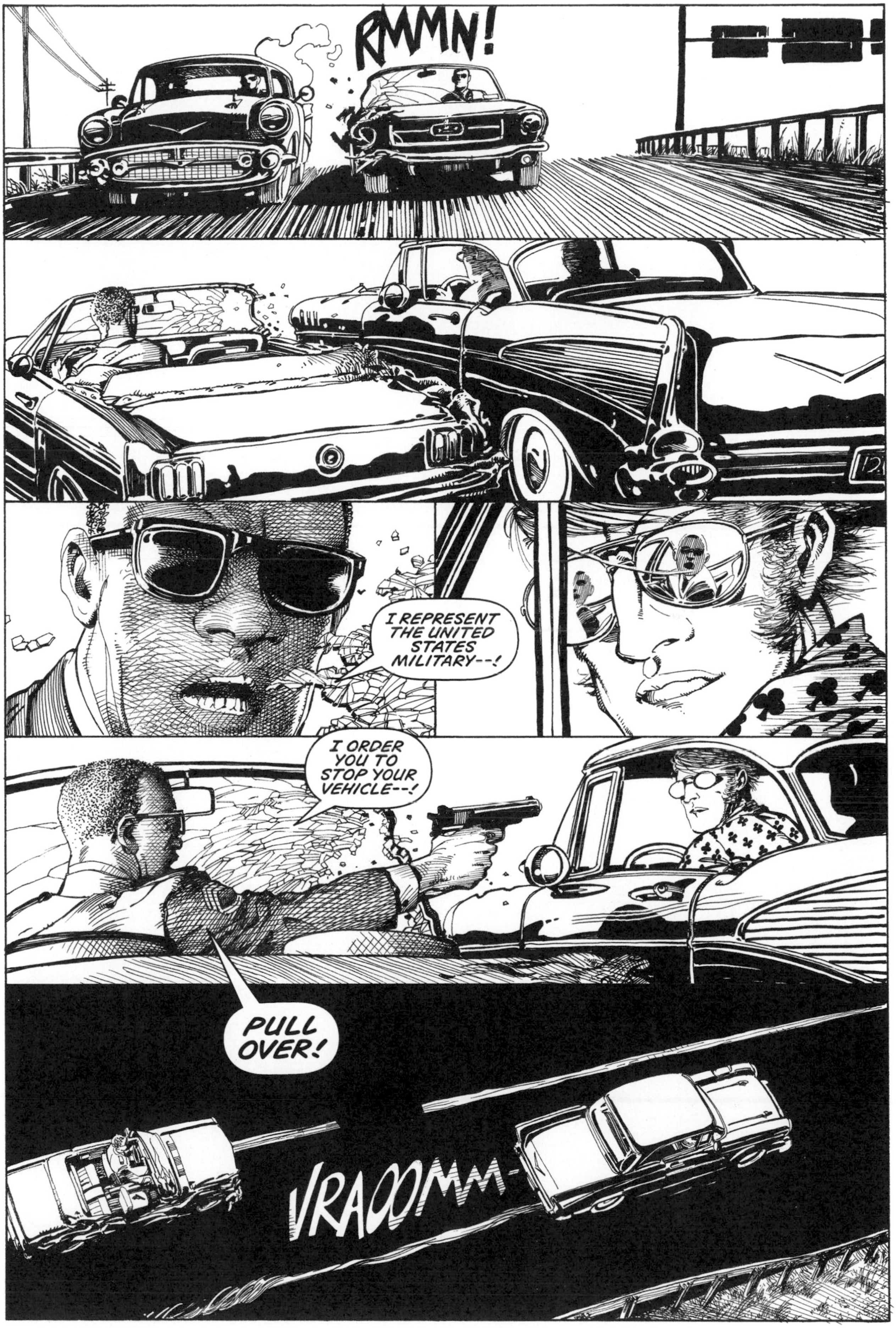
RMMN!
I REPRESENT THE UNITED STATES MILITARY--!
I ORDER YOU TO STOP YOUR VEHICLE--!
PULL OVER!
VRAOOMM-

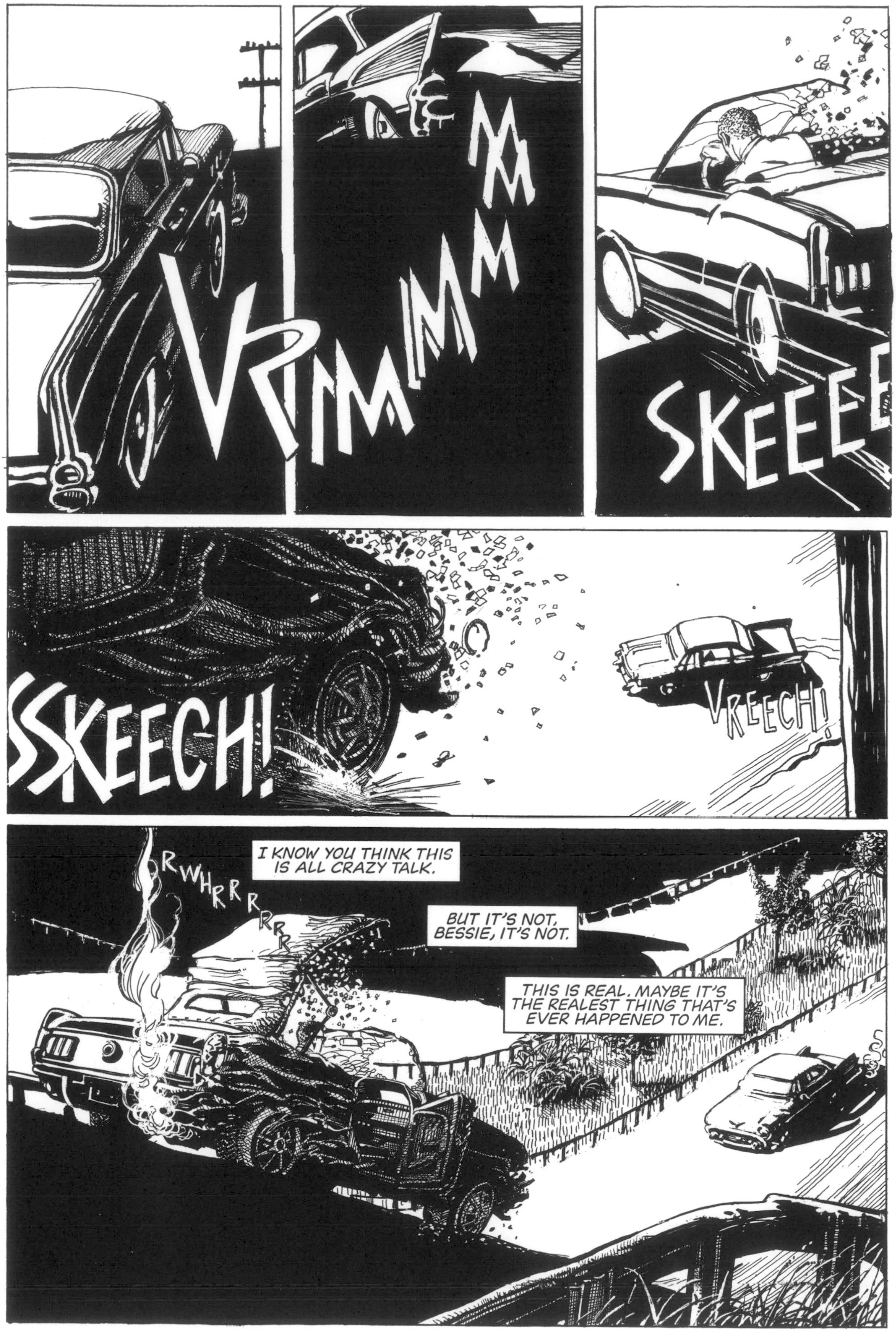
VRMMMMMMMM
SKEEEE
SKEECH!
VREECH!
RWHRRRRR
I KNOW YOU THINK THIS IS ALL CRAZY TALK.
BUT IT'S NOT, BESSIE, IT'S NOT.
THIS IS REAL. MAYBE IT'S THE REALEST THING THAT'S EVER HAPPENED TO ME.

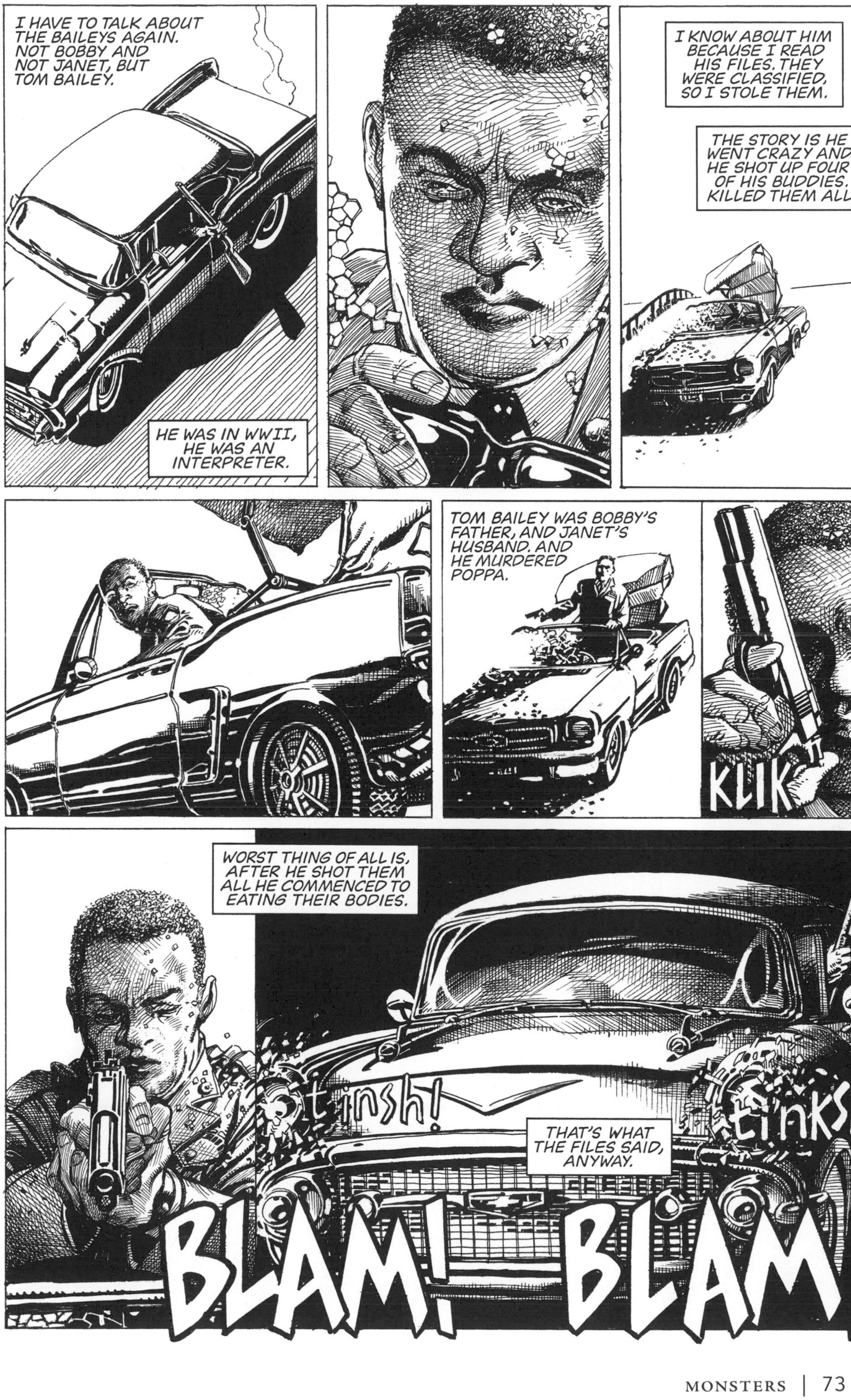
I HAVE TO TALK ABOUT THE BAILEYS AGAIN. NOT BOBBY AND NOT JANET, BUT TOM BAILEY.
HE WAS IN WWII, HE WAS AN INTERPRETER.
I KNOW ABOUT HIM BECAUSE I READ HIS FILES. THEY WERE CLASSIFIED, SO I STOLE THEM.
THE STORY IS HE WENT CRAZY AND HE SHOT UP FOUR OF HIS BUDDIES. KILLED THEM ALL.
TOM BAILEY WAS BOBBY'S FATHER, AND JANET'S HUSBAND. AND HE MURDERED POPPA.
KLIK
WORST THING OF ALL IS, AFTER HE SHOT THEM ALL HE COMMENCED TO EATING THEIR BODIES.
tinsh!
tinkSh!
THAT'S WHAT THE FILES SAID, ANYWAY.
BLAM! BLAM!

HE WAS KEPT IN DETENTION FOR A COUPLE OF YEARS. FOR ALL THE GOOD THAT DID.

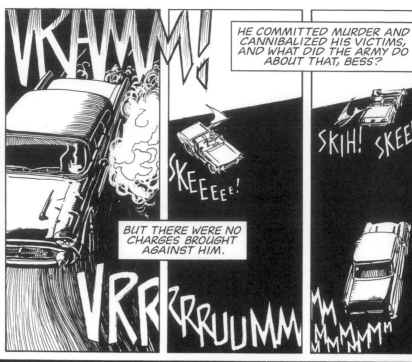

VRAMM!

SKEEEEE!

VRRRRRUMM

HE COMMITTED MURDER AND CANNIBALIZED HIS VICTIMS, AND WHAT DID THE ARMY DO ABOUT THAT, BESS?

BUT THERE WERE NO CHARGES BROUGHT AGAINST HIM.

SKIH! SKEEEE

VRMMMM

RRRRRMMMMMMMM!

THEY SLAPPED A MEDAL ON HIM AND SENT HIM HOME LIKE NOTHING EVER HAPPENED.

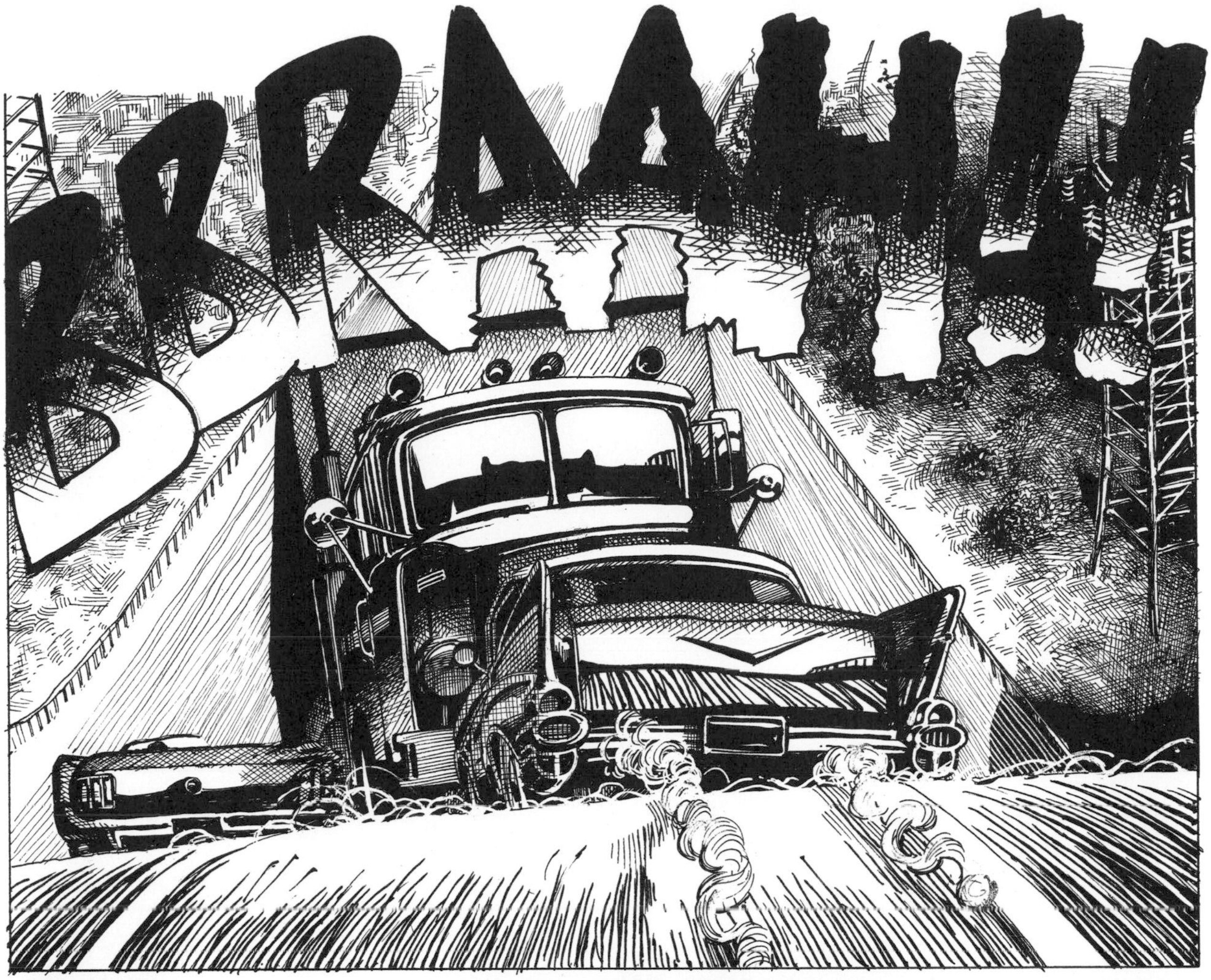
BRRAAH!!!

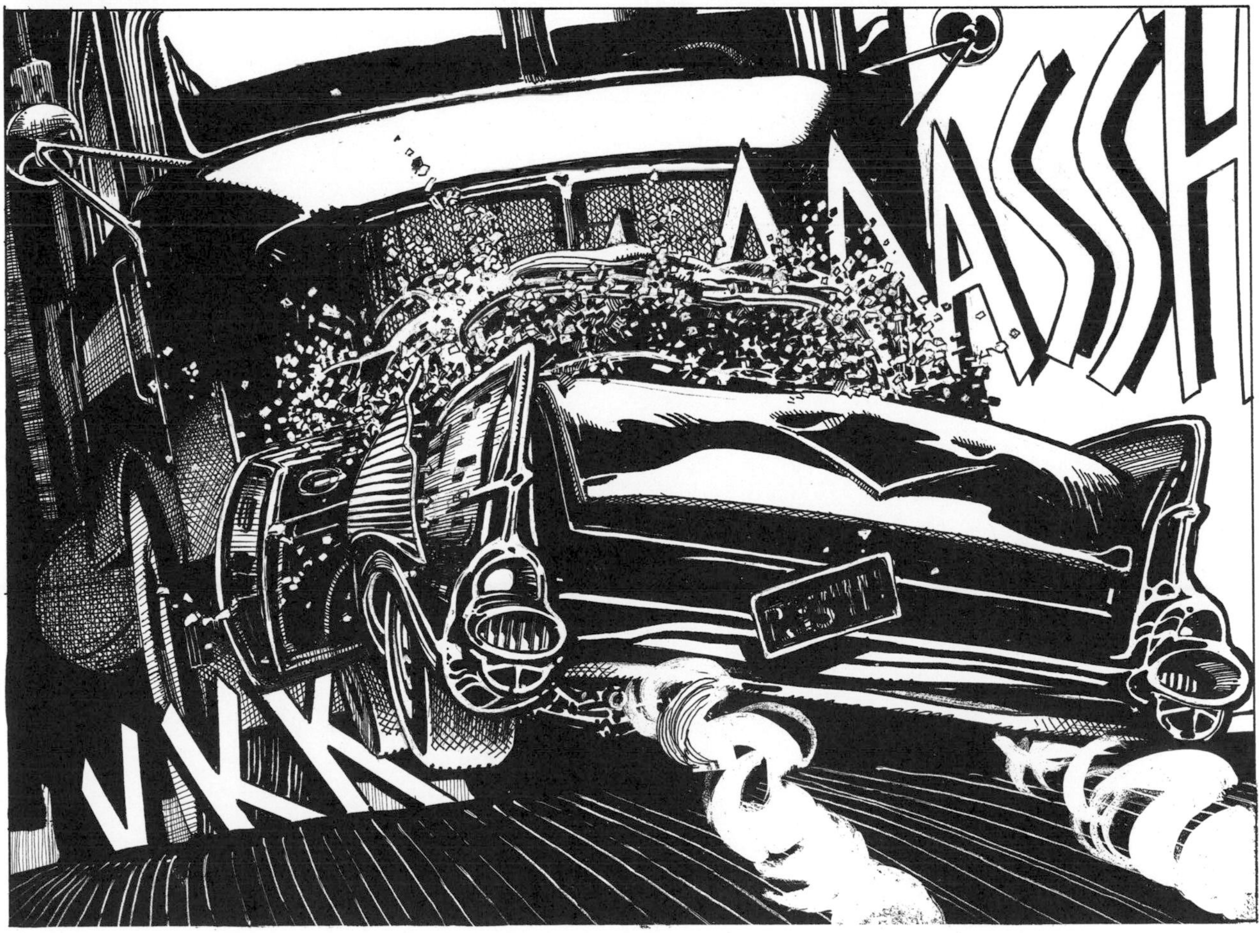
AAASSH
VKK

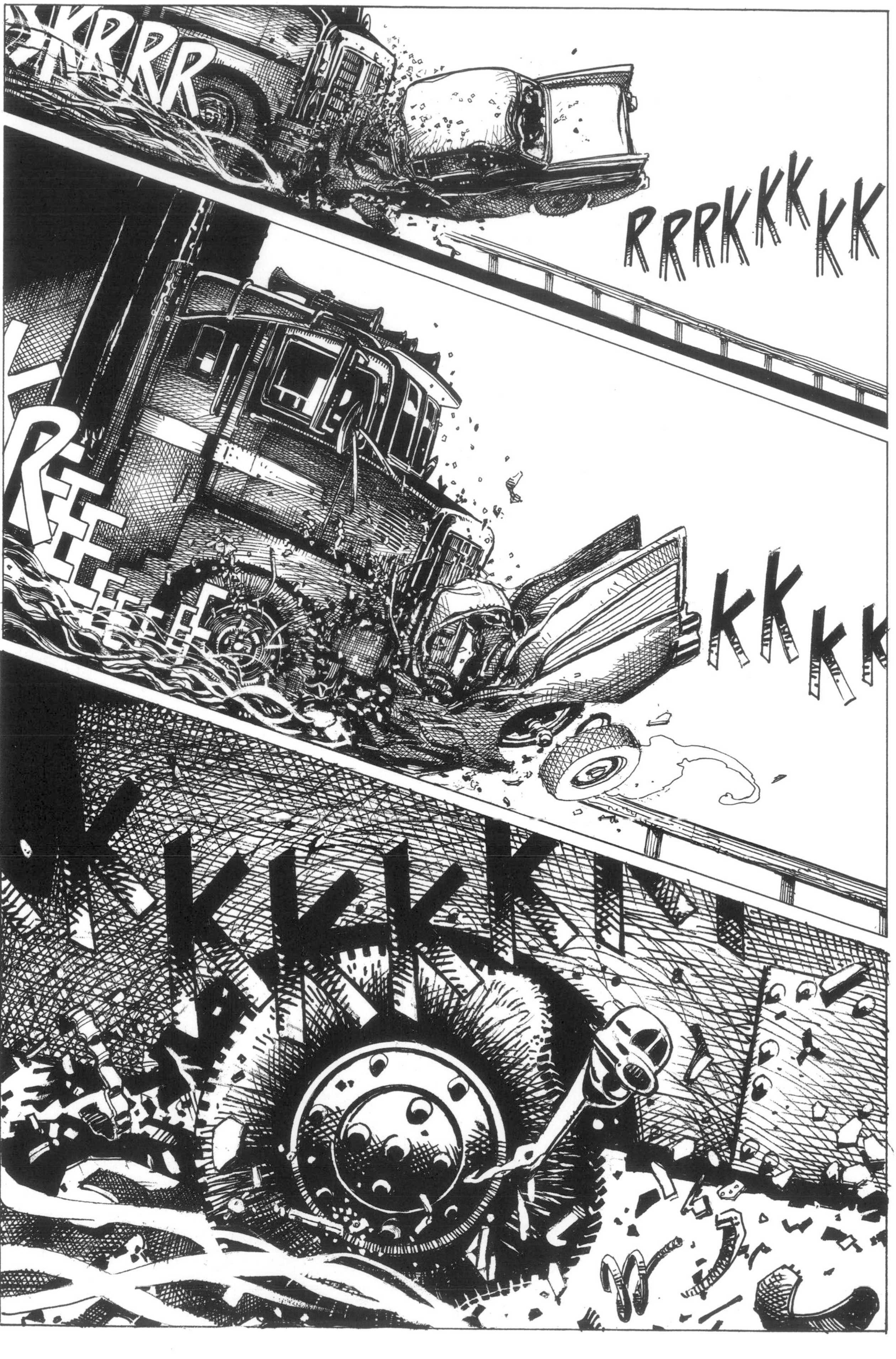
RRRKKKKK
KKKKK

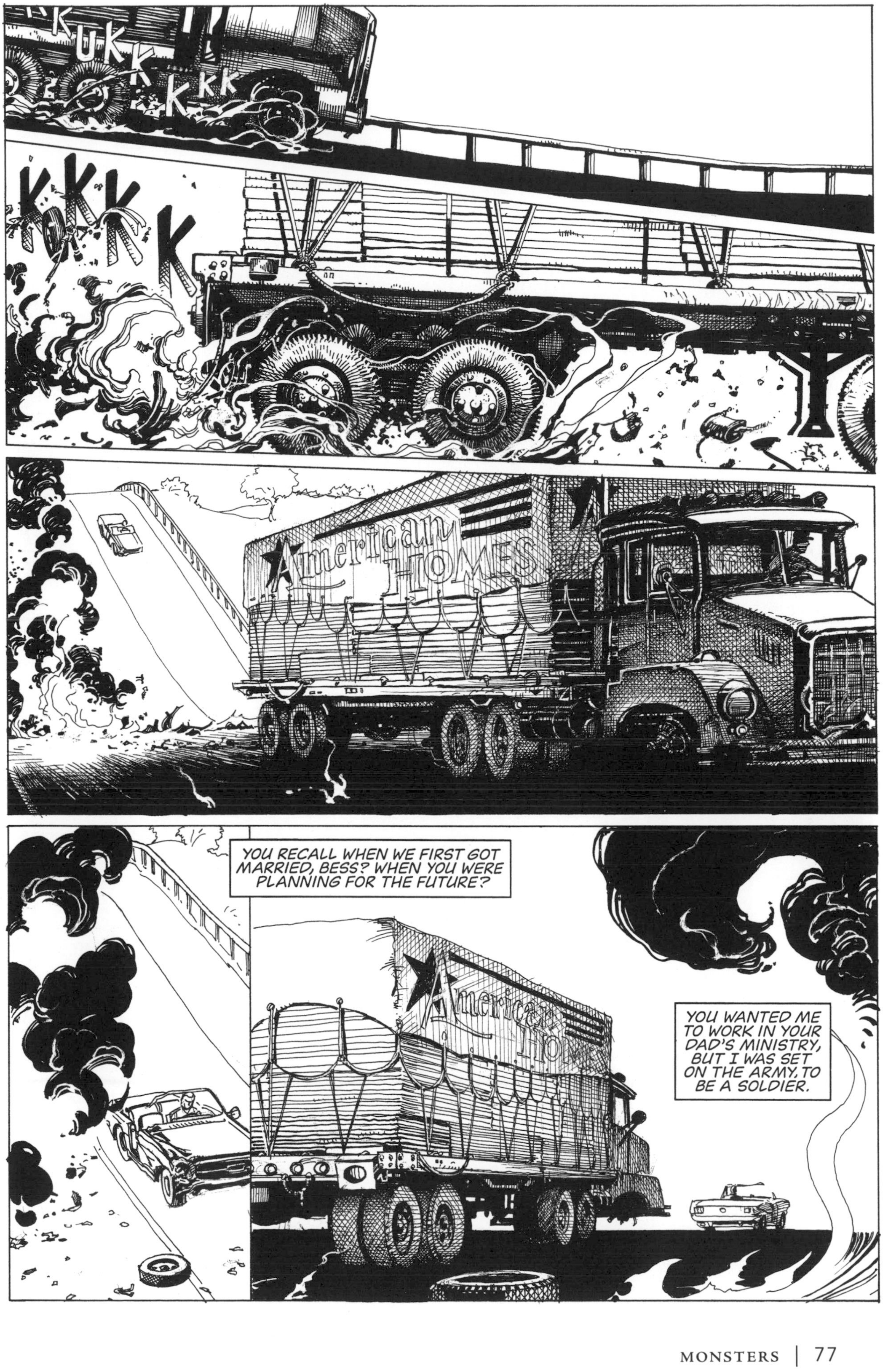

KUKKKKKK
KKKKK
AMERICAN HOMES
YOU RECALL WHEN WE FIRST GOT MARRIED, BESS? WHEN YOU WERE PLANNING FOR THE FUTURE?
YOU WANTED ME TO WORK IN YOUR DAD'S MINISTRY, BUT I WAS SET ON THE ARMY, TO BE A SOLDIER.

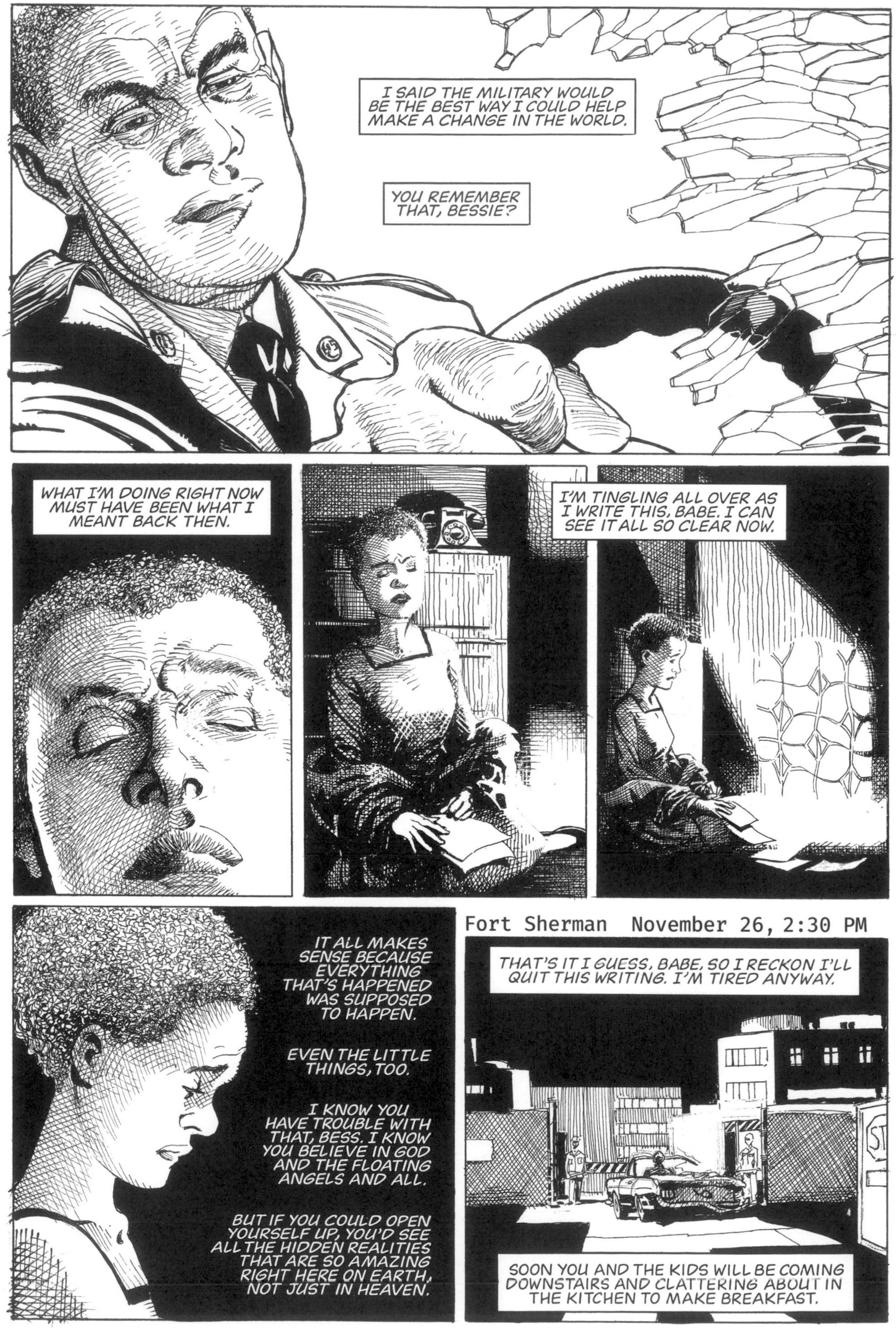
I SAID THE MILITARY WOULD BE THE BEST WAY I COULD HELP MAKE A CHANGE IN THE WORLD.
YOU REMEMBER THAT, BESSIE?
WHAT I'M DOING RIGHT NOW MUST HAVE BEEN WHAT I MEANT BACK THEN.
I'M TINGLING ALL OVER AS I WRITE THIS, BABE. I CAN SEE IT ALL SO CLEAR NOW.
IT ALL MAKES SENSE BECAUSE EVERYTHING THAT'S HAPPENED WAS SUPPOSED TO HAPPEN.
EVEN THE LITTLE THINGS, TOO.
I KNOW YOU HAVE TROUBLE WITH THAT, BESS. I KNOW YOU BELIEVE IN GOD AND THE FLOATING ANGELS AND ALL.
BUT IF YOU COULD OPEN YOURSELF UP, YOU'D SEE ALL THE HIDDEN REALITIES THAT ARE SO AMAZING RIGHT HERE ON EARTH, NOT JUST IN HEAVEN.
Fort Sherman November 26, 2:30 PM
THAT'S IT I GUESS, BABE, SO I RECKON I'LL QUIT THIS WRITING. I'M TIRED ANYWAY.
SOON YOU AND THE KIDS WILL BE COMING DOWNSTAIRS AND CLATTERING ABOUT IN THE KITCHEN TO MAKE BREAKFAST.

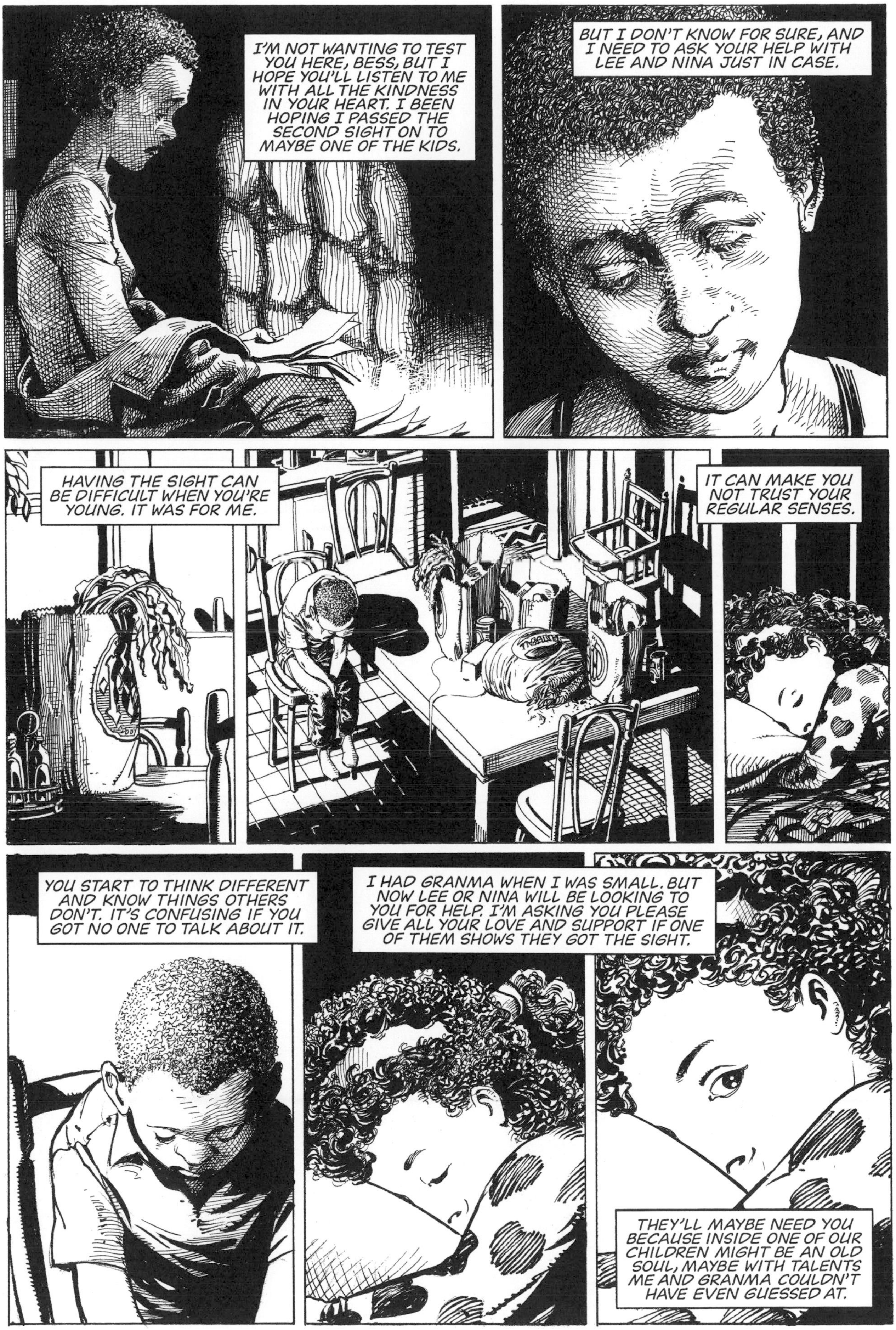
I'M NOT WANTING TO TEST YOU HERE, BESS, BUT I HOPE YOU'LL LISTEN TO ME WITH ALL THE KINDNESS IN YOUR HEART. I BEEN HOPING I PASSED THE SECOND SIGHT ON TO MAYBE ONE OF THE KIDS.
BUT I DON'T KNOW FOR SURE, AND I NEED TO ASK YOUR HELP WITH LEE AND NINA JUST IN CASE.
HAVING THE SIGHT CAN BE DIFFICULT WHEN YOU'RE YOUNG. IT WAS FOR ME.
IT CAN MAKE YOU NOT TRUST YOUR REGULAR SENSES.
YOU START TO THINK DIFFERENT AND KNOW THINGS OTHERS DON'T. IT'S CONFUSING IF YOU GOT NO ONE TO TALK ABOUT IT.
I HAD GRANMA WHEN I WAS SMALL. BUT NOW LEE OR NINA WILL BE LOOKING TO YOU FOR HELP. I'M ASKING YOU PLEASE GIVE ALL YOUR LOVE AND SUPPORT IF ONE OF THEM SHOWS THEY GOT THE SIGHT.
THEY'LL MAYBE NEED YOU BECAUSE INSIDE ONE OF OUR CHILDREN MIGHT BE AN OLD SOUL, MAYBE WITH TALENTS ME AND GRANMA COULDN'T HAVE EVEN GUESSED AT.

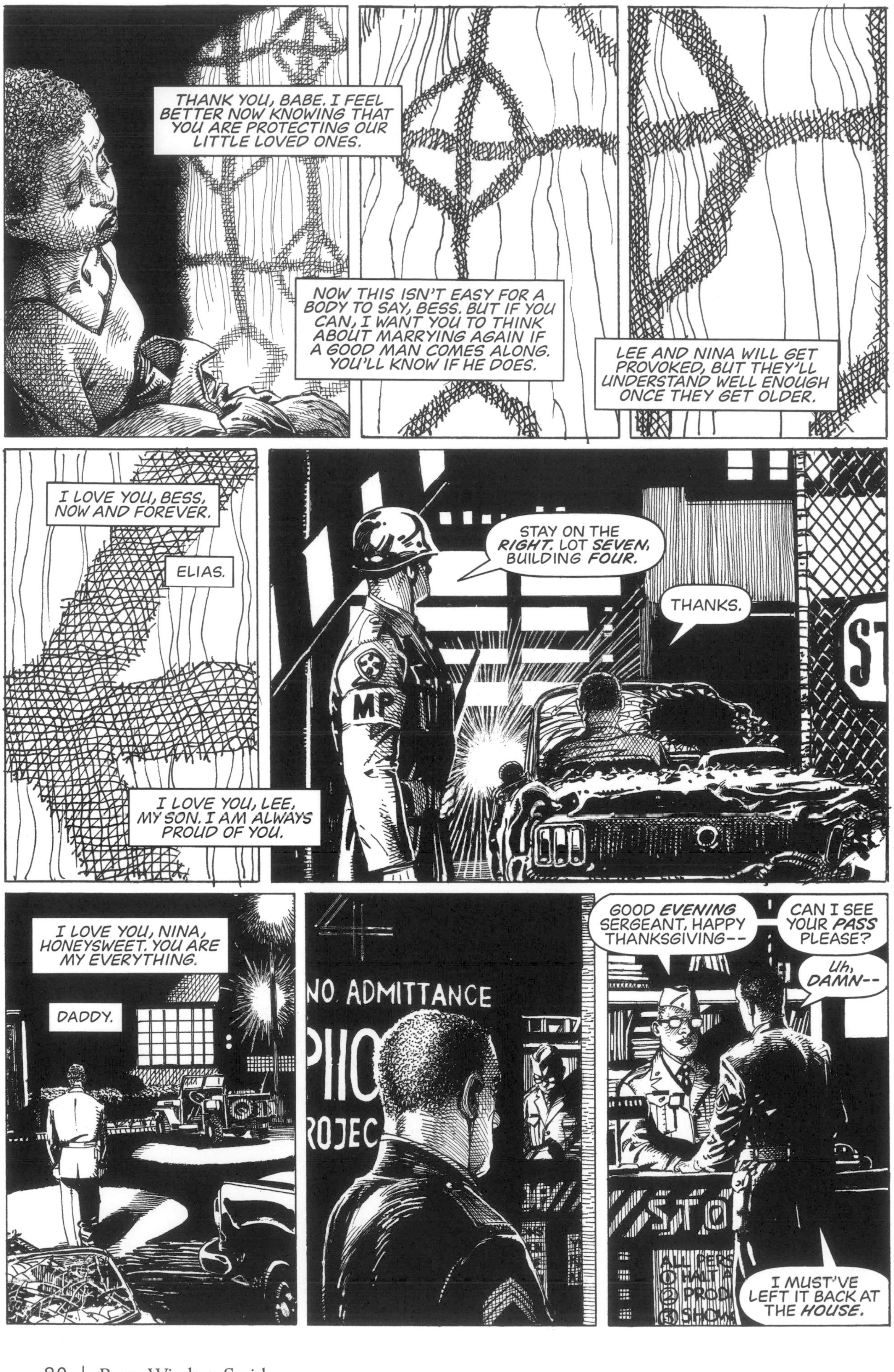
THANK YOU, BABE. I FEEL BETTER NOW KNOWING THAT YOU ARE PROTECTING OUR LITTLE LOVED ONES.
NOW THIS ISN'T EASY FOR A BODY TO SAY, BESS. BUT IF YOU CAN, I WANT YOU TO THINK ABOUT MARRYING AGAIN IF A GOOD MAN COMES ALONG. YOU'LL KNOW IF HE DOES.
LEE AND NINA WILL GET PROVOKED, BUT THEY'LL UNDERSTAND WELL ENOUGH ONCE THEY GET OLDER.
I LOVE YOU, BESS, NOW AND FOREVER.
ELIAS.
I LOVE YOU, LEE, MY SON. I AM ALWAYS PROUD OF YOU.
STAY ON THE RIGHT. LOT SEVEN, BUILDING FOUR.
THANKS.
MP
I LOVE YOU, NINA, HONEYSWEET. YOU ARE MY EVERYTHING.
DADDY.
NO. ADMITTANCE
GOOD EVENING SERGEANT, HAPPY THANKSGIVING--
CAN I SEE YOUR PASS PLEASE?
Uh, DAMN--
I MUST'VE LEFT IT BACK AT THE HOUSE.

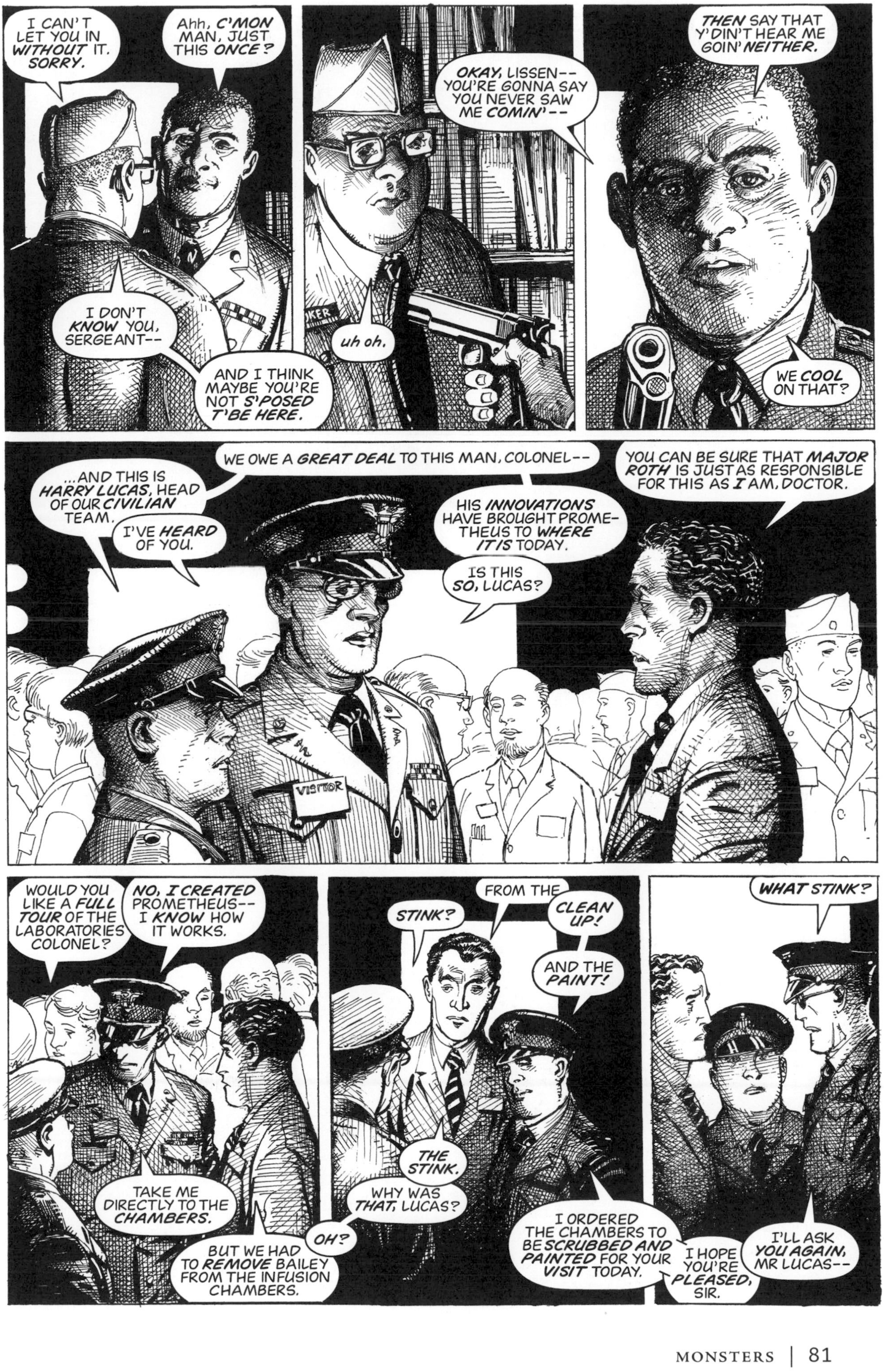
I CAN'T LET YOU IN WITHOUT IT. SORRY.
Ahh, C'MON MAN, JUST THIS ONCE?
I DON'T KNOW YOU, SERGEANT--
AND I THINK MAYBE YOU'RE NOT S'POSED T'BE HERE.
OKAY, LISSEN-- YOU'RE GONNA SAY YOU NEVER SAW ME COMIN'--
uh oh.
THEN SAY THAT Y'DIN'T HEAR ME GOIN' NEITHER.
WE COOL ON THAT?
...AND THIS IS HARRY LUCAS, HEAD OF OUR CIVILIAN TEAM.
WE OWE A GREAT DEAL TO THIS MAN, COLONEL--
I'VE HEARD OF YOU.
HIS INNOVATIONS HAVE BROUGHT PROMETHEUS TO WHERE IT IS TODAY.
IS THIS SO, LUCAS?
YOU CAN BE SURE THAT MAJOR ROTH IS JUST AS RESPONSIBLE FOR THIS AS I AM, DOCTOR.
VISITOR
WOULD YOU LIKE A FULL TOUR OF THE LABORATORIES COLONEL?
NO, I CREATED PROMETHEUS-- I KNOW HOW IT WORKS.
TAKE ME DIRECTLY TO THE CHAMBERS.
OH?
BUT WE HAD TO REMOVE BAILEY FROM THE INFUSION CHAMBERS.
STINK?
FROM THE CLEAN UP!
AND THE PAINT!
THE STINK.
WHY WAS THAT, LUCAS?
I ORDERED THE CHAMBERS TO BE SCRUBBED AND PAINTED FOR YOUR VISIT TODAY.
I HOPE YOU'RE PLEASED, SIR.
WHAT STINK?
I'LL ASK YOU AGAIN, MR LUCAS--

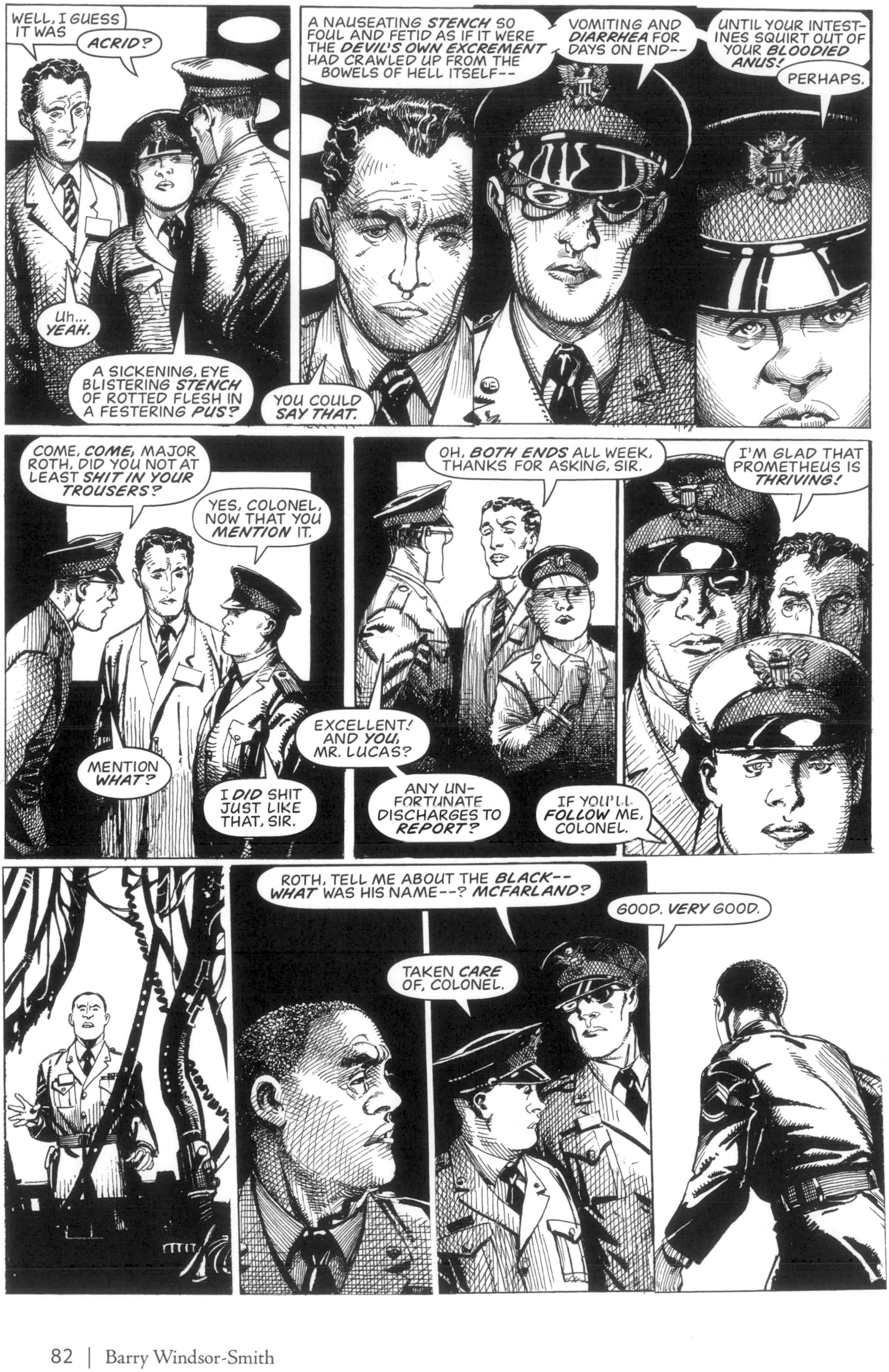
WELL, I GUESS IT WAS
ACRID?
Uh... YEAH.
A SICKENING, EYE BLISTERING STENCH OF ROTTED FLESH IN A FESTERING PUS?
A NAUSEATING STENCH SO FOUL AND FETID AS IF IT WERE THE DEVIL'S OWN EXCREMENT HAD CRAWLED UP FROM THE BOWELS OF HELL ITSELF--
YOU COULD SAY THAT.
VOMITING AND DIARRHEA FOR DAYS ON END--
UNTIL YOUR INTESTINES SQUIRT OUT OF YOUR BLOODIED ANUS!
PERHAPS.
COME, COME, MAJOR ROTH, DID YOU NOT AT LEAST SHIT IN YOUR TROUSERS?
YES, COLONEL, NOW THAT YOU MENTION IT.
MENTION WHAT?
I DID SHIT JUST LIKE THAT, SIR.
OH, BOTH ENDS ALL WEEK, THANKS FOR ASKING, SIR.
EXCELLENT! AND YOU, MR. LUCAS?
ANY UNFORTUNATE DISCHARGES TO REPORT?
I'M GLAD THAT PROMETHEUS IS THRIVING!
IF YOU'LL FOLLOW ME, COLONEL.
ROTH, TELL ME ABOUT THE BLACK-- WHAT WAS HIS NAME--? MCFARLAND?
TAKEN CARE OF, COLONEL.
GOOD. VERY GOOD.

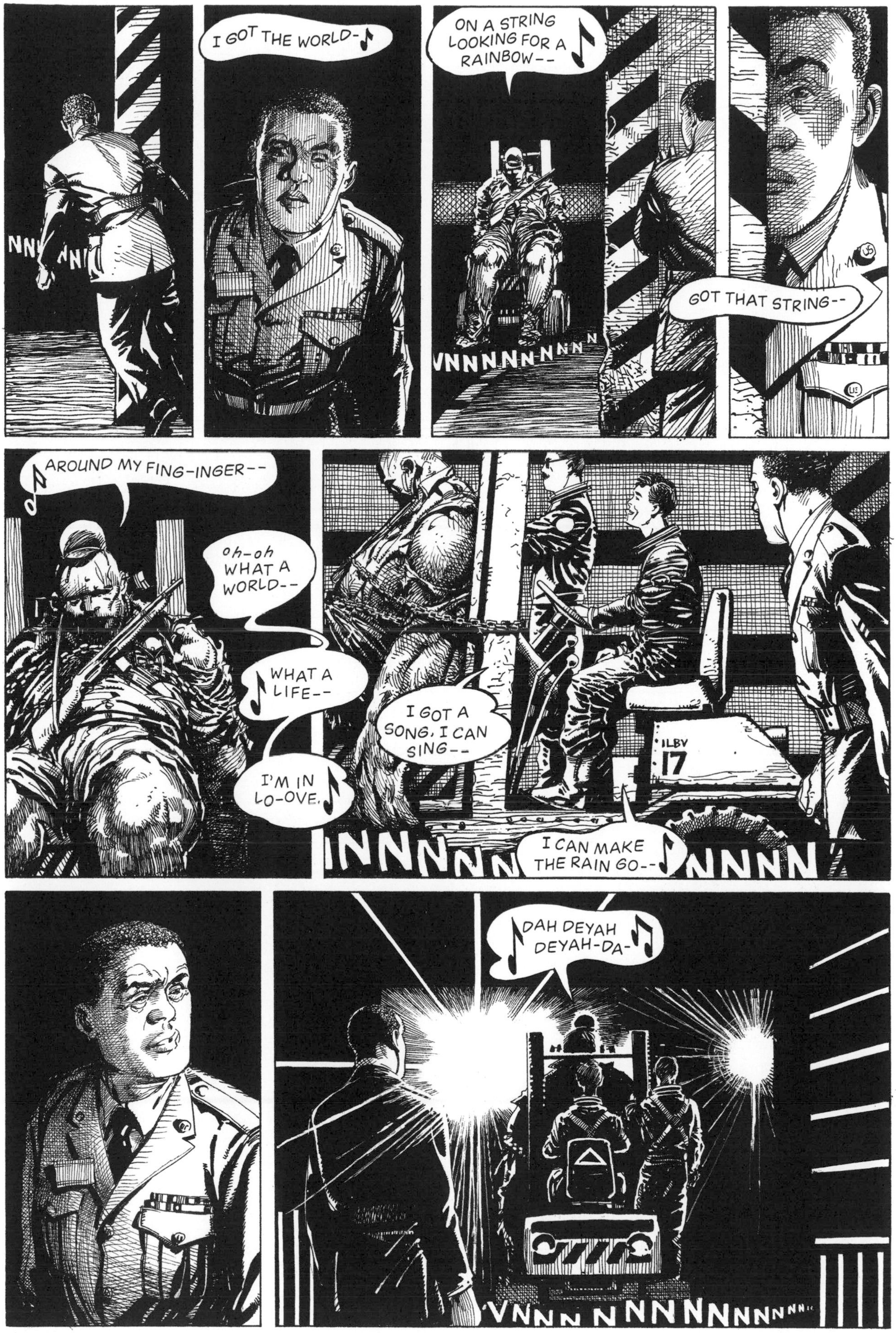
NNNNI
I GOT THE WORLD--
ON A STRING LOOKING FOR A RAINBOW--
VNNNNN-NNNN
GOT THAT STRING--
AROUND MY FING-INGER--
oh-oh WHAT A WORLD--
WHAT A LIFE--
I'M IN LO-OVE.
I GOT A SONG, I CAN SING--
ILBV 17
INNNNN
I CAN MAKE THE RAIN GO--
NNNN
DAH DEYAH DEYAH-DA-
VNNN NNNNNNNNN

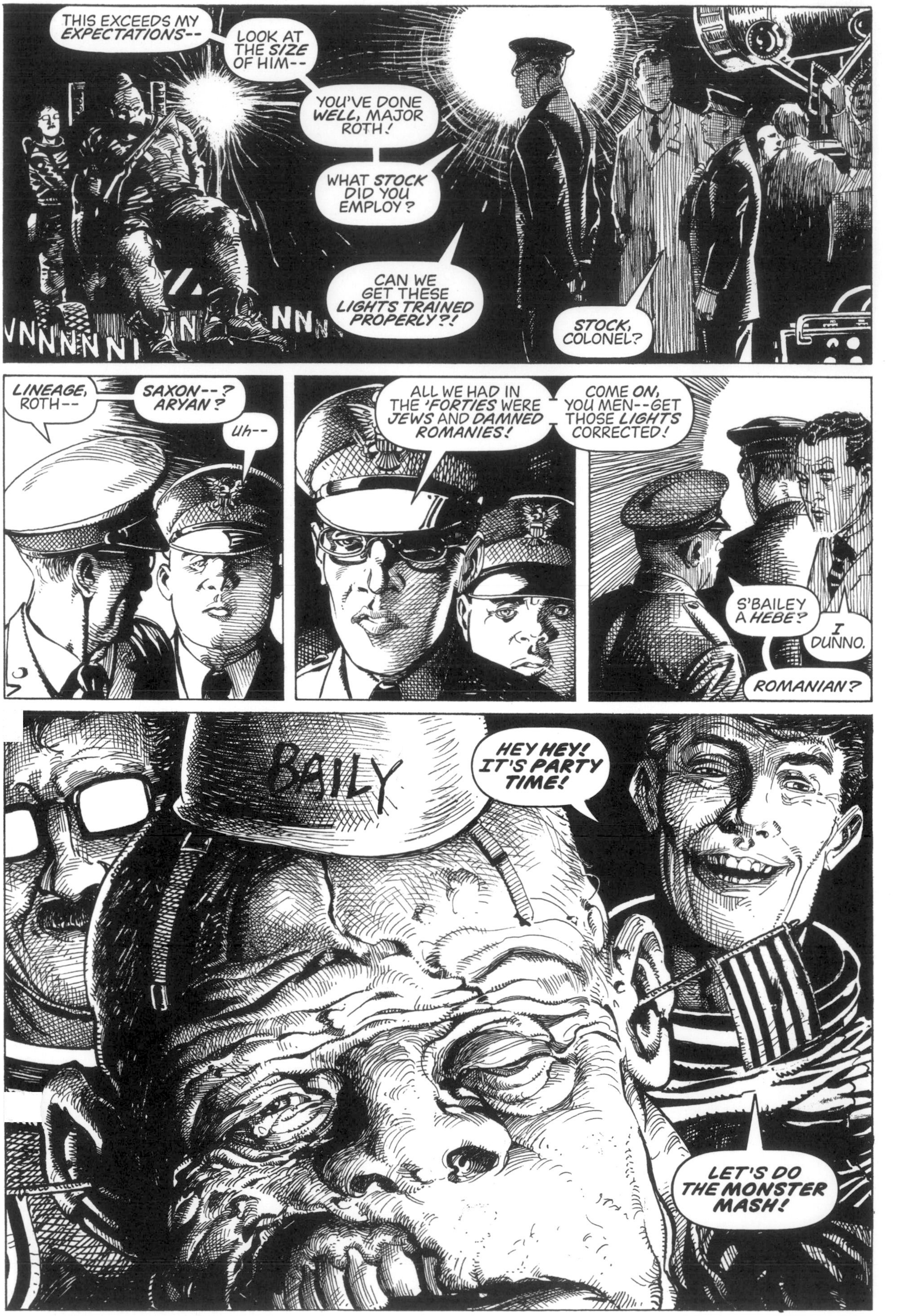
THIS EXCEEDS MY EXPECTATIONS--
LOOK AT THE SIZE OF HIM--
YOU'VE DONE WELL, MAJOR ROTH!
WHAT STOCK DID YOU EMPLOY?
CAN WE GET THESE LIGHTS TRAINED PROPERLY?!
STOCK, COLONEL?
NNNNNNN
LINEAGE, ROTH--
SAXON--? ARYAN?
Uh--
ALL WE HAD IN THE 'FORTIES WERE JEWS AND DAMNED ROMANIES!
COME ON, YOU MEN--GET THOSE LIGHTS CORRECTED!
S'BAILEY A HEBE?
I DUNNO.
ROMANIAN?
BAILY
HEY HEY! IT'S PARTY TIME!
LET'S DO THE MONSTER MASH!

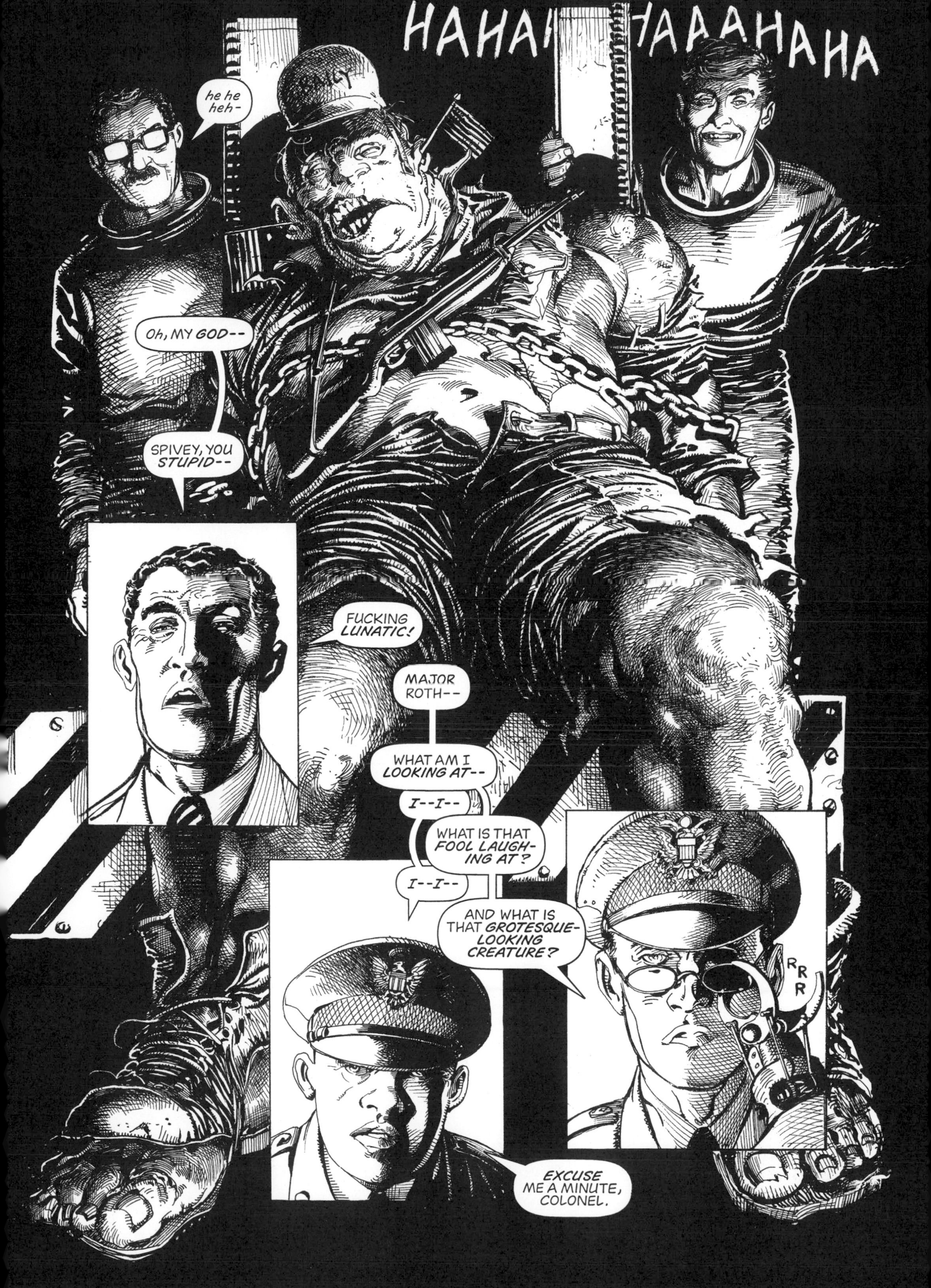
HAHAHAAAAHAHA
he he heh-
Oh, MY GOD--
SPIVEY, YOU STUPID--
FUCKING LUNATIC!
MAJOR ROTH--
WHAT AM I LOOKING AT--
I--I--
WHAT IS THAT FOOL LAUGHING AT?
I--I--
AND WHAT IS THAT GROTESQUE-LOOKING CREATURE?
RRR
EXCUSE ME A MINUTE, COLONEL.

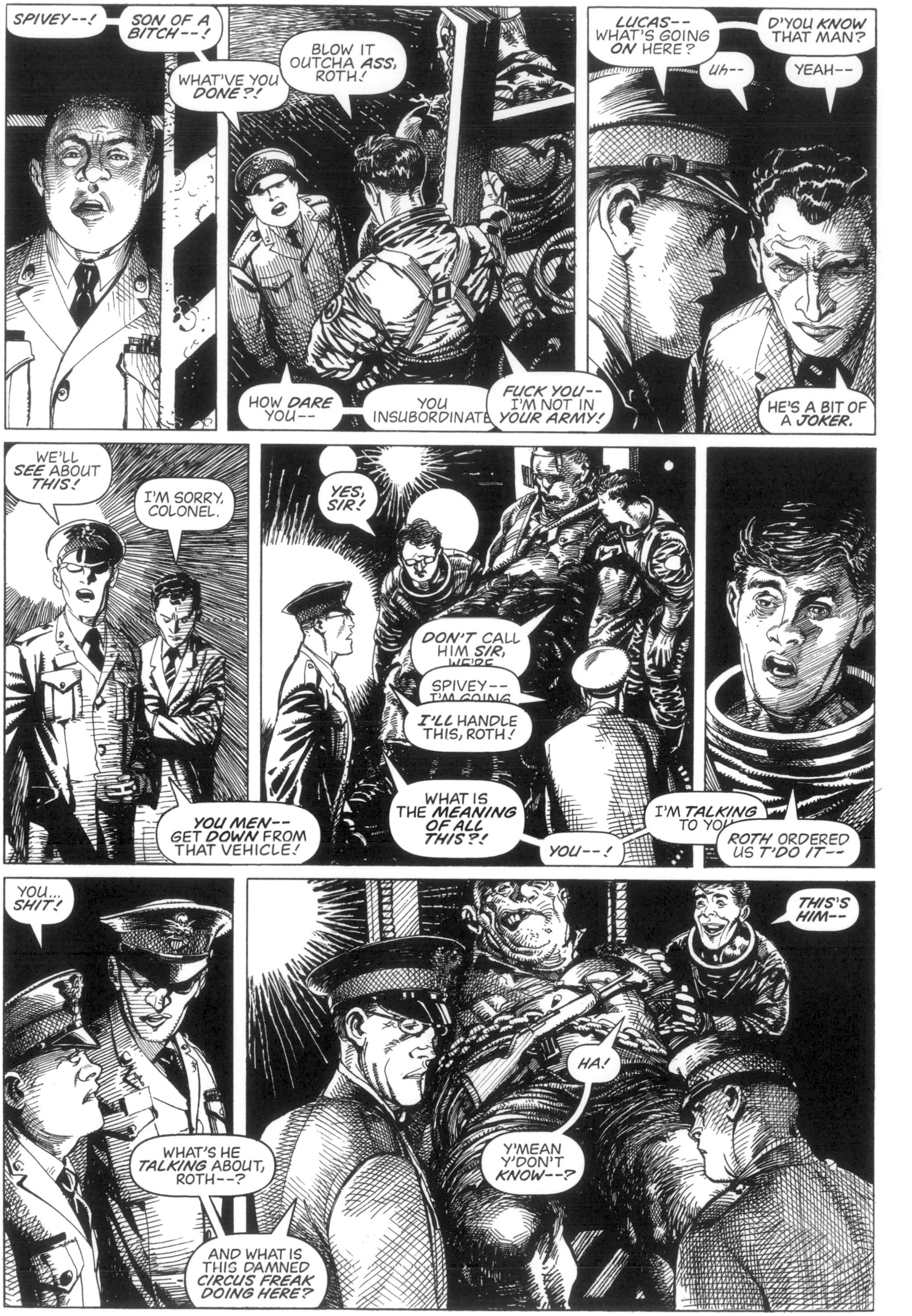
SPIVEY--!
SON OF A BITCH--!
WHAT'VE YOU DONE?!
BLOW IT OUTCHA ASS, ROTH!
HOW DARE YOU--
YOU INSUBORDINATE
FUCK YOU-- I'M NOT IN YOUR ARMY!
LUCAS-- WHAT'S GOING ON HERE?
D'YOU KNOW THAT MAN?
Uh--
YEAH--
HE'S A BIT OF A JOKER.
WE'LL SEE ABOUT THIS!
I'M SORRY, COLONEL.
YOU MEN-- GET DOWN FROM THAT VEHICLE!
YES, SIR!
DON'T CALL HIM SIR,
SPIVEY--
I'LL HANDLE THIS, ROTH!
WHAT IS THE MEANING OF ALL THIS?!
YOU--!
I'M TALKING
ROTH ORDERED US T'DO IT--
YOU... SHIT!
THIS'S HIM--
HA!
WHAT'S HE TALKING ABOUT, ROTH--?
Y'MEAN Y'DON'T KNOW--?
AND WHAT IS THIS DAMNED CIRCUS FREAK DOING HERE?

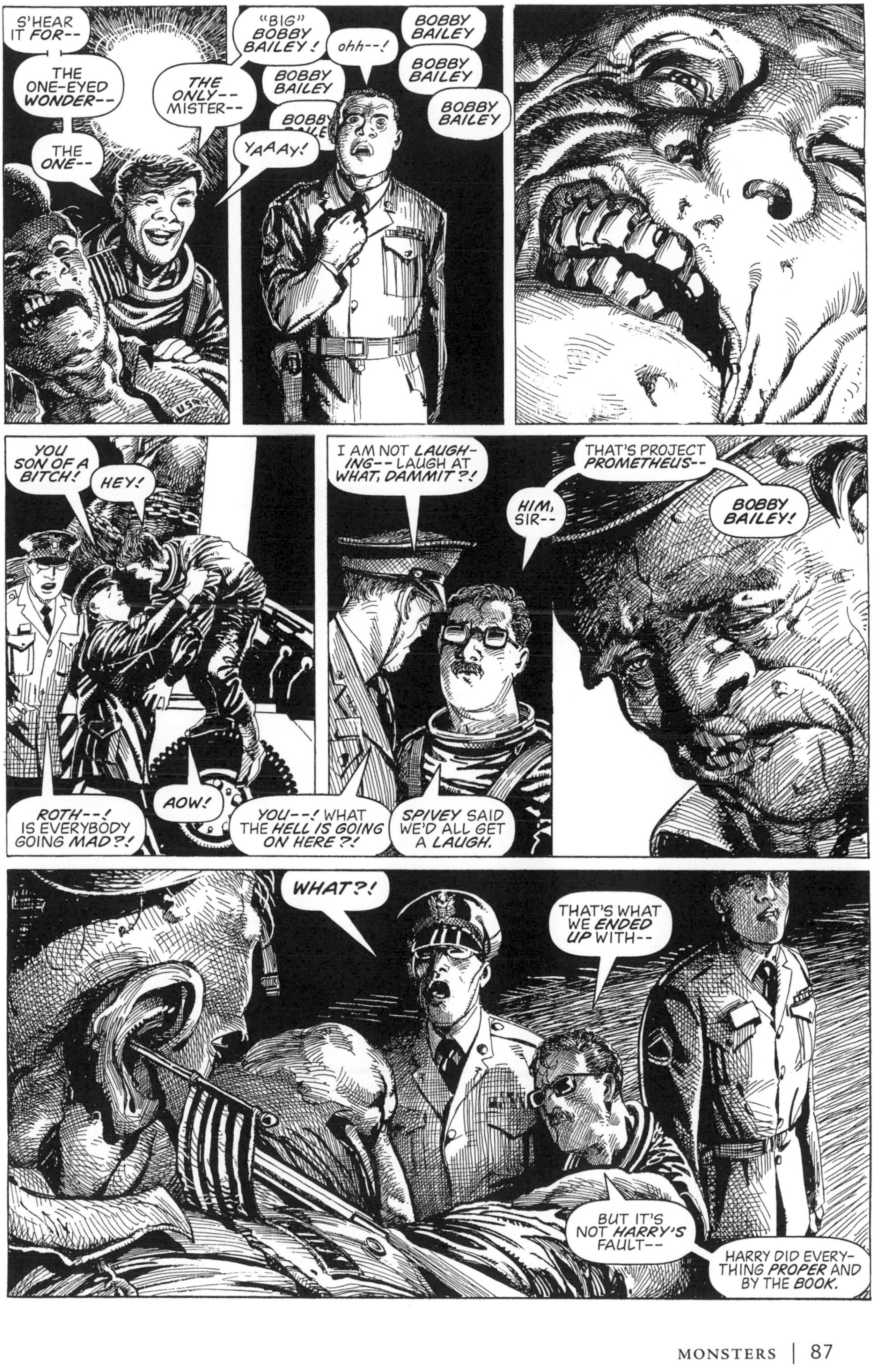
S'HEAR IT FOR--
THE ONE-EYED WONDER--
THE ONE--
THE ONLY-- MISTER--
"BIG" BOBBY BAILEY!
ohh--!
BOBBY BAILEY
BOBBY BAILEY
YAAAY!
BOBBY BAILEY
BOBBY BAILEY
BOBBY BAILEY
YOU SON OF A BITCH!
HEY!
ROTH--! IS EVERYBODY GOING MAD?!
AOW!
YOU--! WHAT THE HELL IS GOING ON HERE?!
I AM NOT LAUGHING-- LAUGH AT WHAT, DAMMIT?!
SPIVEY SAID WE'D ALL GET A LAUGH.
HIM, SIR--
THAT'S PROJECT PROMETHEUS--
BOBBY BAILEY!
WHAT?!
THAT'S WHAT WE ENDED UP WITH--
BUT IT'S NOT HARRY'S FAULT--
HARRY DID EVERYTHING PROPER AND BY THE BOOK.

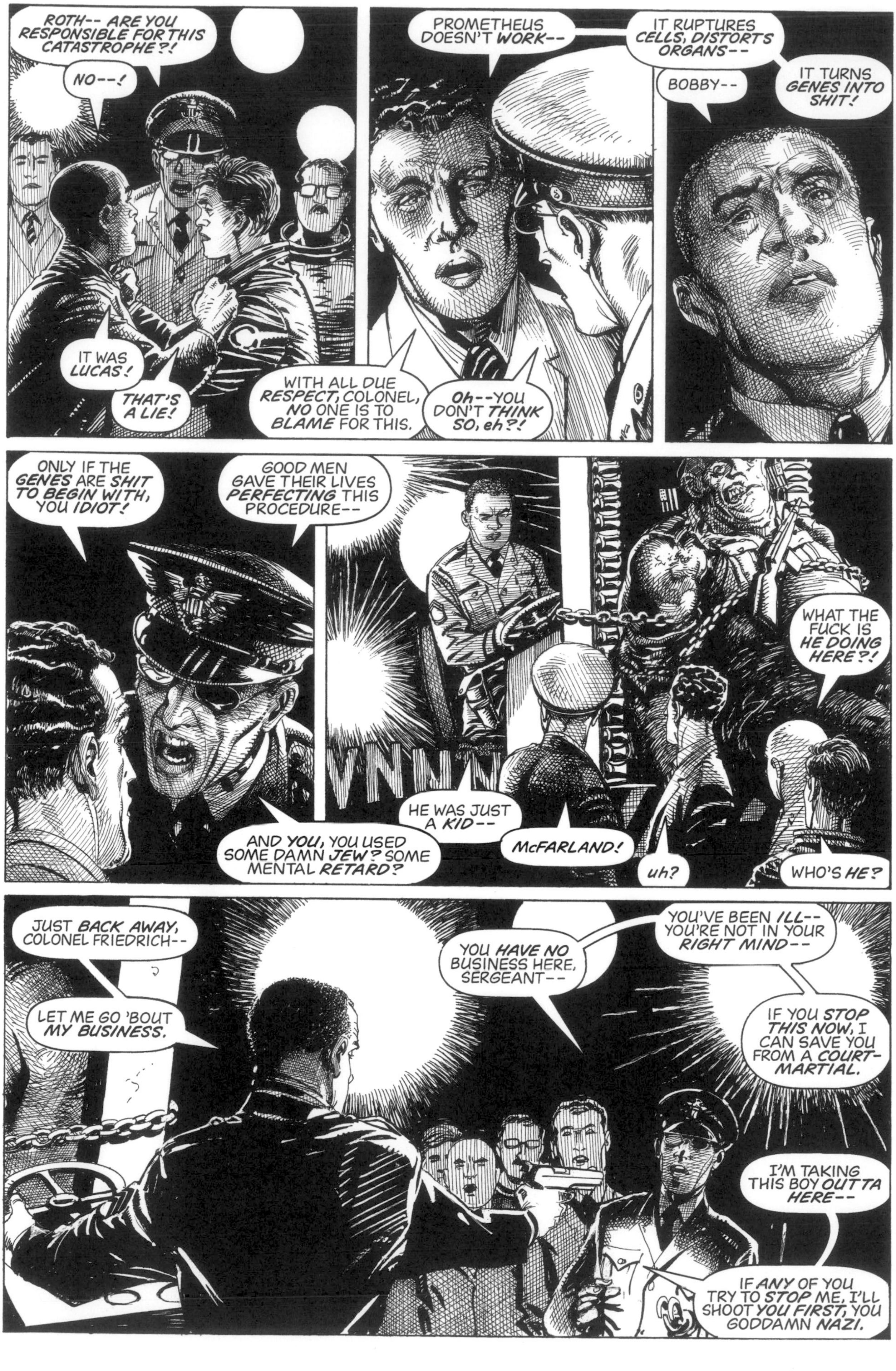
ROTH-- ARE YOU RESPONSIBLE FOR THIS CATASTROPHE?!
NO--!
IT WAS LUCAS!
THAT'S A LIE!
PROMETHEUS DOESN'T WORK--
IT RUPTURES CELLS, DISTORTS ORGANS--
WITH ALL DUE RESPECT, COLONEL, NO ONE IS TO BLAME FOR THIS.
Oh--YOU DON'T THINK SO, eh?!
BOBBY--
IT TURNS GENES INTO SHIT!
ONLY IF THE GENES ARE SHIT TO BEGIN WITH, YOU IDIOT!
GOOD MEN GAVE THEIR LIVES PERFECTING THIS PROCEDURE--
AND YOU, YOU USED SOME DAMN JEW? SOME MENTAL RETARD?
HE WAS JUST A KID--
VNNN
McFARLAND!
WHAT THE FUCK IS HE DOING HERE?!
uh?
WHO'S HE?
JUST BACK AWAY, COLONEL FRIEDRICH--
LET ME GO 'BOUT MY BUSINESS.
YOU HAVE NO BUSINESS HERE, SERGEANT--
YOU'VE BEEN ILL-- YOU'RE NOT IN YOUR RIGHT MIND--
IF YOU STOP THIS NOW, I CAN SAVE YOU FROM A COURT-MARTIAL.
I'M TAKING THIS BOY OUTTA HERE--
IF ANY OF YOU TRY TO STOP ME, I'LL SHOOT YOU FIRST, YOU GODDAMN NAZI.

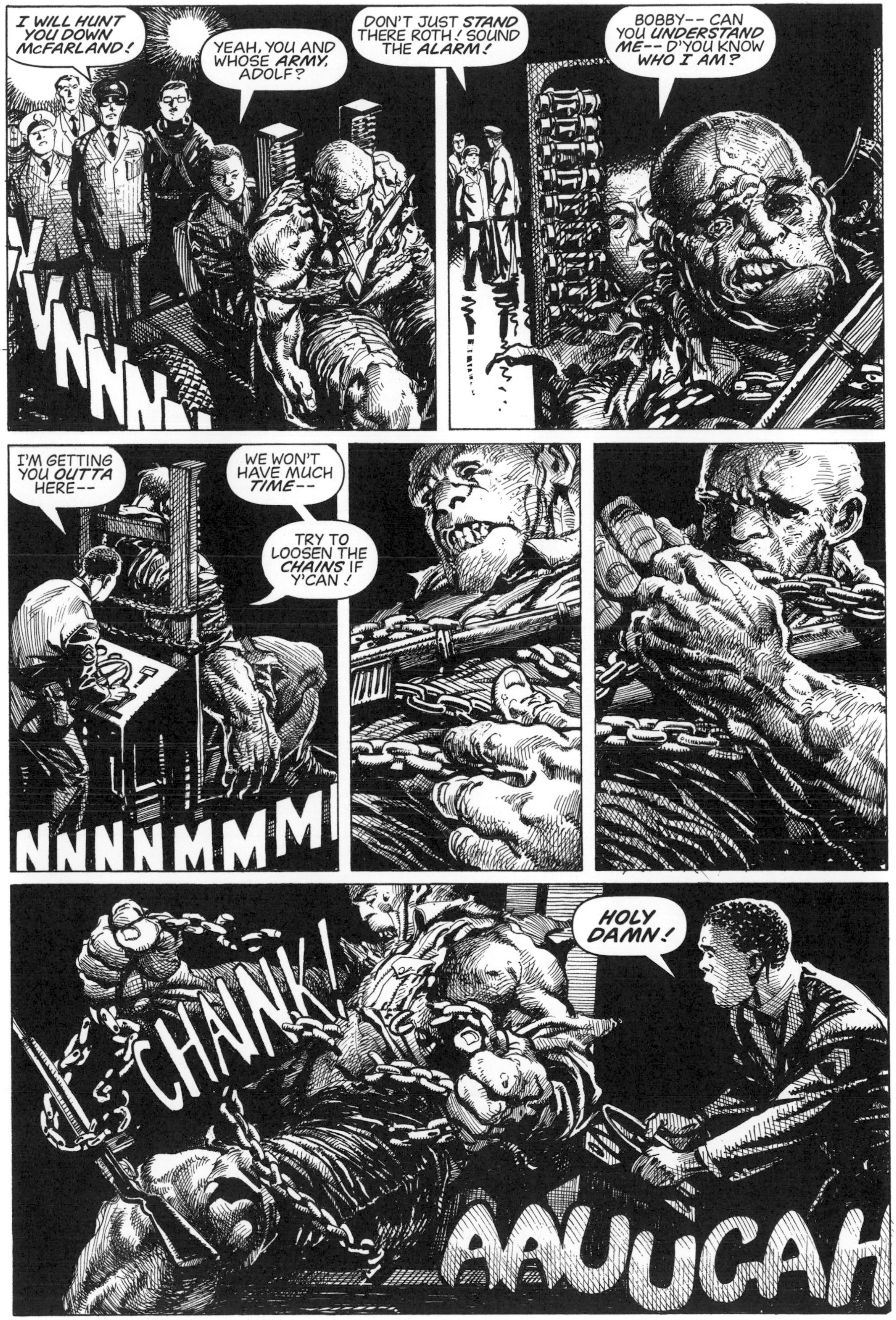
I WILL HUNT YOU DOWN McFARLAND!
YEAH, YOU AND WHOSE ARMY, ADOLF?
VNNNN
DON'T JUST STAND THERE ROTH! SOUND THE ALARM!
BOBBY-- CAN YOU UNDERSTAND ME-- D'YOU KNOW WHO I AM?
I'M GETTING YOU OUTTA HERE--
WE WON'T HAVE MUCH TIME--
TRY TO LOOSEN THE CHAINS IF Y'CAN!
NNNNMMMM
CHANK!
HOLY DAMN!
AAUUGAH

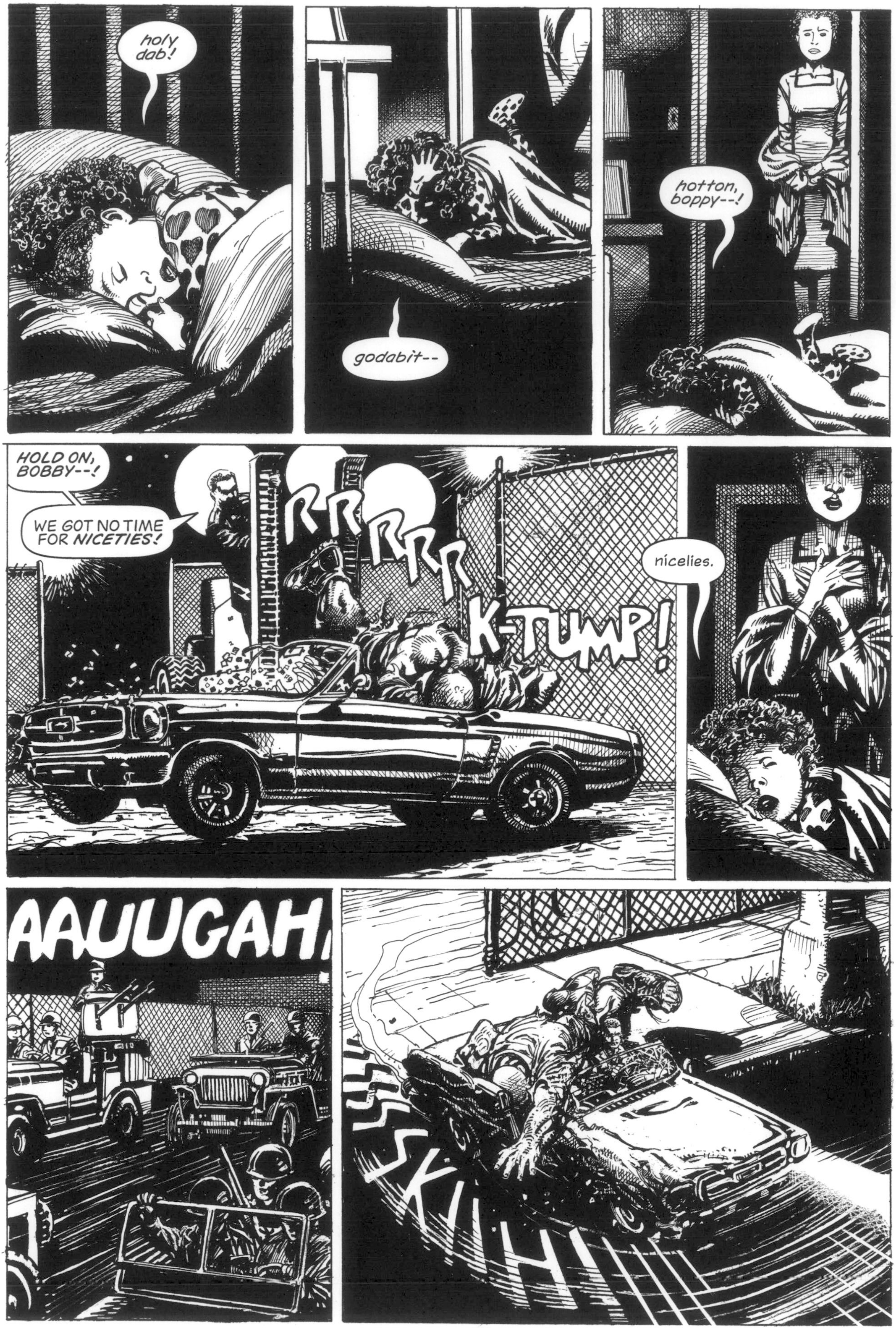

holy dab!
godabit--
hotton, boppy--!
HOLD ON, BOBBY--!
WE GOT NO TIME FOR NICETIES!
RRRRRR
K-TUMP!
nicelies.
AAUUGAH!
SKIIIH!

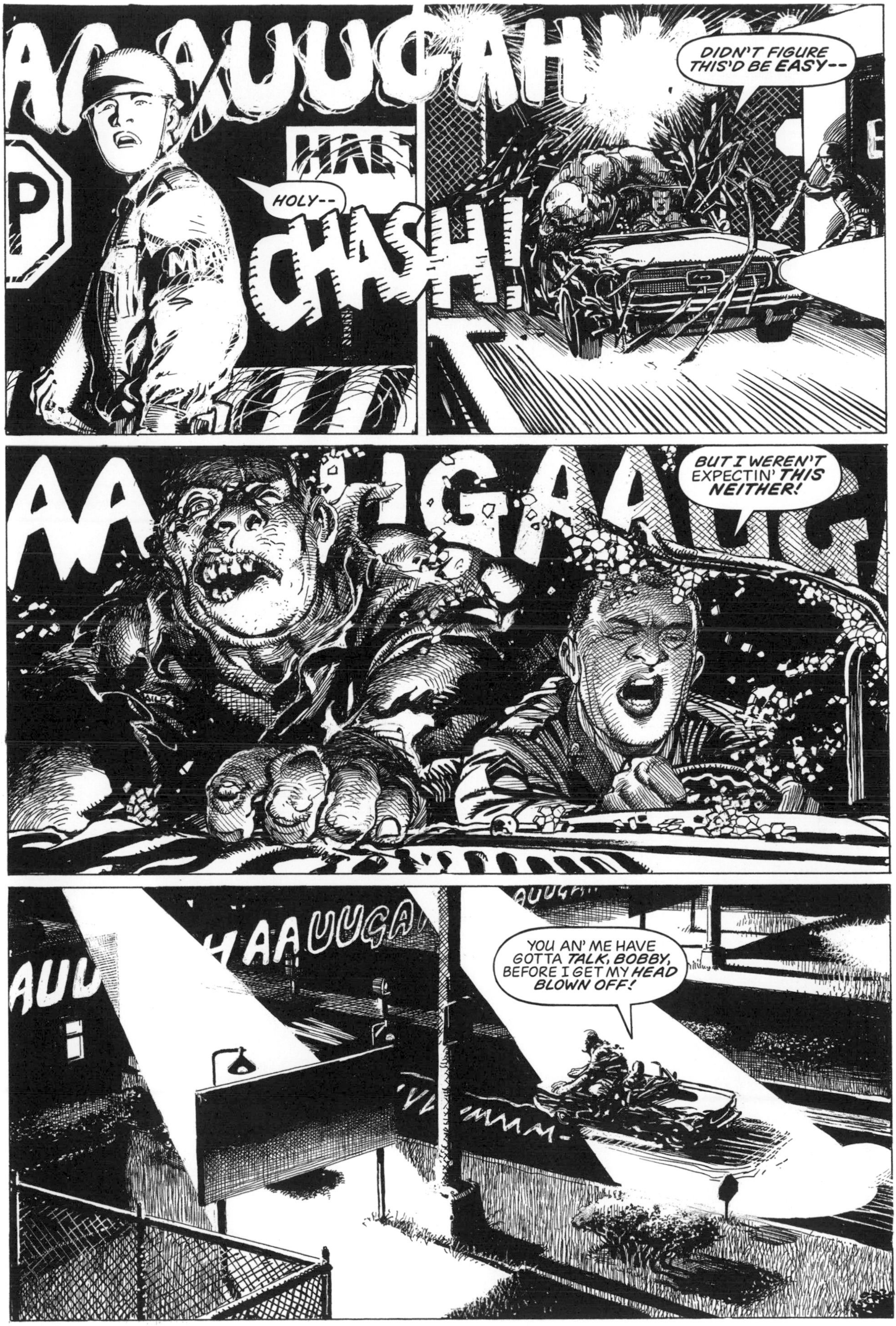
AAAUUGAH
HALT
HOLY--
CHASH!
DIDN'T FIGURE THIS'D BE EASY--
BUT I WEREN'T EXPECTIN' THIS NEITHER!
YOU AN' ME HAVE GOTTA TALK, BOBBY, BEFORE I GET MY HEAD BLOWN OFF!

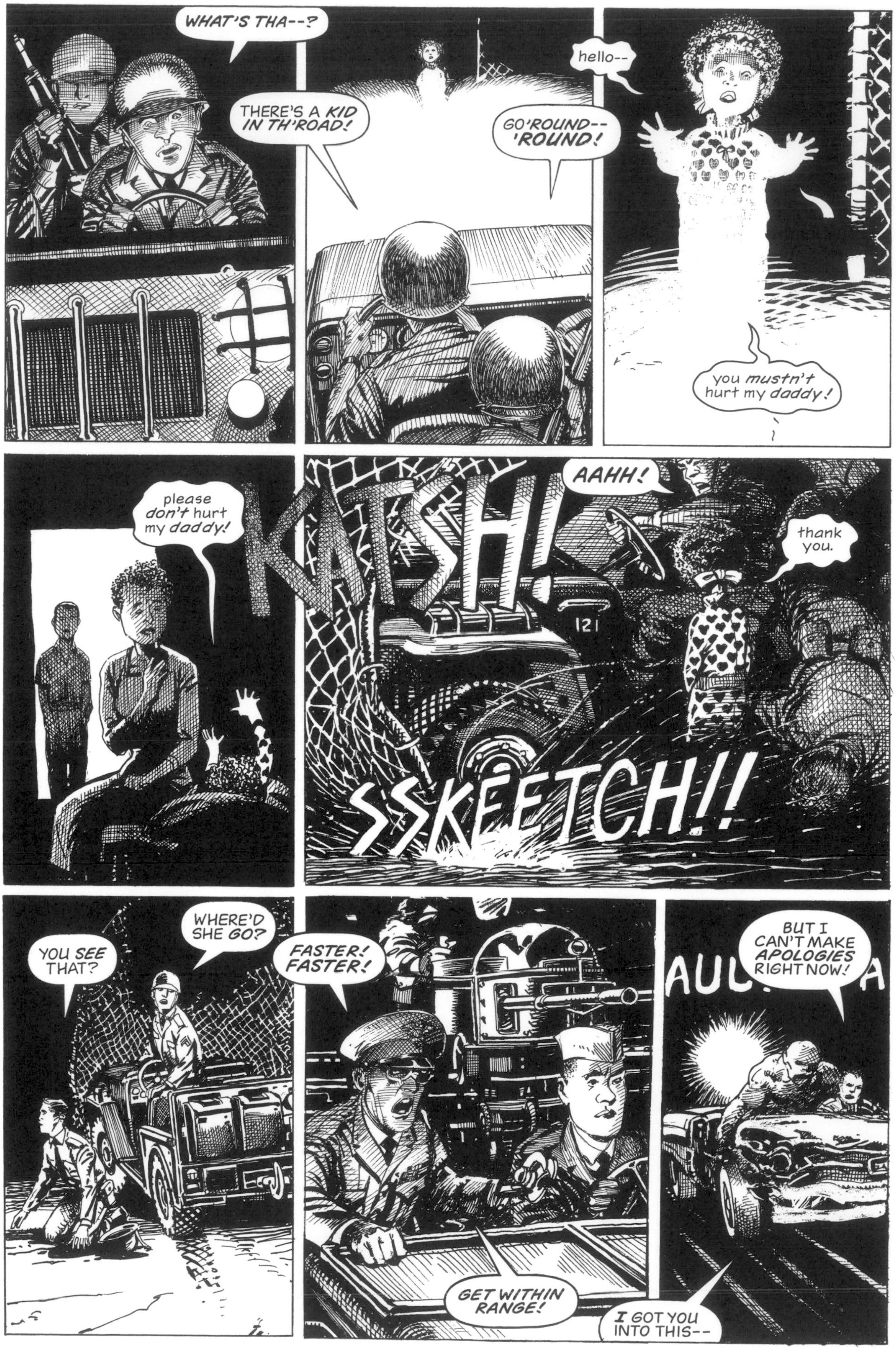

WHAT'S THA--?
THERE'S A KID IN TH'ROAD!
GO'ROUND-- 'ROUND!
hello--
you mustn't hurt my daddy!
please don't hurt my daddy!
KATSH!
AAHH!
thank you.
SSKEETCH!!
WHERE'D SHE GO?
YOU SEE THAT?
FASTER! FASTER!
GET WITHIN RANGE!
BUT I CAN'T MAKE APOLOGIES RIGHT NOW!
I GOT YOU INTO THIS--

I WON'T ASK YOU TO FORGIVE ME FOR WHAT'S HAPPENED--
AND I CAN'T PRETEND THAT I HAD NO CHOICE EITHER--
BUT AS CRAZY AS IT'S GONNA SOUND--
YOU AN' ME ARE CONNECTED TOGETHER--
YUNNER -STAN?
I MEAN THERE'S SOME PURPOSE IN ALL THIS!
GUNNER-- GET THAT DRIVER!
BEG Y'PARDON, SIR, BUT THAT MAN THERE'S ON A SPIRITUAL MISSION!
DON'T QUESTION MY ORDERS, SHOOT THAT NIGGER!
AND EVERYTHING THAT'S HAPPENING IS SUPPOSED TO
POK
POKKAPOKKA!
daddy!
daddyyy!
daddyyy!

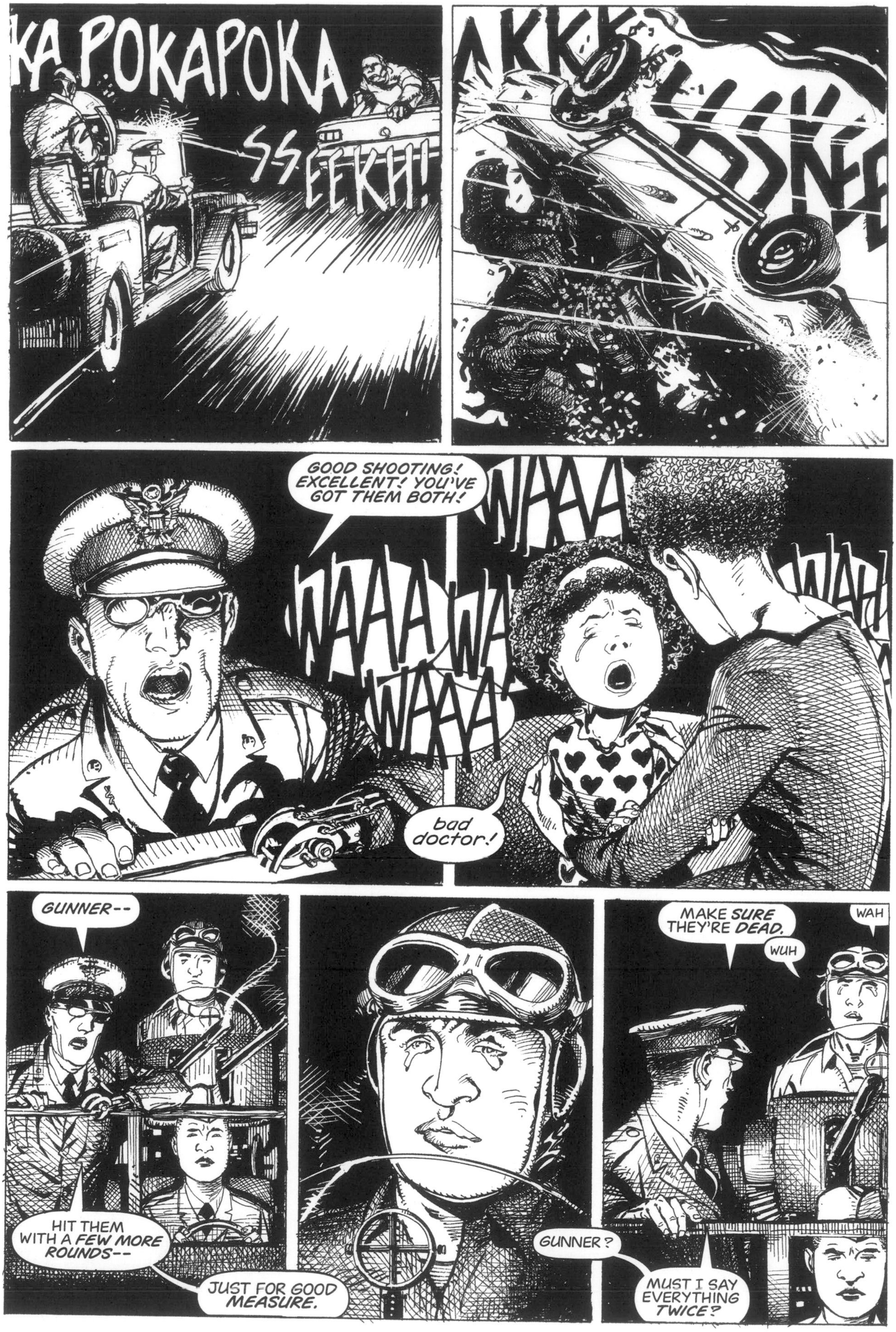
KA POKAPOKA
SSEEKH!
GOOD SHOOTING! EXCELLENT! YOU'VE GOT THEM BOTH!
WAAA
WAAA WA WAAA
bad doctor!
GUNNER--
HIT THEM WITH A FEW MORE ROUNDS--
JUST FOR GOOD MEASURE.
MAKE SURE THEY'RE DEAD.
WAH
WUH
GUNNER?
MUST I SAY EVERYTHING TWICE?

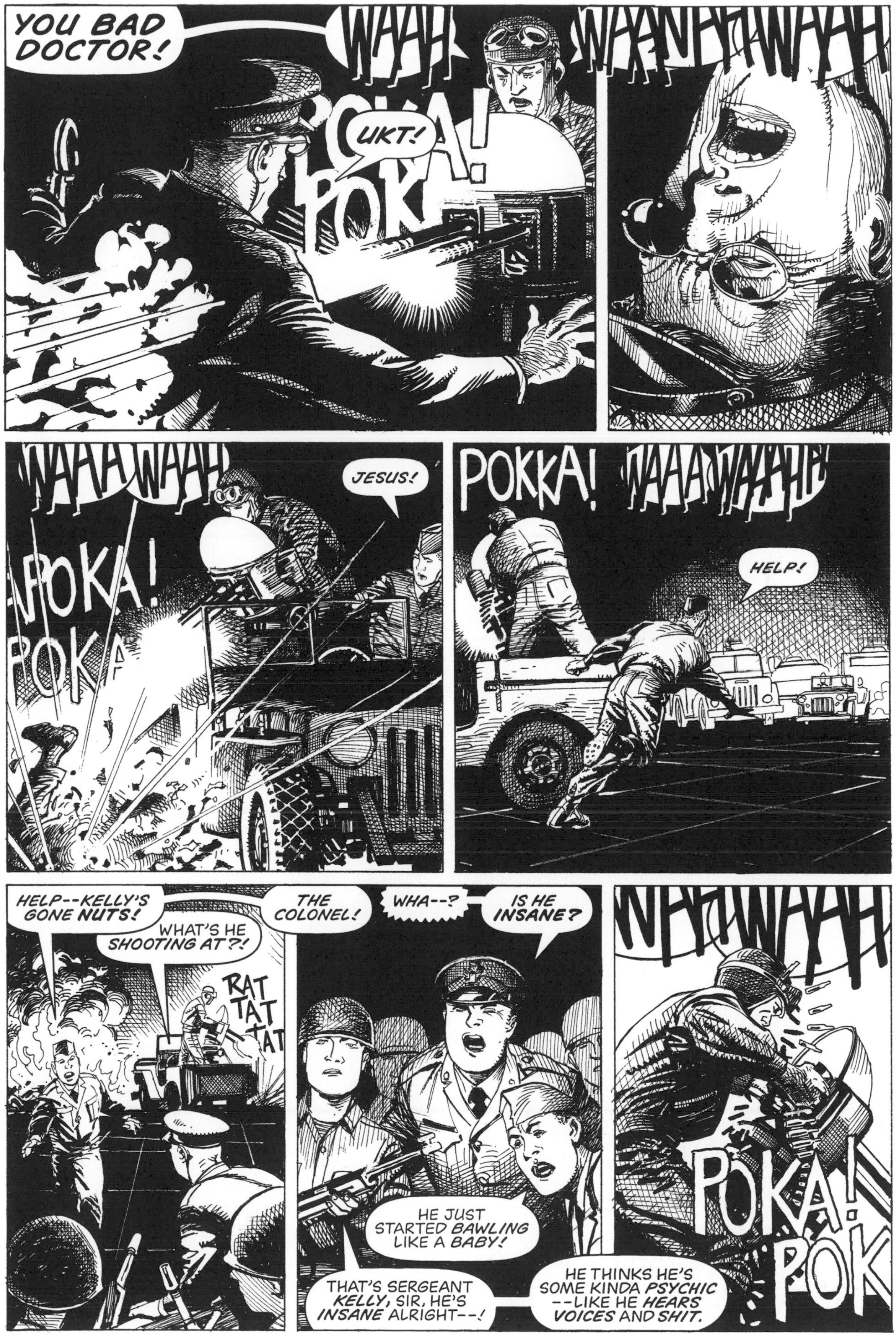
YOU BAD DOCTOR!
WAAH
WAAH WAAH WAAH
POKA!
UKT!
POK
WAAA WAAH
JESUS!
POKA!
POKA
POKKA!
WAAA WAAH
HELP!
HELP--KELLY'S GONE NUTS!
WHAT'S HE SHOOTING AT?!
RAT TAT TAT
THE COLONEL!
WHA--?
IS HE INSANE?
HE JUST STARTED BAWLING LIKE A BABY!
THAT'S SERGEANT KELLY, SIR, HE'S INSANE ALRIGHT--!
HE THINKS HE'S SOME KINDA PSYCHIC --LIKE HE HEARS VOICES AND SHIT.
WAAH WAAH
POKA!
POK

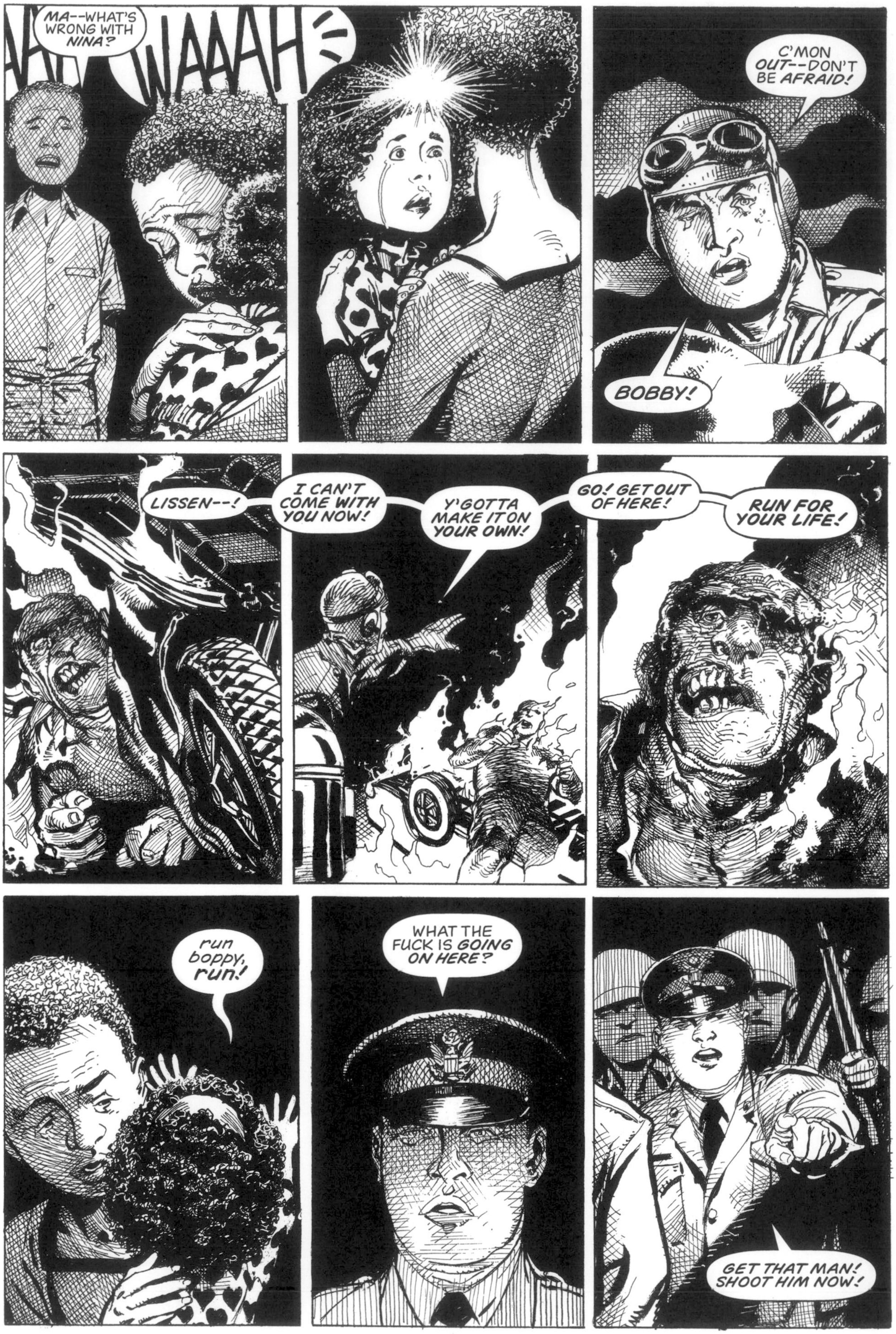
MA--WHAT'S WRONG WITH NINA?
WAAAH
C'MON OUT--DON'T BE AFRAID!
BOBBY!
LISSEN--!
I CAN'T COME WITH YOU NOW!
Y'GOTTA MAKE IT ON YOUR OWN!
GO! GET OUT OF HERE!
RUN FOR YOUR LIFE!
run boppy, run!
WHAT THE FUCK IS GOING ON HERE?
GET THAT MAN! SHOOT HIM NOW!

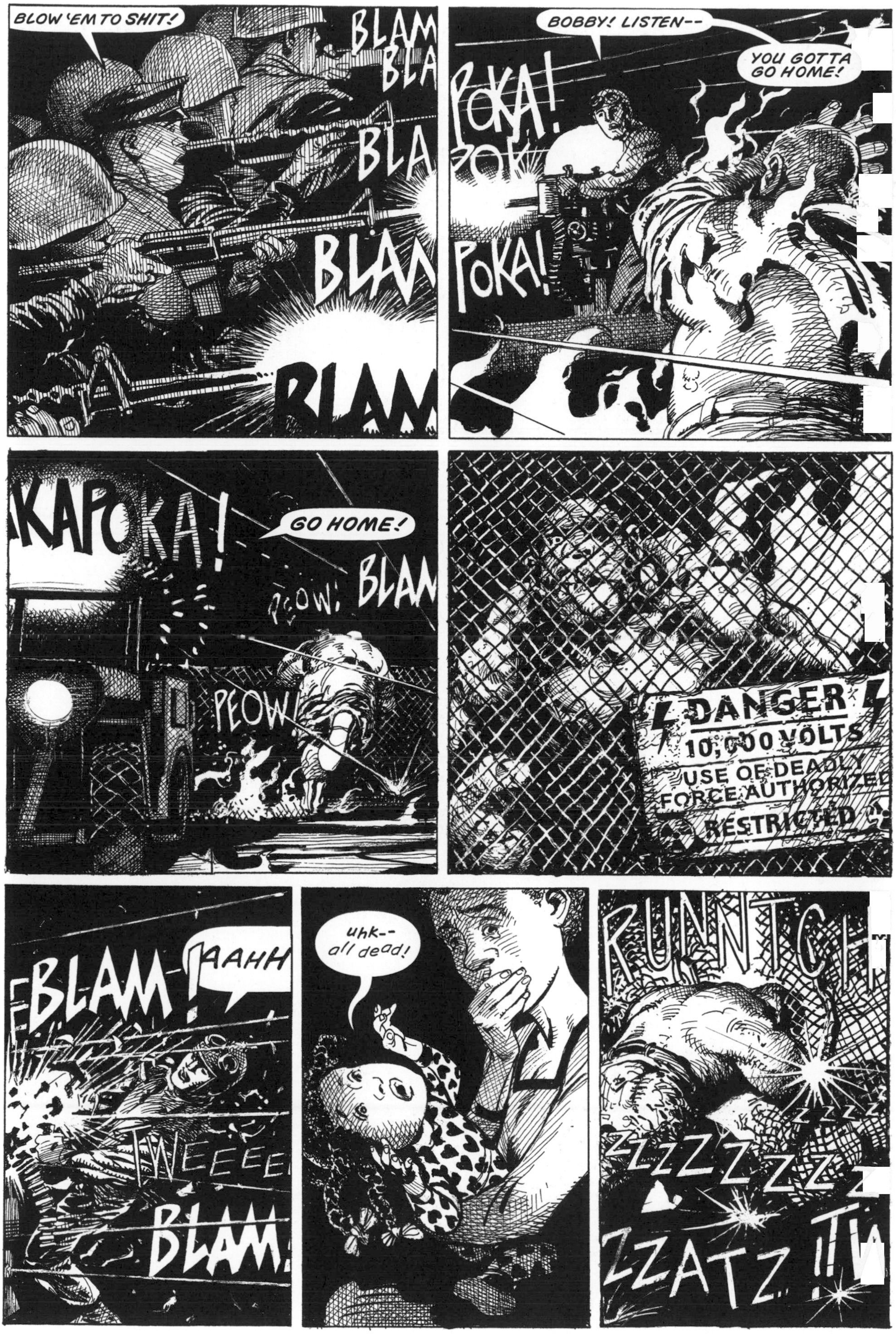
BLOW 'EM TO SHIT!
BLAM
BLA
BLA
BLAM
BLAM
BOBBY! LISTEN--
YOU GOTTA GO HOME!
POKA!
POKA!
KAPOKA!
GO HOME!
BLAM
PEOW!
PEOW!
DANGER
10,000 VOLTS
USE OF DEADLY FORCE AUTHORIZED
RESTRICTED
BLAM!
AAHH
TWEEEE
BLAM!
uhk-- all dead!
RUNNTCH
ZZZZZZZ
ZZATZ

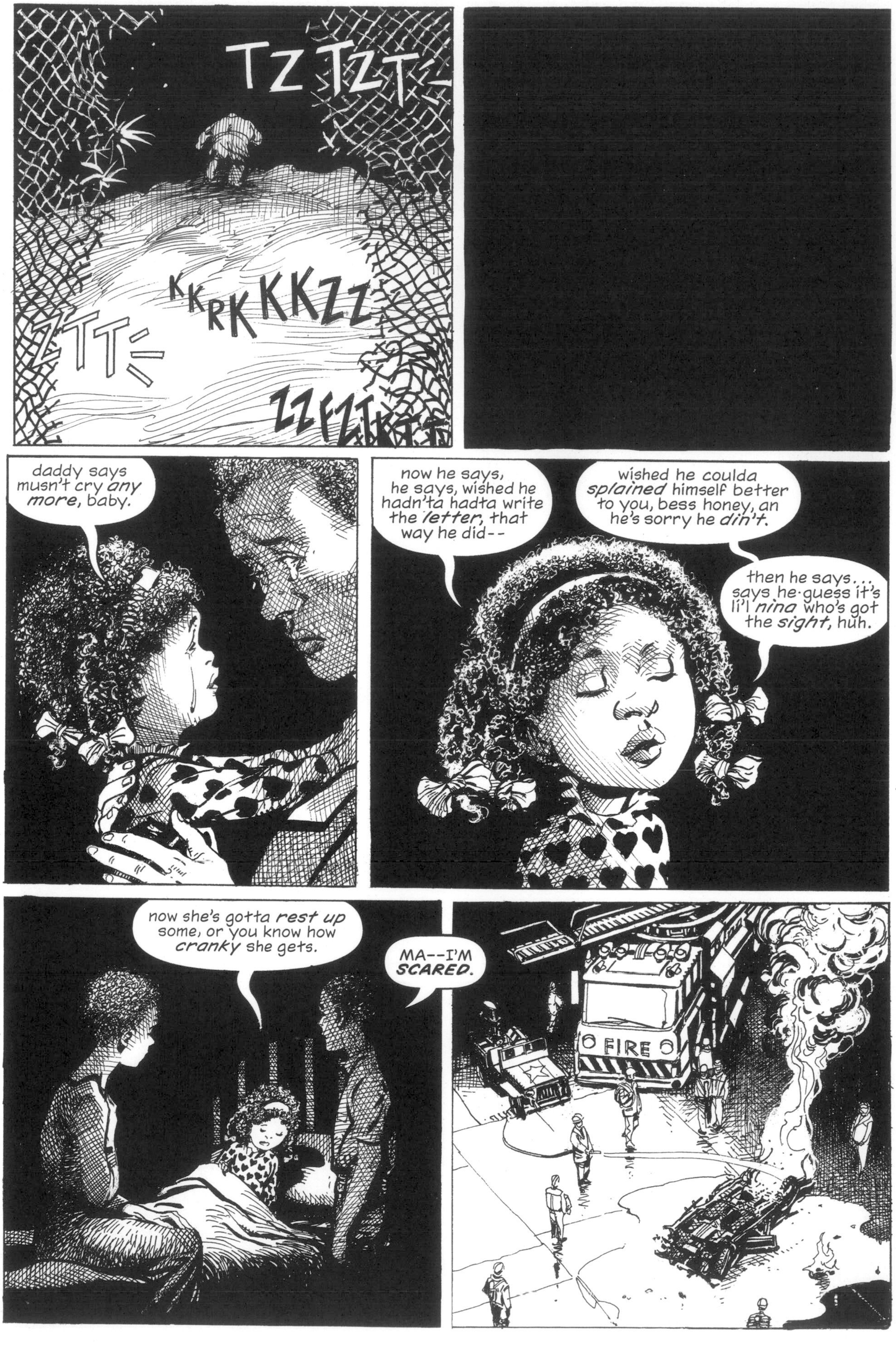
TZ TZT
KKRKKKZZ
ZTT
ZZFZT
daddy says musn't cry *any more*, baby.
now he says, he says, wished he hadn'ta hadta write the *letter*, that way he did--
wished he coulda *splained* himself better to you, bess honey, an he's sorry he *din't*.
then he says... says he guess it's li'l *nina* who's got the *sight*, huh.
now she's gotta *rest up* some, or you know how *cranky* she gets.
MA--I'M *SCARED*.
FIRE

...but daddy, i can't see you.
I'M RIGHT HERE, ANGEL.
y'hidin'?
YEAH--YOU WOULDN'T WANNA SEE ME LIKE THIS, NINA.
why-y-y?
I'M JUST A BIT BANGED UP NOW, SWEET.
does it hurt, daddy?
NOT ANY MORE--I'M FINE NOW...
daddy--?
are you in heaven?
NO, NINA --I'M NOT IN HEAVEN
then where are you?
I'M IN YOUR DREAM, HONEY-SWEET.
did bad doctor go to hell?
NO--
THERE IS NO HELL--
HE JUST WENT...SOME-WHERE ELSE.
NINA--
yes, daddy?
I NEED YOU TO HELP ME, BABE.
oka-a-aY♪
IT'S ABOUT BOBBY.
WILL YOU LISSEN CAREFULLY, HONEY?

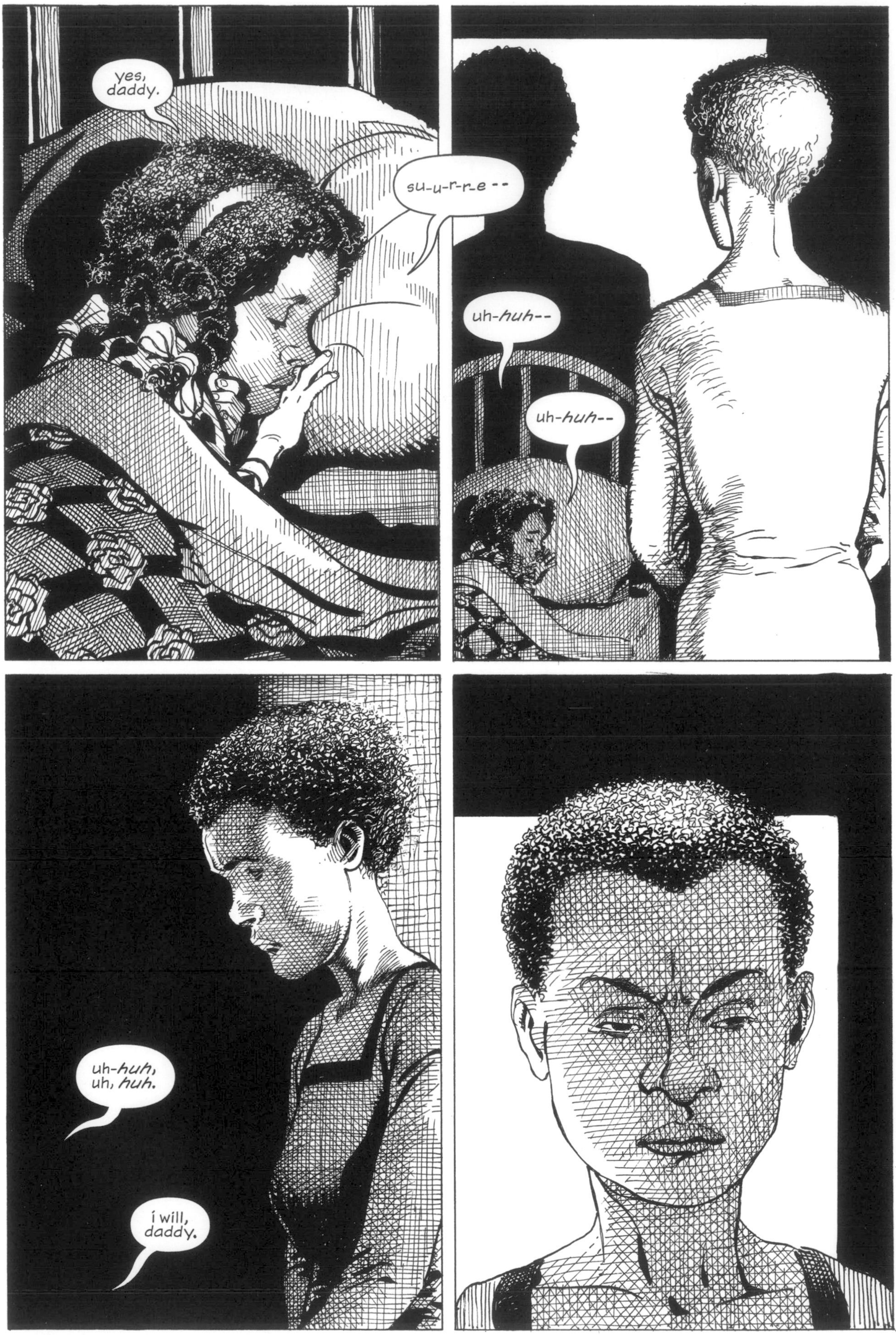
yes, daddy.
su-u-r-r-e --
uh-*huh*--
uh-*huh*--
uh-*huh*, uh, *huh*.
i will, daddy.

1965 One year later, Providence Hills, Ohio Wednesday, November 24

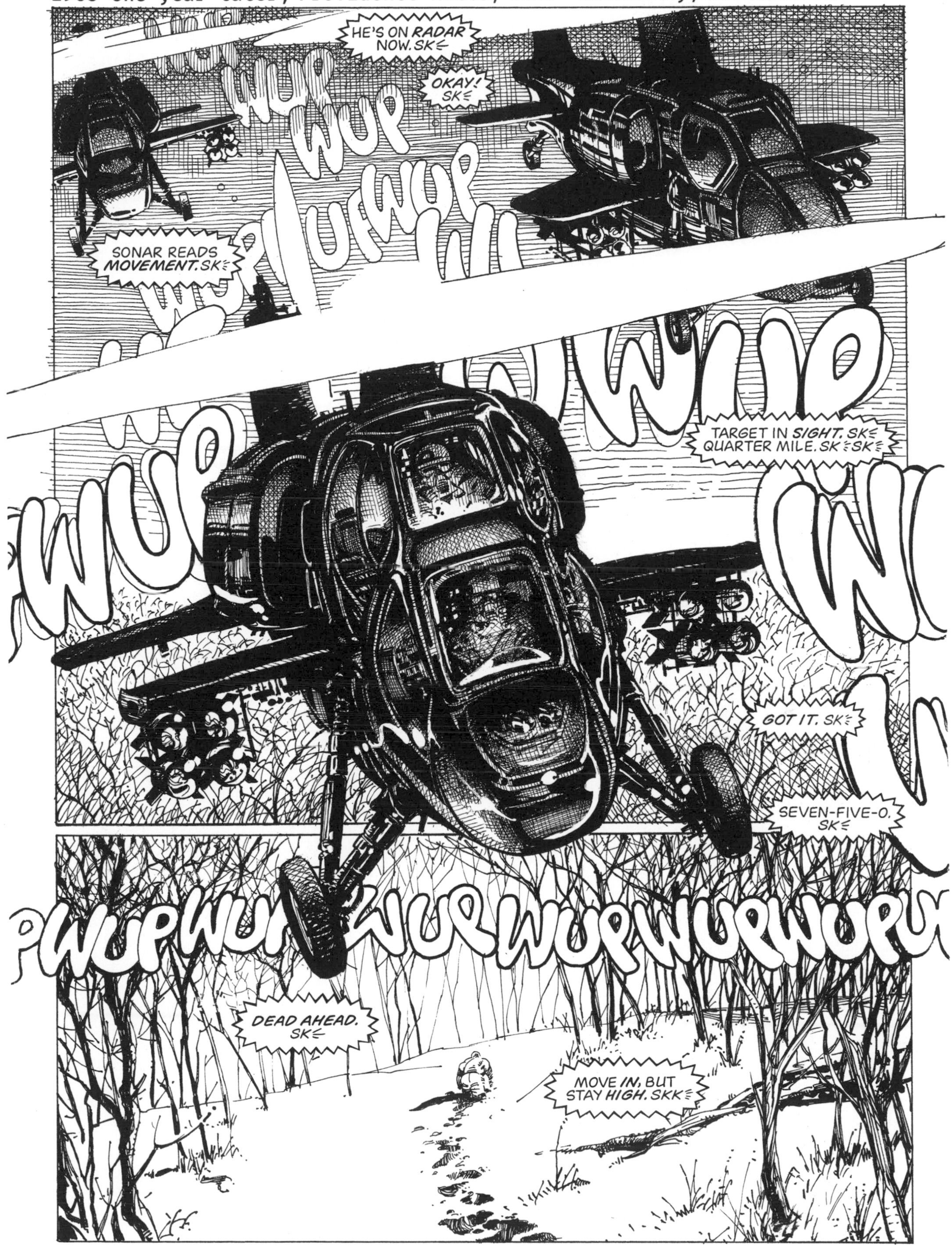
HE'S ON RADAR NOW. SK
OKAY! SK
SONAR READS MOVEMENT. SK
TARGET IN SIGHT. SK QUARTER MILE. SK SK
GOT IT. SK
SEVEN-FIVE-O. SK
WUP WUP WUP WUP WUP WUP
DEAD AHEAD. SK
MOVE IN, BUT STAY HIGH. SKK

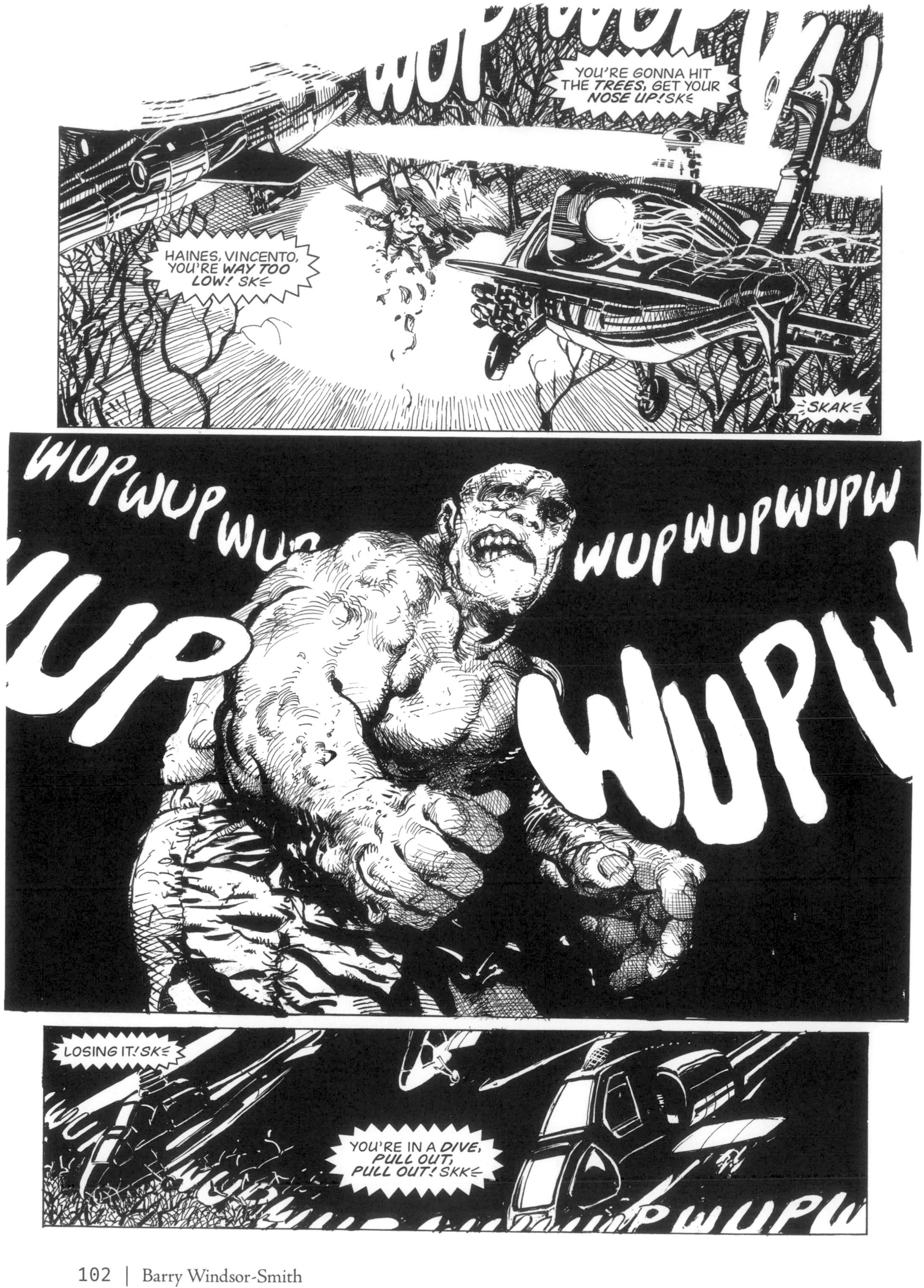
YOU'RE GONNA HIT THE *TREES*, GET YOUR *NOSE UP!* SK
HAINES, VINCENTO, YOU'RE *WAY TOO LOW!* SK
SKAK
WUP WUP WU
WUP WUP WUPW
WUP
WUP
LOSING IT! SK
YOU'RE IN A *DIVE*, *PULL OUT*, *PULL OUT!* SKK
PWUPW

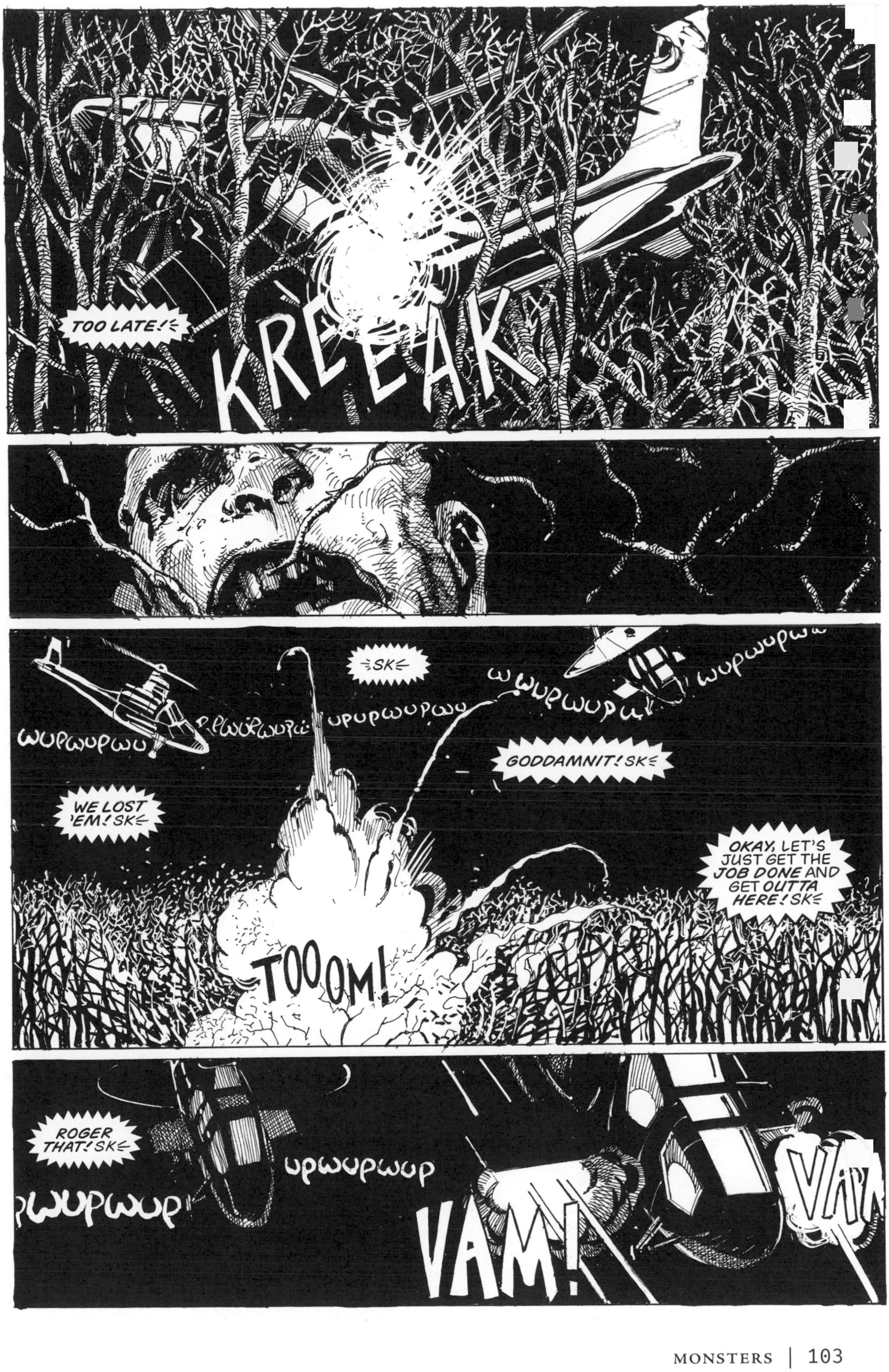
TOO LATE!
KREEAK
SK
WUPWUPWU
UPUPWUPWU
WUPWUPWUPWUP
WUPWUPWU
GODDAMNIT! SK
WE LOST 'EM! SK
OKAY, LET'S JUST GET THE JOB DONE AND GET OUTTA HERE! SK
TOOOM!
ROGER THAT! SK
UPWUPWUP
WUPWUP
VAM!

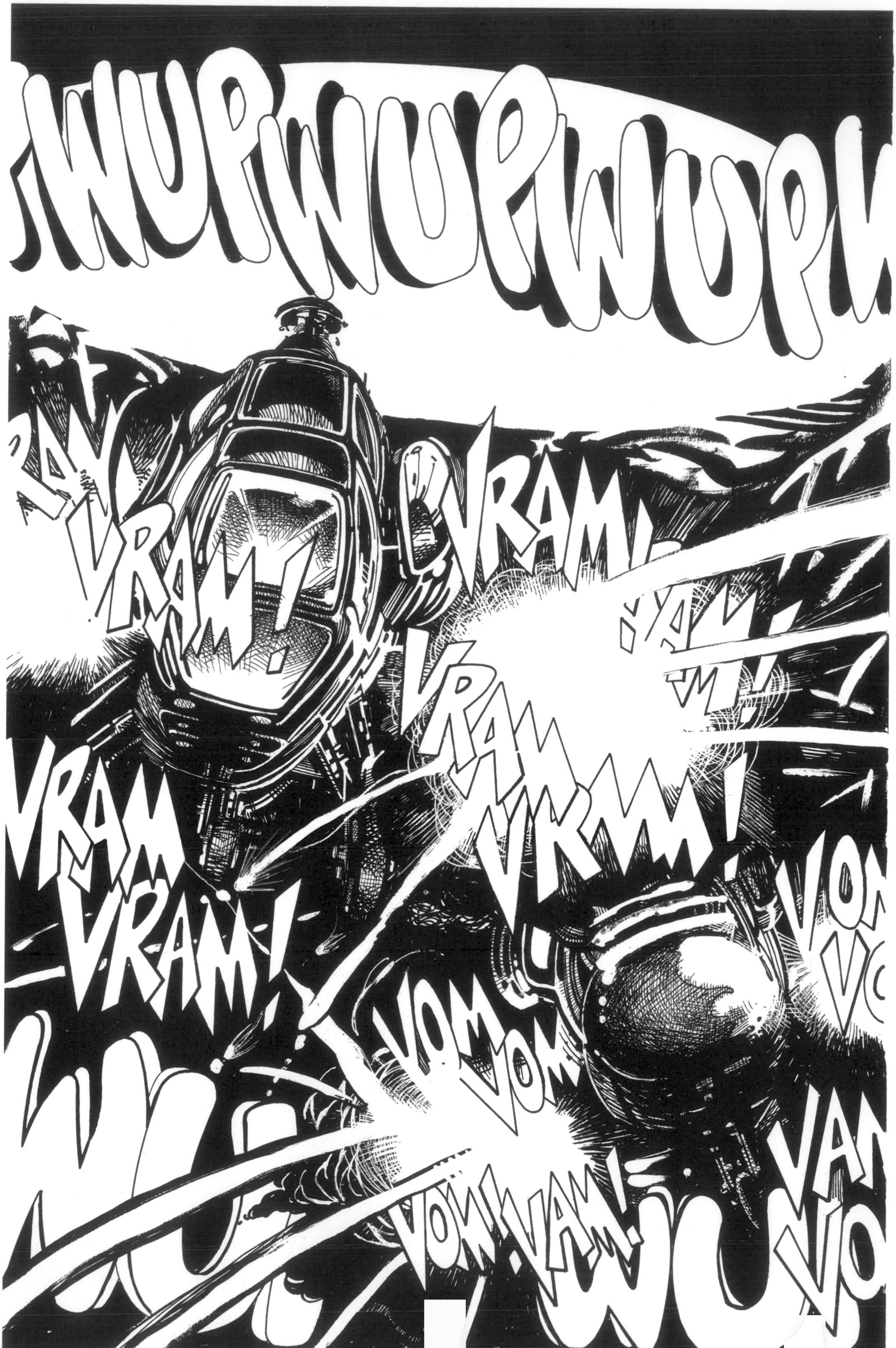

WUP WUP WUP
VRAM!
VRAM!
VRAM!
VRAM!
VRAM
VRAM!
VOM VOM
VOM! VAM!

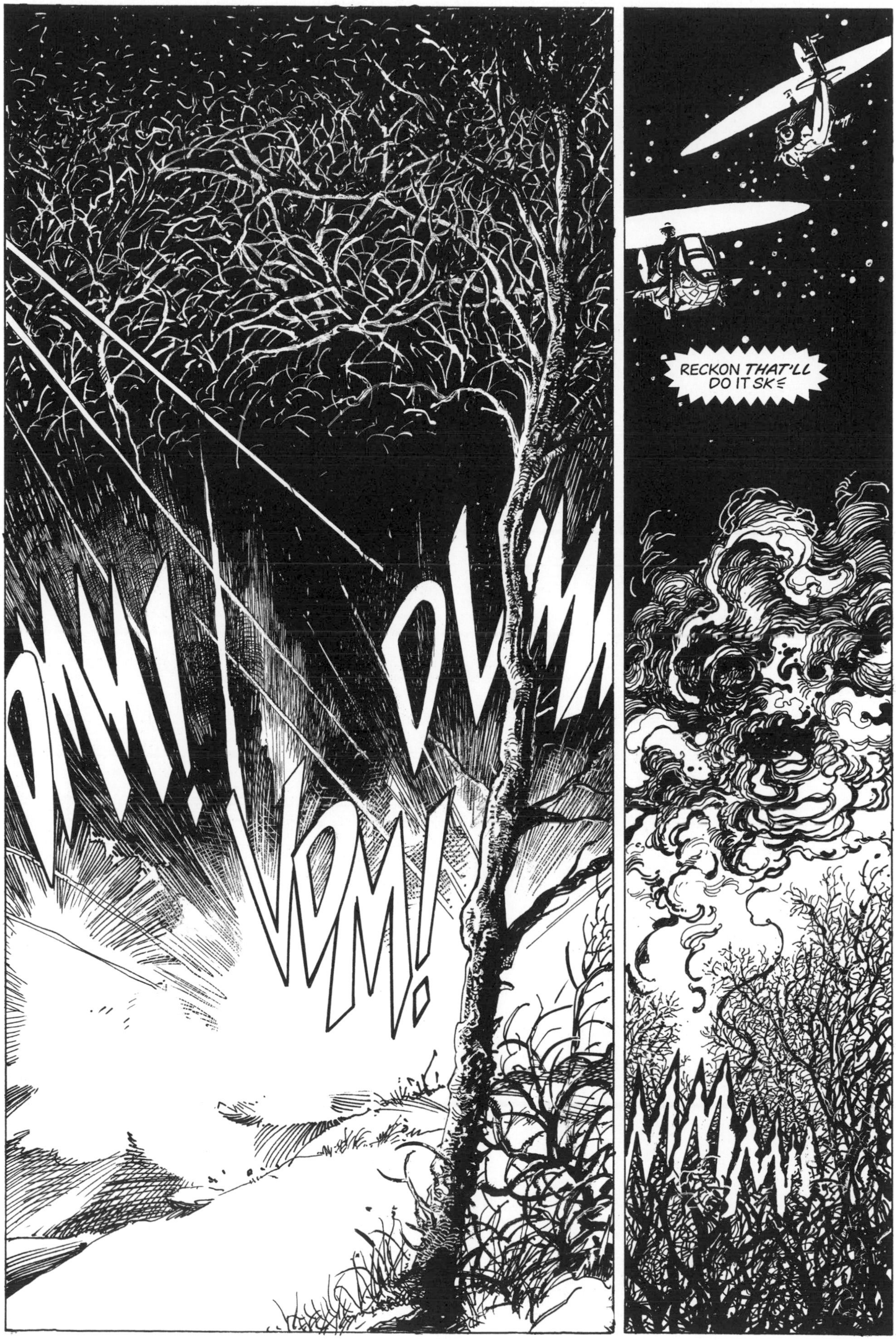
RECKON *THAT'LL* DO IT SK

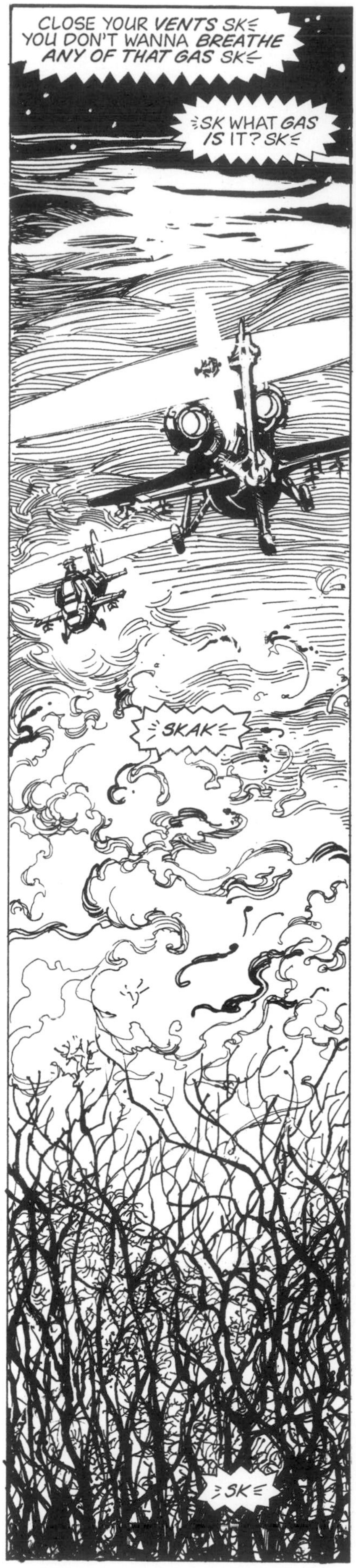
CLOSE YOUR VENTS SK
YOU DON'T WANNA BREATHE ANY OF THAT GAS SK
SK WHAT GAS IS IT? SK
SKAK
SK

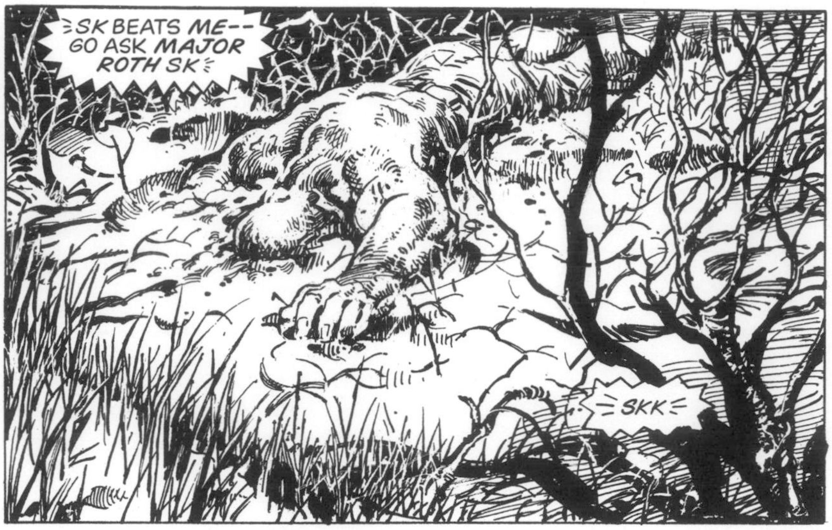
SK BEATS ME-- GO ASK MAJOR ROTH SK
SKK

Outskirts of Providence Hills

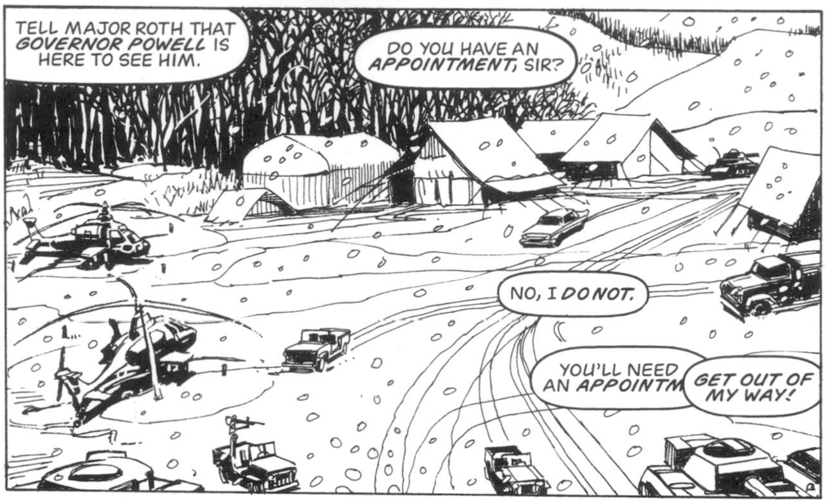
TELL MAJOR ROTH THAT GOVERNOR POWELL IS HERE TO SEE HIM.
DO YOU HAVE AN APPOINTMENT, SIR?
NO, I DO NOT.
YOU'LL NEED AN APPOINTM
GET OUT OF MY WAY!

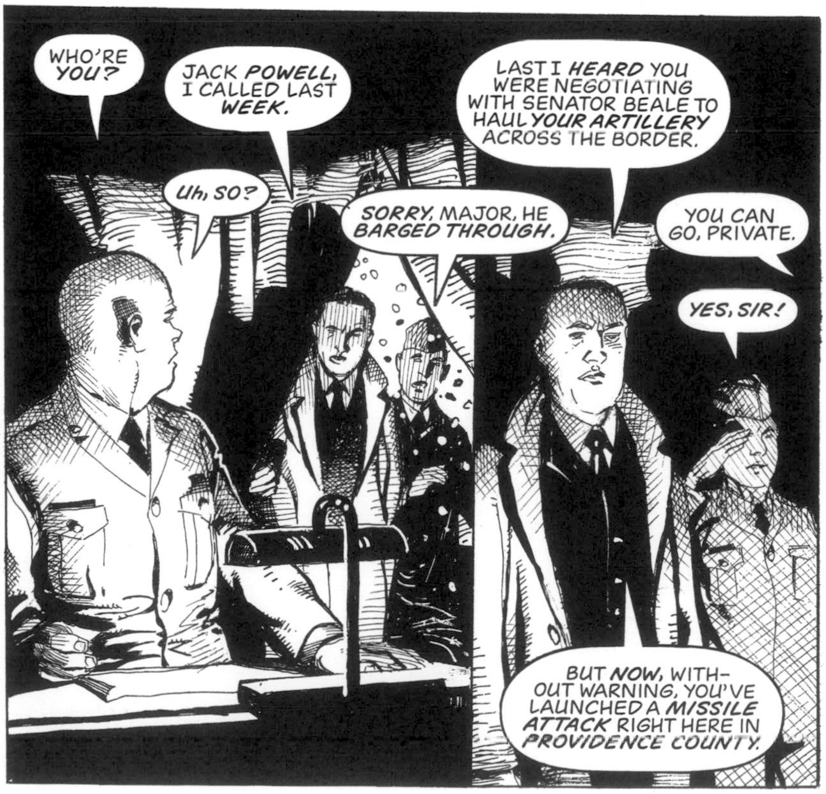
WHO'RE YOU?
JACK POWELL, I CALLED LAST WEEK.
Uh, SO?
SORRY, MAJOR, HE BARGED THROUGH.
LAST I HEARD YOU WERE NEGOTIATING WITH SENATOR BEALE TO HAUL YOUR ARTILLERY ACROSS THE BORDER.
YOU CAN GO, PRIVATE.
YES, SIR!
BUT NOW, WITH-OUT WARNING, YOU'VE LAUNCHED A MISSILE ATTACK RIGHT HERE IN PROVIDENCE COUNTY.

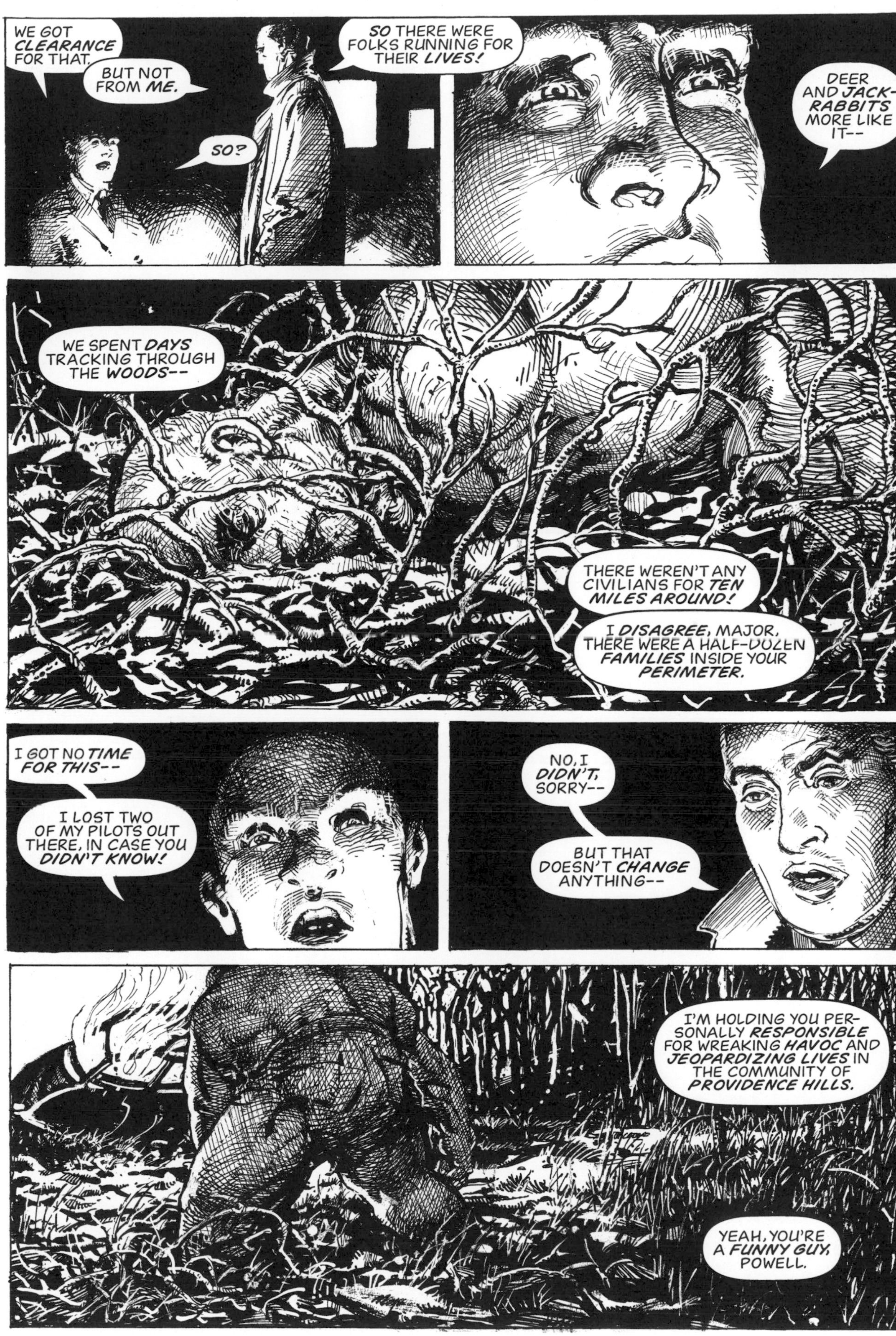
WE GOT CLEARANCE FOR THAT.
BUT NOT FROM ME.
SO?
SO THERE WERE FOLKS RUNNING FOR THEIR LIVES!
DEER AND JACK-RABBITS MORE LIKE IT--
WE SPENT DAYS TRACKING THROUGH THE WOODS--
THERE WEREN'T ANY CIVILIANS FOR TEN MILES AROUND!
I DISAGREE, MAJOR. THERE WERE A HALF-DOZEN FAMILIES INSIDE YOUR PERIMETER.
I GOT NO TIME FOR THIS--
I LOST TWO OF MY PILOTS OUT THERE, IN CASE YOU DIDN'T KNOW!
NO, I DIDN'T, SORRY--
BUT THAT DOESN'T CHANGE ANYTHING--
I'M HOLDING YOU PERSONALLY RESPONSIBLE FOR WREAKING HAVOC AND JEOPARDIZING LIVES IN THE COMMUNITY OF PROVIDENCE HILLS.
YEAH, YOU'RE A FUNNY GUY, POWELL.

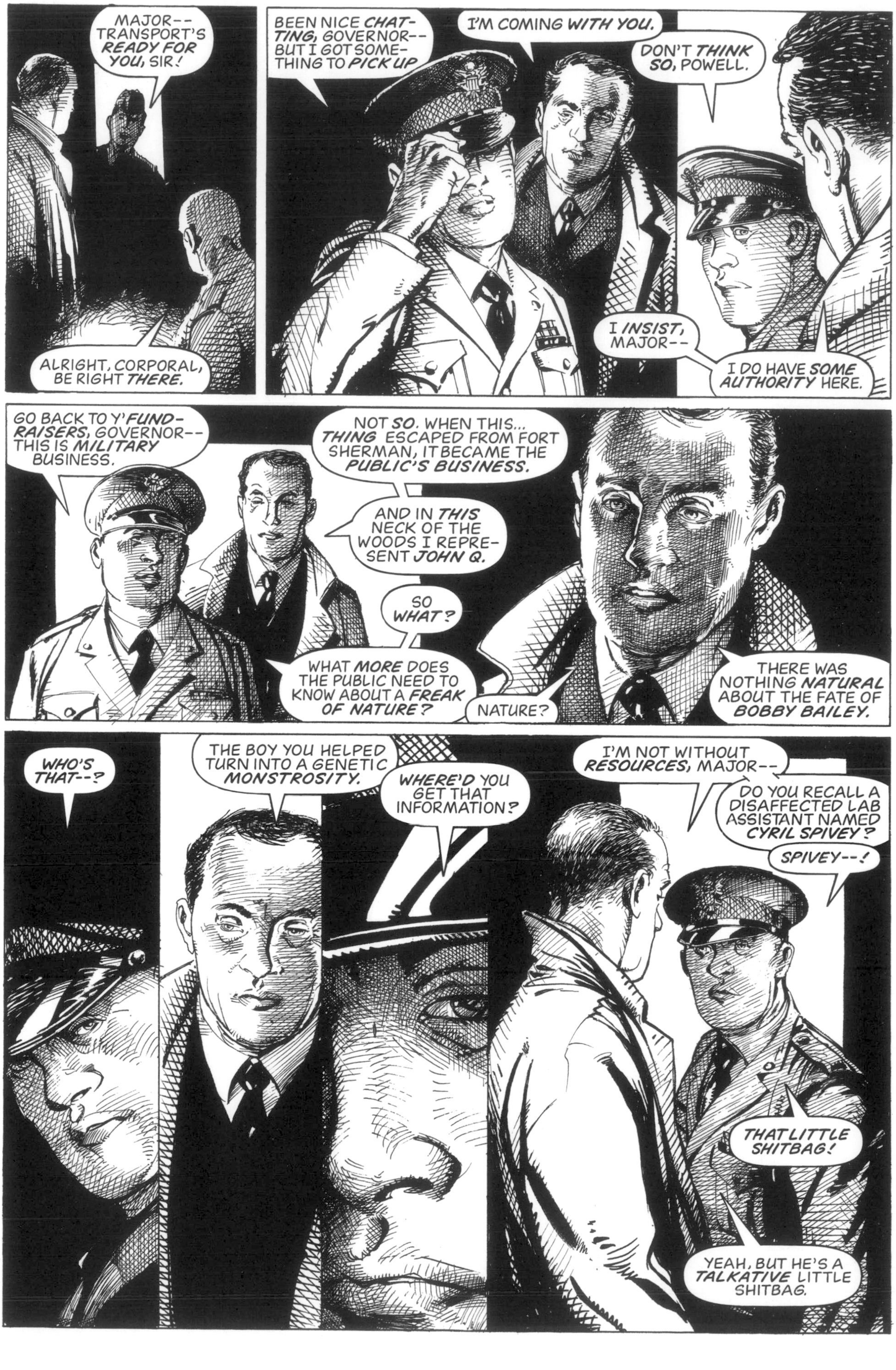
MAJOR--
TRANSPORT'S READY FOR YOU, SIR!
ALRIGHT, CORPORAL, BE RIGHT THERE.
BEEN NICE CHATTING, GOVERNOR-- BUT I GOT SOMETHING TO PICK UP
I'M COMING WITH YOU.
DON'T THINK SO, POWELL.
I INSIST, MAJOR--
I DO HAVE SOME AUTHORITY HERE.
GO BACK TO Y' FUND-RAISERS, GOVERNOR-- THIS IS MILITARY BUSINESS.
NOT SO. WHEN THIS... THING ESCAPED FROM FORT SHERMAN, IT BECAME THE PUBLIC'S BUSINESS.
AND IN THIS NECK OF THE WOODS I REPRESENT JOHN Q.
SO WHAT?
WHAT MORE DOES THE PUBLIC NEED TO KNOW ABOUT A FREAK OF NATURE?
NATURE?
THERE WAS NOTHING NATURAL ABOUT THE FATE OF BOBBY BAILEY.
WHO'S THAT--?
THE BOY YOU HELPED TURN INTO A GENETIC MONSTROSITY.
WHERE'D YOU GET THAT INFORMATION?
I'M NOT WITHOUT RESOURCES, MAJOR--
DO YOU RECALL A DISAFFECTED LAB ASSISTANT NAMED CYRIL SPIVEY?
SPIVEY--!
THAT LITTLE SHITBAG!
YEAH, BUT HE'S A TALKATIVE LITTLE SHITBAG.

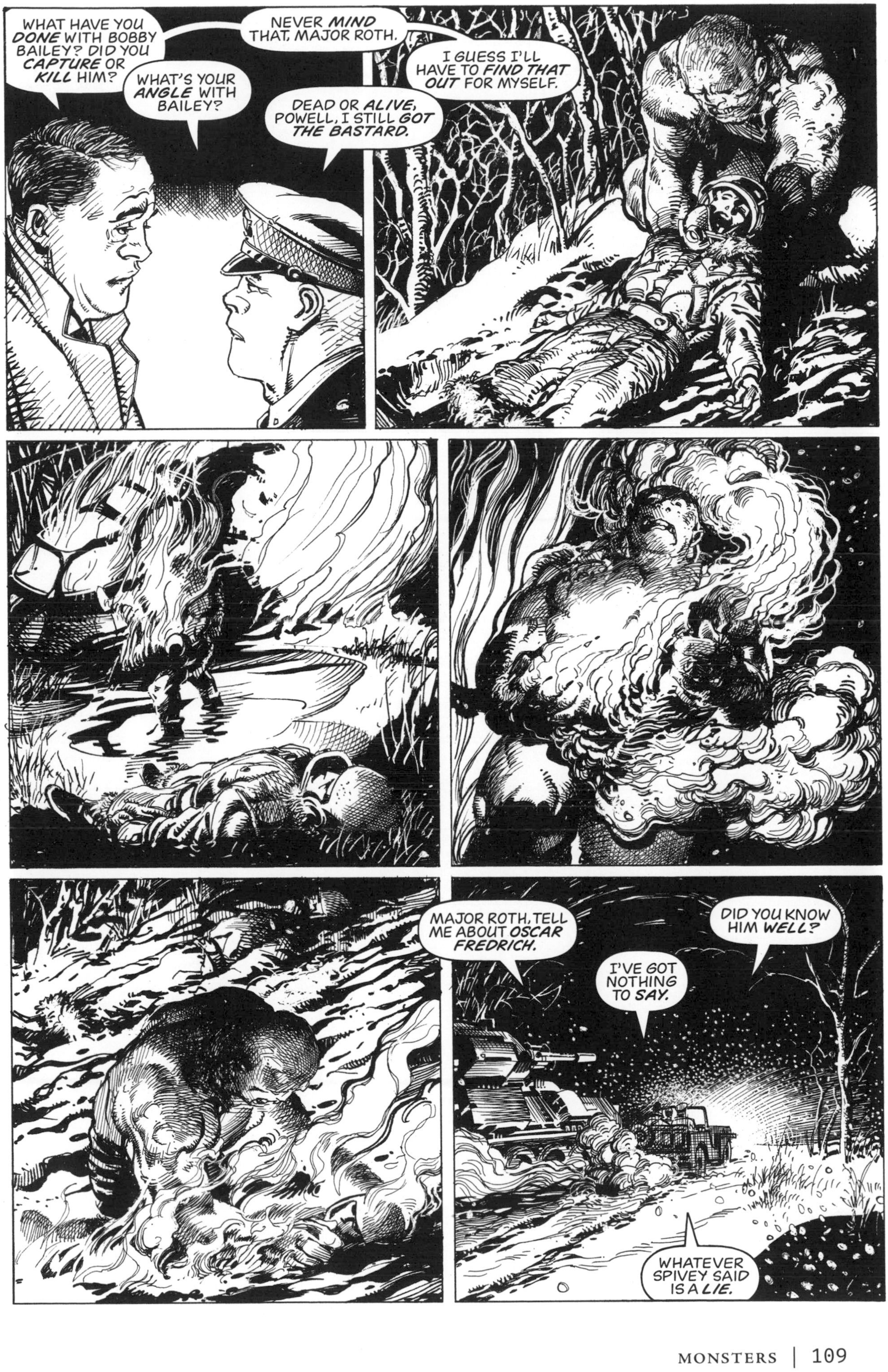
WHAT HAVE YOU DONE WITH BOBBY BAILEY? DID YOU CAPTURE OR KILL HIM?
NEVER MIND THAT, MAJOR ROTH.
WHAT'S YOUR ANGLE WITH BAILEY?
DEAD OR ALIVE, POWELL, I STILL GOT THE BASTARD.
I GUESS I'LL HAVE TO FIND THAT OUT FOR MYSELF.
MAJOR ROTH, TELL ME ABOUT OSCAR FREDRICH.
I'VE GOT NOTHING TO SAY.
DID YOU KNOW HIM WELL?
WHATEVER SPIVEY SAID IS A LIE.

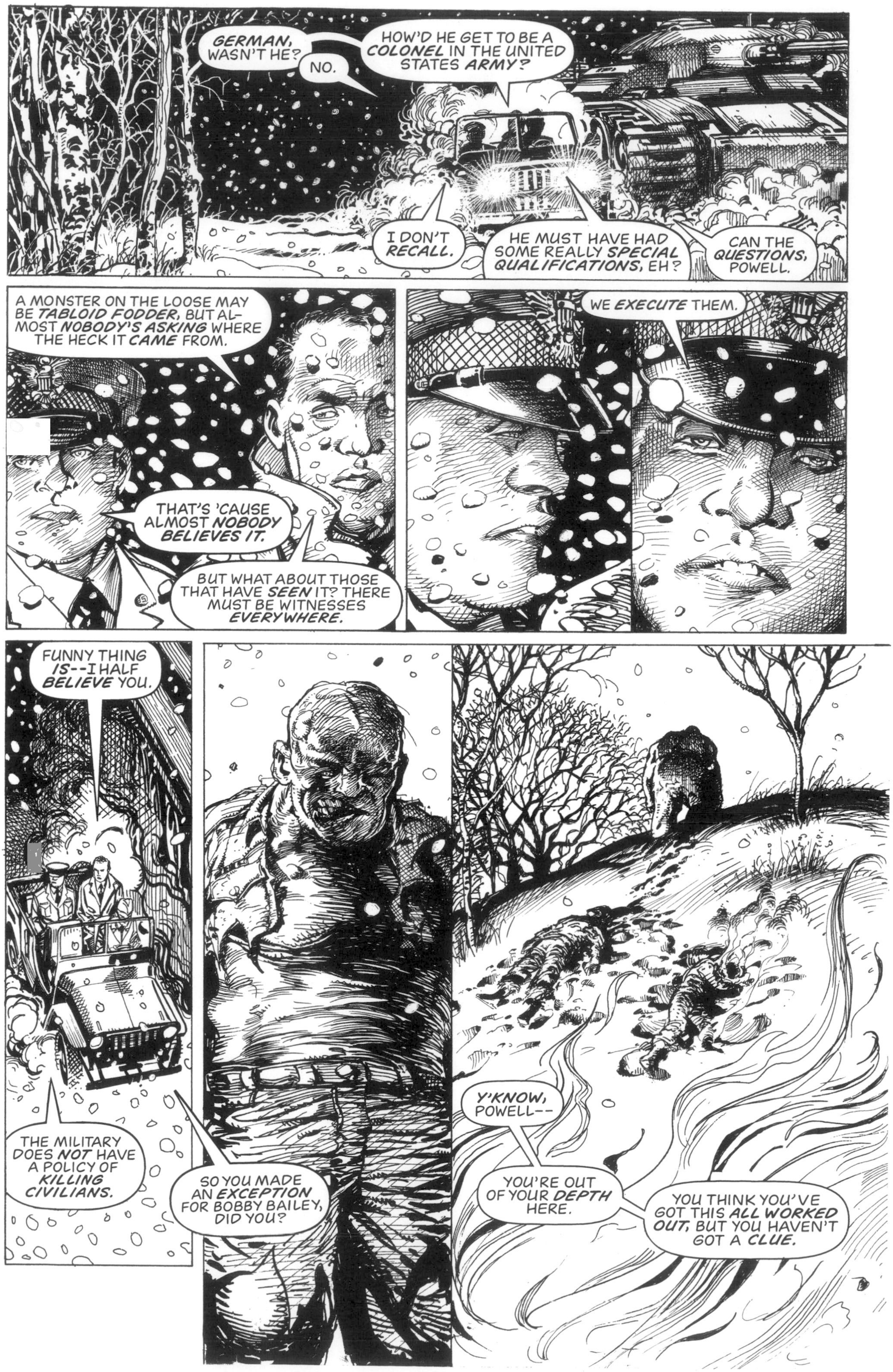
GERMAN, WASN'T HE?
NO.
HOW'D HE GET TO BE A COLONEL IN THE UNITED STATES ARMY?
I DON'T RECALL.
HE MUST HAVE HAD SOME REALLY SPECIAL QUALIFICATIONS, EH?
CAN THE QUESTIONS, POWELL.
A MONSTER ON THE LOOSE MAY BE TABLOID FODDER, BUT ALMOST NOBODY'S ASKING WHERE THE HECK IT CAME FROM.
THAT'S 'CAUSE ALMOST NOBODY BELIEVES IT.
BUT WHAT ABOUT THOSE THAT HAVE SEEN IT? THERE MUST BE WITNESSES EVERYWHERE.
WE EXECUTE THEM.
FUNNY THING IS--I HALF BELIEVE YOU.
THE MILITARY DOES NOT HAVE A POLICY OF KILLING CIVILIANS.
SO YOU MADE AN EXCEPTION FOR BOBBY BAILEY, DID YOU?
Y'KNOW, POWELL--
YOU'RE OUT OF YOUR DEPTH HERE.
YOU THINK YOU'VE GOT THIS ALL WORKED OUT, BUT YOU HAVEN'T GOT A CLUE.

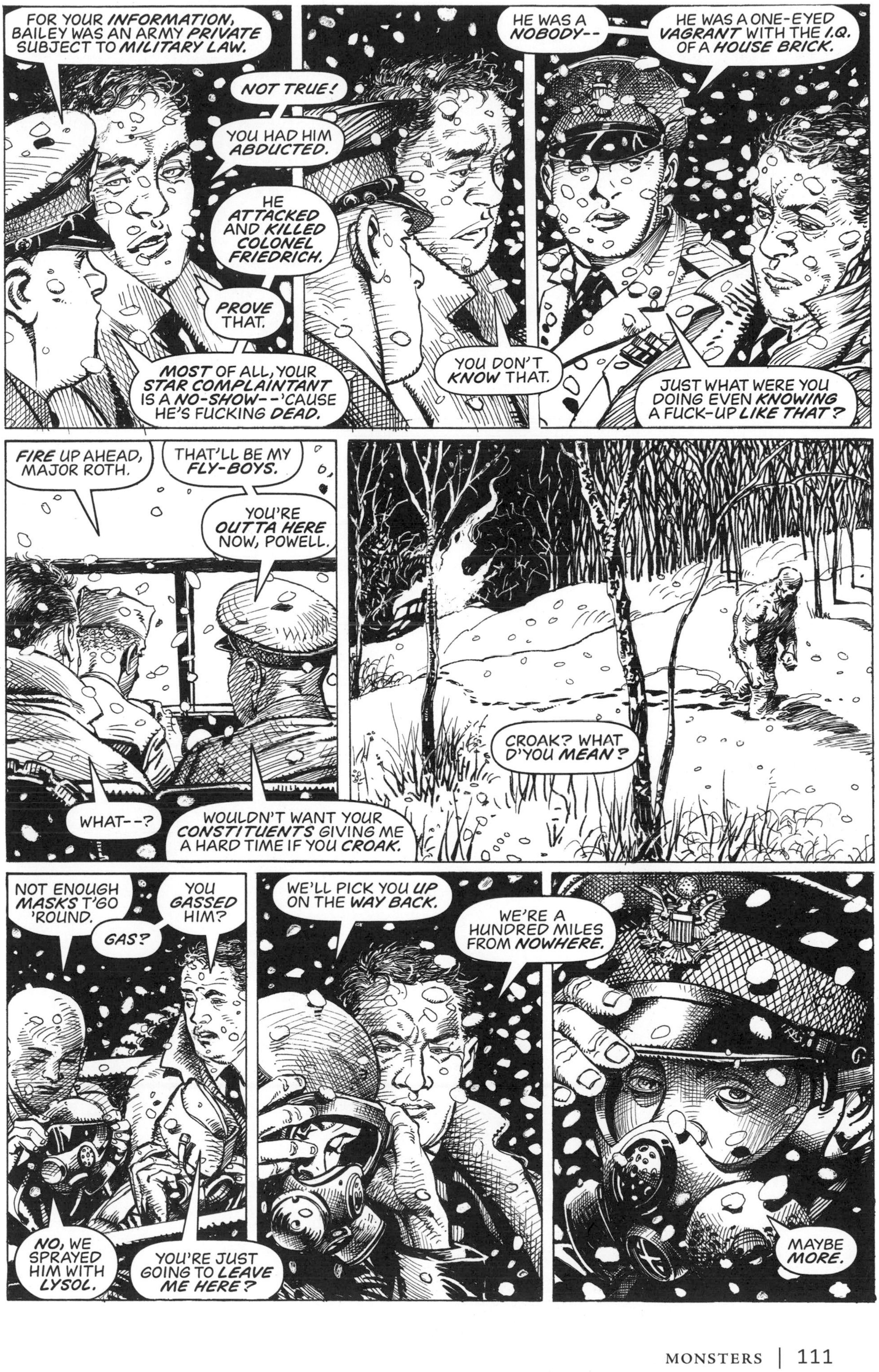

FOR YOUR INFORMATION, BAILEY WAS AN ARMY PRIVATE SUBJECT TO MILITARY LAW.
NOT TRUE!
YOU HAD HIM ABDUCTED.
HE ATTACKED AND KILLED COLONEL FRIEDRICH.
PROVE THAT.
MOST OF ALL, YOUR STAR COMPLAINTANT IS A NO-SHOW--'CAUSE HE'S FUCKING DEAD.
YOU DON'T KNOW THAT.
HE WAS A NOBODY--
HE WAS A ONE-EYED VAGRANT WITH THE I.Q. OF A HOUSE BRICK.
JUST WHAT WERE YOU DOING EVEN KNOWING A FUCK-UP LIKE THAT?
FIRE UP AHEAD, MAJOR ROTH.
THAT'LL BE MY FLY-BOYS.
YOU'RE OUTTA HERE NOW, POWELL.
WHAT--?
WOULDN'T WANT YOUR CONSTITUENTS GIVING ME A HARD TIME IF YOU CROAK.
CROAK? WHAT D'YOU MEAN?
NOT ENOUGH MASKS T'GO 'ROUND.
YOU GASSED HIM?
GAS?
NO, WE SPRAYED HIM WITH LYSOL.
YOU'RE JUST GOING TO LEAVE ME HERE?
WE'LL PICK YOU UP ON THE WAY BACK.
WE'RE A HUNDRED MILES FROM NOWHERE.
MAYBE MORE.

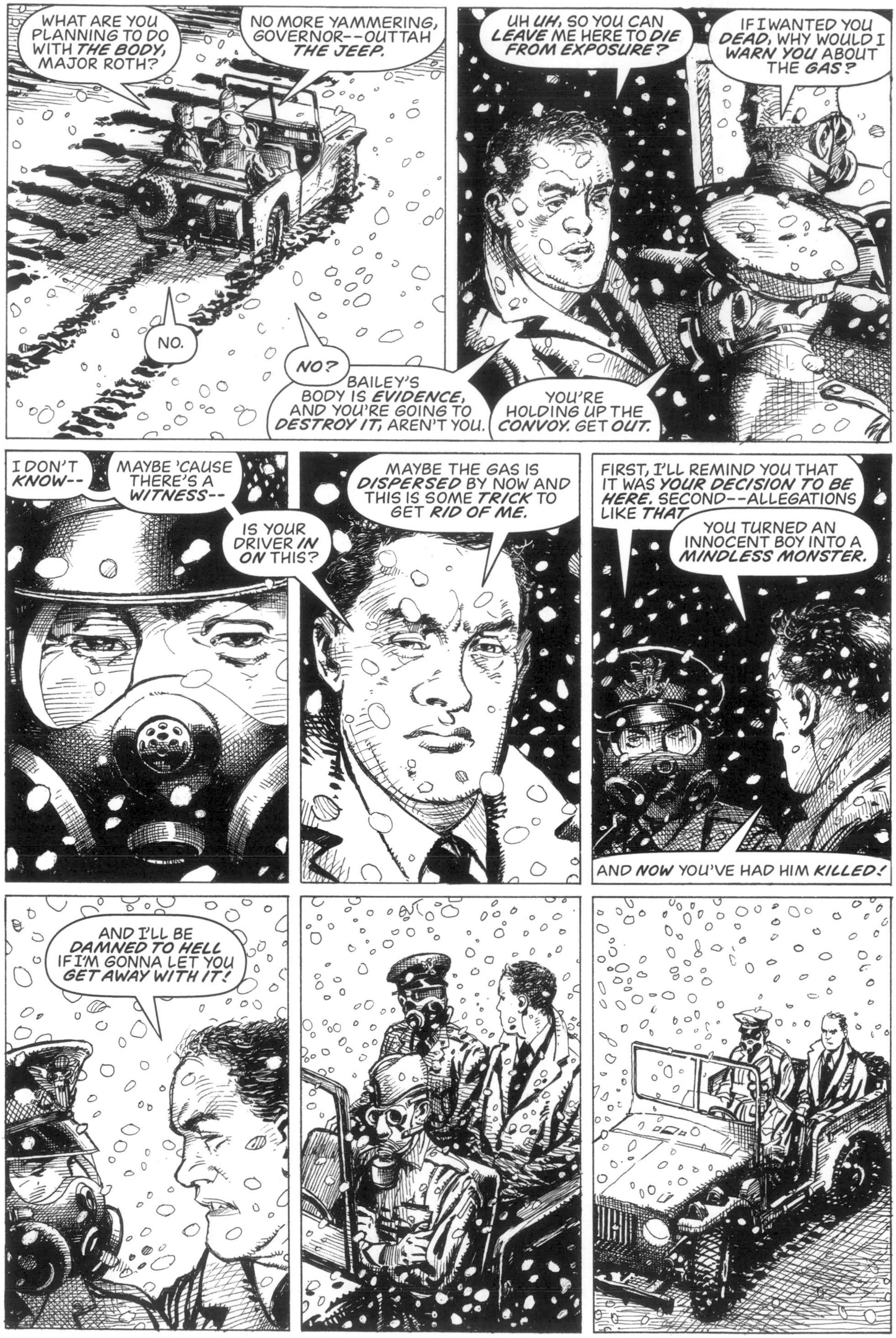
WHAT ARE YOU PLANNING TO DO WITH THE BODY, MAJOR ROTH?
NO MORE YAMMERING, GOVERNOR--OUTTAH THE JEEP.
NO.
NO?
BAILEY'S BODY IS EVIDENCE, AND YOU'RE GOING TO DESTROY IT, AREN'T YOU.
UH UH, SO YOU CAN LEAVE ME HERE TO DIE FROM EXPOSURE?
IF I WANTED YOU DEAD, WHY WOULD I WARN YOU ABOUT THE GAS?
YOU'RE HOLDING UP THE CONVOY. GET OUT.
I DON'T KNOW--
MAYBE 'CAUSE THERE'S A WITNESS--
IS YOUR DRIVER IN ON THIS?
MAYBE THE GAS IS DISPERSED BY NOW AND THIS IS SOME TRICK TO GET RID OF ME.
FIRST, I'LL REMIND YOU THAT IT WAS YOUR DECISION TO BE HERE. SECOND--ALLEGATIONS LIKE THAT.
YOU TURNED AN INNOCENT BOY INTO A MINDLESS MONSTER.
AND NOW YOU'VE HAD HIM KILLED!
AND I'LL BE DAMNED TO HELL IF I'M GONNA LET YOU GET AWAY WITH IT!

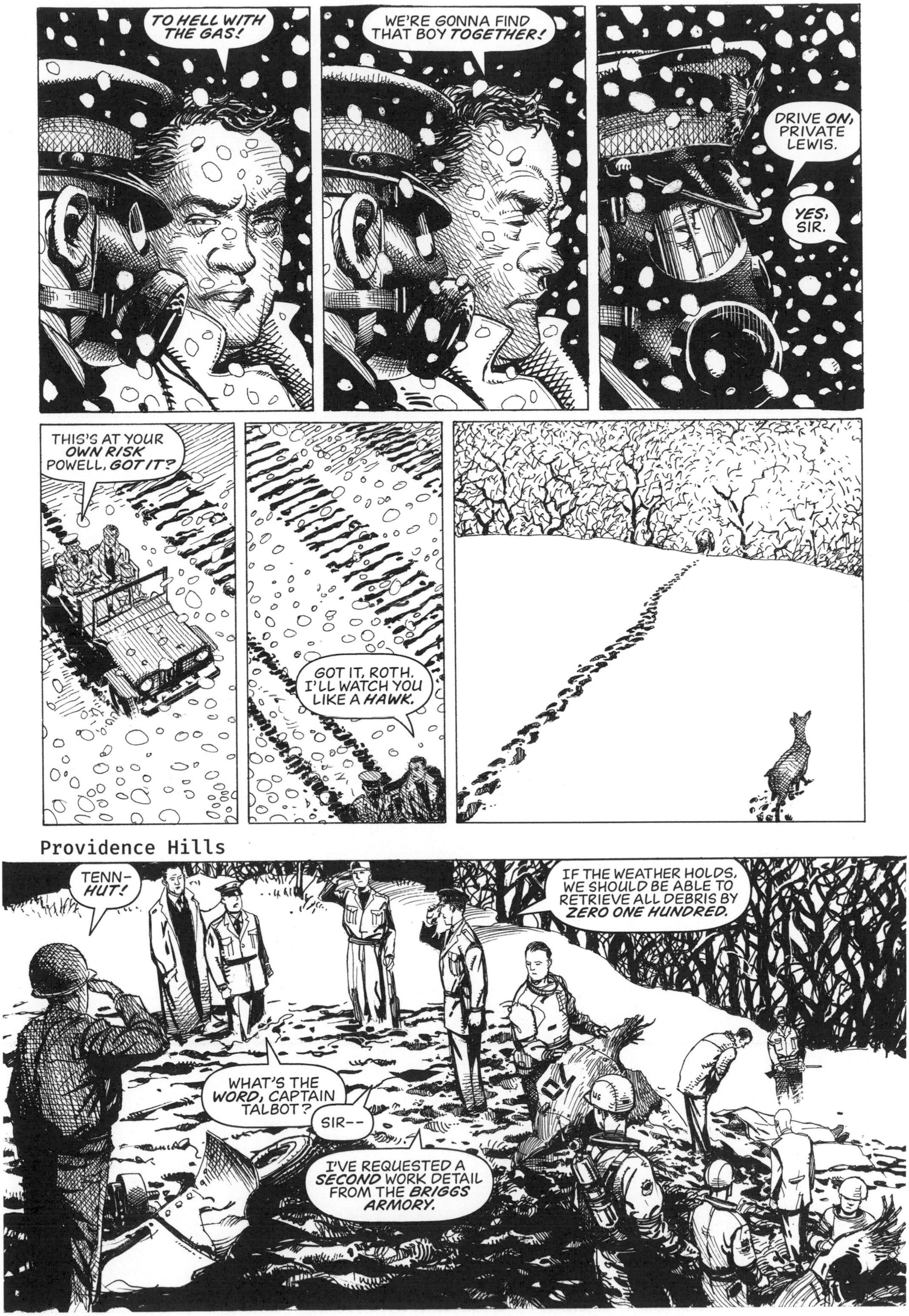
TO HELL WITH THE GAS!
WE'RE GONNA FIND THAT BOY TOGETHER!
DRIVE ON, PRIVATE LEWIS.
YES, SIR.
THIS'S AT YOUR OWN RISK POWELL, GOT IT?
GOT IT, ROTH. I'LL WATCH YOU LIKE A HAWK.
Providence Hills
TENN-HUT!
IF THE WEATHER HOLDS, WE SHOULD BE ABLE TO RETRIEVE ALL DEBRIS BY ZERO ONE HUNDRED.
WHAT'S THE WORD, CAPTAIN TALBOT?
SIR--
I'VE REQUESTED A SECOND WORK DETAIL FROM THE BRIGGS ARMORY.

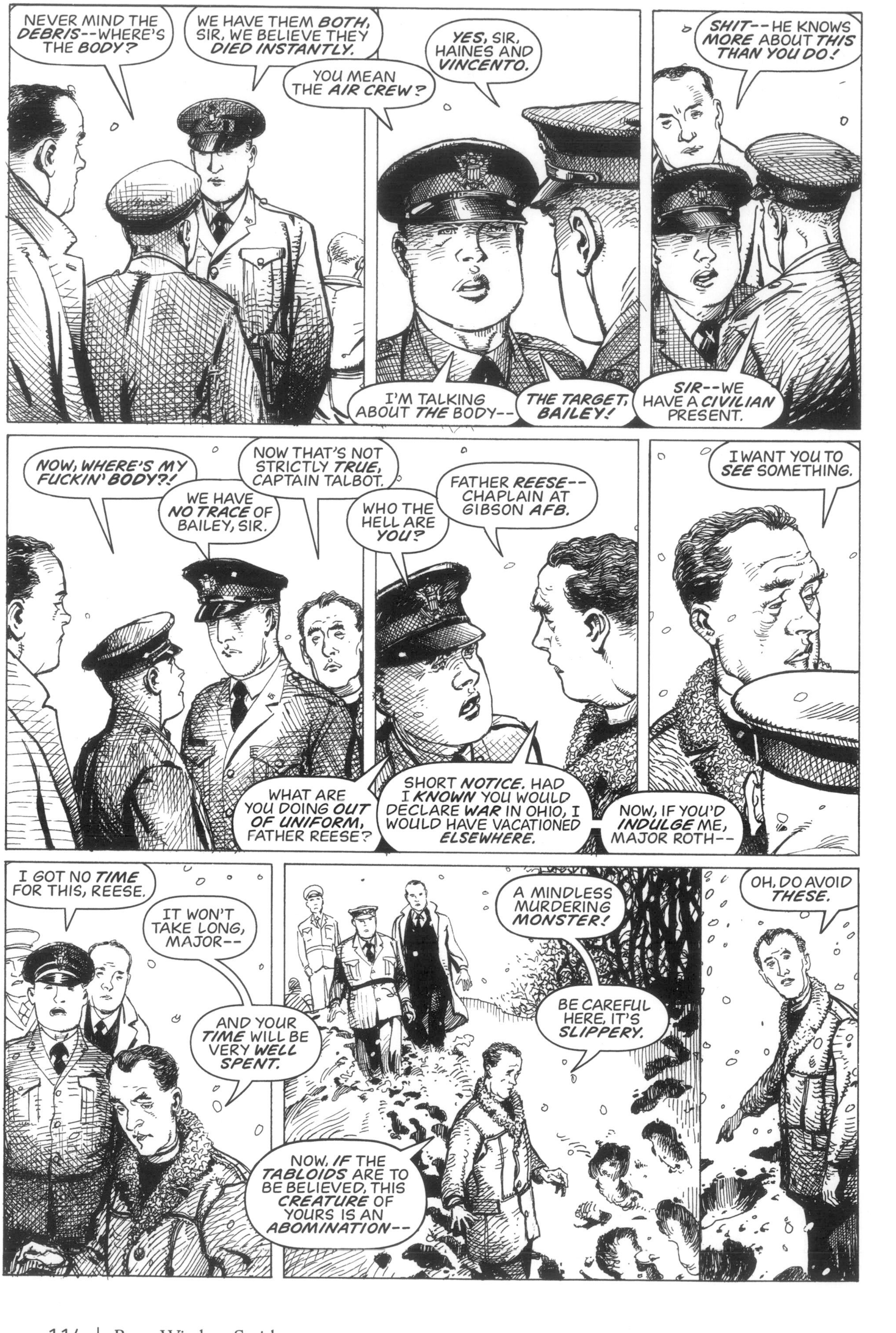
NEVER MIND THE DEBRIS--WHERE'S THE BODY?
WE HAVE THEM BOTH, SIR, WE BELIEVE THEY DIED INSTANTLY.
YOU MEAN THE AIR CREW?
YES, SIR, HAINES AND VINCENTO.
I'M TALKING ABOUT THE BODY--
THE TARGET, BAILEY!
SHIT--HE KNOWS MORE ABOUT THIS THAN YOU DO!
SIR--WE HAVE A CIVILIAN PRESENT.
NOW, WHERE'S MY FUCKIN' BODY?!
WE HAVE NO TRACE OF BAILEY, SIR.
NOW THAT'S NOT STRICTLY TRUE, CAPTAIN TALBOT.
WHO THE HELL ARE YOU?
FATHER REESE--CHAPLAIN AT GIBSON AFB.
WHAT ARE YOU DOING OUT OF UNIFORM, FATHER REESE?
SHORT NOTICE. HAD I KNOWN YOU WOULD DECLARE WAR IN OHIO, I WOULD HAVE VACATIONED ELSEWHERE.
I WANT YOU TO SEE SOMETHING.
NOW, IF YOU'D INDULGE ME, MAJOR ROTH--
I GOT NO TIME FOR THIS, REESE.
IT WON'T TAKE LONG, MAJOR--
AND YOUR TIME WILL BE VERY WELL SPENT.
NOW, IF THE TABLOIDS ARE TO BE BELIEVED, THIS CREATURE OF YOURS IS AN ABOMINATION--
A MINDLESS MURDERING MONSTER!
BE CAREFUL HERE, IT'S SLIPPERY.
OH, DO AVOID THESE.

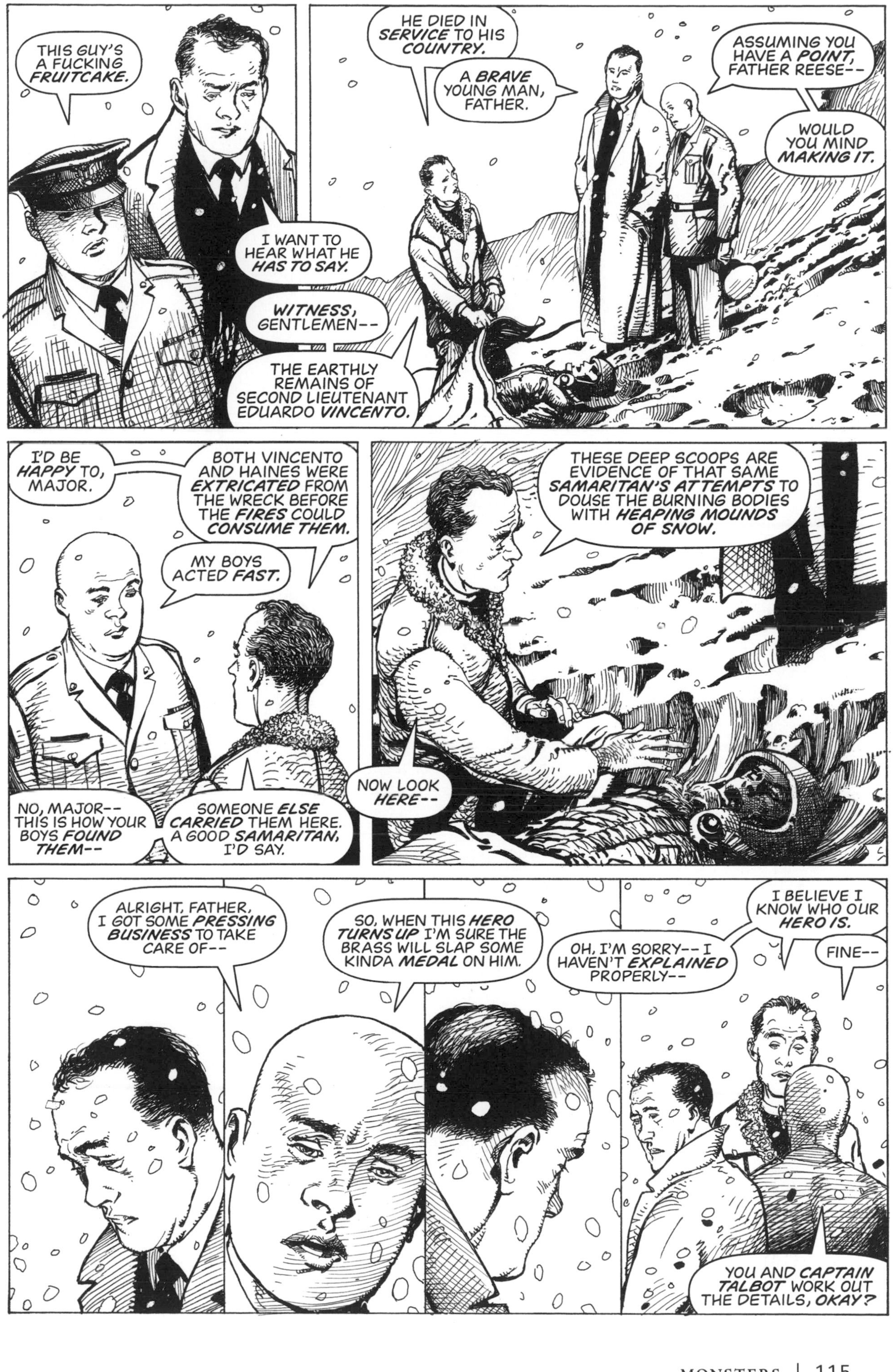
THIS GUY'S A FUCKING FRUITCAKE.
I WANT TO HEAR WHAT HE HAS TO SAY.
HE DIED IN SERVICE TO HIS COUNTRY.
A BRAVE YOUNG MAN, FATHER.
ASSUMING YOU HAVE A POINT, FATHER REESE--
WOULD YOU MIND MAKING IT.
WITNESS, GENTLEMEN--
THE EARTHLY REMAINS OF SECOND LIEUTENANT EDUARDO VINCENTO.
I'D BE HAPPY TO, MAJOR.
BOTH VINCENTO AND HAINES WERE EXTRICATED FROM THE WRECK BEFORE THE FIRES COULD CONSUME THEM.
MY BOYS ACTED FAST.
NO, MAJOR-- THIS IS HOW YOUR BOYS FOUND THEM--
SOMEONE ELSE CARRIED THEM HERE. A GOOD SAMARITAN, I'D SAY.
NOW LOOK HERE--
THESE DEEP SCOOPS ARE EVIDENCE OF THAT SAME SAMARITAN'S ATTEMPTS TO DOUSE THE BURNING BODIES WITH HEAPING MOUNDS OF SNOW.
ALRIGHT, FATHER, I GOT SOME PRESSING BUSINESS TO TAKE CARE OF--
SO, WHEN THIS HERO TURNS UP I'M SURE THE BRASS WILL SLAP SOME KINDA MEDAL ON HIM.
OH, I'M SORRY-- I HAVEN'T EXPLAINED PROPERLY--
I BELIEVE I KNOW WHO OUR HERO IS.
FINE--
YOU AND CAPTAIN TALBOT WORK OUT THE DETAILS, OKAY?

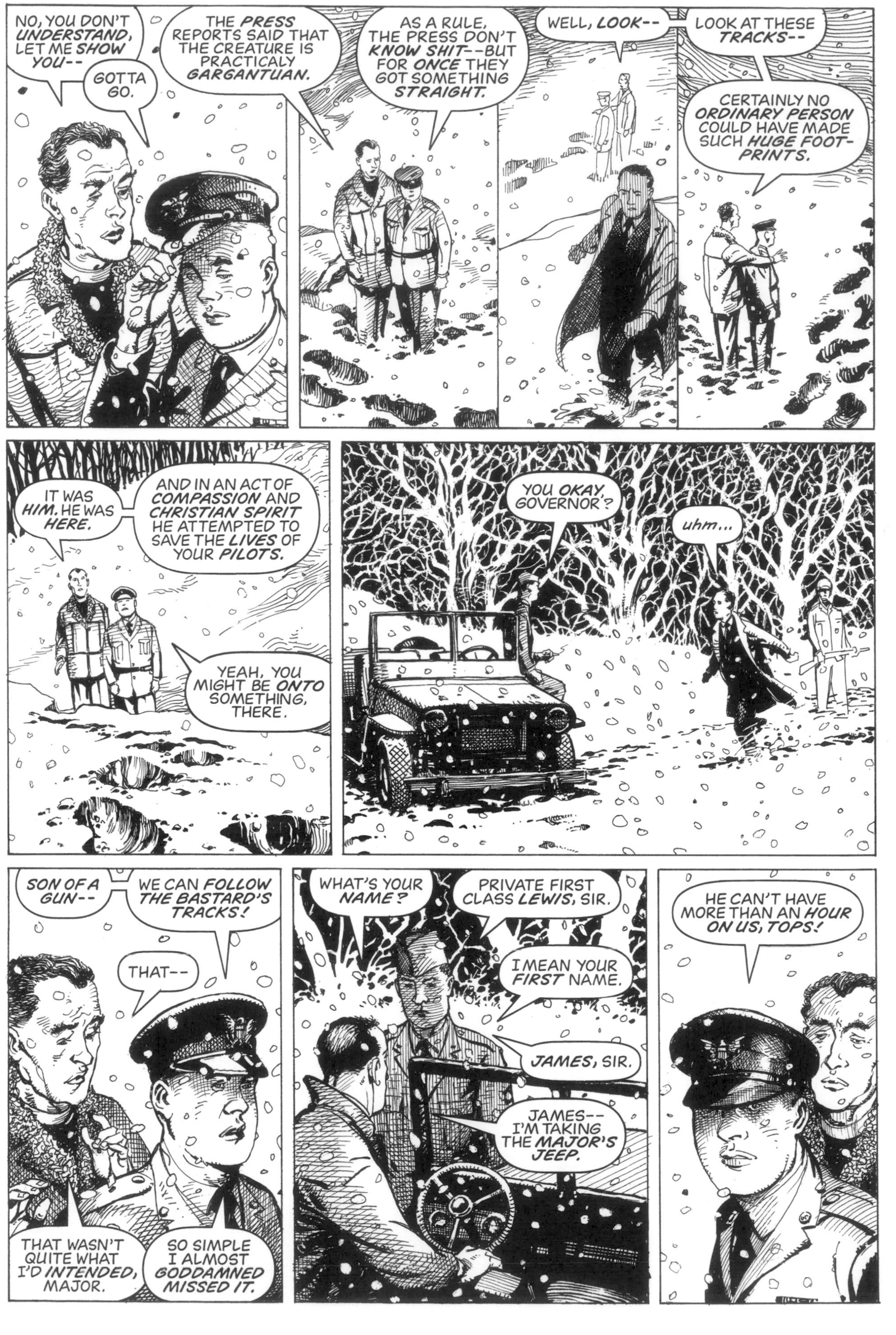
NO, YOU DON'T UNDERSTAND, LET ME SHOW YOU--
GOTTA GO.
THE PRESS REPORTS SAID THAT THE CREATURE IS PRACTICALY GARGANTUAN.
AS A RULE, THE PRESS DON'T KNOW SHIT--BUT FOR ONCE THEY GOT SOMETHING STRAIGHT.
WELL, LOOK--
LOOK AT THESE TRACKS--
CERTAINLY NO ORDINARY PERSON COULD HAVE MADE SUCH HUGE FOOT-PRINTS.
IT WAS HIM. HE WAS HERE.
AND IN AN ACT OF COMPASSION AND CHRISTIAN SPIRIT HE ATTEMPTED TO SAVE THE LIVES OF YOUR PILOTS.
YEAH, YOU MIGHT BE ONTO SOMETHING, THERE.
YOU OKAY, GOVERNOR?
uhm...
SON OF A GUN--
WE CAN FOLLOW THE BASTARD'S TRACKS!
THAT--
THAT WASN'T QUITE WHAT I'D INTENDED, MAJOR.
SO SIMPLE I ALMOST GODDAMNED MISSED IT.
WHAT'S YOUR NAME?
PRIVATE FIRST CLASS LEWIS, SIR.
I MEAN YOUR FIRST NAME.
JAMES, SIR.
JAMES-- I'M TAKING THE MAJOR'S JEEP.
HE CAN'T HAVE MORE THAN AN HOUR ON US, TOPS!

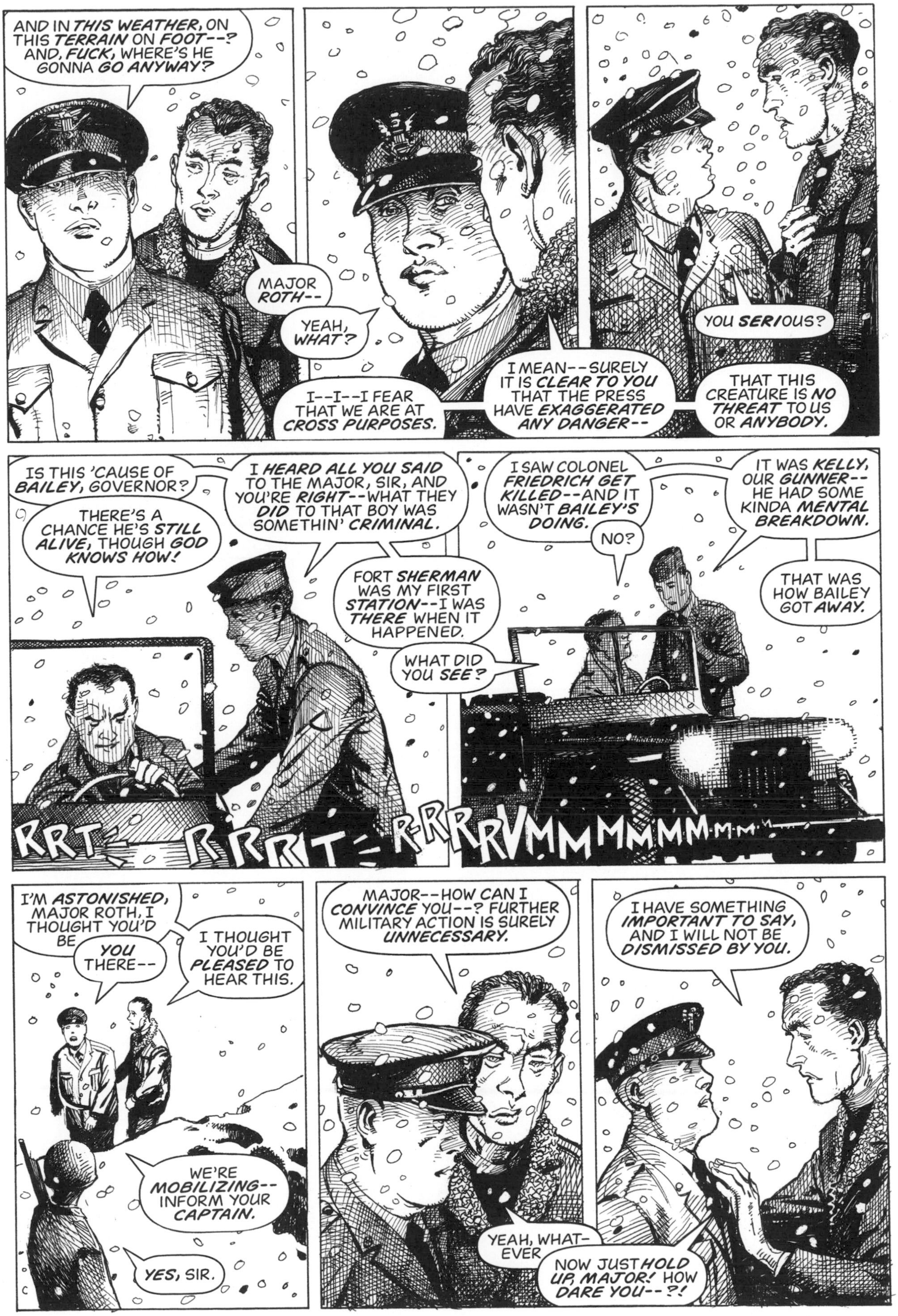
AND IN THIS WEATHER, ON THIS TERRAIN ON FOOT--? AND, FUCK, WHERE'S HE GONNA GO ANYWAY?
MAJOR ROTH--
YEAH, WHAT?
I--I--I FEAR THAT WE ARE AT CROSS PURPOSES.
I MEAN--SURELY IT IS CLEAR TO YOU THAT THE PRESS HAVE EXAGGERATED ANY DANGER--
YOU SERIOUS?
THAT THIS CREATURE IS NO THREAT TO US OR ANYBODY.
IS THIS 'CAUSE OF BAILEY, GOVERNOR?
THERE'S A CHANCE HE'S STILL ALIVE, THOUGH GOD KNOWS HOW!
I HEARD ALL YOU SAID TO THE MAJOR, SIR, AND YOU'RE RIGHT--WHAT THEY DID TO THAT BOY WAS SOMETHIN' CRIMINAL.
FORT SHERMAN WAS MY FIRST STATION--I WAS THERE WHEN IT HAPPENED.
WHAT DID YOU SEE?
RRT
RRRT
RRRRVMMMMMMM·M·M
I SAW COLONEL FRIEDRICH GET KILLED--AND IT WASN'T BAILEY'S DOING.
NO?
IT WAS KELLY, OUR GUNNER--HE HAD SOME KINDA MENTAL BREAKDOWN.
THAT WAS HOW BAILEY GOT AWAY.
I'M ASTONISHED, MAJOR ROTH, I THOUGHT YOU'D BE
YOU THERE--
I THOUGHT YOU'D BE PLEASED TO HEAR THIS.
WE'RE MOBILIZING--INFORM YOUR CAPTAIN.
YES, SIR.
MAJOR--HOW CAN I CONVINCE YOU--? FURTHER MILITARY ACTION IS SURELY UNNECESSARY.
YEAH, WHATEVER
I HAVE SOMETHING IMPORTANT TO SAY, AND I WILL NOT BE DISMISSED BY YOU.
NOW JUST HOLD UP, MAJOR! HOW DARE YOU--?!

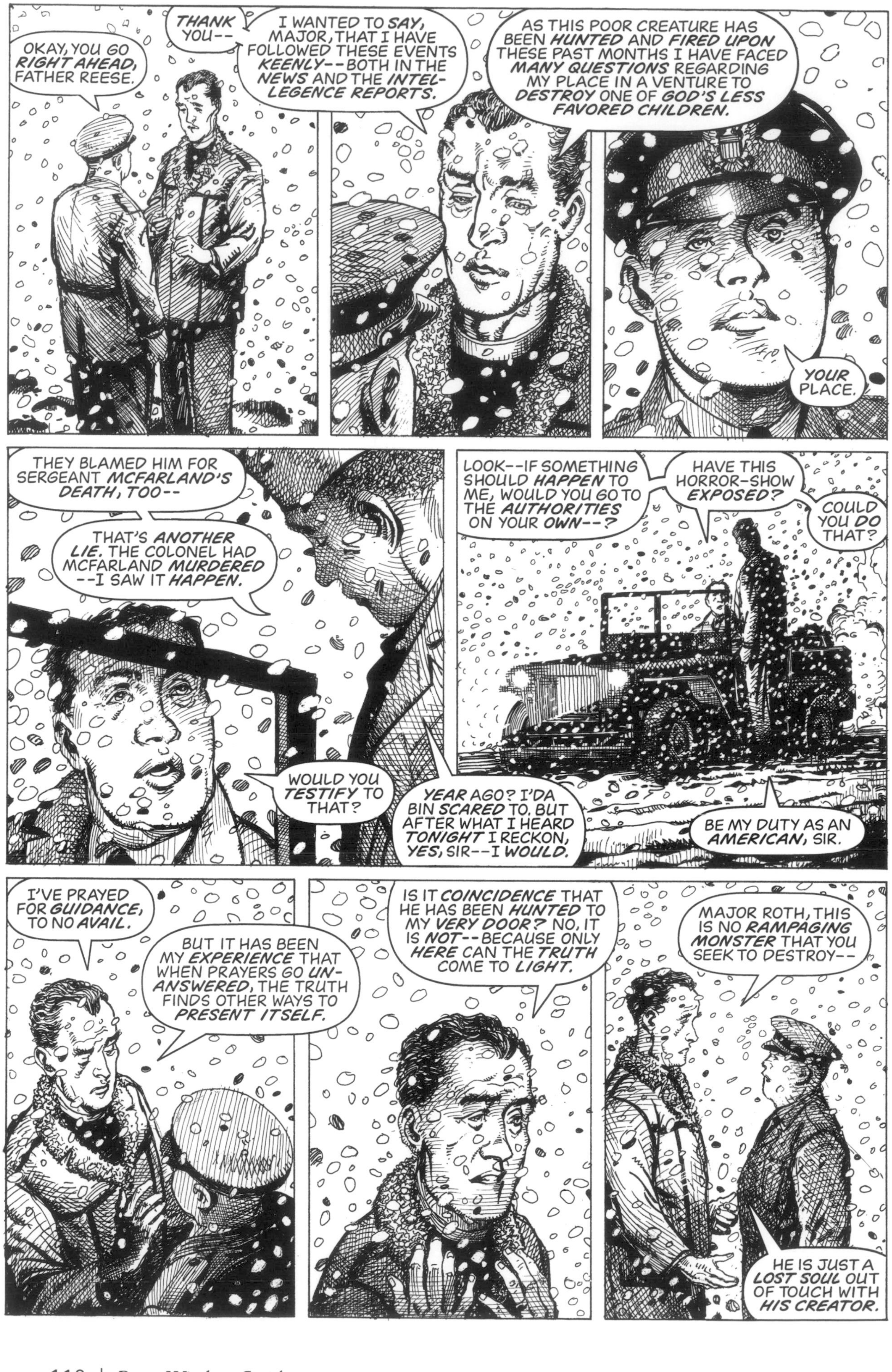
OKAY, YOU GO RIGHT AHEAD, FATHER REESE.
THANK YOU--
I WANTED TO SAY, MAJOR, THAT I HAVE FOLLOWED THESE EVENTS KEENLY--BOTH IN THE NEWS AND THE INTELLEGENCE REPORTS.
AS THIS POOR CREATURE HAS BEEN HUNTED AND FIRED UPON THESE PAST MONTHS I HAVE FACED MANY QUESTIONS REGARDING MY PLACE IN A VENTURE TO DESTROY ONE OF GOD'S LESS FAVORED CHILDREN.
YOUR PLACE.
THEY BLAMED HIM FOR SERGEANT MCFARLAND'S DEATH, TOO--
THAT'S ANOTHER LIE. THE COLONEL HAD MCFARLAND MURDERED --I SAW IT HAPPEN.
WOULD YOU TESTIFY TO THAT?
YEAR AGO? I'DA BIN SCARED TO, BUT AFTER WHAT I HEARD TONIGHT I RECKON, YES, SIR--I WOULD.
LOOK--IF SOMETHING SHOULD HAPPEN TO ME, WOULD YOU GO TO THE AUTHORITIES ON YOUR OWN--?
HAVE THIS HORROR-SHOW EXPOSED?
COULD YOU DO THAT?
BE MY DUTY AS AN AMERICAN, SIR.
I'VE PRAYED FOR GUIDANCE, TO NO AVAIL.
BUT IT HAS BEEN MY EXPERIENCE THAT WHEN PRAYERS GO UNANSWERED, THE TRUTH FINDS OTHER WAYS TO PRESENT ITSELF.
IS IT COINCIDENCE THAT HE HAS BEEN HUNTED TO MY VERY DOOR? NO, IT IS NOT--BECAUSE ONLY HERE CAN THE TRUTH COME TO LIGHT.
MAJOR ROTH, THIS IS NO RAMPAGING MONSTER THAT YOU SEEK TO DESTROY--
HE IS JUST A LOST SOUL OUT OF TOUCH WITH HIS CREATOR.

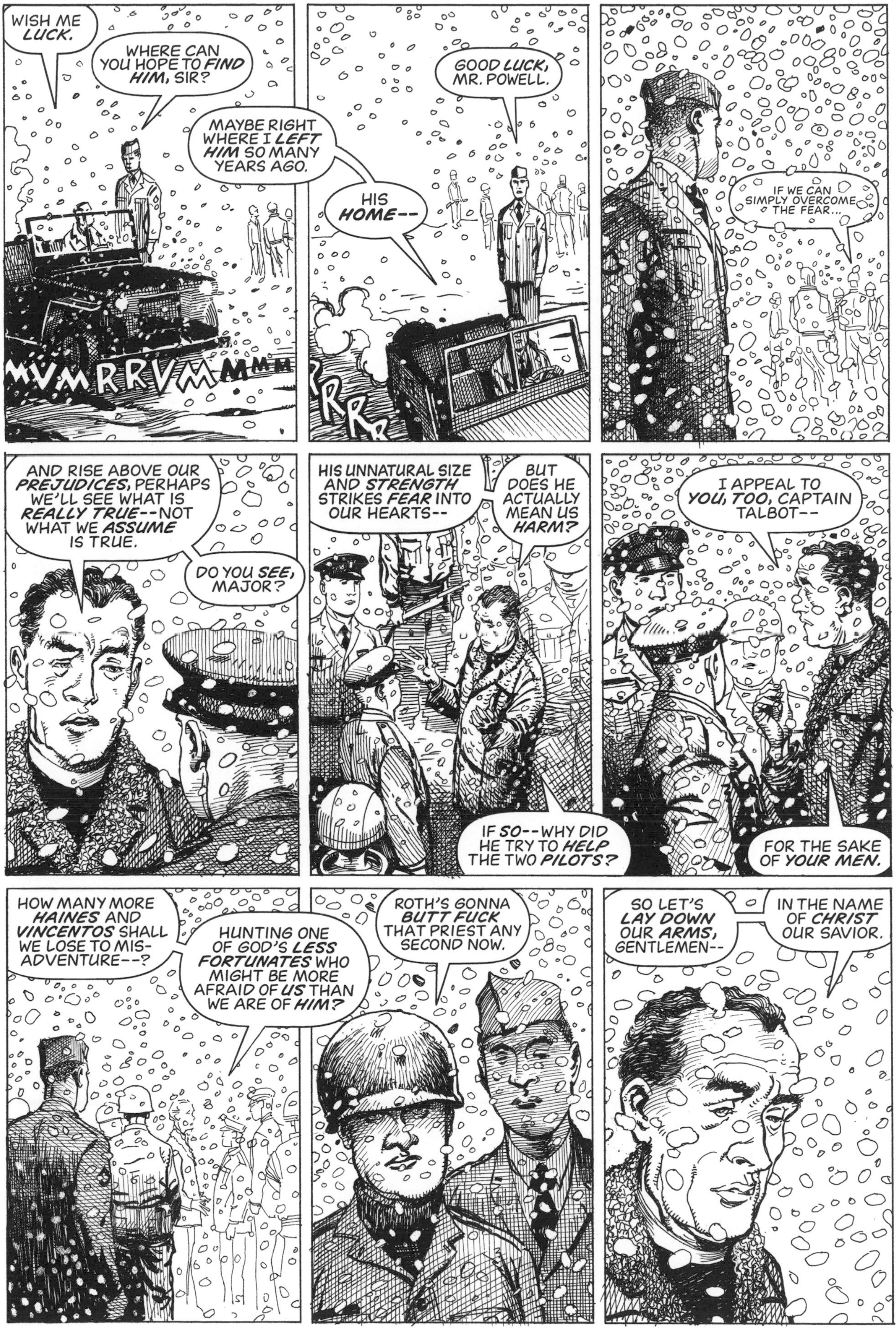
WISH ME LUCK.
WHERE CAN YOU HOPE TO FIND HIM, SIR?
MAYBE RIGHT WHERE I LEFT HIM SO MANY YEARS AGO.
HIS HOME--
MVMRRRVMMMM
RRR
GOOD LUCK, MR. POWELL.
IF WE CAN SIMPLY OVERCOME THE FEAR...
AND RISE ABOVE OUR PREJUDICES, PERHAPS WE'LL SEE WHAT IS REALLY TRUE--NOT WHAT WE ASSUME IS TRUE.
DO YOU SEE, MAJOR?
HIS UNNATURAL SIZE AND STRENGTH STRIKES FEAR INTO OUR HEARTS--
BUT DOES HE ACTUALLY MEAN US HARM?
IF SO--WHY DID HE TRY TO HELP THE TWO PILOTS?
I APPEAL TO YOU, TOO, CAPTAIN TALBOT--
FOR THE SAKE OF YOUR MEN.
HOW MANY MORE HAINES AND VINCENTOS SHALL WE LOSE TO MIS-ADVENTURE--?
HUNTING ONE OF GOD'S LESS FORTUNATES WHO MIGHT BE MORE AFRAID OF US THAN WE ARE OF HIM?
ROTH'S GONNA BUTT FUCK THAT PRIEST ANY SECOND NOW.
SO LET'S LAY DOWN OUR ARMS, GENTLEMEN--
IN THE NAME OF CHRIST OUR SAVIOR.

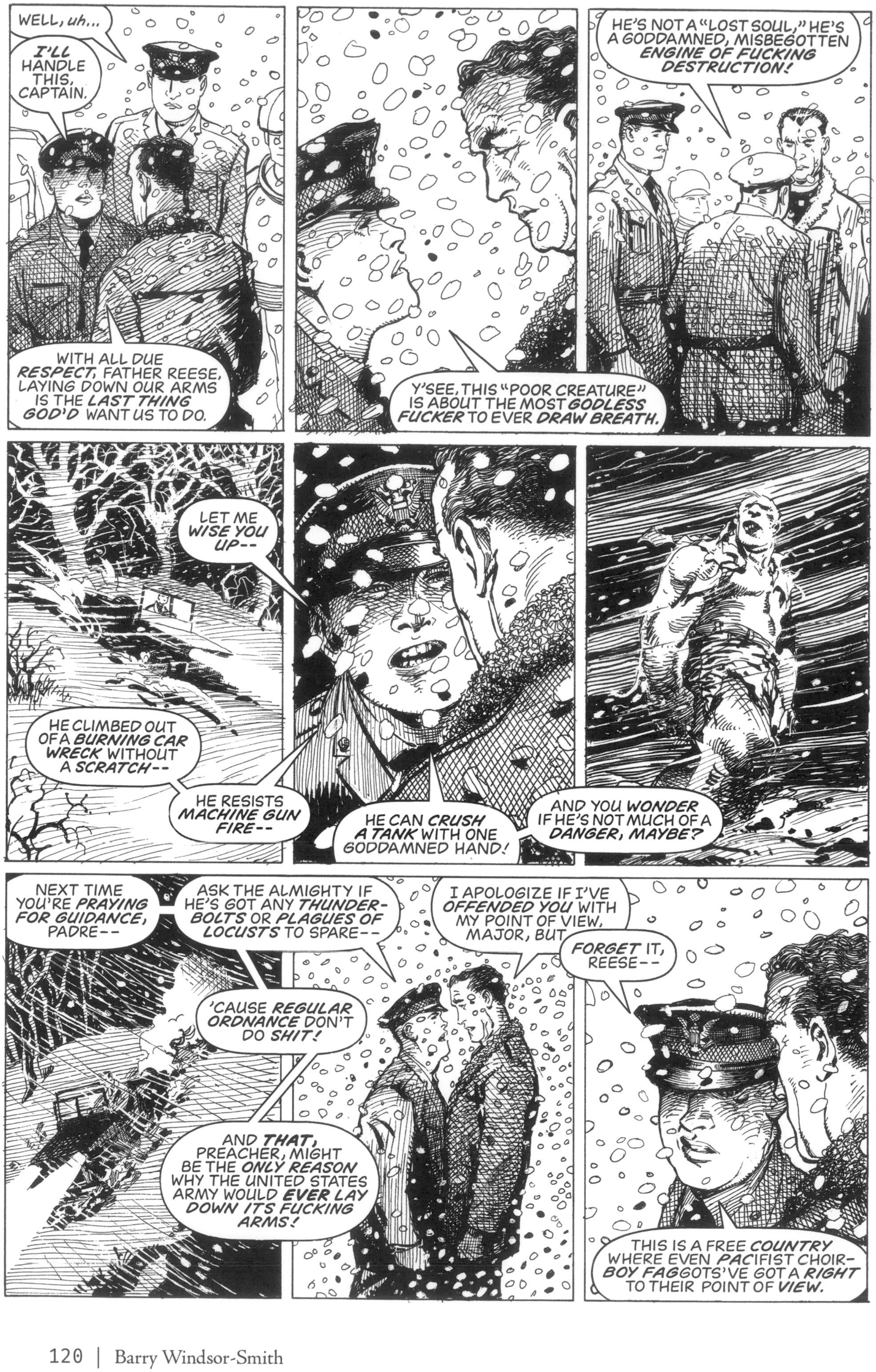
WELL, uh...
I'LL HANDLE THIS, CAPTAIN.
WITH ALL DUE RESPECT, FATHER REESE, LAYING DOWN OUR ARMS IS THE LAST THING GOD'D WANT US TO DO.
Y'SEE, THIS "POOR CREATURE" IS ABOUT THE MOST GODLESS FUCKER TO EVER DRAW BREATH.
HE'S NOT A "LOST SOUL," HE'S A GODDAMNED, MISBEGOTTEN ENGINE OF FUCKING DESTRUCTION!
LET ME WISE YOU UP--
HE CLIMBED OUT OF A BURNING CAR WRECK WITHOUT A SCRATCH--
HE RESISTS MACHINE GUN FIRE--
HE CAN CRUSH A TANK WITH ONE GODDAMNED HAND!
AND YOU WONDER IF HE'S NOT MUCH OF A DANGER, MAYBE?
NEXT TIME YOU'RE PRAYING FOR GUIDANCE, PADRE--
ASK THE ALMIGHTY IF HE'S GOT ANY THUNDER-BOLTS OR PLAGUES OF LOCUSTS TO SPARE--
'CAUSE REGULAR ORDNANCE DON'T DO SHIT!
AND THAT, PREACHER, MIGHT BE THE ONLY REASON WHY THE UNITED STATES ARMY WOULD EVER LAY DOWN ITS FUCKING ARMS!
I APOLOGIZE IF I'VE OFFENDED YOU WITH MY POINT OF VIEW, MAJOR, BUT
FORGET IT, REESE--
THIS IS A FREE COUNTRY WHERE EVEN PACIFIST CHOIR-BOY FAGGOTS'VE GOT A RIGHT TO THEIR POINT OF VIEW.

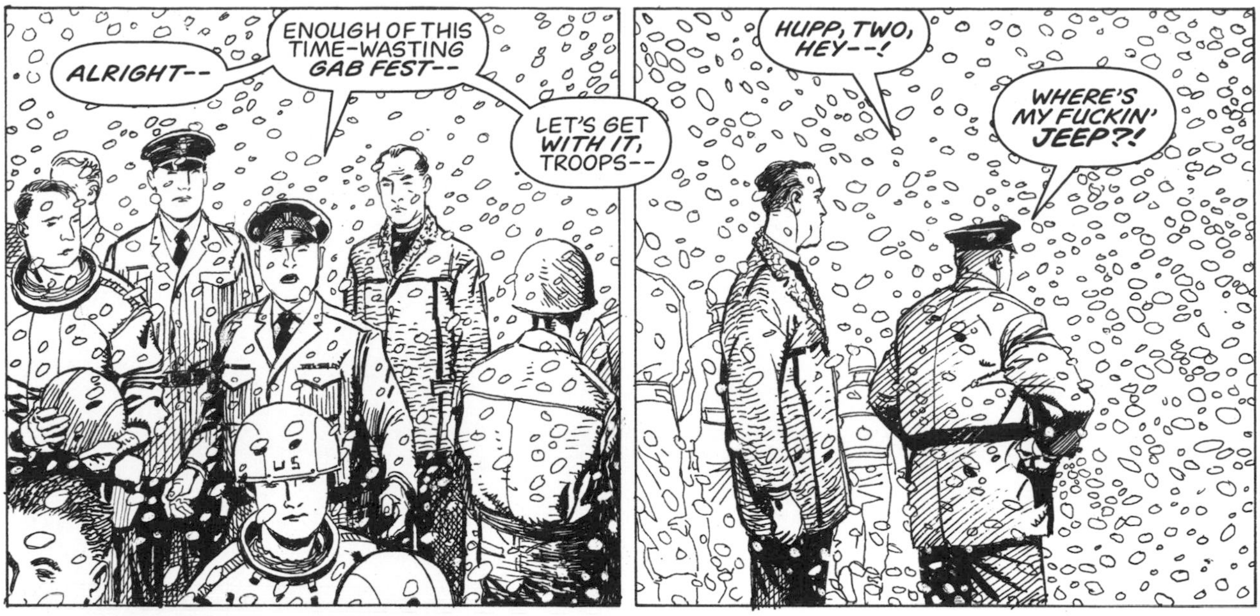
ALRIGHT--
ENOUGH OF THIS TIME-WASTING GAB FEST--
LET'S GET WITH IT, TROOPS--
HUPP, TWO, HEY--!
WHERE'S MY FUCKIN' JEEP?!

Providence Hills Thursday, November 25

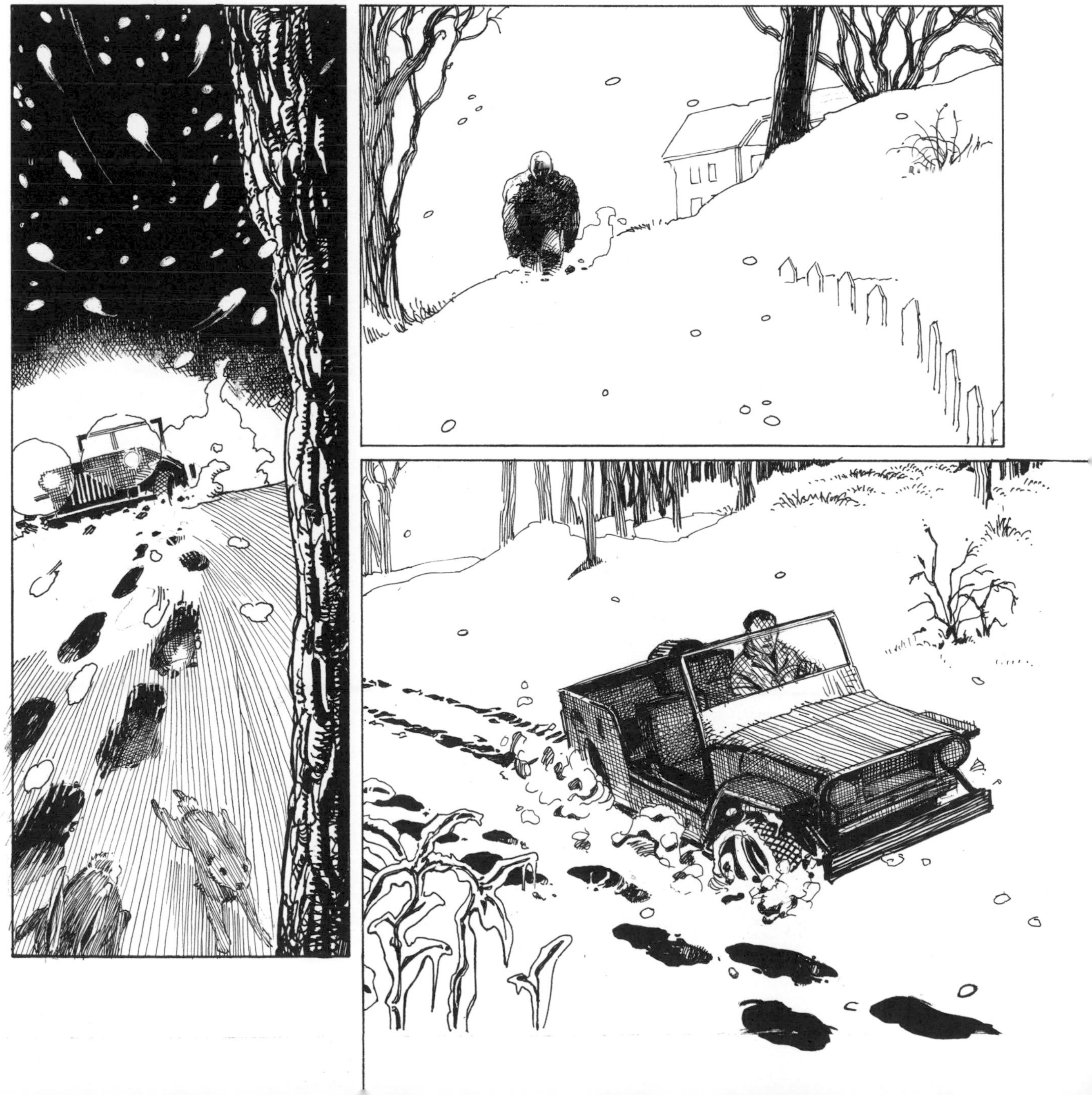

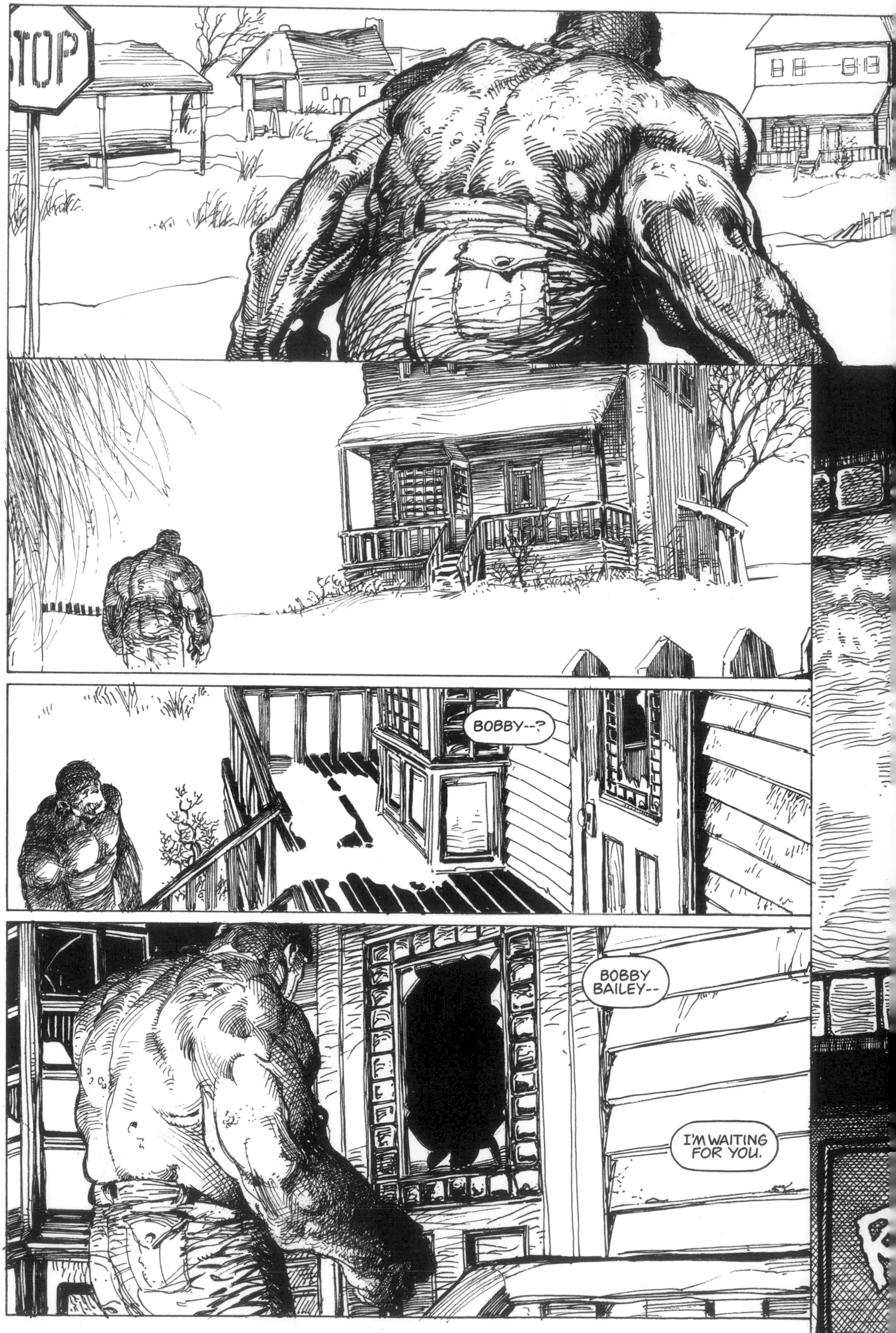
STOP
BOBBY--?
BOBBY BAILEY--
I'M WAITING FOR YOU.

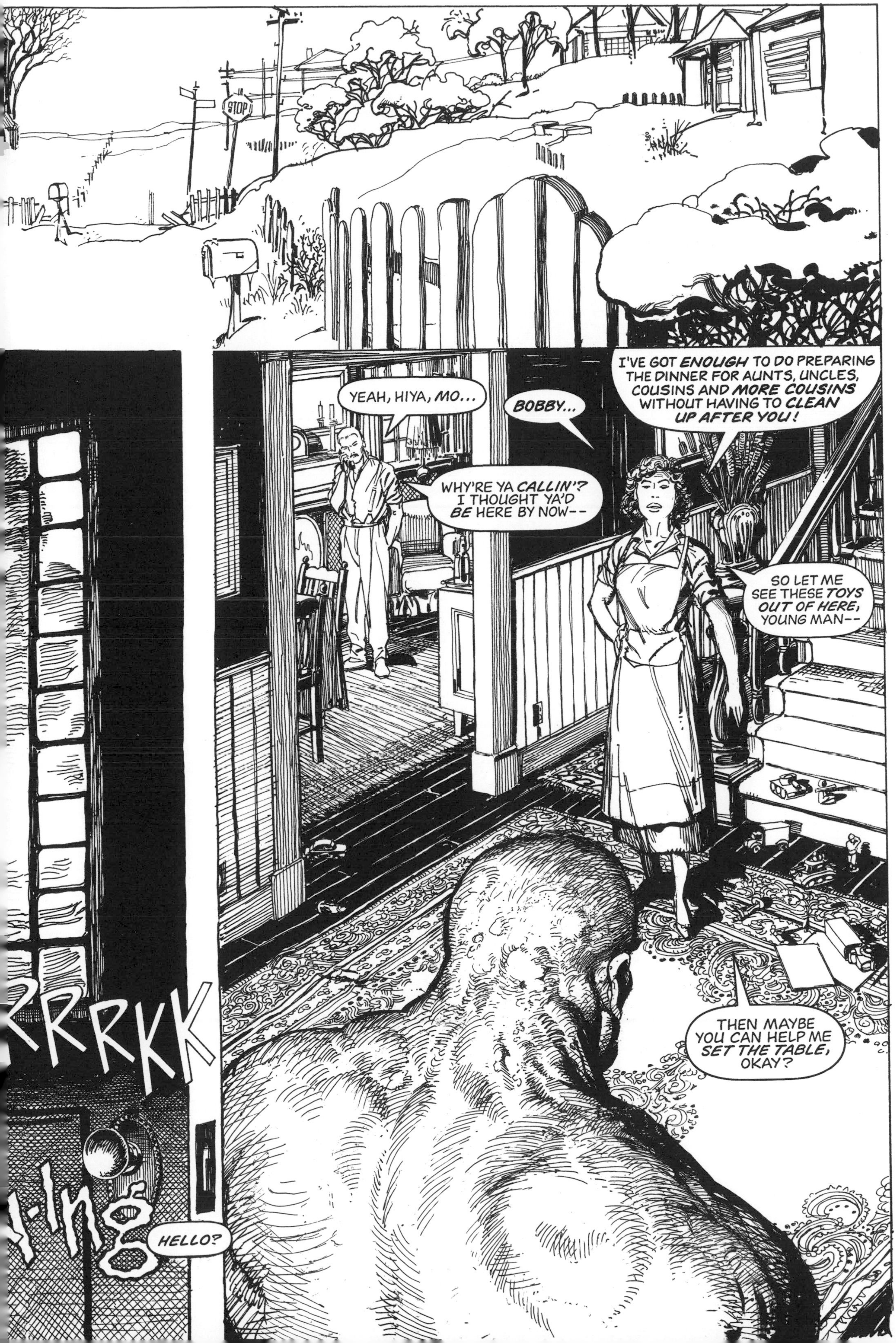

RRRKK
HELLO?
YEAH, HIYA, MO...
BOBBY...
WHY'RE YA CALLIN'? I THOUGHT YA'D BE HERE BY NOW--
I'VE GOT ENOUGH TO DO PREPARING THE DINNER FOR AUNTS, UNCLES, COUSINS AND MORE COUSINS WITHOUT HAVING TO CLEAN UP AFTER YOU!
SO LET ME SEE THESE TOYS OUT OF HERE, YOUNG MAN--
THEN MAYBE YOU CAN HELP ME SET THE TABLE, OKAY?

1949 The Bailey home Thursday, November 24

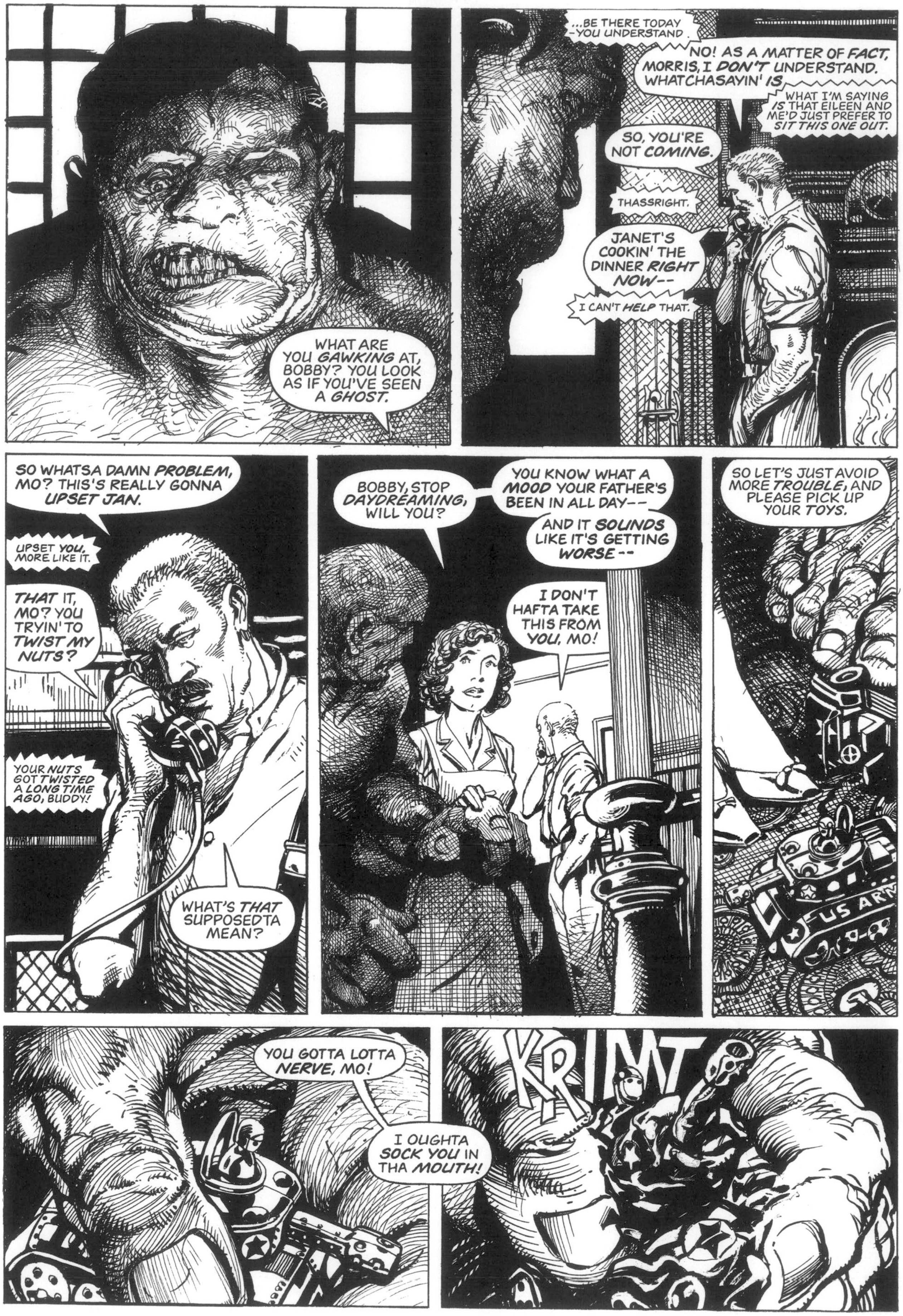

WHAT ARE YOU GAWKING AT, BOBBY? YOU LOOK AS IF YOU'VE SEEN A GHOST.
...BE THERE TODAY —YOU UNDERSTAND.
NO! AS A MATTER OF FACT, MORRIS, I DON'T UNDERSTAND. WHATCHASAYIN' IS
WHAT I'M SAYING IS THAT EILEEN AND ME'D JUST PREFER TO SIT THIS ONE OUT.
SO, YOU'RE NOT COMING.
THASSRIGHT.
JANET'S COOKIN' THE DINNER RIGHT NOW--
I CAN'T HELP THAT.
SO WHATSA DAMN PROBLEM, MO? THIS'S REALLY GONNA UPSET JAN.
UPSET YOU, MORE LIKE IT.
THAT IT, MO? YOU TRYIN' TO TWIST MY NUTS?
YOUR NUTS GOT TWISTED A LONG TIME AGO, BUDDY!
WHAT'S THAT SUPPOSEDTA MEAN?
BOBBY, STOP DAYDREAMING, WILL YOU?
YOU KNOW WHAT A MOOD YOUR FATHER'S BEEN IN ALL DAY--
AND IT SOUNDS LIKE IT'S GETTING WORSE--
I DON'T HAFTA TAKE THIS FROM YOU, MO!
SO LET'S JUST AVOID MORE TROUBLE, AND PLEASE PICK UP YOUR TOYS.
YOU GOTTA LOTTA NERVE, MO!
I OUGHTA SOCK YOU IN THA MOUTH!
KRIMT

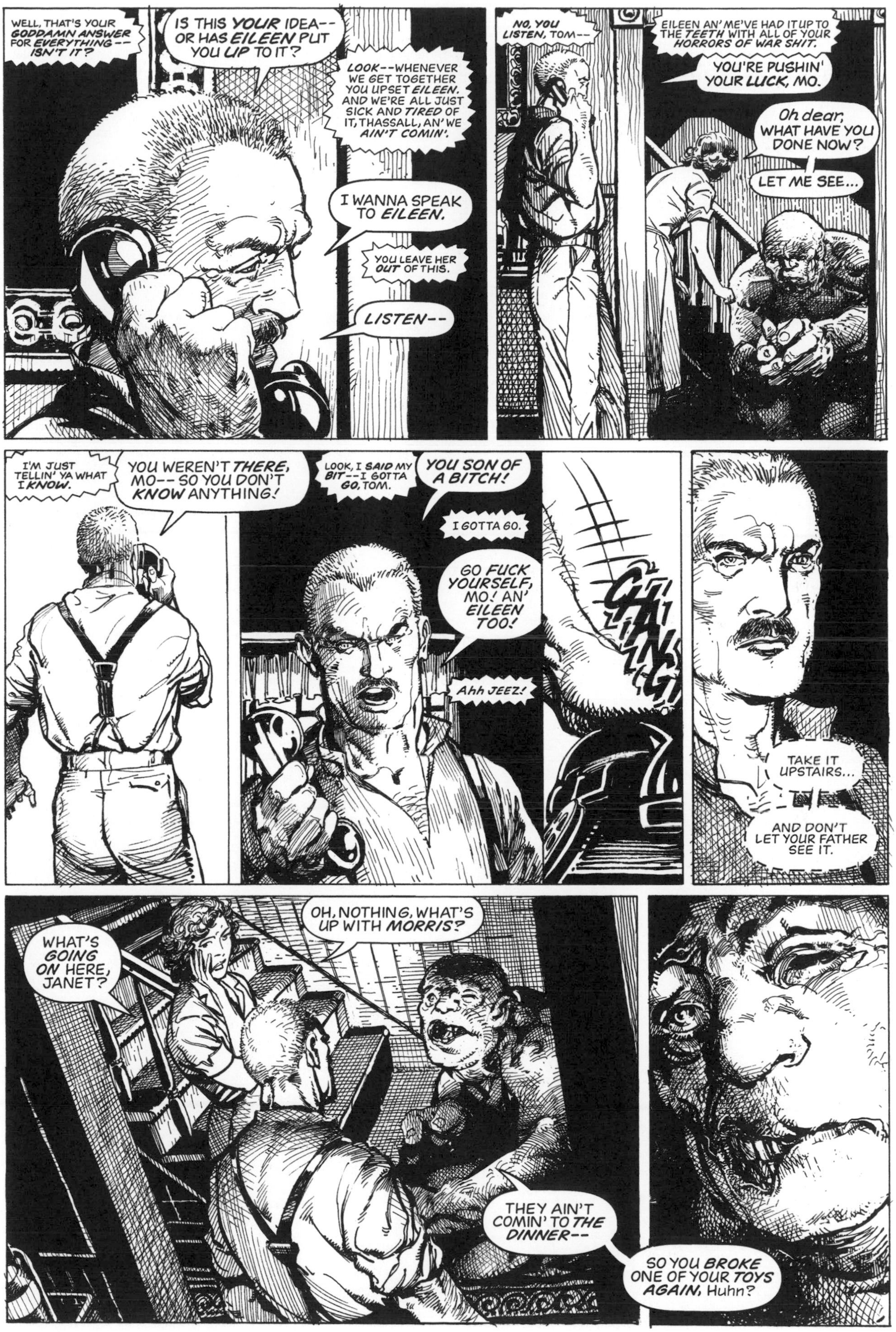
WELL, THAT'S YOUR GODDAMN ANSWER FOR EVERYTHING-- ISN'T IT?
IS THIS YOUR IDEA-- OR HAS EILEEN PUT YOU UP TO IT?
LOOK--WHENEVER WE GET TOGETHER YOU UPSET EILEEN. AND WE'RE ALL JUST SICK AND TIRED OF IT, THASSALL, AN' WE AIN'T COMIN'.
I WANNA SPEAK TO EILEEN.
YOU LEAVE HER OUT OF THIS.
LISTEN--
NO, YOU LISTEN, TOM--
EILEEN AN' ME'VE HAD IT UP TO THE TEETH WITH ALL OF YOUR HORRORS OF WAR SHIT.
YOU'RE PUSHIN' YOUR LUCK, MO.
Oh dear, WHAT HAVE YOU DONE NOW?
LET ME SEE...
I'M JUST TELLIN' YA WHAT I KNOW.
YOU WEREN'T THERE, MO-- SO YOU DON'T KNOW ANYTHING!
LOOK, I SAID MY BIT--I GOTTA GO, TOM.
YOU SON OF A BITCH!
I GOTTA GO.
GO FUCK YOURSELF, MO! AN' EILEEN TOO!
Ahh JEEZ!
TAKE IT UPSTAIRS...
AND DON'T LET YOUR FATHER SEE IT.
WHAT'S GOING ON HERE, JANET?
OH, NOTHING, WHAT'S UP WITH MORRIS?
THEY AIN'T COMIN' TO THE DINNER--
SO YOU BROKE ONE OF YOUR TOYS AGAIN, Huhn?

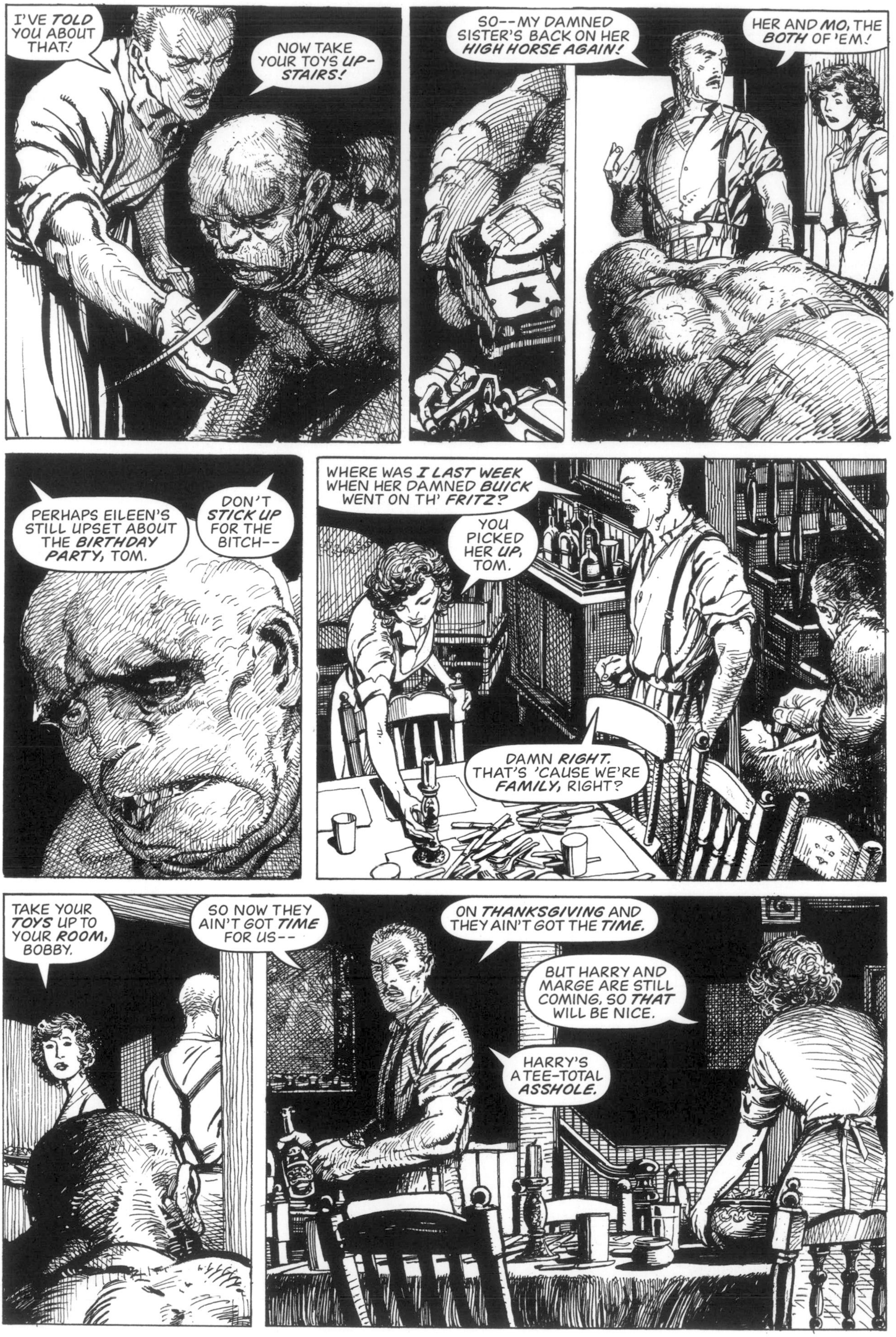
I'VE TOLD YOU ABOUT THAT!
NOW TAKE YOUR TOYS UP-STAIRS!
SO--MY DAMNED SISTER'S BACK ON HER HIGH HORSE AGAIN!
HER AND MO, THE BOTH OF 'EM!
PERHAPS EILEEN'S STILL UPSET ABOUT THE BIRTHDAY PARTY, TOM.
DON'T STICK UP FOR THE BITCH--
WHERE WAS I LAST WEEK WHEN HER DAMNED BUICK WENT ON TH' FRITZ?
YOU PICKED HER UP, TOM.
DAMN RIGHT. THAT'S 'CAUSE WE'RE FAMILY, RIGHT?
TAKE YOUR TOYS UP TO YOUR ROOM, BOBBY.
SO NOW THEY AIN'T GOT TIME FOR US--
ON THANKSGIVING AND THEY AIN'T GOT THE TIME.
BUT HARRY AND MARGE ARE STILL COMING, SO THAT WILL BE NICE.
HARRY'S A TEE-TOTAL ASSHOLE.

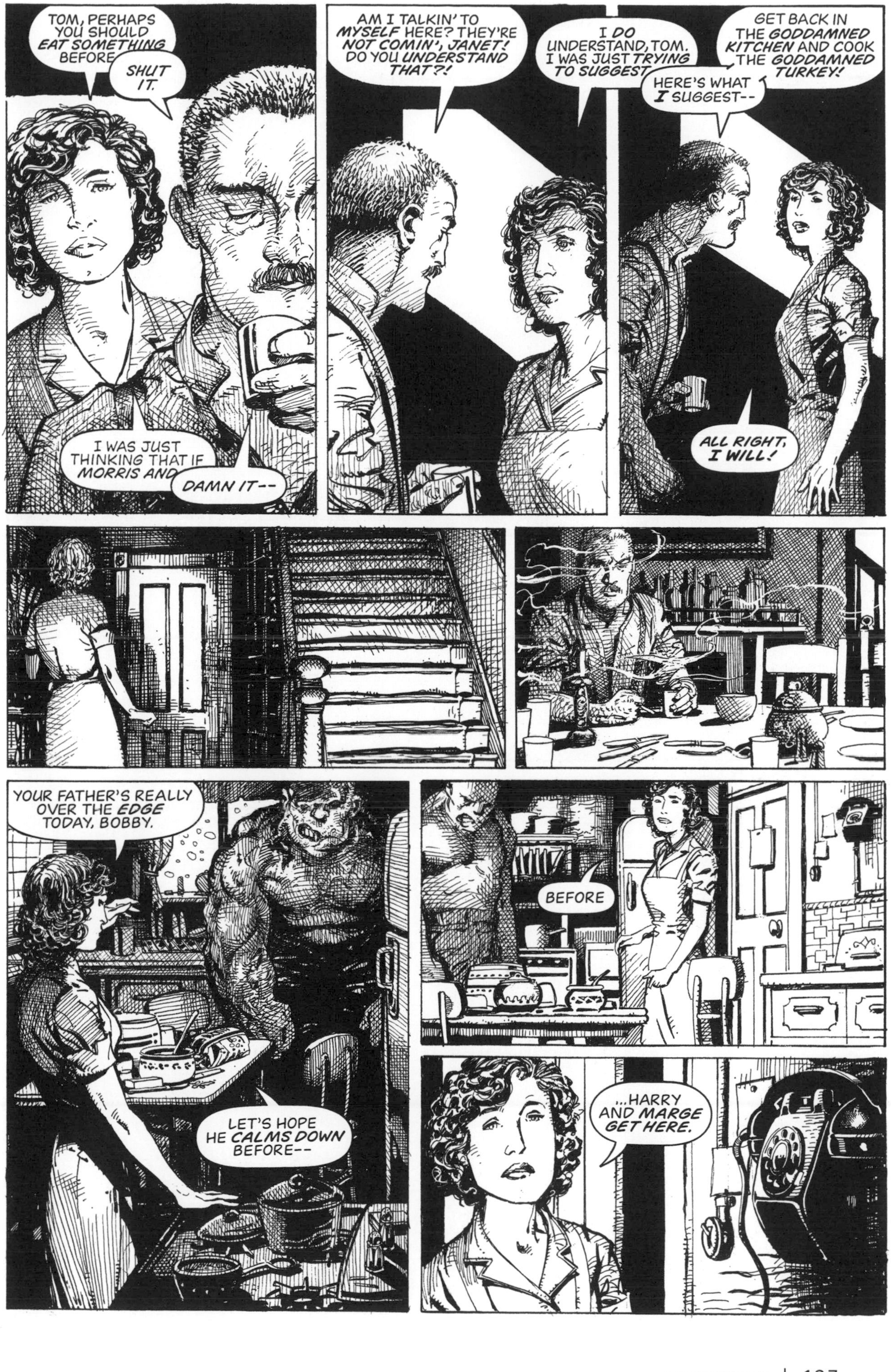

TOM, PERHAPS YOU SHOULD EAT SOMETHING BEFORE
SHUT IT.
I WAS JUST THINKING THAT IF MORRIS AND
DAMN IT--
AM I TALKIN' TO MYSELF HERE? THEY'RE NOT COMIN', JANET! DO YOU UNDERSTAND THAT?!
I DO UNDERSTAND, TOM. I WAS JUST TRYING TO SUGGEST
HERE'S WHAT I SUGGEST--
GET BACK IN THE GODDAMNED KITCHEN AND COOK THE GODDAMNED TURKEY!
ALL RIGHT, I WILL!
YOUR FATHER'S REALLY OVER THE EDGE TODAY, BOBBY.
LET'S HOPE HE CALMS DOWN BEFORE--
BEFORE
...HARRY AND MARGE GET HERE.

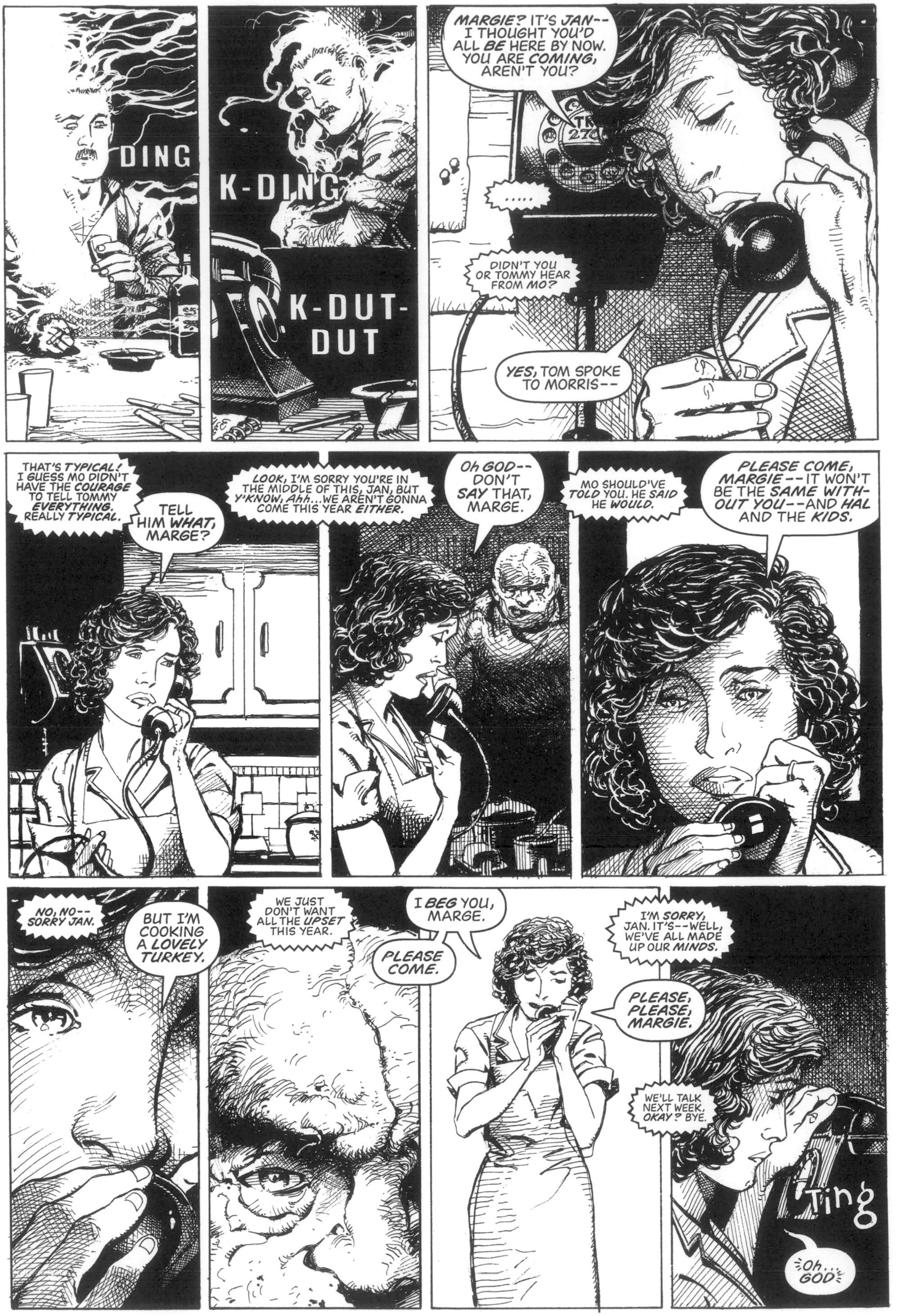

DING
K-DING
K-DUT-DUT
MARGIE? IT'S JAN--I THOUGHT YOU'D ALL BE HERE BY NOW. YOU ARE COMING, AREN'T YOU?
.....
DIDN'T YOU OR TOMMY HEAR FROM MO?
YES, TOM SPOKE TO MORRIS--
THAT'S TYPICAL! I GUESS MO DIDN'T HAVE THE COURAGE TO TELL TOMMY EVERYTHING. REALLY TYPICAL.
TELL HIM WHAT, MARGE?
LOOK, I'M SORRY YOU'RE IN THE MIDDLE OF THIS, JAN, BUT Y'KNOW, Ahh...WE AREN'T GONNA COME THIS YEAR EITHER.
Oh GOD--DON'T SAY THAT, MARGE.
MO SHOULD'VE TOLD YOU. HE SAID HE WOULD.
PLEASE COME, MARGIE--IT WON'T BE THE SAME WITHOUT YOU--AND HAL AND THE KIDS.
NO, NO--SORRY JAN.
BUT I'M COOKING A LOVELY TURKEY.
WE JUST DON'T WANT ALL THE UPSET THIS YEAR.
I BEG YOU, MARGE.
PLEASE COME.
I'M SORRY, JAN. IT'S--WELL, WE'VE ALL MADE UP OUR MINDS.
PLEASE, PLEASE, MARGIE.
WE'LL TALK NEXT WEEK, OKAY? BYE.
Ting
Oh... GOD

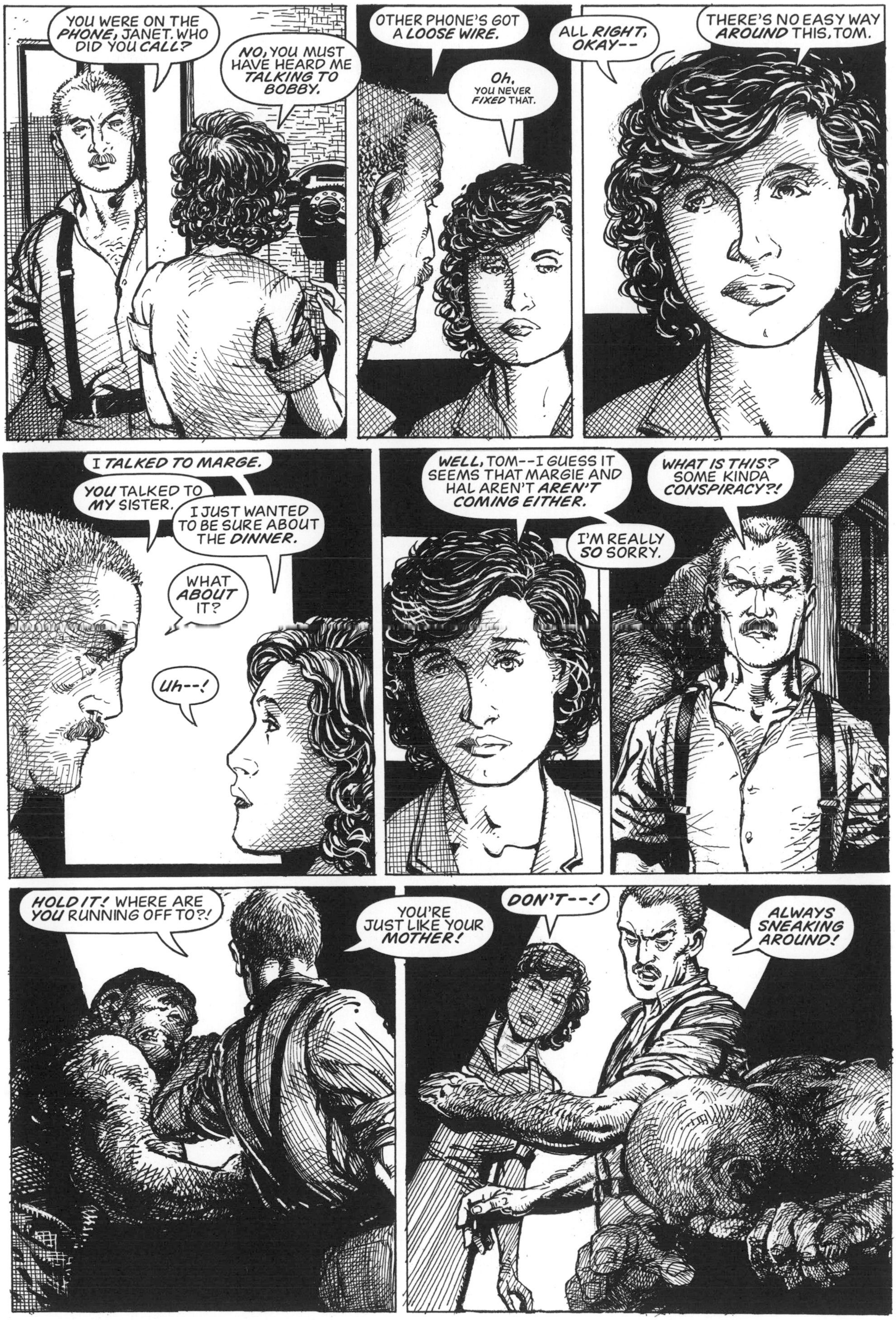
YOU WERE ON THE PHONE, JANET. WHO DID YOU CALL?
NO, YOU MUST HAVE HEARD ME TALKING TO BOBBY.
OTHER PHONE'S GOT A LOOSE WIRE.
Oh, YOU NEVER FIXED THAT.
ALL RIGHT, OKAY--
THERE'S NO EASY WAY AROUND THIS, TOM.
I TALKED TO MARGE.
YOU TALKED TO MY SISTER.
I JUST WANTED TO BE SURE ABOUT THE DINNER.
WHAT ABOUT IT?
Uh--!
WELL, TOM--I GUESS IT SEEMS THAT MARGIE AND HAL AREN'T AREN'T COMING EITHER.
I'M REALLY SO SORRY.
WHAT IS THIS? SOME KINDA CONSPIRACY?!
HOLD IT! WHERE ARE YOU RUNNING OFF TO?!
YOU'RE JUST LIKE YOUR MOTHER!
DON'T--!
ALWAYS SNEAKING AROUND!

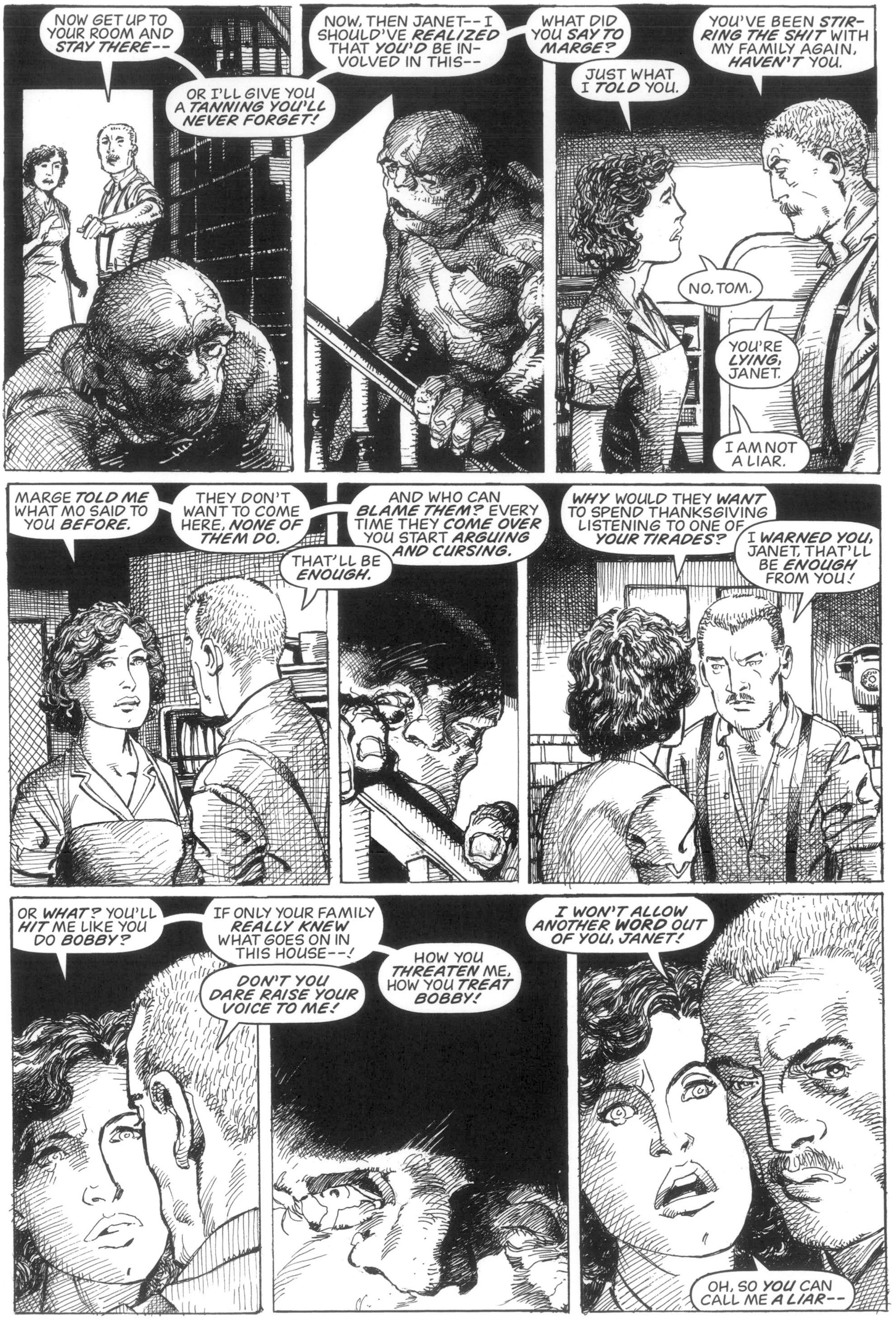
NOW GET UP TO YOUR ROOM AND STAY THERE--
OR I'LL GIVE YOU A TANNING YOU'LL NEVER FORGET!
NOW, THEN JANET--I SHOULD'VE REALIZED THAT YOU'D BE INVOLVED IN THIS--
WHAT DID YOU SAY TO MARGE?
JUST WHAT I TOLD YOU.
YOU'VE BEEN STIRRING THE SHIT WITH MY FAMILY AGAIN, HAVEN'T YOU.
NO, TOM.
YOU'RE LYING, JANET.
I AM NOT A LIAR.
MARGE TOLD ME WHAT MO SAID TO YOU BEFORE.
THEY DON'T WANT TO COME HERE. NONE OF THEM DO.
AND WHO CAN BLAME THEM? EVERY TIME THEY COME OVER YOU START ARGUING AND CURSING.
THAT'LL BE ENOUGH.
WHY WOULD THEY WANT TO SPEND THANKSGIVING LISTENING TO ONE OF YOUR TIRADES?
I WARNED YOU, JANET. THAT'LL BE ENOUGH FROM YOU!
OR WHAT? YOU'LL HIT ME LIKE YOU DO BOBBY?
IF ONLY YOUR FAMILY REALLY KNEW WHAT GOES ON IN THIS HOUSE--!
DON'T YOU DARE RAISE YOUR VOICE TO ME!
HOW YOU THREATEN ME, HOW YOU TREAT BOBBY!
I WON'T ALLOW ANOTHER WORD OUT OF YOU, JANET!
OH, SO YOU CAN CALL ME A LIAR--

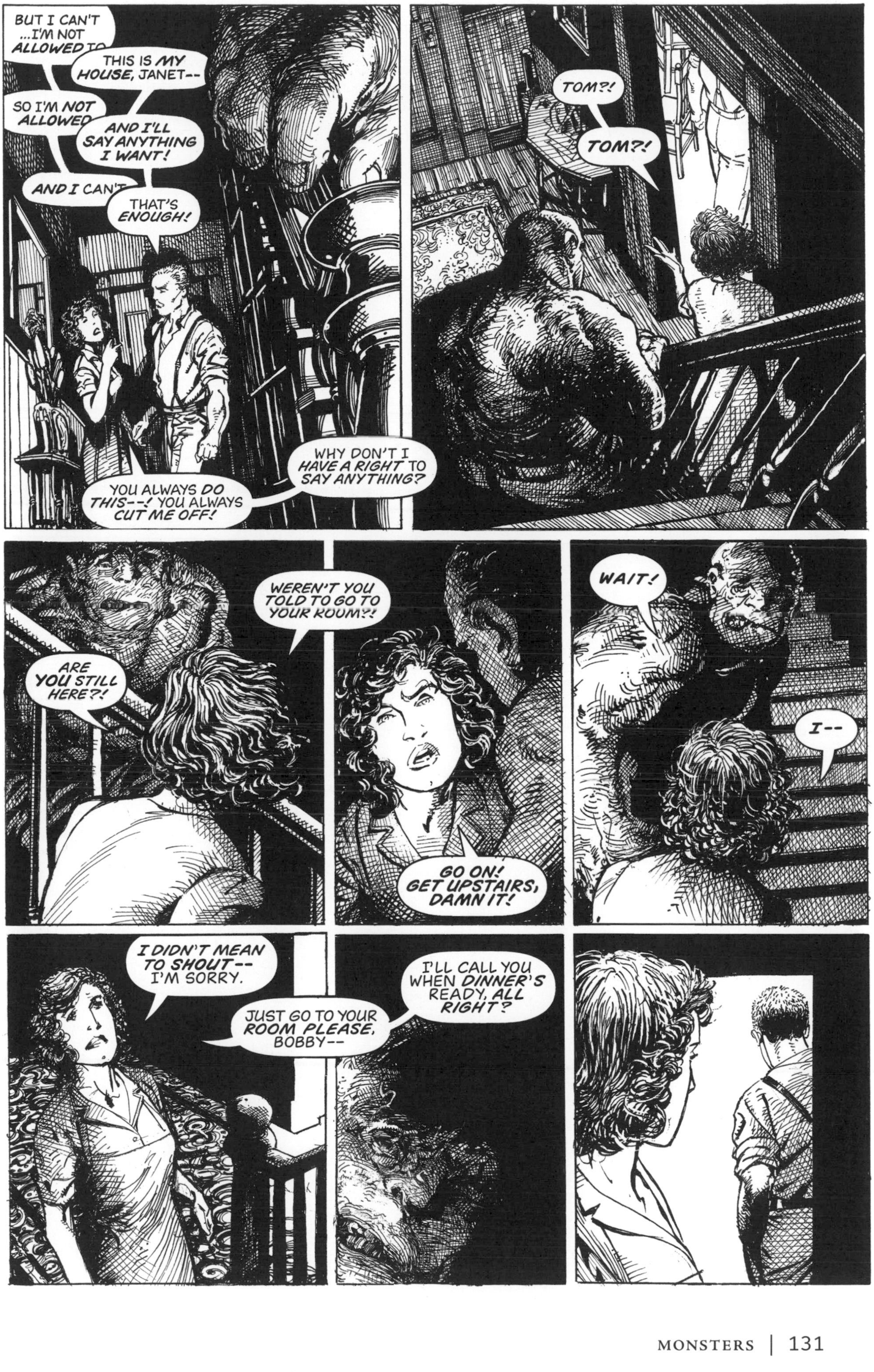
BUT I CAN'T ...I'M NOT ALLOWED TO
THIS IS MY HOUSE, JANET--
SO I'M NOT ALLOWED
AND I'LL SAY ANYTHING I WANT!
AND I CAN'T
THAT'S ENOUGH!
WHY DON'T I HAVE A RIGHT TO SAY ANYTHING?
YOU ALWAYS DO THIS--! YOU ALWAYS CUT ME OFF!
TOM?!
TOM?!
ARE YOU STILL HERE?!
WEREN'T YOU TOLD TO GO TO YOUR ROOM?!
GO ON! GET UPSTAIRS, DAMN IT!
WAIT!
I--
I DIDN'T MEAN TO SHOUT-- I'M SORRY.
JUST GO TO YOUR ROOM PLEASE, BOBBY--
I'LL CALL YOU WHEN DINNER'S READY, ALL RIGHT?

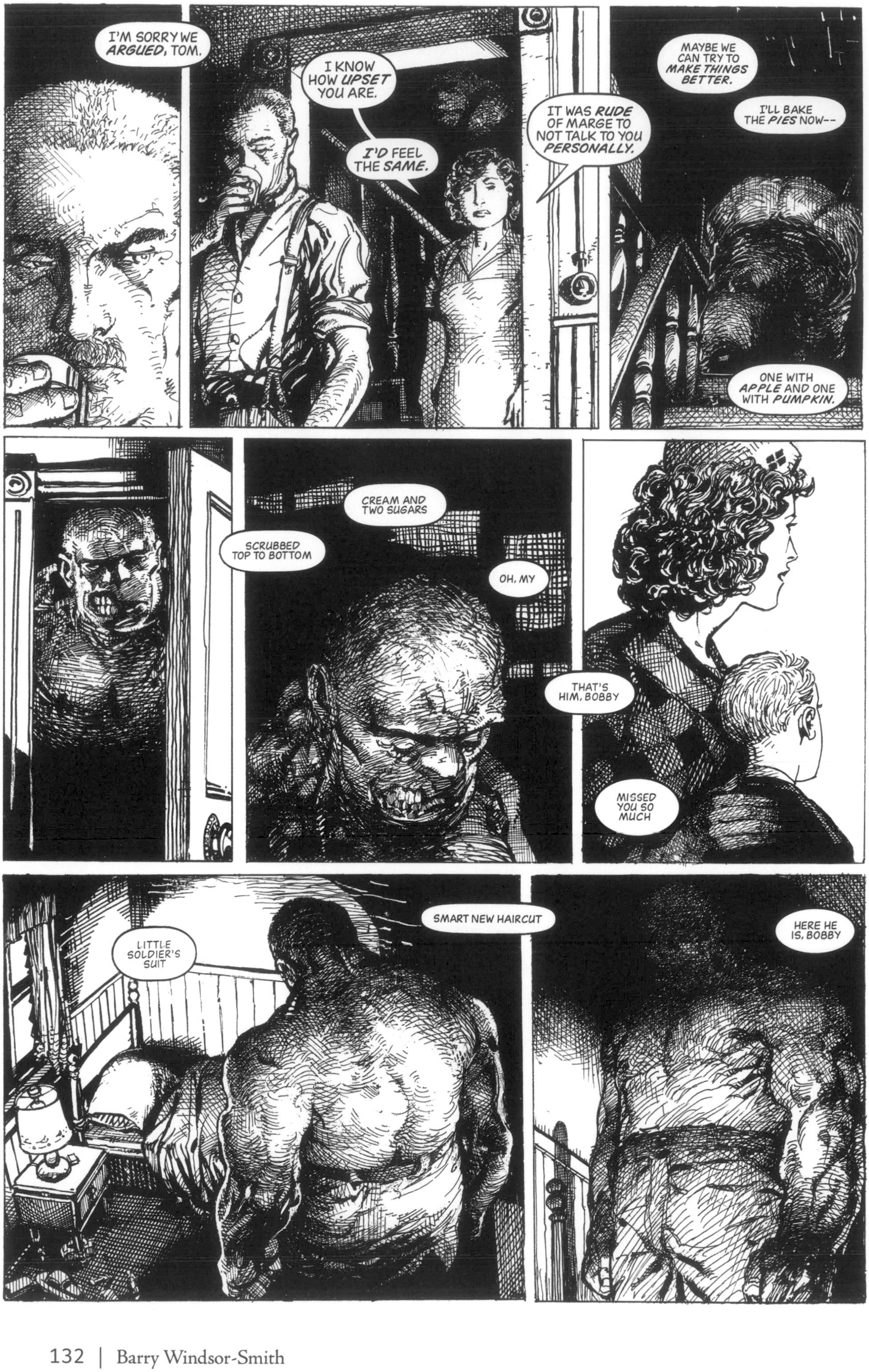
I'M SORRY WE ARGUED, TOM.
I KNOW HOW UPSET YOU ARE.
I'D FEEL THE SAME.
IT WAS RUDE OF MARGE TO NOT TALK TO YOU PERSONALLY.
MAYBE WE CAN TRY TO MAKE THINGS BETTER.
I'LL BAKE THE PIES NOW--
ONE WITH APPLE AND ONE WITH PUMPKIN.
CREAM AND TWO SUGARS
SCRUBBED TOP TO BOTTOM
OH, MY
THAT'S HIM, BOBBY
MISSED YOU SO MUCH
LITTLE SOLDIER'S SUIT
SMART NEW HAIRCUT
HERE HE IS, BOBBY

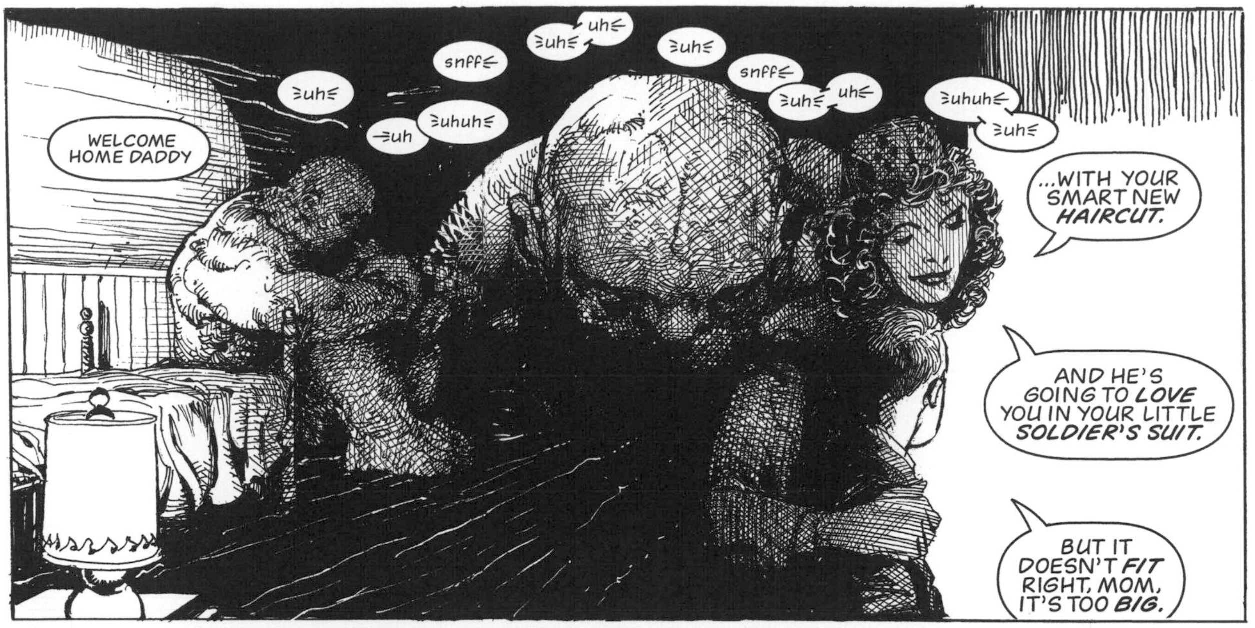
WELCOME HOME DADDY
uh
uh
uhuh
snff
uh
uh
uh
snff
uh
uh
uhuh
uh
...WITH YOUR SMART NEW HAIRCUT.
AND HE'S GOING TO LOVE YOU IN YOUR LITTLE SOLDIER'S SUIT.
BUT IT DOESN'T FIT RIGHT, MOM. IT'S TOO BIG.

1949 St. Claire Railroad Station, Providence, Ohio Friday, March 4

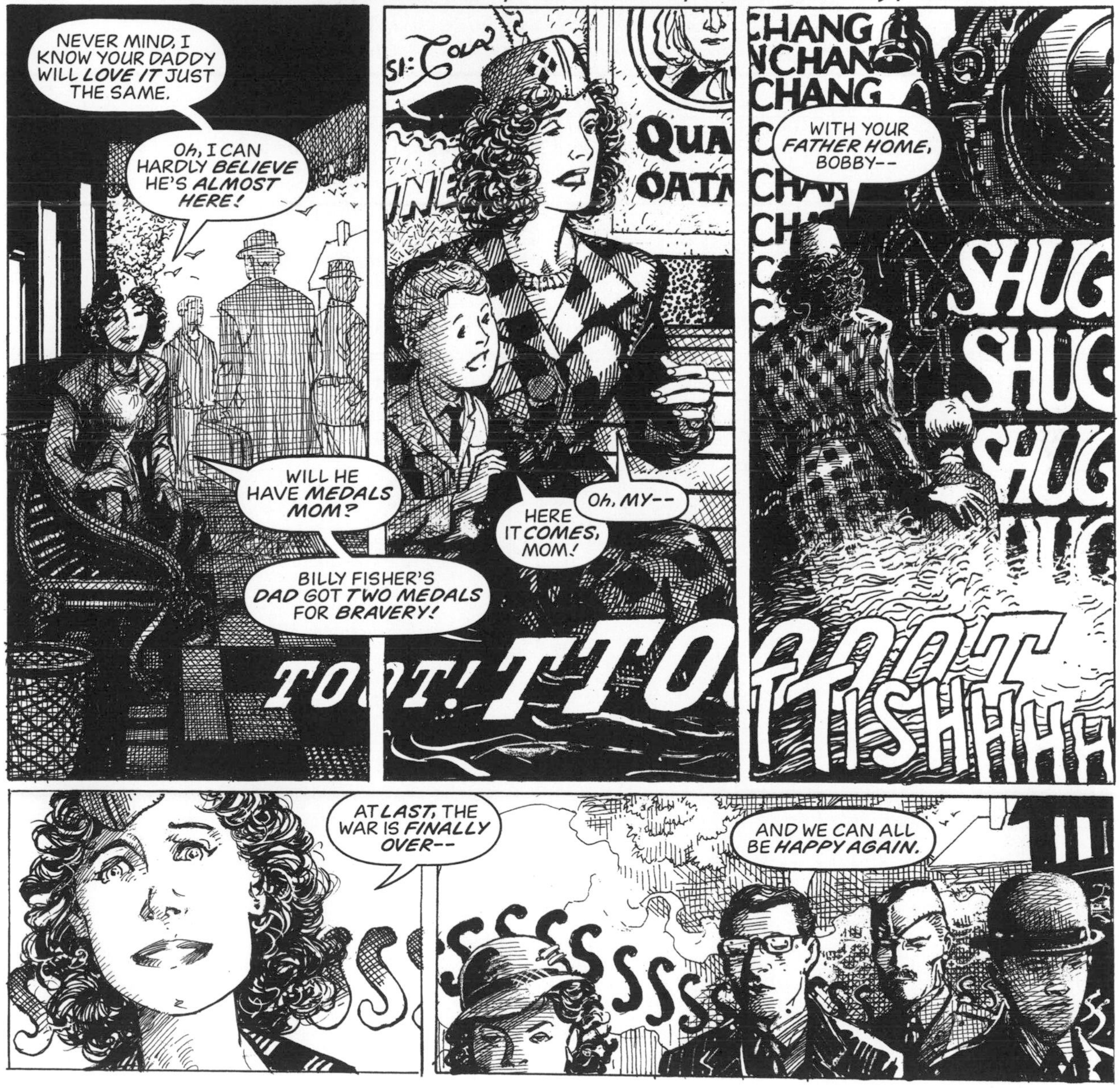
NEVER MIND, I KNOW YOUR DADDY WILL LOVE IT JUST THE SAME.
Oh, I CAN HARDLY BELIEVE HE'S ALMOST HERE!
WILL HE HAVE MEDALS MOM?
BILLY FISHER'S DAD GOT TWO MEDALS FOR BRAVERY!
TOOT!
HERE IT COMES, MOM!
Oh, MY--
TTOOOOOT
WITH YOUR FATHER HOME, BOBBY--
SHUG
SHUG
SHUG
TISHHHH
AT LAST, THE WAR IS FINALLY OVER--
AND WE CAN ALL BE HAPPY AGAIN.

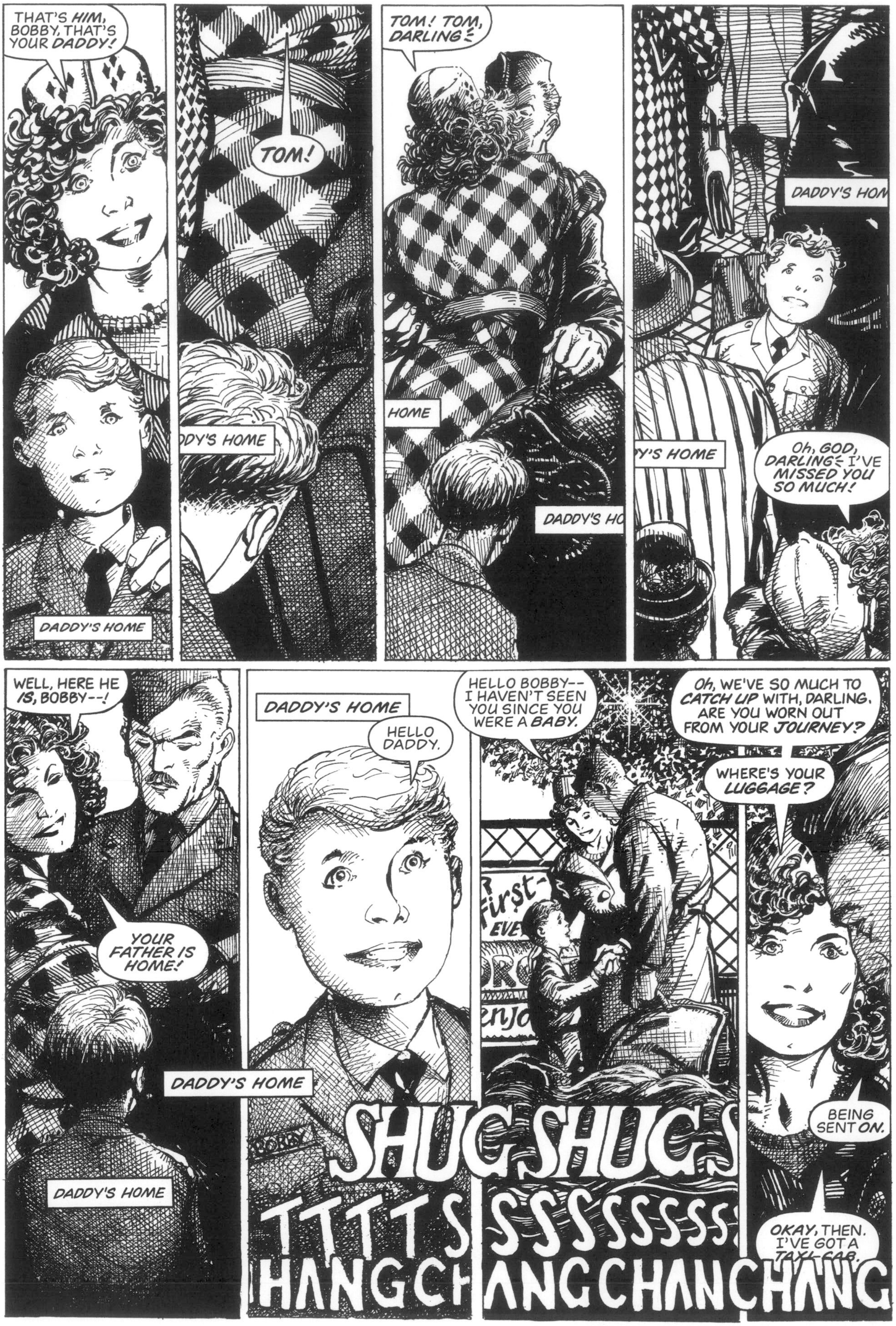
THAT'S HIM, BOBBY, THAT'S YOUR DADDY!
DADDY'S HOME
TOM!
DDY'S HOME
TOM! TOM, DARLING...
HOME
DADDY'S HO
DADDY'S HOM
Y'S HOME
Oh, GOD, DARLING... I'VE MISSED YOU SO MUCH!
WELL, HERE HE IS, BOBBY--!
YOUR FATHER IS HOME!
DADDY'S HOME
DADDY'S HOME
DADDY'S HOME
HELLO DADDY.
BOBBY
HELLO BOBBY-- I HAVEN'T SEEN YOU SINCE YOU WERE A BABY.
First-
EVE
Oh, WE'VE SO MUCH TO CATCH UP WITH, DARLING. ARE YOU WORN OUT FROM YOUR JOURNEY?
WHERE'S YOUR LUGGAGE?
BEING SENT ON.
OKAY, THEN. I'VE GOT A TAXI-CAB.
SHUG SHUG S
TTTTS SSSSSSS
HANGCHANGCHANCHANG

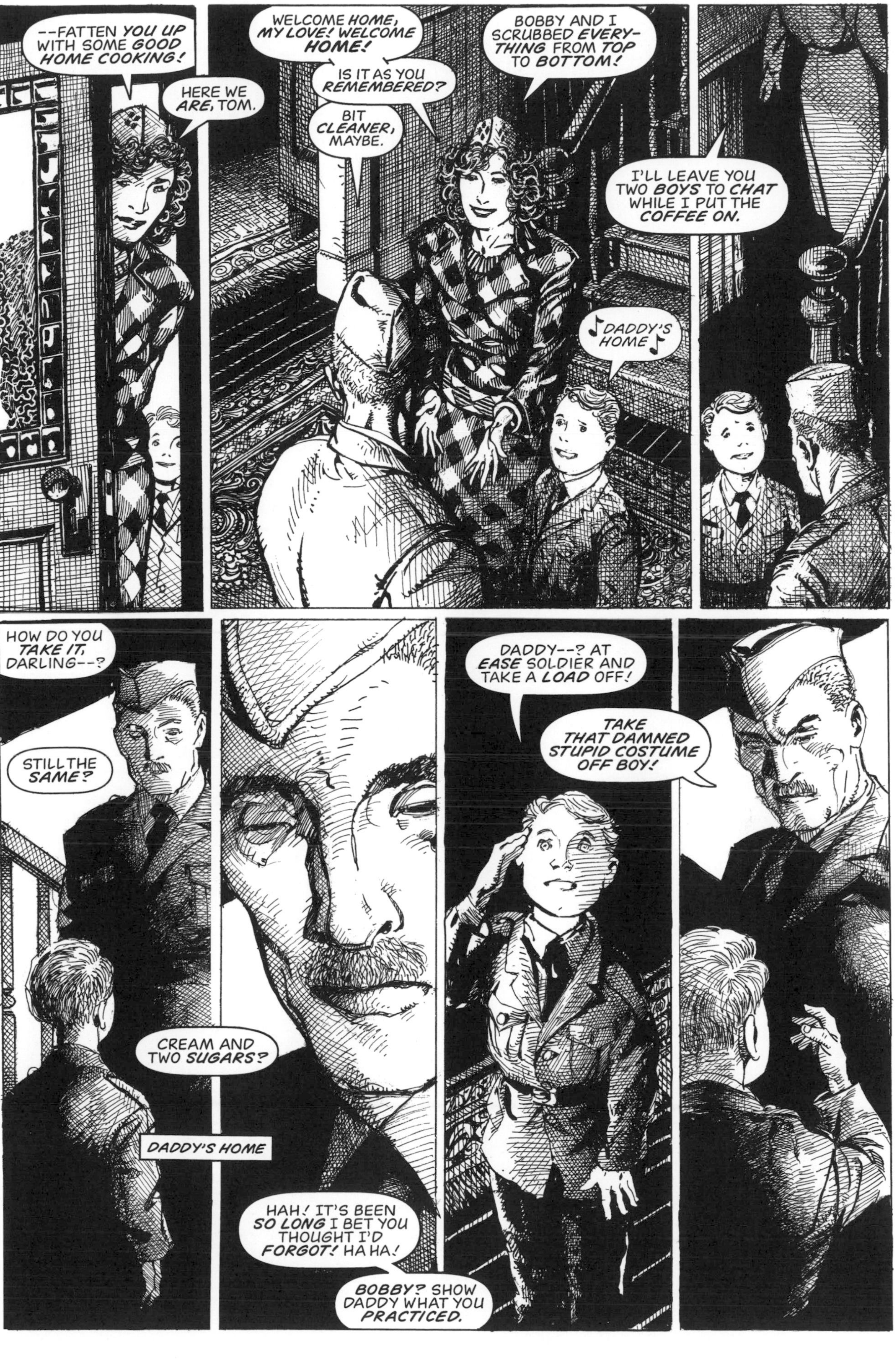

--FATTEN YOU UP WITH SOME GOOD HOME COOKING!
HERE WE ARE, TOM.
WELCOME HOME, MY LOVE! WELCOME HOME!
IS IT AS YOU REMEMBERED?
BIT CLEANER, MAYBE.
BOBBY AND I SCRUBBED EVERY-THING FROM TOP TO BOTTOM!
DADDY'S HOME
I'LL LEAVE YOU TWO BOYS TO CHAT WHILE I PUT THE COFFEE ON.
HOW DO YOU TAKE IT, DARLING--?
STILL THE SAME?
CREAM AND TWO SUGARS?
DADDY'S HOME
HAH! IT'S BEEN SO LONG I BET YOU THOUGHT I'D FORGOT! HA HA!
BOBBY? SHOW DADDY WHAT YOU PRACTICED.
DADDY--? AT EASE SOLDIER AND TAKE A LOAD OFF!
TAKE THAT DAMNED STUPID COSTUME OFF BOY!

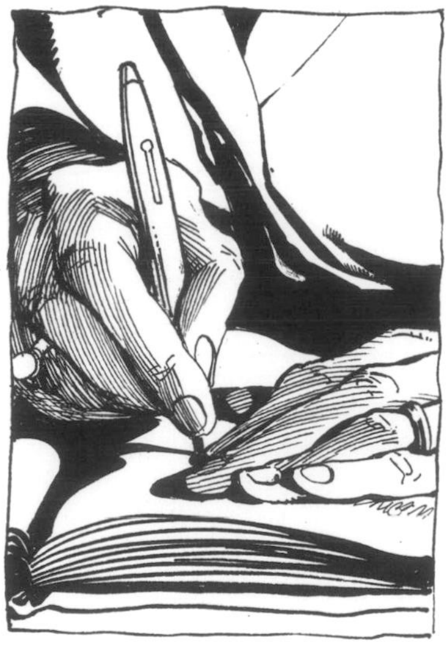

March 5, 1949

Well, it's finally happened. <u>Tom is HOME!!</u> Bobby and I picked him up at the station.

I made an early dinner of a T-Bone and garlic mash (his favorite) with apple pie and cream. He loved it and couldn't get enough, so I gave him the last of mine. He was so worn out he went straight to bed without even undressing. This morning he had some coffee and went back to sleep for the whole day.

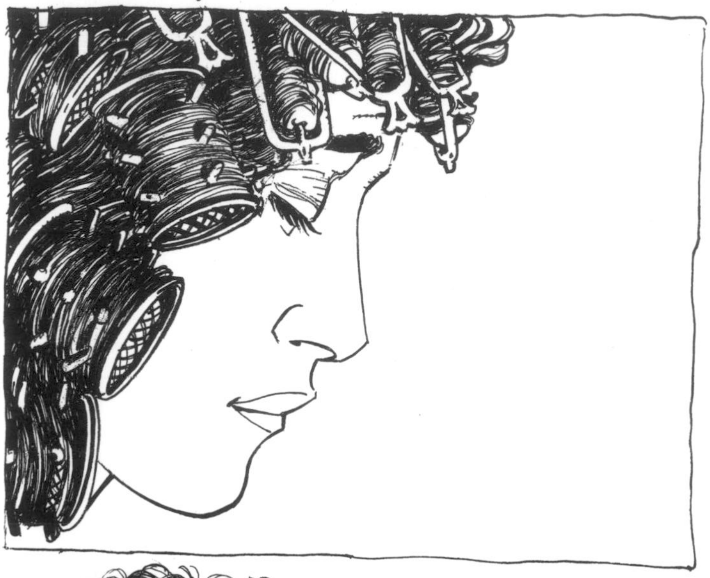

It's a bit disturbing to see Tom with grey hair (well, it's white I guess), and he's lost so much weight, too, but he'll soon put that back on. I do like his new mustache, very debonair I think, a bit like Clark Gable.

I talked with Harry & Marge and they said they and Mo & Eileen are all on for a reunion next Saturday. Marge said she'd do all the cooking, and she and Ei will do the dishes. How nice! It'll be a great old time.

I can't hardly believe that Tom's back home after all these years. Thank you God for being so benevolent and so everything. You have answered my prayers.

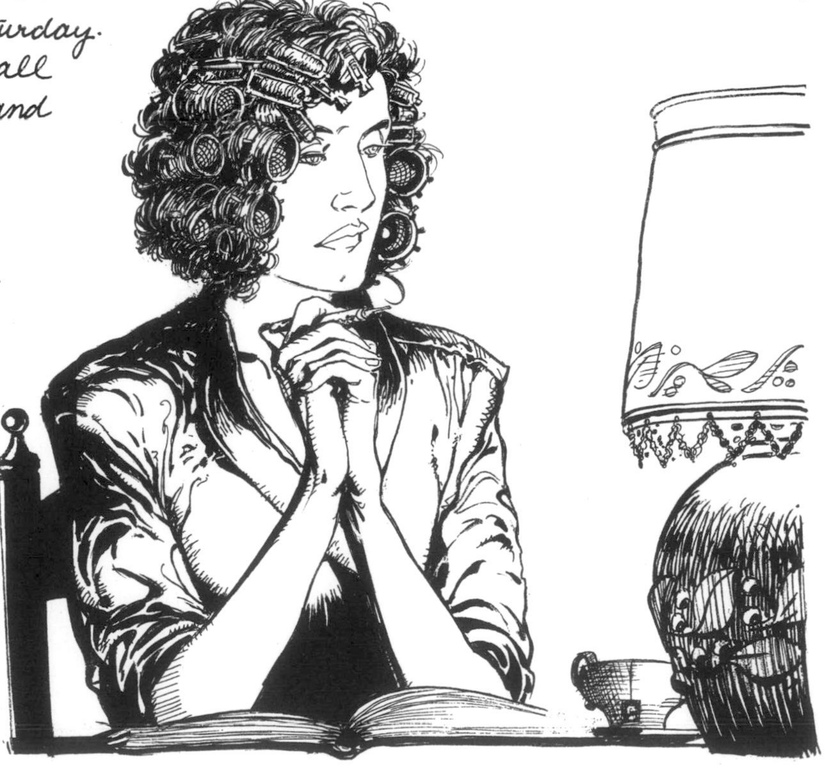

Saturday, April 2

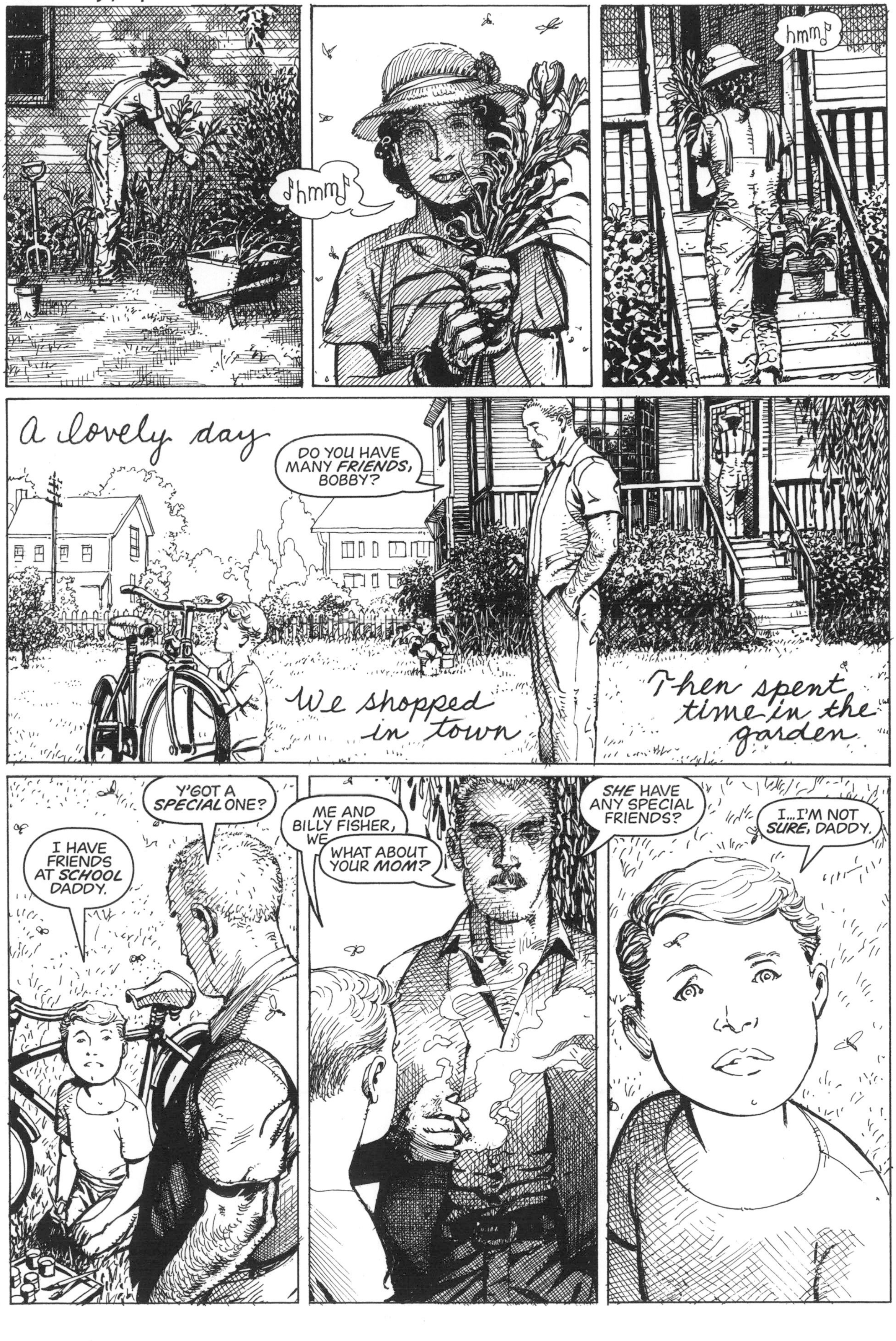
hmm
hmm
hmm
a lovely day
DO YOU HAVE MANY *FRIENDS*, BOBBY?
We shopped in town
Then spent time in the garden
I HAVE FRIENDS AT *SCHOOL* DADDY.
Y'GOT A *SPECIAL* ONE?
ME AND BILLY FISHER, WE
WHAT ABOUT YOUR *MOM*?
SHE HAVE ANY SPECIAL FRIENDS?
I...I'M NOT *SURE*, DADDY.

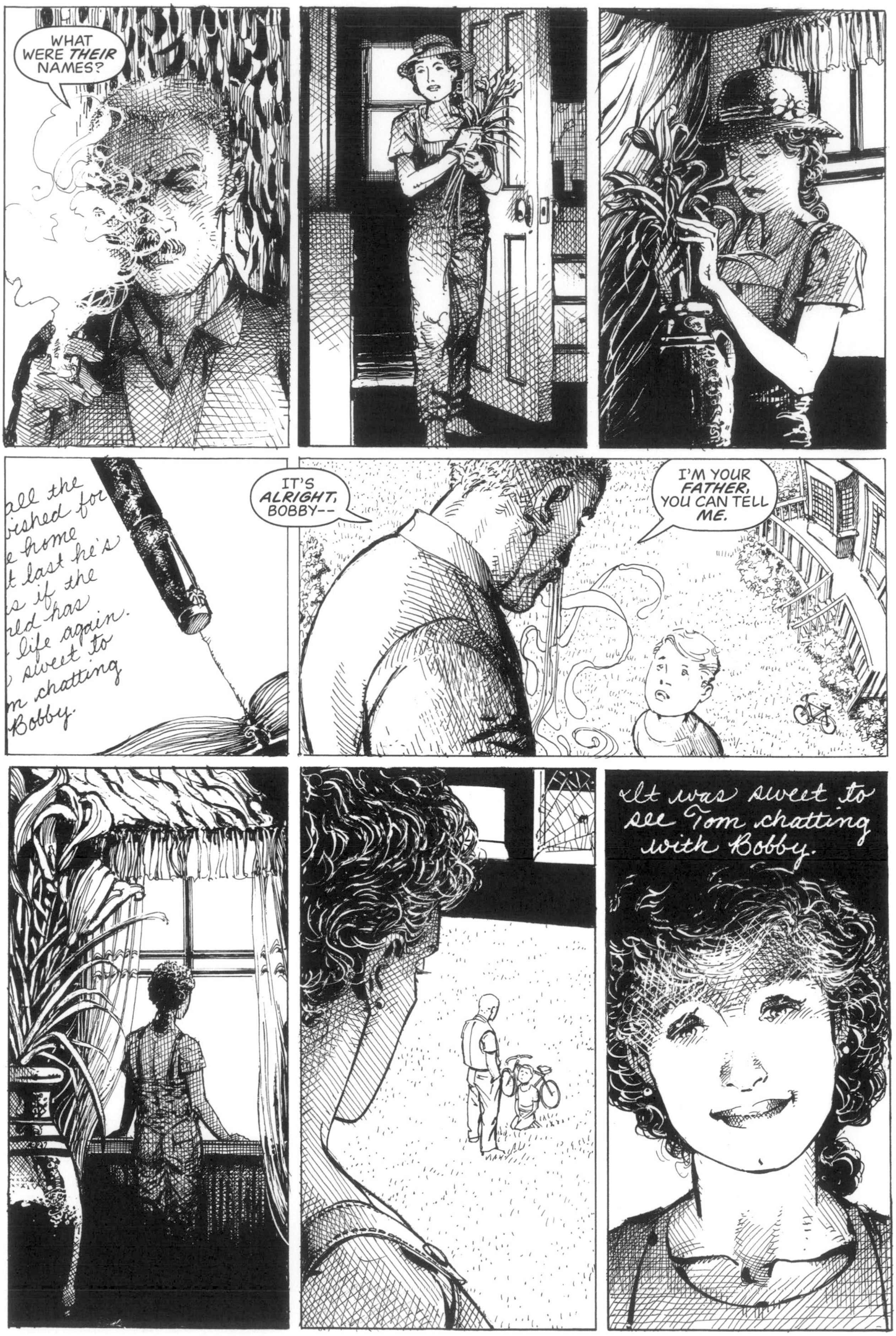

WHAT WERE *THEIR* NAMES?
all the
ished for
home
last he's
if the
has
life again.
sweet to
chatting
Bobby.
IT'S *ALRIGHT,* BOBBY--
I'M YOUR *FATHER,* YOU CAN TELL *ME.*
It was sweet to see Tom chatting with Bobby.

Sunday, April 10

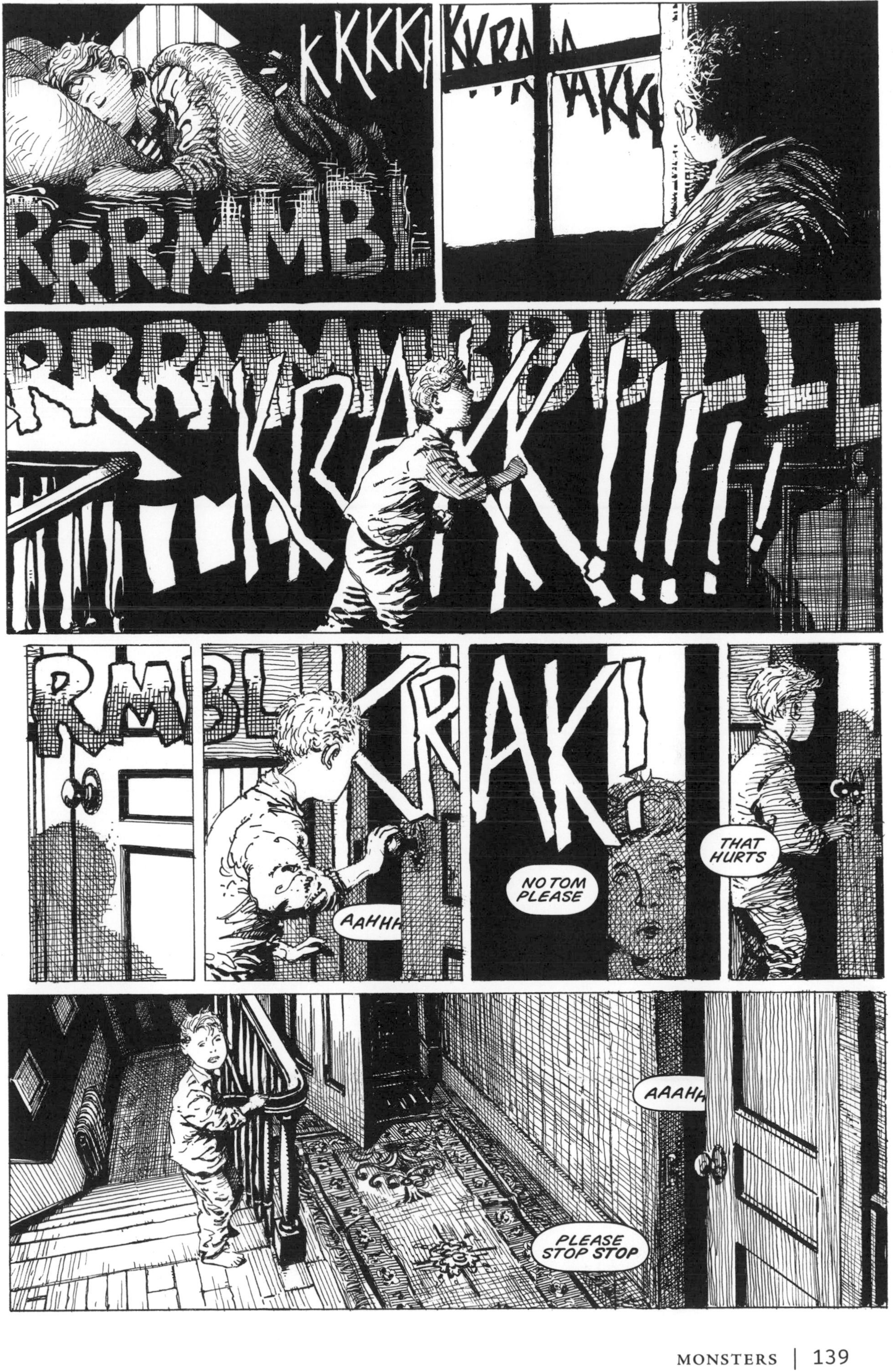
KKKKKKRAM
AKKK
RRRMMB
RRRMMBBLLL
KRAK!!!!!
RMBL
KRAK!
AAHHH
NO TOM PLEASE
THAT HURTS
AAAHH
PLEASE STOP STOP

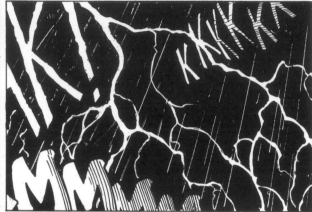

April 13,
There's been such stormy weather
all week long. Thunder and
lightning all through the night
sometimes. Poor Bobby has been
so upset having to stay in his
room all alone.

April 20,

Haven't written in a while. Tom is
having difficulty settling in. I know
things must seem so strange
after being away so long. I wish
there were more I could do for
him, but I try my best all of
the time. I do wonder how
Tom's nose got broken but I'm
afraid to ask unless I stir up
some memories we are he might
be trying to forget.

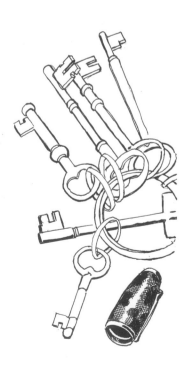

Monday, April 25

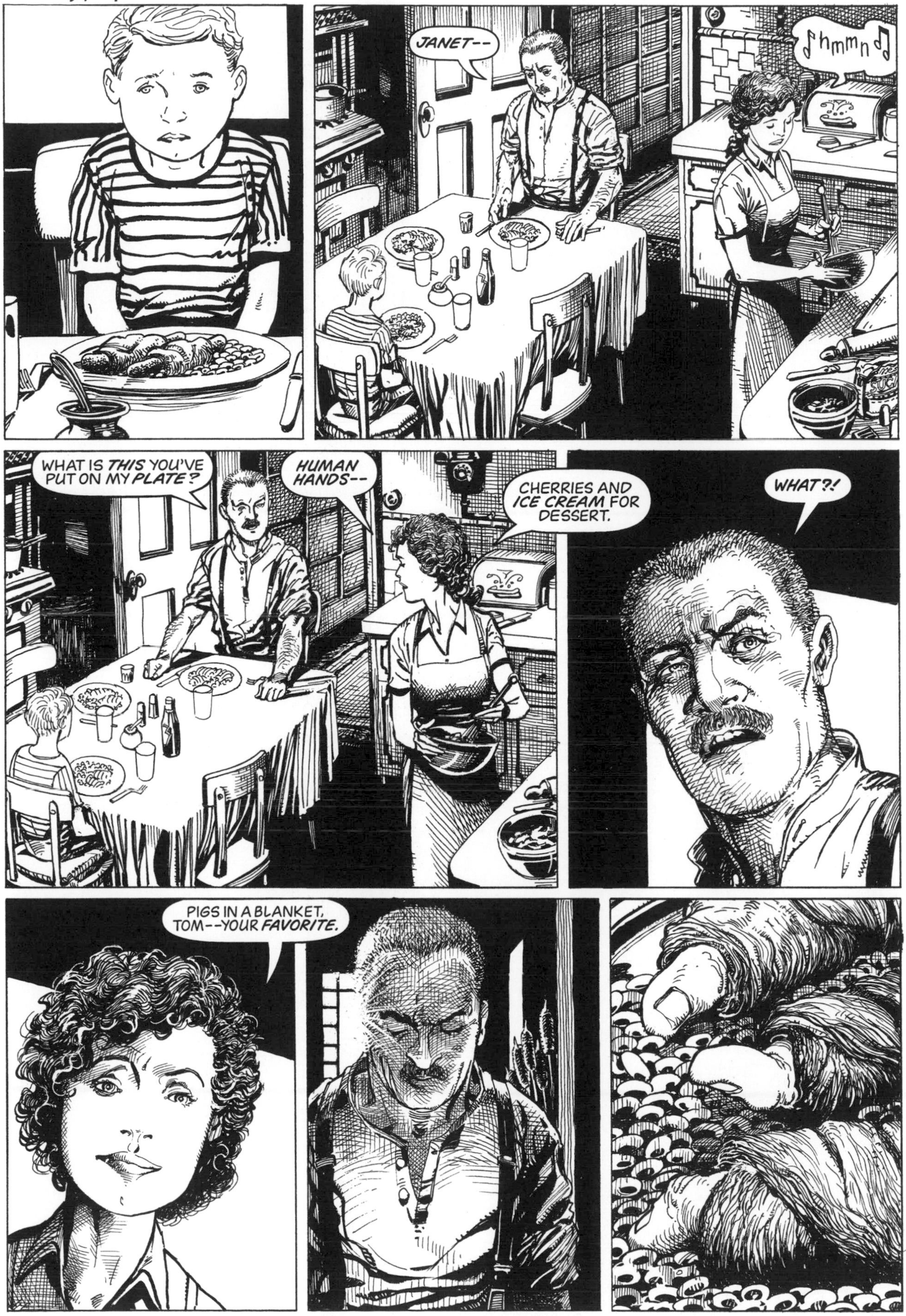
JANET--
hmmn
WHAT IS *THIS* YOU'VE PUT ON MY *PLATE*?
HUMAN HANDS--
CHERRIES AND *ICE CREAM* FOR DESSERT.
WHAT?!
PIGS IN A BLANKET, TOM--YOUR *FAVORITE*.

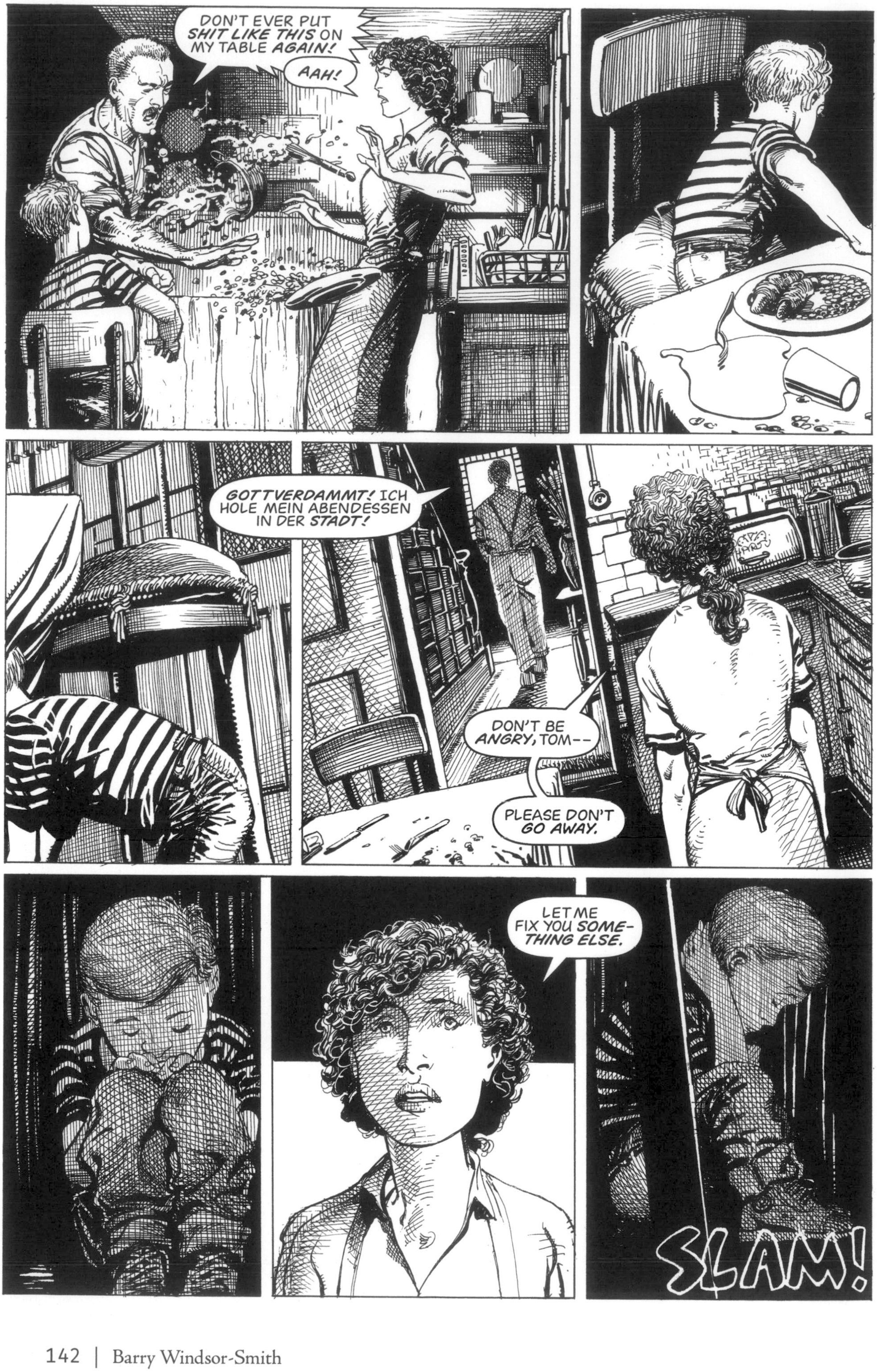
DON'T EVER PUT SHIT LIKE THIS ON MY TABLE AGAIN!
AAH!
GOTTVERDAMMT! ICH HOLE MEIN ABENDESSEN IN DER STADT!
DON'T BE ANGRY, TOM--
PLEASE DON'T GO AWAY.
LET ME FIX YOU SOME-THING ELSE.
SLAM!

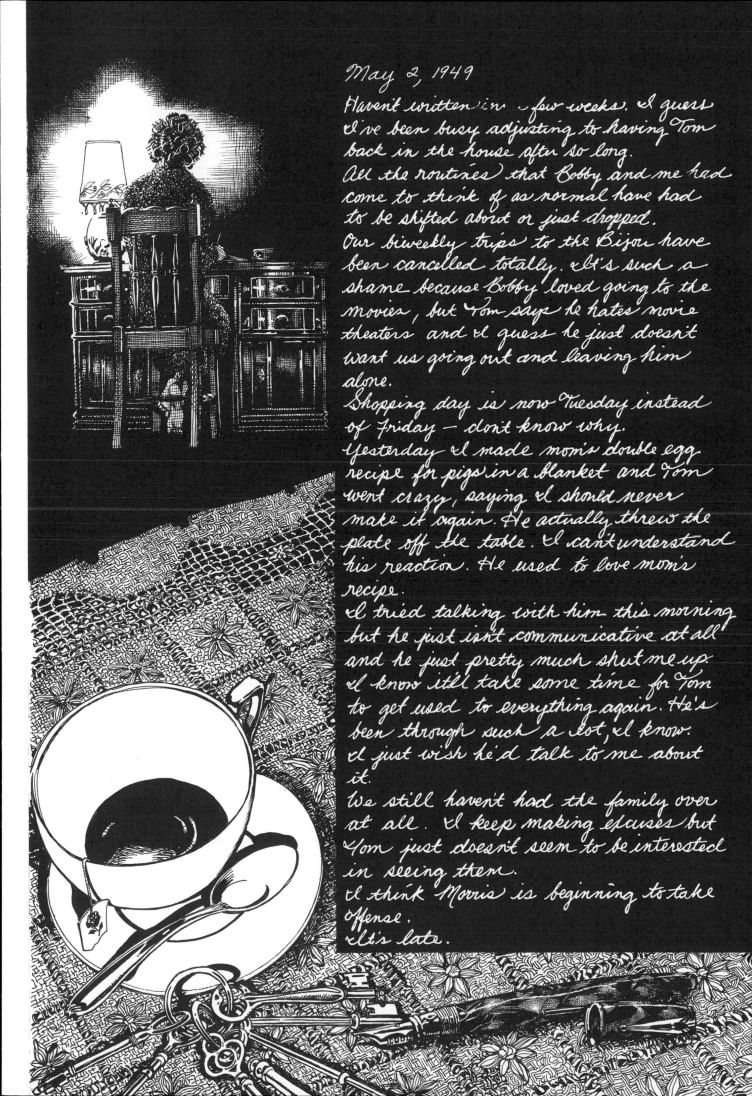

May 2, 1949

Haven't written in a few weeks. I guess
I've been busy adjusting to having Tom
back in the house after so long.
All the routines that Bobby and me had
come to think of as normal have had
to be shifted about or just dropped.
Our biweekly trips to the Bijou have
been cancelled totally. It's such a
shame because Bobby loved going to the
movies, but Tom says he hates movie
theaters and I guess he just doesn't
want us going out and leaving him
alone.
Shopping day is now Tuesday instead
of Friday — don't know why.
Yesterday I made mom's double egg
recipe for pigs in a blanket and Tom
went crazy, saying I should never
make it again. He actually threw the
plate off the table. I can't understand
his reaction. He used to love mom's
recipe.
I tried talking with him this morning
but he just isn't communicative at all
and he just pretty much shut me up.
I know it'll take some time for Tom
to get used to everything again. He's
been through such a lot, I know.
I just wish he'd talk to me about
it.
We still haven't had the family over
at all. I keep making excuses but
Tom just doesn't seem to be interested
in seeing them.
I think Morris is beginning to take
offense.
It's late.

May 11, 1949

It's been such nice weather lately. I caused a little upset yesterday and Tom has been quite annoyed w/me ever since. I mentioned how I thought he should pay a little more attention to Bobby and how left out he feels. Poor Bobby was longing for his Daddy to come home and now that he's here it's as if Tom has no interest in him at all. I can see the look of disappointment on Bobby's face when T ignores him at the dinner table. It's all ~~very painful~~ ~~such a shame~~.

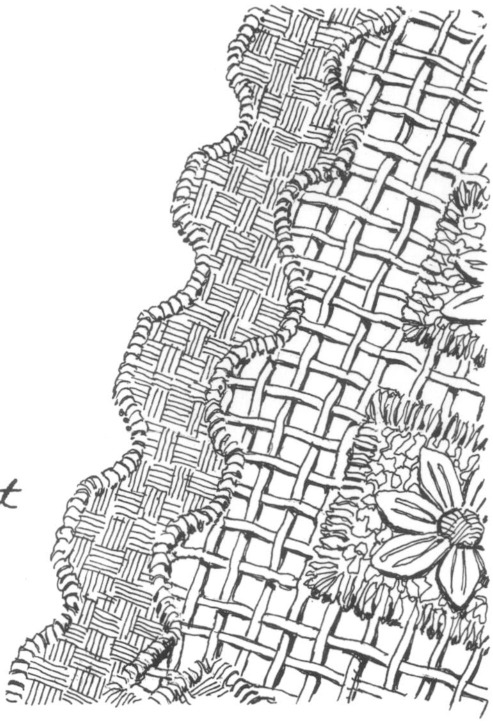

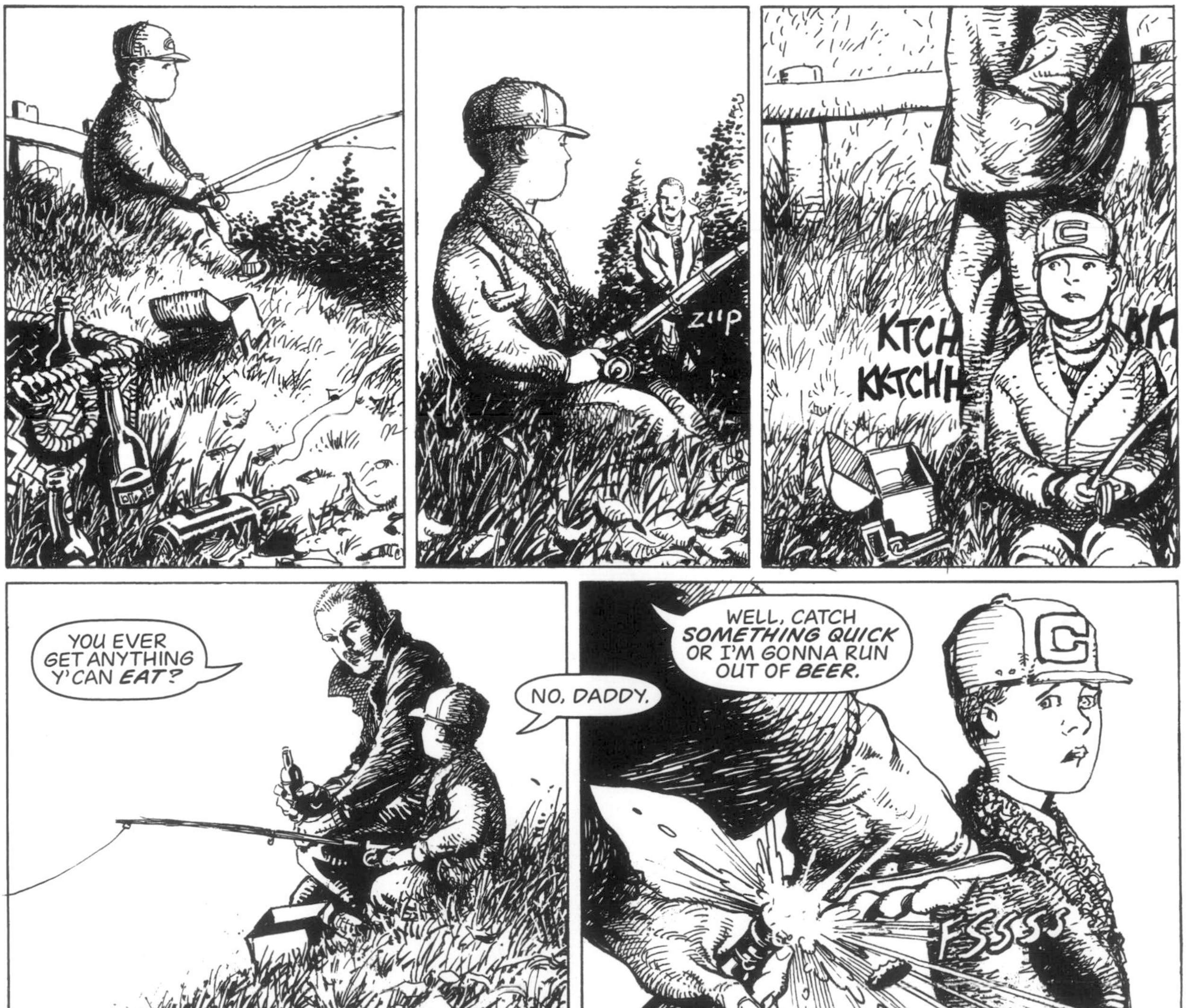
ZIIP
KTCH
KKTCHH
YOU EVER GET ANYTHING Y'CAN *EAT*?
NO, DADDY.
WELL, CATCH *SOMETHING QUICK* OR I'M GONNA RUN OUT OF *BEER*.
FSSSS

I think that Tom really thought about what I said the other day because he actually talked to Bobby this morning and at lunch too. I completely stuck my neck out and suggested to Tom that he go w/ Bobby to his little fishing pond off of Geneva Turnpike.

WHAT'S *THIS*?
WHAT'S *THIS* YOU GOT HERE?
WHERE'D YOU *GET* THIS?
IT SHOOTS *POTATOES*.
I DIDN'T SAY WHADSIT *SHOOTS*--
I SAID WHERE'D YOU *GET* IT FROM?
MMMOM GAVE IT TO ME.
IT'S A *PIECE* OF *SHIT*!

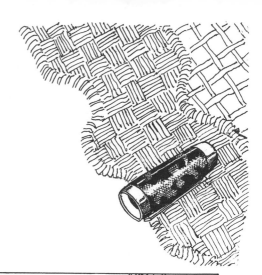

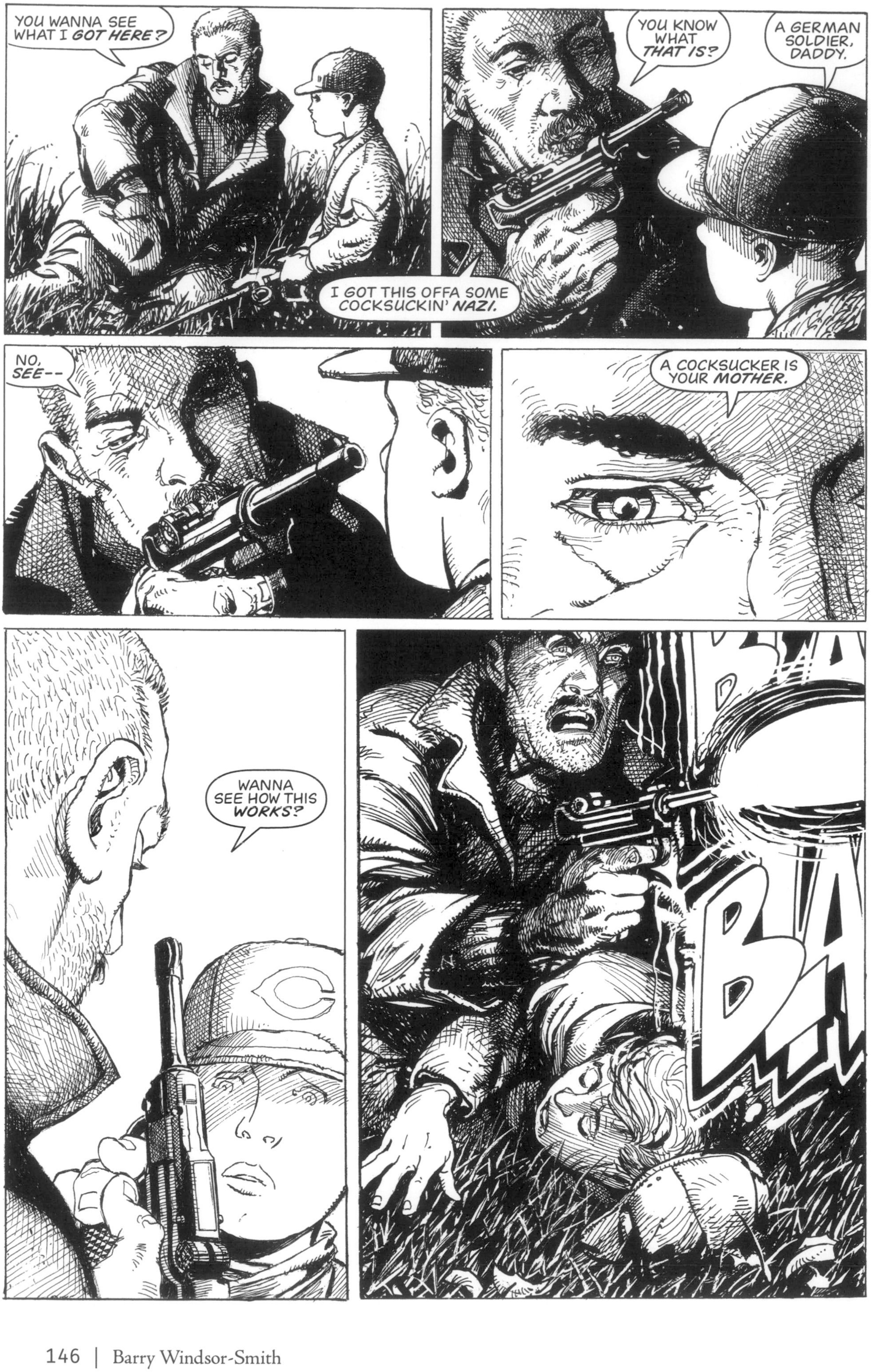
YOU WANNA SEE WHAT I GOT HERE?
YOU KNOW WHAT THAT IS?
A GERMAN SOLDIER, DADDY.
I GOT THIS OFFA SOME COCKSUCKIN' NAZI.
NO, SEE--
A COCKSUCKER IS YOUR MOTHER.
WANNA SEE HOW THIS WORKS?

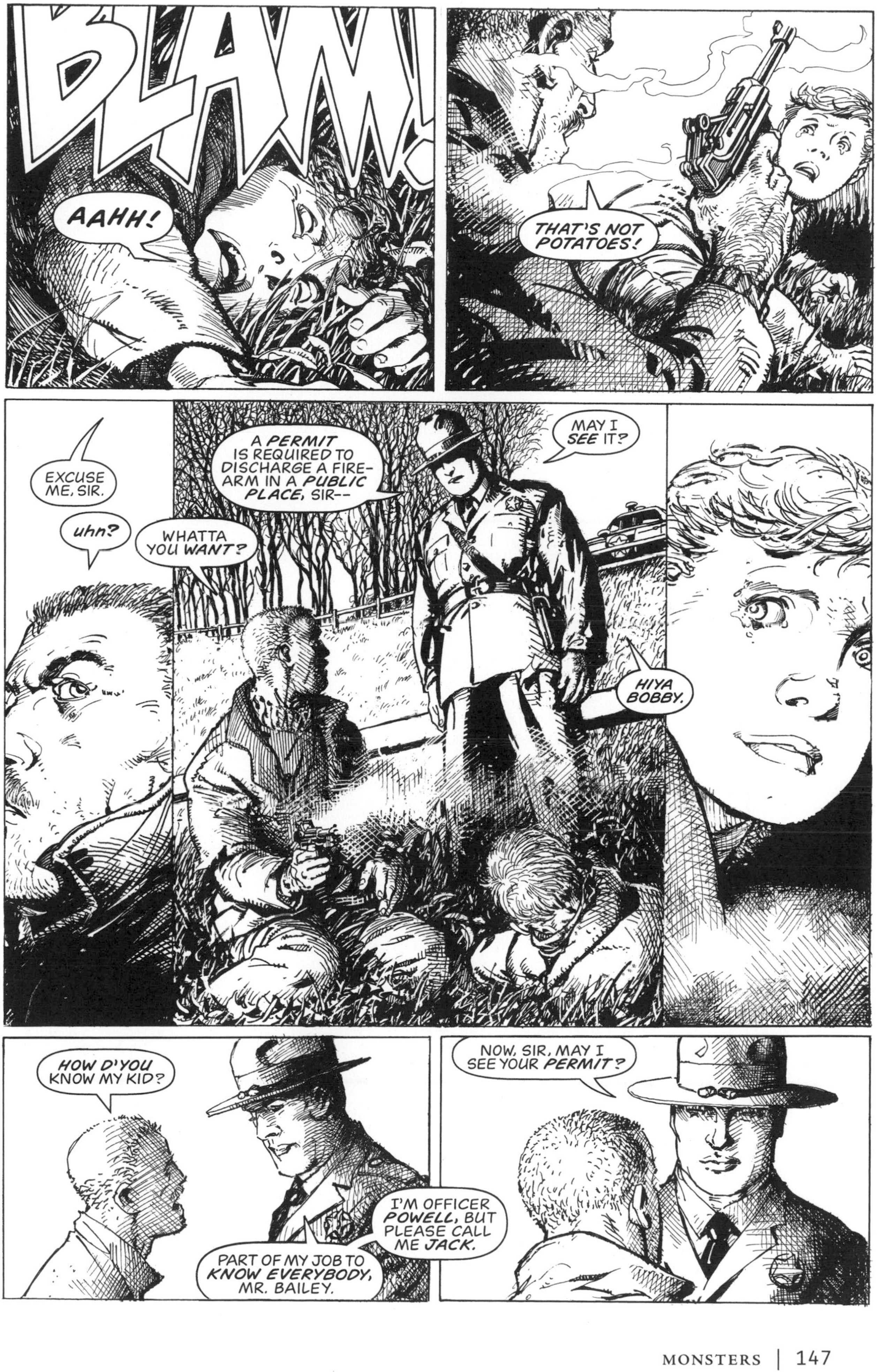
BLAM!
AAHH!
THAT'S NOT POTATOES!
EXCUSE ME, SIR.
uhn?
WHATTA YOU WANT?
A PERMIT IS REQUIRED TO DISCHARGE A FIRE-ARM IN A PUBLIC PLACE, SIR--
MAY I SEE IT?
HIYA BOBBY.
HOW D'YOU KNOW MY KID?
PART OF MY JOB TO KNOW EVERYBODY, MR. BAILEY.
I'M OFFICER POWELL, BUT PLEASE CALL ME JACK.
NOW, SIR, MAY I SEE YOUR PERMIT?

I DIDN'T NEED A PERMIT IN THE *SERVICE*, AN' I DON'T NEED ONE *NOW*.

THAT WAS *WAR TIME*, MR BAILEY--

THINGS ARE *DIFFERENT* NOW.

FOR *SOME*, MAYBE.

THE COUNTY RULING ALLOWS FOR *SEIZURE* OF A FIREARM IMPROPERLY DISCHARGED.

SO WHAT--

YOU THINK YOU'RE *MAN* ENOUGH TO *TAKE MY GUN* FROM ME?

PERHAPS YOU'D BETTER JUST PLACE THE WEAPON ON *THE GROUND*, MR BAILEY.

I'LL PLACE IT IN MY *POCKET*--

WHAT'LL YOU DO ABOUT *THAT*?

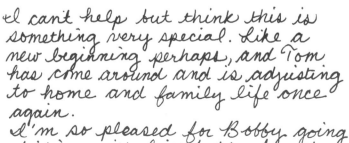

A PERMIT IS *REQUIRED*. DO YOU *HAVE IT* WITH YOU?

NO, I DON'T.

I can't help but think this is something very special. Like a new beginning perhaps, and Tom has come around and is adjusting to home and family life once again.
I'm so pleased for Bobby going fishing with his daddy for the first time.

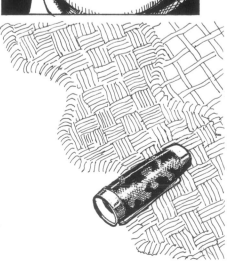

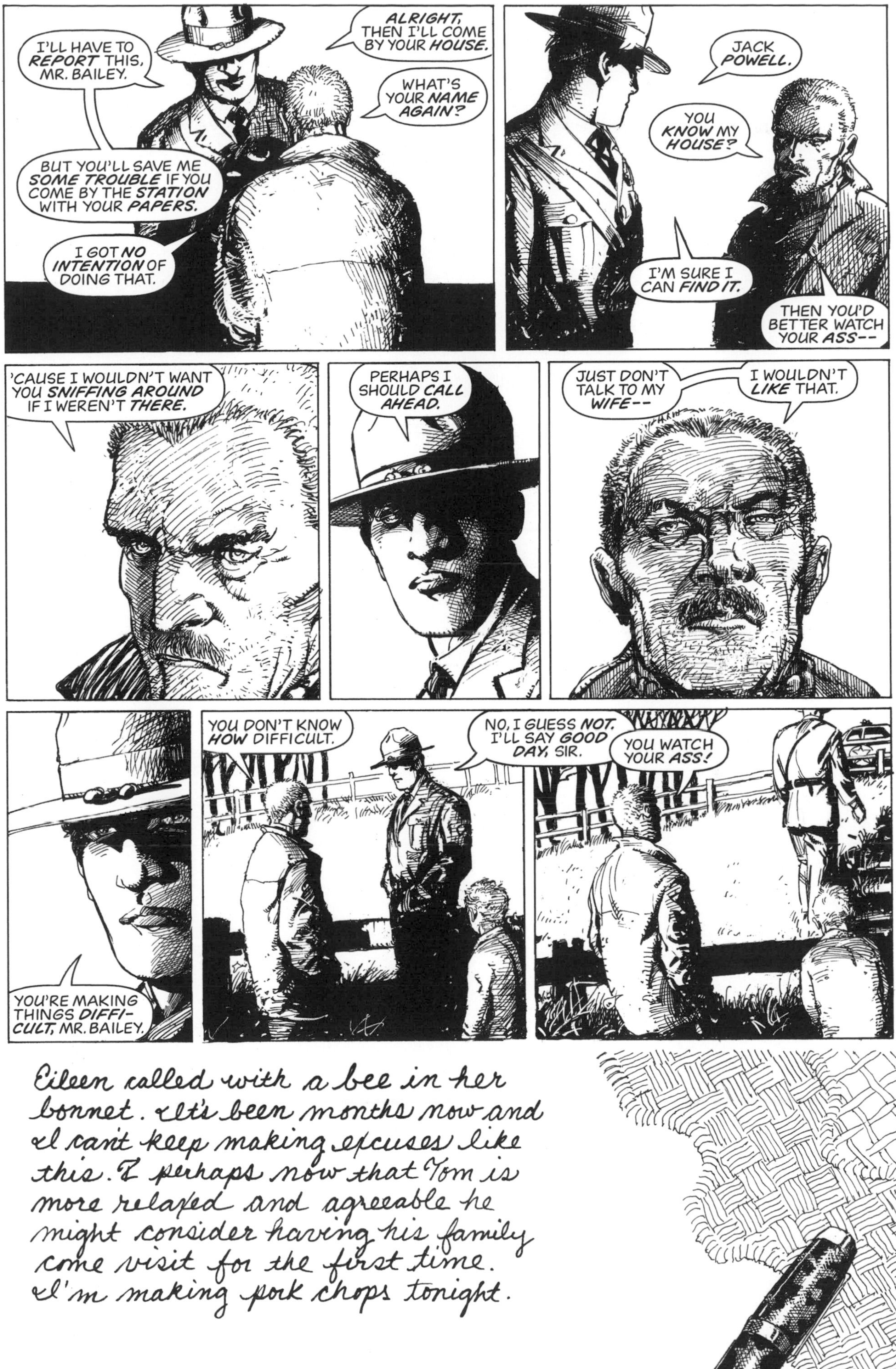

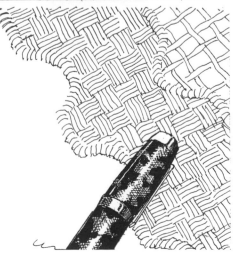

I'LL HAVE TO REPORT THIS, MR. BAILEY.
ALRIGHT, THEN I'LL COME BY YOUR HOUSE.
WHAT'S YOUR NAME AGAIN?
BUT YOU'LL SAVE ME SOME TROUBLE IF YOU COME BY THE STATION WITH YOUR PAPERS.
I GOT NO INTENTION OF DOING THAT.
JACK POWELL.
YOU KNOW MY HOUSE?
I'M SURE I CAN FIND IT.
THEN YOU'D BETTER WATCH YOUR ASS--
'CAUSE I WOULDN'T WANT YOU SNIFFING AROUND IF I WEREN'T THERE.
PERHAPS I SHOULD CALL AHEAD.
JUST DON'T TALK TO MY WIFE--
I WOULDN'T LIKE THAT.
YOU'RE MAKING THINGS DIFFI-CULT, MR. BAILEY.
YOU DON'T KNOW HOW DIFFICULT.
NO, I GUESS NOT. I'LL SAY GOOD DAY, SIR.
YOU WATCH YOUR ASS!
Eileen called with a bee in her bonnet. It's been months now and I can't keep making excuses like this. I perhaps now that Tom is more relaxed and agreeable he might consider having his family come visit for the first time. I'm making pork chops tonight.

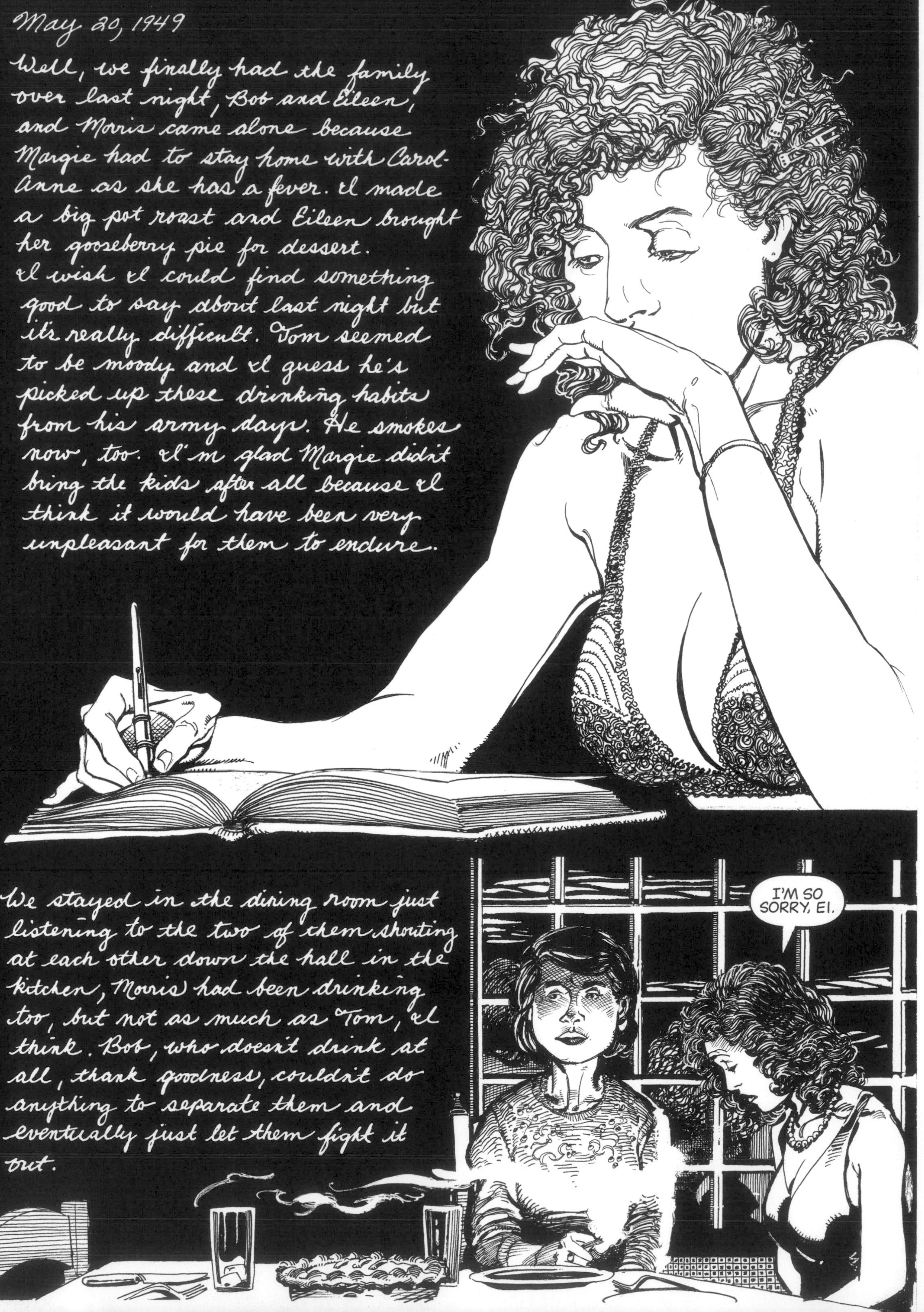
May 20, 1949
Well, we finally had the family over last night, Bob and Eileen, and Morris came alone because Margie had to stay home with Carol-Anne as she has a fever. I made a big pot roast and Eileen brought her gooseberry pie for dessert.
I wish I could find something good to say about last night but it's really difficult. Tom seemed to be moody and I guess he's picked up these drinking habits from his army days. He smokes now, too. I'm glad Margie didn't bring the kids after all because I think it would have been very unpleasant for them to endure.
We stayed in the dining room just listening to the two of them shouting at each other down the hall in the kitchen, Morris had been drinking too, but not as much as Tom, I think. Bob, who doesn't drink at all, thank goodness, couldn't do anything to separate them and eventually just let them fight it out.
I'M SO SORRY, EI.

I sent Bobby to bed early, but I know he must have heard all of the shouting and cursing anyway. I'm so ashamed of the way it went and I must have called Eileen a hundred times today. She keeps saying it's all right but I know it isn't because Morris wouldn't even come to the phone. Tom has been sulky all afternoon and didn't go in to the hardware store like he said he would.
He cut his hand on something in the yard and when I tried to help he pushed me and got really abusive. Tom seems to be having real difficulties settling back into life here w/Bobby and me. I know it's only been a few months and I know everything takes time and I shouldn't worry, but he seems so different nowadays. Not the man who went away to war.

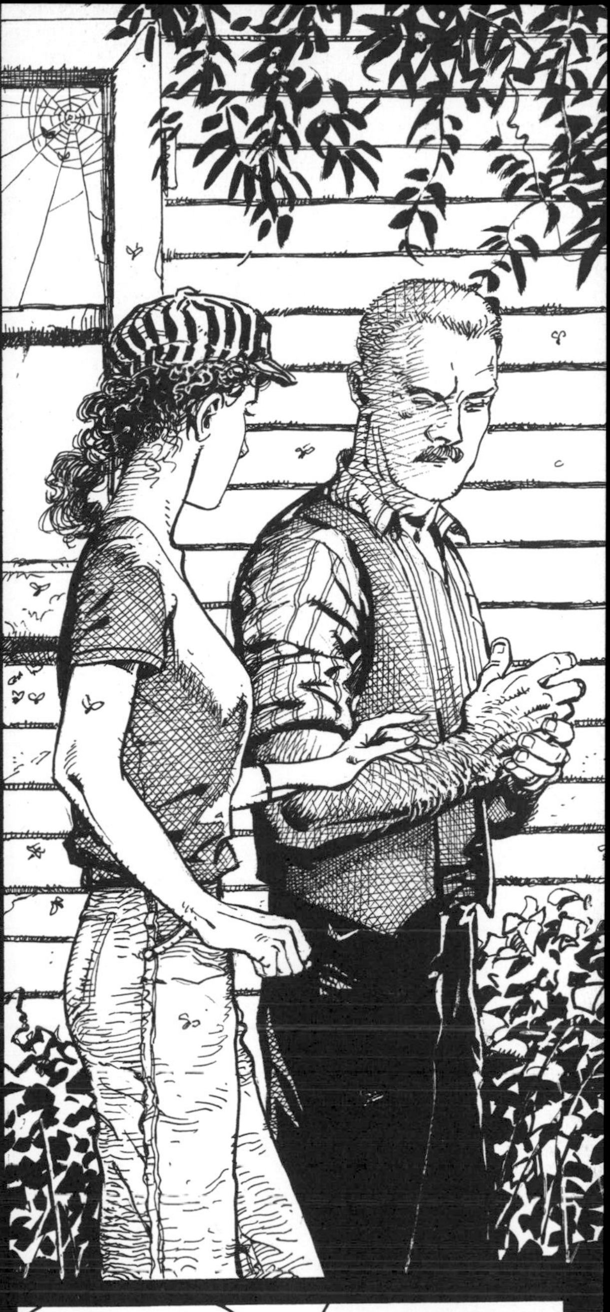

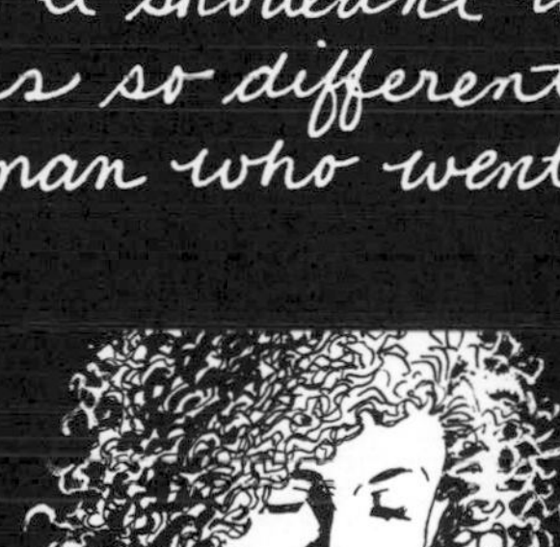

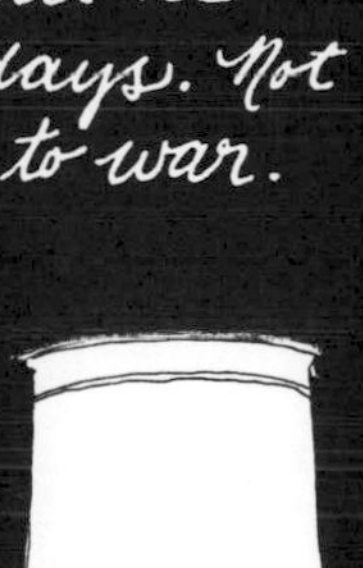

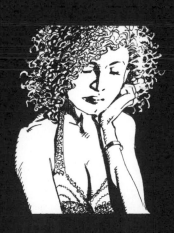

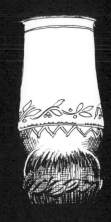

Poor Bobby hurt himself again today. I swear I've never known a child to become so accident prone. I'm leaving his dungarees to soak overnight, but I don't think the blood will come out without a real bleaching.
Been really humid all week.

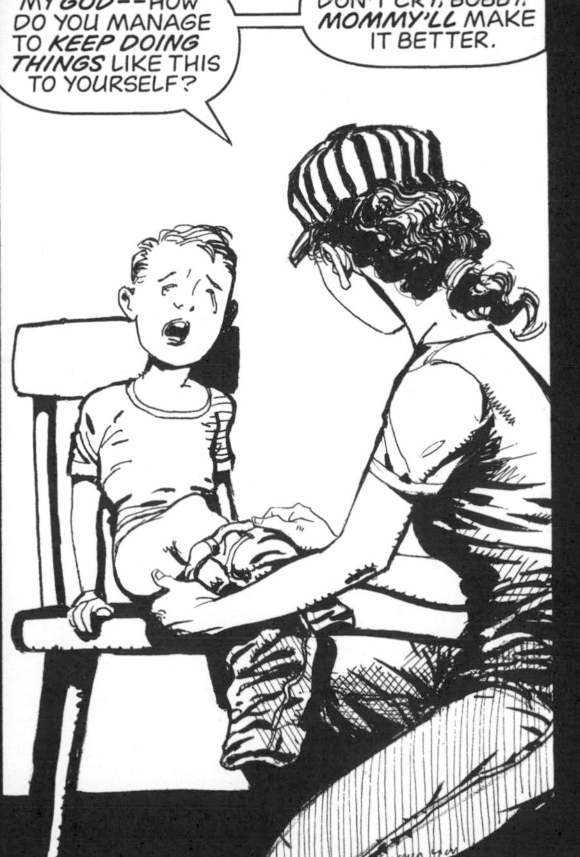
MY GOD--HOW DO YOU MANAGE TO KEEP DOING THINGS LIKE THIS TO YOURSELF?
DON'T CRY, BOBBY. MOMMY'LL MAKE IT BETTER.

1949 Saturday, June 4

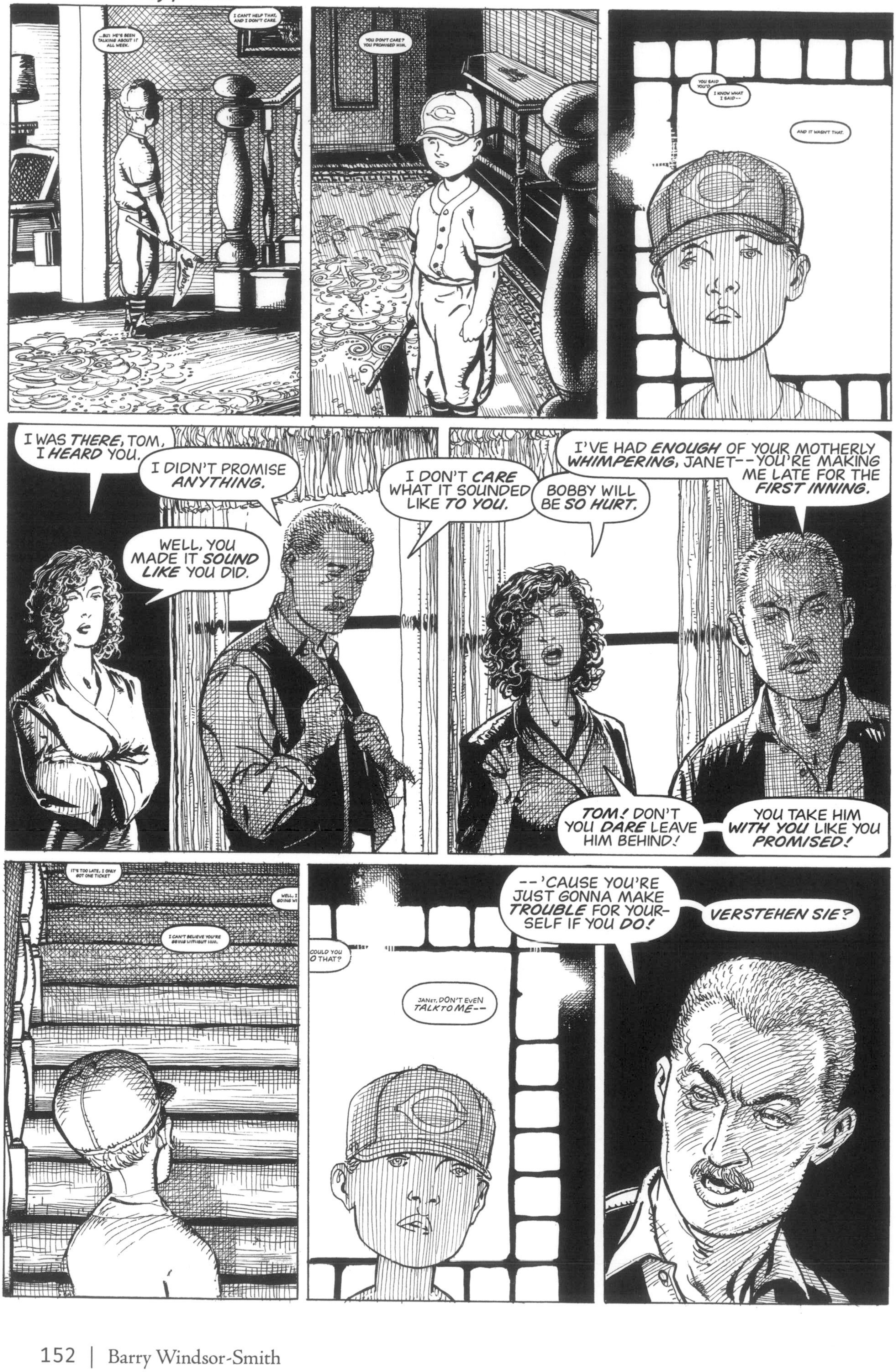

...BUT HE'S BEEN TALKING ABOUT IT ALL WEEK.
I CAN'T HELP THAT, AND I DON'T CARE.
YOU DON'T CARE? YOU PROMISED HIM.
YOU SAID YOU'D
I KNOW WHAT I SAID--
AND IT WASN'T THAT.
I WAS THERE, TOM, I HEARD YOU.
I DIDN'T PROMISE ANYTHING.
WELL, YOU MADE IT SOUND LIKE YOU DID.
I DON'T CARE WHAT IT SOUNDED LIKE TO YOU.
BOBBY WILL BE SO HURT.
I'VE HAD ENOUGH OF YOUR MOTHERLY WHIMPERING, JANET--YOU'RE MAKING ME LATE FOR THE FIRST INNING.
TOM! DON'T YOU DARE LEAVE HIM BEHIND!
YOU TAKE HIM WITH YOU LIKE YOU PROMISED!
IT'S TOO LATE, I ONLY GOT ONE TICKET
I CAN'T BELIEVE YOU'RE GOING WITHOUT HIM.
JANET, DON'T EVEN TALK TO ME--
--'CAUSE YOU'RE JUST GONNA MAKE TROUBLE FOR YOURSELF IF YOU DO!
VERSTEHEN SIE?

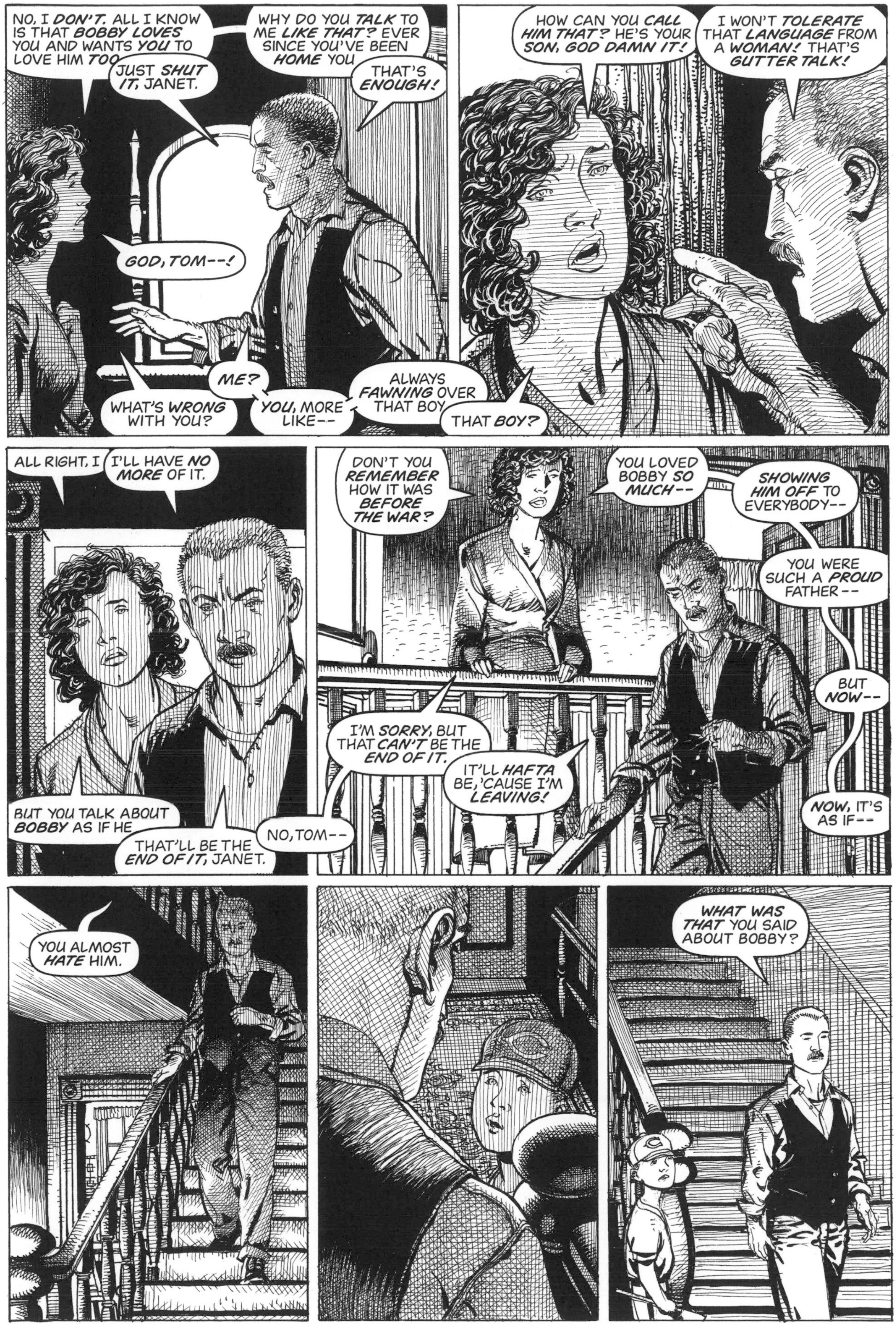
NO, I DON'T. ALL I KNOW IS THAT BOBBY LOVES YOU AND WANTS YOU TO LOVE HIM TOO
WHY DO YOU TALK TO ME LIKE THAT? EVER SINCE YOU'VE BEEN HOME YOU
JUST SHUT IT, JANET.
THAT'S ENOUGH!
GOD, TOM--!
WHAT'S WRONG WITH YOU?
ME?
YOU, MORE LIKE--
ALWAYS FAWNING OVER THAT BOY
THAT BOY?
HOW CAN YOU CALL HIM THAT? HE'S YOUR SON, GOD DAMN IT!
I WON'T TOLERATE THAT LANGUAGE FROM A WOMAN! THAT'S GUTTER TALK!
ALL RIGHT, I
I'LL HAVE NO MORE OF IT.
BUT YOU TALK ABOUT BOBBY AS IF HE
THAT'LL BE THE END OF IT, JANET.
NO, TOM--
DON'T YOU REMEMBER HOW IT WAS BEFORE THE WAR?
YOU LOVED BOBBY SO MUCH--
SHOWING HIM OFF TO EVERYBODY--
YOU WERE SUCH A PROUD FATHER--
BUT NOW--
NOW, IT'S AS IF--
I'M SORRY, BUT THAT CAN'T BE THE END OF IT.
IT'LL HAFTA BE, 'CAUSE I'M LEAVING!
YOU ALMOST HATE HIM.
WHAT WAS THAT YOU SAID ABOUT BOBBY?

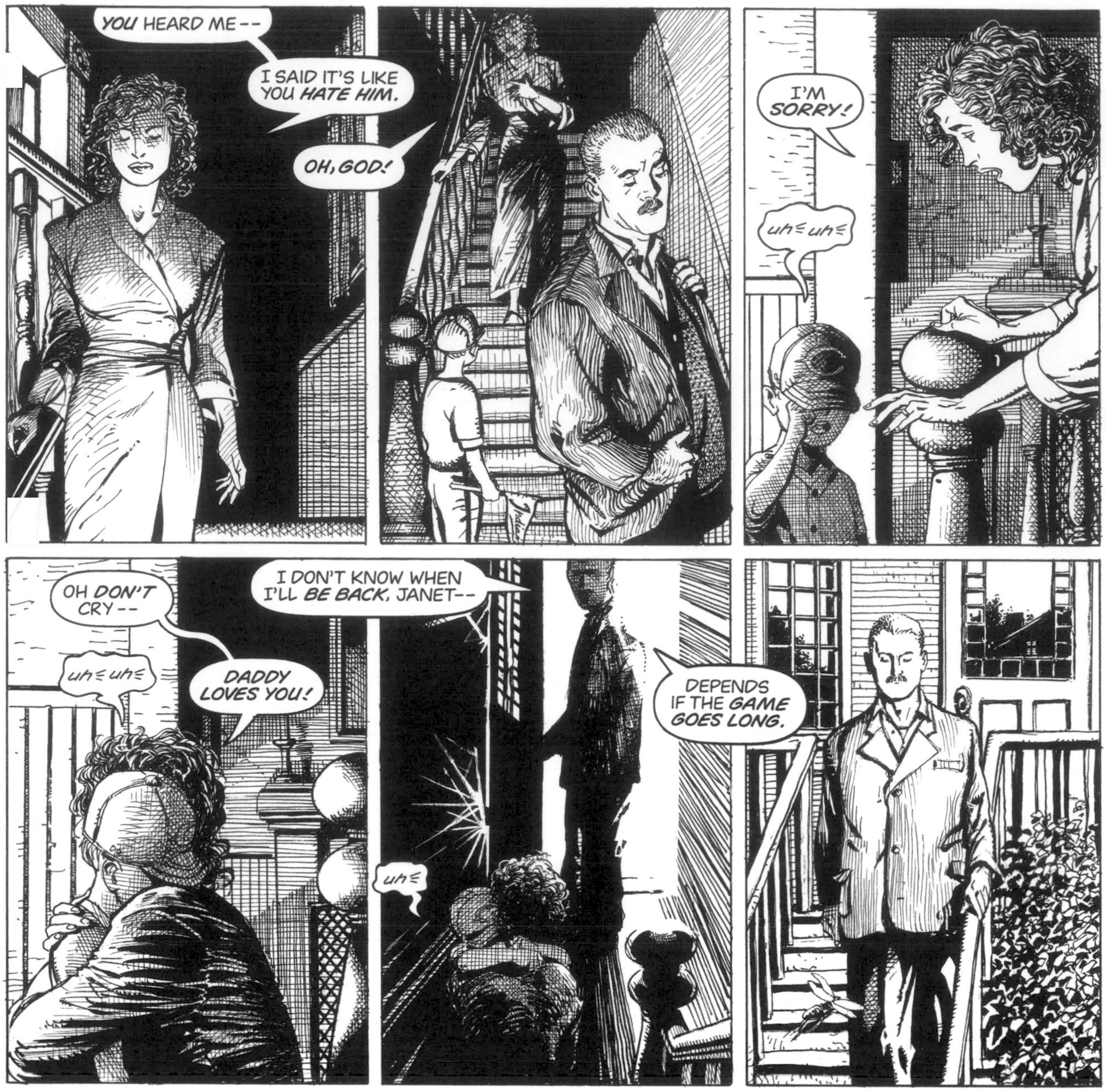
YOU HEARD ME--
I SAID IT'S LIKE YOU HATE HIM.
OH, GOD!
I'M SORRY!
uh uh
OH DON'T CRY--
uh uh
DADDY LOVES YOU!
I DON'T KNOW WHEN I'LL BE BACK, JANET--
uh
DEPENDS IF THE GAME GOES LONG.

June 5

Seems that every time I sit with this diary nowadays there's new trouble to write about. ~~It's almost as if Tom is~~ ~~[illegible] determined to~~ It's almost as if Tom would rather not have come home at all. We seem to be constantly at odds with each other. It seems to me that he'll deliberately say something, make some statement or something, only to contradict it later on after I have ~~believed~~. He keeps doing this all of the time. It's like he wants to drive me crazy. So far, this has just been confusing

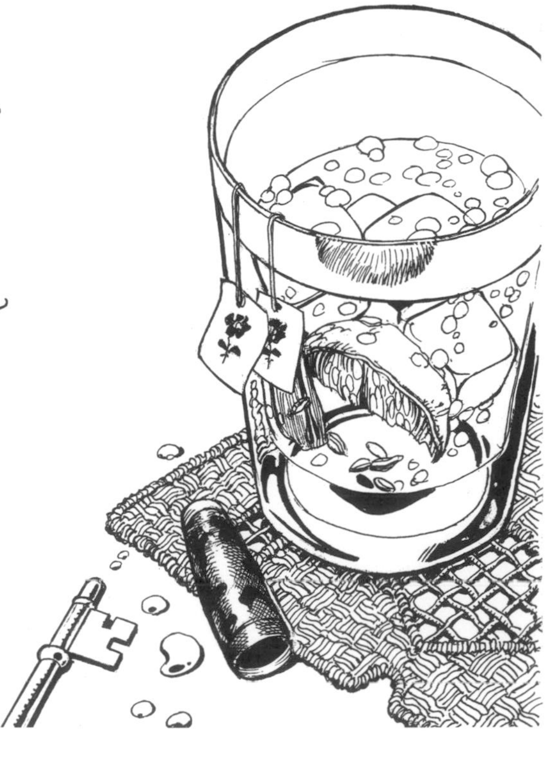

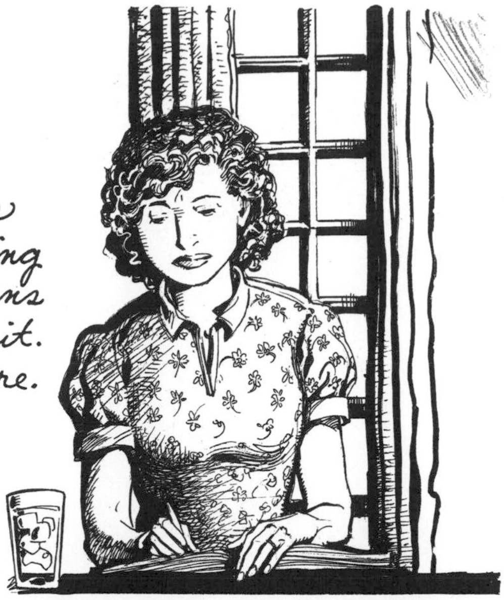

But now I can't help but think that Tom is being deliberately vindictive. After promising Bobby that he'd take him along to the Indians game today, T just outright refused to do it. He just walked out leaving B standing there. What a really cruel thing to do.
Poor little Bobby, all dressed up with his cap and pennant. We both sat on the stairs and cried together. Poor baby. I do so wish there were more children of Bobby's age in the neighborhood. I'm sure he must get so lonely playing all by himself during summer recess. He's too small to be going off on his own, so he only has the front yard to play in. Carol-Anne is the only other child around here, but Margie (or maybe Harry) ~~does~~ (or both, come to think of it) doesn't seem to like the idea of them playing together. Perhaps this is because of Tom (?). He's been so antagonistic toward both of them since he came home. How could a man change so much, I wonder? It's not as if T was a tank commander or anything, he was just a German translator. How much awfulness could he have been a party to if he was just a translator? Tom won't talk about it at all, and I am afraid to ask anymore. It's disturbing to

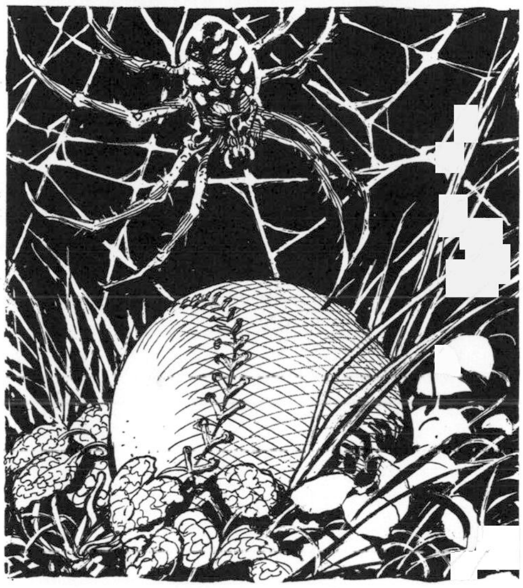

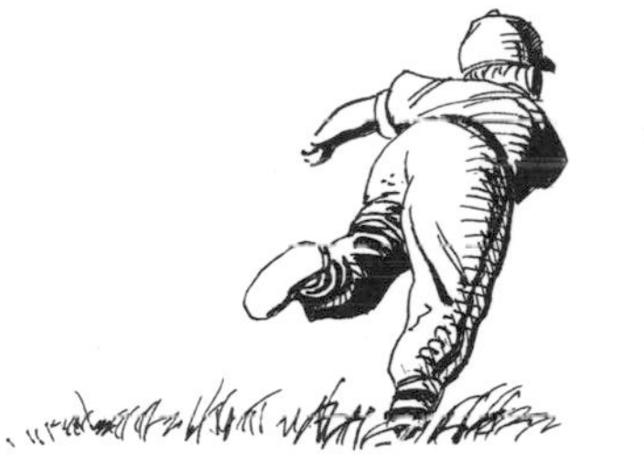

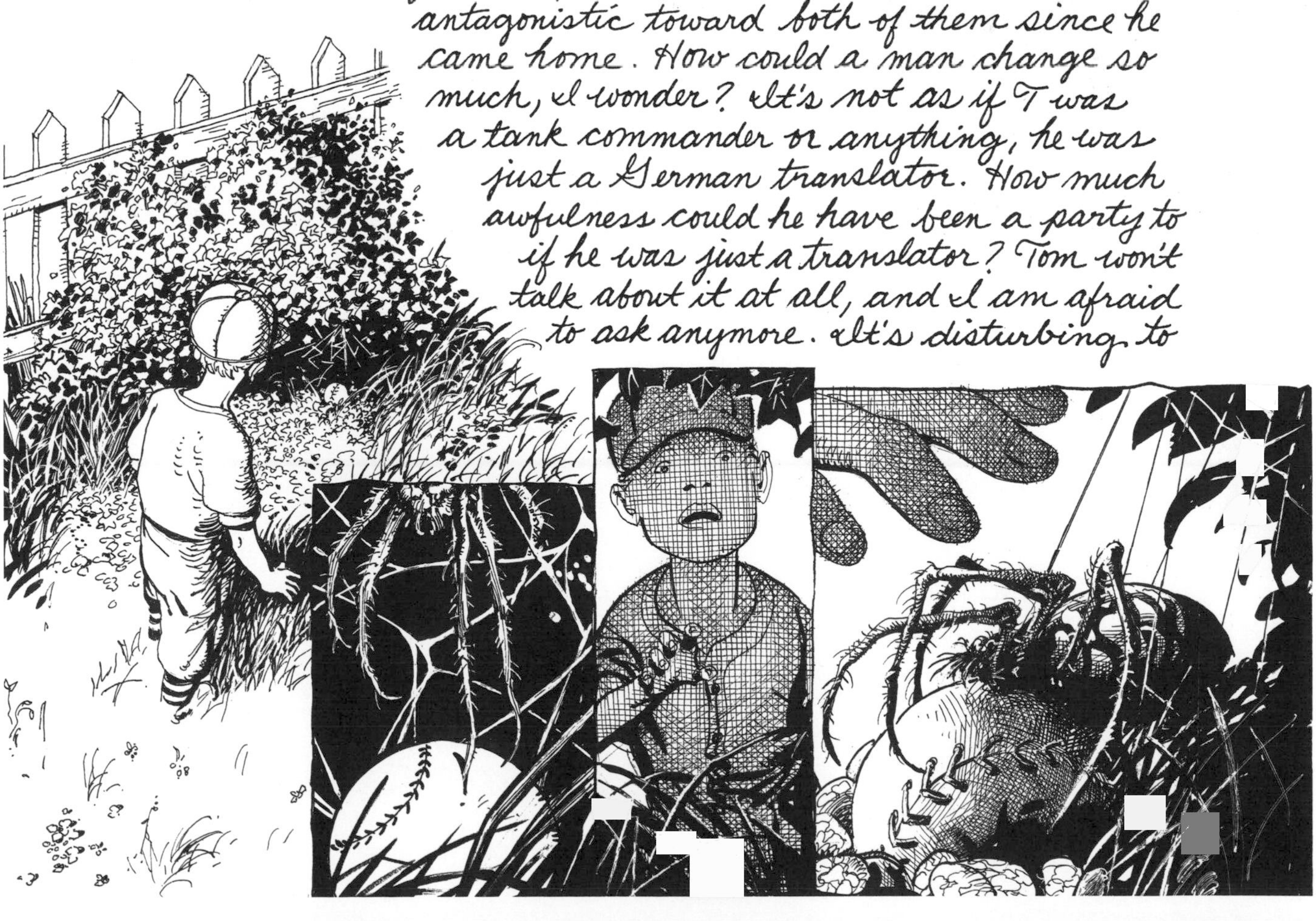

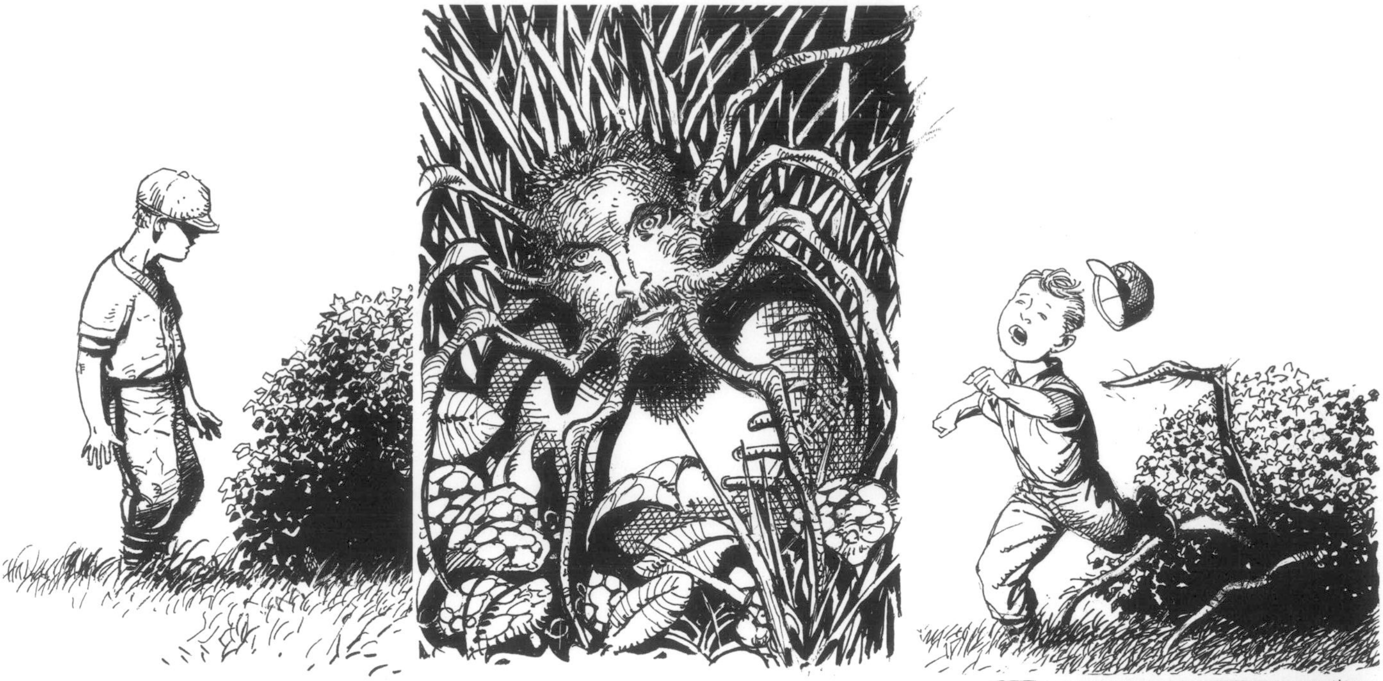

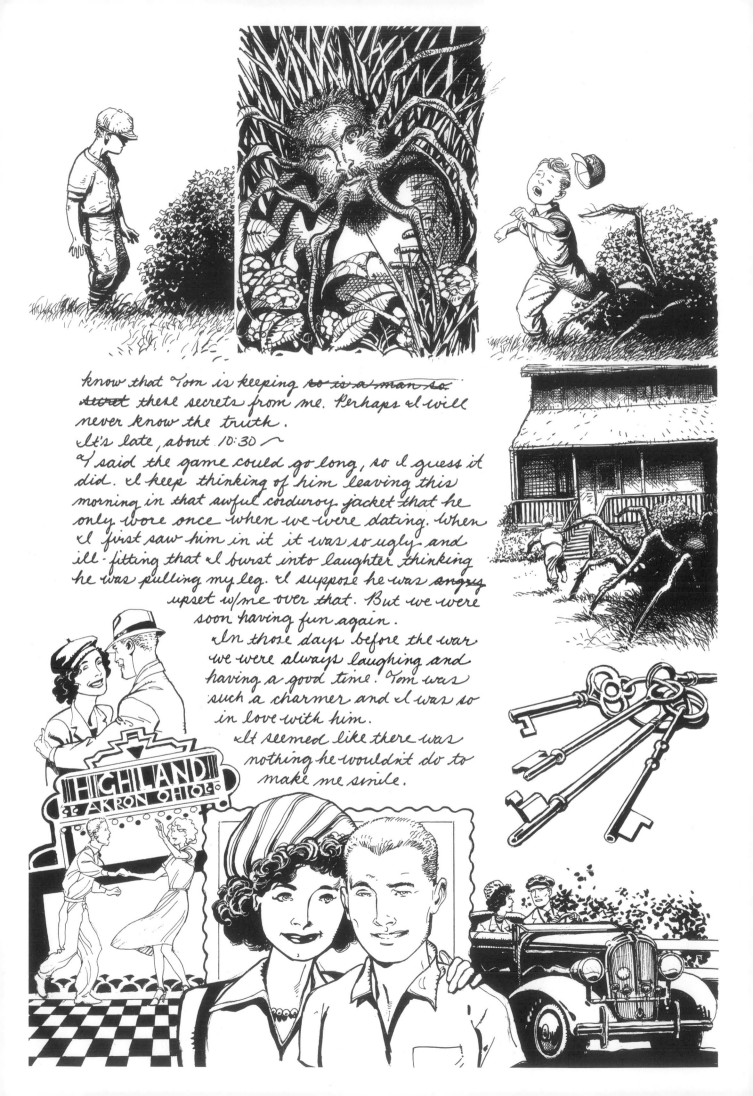

know that Tom is keeping ~~so is a man so stout~~ these secrets from me. Perhaps I will never know the truth.

It's late, about 10:30 ~

I said the game could go long, so I guess it did. I keep thinking of him leaving this morning in that awful corduroy jacket that he only wore once when we were dating. When I first saw him in it it was so ugly and ill-fitting that I burst into laughter thinking he was pulling my leg. I suppose he was ~~angry~~ upset w/me over that. But we were soon having fun again.

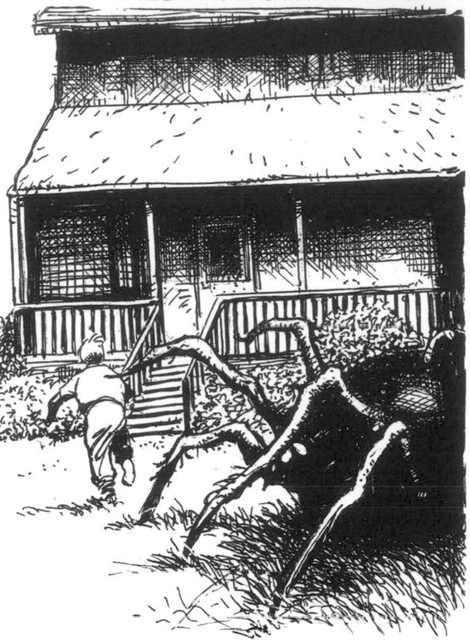

In those days before the war we were always laughing and having a good time. Tom was such a charmer and I was so in love with him.

It seemed like there was nothing he wouldn't do to make me smile.

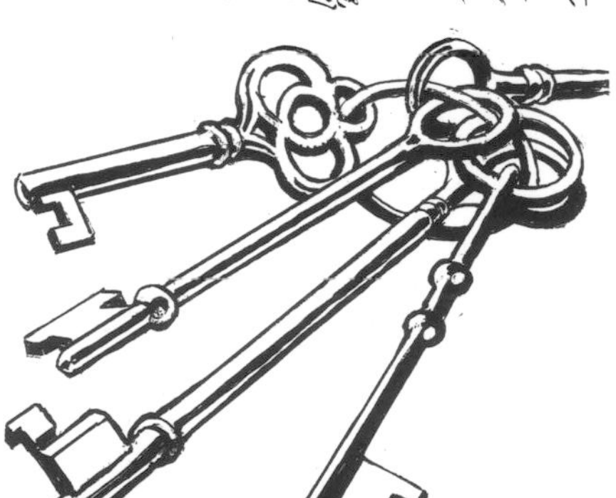

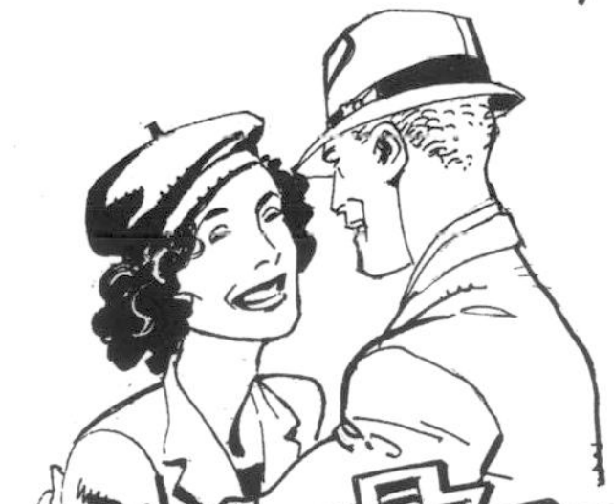

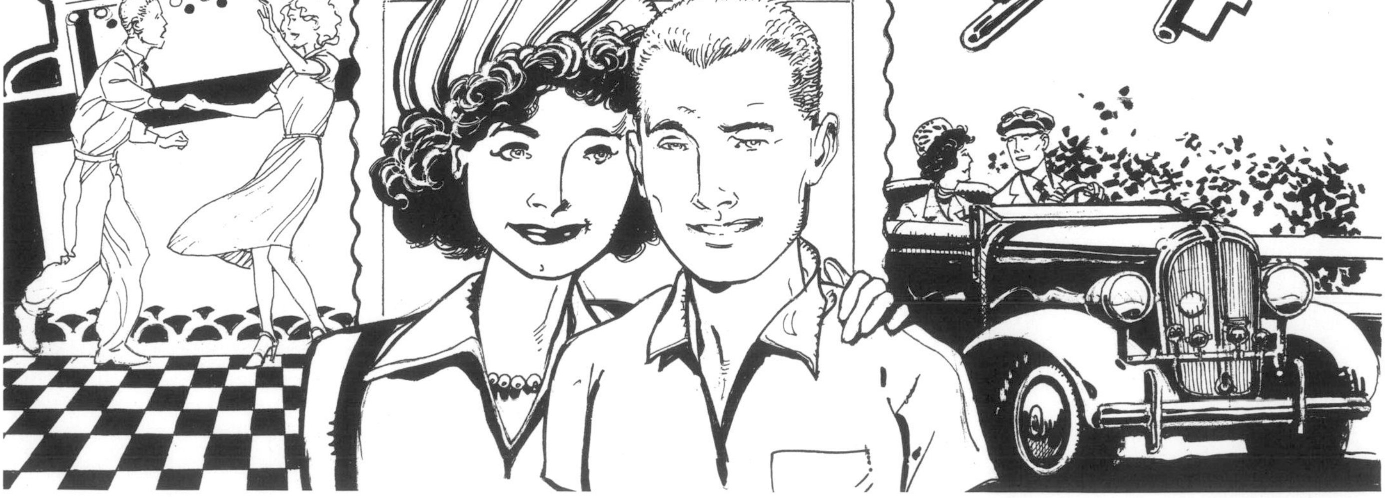
HIGHLAND
AKRON OHIO

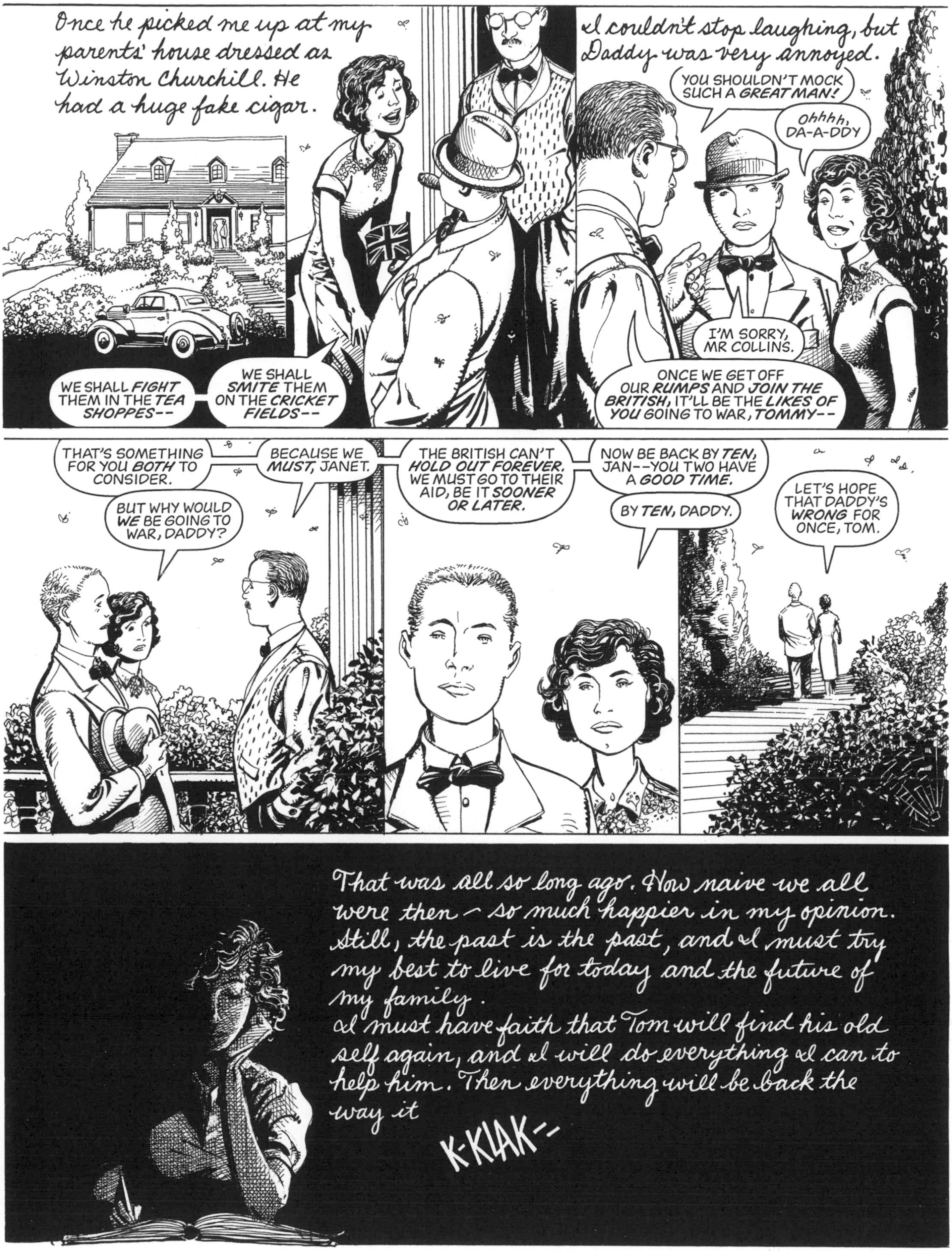

Once he picked me up at my parents' house dressed as Winston Churchill. He had a huge fake cigar.
WE SHALL FIGHT THEM IN THE TEA SHOPPES--
WE SHALL SMITE THEM ON THE CRICKET FIELDS--
I couldn't stop laughing, but Daddy was very annoyed.
YOU SHOULDN'T MOCK SUCH A GREAT MAN!
Ohhhh, DA-A-DDY
I'M SORRY, MR COLLINS.
ONCE WE GET OFF OUR RUMPS AND JOIN THE BRITISH, IT'LL BE THE LIKES OF YOU GOING TO WAR, TOMMY--
THAT'S SOMETHING FOR YOU BOTH TO CONSIDER.
BUT WHY WOULD WE BE GOING TO WAR, DADDY?
BECAUSE WE MUST, JANET.
THE BRITISH CAN'T HOLD OUT FOREVER. WE MUST GO TO THEIR AID, BE IT SOONER OR LATER.
NOW BE BACK BY TEN, JAN--YOU TWO HAVE A GOOD TIME.
BY TEN, DADDY.
LET'S HOPE THAT DADDY'S WRONG FOR ONCE, TOM.
That was all so long ago. How naive we all were then - so much happier in my opinion. Still, the past is the past, and I must try my best to live for today and the future of my family.
I must have faith that Tom will find his old self again, and I will do everything I can to help him. Then everything will be back the way it
K-KLAK--

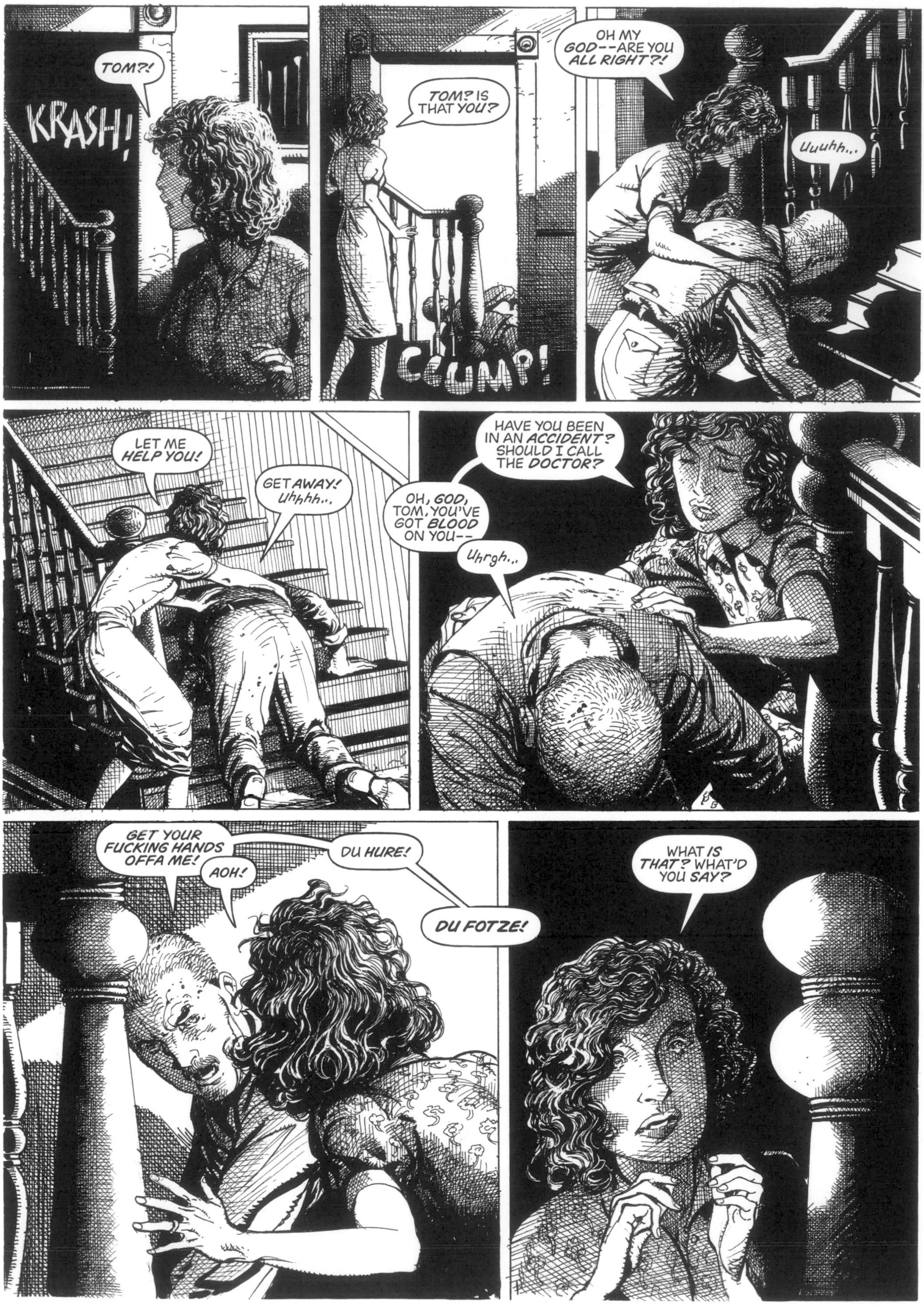

TOM?!
KRASH!
TOM? IS THAT YOU?
CCUMP!
OH MY GOD--ARE YOU ALL RIGHT?!
Uuuhh...
LET ME HELP YOU!
GET AWAY! Uhhhh...
HAVE YOU BEEN IN AN ACCIDENT? SHOULD I CALL THE DOCTOR?
OH, GOD, TOM, YOU'VE GOT BLOOD ON YOU--
Uhrgh...
GET YOUR FUCKING HANDS OFFA ME!
AOH!
DU HURE!
DU FOTZE!
WHAT IS THAT? WHAT'D YOU SAY?

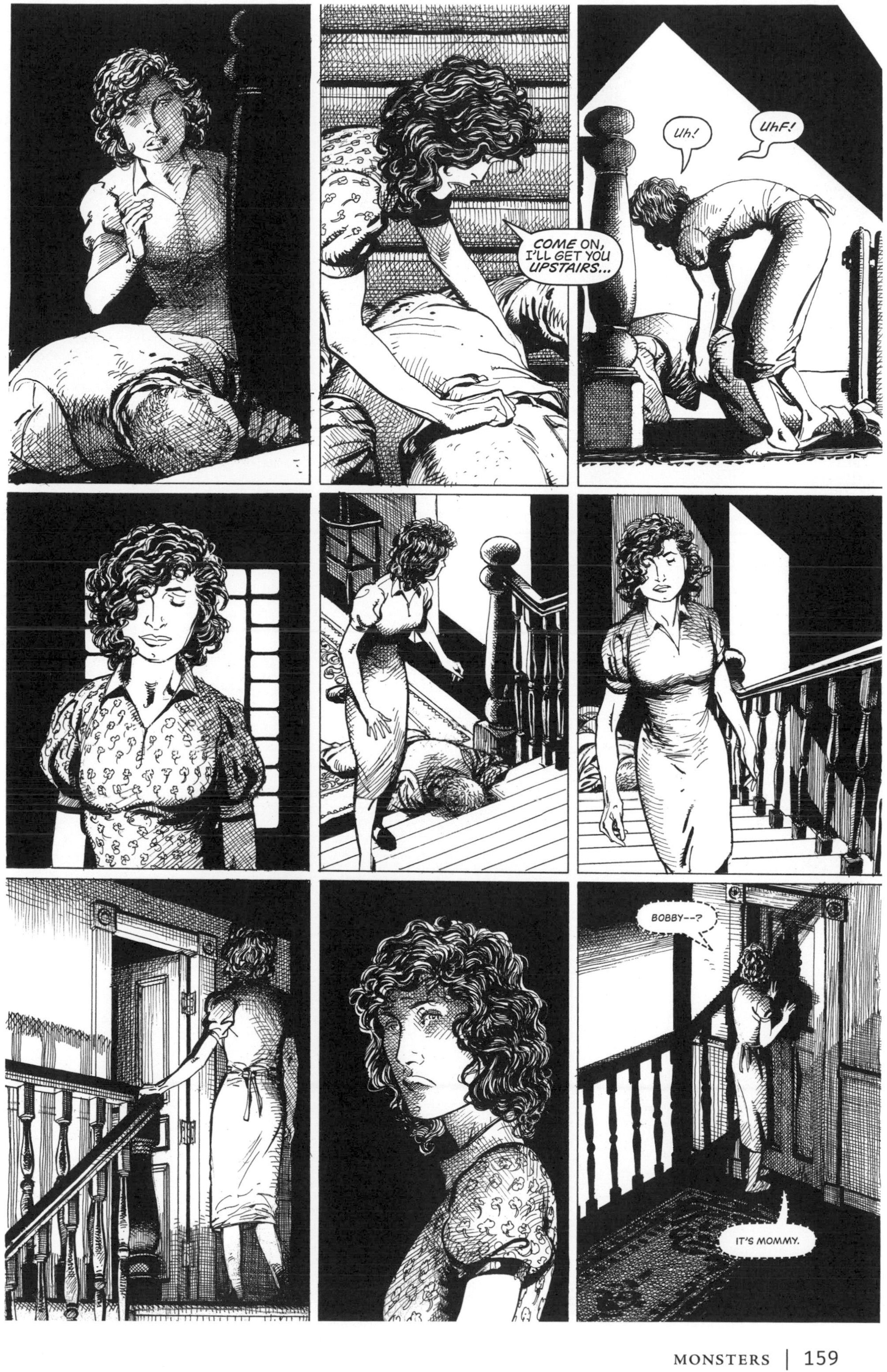
COME ON, I'LL GET YOU UPSTAIRS...
Uh!
UhF!
BOBBY--?
IT'S MOMMY.

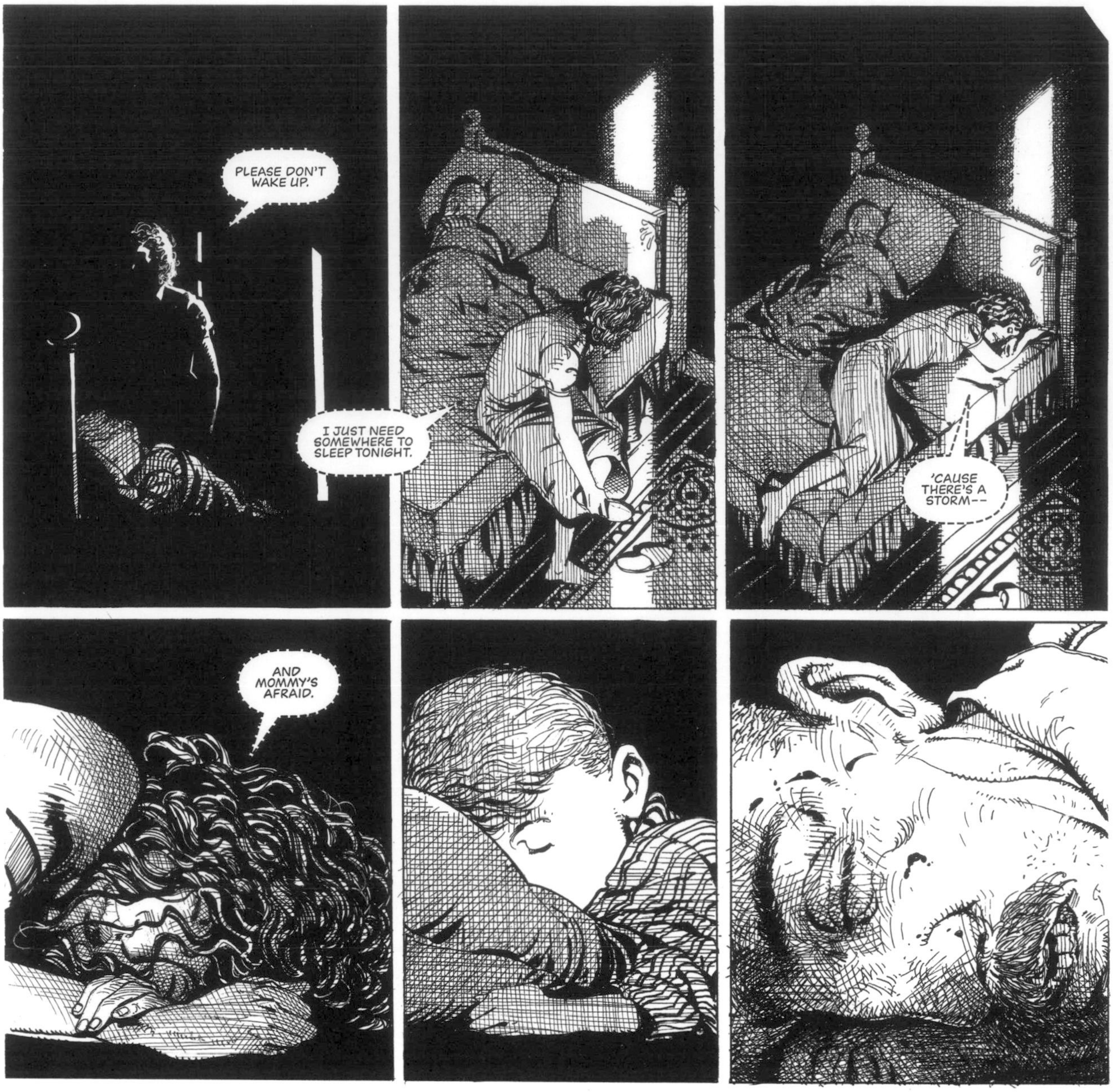
PLEASE DON'T WAKE UP.
I JUST NEED SOMEWHERE TO SLEEP TONIGHT.
'CAUSE THERE'S A STORM--
AND MOMMY'S AFRAID.

Sunday, June 5

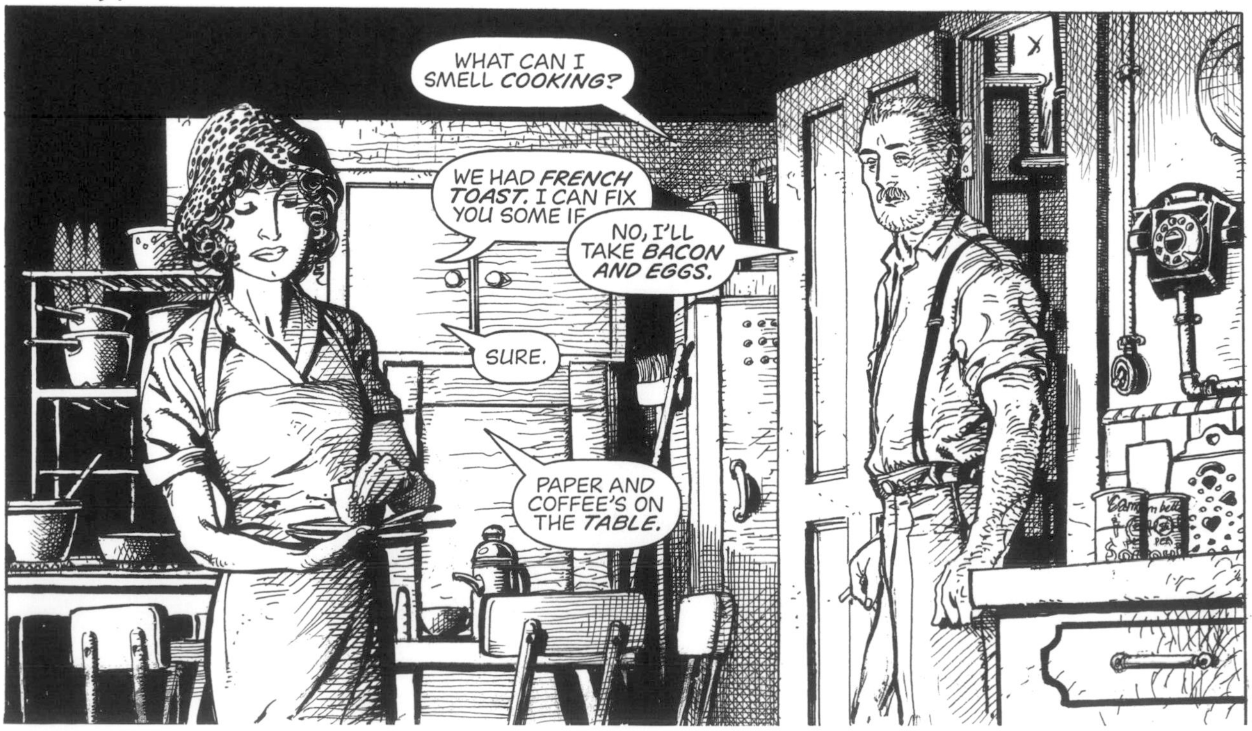
WHAT CAN I SMELL *COOKING*?
WE HAD *FRENCH TOAST*. I CAN FIX YOU SOME IF--
NO, I'LL TAKE *BACON AND EGGS*.
SURE.
PAPER AND COFFEE'S ON THE *TABLE*.

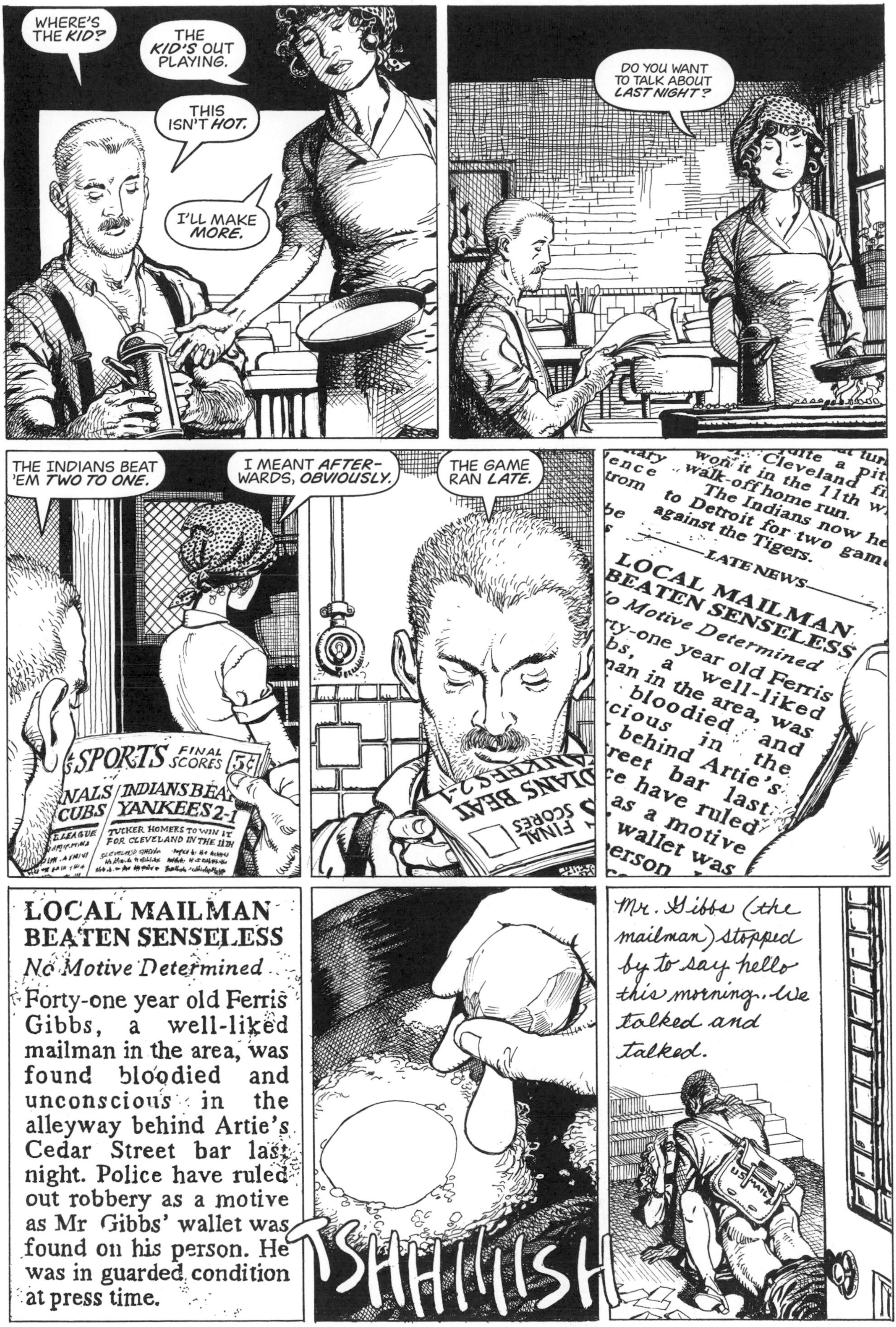
WHERE'S THE *KID?*
THE *KID'S* OUT PLAYING.
THIS ISN'T *HOT.*
I'LL MAKE *MORE.*
DO YOU WANT TO TALK ABOUT *LAST NIGHT?*
THE INDIANS BEAT 'EM *TWO TO ONE.*
I MEANT *AFTER-WARDS, OBVIOUSLY.*
SPORTS FINAL SCORES 5¢
INDIANS BEAT YANKEES 2-1
TUCKER HOMERS TO WIN IT FOR CLEVELAND IN THE 11TH
THE GAME RAN *LATE.*
walk-off home run.
The Indians now
to Detroit for two
against the Tigers.
LATE NEWS
LOCAL MAILMAN BEATEN SENSELESS
LOCAL MAILMAN
BEATEN SENSELESS
No Motive Determined
Forty-one year old Ferris Gibbs, a well-liked mailman in the area, was found bloodied and unconscious in the alleyway behind Artie's Cedar Street bar last night. Police have ruled out robbery as a motive as Mr Gibbs' wallet was found on his person. He was in guarded condition at press time.
TSHHIIISH
Mr. Gibbs (the mailman) stopped by to say hello this morning. We talked and talked.
U.S. MAIL

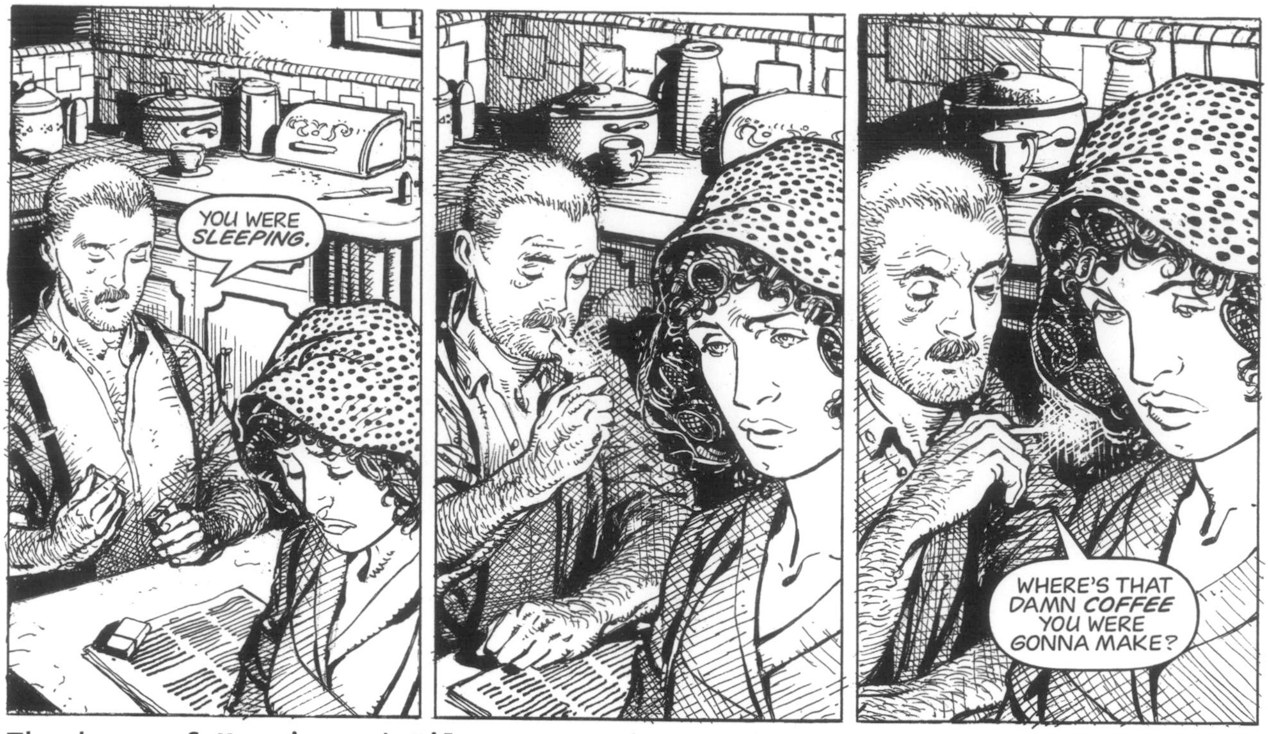
YOU WERE SLEEPING.
WHERE'S THAT DAMN COFFEE YOU WERE GONNA MAKE?

The home of Morris and Eileen Ronsadt Monday, June 6

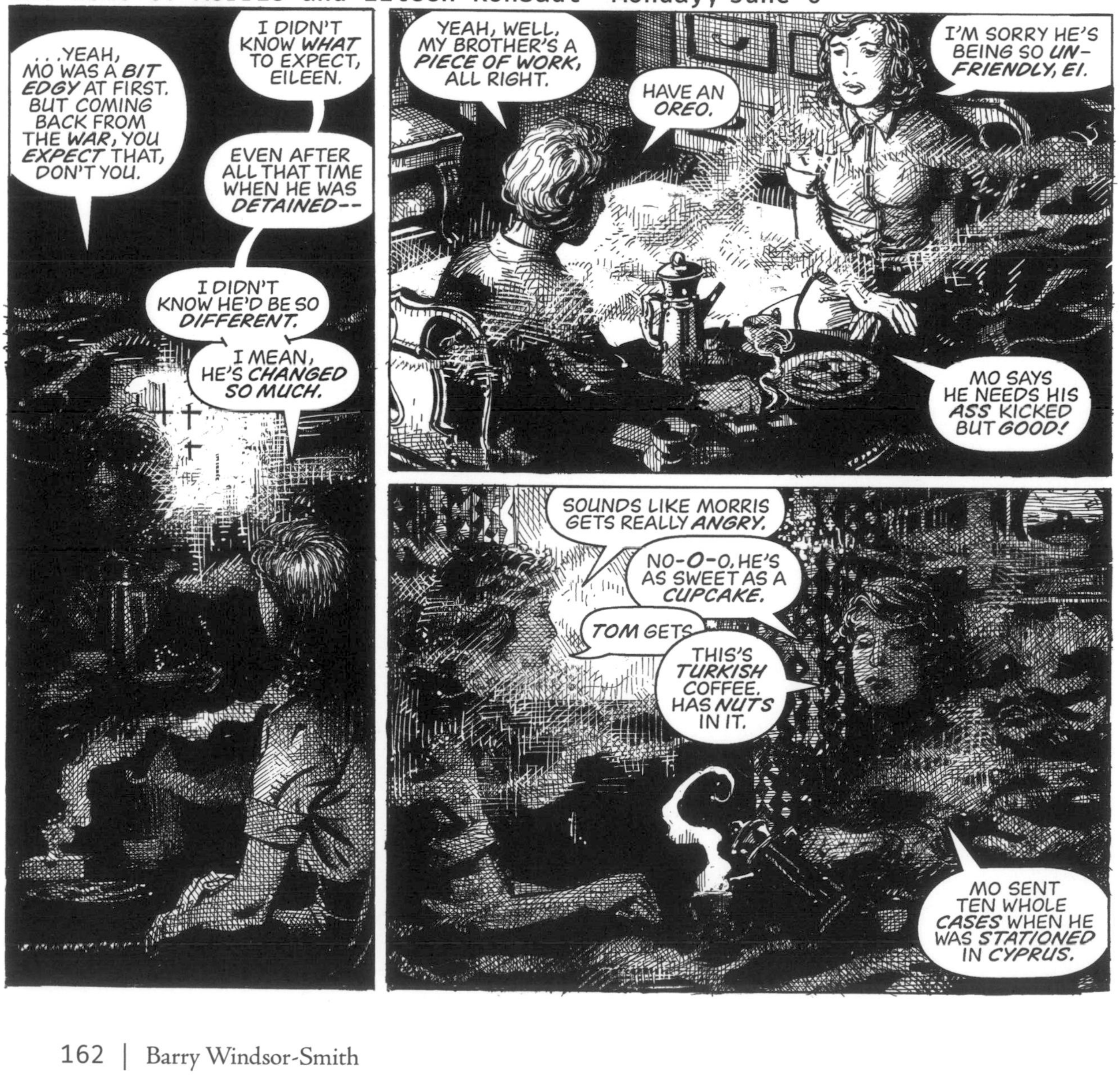
. . .YEAH, MO WAS A BIT EDGY AT FIRST. BUT COMING BACK FROM THE WAR, YOU EXPECT THAT, DON'T YOU.
I DIDN'T KNOW WHAT TO EXPECT, EILEEN.
EVEN AFTER ALL THAT TIME WHEN HE WAS DETAINED--
I DIDN'T KNOW HE'D BE SO DIFFERENT.
I MEAN, HE'S CHANGED SO MUCH.
YEAH, WELL, MY BROTHER'S A PIECE OF WORK, ALL RIGHT.
HAVE AN OREO.
I'M SORRY HE'S BEING SO UN-FRIENDLY, EI.
MO SAYS HE NEEDS HIS ASS KICKED BUT GOOD!
SOUNDS LIKE MORRIS GETS REALLY ANGRY.
NO-O-O, HE'S AS SWEET AS A CUPCAKE.
TOM GETS.
THIS'S TURKISH COFFEE. HAS NUTS IN IT.
MO SENT TEN WHOLE CASES WHEN HE WAS STATIONED IN CYPRUS.

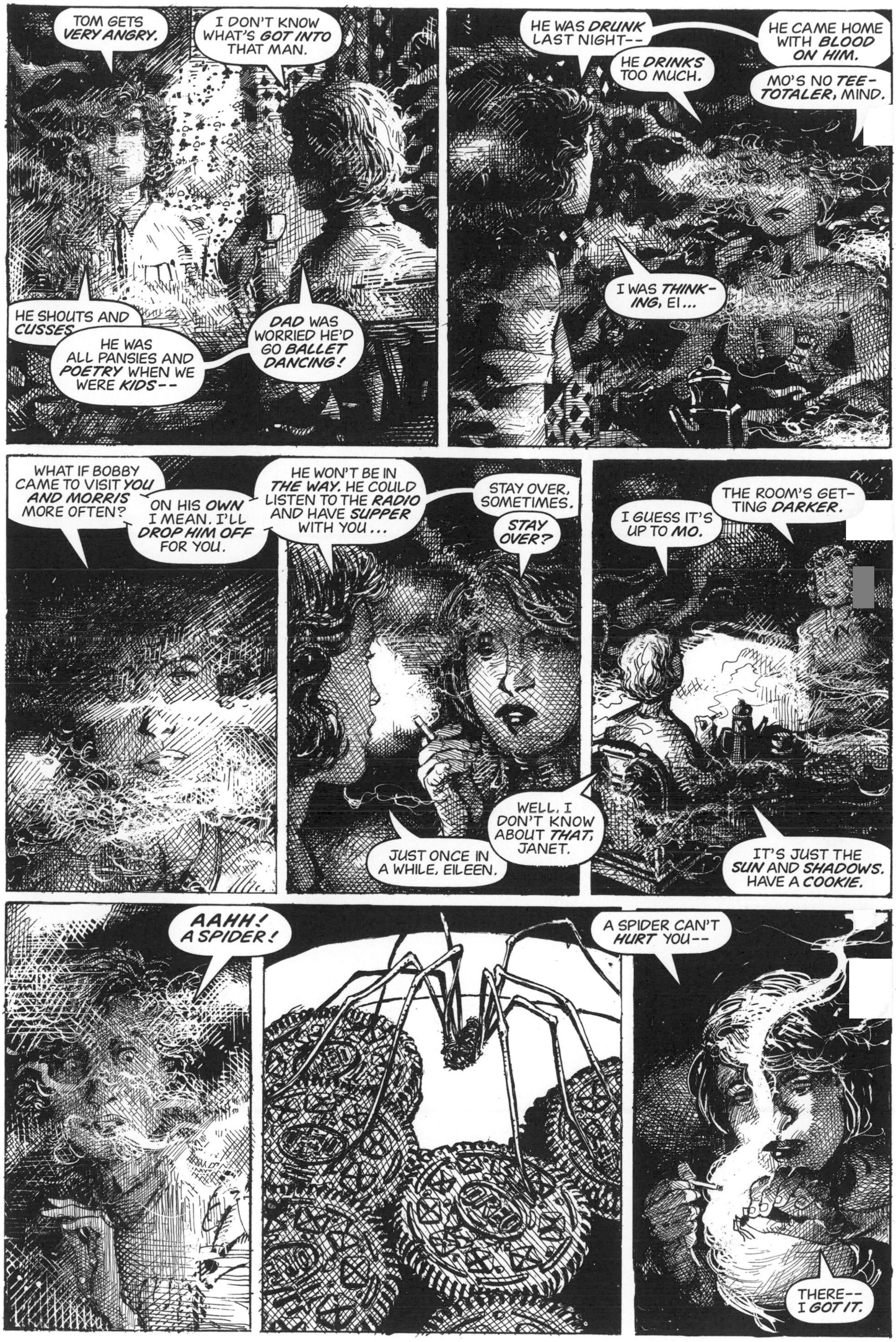

TOM GETS VERY ANGRY.
I DON'T KNOW WHAT'S GOT INTO THAT MAN.
HE SHOUTS AND CUSSES.
HE WAS ALL PANSIES AND POETRY WHEN WE WERE KIDS--
DAD WAS WORRIED HE'D GO BALLET DANCING!
HE WAS DRUNK LAST NIGHT--
HE DRINKS TOO MUCH.
HE CAME HOME WITH BLOOD ON HIM.
MO'S NO TEE-TOTALER, MIND.
I WAS THINK-ING, EI...
WHAT IF BOBBY CAME TO VISIT YOU AND MORRIS MORE OFTEN?
ON HIS OWN I MEAN. I'LL DROP HIM OFF FOR YOU.
HE WON'T BE IN THE WAY. HE COULD LISTEN TO THE RADIO AND HAVE SUPPER WITH YOU...
STAY OVER, SOMETIMES.
STAY OVER?
JUST ONCE IN A WHILE, EILEEN.
WELL, I DON'T KNOW ABOUT THAT, JANET.
I GUESS IT'S UP TO MO.
THE ROOM'S GET-TING DARKER.
IT'S JUST THE SUN AND SHADOWS. HAVE A COOKIE.
AAHH! A SPIDER!
A SPIDER CAN'T HURT YOU--
THERE-- I GOT IT.

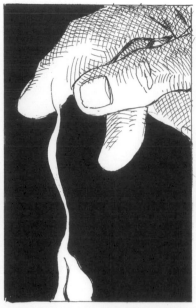

2:31 am

I stopped by Eileen's today and she

I'm more and more concerned about
Tom and I wish I had somebody to
talk to about it. He's been
staying out quite late in the
evenings and usually comes
home smelling of whiskey. He
can be quite beligerent and
I've stopped keeping his plate
warm in the oven.

Tom is just not the man he
was before going to war. He
must have suffered terribly
is all I can think of. His
time in the debriefing
must have been traumatic.
He doesn't act like Tom,
he doesn't talk like Tom.
It's almost as if he
isn't really my husband
at all, just someone who
looks like him if he
were 15 years older.

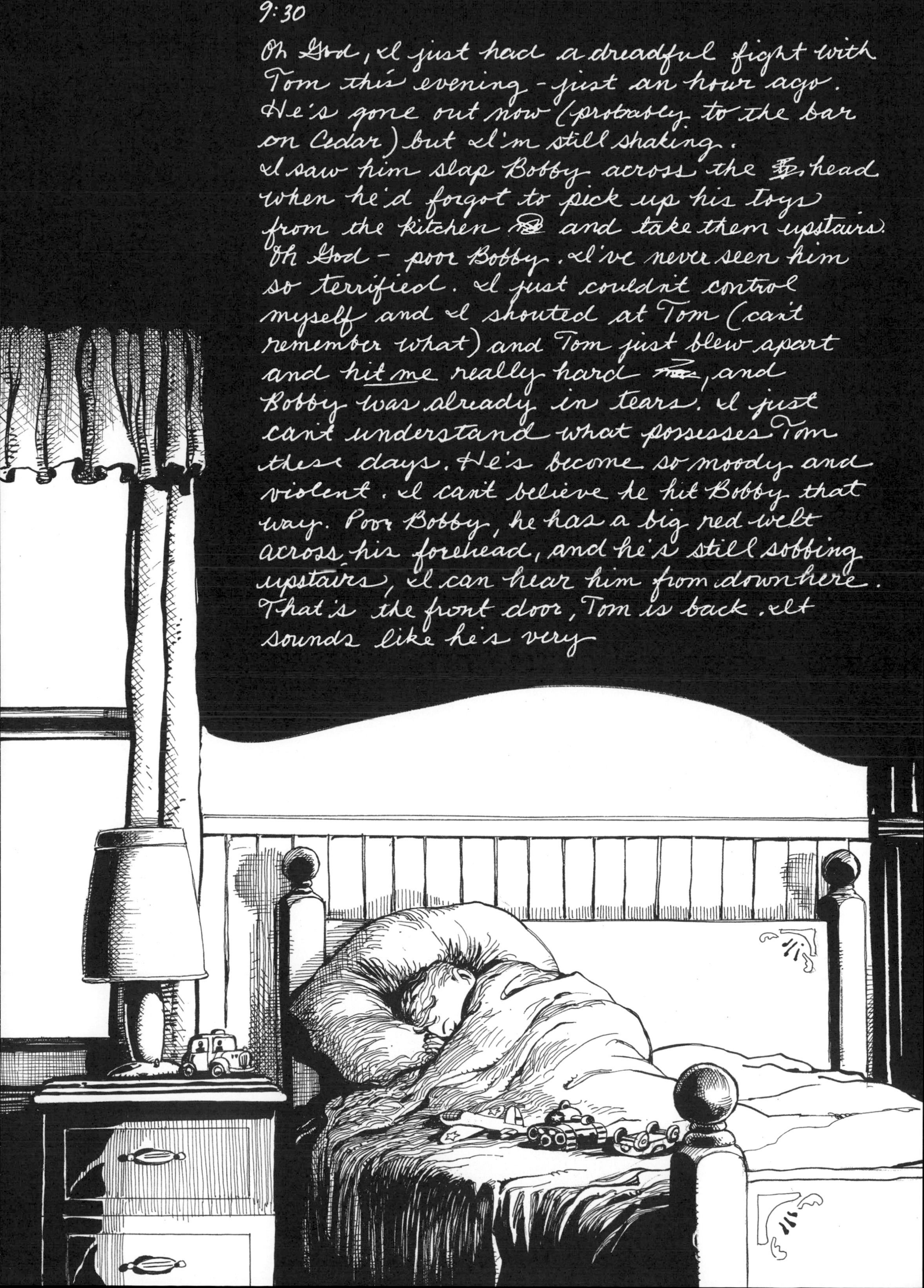
9:30
Oh God, I just had a dreadful fight with Tom this evening - just an hour ago. He's gone out now (probably to the bar on Cedar) but I'm still shaking.
I saw him slap Bobby across the head when he'd forgot to pick up his toys from the kitchen and take them upstairs. Oh God - poor Bobby. I've never seen him so terrified. I just couldn't control myself and I shouted at Tom (can't remember what) and Tom just blew apart and hit me really hard, and Bobby was already in tears. I just can't understand what possesses Tom these days. He's become so moody and violent. I can't believe he hit Bobby that way. Poor Bobby, he has a big red welt across his forehead, and he's still sobbing upstairs, I can hear him from down here. That's the front door, Tom is back. It sounds like he's very

Wednesday, August 10

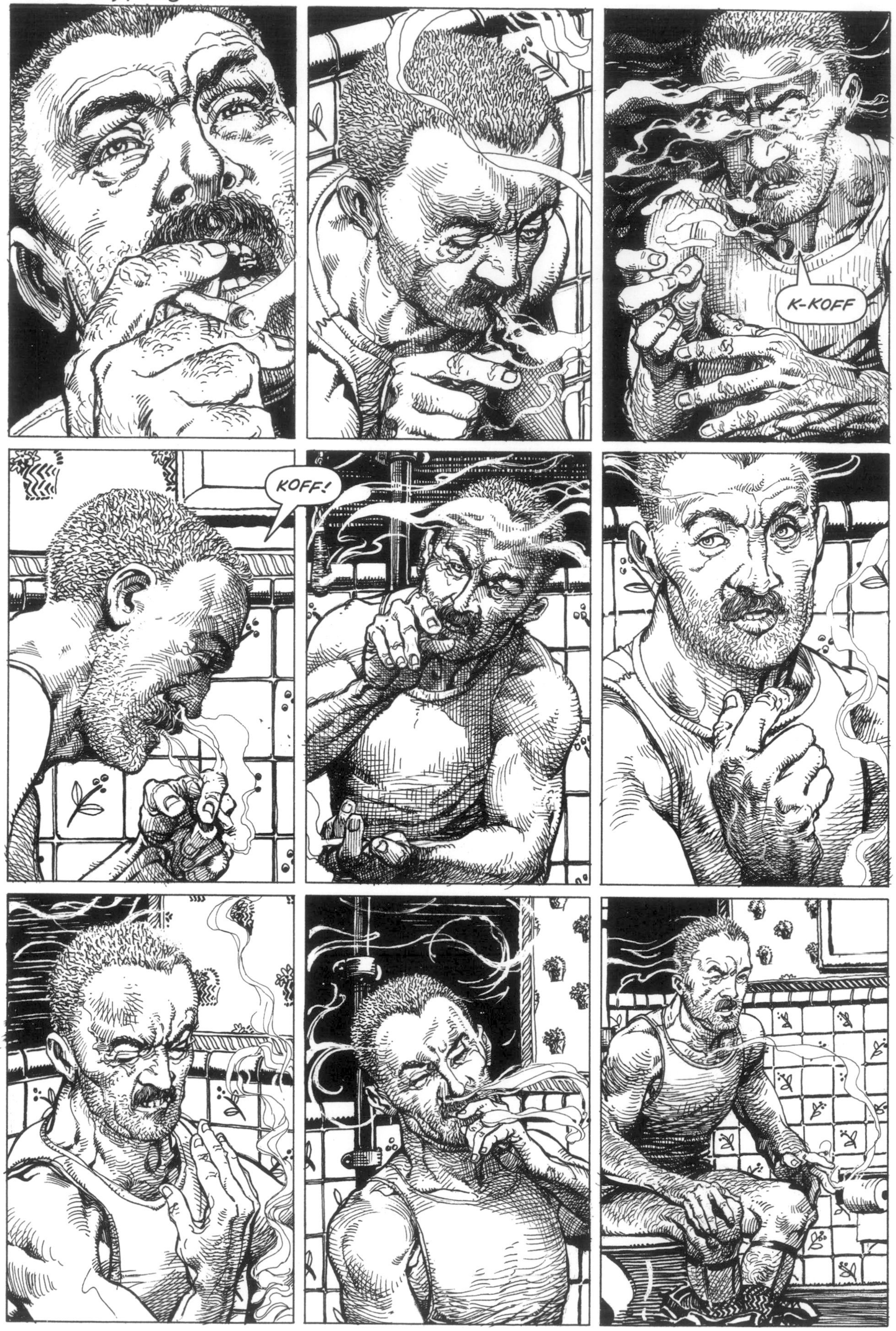
K-KOFF
KOFF!

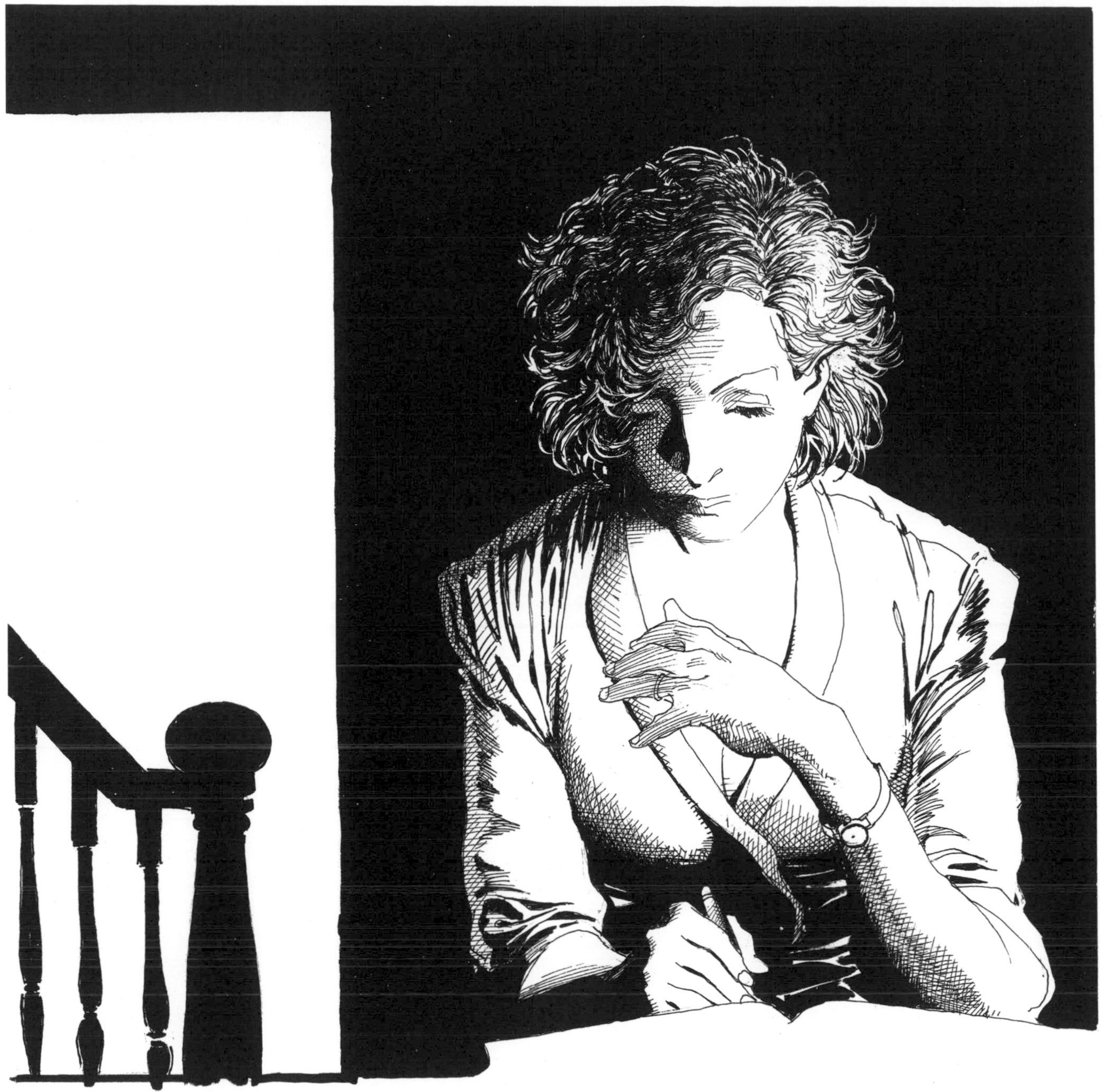

August 17,

We all had the most terrible time last Wednesday. Somehow Bobby fell off his bicycle and hurt his eye.

Bobby had a terrible accident on his bicycle last week. The doctor at the hospital ~~said~~ was worried that B might ~~only~~ have only partial sight in his left eye.

Poor Bobby really hurt himself last week. When he fell of off his bicycle in the garden.

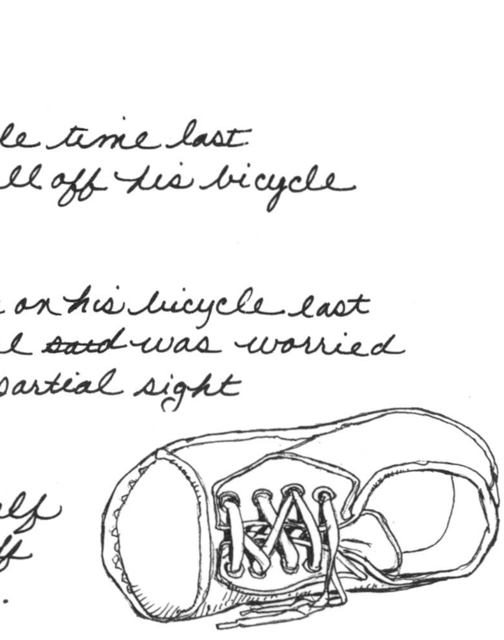

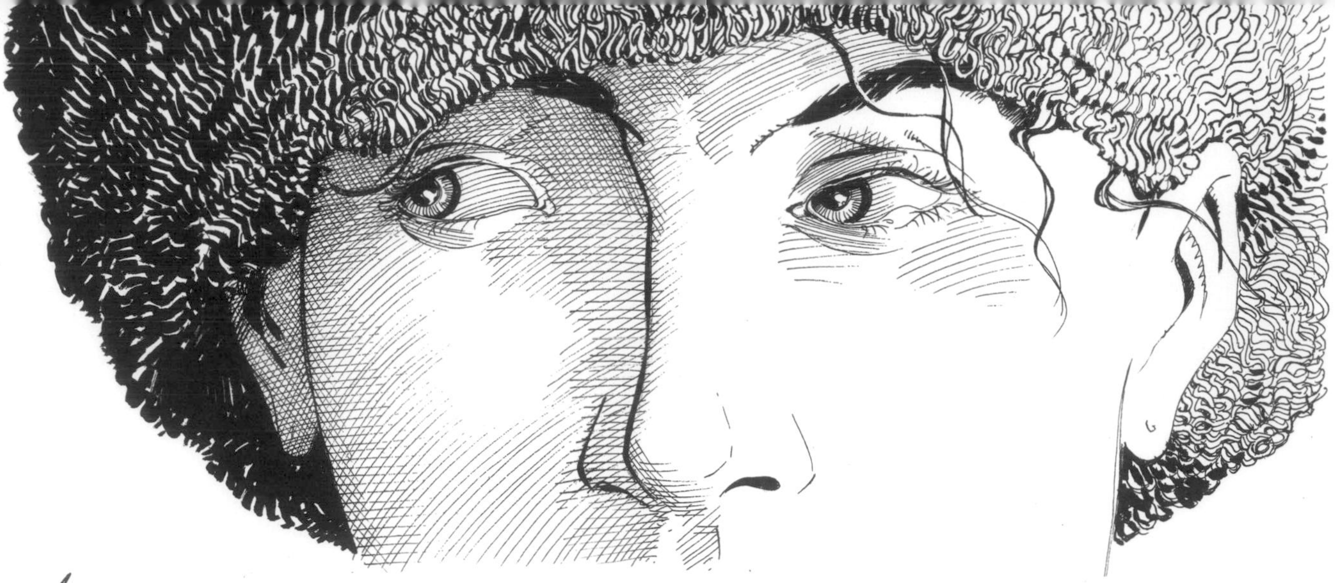

Sept 10, 1949
I haven't written for ages, I can't seem to concentrate long enough. I don't seem to know what I'm doing anymore.
Bobby's second inspection at the eye clinic went poorly today. She said that even the cheapest glass eye was necessary to prevent further loss of tissue and possible diseases. She just wouldn't accept that we can't afford it, and she's right, of course. But I couldn't explain the situation w/Tom to her.
I'll have to find the right time to ask him again, but I just know that it's going to upset the relative calm around here since the bicycle accident.
Tom has been very repentant, I must say. He's brought me flowers a few times and he's even promising to buy B. a new bicycle (although I'd prefer the money to go toward the costs of the eye). But despite this and a few other changes for the better (who knows how long they'll last?), I can't seem to feel ~~cm~~ comfortable around Tom anymore. I pretend that I am — I smile and make chit chat, I cook and sew and all of that, but inside me I feel that a lot has changed.
Something that keeps
He's back, must close
11:30 p.m.
Something that keeps getting to me is that almost every time I notice that Bobby isn't around, or if he isn't where I expected him to be, my heart stops

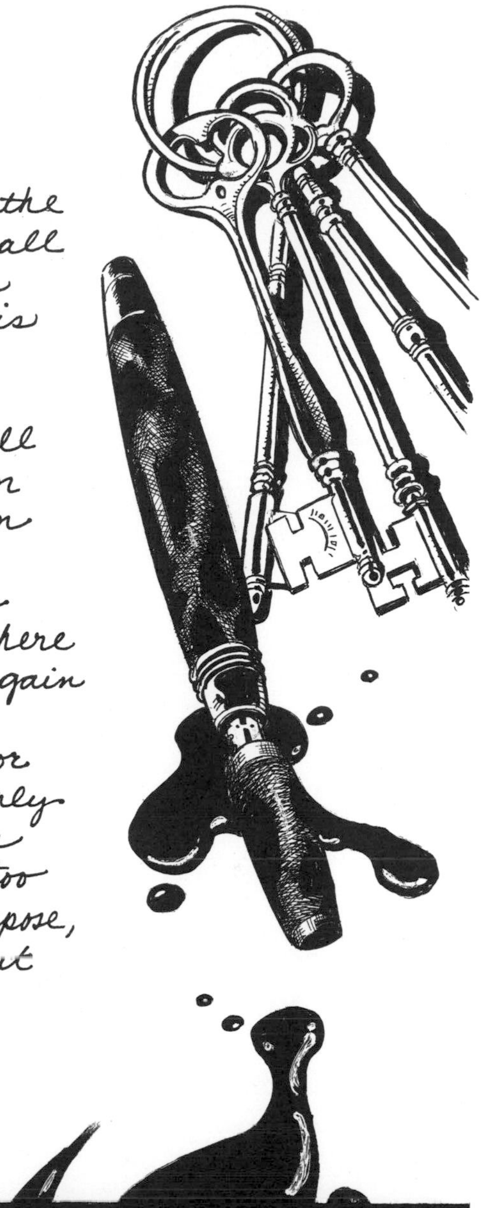

beating. Then I have to run around the house looking for him. I don't dare call out in case Tom realizes that I'm in a complete panic that he's beating his son again.

I still relive it ~~all over again~~ in my dreams. B. with his bloodied face all ~~blown up like a~~ bulging, and Tom screaming some obscenities in German like those newsreels of Hitler at the rallies. I'm almost afraid that I'm shouting in my sleep and Tom lies there wide awake watching me go through it again and again.

I don't know how long it will take for me to get over all of this. And God only knows how Bobby feels. I can't seem to talk to him about it, he's just too young I guess. One good thing, I suppose, is that B. might have been knocked out unconscious through most of it, so perhaps he doesn't remember much. Well that's my hope anyway.

It's midnight, I should turn in.

I hope I don't wake T.

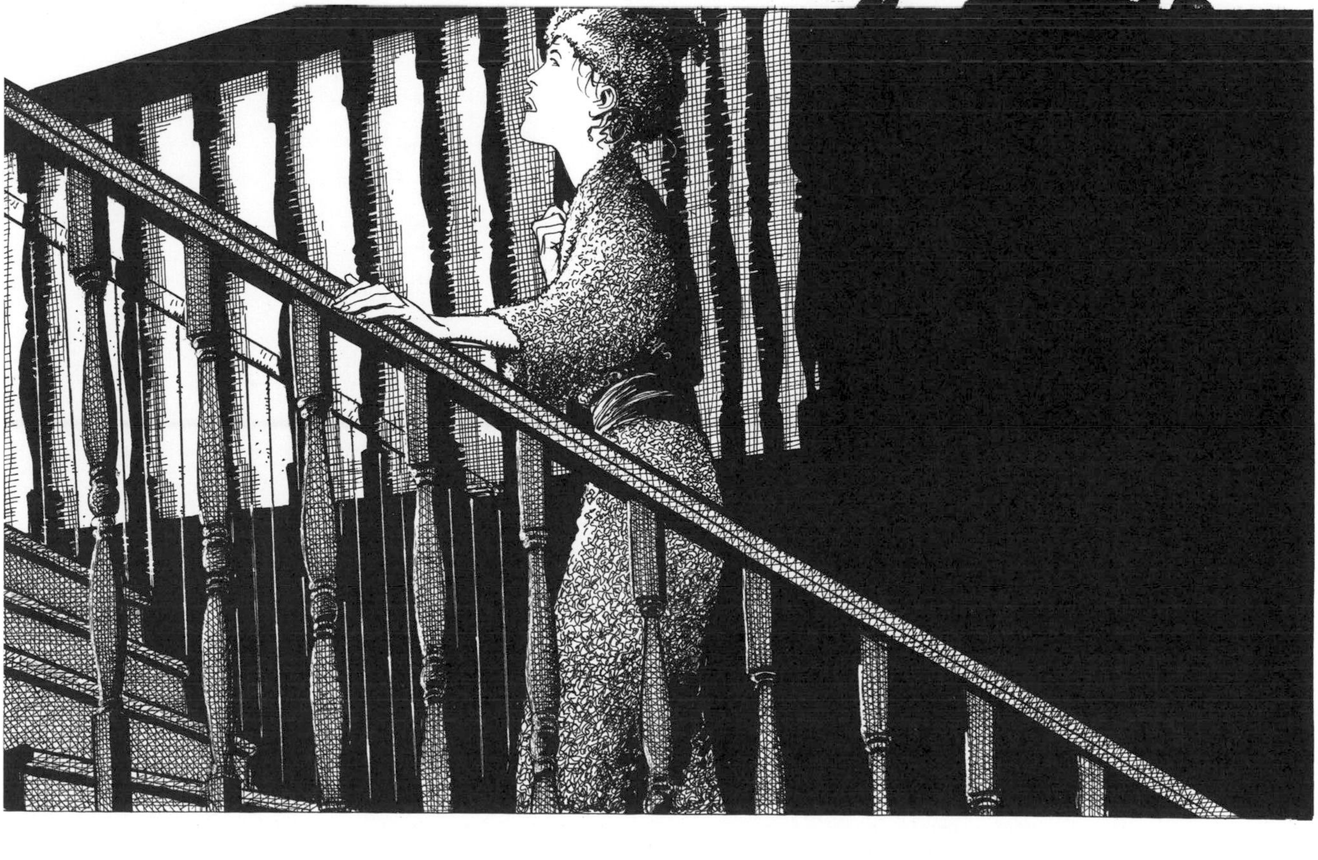

Sunday, September 18

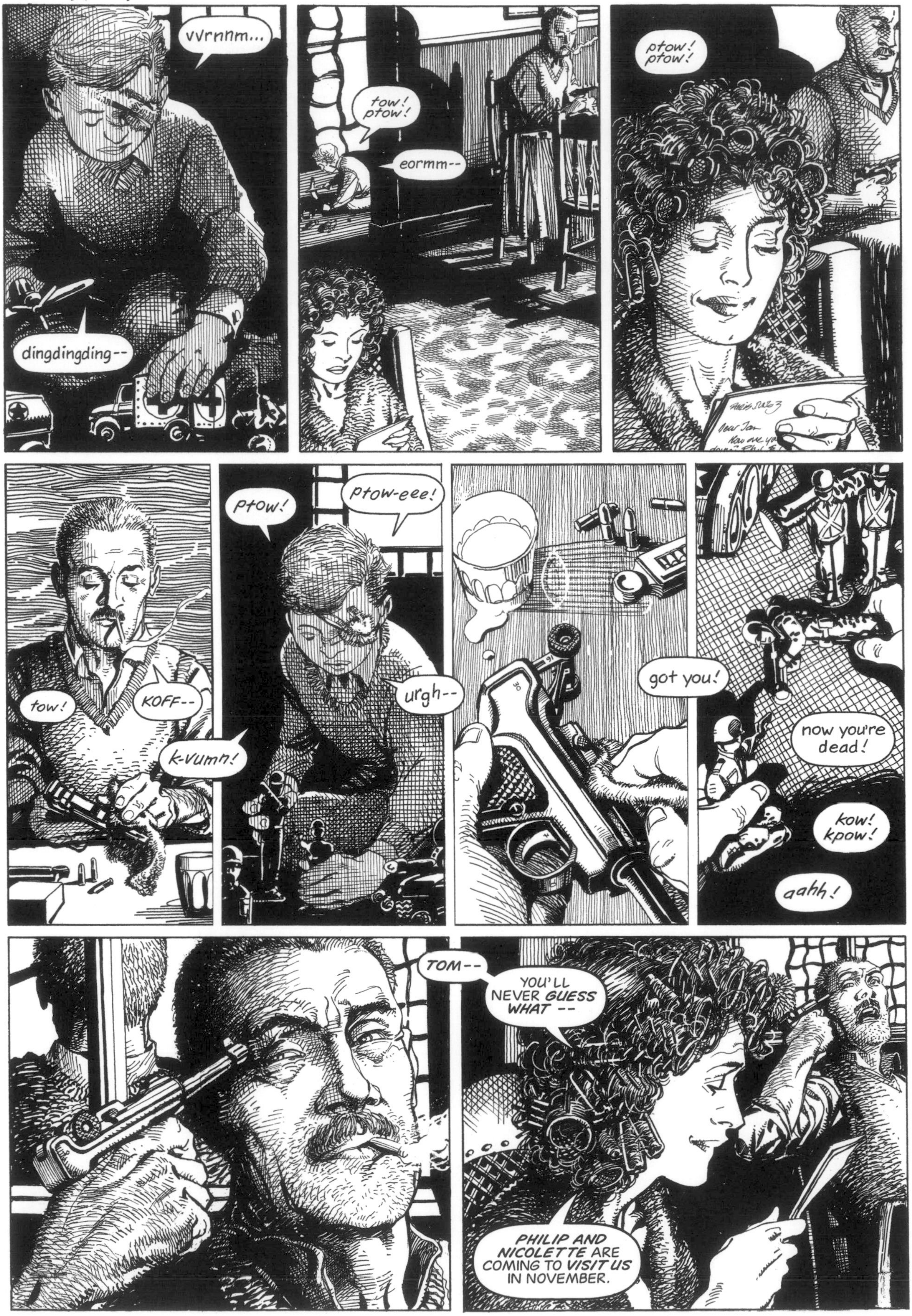
vvrnnm...
dingdingding--
tow! ptow!
eormm--
ptow! ptow!
tow!
KOFF--
k-vumm!
ptow!
ptow-eee!
urgh--
got you!
now you're dead!
kow! kpow!
aahh!
TOM--
YOU'LL NEVER GUESS WHAT --
PHILIP AND NICOLETTE ARE COMING TO VISIT US IN NOVEMBER.

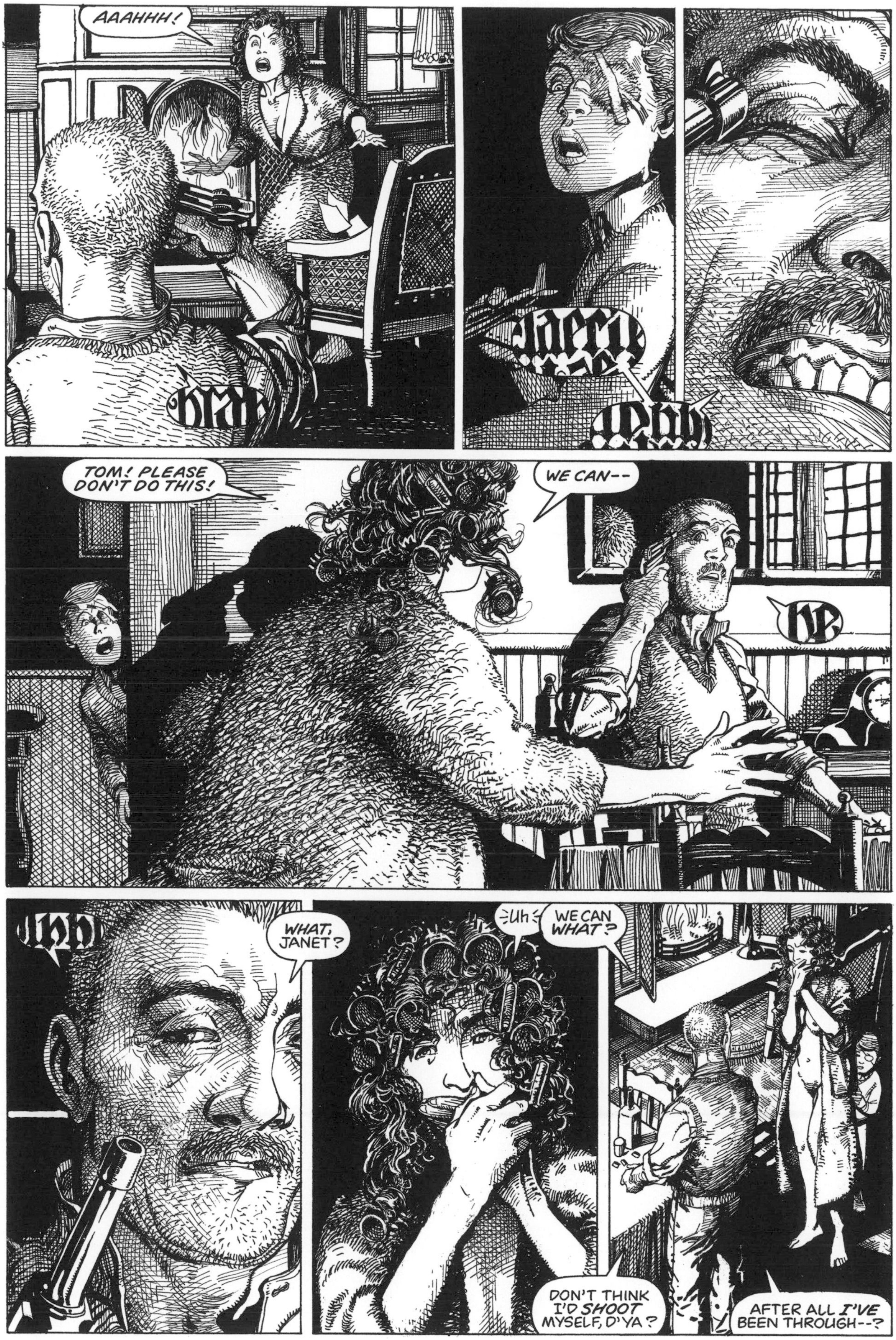
AAAHHH!
TOM! PLEASE DON'T DO THIS!
WE CAN--
WHAT, JANET?
UH
WE CAN WHAT?
DON'T THINK I'D SHOOT MYSELF, D'YA?
AFTER ALL I'VE BEEN THROUGH--?

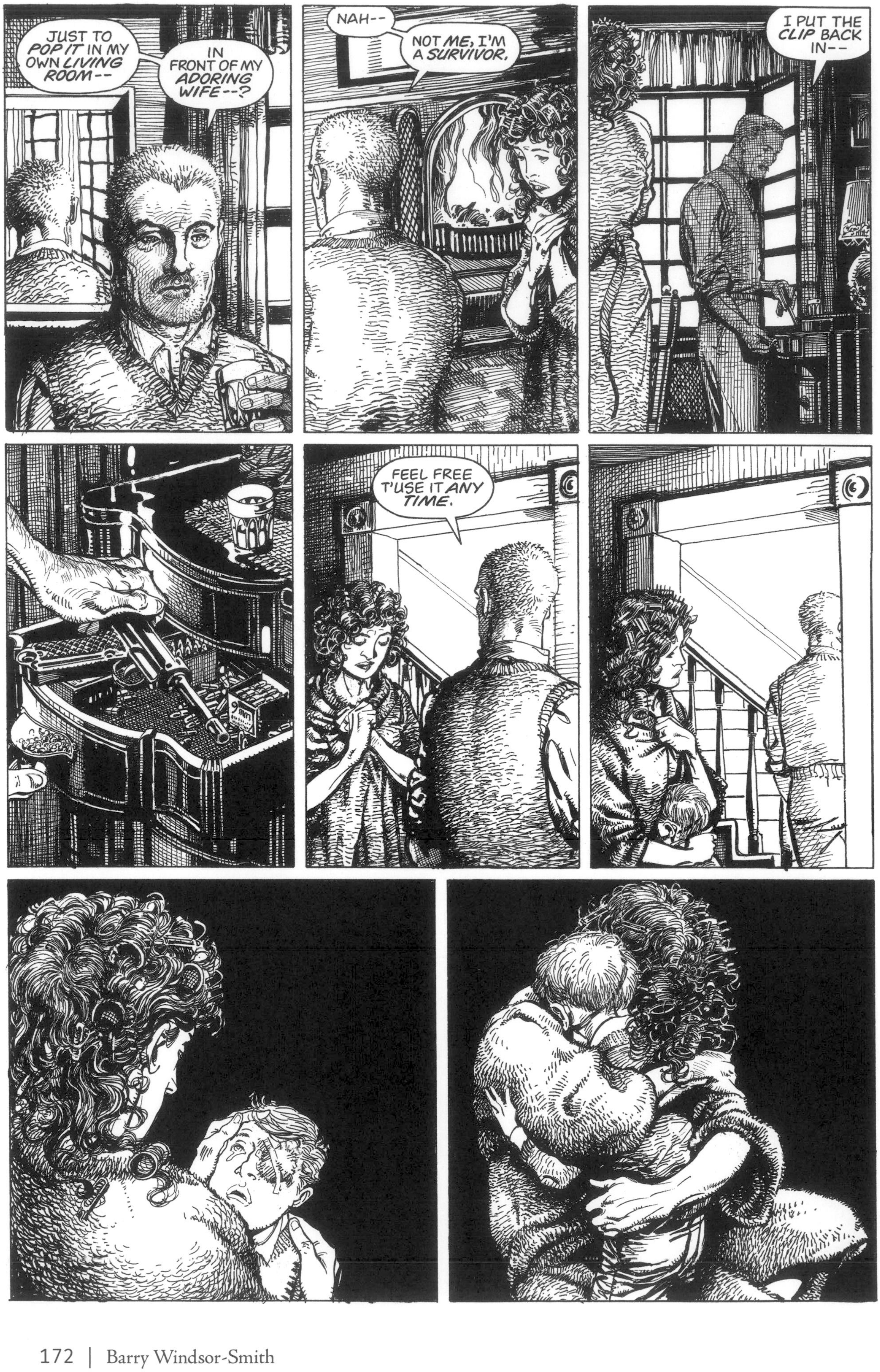
JUST TO POP IT IN MY OWN LIVING ROOM--
IN FRONT OF MY ADORING WIFE--?
NAH--
NOT ME, I'M A SURVIVOR.
I PUT THE CLIP BACK IN--
FEEL FREE T'USE IT ANY TIME.

October 26, 1949

I'm very tired as I write this, so I may not write for long. I ran into Jack today as I was coming out of the market with Bobby. It was so awkward and I didn't know what to say to him at all. He couldn't help but notice the bandages on Bobby's face even though I made him wear that silly hat. I lied and said he'd got into a fight at school, completely forgetting that school doesn't start 'til next week. I don't know if Jack caught that. I should've stuck to the bicycle accident, but I was flustered.

Jack was so wonderful and so concerned for Bobby and me, I just wanted to take him in my arms right then in the street with everybody watching. Jack was telling me where he'd been all these months, and if it was supposed to be Top Secret or something it didn't matter because I wasn't really listening, I was just gazing into his deep brown eyes all the time. I feel so cared for when Jack talks to me. The way he looks at me, I know he's still in love with me and I know no matter that it can never be, that I shall always love that man so much.

Oh dear God, please don't let me even think these sorts of things.

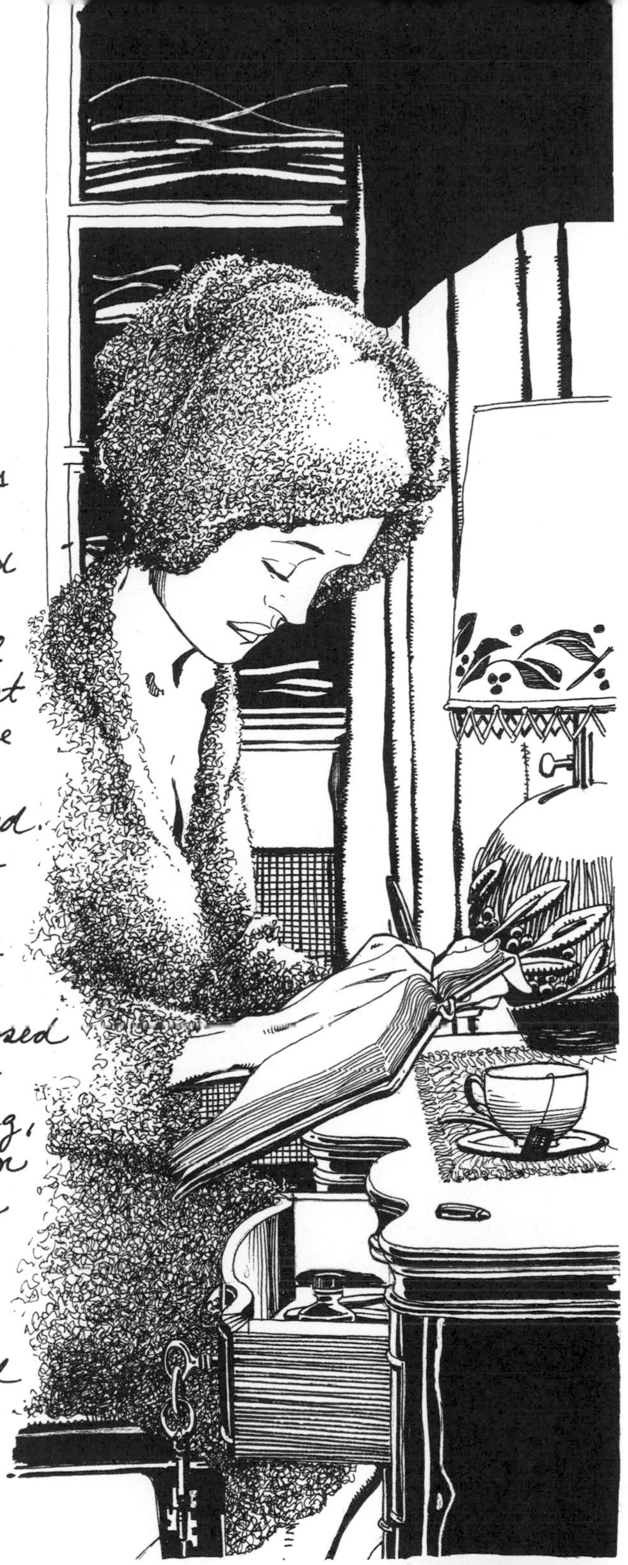

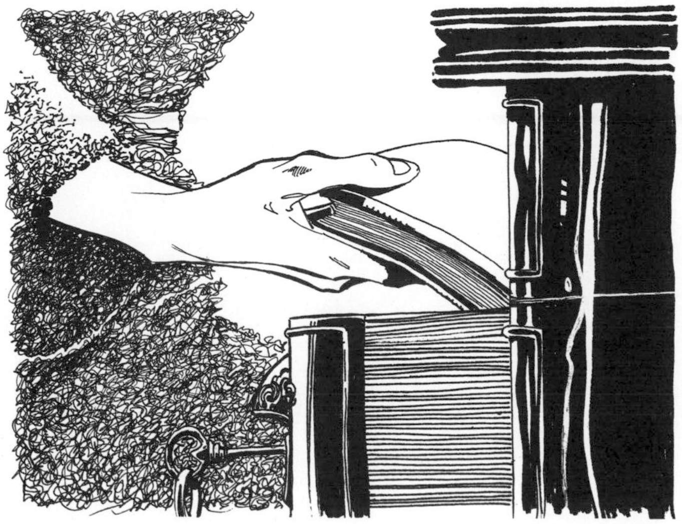

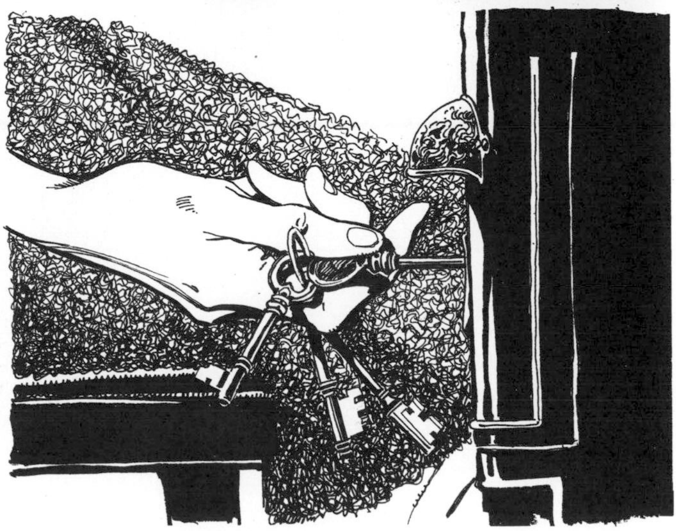

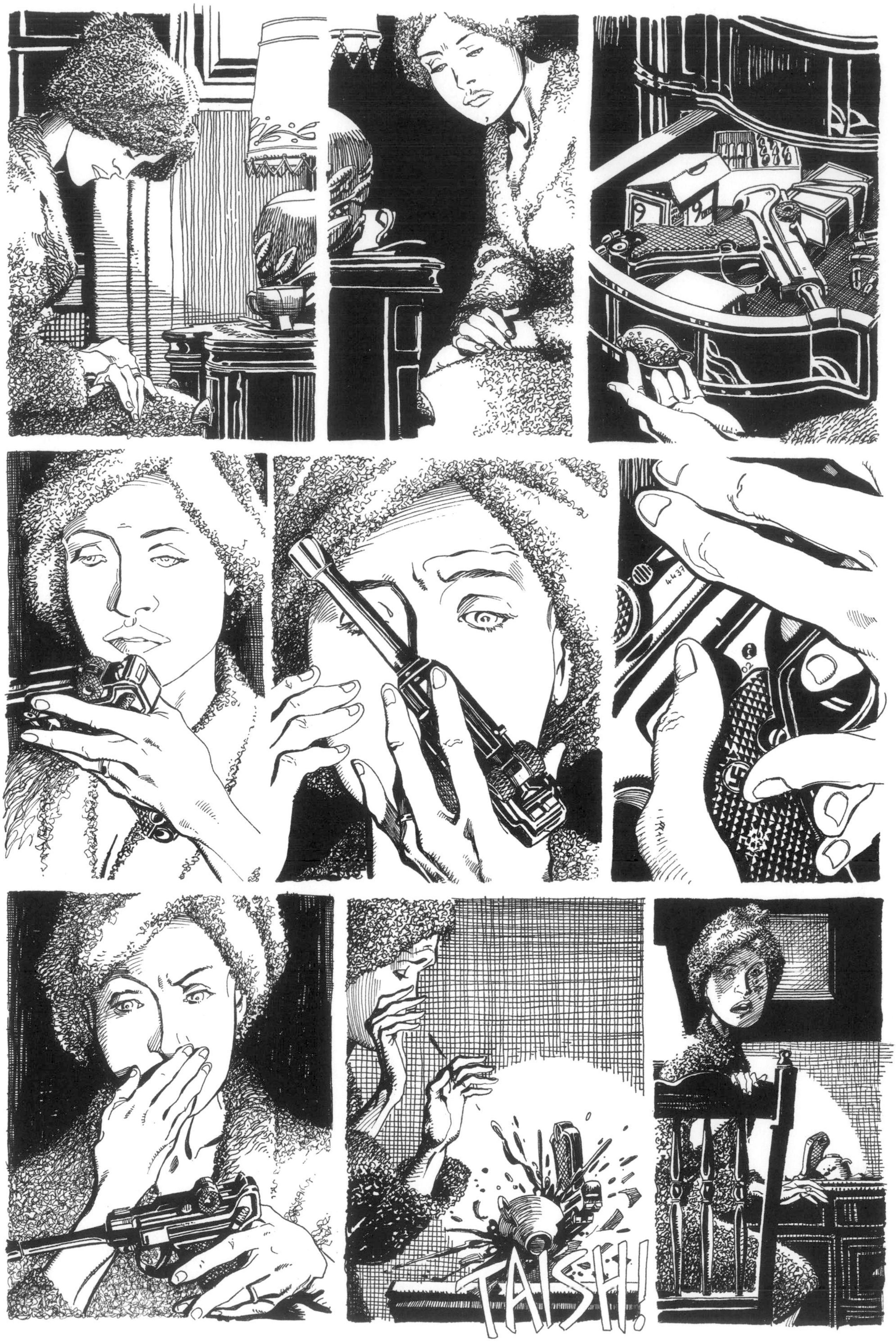
TAISH!

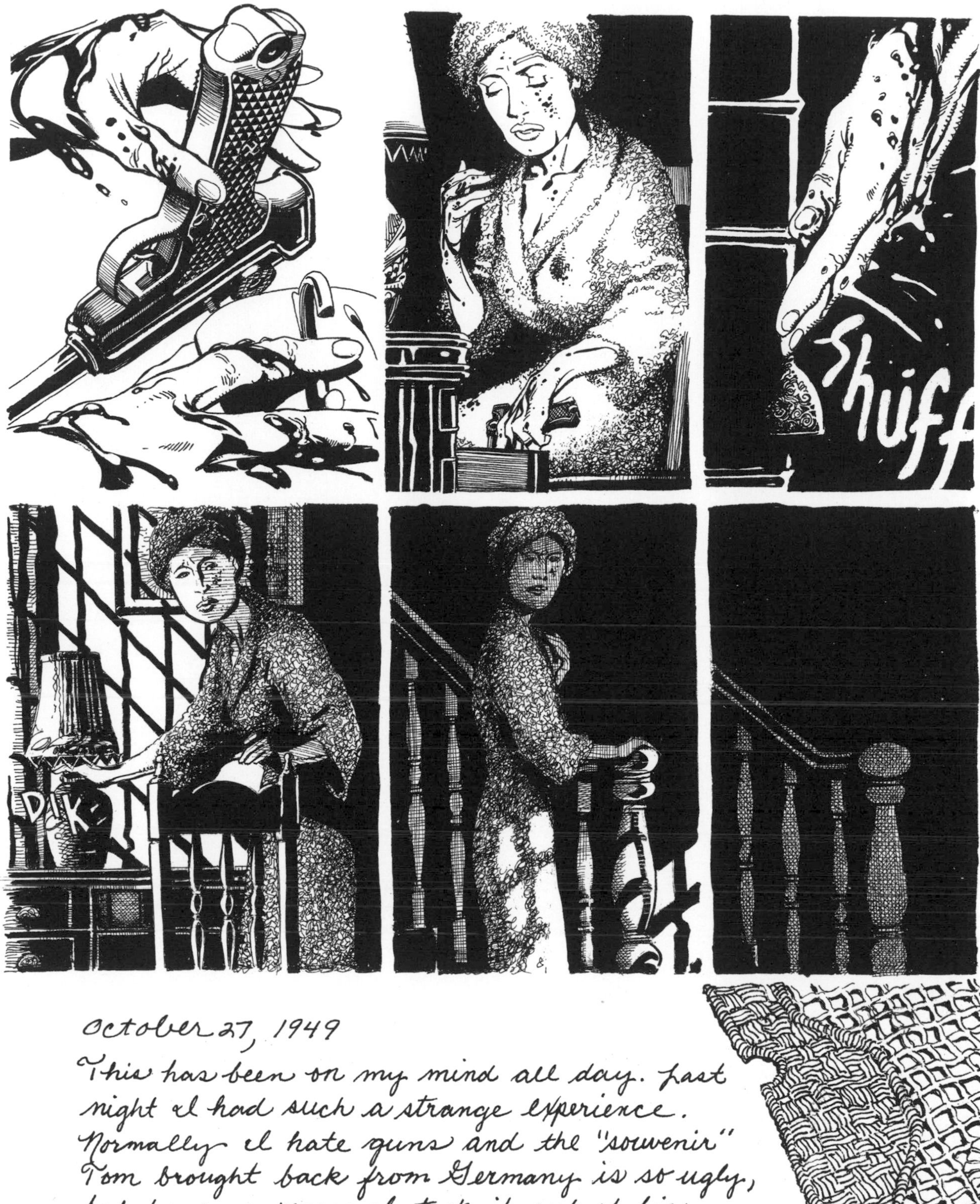
Shuff

October 27, 1949

This has been on my mind all day. Last night I had such a strange experience. Normally I hate guns and the "souvenir" Tom brought back from Germany is so ugly, but for some reason I took it out of his drawer and held it for a while. I just don't know why I did this. The thing frightens me. It has a Nazi sign (insignia or something I can't remember what it's called) right in the middle of the handle, and it's black and heavy like something that's evil.

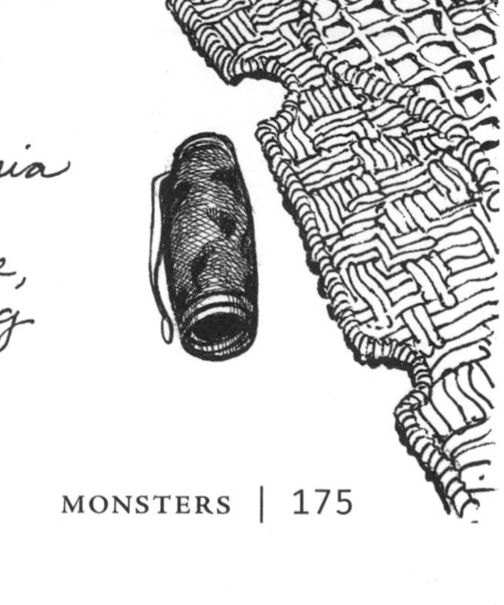

While I was holding it I started to hear voices! I know how ridiculous that sounds, but I can't forget it it and it's worrying me so I thought that writing about it would help somehow. ~~There was~~
I could hear voices of men talking in German. There was a woman, too, who sounded French (or perhaps Swedish like that movie actress), but it was mostly men talking about death. It was their own deaths they were discussing so strangely.

I don't know how I understood them as I don't speak German like Tom does. But I understood them anyway. Talking about death and dying, it was so gruesome and frightening I accidentally dropped the gun. Thank goodness it didn't go off! I don't believe in ghosts, but it was almost like the gun is haunted. That's just ridiculous, I know.
I've just remembered what the French woman said. She said "Spare the boy", or maybe, "Save the boy." What could that have meant? My skin is crawling.

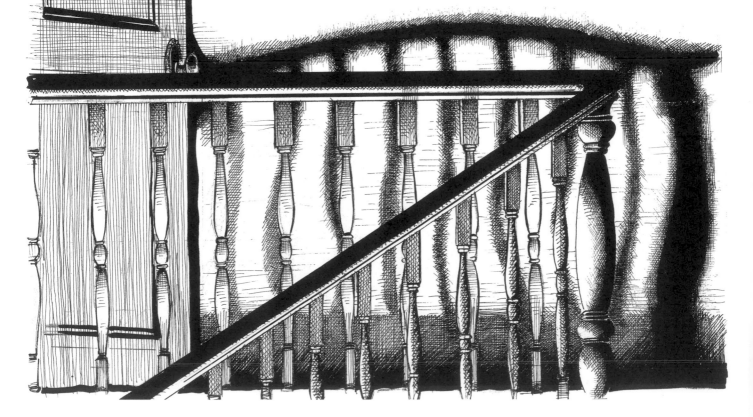

Providence Square Wednesday, October 12

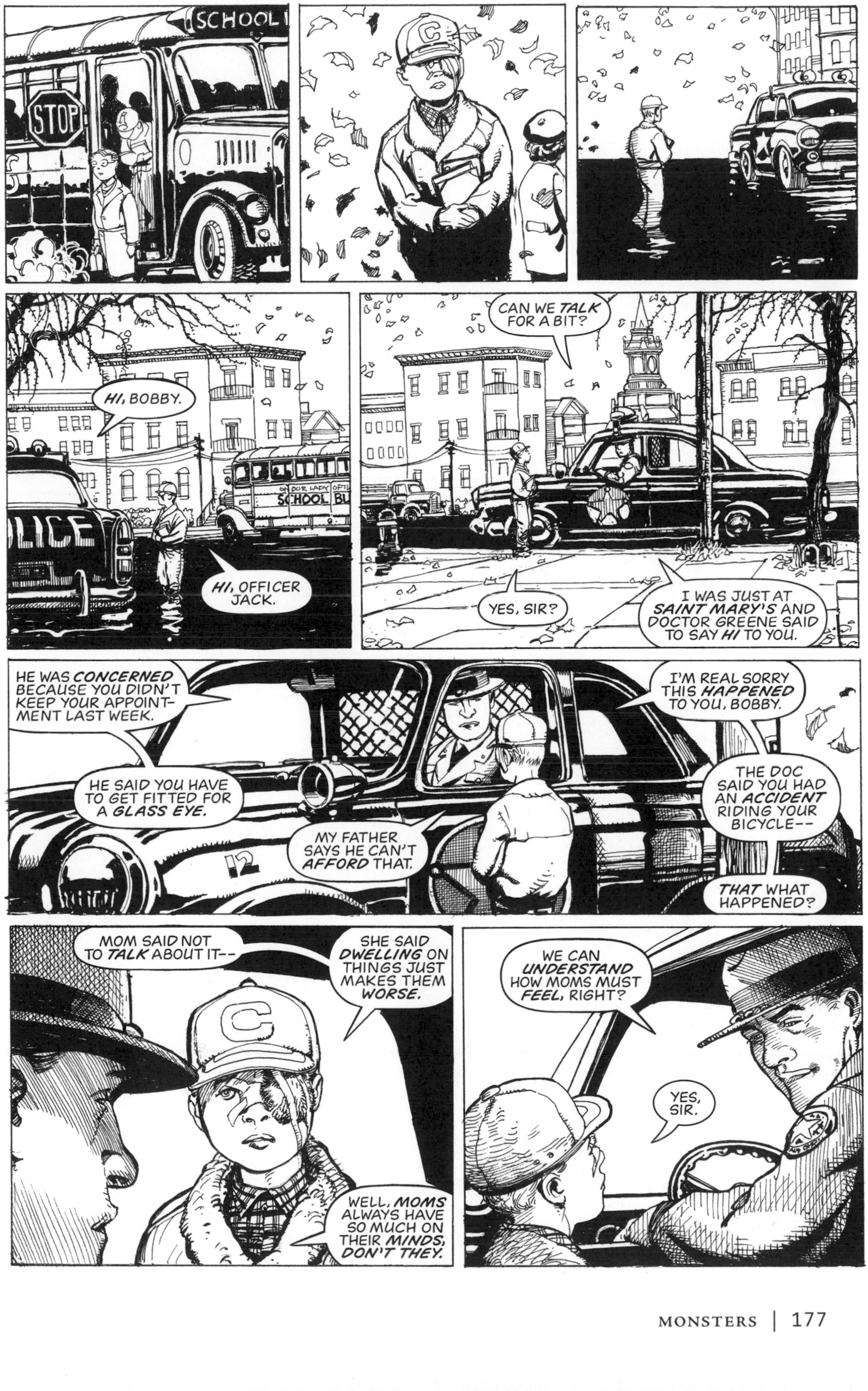
SCHOOL
STOP
HI, BOBBY.
HI, OFFICER JACK.
SCHOOL BU
CAN WE TALK FOR A BIT?
YES, SIR?
I WAS JUST AT SAINT MARY'S AND DOCTOR GREENE SAID TO SAY HI TO YOU.
HE WAS CONCERNED BECAUSE YOU DIDN'T KEEP YOUR APPOINT-MENT LAST WEEK.
HE SAID YOU HAVE TO GET FITTED FOR A GLASS EYE.
MY FATHER SAYS HE CAN'T AFFORD THAT.
I'M REAL SORRY THIS HAPPENED TO YOU, BOBBY.
THE DOC SAID YOU HAD AN ACCIDENT RIDING YOUR BICYCLE--
THAT WHAT HAPPENED?
MOM SAID NOT TO TALK ABOUT IT--
SHE SAID DWELLING ON THINGS JUST MAKES THEM WORSE.
WELL, MOMS ALWAYS HAVE SO MUCH ON THEIR MINDS, DON'T THEY.
WE CAN UNDERSTAND HOW MOMS MUST FEEL, RIGHT?
YES, SIR.

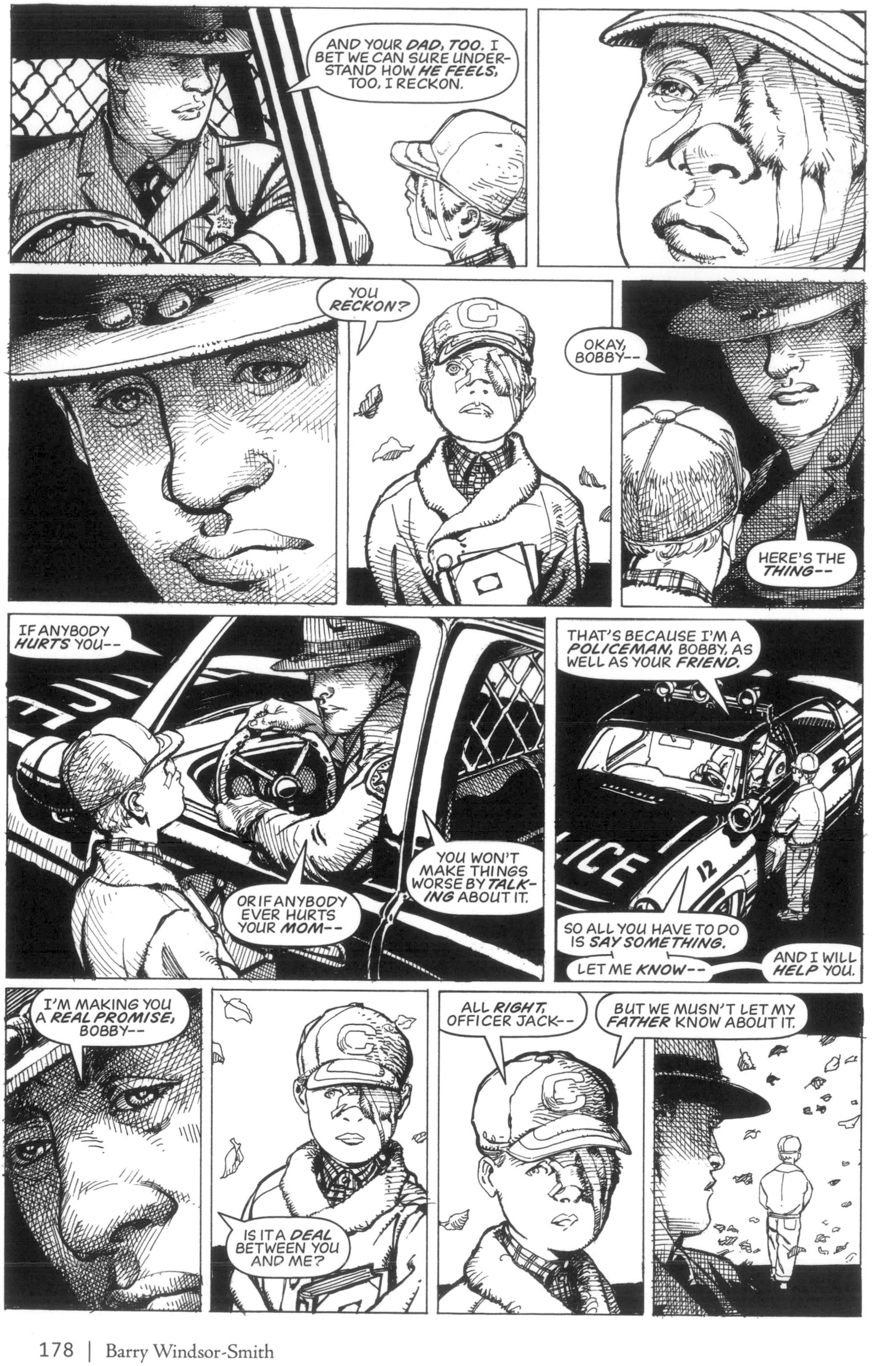

AND YOUR DAD, TOO. I BET WE CAN SURE UNDERSTAND HOW HE FEELS, TOO, I RECKON.
YOU RECKON?
OKAY, BOBBY--
HERE'S THE THING--
IF ANYBODY HURTS YOU--
OR IF ANYBODY EVER HURTS YOUR MOM--
YOU WON'T MAKE THINGS WORSE BY TALKING ABOUT IT.
THAT'S BECAUSE I'M A POLICEMAN, BOBBY, AS WELL AS YOUR FRIEND.
SO ALL YOU HAVE TO DO IS SAY SOMETHING.
LET ME KNOW--
AND I WILL HELP YOU.
POLICE
12
I'M MAKING YOU A REAL PROMISE, BOBBY--
IS IT A DEAL BETWEEN YOU AND ME?
ALL RIGHT, OFFICER JACK--
BUT WE MUSN'T LET MY FATHER KNOW ABOUT IT.

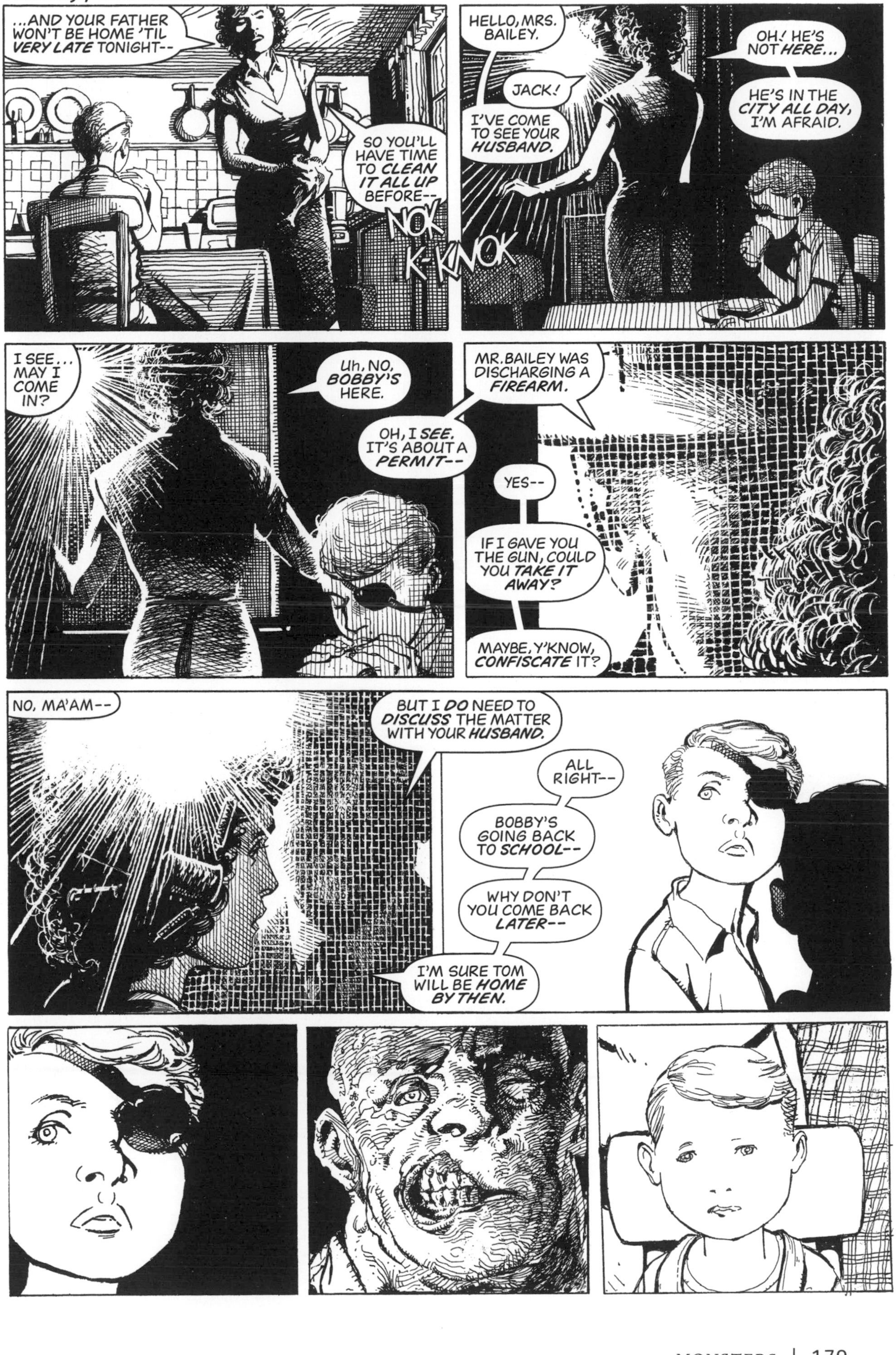
...AND YOUR FATHER WON'T BE HOME 'TIL VERY LATE TONIGHT--
SO YOU'LL HAVE TIME TO CLEAN IT ALL UP BEFORE--
NOK K-KNOK
HELLO, MRS. BAILEY.
JACK!
I'VE COME TO SEE YOUR HUSBAND.
OH! HE'S NOT HERE...
HE'S IN THE CITY ALL DAY, I'M AFRAID.
I SEE... MAY I COME IN?
Uh, NO, BOBBY'S HERE.
MR. BAILEY WAS DISCHARGING A FIREARM.
OH, I SEE. IT'S ABOUT A PERMIT--
YES--
IF I GAVE YOU THE GUN, COULD YOU TAKE IT AWAY?
MAYBE, Y'KNOW, CONFISCATE IT?
NO, MA'AM--
BUT I DO NEED TO DISCUSS THE MATTER WITH YOUR HUSBAND.
ALL RIGHT--
BOBBY'S GOING BACK TO SCHOOL--
WHY DON'T YOU COME BACK LATER--
I'M SURE TOM WILL BE HOME BY THEN.

1947 Two years earlier, the Bailey home Tuesday, December 2

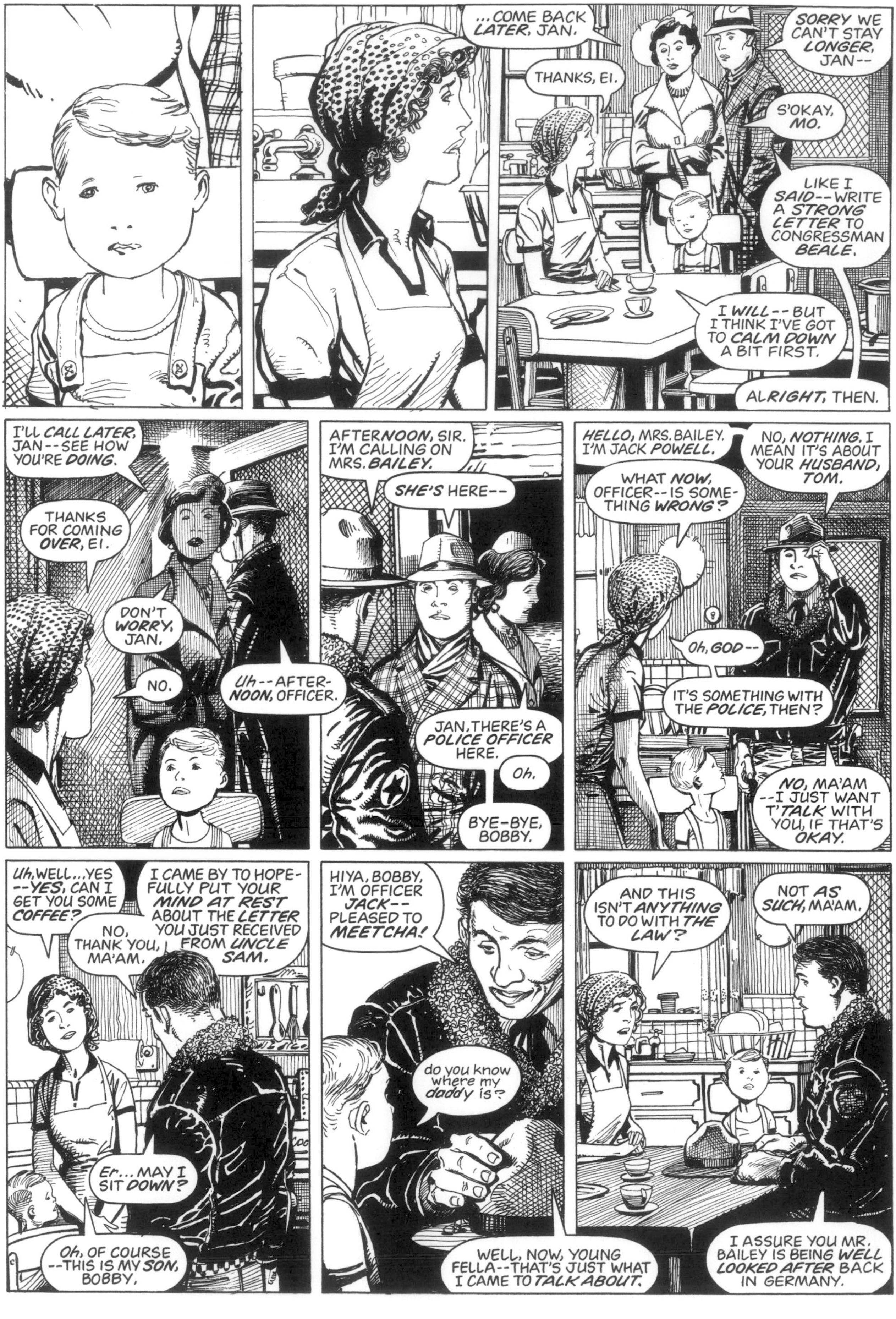

...COME BACK LATER, JAN.
THANKS, EI.
SORRY WE CAN'T STAY LONGER, JAN--
S'OKAY, MO.
LIKE I SAID--WRITE A STRONG LETTER TO CONGRESSMAN BEALE.
I WILL--BUT I THINK I'VE GOT TO CALM DOWN A BIT FIRST.
ALRIGHT, THEN.
I'LL CALL LATER, JAN--SEE HOW YOU'RE DOING.
THANKS FOR COMING OVER, EI.
DON'T WORRY, JAN.
NO.
Uh--AFTERNOON, OFFICER.
AFTERNOON, SIR. I'M CALLING ON MRS. BAILEY.
SHE'S HERE--
JAN, THERE'S A POLICE OFFICER HERE.
Oh.
BYE-BYE, BOBBY.
HELLO, MRS. BAILEY. I'M JACK POWELL.
WHAT NOW, OFFICER--IS SOMETHING WRONG?
NO, NOTHING. I MEAN IT'S ABOUT YOUR HUSBAND, TOM.
Oh, GOD--
IT'S SOMETHING WITH THE POLICE, THEN?
NO, MA'AM--I JUST WANT T'TALK WITH YOU, IF THAT'S OKAY.
Uh, WELL...YES--YES, CAN I GET YOU SOME COFFEE?
NO, THANK YOU, MA'AM.
I CAME BY TO HOPEFULLY PUT YOUR MIND AT REST ABOUT THE LETTER YOU JUST RECEIVED FROM UNCLE SAM.
Er...MAY I SIT DOWN?
Oh, OF COURSE--THIS IS MY SON, BOBBY.
HIYA, BOBBY, I'M OFFICER JACK--PLEASED TO MEETCHA!
do you know where my daddy is?
WELL, NOW, YOUNG FELLA--THAT'S JUST WHAT I CAME TO TALK ABOUT.
AND THIS ISN'T ANYTHING TO DO WITH THE LAW?
NOT AS SUCH, MA'AM.
I ASSURE YOU MR. BAILEY IS BEING WELL LOOKED AFTER BACK IN GERMANY.

Oh, HE'S STILL *THERE*?

YES, MA'AM.

THEY DIDN'T *SAY* THAT.

WHY CAN'T HE *COME HOME* LIKE EVERYBODY ELSE?

IT'S A BIT COMPLICATED...

FROM WHAT I'VE *LEARNED*, HE'S HELPING THE *GOVERNMENT* IN A SPECIAL--*Uh*--

WELL, IT'S A BIT OF A *EUPHEMISM*, BUT IT'S WHAT WE CALL *DEBRIEFING*.

ARE *YOU* WITH THE *GOVERNMENT*?

I'M SORRY-- WHAT *THEY* CALL DEBRIEFING.

SO, WHAT *IS THAT*?

WELL, IT'S LIKE *THIS*, MRS. BAILEY--

WHEN YOUR HUSBAND'S LEAD UNIT FOUND A *COMPOUND* IN GERMANY IN FORTY-FIVE--

THEY'VE...DISCOVERED SOME EVIDENCE OF THE SO-CALLED *WAR CRIMES* THAT'S BEEN IN THE NEWS.

Oh, GOD...

HE'S OKAY, BUT THE BRASS OVER THERE'RE *INVESTIGATING IT* AND THAT'S PRETTY MUCH *IT, REALLY.*

SO THE *UPSHOT* IS THAT MR. BAILEY WILL BE *AIDING* THE S.I.A.

WHAT'S S.I.A.?

SPECIAL INTELLIGENCE AGENCY.

I'VE NEVER *HEARD* OF THAT.

THEY--THEY'RE KINDA *PRIVATE* PEOPLE.

BUT THEY DON'T THINK TOM'S DONE *ANYTHING WRONG*, DO THEY?

I ASSURE YOU, MA'AM, HE'S BEING TREATED *REAL WELL*, DON'T WORRY ABOUT *THAT*.

WELL... WHEN WILL *THIS* BE OVER--?

HARD TO *SAY* JUST NOW, MRS. BAILEY-- THE GOVERNMENT, AS *USUAL*, IS SLOW BUT *THOROUGH*.

IS THERE AN ADDRESS WHERE I CAN *WRITE TO HIM*?

I'LL SEE WHAT THE POWERS THAT *BE* SAY ABOUT *LETTERS*, MRS. BAILEY.

I'LL LET YOU KNOW AS *SOON* AS I *DO*.

WILL YOU BE *BACK*?

YES, AND I PROMISE TO *PHONE AHEAD* NEXT TIME.

THANK YOU FOR YOUR PATIENCE, MRS. BAILEY--

LOOK AFTER YOUR MOM 'TIL YOUR *POP GETS HOME*, BOBBY.

yu-up!

December 8 1947

Along w/the bad news about Tom this afternoon I was visited by a police officer who had information about Tom's current situation in Germany.

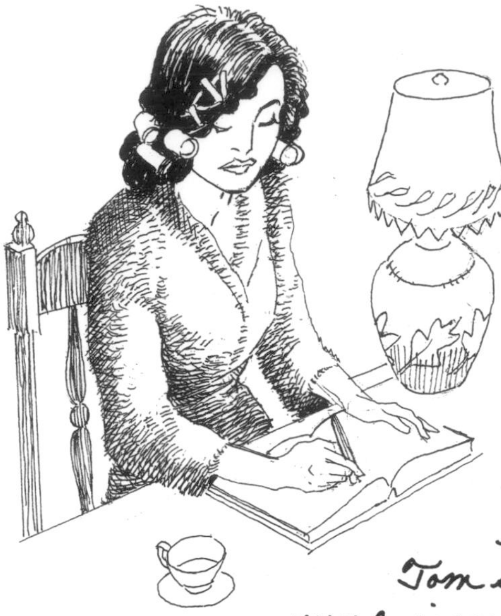

Police officer Powell seems to be working for government or the ~~us~~ army. He told me that Tom is helping out in some ~~im~~ investigation into German war crimes. I can't pretend to understand what that means but it's good to know that if Tom is to be held up it's at least for a good reason. I wonder if this is why Tom stopped writing, because his work is very secret.

Dec 13

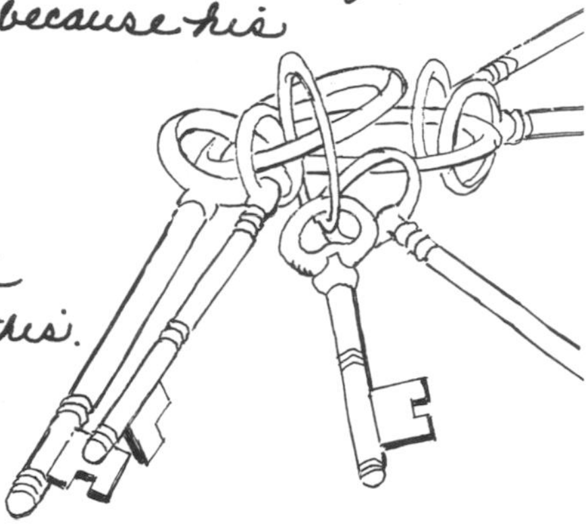

I've been waiting forever to hear from officer Powell again but he hasn't called or come by. I'm feeling very frustrated over this.

Bobby's sniffles are better now. Expected to snow again.

Dec 17 1947

It's christmas week and I've hardly any spirit for it, so to speak. I must try to go shopping at least ~~for~~ to get something for Bobby but I'm afraid to go out incase Officer Powell should phone or visit while I'm away.

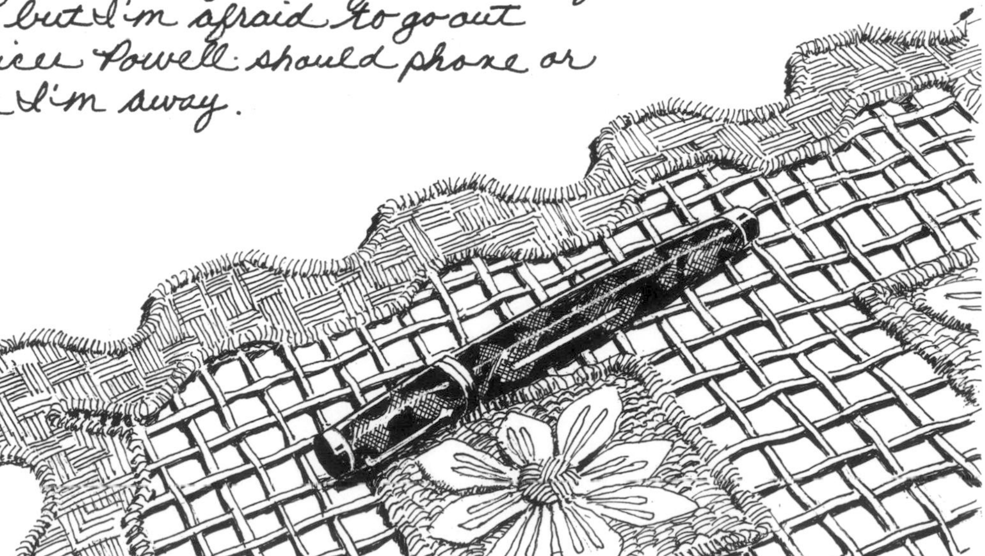

Providence Sheriff's Department Friday, December 19

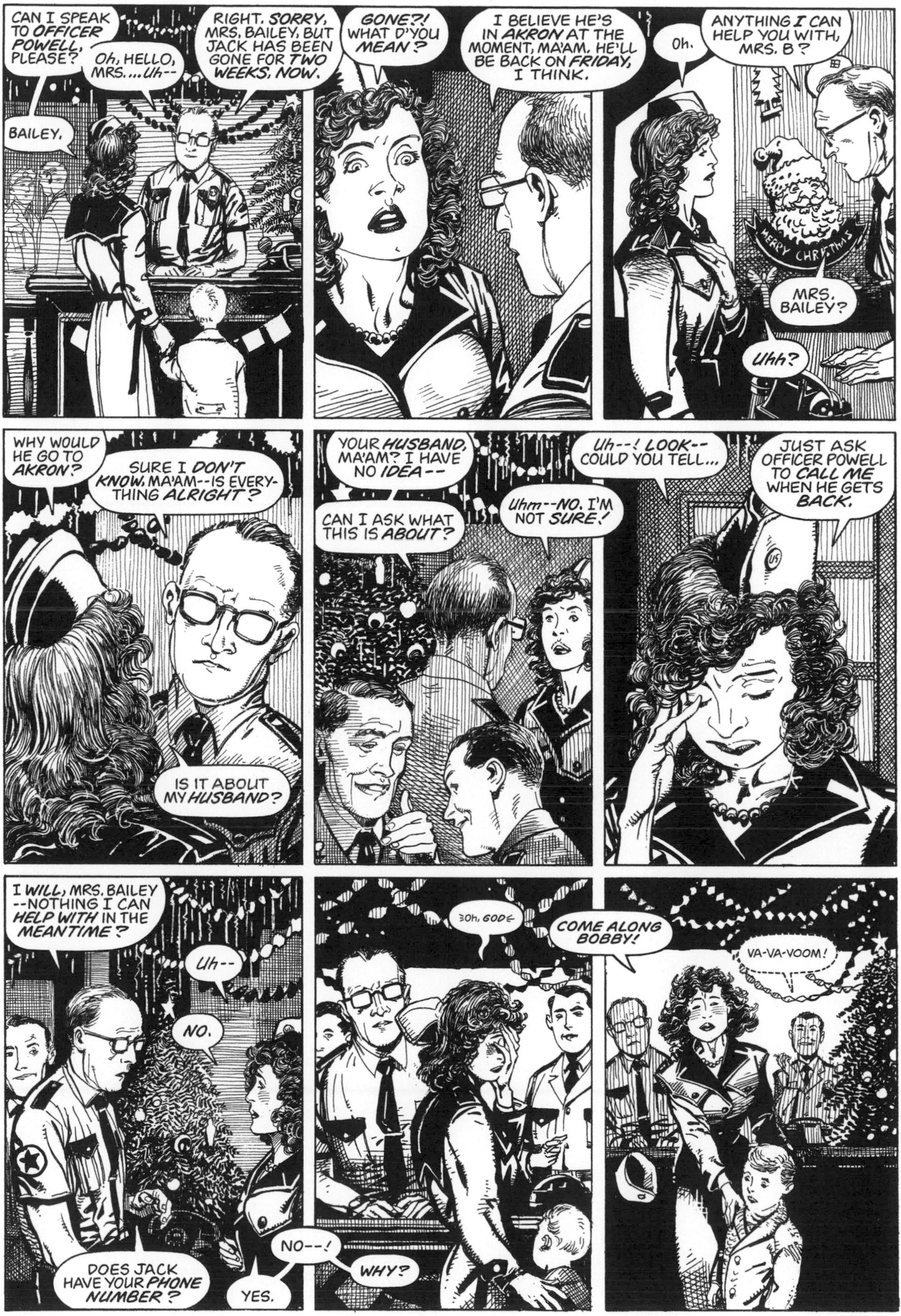

CAN I SPEAK TO OFFICER POWELL, PLEASE?
Oh, HELLO, MRS.... Uh--
BAILEY.
RIGHT. SORRY, MRS. BAILEY, BUT JACK HAS BEEN GONE FOR TWO WEEKS, NOW.
GONE?! WHAT D'YOU MEAN?
I BELIEVE HE'S IN AKRON AT THE MOMENT, MA'AM. HE'LL BE BACK ON FRIDAY, I THINK.
Oh.
ANYTHING I CAN HELP YOU WITH, MRS. B?
MERRY CHRISTMAS
MRS. BAILEY?
Uhh?
WHY WOULD HE GO TO AKRON?
SURE I DON'T KNOW, MA'AM--IS EVERY-THING ALRIGHT?
IS IT ABOUT MY HUSBAND?
YOUR HUSBAND, MA'AM? I HAVE NO IDEA--
CAN I ASK WHAT THIS IS ABOUT?
Uhm--NO. I'M NOT SURE!
Uh--! LOOK--COULD YOU TELL...
JUST ASK OFFICER POWELL TO CALL ME WHEN HE GETS BACK.
I WILL, MRS. BAILEY--NOTHING I CAN HELP WITH IN THE MEANTIME?
Uh--
NO.
DOES JACK HAVE YOUR PHONE NUMBER?
YES.
NO--!
WHY?
Oh, GOD
COME ALONG BOBBY!
VA-VA-VOOM!

1948 The Bailey home, Providence, Ohio Saturday, March 20

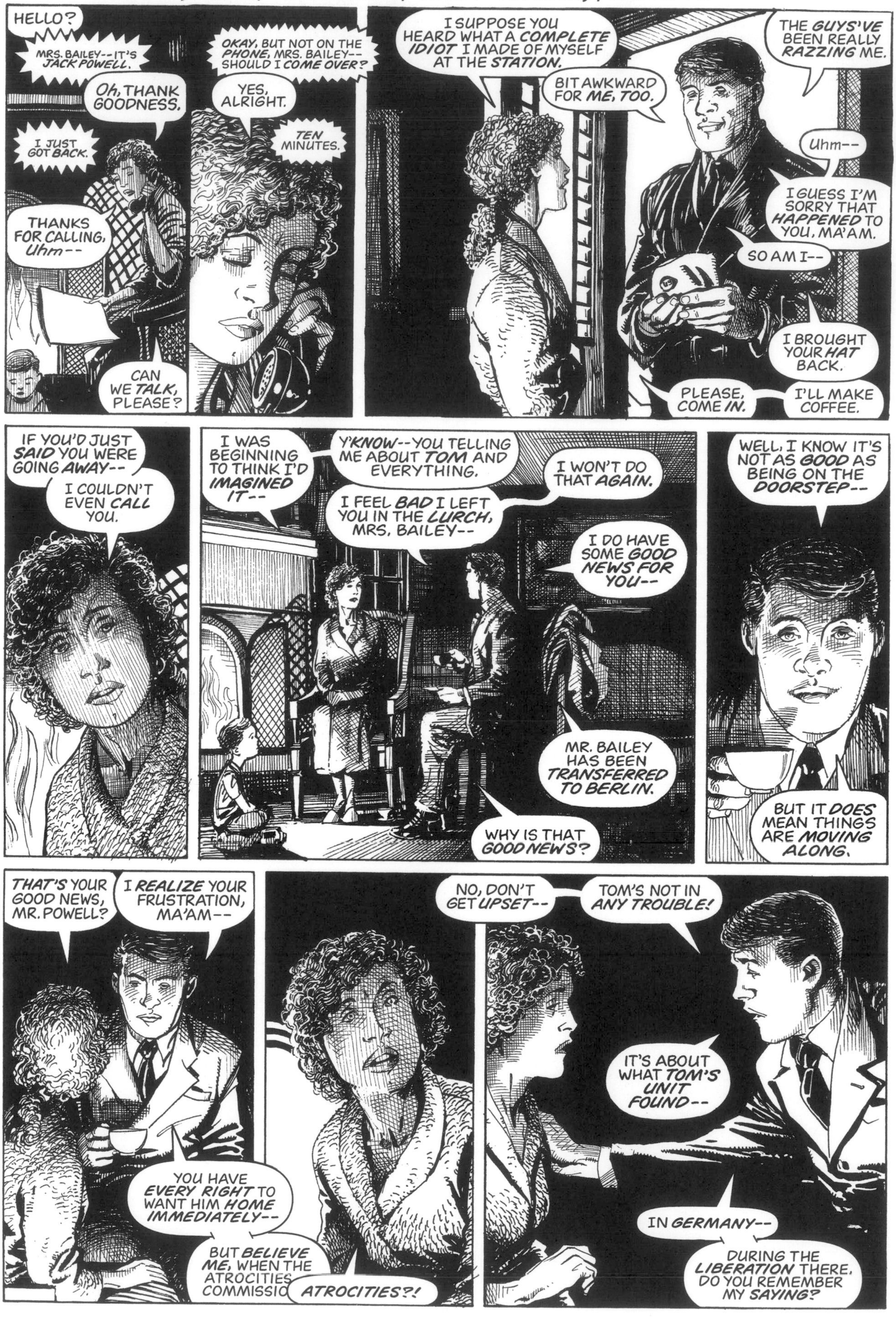

HELLO?
MRS. BAILEY--IT'S JACK POWELL.
Oh, THANK GOODNESS.
I JUST GOT BACK.
THANKS FOR CALLING, Uhm--
CAN WE TALK, PLEASE?
OKAY, BUT NOT ON THE PHONE, MRS. BAILEY--SHOULD I COME OVER?
YES, ALRIGHT.
TEN MINUTES.
I SUPPOSE YOU HEARD WHAT A COMPLETE IDIOT I MADE OF MYSELF AT THE STATION.
BIT AWKWARD FOR ME, TOO.
THE GUYS'VE BEEN REALLY RAZZING ME.
Uhm--
I GUESS I'M SORRY THAT HAPPENED TO YOU, MA'AM.
SO AM I--
I BROUGHT YOUR HAT BACK.
PLEASE, COME IN.
I'LL MAKE COFFEE.
IF YOU'D JUST SAID YOU WERE GOING AWAY--
I COULDN'T EVEN CALL YOU.
I WAS BEGINNING TO THINK I'D IMAGINED IT--
Y'KNOW--YOU TELLING ME ABOUT TOM AND EVERYTHING.
I WON'T DO THAT AGAIN.
I FEEL BAD I LEFT YOU IN THE LURCH, MRS. BAILEY--
I DO HAVE SOME GOOD NEWS FOR YOU--
MR. BAILEY HAS BEEN TRANSFERRED TO BERLIN.
WHY IS THAT GOOD NEWS?
WELL, I KNOW IT'S NOT AS GOOD AS BEING ON THE DOORSTEP--
BUT IT DOES MEAN THINGS ARE MOVING ALONG.
THAT'S YOUR GOOD NEWS, MR. POWELL?
I REALIZE YOUR FRUSTRATION, MA'AM--
YOU HAVE EVERY RIGHT TO WANT HIM HOME IMMEDIATELY--
BUT BELIEVE ME, WHEN THE ATROCITIES COMMISSIO
ATROCITIES?!
NO, DON'T GET UPSET--
TOM'S NOT IN ANY TROUBLE!
IT'S ABOUT WHAT TOM'S UNIT FOUND--
IN GERMANY--
DURING THE LIBERATION THERE, DO YOU REMEMBER MY SAYING?

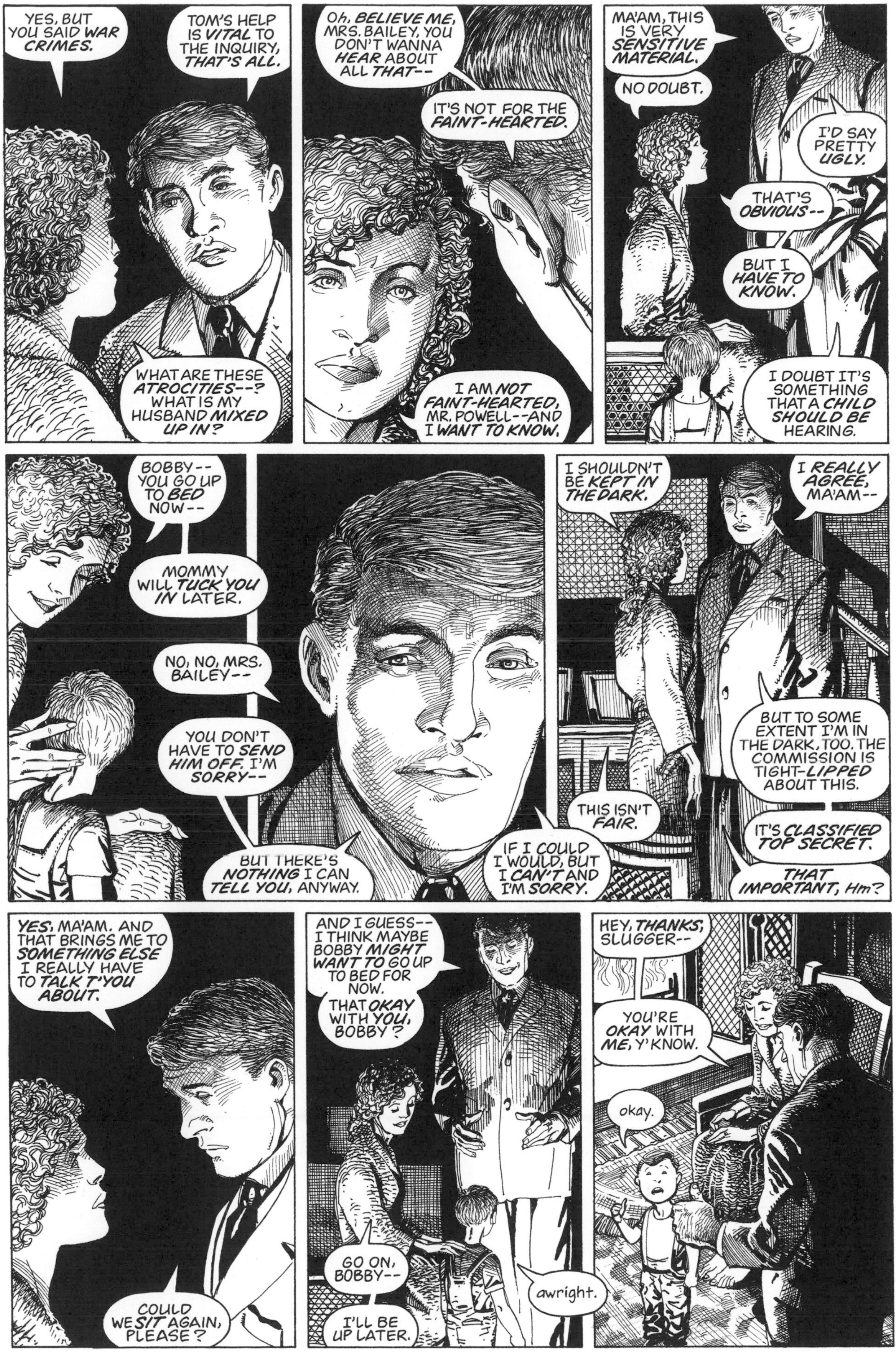
YES, BUT YOU SAID WAR CRIMES.
TOM'S HELP IS VITAL TO THE INQUIRY, THAT'S ALL.
WHAT ARE THESE ATROCITIES--? WHAT IS MY HUSBAND MIXED UP IN?
Oh, BELIEVE ME, MRS. BAILEY, YOU DON'T WANNA HEAR ABOUT ALL THAT--
IT'S NOT FOR THE FAINT-HEARTED.
I AM NOT FAINT-HEARTED, MR. POWELL--AND I WANT TO KNOW.
MA'AM, THIS IS VERY SENSITIVE MATERIAL.
NO DOUBT.
I'D SAY PRETTY UGLY.
THAT'S OBVIOUS--
BUT I HAVE TO KNOW.
I DOUBT IT'S SOMETHING THAT A CHILD SHOULD BE HEARING.
BOBBY-- YOU GO UP TO BED NOW--
MOMMY WILL TUCK YOU IN LATER.
NO, NO, MRS. BAILEY--
YOU DON'T HAVE TO SEND HIM OFF. I'M SORRY--
BUT THERE'S NOTHING I CAN TELL YOU, ANYWAY.
IF I COULD I WOULD, BUT I CAN'T AND I'M SORRY.
I SHOULDN'T BE KEPT IN THE DARK.
I REALLY AGREE, MA'AM--
BUT TO SOME EXTENT I'M IN THE DARK, TOO. THE COMMISSION IS TIGHT-LIPPED ABOUT THIS.
THIS ISN'T FAIR.
IT'S CLASSIFIED TOP SECRET.
THAT IMPORTANT, Hm?
YES, MA'AM. AND THAT BRINGS ME TO SOMETHING ELSE I REALLY HAVE TO TALK T'YOU ABOUT.
COULD WE SIT AGAIN, PLEASE?
AND I GUESS-- I THINK MAYBE BOBBY MIGHT WANT TO GO UP TO BED FOR NOW.
THAT OKAY WITH YOU, BOBBY?
GO ON, BOBBY--
I'LL BE UP LATER.
awright.
HEY, THANKS, SLUGGER--
YOU'RE OKAY WITH ME, Y'KNOW.
okay.

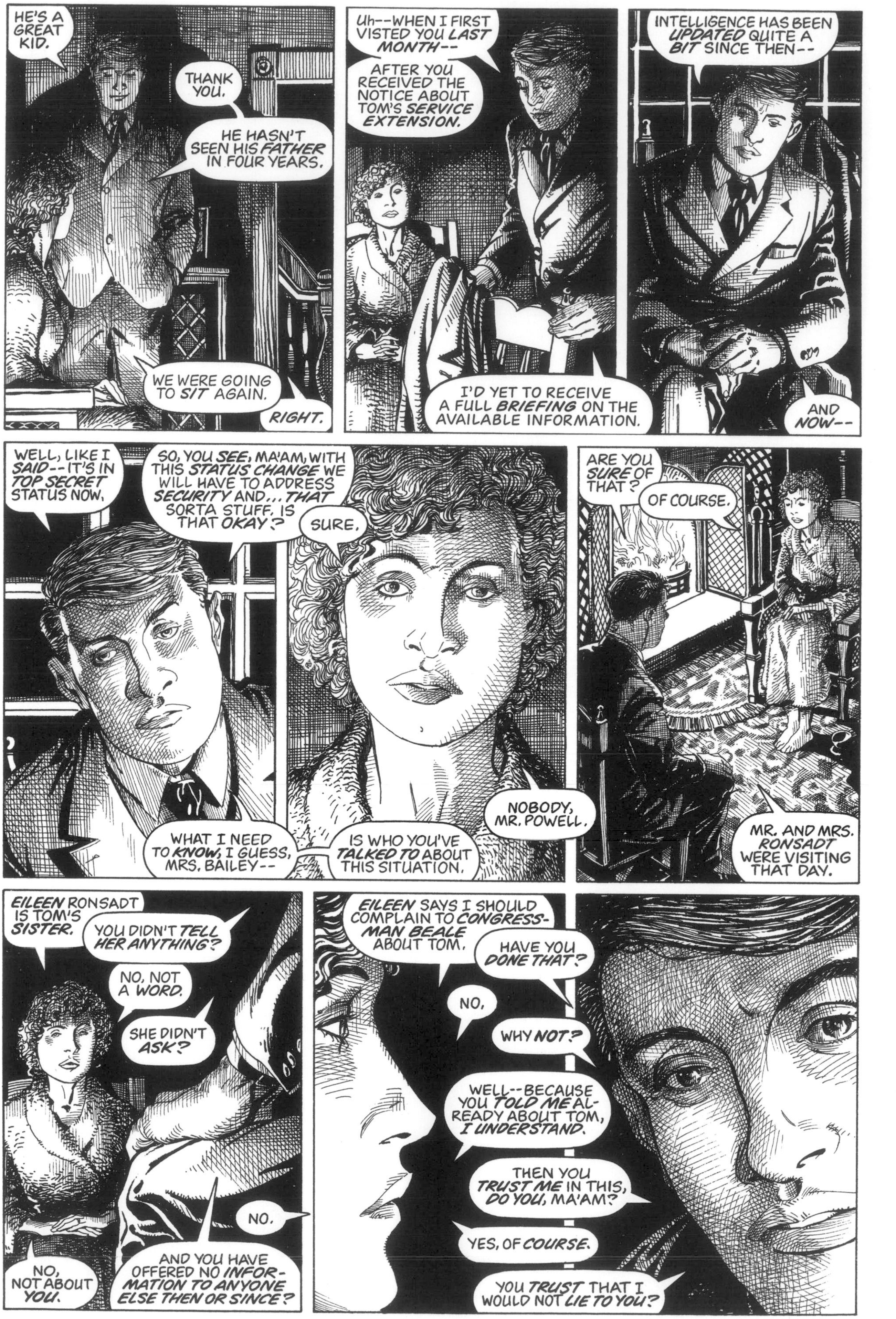
HE'S A GREAT KID.
THANK YOU.
HE HASN'T SEEN HIS FATHER IN FOUR YEARS.
WE WERE GOING TO SIT AGAIN.
RIGHT.
Uh--WHEN I FIRST VISTED YOU LAST MONTH--
AFTER YOU RECEIVED THE NOTICE ABOUT TOM'S SERVICE EXTENSION.
I'D YET TO RECEIVE A FULL BRIEFING ON THE AVAILABLE INFORMATION.
INTELLIGENCE HAS BEEN UPDATED QUITE A BIT SINCE THEN--
AND NOW--
WELL, LIKE I SAID--IT'S IN TOP SECRET STATUS NOW,
SO, YOU SEE, MA'AM, WITH THIS STATUS CHANGE WE WILL HAVE TO ADDRESS SECURITY AND...THAT SORTA STUFF. IS THAT OKAY?
SURE.
WHAT I NEED TO KNOW, I GUESS, MRS. BAILEY--
IS WHO YOU'VE TALKED TO ABOUT THIS SITUATION.
NOBODY, MR. POWELL.
ARE YOU SURE OF THAT?
OF COURSE.
MR. AND MRS. RONSADT WERE VISITING THAT DAY.
EILEEN RONSADT IS TOM'S SISTER.
YOU DIDN'T TELL HER ANYTHING?
NO, NOT A WORD.
SHE DIDN'T ASK?
NO, NOT ABOUT YOU.
AND YOU HAVE OFFERED NO INFORMATION TO ANYONE ELSE THEN OR SINCE?
NO.
EILEEN SAYS I SHOULD COMPLAIN TO CONGRESSMAN BEALE ABOUT TOM.
HAVE YOU DONE THAT?
NO.
WHY NOT?
WELL--BECAUSE YOU TOLD ME ALREADY ABOUT TOM, I UNDERSTAND.
THEN YOU TRUST ME IN THIS, DO YOU, MA'AM?
YES, OF COURSE.
YOU TRUST THAT I WOULD NOT LIE TO YOU?

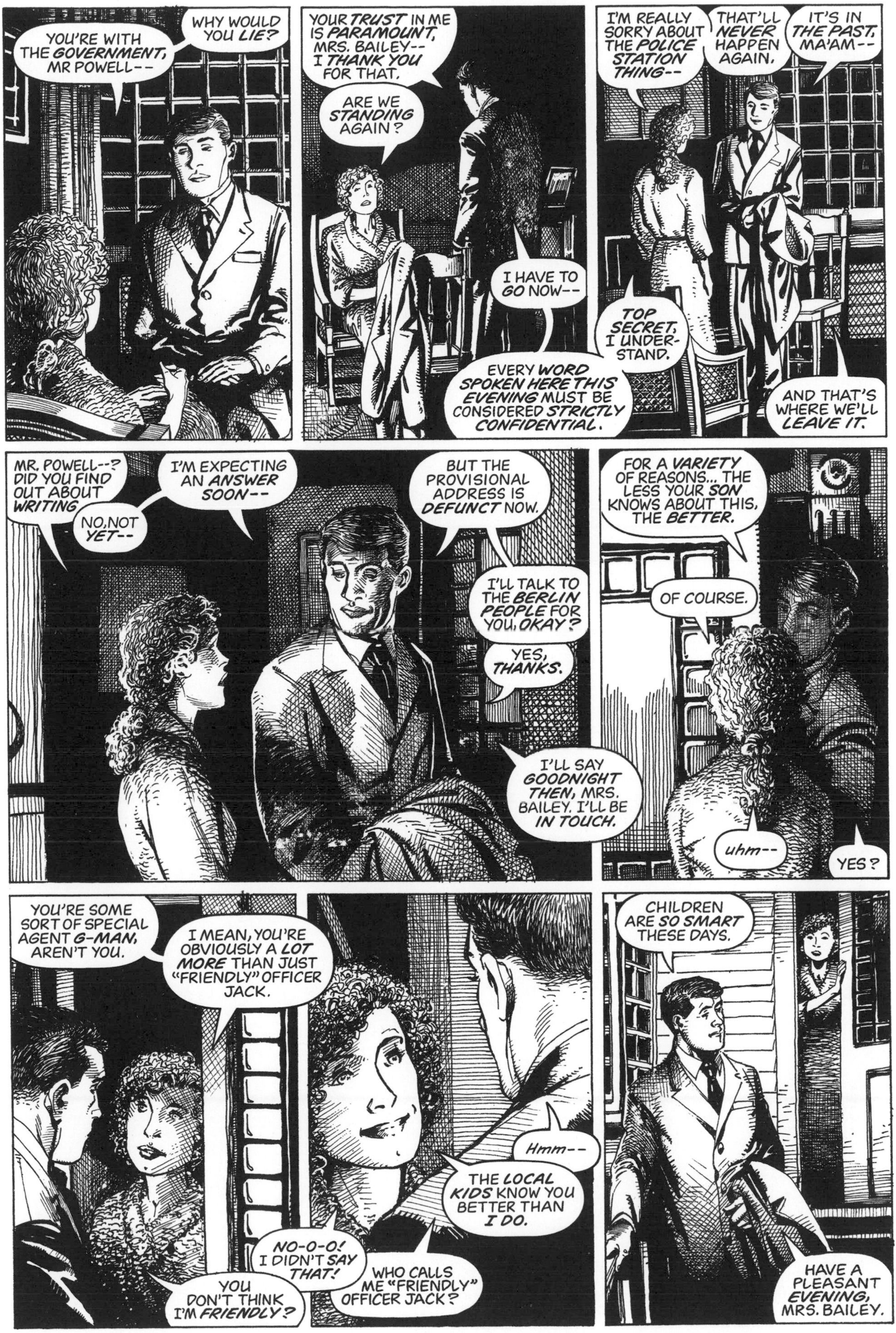
YOU'RE WITH THE GOVERNMENT, MR POWELL--
WHY WOULD YOU LIE?
YOUR TRUST IN ME IS PARAMOUNT, MRS. BAILEY-- I THANK YOU FOR THAT.
ARE WE STANDING AGAIN?
I HAVE TO GO NOW--
EVERY WORD SPOKEN HERE THIS EVENING MUST BE CONSIDERED STRICTLY CONFIDENTIAL.
TOP SECRET, I UNDERSTAND.
I'M REALLY SORRY ABOUT THE POLICE STATION THING--
THAT'LL NEVER HAPPEN AGAIN.
IT'S IN THE PAST, MA'AM--
AND THAT'S WHERE WE'LL LEAVE IT.
MR. POWELL--? DID YOU FIND OUT ABOUT WRITING
NO, NOT YET--
I'M EXPECTING AN ANSWER SOON--
BUT THE PROVISIONAL ADDRESS IS DEFUNCT NOW.
I'LL TALK TO THE BERLIN PEOPLE FOR YOU, OKAY?
YES, THANKS.
I'LL SAY GOODNIGHT THEN, MRS. BAILEY. I'LL BE IN TOUCH.
FOR A VARIETY OF REASONS... THE LESS YOUR SON KNOWS ABOUT THIS, THE BETTER.
OF COURSE.
uhm--
YES?
YOU'RE SOME SORT OF SPECIAL AGENT G-MAN, AREN'T YOU.
I MEAN, YOU'RE OBVIOUSLY A LOT MORE THAN JUST "FRIENDLY" OFFICER JACK.
YOU DON'T THINK I'M FRIENDLY?
NO-O-O! I DIDN'T SAY THAT!
WHO CALLS ME "FRIENDLY" OFFICER JACK?
Hmm--
THE LOCAL KIDS KNOW YOU BETTER THAN I DO.
CHILDREN ARE SO SMART THESE DAYS.
HAVE A PLEASANT EVENING, MRS. BAILEY.

Saturday, March 20

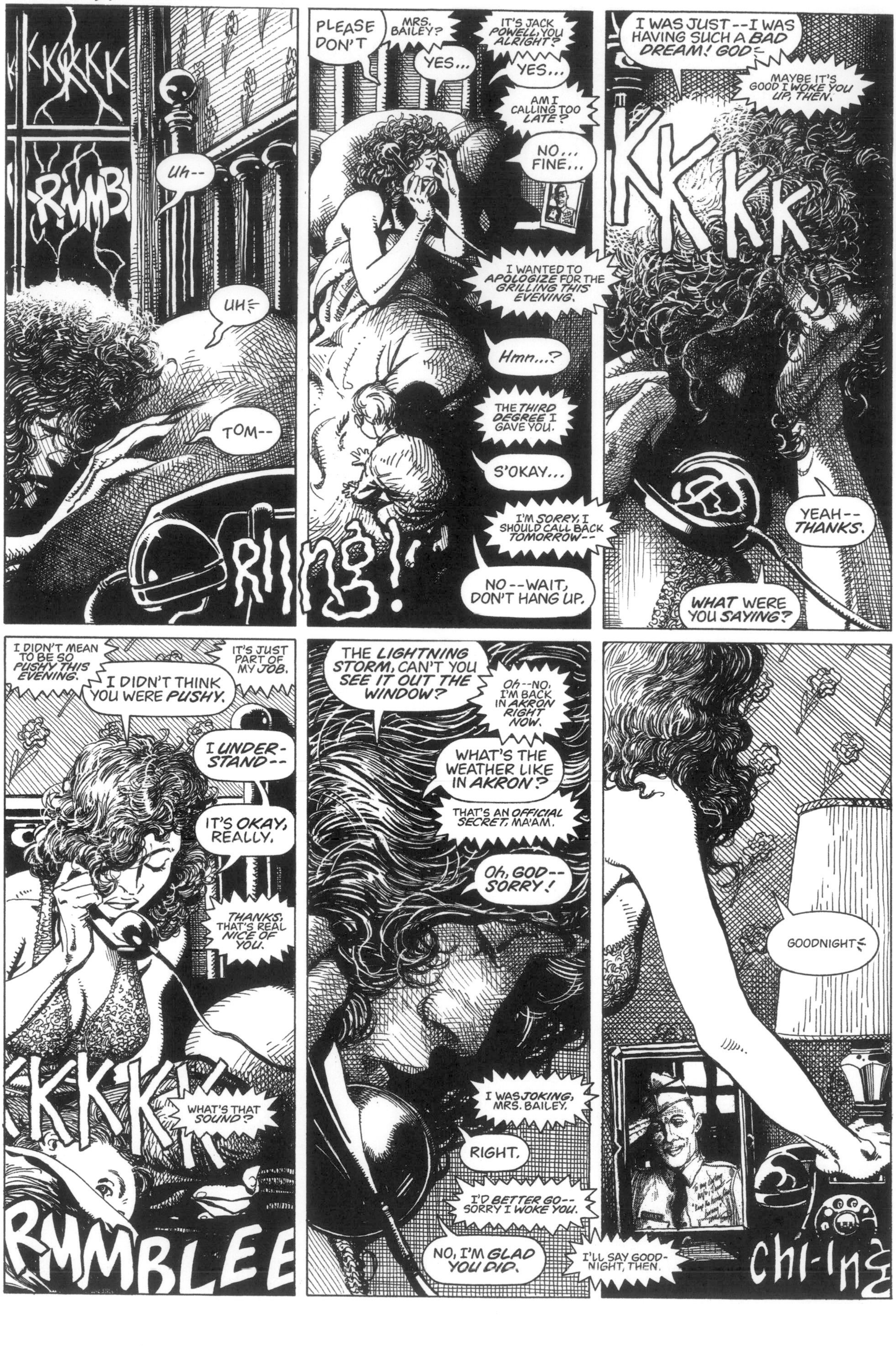
Uh--
UH...
TOM--
RIIING!
PLEASE DON'T
MRS. BAILEY?
YES...
IT'S JACK POWELL, YOU ALRIGHT?
YES...
AM I CALLING TOO LATE?
NO... FINE...
I WANTED TO APOLOGIZE FOR THE GRILLING THIS EVENING.
Hmn...?
THE THIRD DEGREE I GAVE YOU.
S'OKAY...
I'M SORRY, I SHOULD CALL BACK TOMORROW--
NO--WAIT, DON'T HANG UP.
I WAS JUST--I WAS HAVING SUCH A BAD DREAM! GOD...
MAYBE IT'S GOOD I WOKE YOU UP, THEN.
YEAH--THANKS.
WHAT WERE YOU SAYING?
I DIDN'T MEAN TO BE SO PUSHY THIS EVENING.
IT'S JUST PART OF MY JOB.
I DIDN'T THINK YOU WERE PUSHY.
I UNDERSTAND--
IT'S OKAY, REALLY.
THANKS, THAT'S REAL NICE OF YOU.
WHAT'S THAT SOUND?
RMMBLEE
THE LIGHTNING STORM. CAN'T YOU SEE IT OUT THE WINDOW?
Oh--NO, I'M BACK IN AKRON RIGHT NOW.
WHAT'S THE WEATHER LIKE IN AKRON?
THAT'S AN OFFICIAL SECRET, MA'AM.
Oh, GOD--SORRY!
I WAS JOKING, MRS. BAILEY.
RIGHT.
I'D BETTER GO--SORRY I WOKE YOU.
NO, I'M GLAD YOU DID.
I'LL SAY GOOD-NIGHT, THEN.
GOODNIGHT...

Sunday, April 4

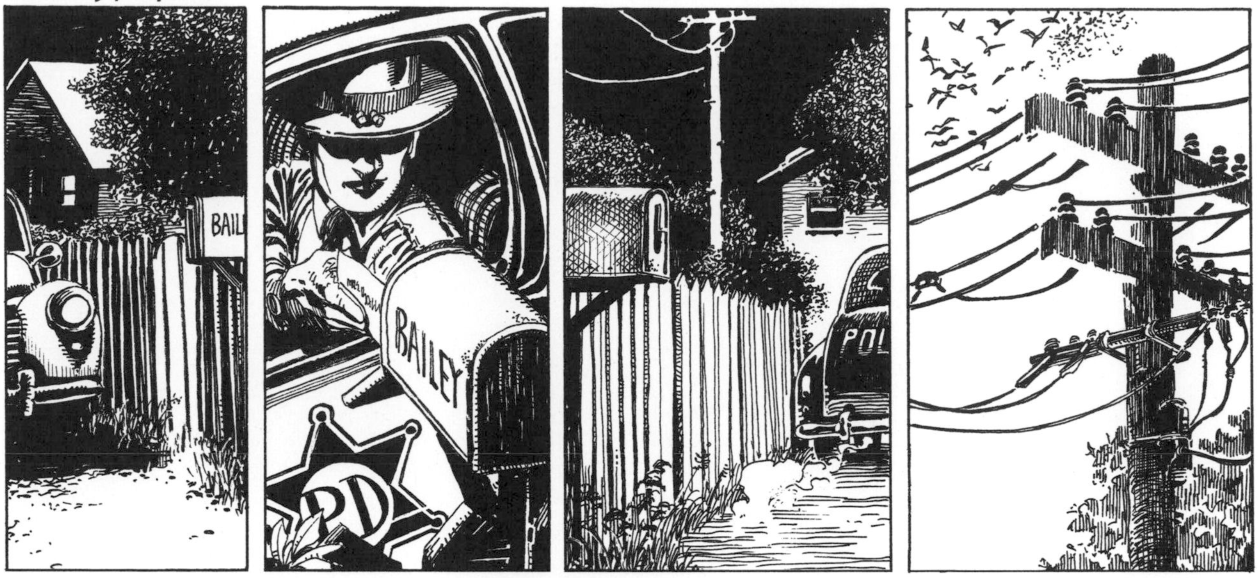
BAILEY
BAILEY
PD
POL

Monday, April 5

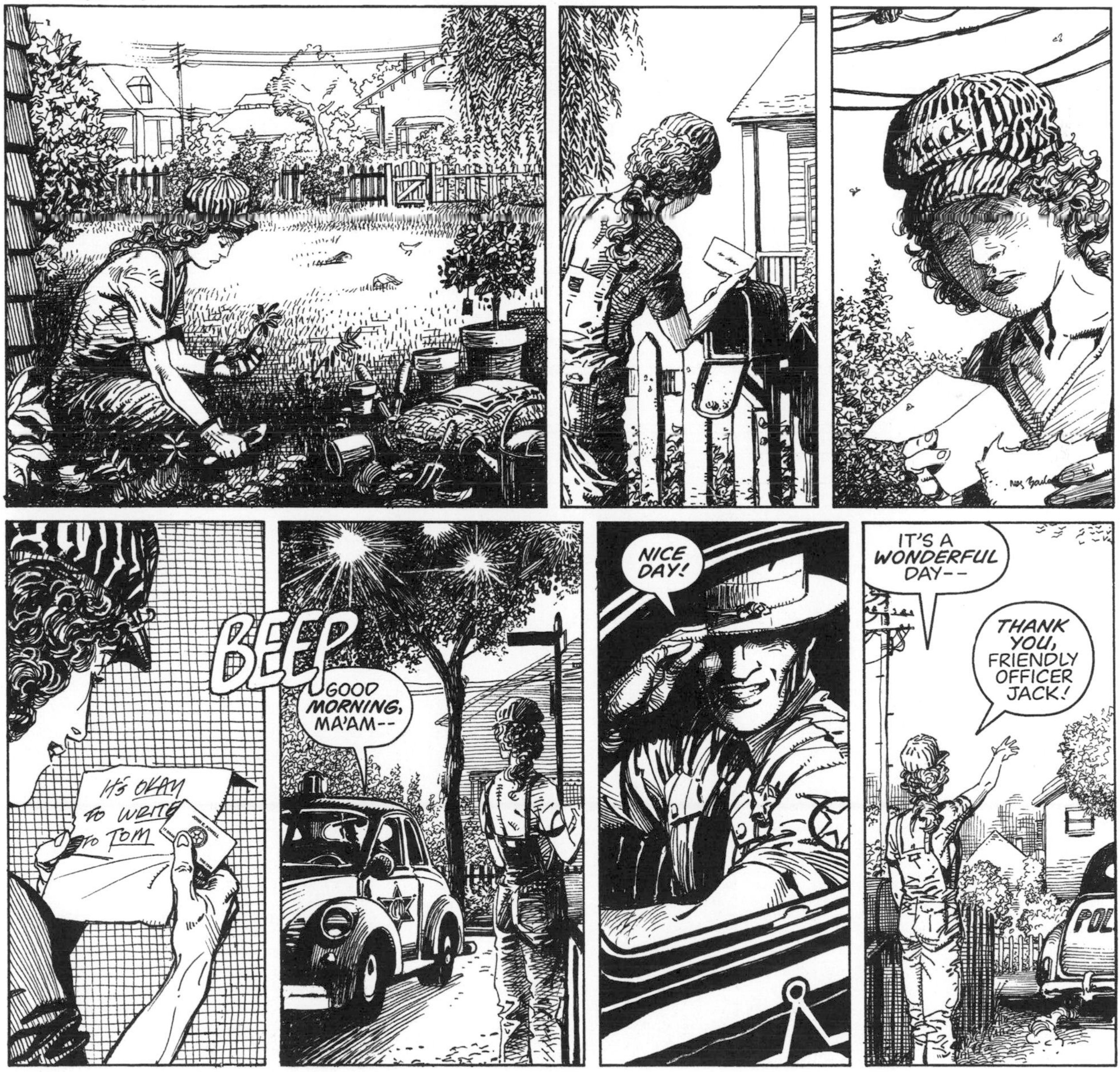
IT'S OKAY TO WRITE TO TOM
BEEP
GOOD MORNING, MA'AM--
NICE DAY!
IT'S A WONDERFUL DAY--
THANK YOU, FRIENDLY OFFICER JACK!
POL

WHAT DO YOU *MEAN*?

WELL, IF *I* DON'T-- SOMEBODY AT THE *DEPARTMENT* WILL *DO* IT.

I HOPE YOU REALIZE, MRS. BAILEY, THAT I'M ONLY *DOING MY JOB*, HERE.

YES.

THEN MAY I *ASK*... JUST HOW PRIVATE *IS IT*?

QUITE A *BIT*, I GUESS.

MAYBE A *TEENSY* MORE.

BUT-- IT'S FOR *TOM.*

YES, BUT

IT'S *PRIVATE*--

I DIDN'T THINK THAT ANYBODY BUT MY *HUSBAND* WOULD BE *READING* IT.

ALL RIGHT, *I UNDERSTAND.* THEN I'LL *HAVE* TO SKIP MY *INPUT* ON THIS.

BUT AS A *COURTESY*, I WILL BE SURE TO *DELIVER IT* TO THE DEPARTMENT *MYSELF.*

THE CENSORS THERE ARE *DISCREET* BY NATURE, I *ASSURE* YOU.

I DON'T FEEL *AT ALL COMFORTABLE* WITH THIS. I MEAN--

DOES THIS *HAVE TO* HAPPEN?

IT CAN HAPPEN *NO OTHER WAY*, MA'AM.

BUT I'LL BE SO *EMBARRASSED!*

HERE'S AN *IDEA*-- WHY DON'T YOU JUST WRITE *ANOTHER LETTER?*

Y'KNOW, SOME OF THE

LEAVE *OUT* SOME OF THE...

GIVE!

SORRY FOR *GRABBING.*

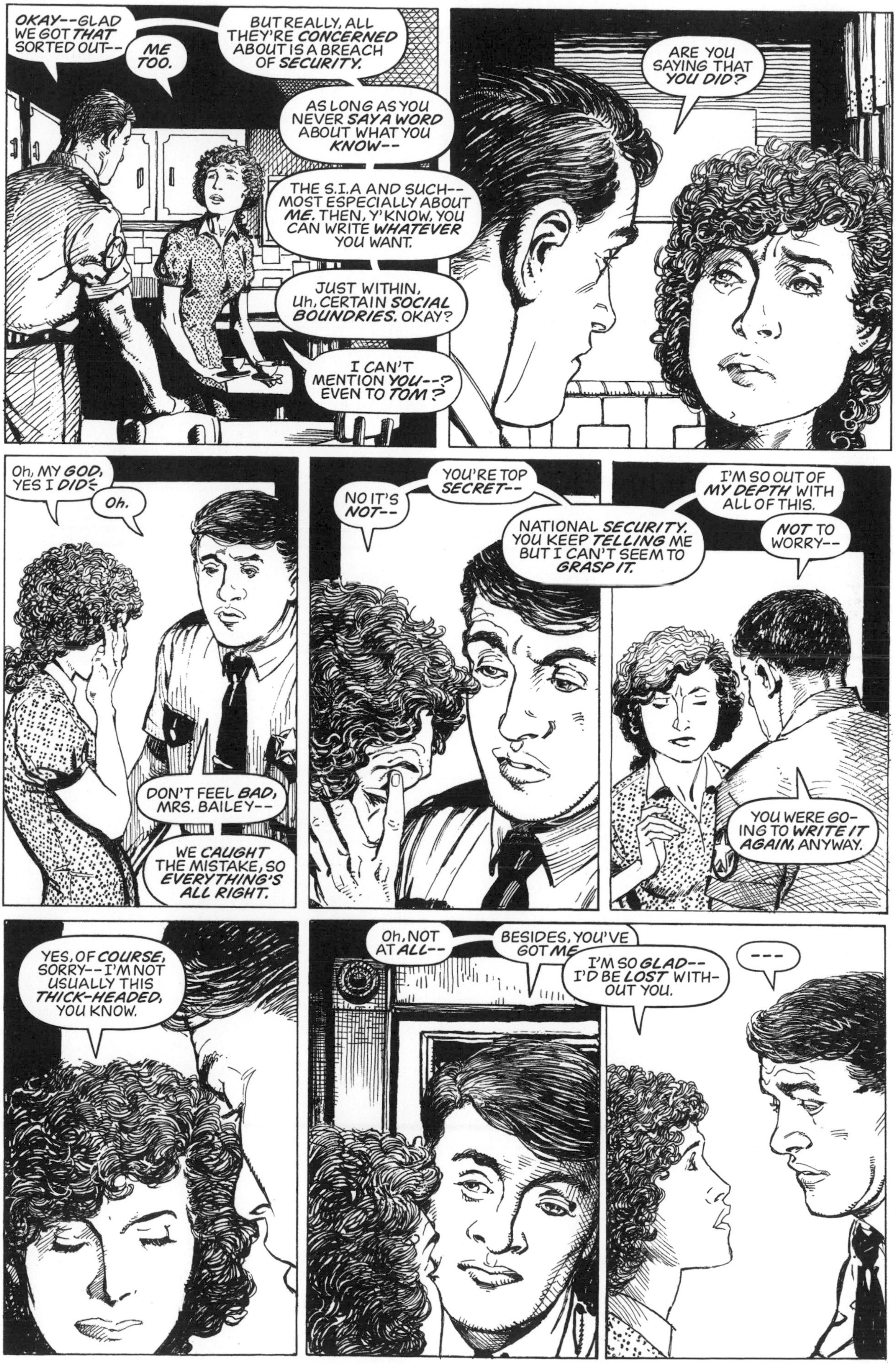
OKAY--GLAD WE GOT THAT SORTED OUT--
ME TOO.
BUT REALLY, ALL THEY'RE CONCERNED ABOUT IS A BREACH OF SECURITY.
AS LONG AS YOU NEVER SAY A WORD ABOUT WHAT YOU KNOW--
THE S.I.A AND SUCH--MOST ESPECIALLY ABOUT ME. THEN, Y'KNOW, YOU CAN WRITE WHATEVER YOU WANT.
JUST WITHIN, Uh, CERTAIN SOCIAL BOUNDRIES. OKAY?
I CAN'T MENTION YOU--? EVEN TO TOM?
ARE YOU SAYING THAT YOU DID?
Oh, MY GOD, YES I DID<
Oh.
DON'T FEEL BAD, MRS. BAILEY--
WE CAUGHT THE MISTAKE, SO EVERYTHING'S ALL RIGHT.
NO IT'S NOT--
YOU'RE TOP SECRET--
NATIONAL SECURITY. YOU KEEP TELLING ME BUT I CAN'T SEEM TO GRASP IT.
I'M SO OUT OF MY DEPTH WITH ALL OF THIS.
NOT TO WORRY--
YOU WERE GOING TO WRITE IT AGAIN, ANYWAY.
YES, OF COURSE, SORRY--I'M NOT USUALLY THIS THICK-HEADED, YOU KNOW.
Oh, NOT AT ALL--
BESIDES, YOU'VE GOT ME.
I'M SO GLAD--I'D BE LOST WITHOUT YOU.

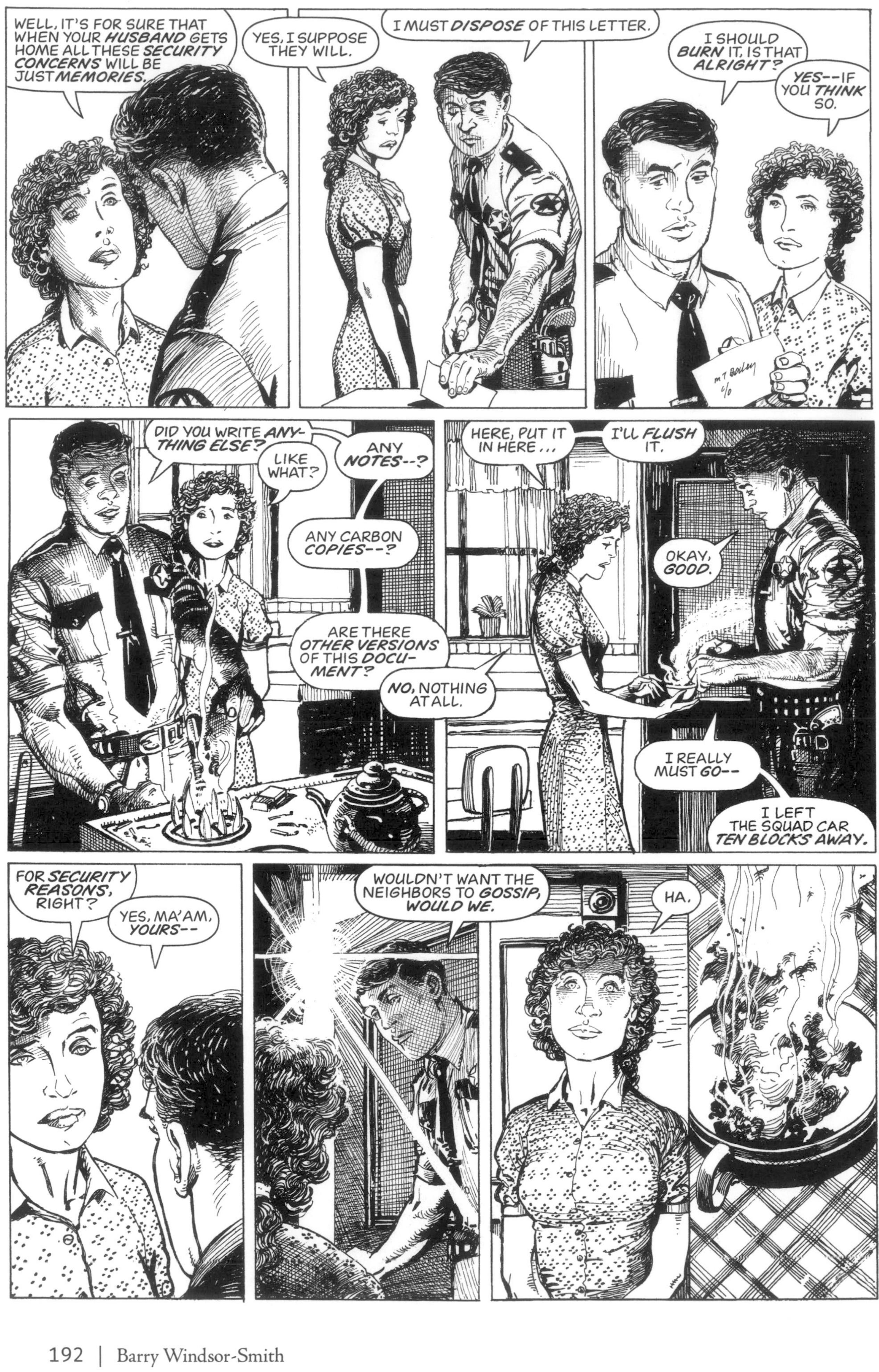
WELL, IT'S FOR SURE THAT WHEN YOUR HUSBAND GETS HOME ALL THESE SECURITY CONCERNS WILL BE JUST MEMORIES.
YES, I SUPPOSE THEY WILL.
I MUST DISPOSE OF THIS LETTER.
I SHOULD BURN IT, IS THAT ALRIGHT?
YES--IF YOU THINK SO.
DID YOU WRITE ANYTHING ELSE?
LIKE WHAT?
ANY NOTES--?
ANY CARBON COPIES--?
ARE THERE OTHER VERSIONS OF THIS DOCUMENT?
NO, NOTHING AT ALL.
HERE, PUT IT IN HERE...
I'LL FLUSH IT.
OKAY, GOOD.
I REALLY MUST GO--
I LEFT THE SQUAD CAR TEN BLOCKS AWAY.
FOR SECURITY REASONS, RIGHT?
YES, MA'AM, YOURS--
WOULDN'T WANT THE NEIGHBORS TO GOSSIP, WOULD WE.
HA.

1948 Tuesday, June 1

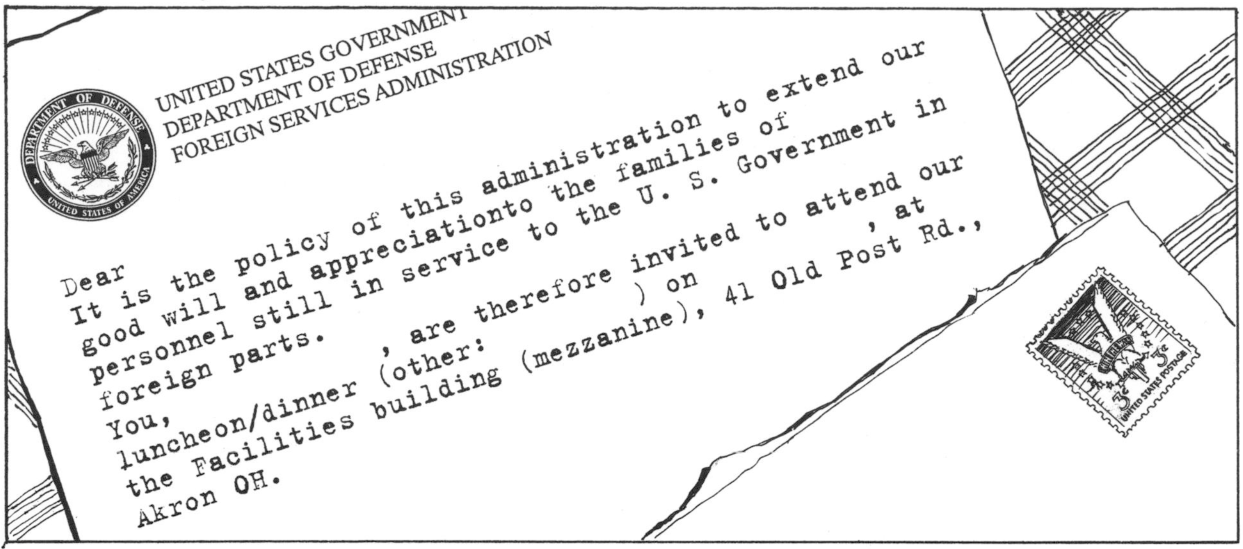
UNITED STATES GOVERNMENT
DEPARTMENT OF DEFENSE
FOREIGN SERVICES ADMINISTRATION
DEPARTMENT OF DEFENSE
UNITED STATES OF AMERICA
Dear
It is the policy of this administration to extend our good will and appreciationto the families of personnel still in service to the U. S. Government in foreign parts.
You, , are therefore invited to attend our luncheon/dinner (other:) on , at the Facilities building (mezzanine), 41 Old Post Rd., Akron OH.

St. Claire bus station Saturday, June 5

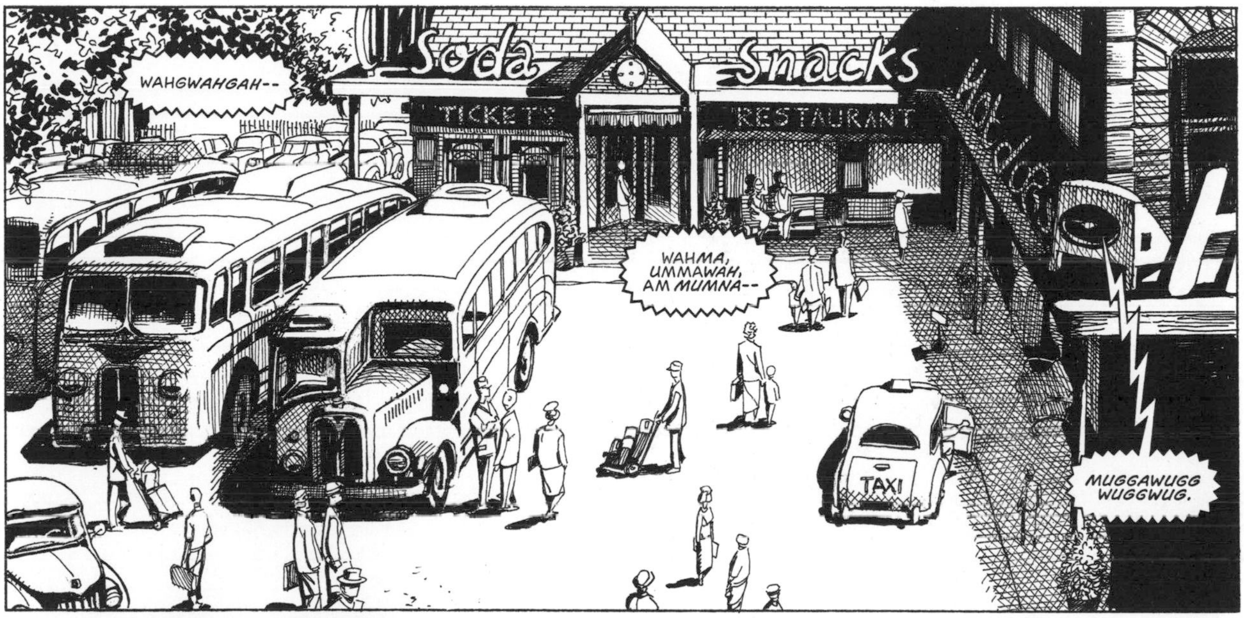
Soda
Snacks
TICKETS
RESTAURANT
WAHGWAHGAH--
WAHMA, UMMAWAH, AM MUMNA--
TAXI
MUGGAWUGG WUGGWUG.

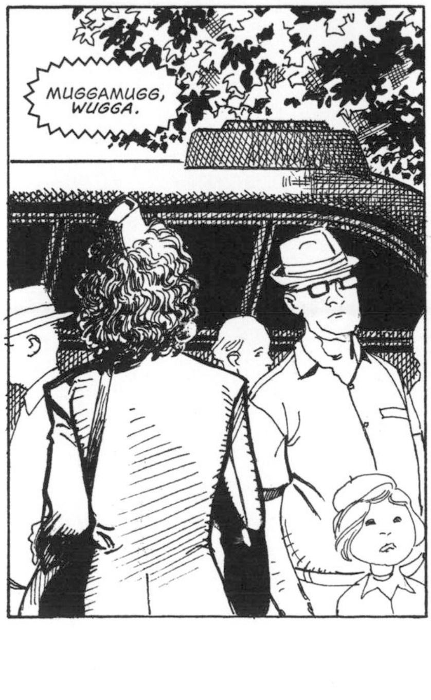
MUGGAMUGG, WUGGA.

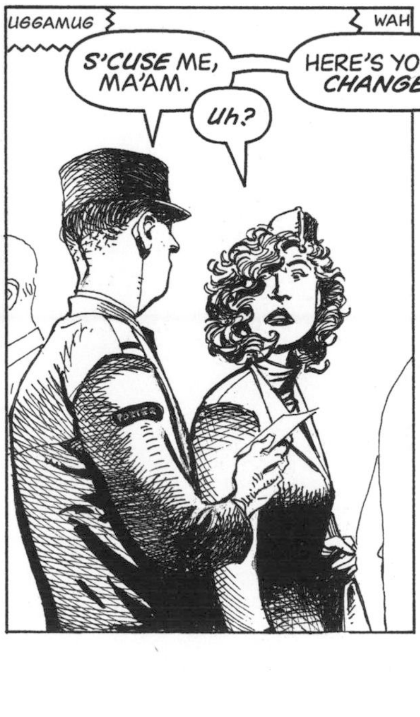
UGGAMUG
WAH
S'CUSE ME, MA'AM.
Uh?
HERE'S YOUR CHANGE.

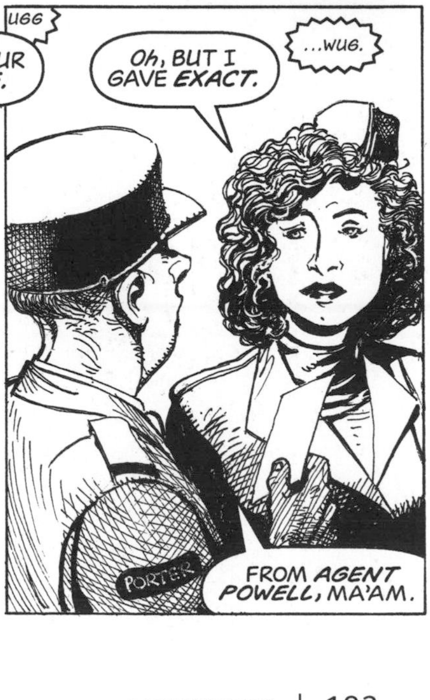
UGG
Oh, BUT I GAVE EXACT.
...WUG.
PORTER
FROM AGENT POWELL, MA'AM.

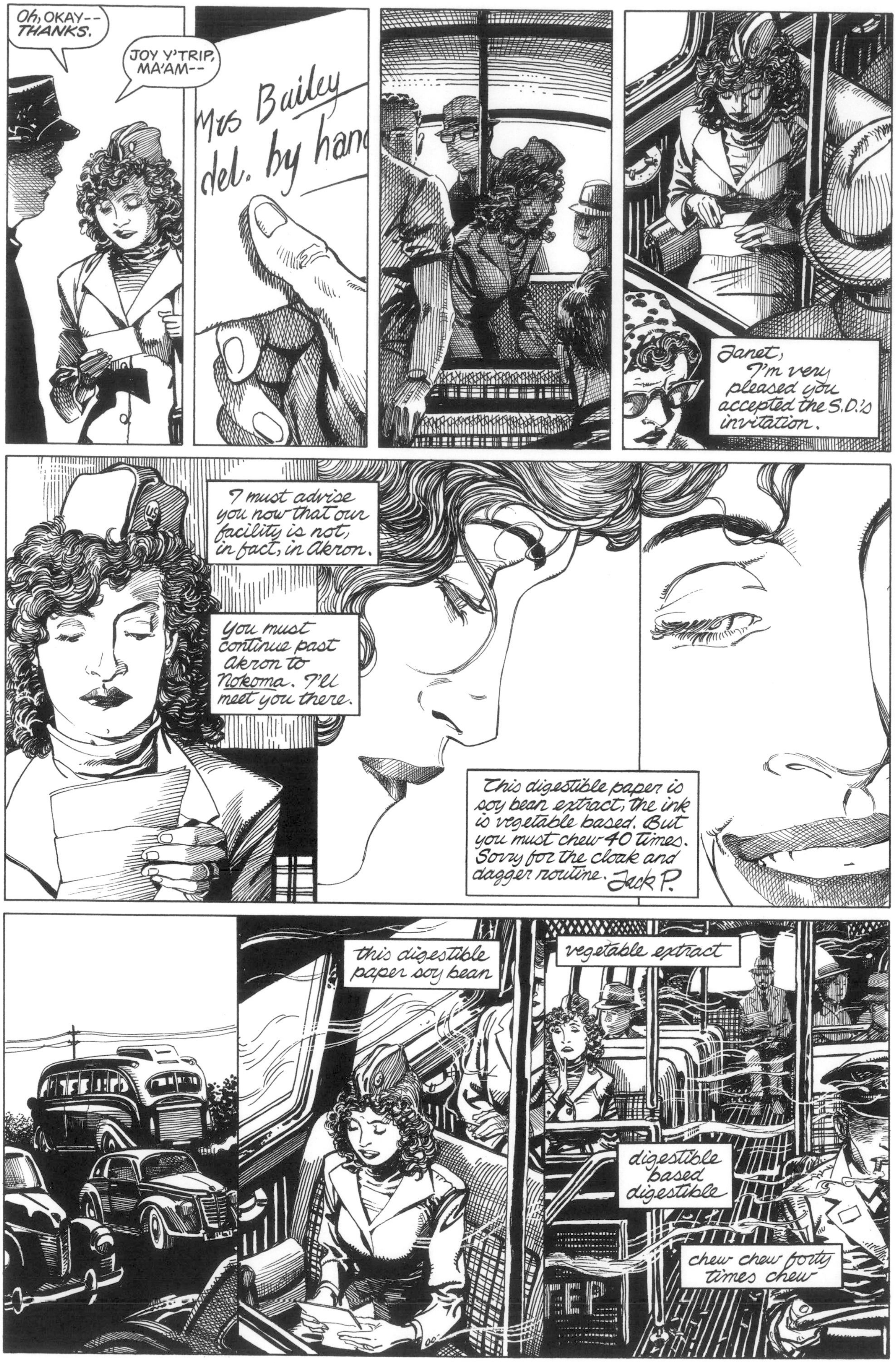

Oh, OKAY-- THANKS.
JOY Y'TRIP, MA'AM--
Mrs Bailey del. by hand
Janet, I'm very pleased you accepted the S.D.'s invitation.
I must advise you now that our facility is not, in fact, in Akron.
You must continue past Akron to Nokoma. I'll meet you there.
This digestible paper is soy bean extract, the ink is vegetable based. But you must chew 40 times. Sorry for the cloak and dagger routine. Jack P.
this digestible paper soy bean
vegetable extract
digestible based digestible
chew chew forty times chew

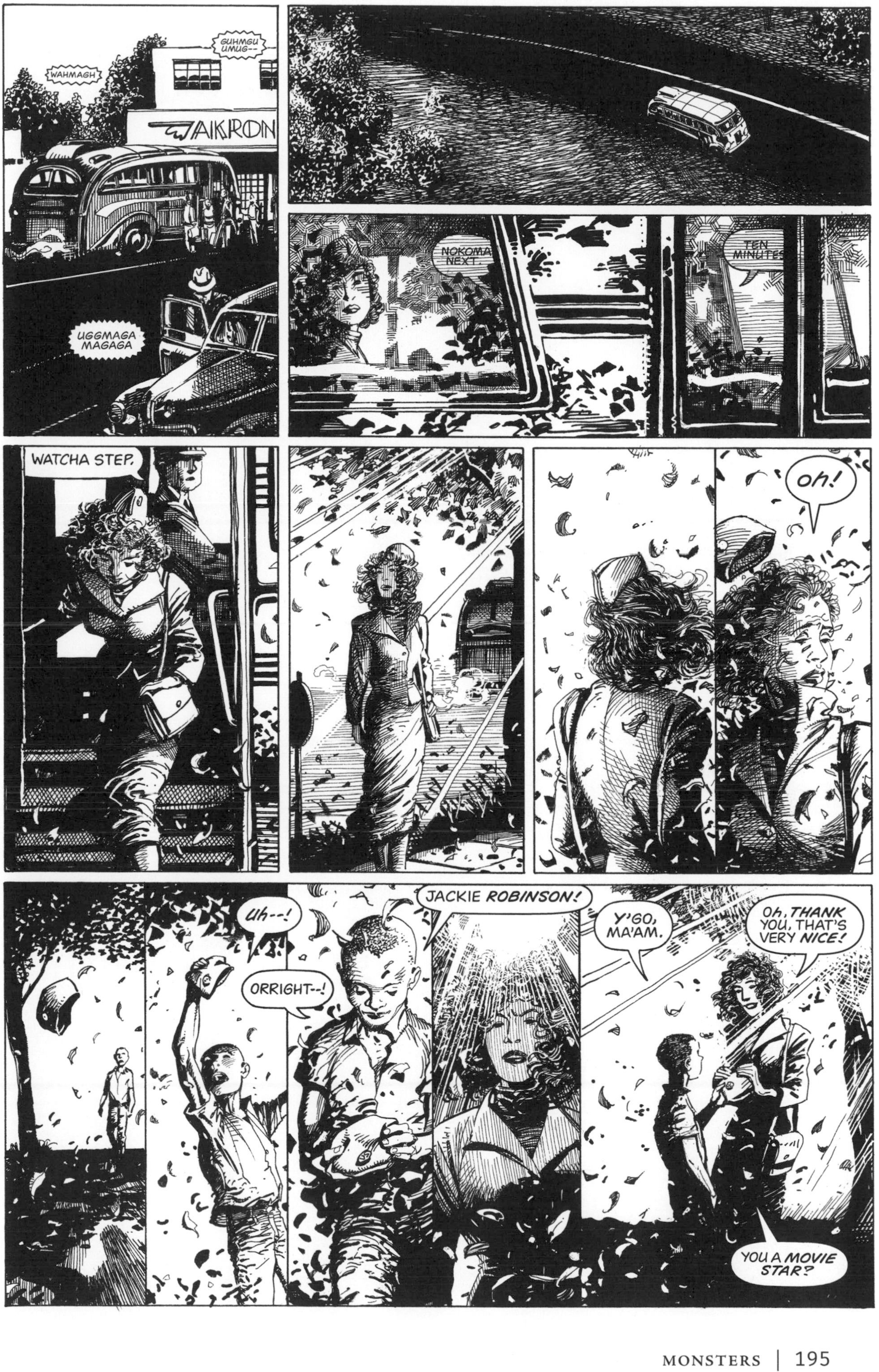
WAHMAGH
GUHMGU UMUG--
AKRON
UGGMAGA MAGAGA
NOKOMA NEXT.
TEN MINUTES.
WATCHA STEP.
Oh!
Uh--!
ORRIGHT--!
JACKIE ROBINSON!
Y'GO, MA'AM.
Oh, THANK YOU, THAT'S VERY NICE!
YOU A MOVIE STAR?

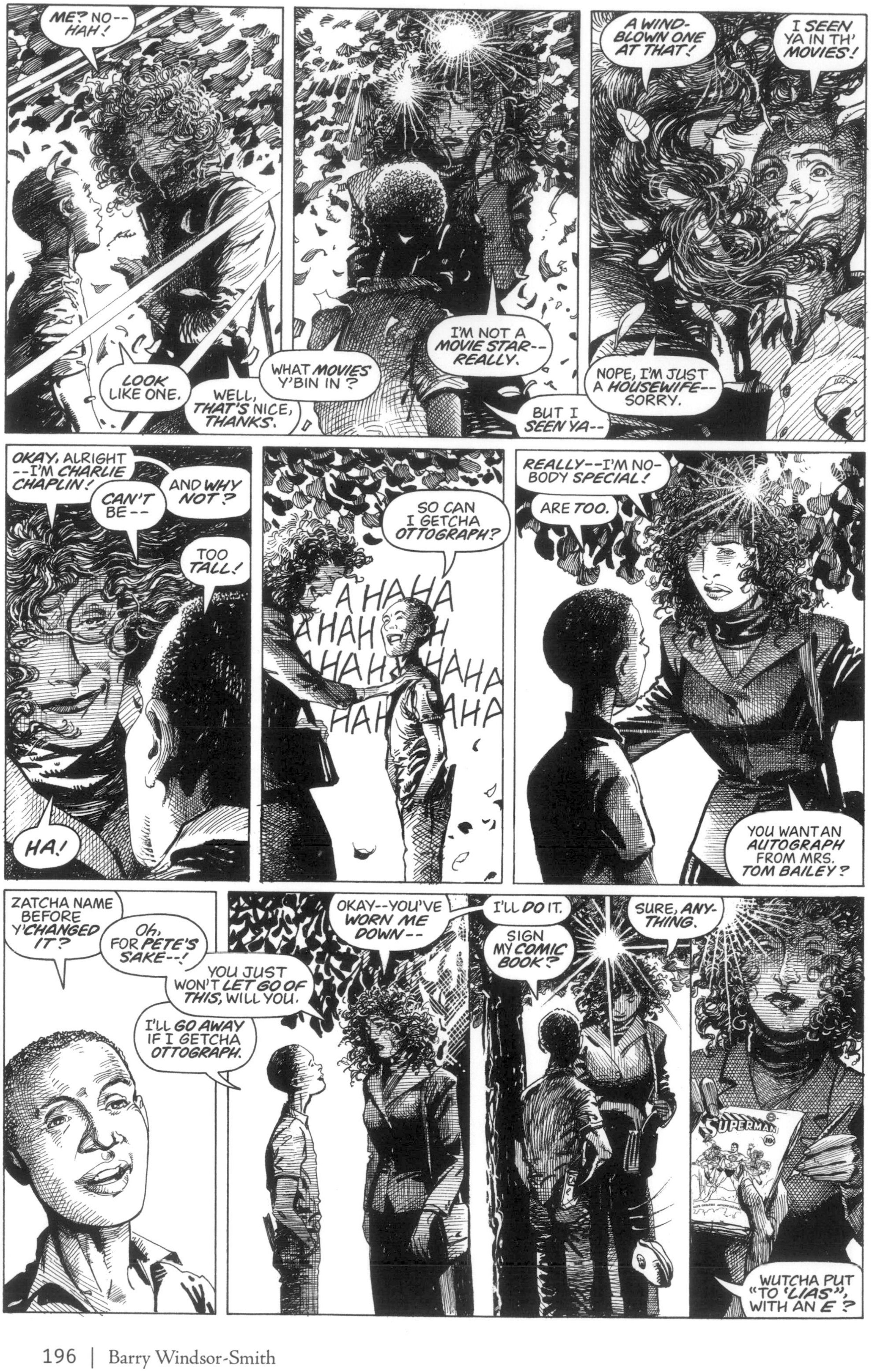
ME? NO--HAH!
LOOK LIKE ONE.
WELL, THAT'S NICE, THANKS.
WHAT MOVIES Y'BIN IN?
I'M NOT A MOVIE STAR--REALLY.
BUT I SEEN YA--
A WIND-BLOWN ONE AT THAT!
I SEEN YA IN TH' MOVIES!
NOPE, I'M JUST A HOUSEWIFE--SORRY.
OKAY, ALRIGHT--I'M CHARLIE CHAPLIN!
CAN'T BE--
AND WHY NOT?
TOO TALL!
HA!
SO CAN I GETCHA OTTOGRAPH?
A HAHA AHAH AHAH HAHA HAH AHA
REALLY--I'M NOBODY SPECIAL!
ARE TOO.
YOU WANT AN AUTOGRAPH FROM MRS. TOM BAILEY?
ZATCHA NAME BEFORE Y'CHANGED IT?
Oh, FOR PETE'S SAKE--!
YOU JUST WON'T LET GO OF THIS, WILL YOU.
I'LL GO AWAY IF I GETCHA OTTOGRAPH.
OKAY--YOU'VE WORN ME DOWN--
I'LL DO IT.
SIGN MY COMIC BOOK?
SURE, ANYTHING.
SUPERMAN
WUTCHA PUT "TO 'LIAS", WITH AN E?

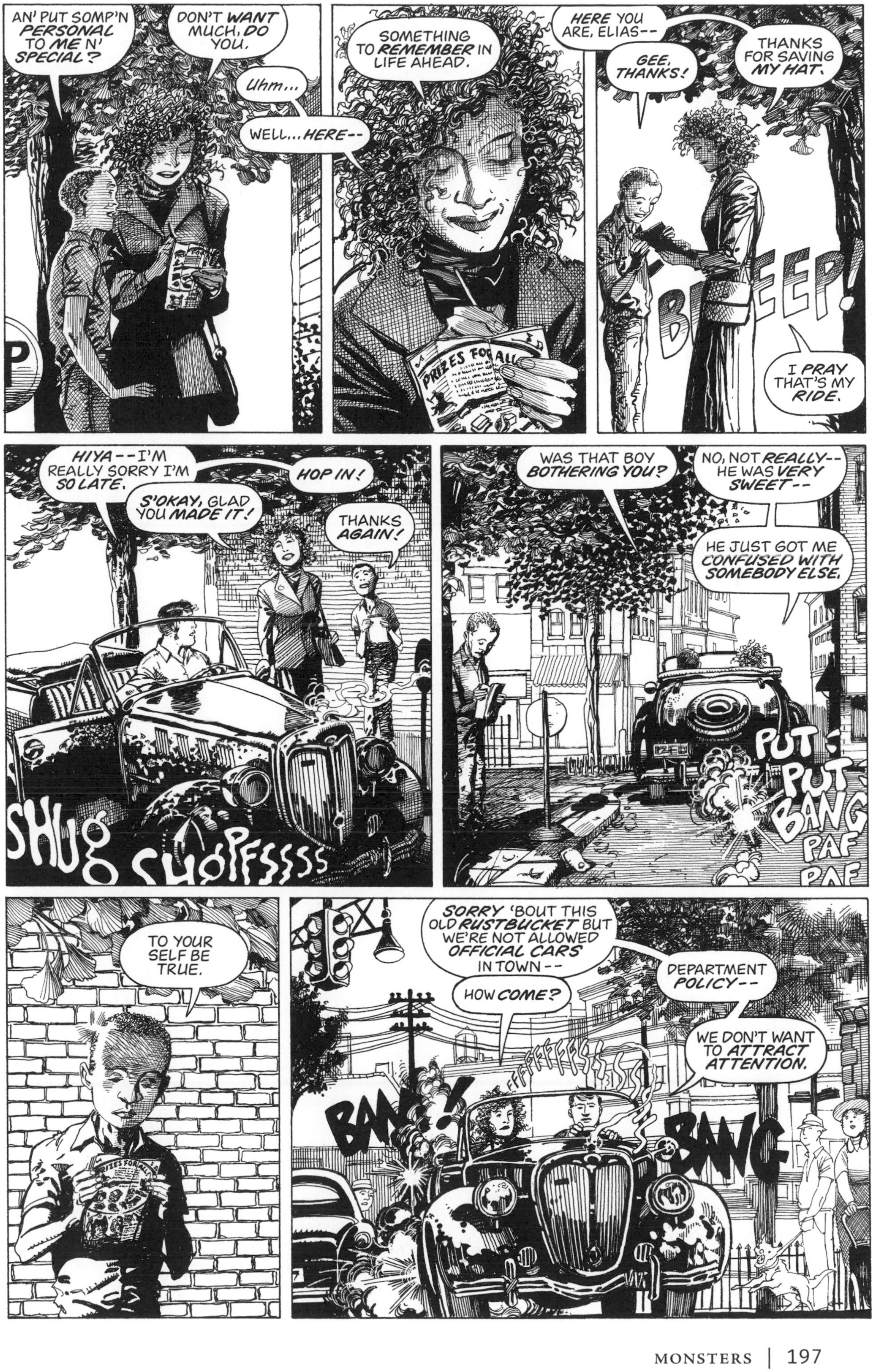
AN' PUT SOMP'N PERSONAL TO ME N' SPECIAL?
DON'T WANT MUCH, DO YOU.
Uhm...
WELL... HERE--
SOMETHING TO REMEMBER IN LIFE AHEAD.
PRIZES FOR ALL
HERE YOU ARE, ELIAS--
GEE, THANKS!
THANKS FOR SAVING MY HAT.
BEEEP!
I PRAY THAT'S MY RIDE.
HIYA--I'M REALLY SORRY I'M SO LATE.
HOP IN!
S'OKAY, GLAD YOU MADE IT!
THANKS AGAIN!
SHUG
SHOFSSSS
WAS THAT BOY BOTHERING YOU?
NO, NOT REALLY-- HE WAS VERY SWEET--
HE JUST GOT ME CONFUSED WITH SOMEBODY ELSE.
PUT-PUT
BANG
PAF
PAF
TO YOUR SELF BE TRUE.
SORRY 'BOUT THIS OLD RUSTBUCKET BUT WE'RE NOT ALLOWED OFFICIAL CARS IN TOWN--
HOW COME?
DEPARTMENT POLICY--
WE DON'T WANT TO ATTRACT ATTENTION.
BANG!
BANG

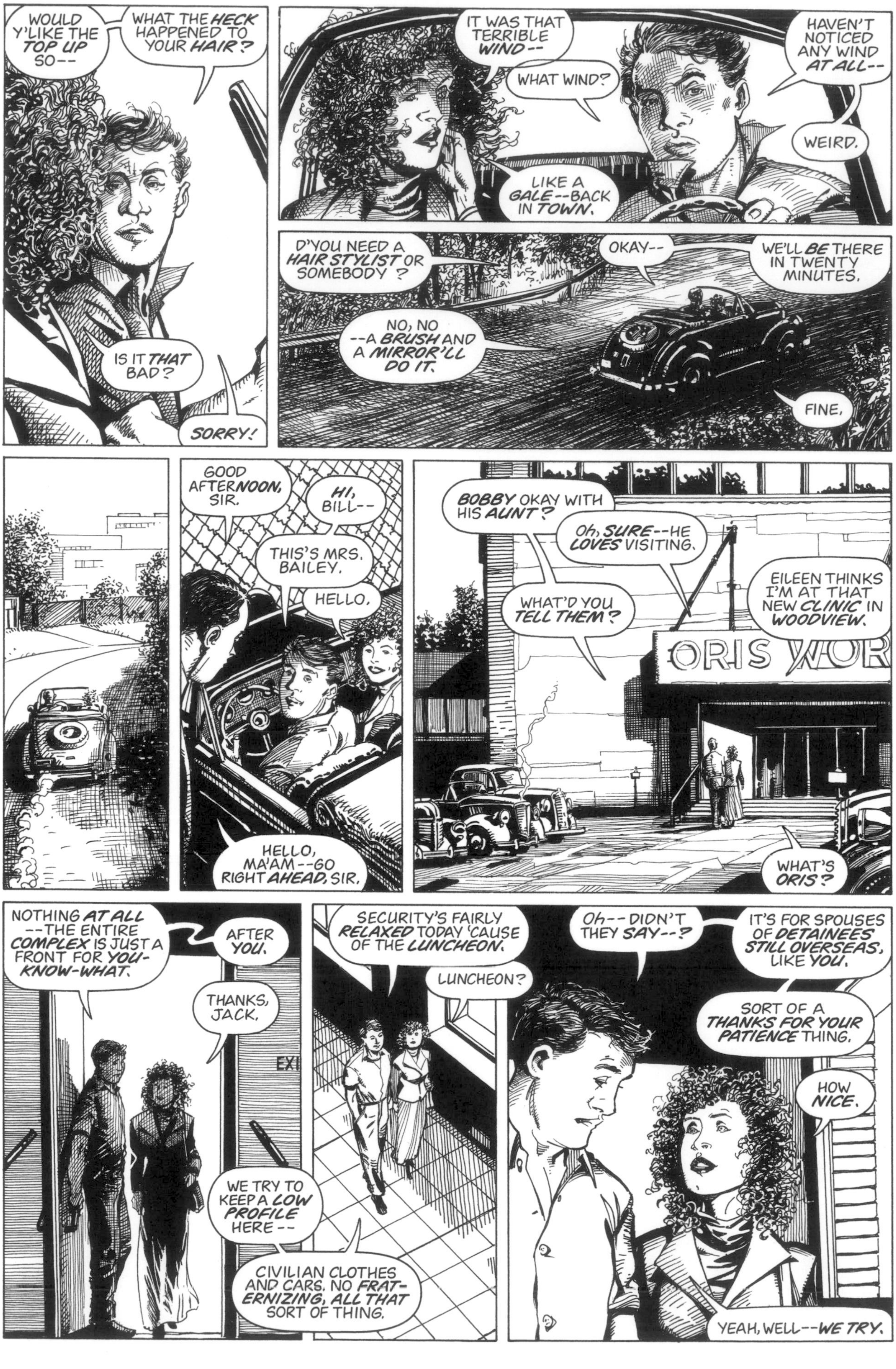
WOULD Y'LIKE THE TOP UP SO--
WHAT THE HECK HAPPENED TO YOUR HAIR?
IS IT THAT BAD?
SORRY!
IT WAS THAT TERRIBLE WIND--
WHAT WIND?
LIKE A GALE--BACK IN TOWN.
HAVEN'T NOTICED ANY WIND AT ALL--
WEIRD.
D'YOU NEED A HAIR STYLIST OR SOMEBODY?
NO, NO --A BRUSH AND A MIRROR'LL DO IT.
OKAY--
WE'LL BE THERE IN TWENTY MINUTES.
FINE.
GOOD AFTERNOON, SIR.
HI, BILL--
THIS'S MRS. BAILEY.
HELLO.
HELLO, MA'AM--GO RIGHT AHEAD, SIR.
BOBBY OKAY WITH HIS AUNT?
Oh, SURE--HE LOVES VISITING.
WHAT'D YOU TELL THEM?
EILEEN THINKS I'M AT THAT NEW CLINIC IN WOODVIEW.
ORIS WOR
WHAT'S ORIS?
NOTHING AT ALL--THE ENTIRE COMPLEX IS JUST A FRONT FOR YOU-KNOW-WHAT.
AFTER YOU.
THANKS, JACK.
EXI
WE TRY TO KEEP A LOW PROFILE HERE--
CIVILIAN CLOTHES AND CARS. NO FRATERNIZING, ALL THAT SORT OF THING.
SECURITY'S FAIRLY RELAXED TODAY 'CAUSE OF THE LUNCHEON.
LUNCHEON?
Oh--DIDN'T THEY SAY--?
IT'S FOR SPOUSES OF DETAINEES STILL OVERSEAS, LIKE YOU.
SORT OF A THANKS FOR YOUR PATIENCE THING.
HOW NICE.
YEAH, WELL--WE TRY.

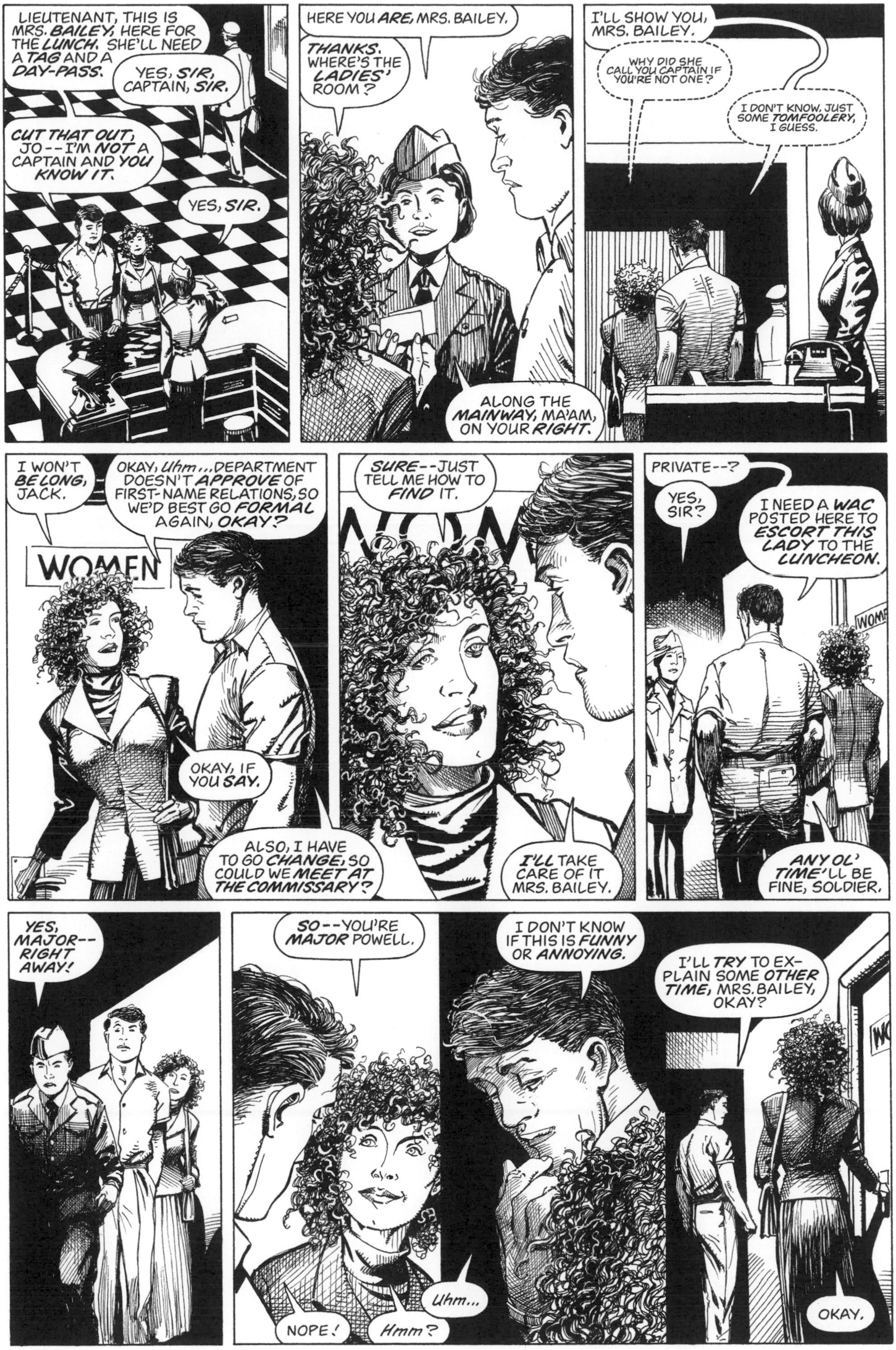
LIEUTENANT, THIS IS MRS. BAILEY, HERE FOR THE LUNCH. SHE'LL NEED A TAG AND A DAY-PASS.
YES, SIR, CAPTAIN, SIR.
CUT THAT OUT, JO--I'M NOT A CAPTAIN AND YOU KNOW IT.
YES, SIR.
HERE YOU ARE, MRS. BAILEY.
THANKS. WHERE'S THE LADIES' ROOM?
ALONG THE MAINWAY, MA'AM, ON YOUR RIGHT.
I'LL SHOW YOU, MRS. BAILEY.
WHY DID SHE CALL YOU CAPTAIN IF YOU'RE NOT ONE?
I DON'T KNOW. JUST SOME TOMFOOLERY, I GUESS.
I WON'T BE LONG, JACK.
OKAY, Uhm... DEPARTMENT DOESN'T APPROVE OF FIRST-NAME RELATIONS, SO WE'D BEST GO FORMAL AGAIN, OKAY?
WOMEN
OKAY, IF YOU SAY.
ALSO, I HAVE TO GO CHANGE, SO COULD WE MEET AT THE COMMISSARY?
SURE--JUST TELL ME HOW TO FIND IT.
I'LL TAKE CARE OF IT MRS. BAILEY.
PRIVATE--?
YES, SIR?
I NEED A WAC POSTED HERE TO ESCORT THIS LADY TO THE LUNCHEON.
ANY OL' TIME'LL BE FINE, SOLDIER.
YES, MAJOR--RIGHT AWAY!
SO--YOU'RE MAJOR POWELL.
I DON'T KNOW IF THIS IS FUNNY OR ANNOYING.
NOPE!
Hmm?
Uhm...
I'LL TRY TO EXPLAIN SOME OTHER TIME, MRS. BAILEY, OKAY?
OKAY.

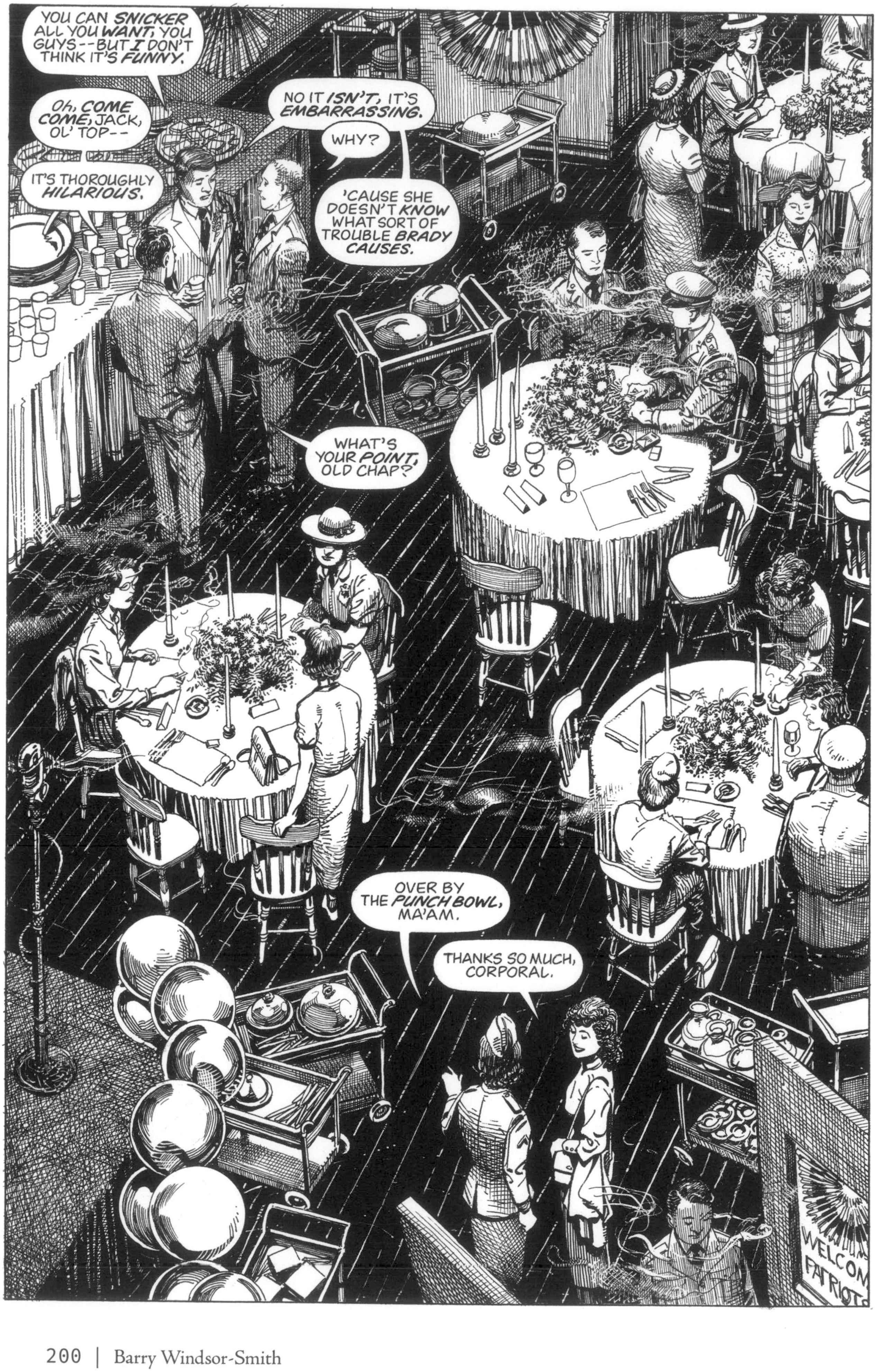
YOU CAN SNICKER ALL YOU WANT, YOU GUYS--BUT I DON'T THINK IT'S FUNNY.
Oh, COME COME, JACK, OL' TOP--
IT'S THOROUGHLY HILARIOUS.
NO IT ISN'T, IT'S EMBARRASSING.
WHY?
'CAUSE SHE DOESN'T KNOW WHAT SORT OF TROUBLE BRADY CAUSES.
WHAT'S YOUR POINT, OLD CHAP?
OVER BY THE PUNCH BOWL, MA'AM.
THANKS SO MUCH, CORPORAL.
WELCOM
PATRIOT

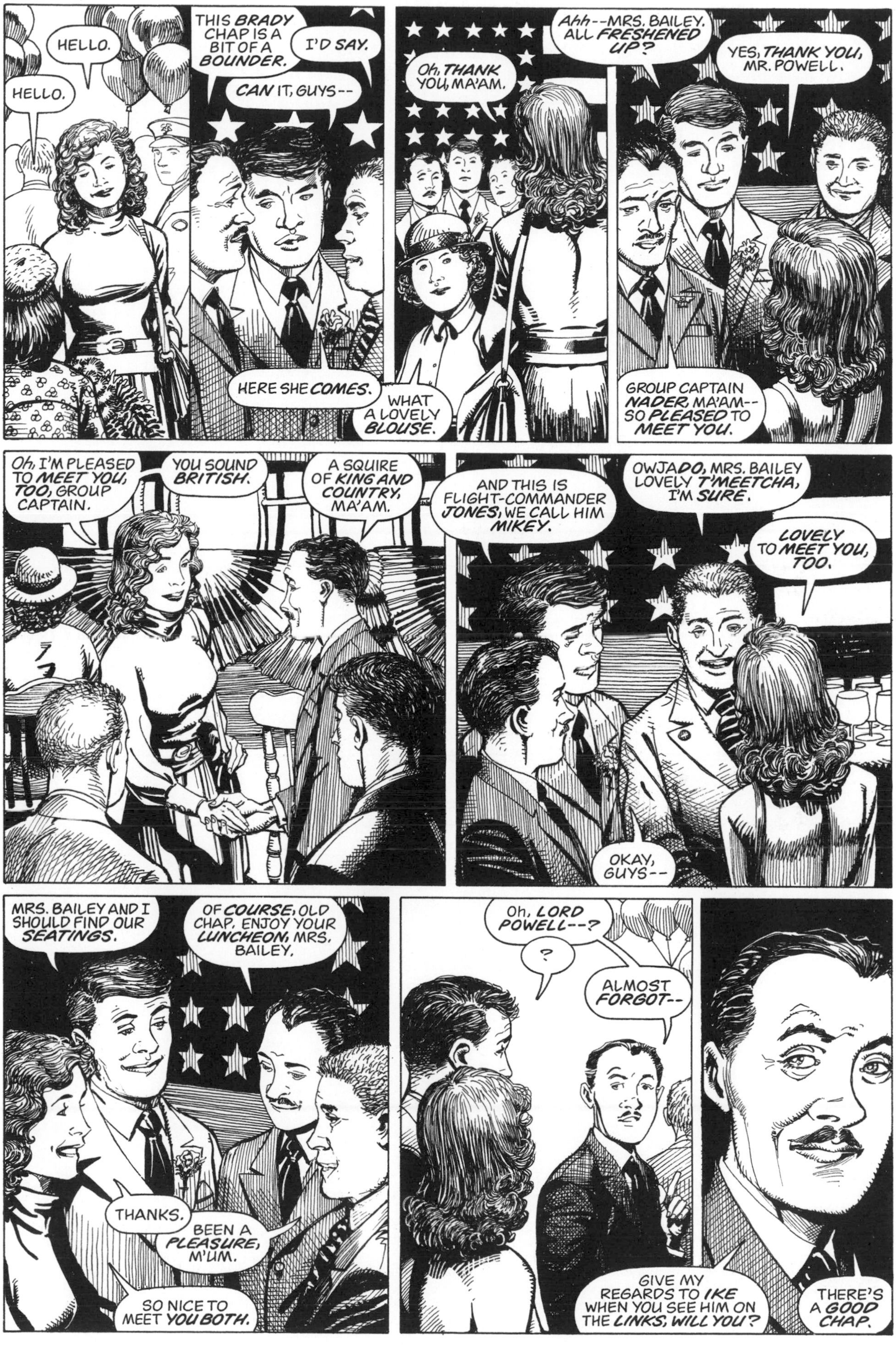
HELLO.
HELLO.
THIS BRADY CHAP IS A BIT OF A BOUNDER.
I'D SAY.
CAN IT, GUYS--
HERE SHE COMES.
Oh, THANK YOU, MA'AM.
WHAT A LOVELY BLOUSE.
Ahh--MRS. BAILEY. ALL FRESHENED UP?
YES, THANK YOU, MR. POWELL.
GROUP CAPTAIN NADER, MA'AM--SO PLEASED TO MEET YOU.
Oh, I'M PLEASED TO MEET YOU, TOO, GROUP CAPTAIN.
YOU SOUND BRITISH.
A SQUIRE OF KING AND COUNTRY, MA'AM.
AND THIS IS FLIGHT-COMMANDER JONES, WE CALL HIM MIKEY.
OWJADO, MRS. BAILEY LOVELY T'MEETCHA, I'M SURE.
LOVELY TO MEET YOU, TOO.
OKAY, GUYS--
MRS. BAILEY AND I SHOULD FIND OUR SEATINGS.
OF COURSE, OLD CHAP. ENJOY YOUR LUNCHEON, MRS. BAILEY.
THANKS.
BEEN A PLEASURE, M'UM.
SO NICE TO MEET YOU BOTH.
Oh, LORD POWELL--?
?
ALMOST FORGOT--
GIVE MY REGARDS TO IKE WHEN YOU SEE HIM ON THE LINKS, WILL YOU?
THERE'S A GOOD CHAP.

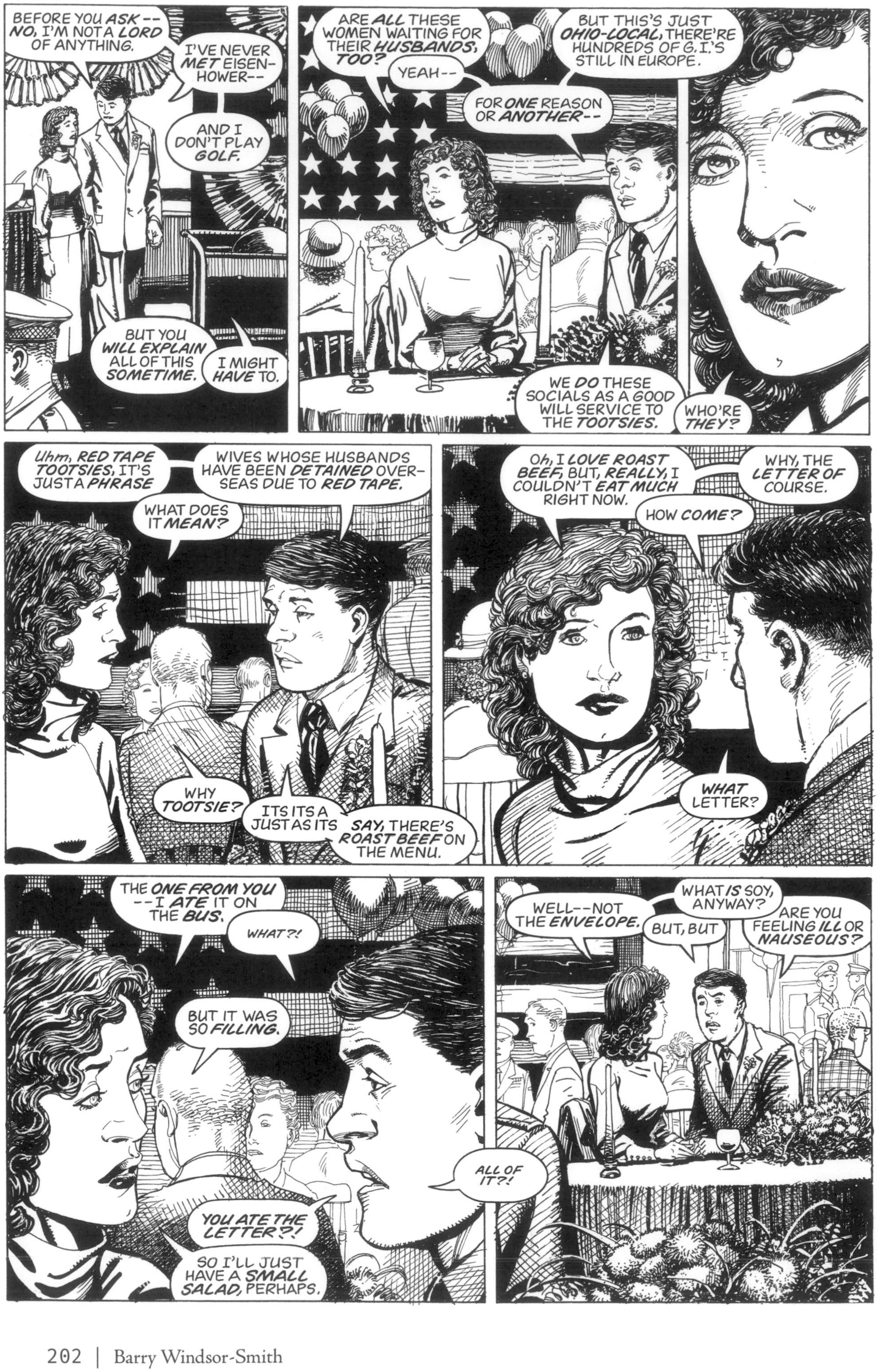
BEFORE YOU ASK -- NO, I'M NOT A LORD OF ANYTHING.
I'VE NEVER MET EISEN-HOWER--
AND I DON'T PLAY GOLF.
BUT YOU WILL EXPLAIN ALL OF THIS SOMETIME.
I MIGHT HAVE TO.
ARE ALL THESE WOMEN WAITING FOR THEIR HUSBANDS, TOO?
YEAH--
BUT THIS'S JUST OHIO-LOCAL, THERE'RE HUNDREDS OF G.I.'S STILL IN EUROPE.
FOR ONE REASON OR ANOTHER--
WE DO THESE SOCIALS AS A GOOD WILL SERVICE TO THE TOOTSIES.
WHO'RE THEY?
Uhm, RED TAPE TOOTSIES, IT'S JUST A PHRASE
WIVES WHOSE HUSBANDS HAVE BEEN DETAINED OVER-SEAS DUE TO RED TAPE.
WHAT DOES IT MEAN?
WHY TOOTSIE?
ITS ITS A JUST AS ITS
SAY, THERE'S ROAST BEEF ON THE MENU.
Oh, I LOVE ROAST BEEF, BUT, REALLY, I COULDN'T EAT MUCH RIGHT NOW.
HOW COME?
WHY, THE LETTER OF COURSE.
WHAT LETTER?
THE ONE FROM YOU --I ATE IT ON THE BUS.
WHAT?!
BUT IT WAS SO FILLING.
ALL OF IT?!
YOU ATE THE LETTER?!
SO I'LL JUST HAVE A SMALL SALAD, PERHAPS.
WELL--NOT THE ENVELOPE.
WHAT IS SOY, ANYWAY?
BUT, BUT
ARE YOU FEELING ILL OR NAUSEOUS?

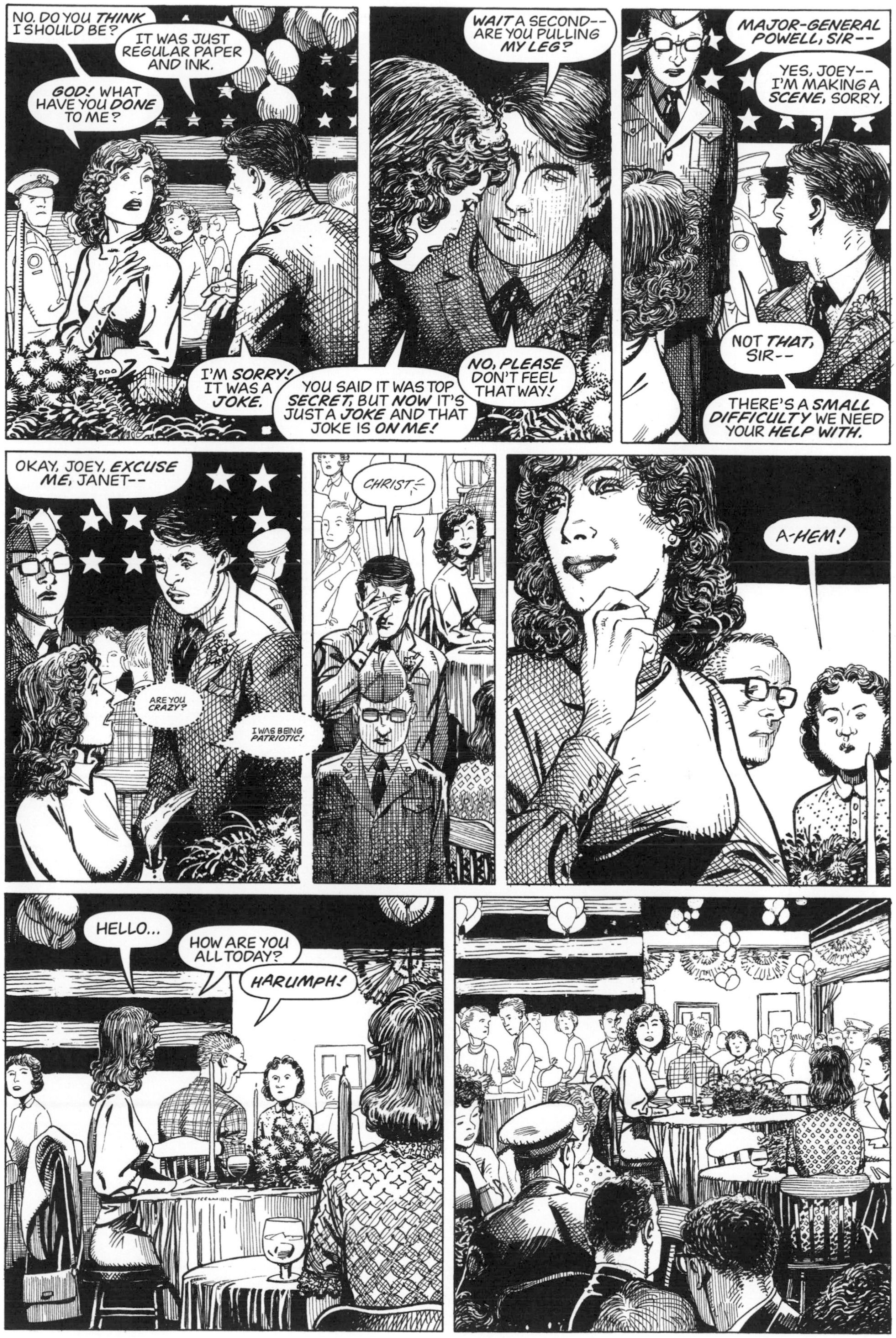
NO. DO YOU THINK I SHOULD BE?
IT WAS JUST REGULAR PAPER AND INK.
GOD! WHAT HAVE YOU DONE TO ME?
I'M SORRY! IT WAS A JOKE.
YOU SAID IT WAS TOP SECRET, BUT NOW IT'S JUST A JOKE AND THAT JOKE IS ON ME!
WAIT A SECOND-- ARE YOU PULLING MY LEG?
NO, PLEASE DON'T FEEL THAT WAY!
MAJOR-GENERAL POWELL, SIR--
YES, JOEY-- I'M MAKING A SCENE, SORRY.
NOT THAT, SIR--
THERE'S A SMALL DIFFICULTY WE NEED YOUR HELP WITH.
OKAY, JOEY, EXCUSE ME, JANET--
ARE YOU CRAZY?
I WAS BEING PATRIOTIC!
CHRIST
A-HEM!
HELLO...
HOW ARE YOU ALL TODAY?
HARUMPH!

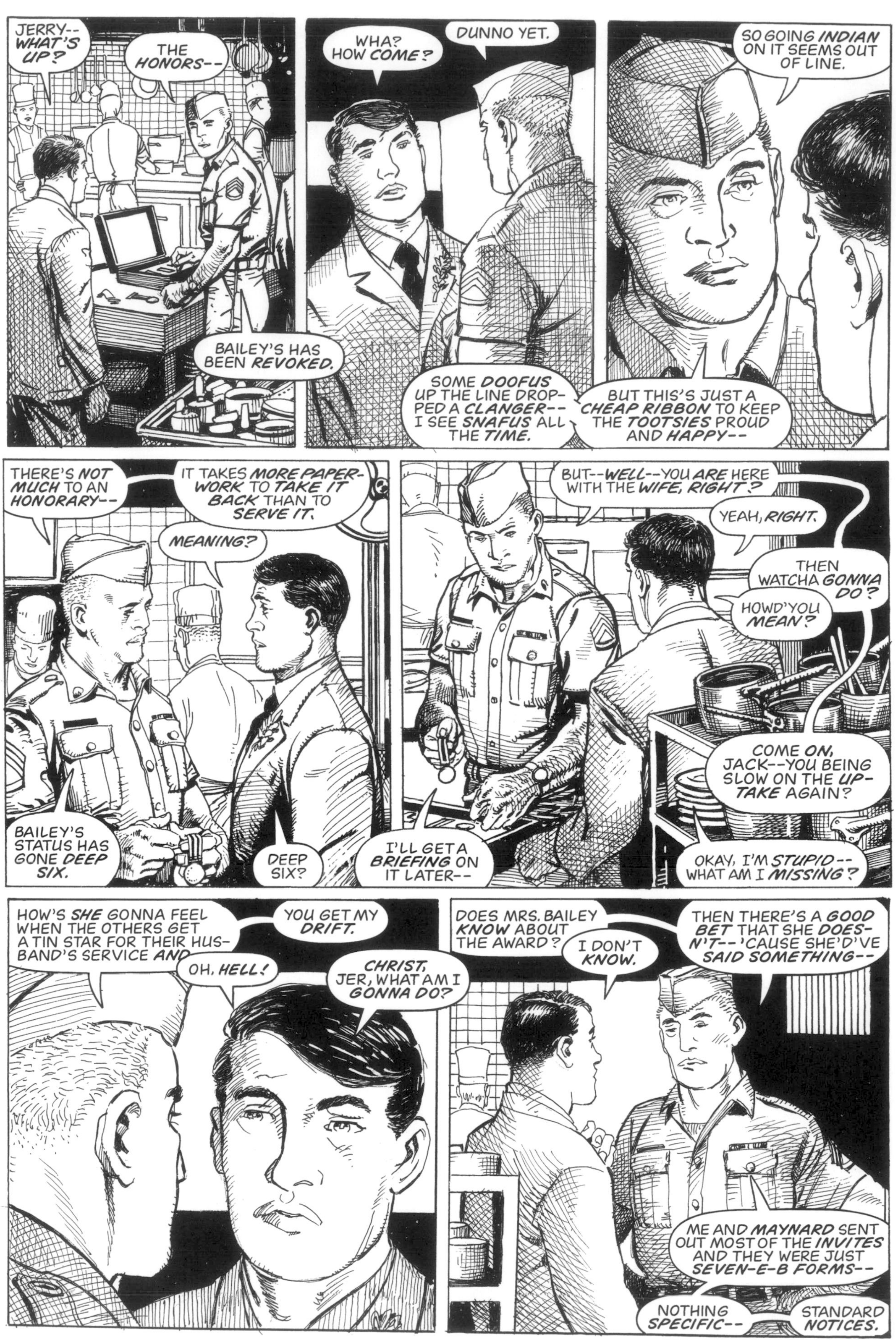

JERRY-- WHAT'S UP?
THE HONORS--
BAILEY'S HAS BEEN REVOKED.
WHA? HOW COME?
DUNNO YET.
SOME DOOFUS UP THE LINE DROPPED A CLANGER-- I SEE SNAFUS ALL THE TIME.
SO GOING INDIAN ON IT SEEMS OUT OF LINE.
BUT THIS'S JUST A CHEAP RIBBON TO KEEP THE TOOTSIES PROUD AND HAPPY--
THERE'S NOT MUCH TO AN HONORARY--
IT TAKES MORE PAPERWORK TO TAKE IT BACK THAN TO SERVE IT.
MEANING?
BAILEY'S STATUS HAS GONE DEEP SIX.
DEEP SIX?
I'LL GET A BRIEFING ON IT LATER--
BUT--WELL--YOU ARE HERE WITH THE WIFE, RIGHT?
YEAH, RIGHT.
THEN WATCHA GONNA DO?
HOWD'YOU MEAN?
COME ON, JACK--YOU BEING SLOW ON THE UPTAKE AGAIN?
OKAY, I'M STUPID-- WHAT AM I MISSING?
HOW'S SHE GONNA FEEL WHEN THE OTHERS GET A TIN STAR FOR THEIR HUSBAND'S SERVICE AND--
YOU GET MY DRIFT.
OH, HELL!
CHRIST, JER, WHAT AM I GONNA DO?
DOES MRS. BAILEY KNOW ABOUT THE AWARD?
I DON'T KNOW.
THEN THERE'S A GOOD BET THAT SHE DOESN'T-- 'CAUSE SHE'D'VE SAID SOMETHING--
ME AND MAYNARD SENT OUT MOST OF THE INVITES AND THEY WERE JUST SEVEN-E-B FORMS--
NOTHING SPECIFIC--
STANDARD NOTICES.

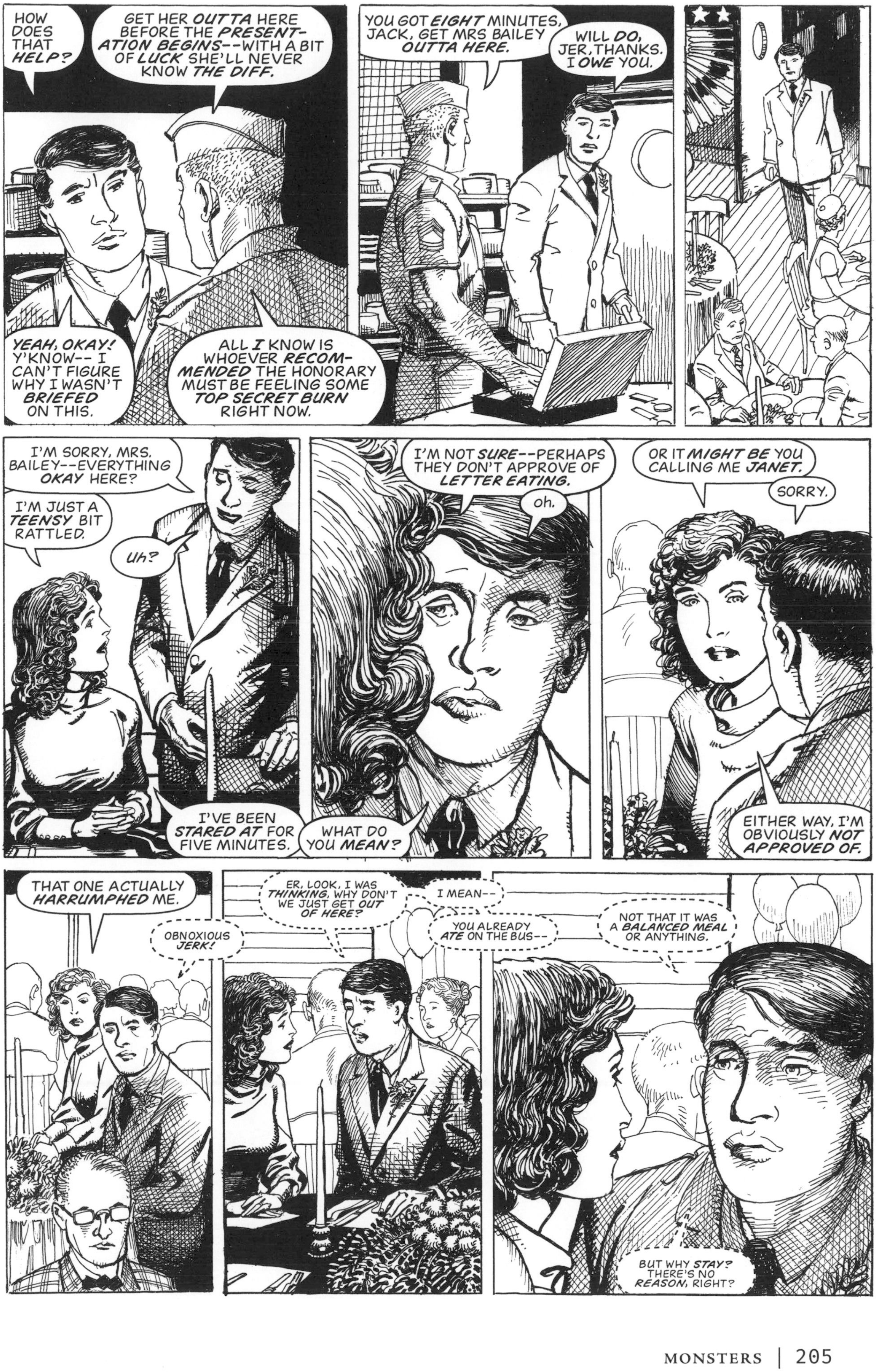
HOW DOES THAT HELP?
GET HER OUTTA HERE BEFORE THE PRESENTATION BEGINS--WITH A BIT OF LUCK SHE'LL NEVER KNOW THE DIFF.
YEAH, OKAY! Y'KNOW-- I CAN'T FIGURE WHY I WASN'T BRIEFED ON THIS.
ALL I KNOW IS WHOEVER RECOMMENDED THE HONORARY MUST BE FEELING SOME TOP SECRET BURN RIGHT NOW.
YOU GOT EIGHT MINUTES, JACK, GET MRS BAILEY OUTTA HERE.
WILL DO, JER, THANKS. I OWE YOU.
I'M SORRY, MRS. BAILEY--EVERYTHING OKAY HERE?
I'M JUST A TEENSY BIT RATTLED.
Uh?
I'VE BEEN STARED AT FOR FIVE MINUTES.
WHAT DO YOU MEAN?
I'M NOT SURE--PERHAPS THEY DON'T APPROVE OF LETTER EATING.
oh.
OR IT MIGHT BE YOU CALLING ME JANET.
SORRY.
EITHER WAY, I'M OBVIOUSLY NOT APPROVED OF.
THAT ONE ACTUALLY HARRUMPHED ME.
OBNOXIOUS JERK!
ER, LOOK, I WAS THINKING, WHY DON'T WE JUST GET OUT OF HERE?
I MEAN--
YOU ALREADY ATE ON THE BUS--
NOT THAT IT WAS A BALANCED MEAL OR ANYTHING.
BUT WHY STAY? THERE'S NO REASON, RIGHT?

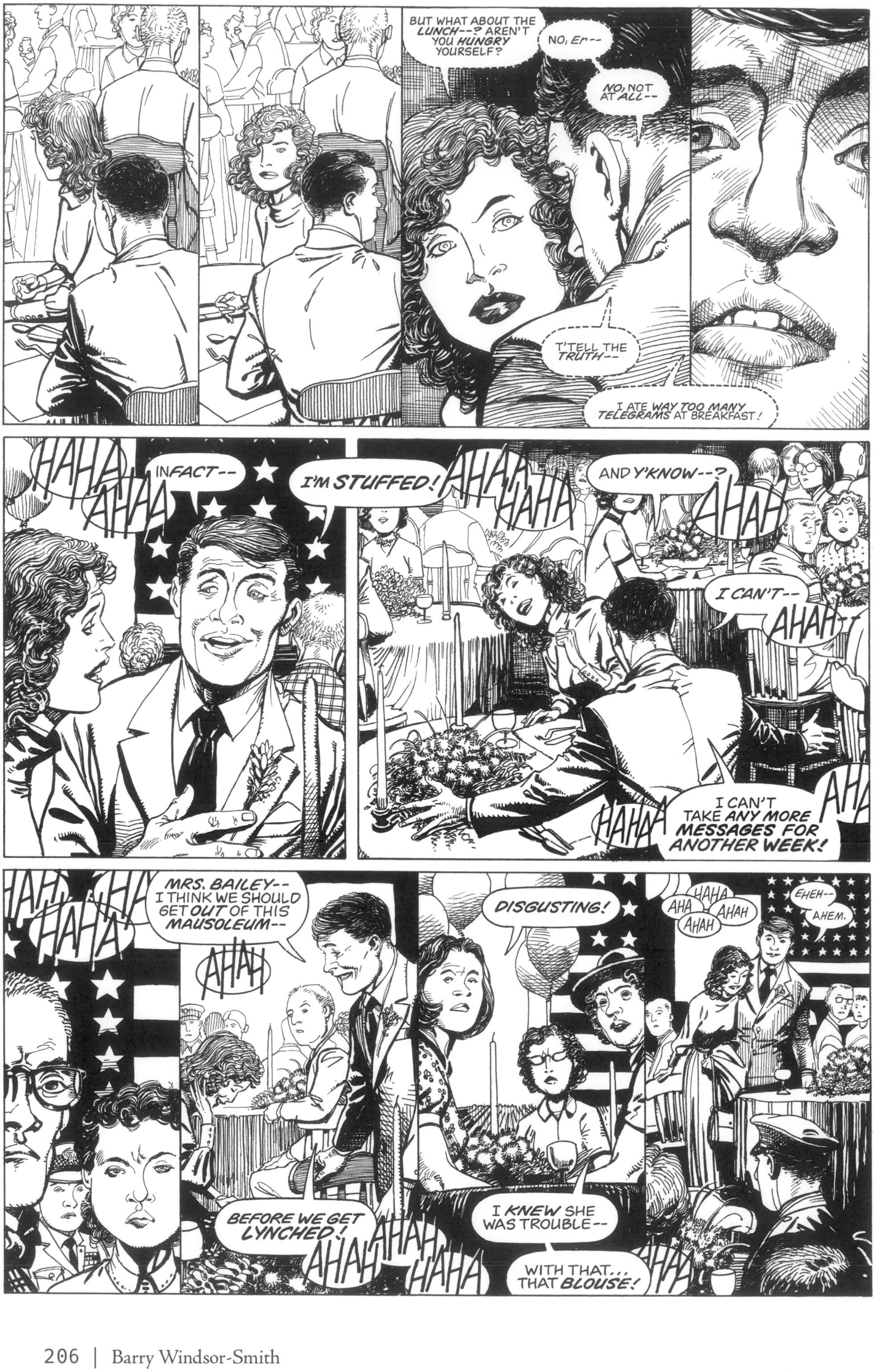
BUT WHAT ABOUT THE LUNCH--? AREN'T YOU HUNGRY YOURSELF?
NO, Er--
NO, NOT AT ALL--
T'TELL THE TRUTH--
I ATE WAY TOO MANY TELEGRAMS AT BREAKFAST!
HAHA AHAA
INFACT--
I'M STUFFED!
AHAA HAHA
AND Y'KNOW--?
AHAH
I CAN'T--
AHAH
HAHA
I CAN'T TAKE ANY MORE MESSAGES FOR ANOTHER WEEK!
AHA
HAHA HAHA
MRS. BAILEY-- I THINK WE SHOULD GET OUT OF THIS MAUSOLEUM--
AHAH
BEFORE WE GET LYNCHED!
AHAH AHAH HAHA
DISGUSTING!
I KNEW SHE WAS TROUBLE--
WITH THAT... THAT BLOUSE!
AHA HAHA AHAH AHAH
EHEH-- AHEM.

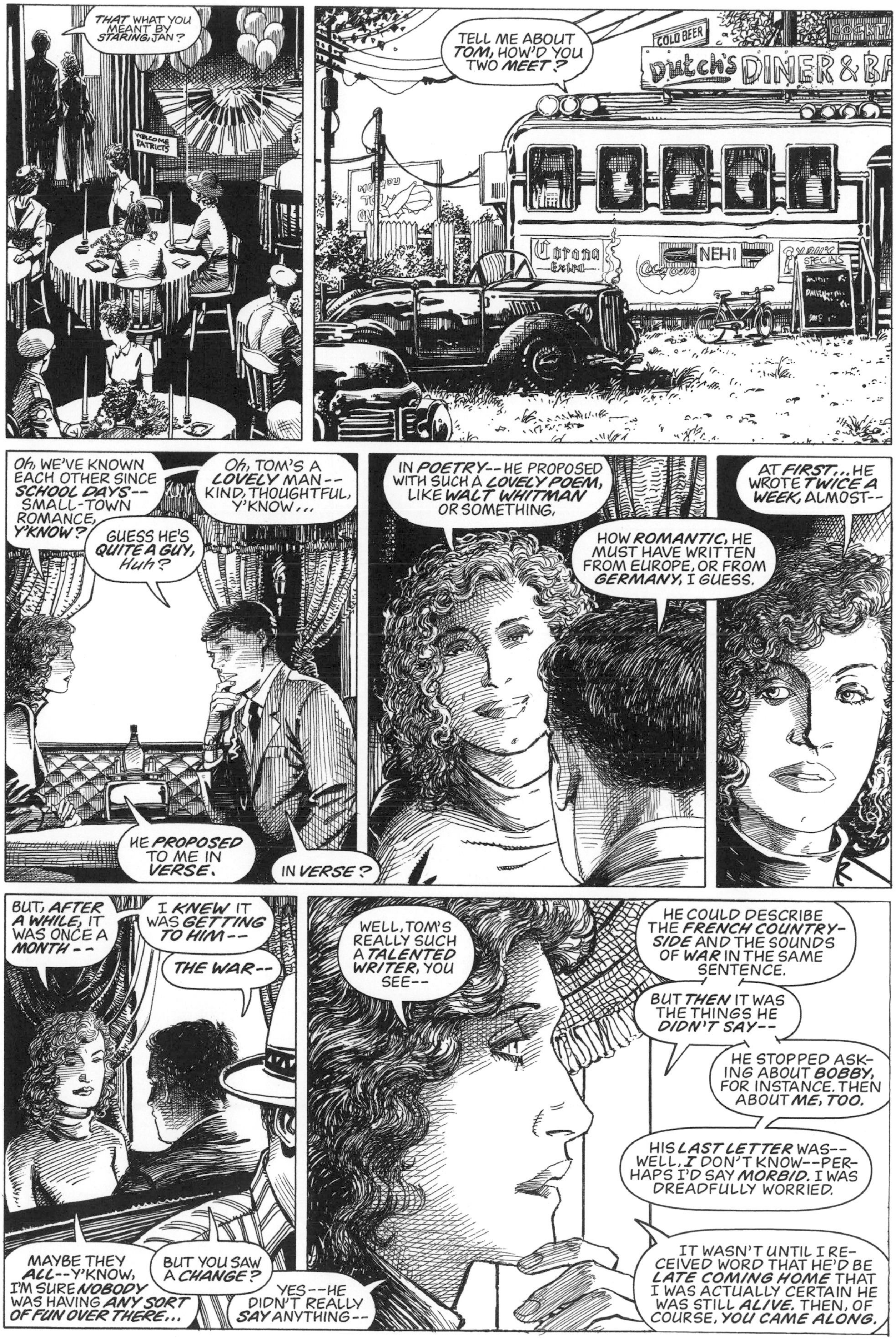
THAT WHAT YOU MEANT BY STARING, JAN?
WELCOME PATRIOTS
TELL ME ABOUT TOM, HOW'D YOU TWO MEET?
COLD BEER
Dutch's DINER & BA
Corona Extra
NEHI
SPECIALS
Oh, WE'VE KNOWN EACH OTHER SINCE SCHOOL DAYS-- SMALL-TOWN ROMANCE, Y'KNOW?
Oh, TOM'S A LOVELY MAN-- KIND, THOUGHTFUL, Y'KNOW...
GUESS HE'S QUITE A GUY, Huh?
HE PROPOSED TO ME IN VERSE.
IN VERSE?
IN POETRY--HE PROPOSED WITH SUCH A LOVELY POEM, LIKE WALT WHITMAN OR SOMETHING.
HOW ROMANTIC. HE MUST HAVE WRITTEN FROM EUROPE, OR FROM GERMANY, I GUESS.
AT FIRST... HE WROTE TWICE A WEEK, ALMOST--
BUT, AFTER A WHILE, IT WAS ONCE A MONTH--
I KNEW IT WAS GETTING TO HIM--
THE WAR--
MAYBE THEY ALL--Y'KNOW, I'M SURE NOBODY WAS HAVING ANY SORT OF FUN OVER THERE...
BUT YOU SAW A CHANGE?
YES--HE DIDN'T REALLY SAY ANYTHING--
WELL, TOM'S REALLY SUCH A TALENTED WRITER, YOU SEE--
HE COULD DESCRIBE THE FRENCH COUNTRY-SIDE AND THE SOUNDS OF WAR IN THE SAME SENTENCE.
BUT THEN IT WAS THE THINGS HE DIDN'T SAY--
HE STOPPED ASKING ABOUT BOBBY, FOR INSTANCE. THEN ABOUT ME, TOO.
HIS LAST LETTER WAS-- WELL, I DON'T KNOW--PERHAPS I'D SAY MORBID. I WAS DREADFULLY WORRIED.
IT WASN'T UNTIL I RECEIVED WORD THAT HE'D BE LATE COMING HOME THAT I WAS ACTUALLY CERTAIN HE WAS STILL ALIVE. THEN, OF COURSE, YOU CAME ALONG.

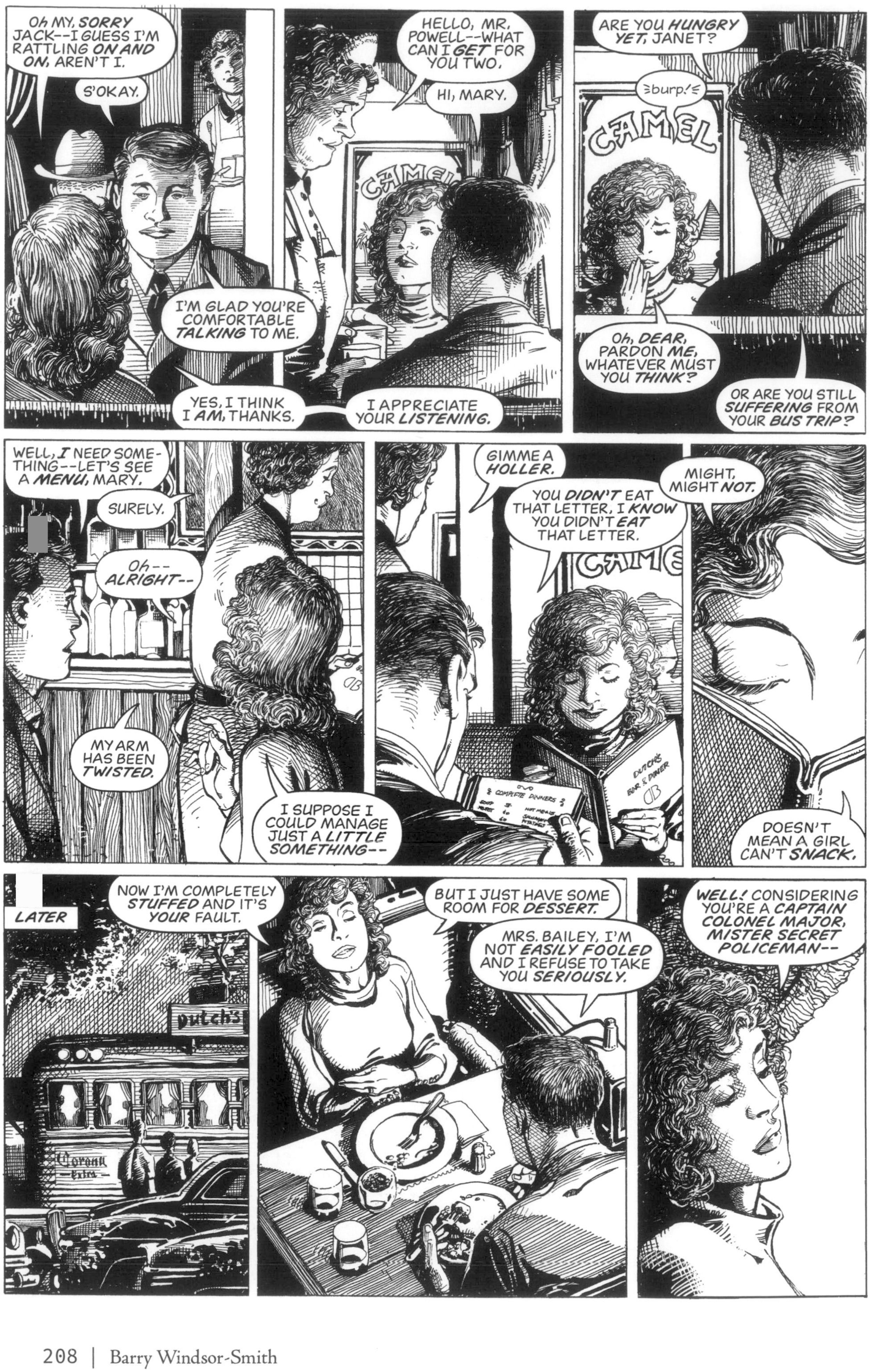
Oh MY, SORRY JACK--I GUESS I'M RATTLING ON AND ON, AREN'T I.
S'OKAY.
I'M GLAD YOU'RE COMFORTABLE TALKING TO ME.
YES, I THINK I AM, THANKS.
I APPRECIATE YOUR LISTENING.
HELLO, MR. POWELL--WHAT CAN I GET FOR YOU TWO.
HI, MARY.
CAMEL
ARE YOU HUNGRY YET, JANET?
burp!
CAMEL
Oh, DEAR, PARDON ME, WHATEVER MUST YOU THINK?
OR ARE YOU STILL SUFFERING FROM YOUR BUS TRIP?
WELL, I NEED SOMETHING--LET'S SEE A MENU, MARY.
SURELY.
Oh-- ALRIGHT--
MY ARM HAS BEEN TWISTED.
I SUPPOSE I COULD MANAGE JUST A LITTLE SOMETHING--
GIMME A HOLLER.
YOU DIDN'T EAT THAT LETTER. I KNOW YOU DIDN'T EAT THAT LETTER.
MIGHT. MIGHT NOT.
DOESN'T MEAN A GIRL CAN'T SNACK.
LATER
NOW I'M COMPLETELY STUFFED AND IT'S YOUR FAULT.
BUT I JUST HAVE SOME ROOM FOR DESSERT.
MRS. BAILEY, I'M NOT EASILY FOOLED AND I REFUSE TO TAKE YOU SERIOUSLY.
WELL! CONSIDERING YOU'RE A CAPTAIN COLONEL MAJOR, MISTER SECRET POLICEMAN--

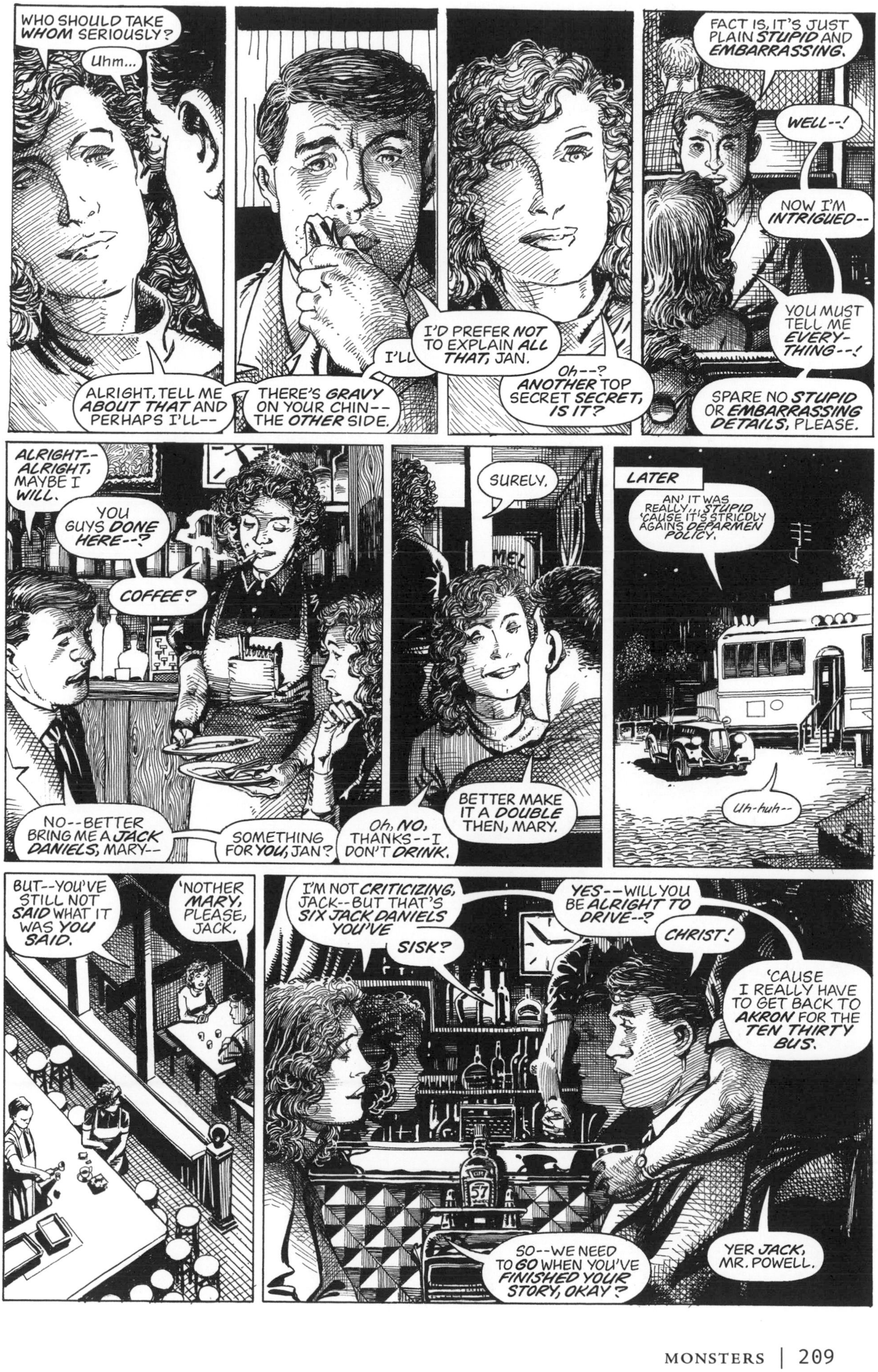
WHO SHOULD TAKE WHOM SERIOUSLY?
Uhm...
ALRIGHT, TELL ME ABOUT THAT AND PERHAPS I'LL--
THERE'S GRAVY ON YOUR CHIN-- THE OTHER SIDE.
I'LL
I'D PREFER NOT TO EXPLAIN ALL THAT, JAN.
Oh--? ANOTHER TOP SECRET SECRET, IS IT?
FACT IS, IT'S JUST PLAIN STUPID AND EMBARRASSING.
WELL--!
NOW I'M INTRIGUED--
YOU MUST TELL ME EVERY-THING--!
SPARE NO STUPID OR EMBARRASSING DETAILS, PLEASE.
ALRIGHT-- ALRIGHT, MAYBE I WILL.
YOU GUYS DONE HERE--?
COFFEE?
NO--BETTER BRING ME A JACK DANIELS, MARY--
SOMETHING FOR YOU, JAN?
Oh, NO, THANKS--I DON'T DRINK.
SURELY.
BETTER MAKE IT A DOUBLE THEN, MARY.
LATER
AN' IT WAS REALLY... STUPID 'CAUSE IT'S STRICDLY AGAINS DEPARMEN POLICY.
Uh-huh--
BUT--YOU'VE STILL NOT SAID WHAT IT WAS YOU SAID.
'NOTHER MARY, PLEASE, JACK.
I'M NOT CRITICIZING, JACK--BUT THAT'S SIX JACK DANIELS YOU'VE
SISK?
YES--WILL YOU BE ALRIGHT TO DRIVE--?
CHRIST!
'CAUSE I REALLY HAVE TO GET BACK TO AKRON FOR THE TEN THIRTY BUS.
SO--WE NEED TO GO WHEN YOU'VE FINISHED YOUR STORY, OKAY?
YER JACK, MR. POWELL.

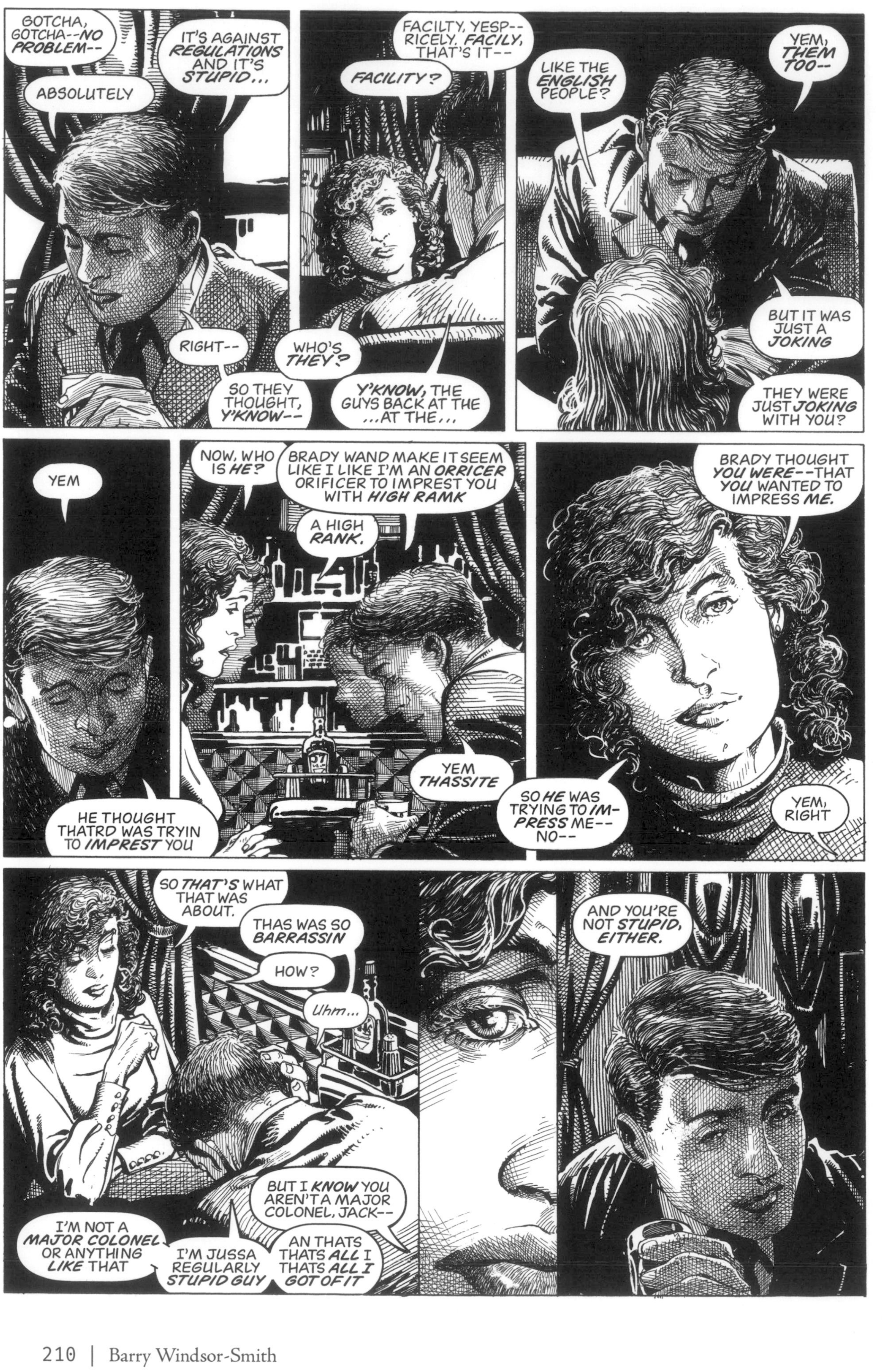
GOTCHA, GOTCHA--NO PROBLEM--
IT'S AGAINST REGULATIONS AND IT'S STUPID...
ABSOLUTELY
RIGHT--
SO THEY THOUGHT, Y'KNOW--
FACILTY, YESP--RICELY. FACILY, THAT'S IT--
FACILITY?
WHO'S THEY?
Y'KNOW, THE GUYS BACK AT THE ...AT THE...
LIKE THE ENGLISH PEOPLE?
YEM, THEM TOO--
BUT IT WAS JUST A JOKING
THEY WERE JUST JOKING WITH YOU?
YEM
HE THOUGHT THATRD WAS TRYIN TO IMPRESS YOU
NOW, WHO IS HE?
BRADY WAND MAKE IT SEEM LIKE I LIKE I'M AN ORRICER ORIFICER TO IMPRESS YOU WITH HIGH RAMK
A HIGH RANK.
YEM THASSITE
BRADY THOUGHT YOU WERE--THAT YOU WANTED TO IMPRESS ME.
SO HE WAS TRYING TO IMPRESS ME--NO--
YEM, RIGHT
SO THAT'S WHAT THAT WAS ABOUT.
THAS WAS SO BARRASSIN
HOW?
Uhm...
I'M NOT A MAJOR COLONEL OR ANYTHING LIKE THAT
I'M JUSSA REGULARLY STUPID GUY
BUT I KNOW YOU AREN'T A MAJOR COLONEL, JACK--
AN THATS THATS ALL I THATS ALL I GOT OF IT
AND YOU'RE NOT STUPID, EITHER.

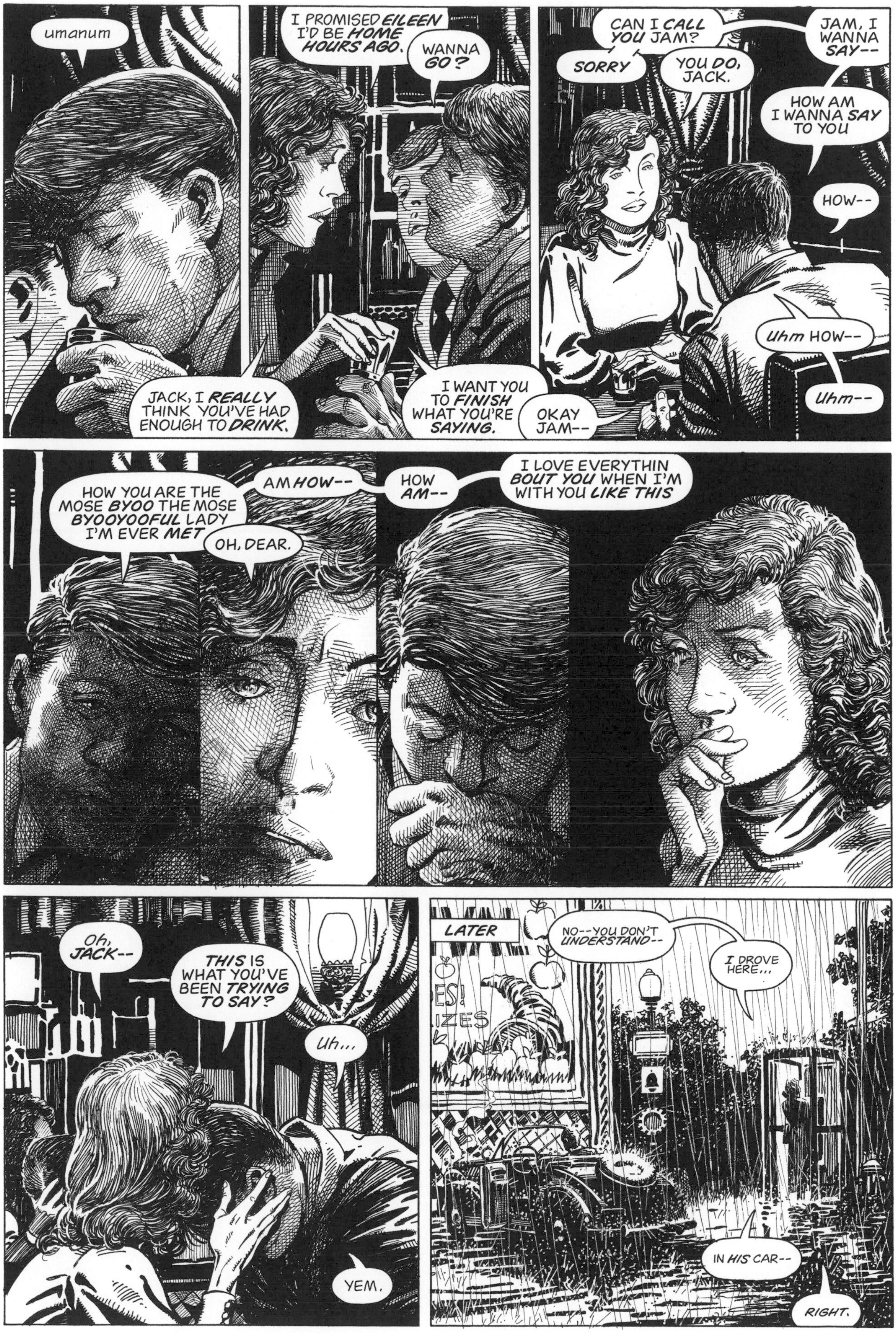
umanum
JACK, I REALLY THINK YOU'VE HAD ENOUGH TO DRINK.
I PROMISED EILEEN I'D BE HOME HOURS AGO.
WANNA GO?
I WANT YOU TO FINISH WHAT YOU'RE SAYING.
CAN I CALL YOU JAM?
SORRY
YOU DO, JACK.
OKAY JAM--
JAM, I WANNA SAY--
HOW AM I WANNA SAY TO YOU
HOW--
Uhm HOW--
Uhm--
HOW YOU ARE THE MOSE BYOO THE MOSE BYOOYOOFUL LADY I'M EVER MET
AM HOW--
OH, DEAR.
HOW AM--
I LOVE EVERYTHIN BOUT YOU WHEN I'M WITH YOU LIKE THIS
Oh, JACK--
THIS is WHAT YOU'VE BEEN TRYING TO SAY?
Uh...
YEM.
LATER
NO--YOU DON'T UNDERSTAND--
I DROVE HERE...
IN HIS CAR--
RIGHT.

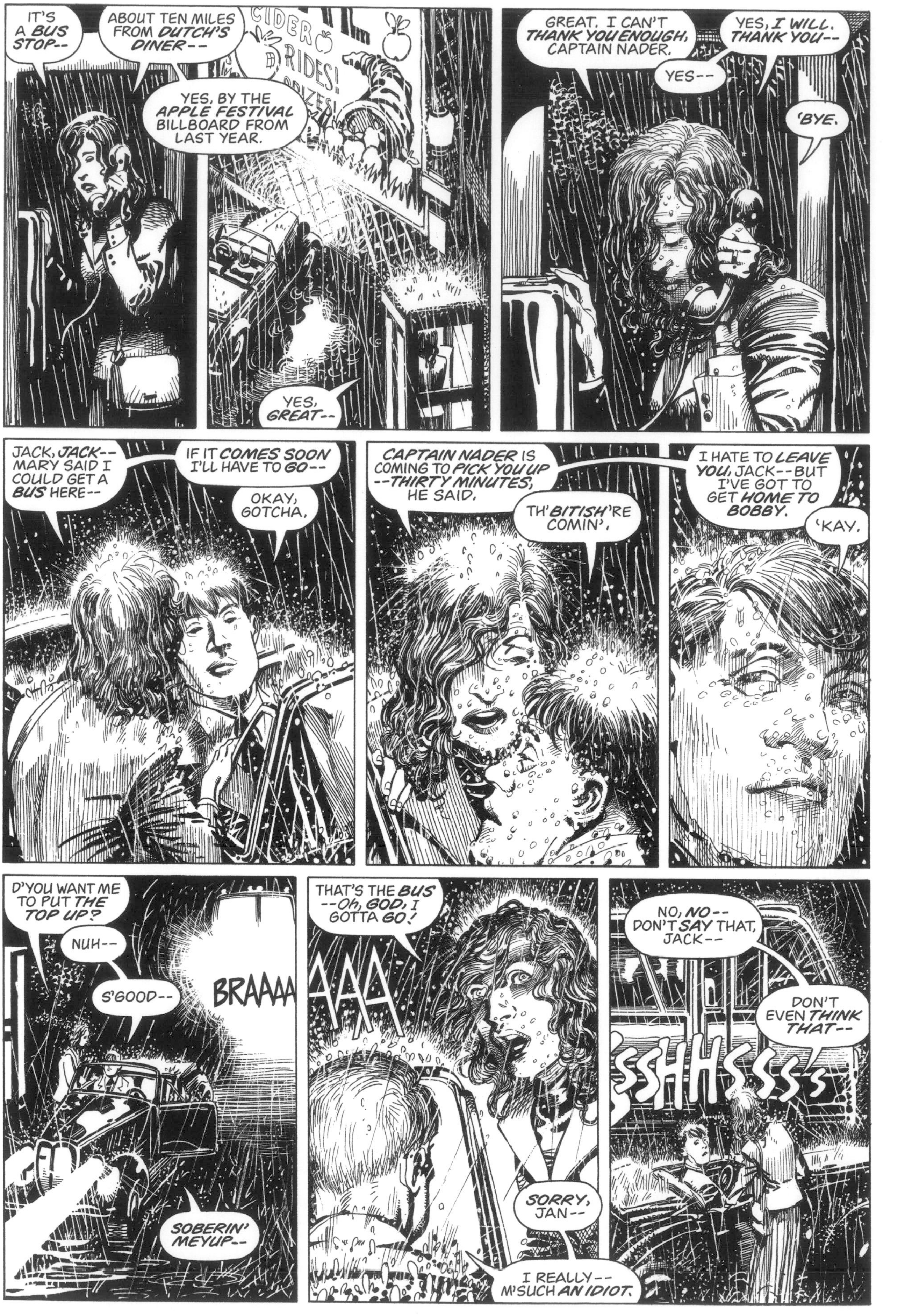
IT'S A BUS STOP--
ABOUT TEN MILES FROM DUTCH'S DINER--
YES, BY THE APPLE FESTIVAL BILLBOARD FROM LAST YEAR.
CIDER
RIDES!
YES, GREAT--
GREAT. I CAN'T THANK YOU ENOUGH, CAPTAIN NADER.
YES--
YES, I WILL. THANK YOU--
'BYE.
JACK, JACK-- MARY SAID I COULD GET A BUS HERE--
IF IT COMES SOON I'LL HAVE TO GO--
OKAY, GOTCHA.
CAPTAIN NADER IS COMING TO PICK YOU UP --THIRTY MINUTES, HE SAID.
TH' BITISH'RE COMIN'.
I HATE TO LEAVE YOU, JACK--BUT I'VE GOT TO GET HOME TO BOBBY.
'KAY.
D'YOU WANT ME TO PUT THE TOP UP?
NUH--
S'GOOD--
BRAAAAAAA
SOBERIN' MEYUP--
THAT'S THE BUS --Oh, GOD, I GOTTA GO!
SORRY, JAN--
I REALLY-- M'SUCH AN IDIOT.
NO, NO-- DON'T SAY THAT, JACK--
DON'T EVEN THINK THAT--
SSHHSSSS

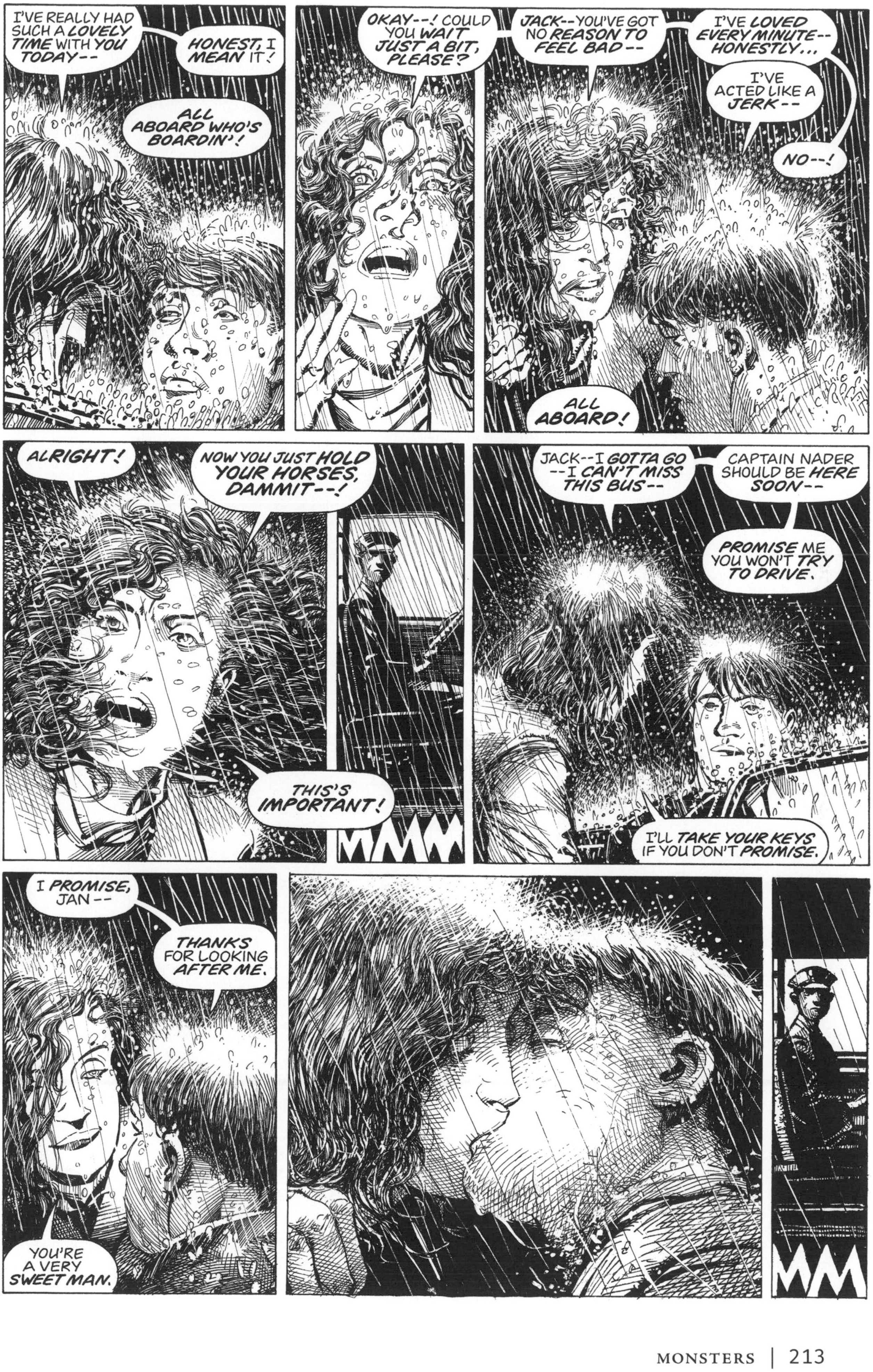
I'VE REALLY HAD SUCH A LOVELY TIME WITH YOU TODAY--
HONEST, I MEAN IT!
ALL ABOARD WHO'S BOARDIN'!
OKAY--! COULD YOU WAIT JUST A BIT, PLEASE?
JACK--YOU'VE GOT NO REASON TO FEEL BAD--
I'VE LOVED EVERY MINUTE--HONESTLY...
I'VE ACTED LIKE A JERK--
NO--!
ALL ABOARD!
ALRIGHT!
NOW YOU JUST HOLD YOUR HORSES, DAMMIT--!
THIS'S IMPORTANT!
MMM
JACK--I GOTTA GO--I CAN'T MISS THIS BUS--
CAPTAIN NADER SHOULD BE HERE SOON--
PROMISE ME YOU WON'T TRY TO DRIVE.
I'LL TAKE YOUR KEYS IF YOU DON'T PROMISE.
I PROMISE, JAN--
THANKS FOR LOOKING AFTER ME.
YOU'RE A VERY SWEET MAN.
MM

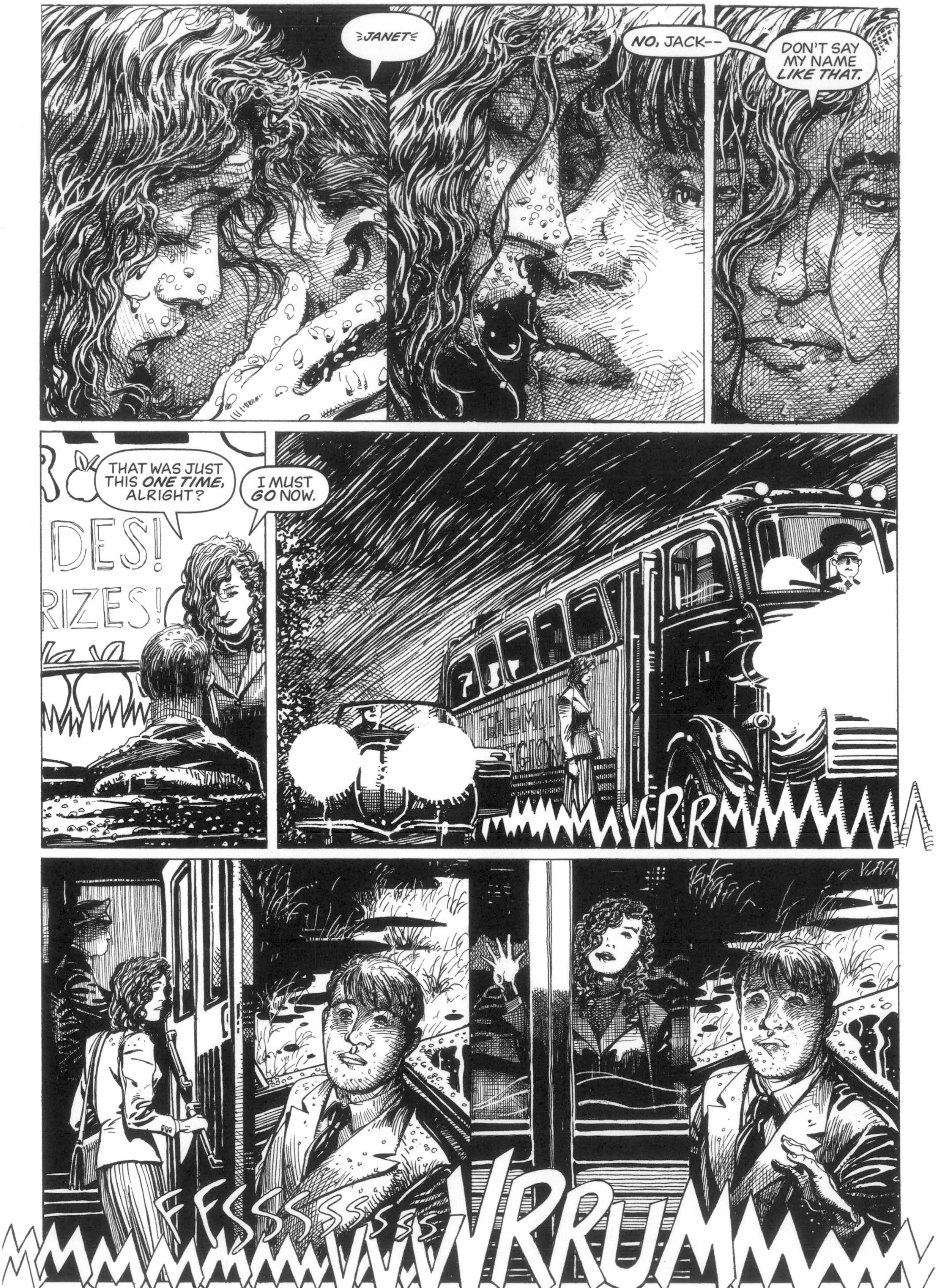
JANET
NO, JACK--
DON'T SAY MY NAME LIKE THAT.
THAT WAS JUST THIS ONE TIME, ALRIGHT?
I MUST GO NOW.
DES!
RIZES!
WRRMMMMMM
FFSSSSSSSS
MMMMMMVVVVRRUMMMM

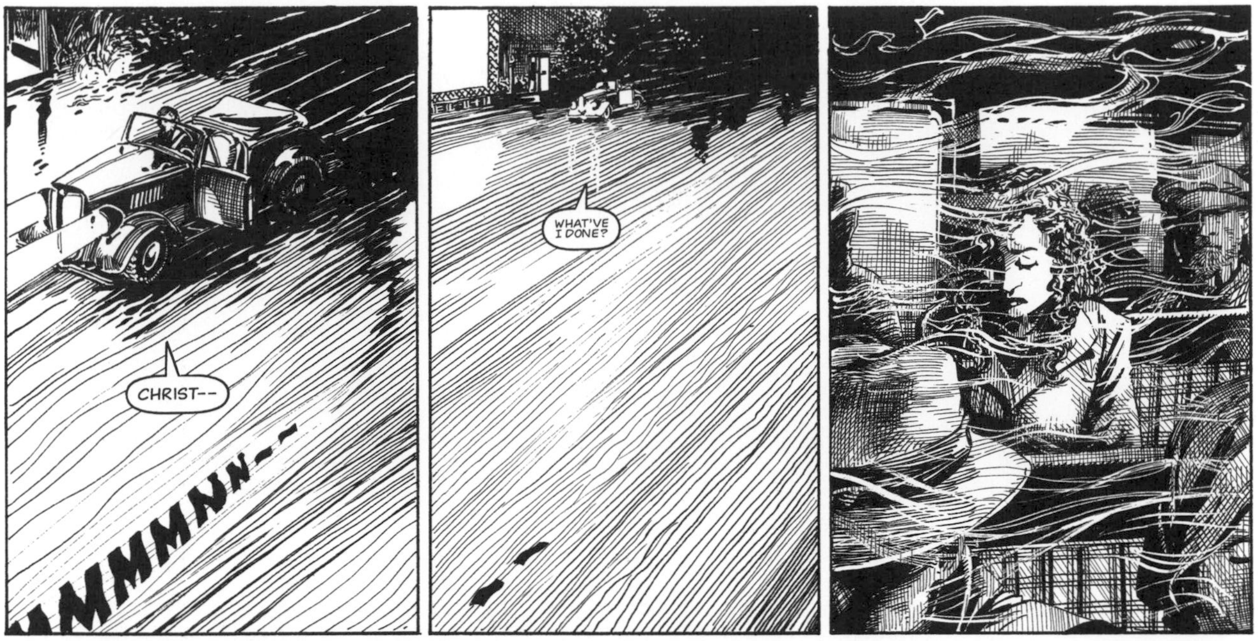
CHRIST--
MMMMMNN--
WHAT'VE I DONE?

The John E. Powell residence Sunday, July 25

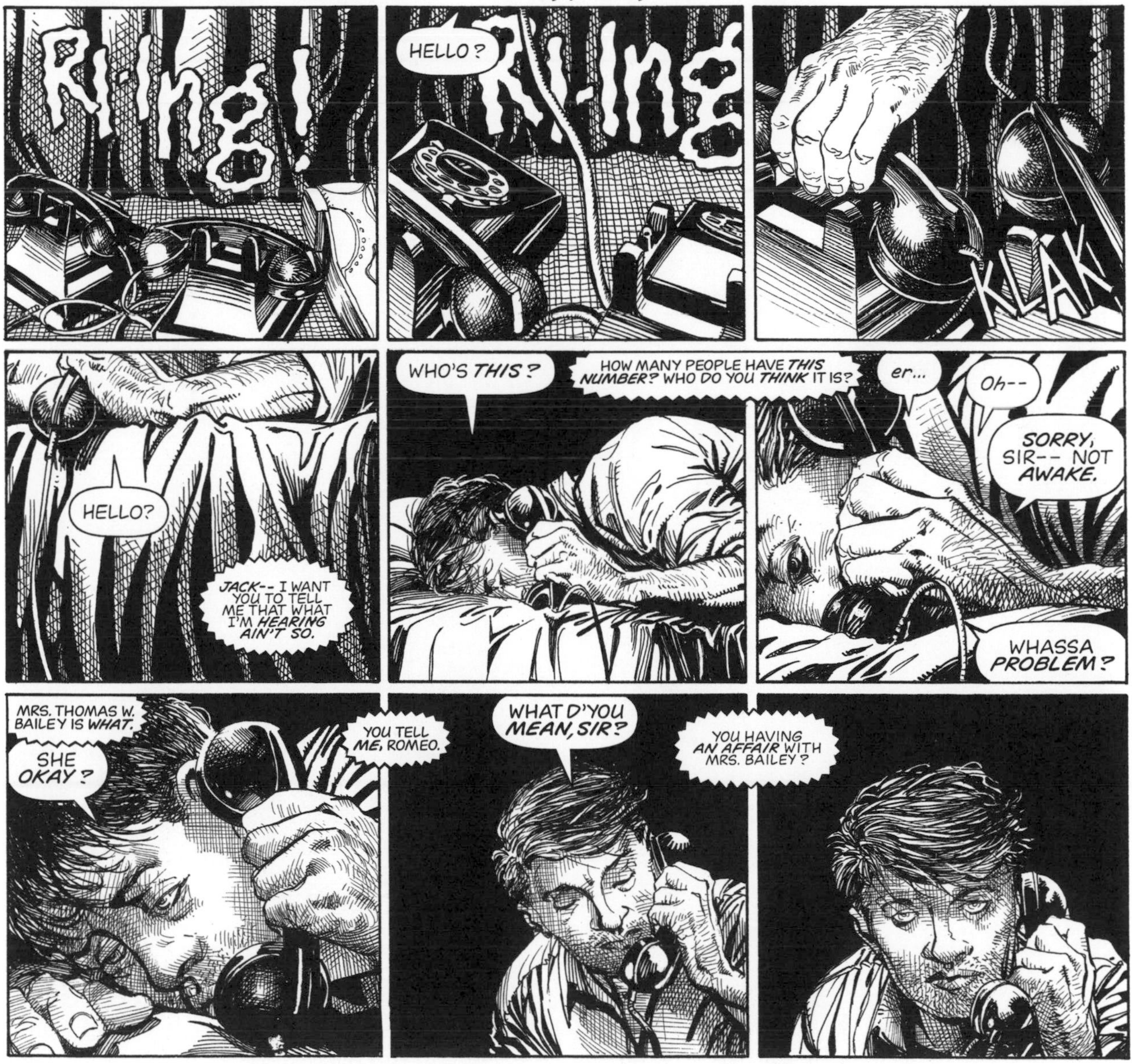
RI-ING!
HELLO?
RI-ING
KLAK
HELLO?
JACK-- I WANT YOU TO TELL ME THAT WHAT I'M HEARING AIN'T SO.
WHO'S THIS?
HOW MANY PEOPLE HAVE THIS NUMBER? WHO DO YOU THINK IT IS?
er...
Oh--
SORRY, SIR-- NOT AWAKE.
WHASSA PROBLEM?
MRS. THOMAS W. BAILEY IS WHAT.
SHE OKAY?
YOU TELL ME, ROMEO.
WHAT D'YOU MEAN, SIR?
YOU HAVING AN AFFAIR WITH MRS. BAILEY?

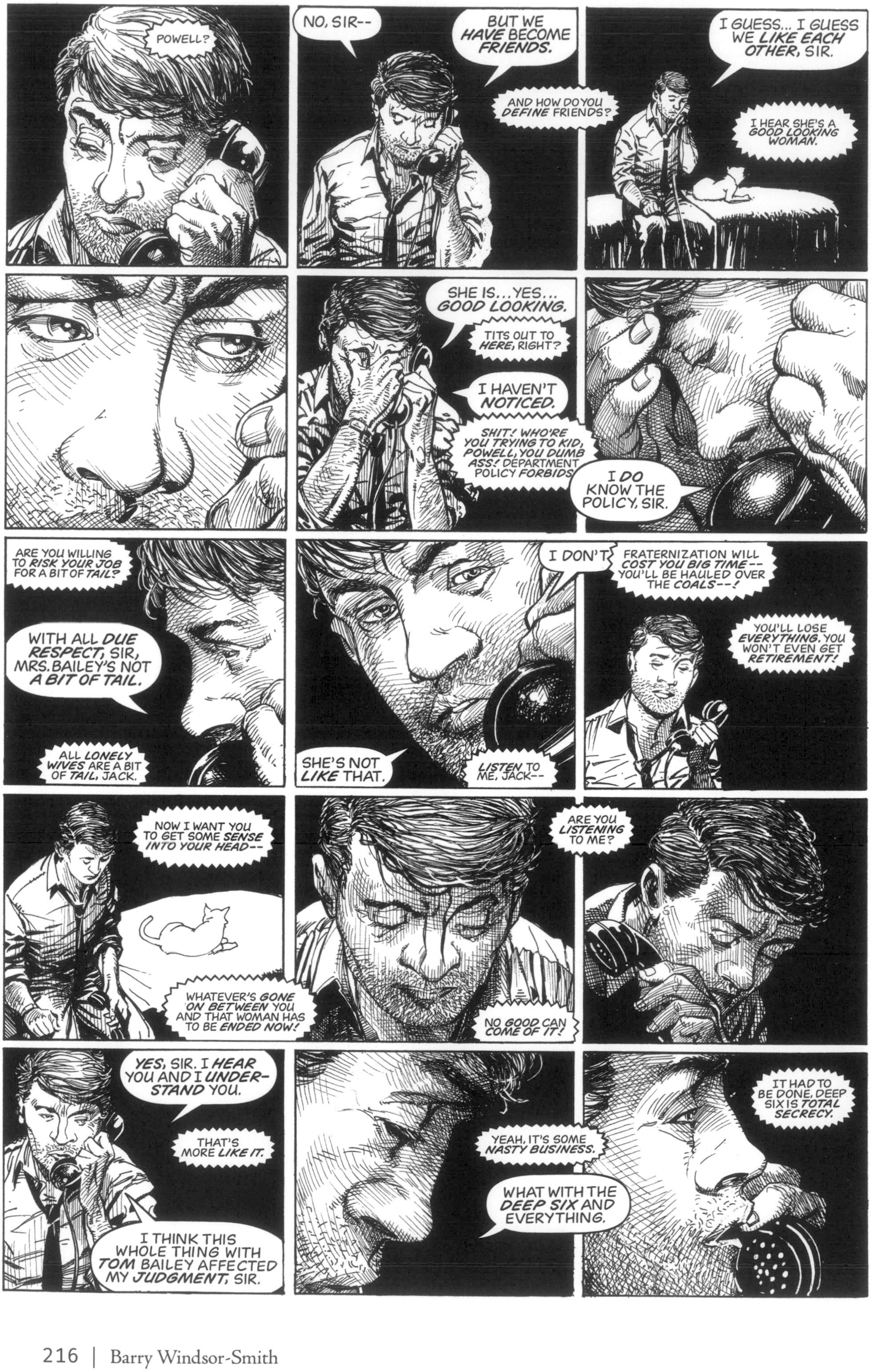
POWELL?
NO, SIR--
BUT WE HAVE BECOME FRIENDS.
AND HOW DO YOU DEFINE FRIENDS?
I GUESS... I GUESS WE LIKE EACH OTHER, SIR.
I HEAR SHE'S A GOOD LOOKING WOMAN.
SHE IS... YES... GOOD LOOKING.
TITS OUT TO HERE, RIGHT?
I HAVEN'T NOTICED.
SHIT! WHO'RE YOU TRYING TO KID, POWELL, YOU DUMB ASS! DEPARTMENT POLICY FORBIDS
I DO KNOW THE POLICY, SIR.
ARE YOU WILLING TO RISK YOUR JOB FOR A BIT OF TAIL?
WITH ALL DUE RESPECT, SIR, MRS. BAILEY'S NOT A BIT OF TAIL.
ALL LONELY WIVES ARE A BIT OF TAIL, JACK.
I DON'T
SHE'S NOT LIKE THAT.
LISTEN TO ME, JACK--
FRATERNIZATION WILL COST YOU BIG TIME-- YOU'LL BE HAULED OVER THE COALS--!
YOU'LL LOSE EVERYTHING. YOU WON'T EVEN GET RETIREMENT!
NOW I WANT YOU TO GET SOME SENSE INTO YOUR HEAD--
WHATEVER'S GONE 'ON BETWEEN YOU AND THAT WOMAN HAS TO BE ENDED NOW!
NO GOOD CAN COME OF IT!
ARE YOU LISTENING TO ME?
YES, SIR. I HEAR YOU AND I UNDER-STAND YOU.
THAT'S MORE LIKE IT.
I THINK THIS WHOLE THING WITH TOM BAILEY AFFECTED MY JUDGMENT, SIR.
YEAH, IT'S SOME NASTY BUSINESS.
WHAT WITH THE DEEP SIX AND EVERYTHING.
IT HAD TO BE DONE. DEEP SIX IS TOTAL SECRECY.

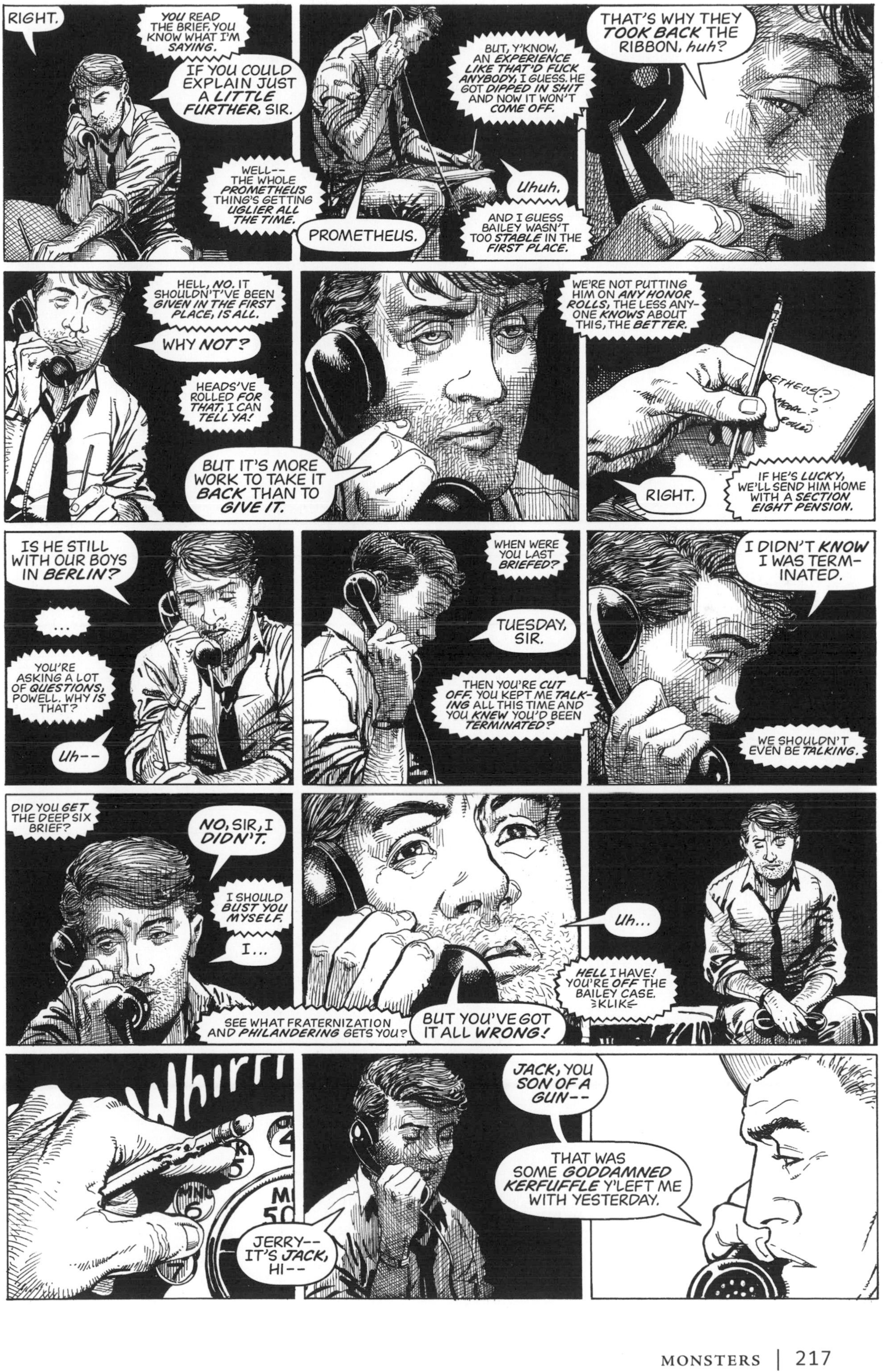

RIGHT.
YOU READ THE BRIEF. YOU KNOW WHAT I'M SAYING.
IF YOU COULD EXPLAIN JUST A LITTLE FURTHER, SIR.
WELL-- THE WHOLE PROMETHEUS THING'S GETTING UGLIER ALL THE TIME.
PROMETHEUS.
BUT, Y'KNOW, AN EXPERIENCE LIKE THAT'D FUCK ANYBODY, I GUESS. HE GOT DIPPED IN SHIT AND NOW IT WON'T COME OFF.
Uhuh.
AND I GUESS BAILEY WASN'T TOO STABLE IN THE FIRST PLACE.
THAT'S WHY THEY TOOK BACK THE RIBBON, huh?
HELL, NO. IT SHOULDN'T'VE BEEN GIVEN IN THE FIRST PLACE, IS ALL.
WHY NOT?
HEADS'VE ROLLED FOR THAT, I CAN TELL YA!
BUT IT'S MORE WORK TO TAKE IT BACK THAN TO GIVE IT.
WE'RE NOT PUTTING HIM ON ANY HONOR ROLLS, THE LESS ANYONE KNOWS ABOUT THIS, THE BETTER.
RIGHT.
IF HE'S LUCKY, WE'LL SEND HIM HOME WITH A SECTION EIGHT PENSION.
IS HE STILL WITH OUR BOYS IN BERLIN?
...
YOU'RE ASKING A LOT OF QUESTIONS, POWELL. WHY IS THAT?
Uh--
WHEN WERE YOU LAST BRIEFED?
TUESDAY, SIR.
THEN YOU'RE CUT OFF. YOU KEPT ME TALKING ALL THIS TIME AND YOU KNEW YOU'D BEEN TERMINATED?
I DIDN'T KNOW I WAS TERMINATED.
WE SHOULDN'T EVEN BE TALKING.
DID YOU GET THE DEEP SIX BRIEF?
NO, SIR, I DIDN'T.
I SHOULD BUST YOU MYSELF.
I...
SEE WHAT FRATERNIZATION AND PHILANDERING GETS YOU?
Uh...
BUT YOU'VE GOT IT ALL WRONG!
HELL I HAVE! YOU'RE OFF THE BAILEY CASE.
KLIK
Whirrr
JERRY-- IT'S JACK, HI--
JACK, YOU SON OF A GUN--
THAT WAS SOME GODDAMNED KERFUFFLE Y'LEFT ME WITH YESTERDAY.

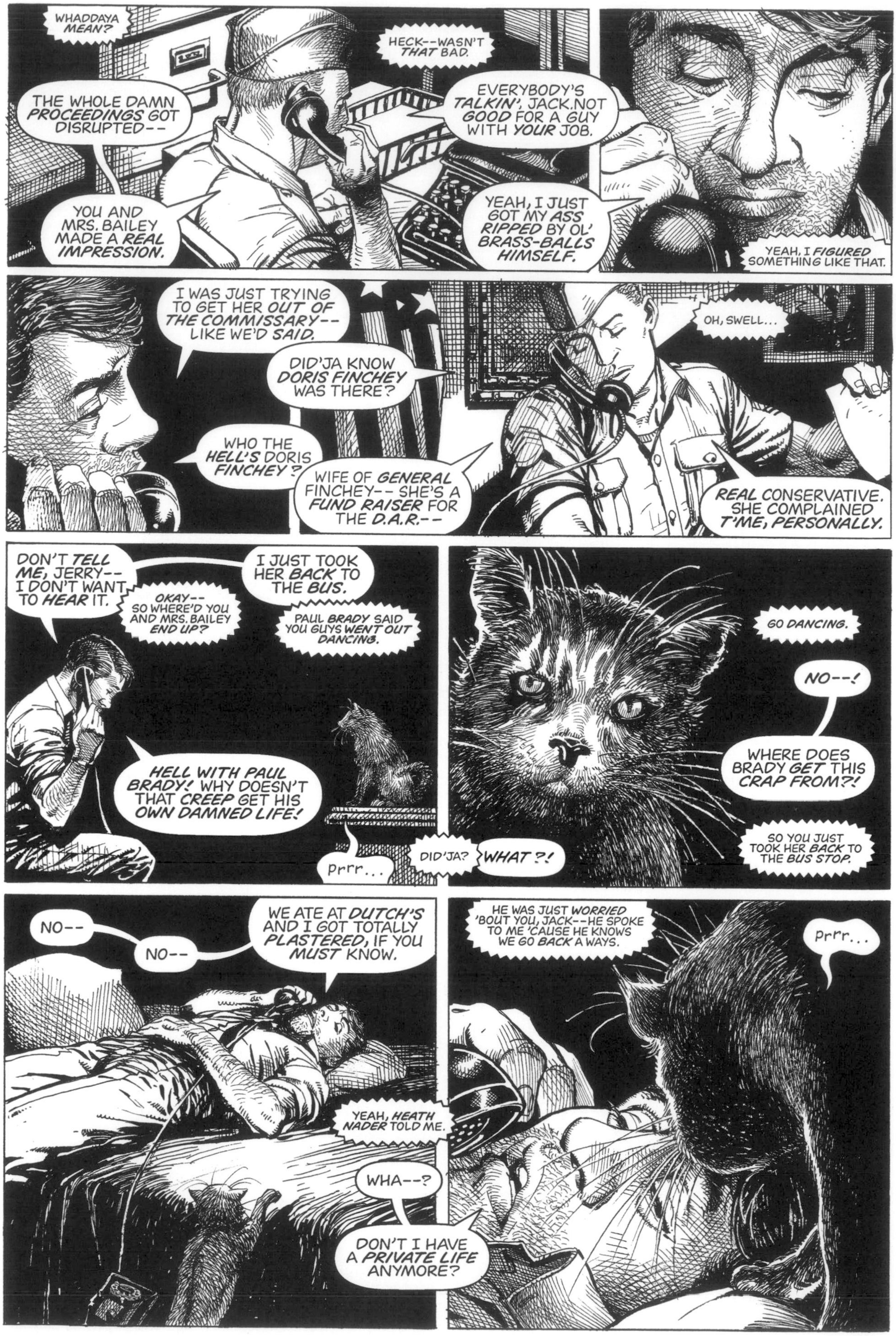
WHADDAYA MEAN?
THE WHOLE DAMN PROCEEDINGS GOT DISRUPTED--
YOU AND MRS. BAILEY MADE A REAL IMPRESSION.
HECK--WASN'T THAT BAD.
EVERYBODY'S TALKIN', JACK. NOT GOOD FOR A GUY WITH YOUR JOB.
YEAH, I JUST GOT MY ASS RIPPED BY OL' BRASS-BALLS HIMSELF.
YEAH, I FIGURED SOMETHING LIKE THAT.
I WAS JUST TRYING TO GET HER OUT OF THE COMMISSARY-- LIKE WE'D SAID.
DID'JA KNOW DORIS FINCHEY WAS THERE?
WHO THE HELL'S DORIS FINCHEY?
WIFE OF GENERAL FINCHEY-- SHE'S A FUND RAISER FOR THE D.A.R.--
OH, SWELL...
REAL CONSERVATIVE. SHE COMPLAINED T'ME, PERSONALLY.
DON'T TELL ME, JERRY-- I DON'T WANT TO HEAR IT.
I JUST TOOK HER BACK TO THE BUS.
OKAY-- SO WHERE'D YOU AND MRS. BAILEY END UP?
PAUL BRADY SAID YOU GUYS WENT OUT DANCING.
HELL WITH PAUL BRADY! WHY DOESN'T THAT CREEP GET HIS OWN DAMNED LIFE!
prrr...
DID'JA?
WHAT?!
GO DANCING.
NO--!
WHERE DOES BRADY GET THIS CRAP FROM?!
SO YOU JUST TOOK HER BACK TO THE BUS STOP.
NO--
NO--
WE ATE AT DUTCH'S AND I GOT TOTALLY PLASTERED, IF YOU MUST KNOW.
YEAH, HEATH NADER TOLD ME.
WHA--?
DON'T I HAVE A PRIVATE LIFE ANYMORE?
HE WAS JUST WORRIED 'BOUT YOU, JACK--HE SPOKE TO ME 'CAUSE HE KNOWS WE GO BACK A WAYS.
prrr...

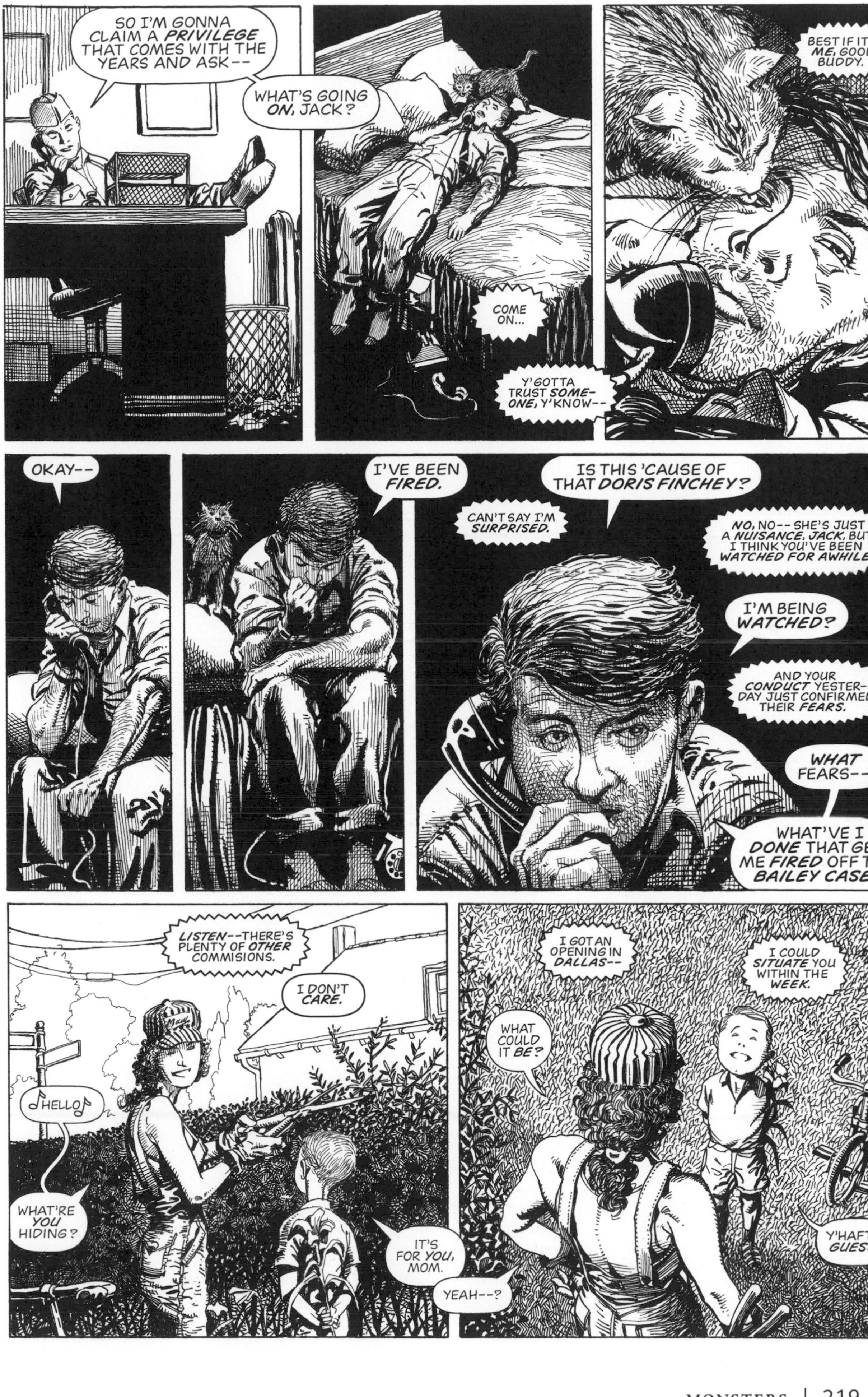
SO I'M GONNA CLAIM A PRIVILEGE THAT COMES WITH THE YEARS AND ASK--
WHAT'S GOING ON, JACK?
COME ON...
Y'GOTTA TRUST SOME-ONE, Y'KNOW--
BEST IF IT'S ME, GOOD BUDDY.
OKAY--
I'VE BEEN FIRED.
IS THIS 'CAUSE OF THAT DORIS FINCHEY?
CAN'T SAY I'M SURPRISED.
NO, NO--SHE'S JUST A NUISANCE, JACK, BUT I THINK YOU'VE BEEN WATCHED FOR AWHILE.
I'M BEING WATCHED?
AND YOUR CONDUCT YESTER-DAY JUST CONFIRMED THEIR FEARS.
WHAT FEARS--?
WHAT'VE I DONE THAT GETS ME FIRED OFF THE BAILEY CASE?
LISTEN--THERE'S PLENTY OF OTHER COMMISIONS.
I DON'T CARE.
HELLO
WHAT'RE YOU HIDING?
IT'S FOR YOU, MOM.
YEAH--?
I GOT AN OPENING IN DALLAS--
I COULD SITUATE YOU WITHIN THE WEEK.
WHAT COULD IT BE?
Y'HAFTA GUESS.

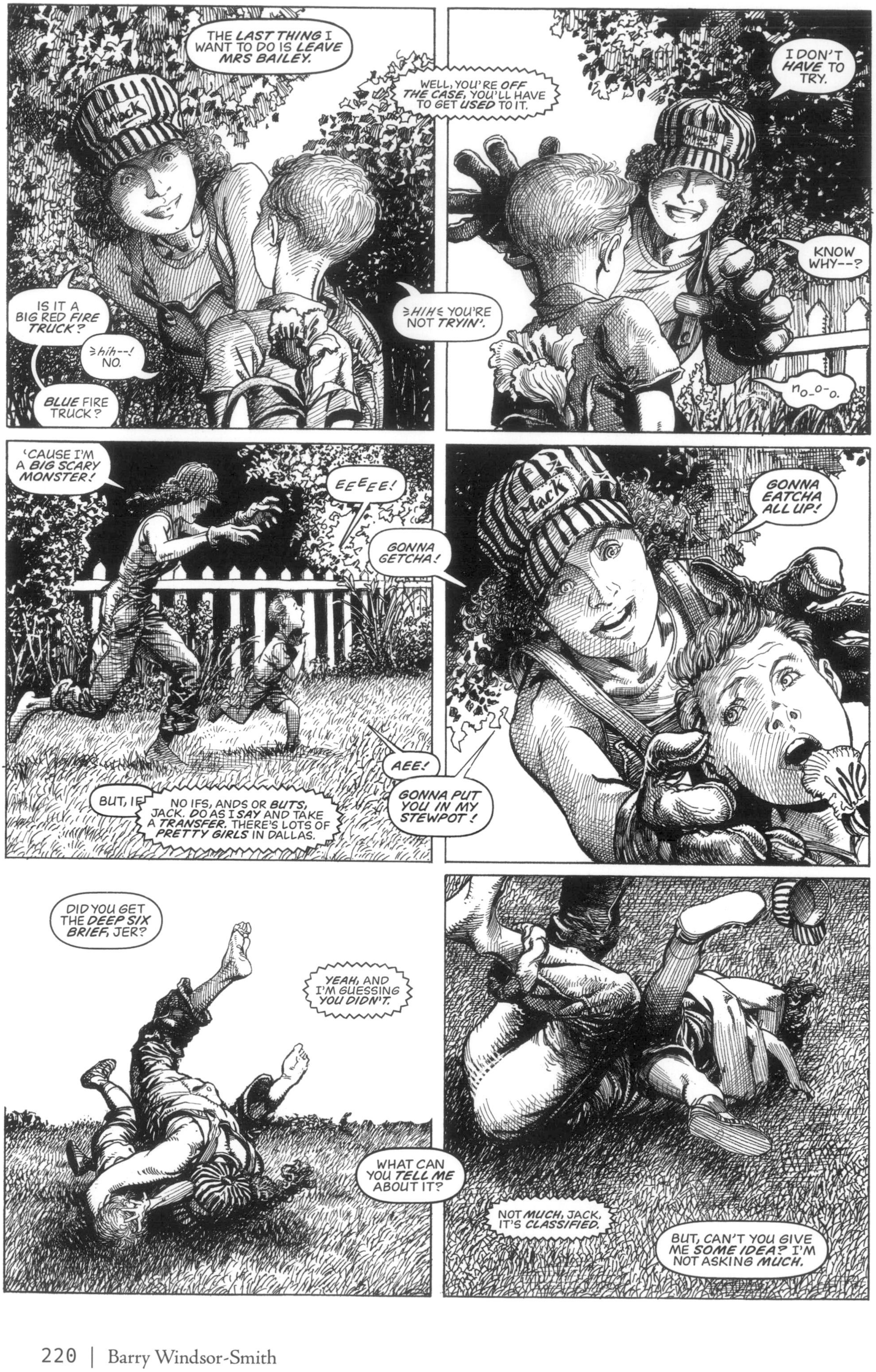

THE LAST THING I WANT TO DO IS LEAVE MRS BAILEY.
WELL, YOU'RE OFF THE CASE, YOU'LL HAVE TO GET USED TO IT.
IS IT A BIG RED FIRE TRUCK?
hih--! NO.
BLUE FIRE TRUCK?
HIH YOU'RE NOT TRYIN'.
I DON'T HAVE TO TRY.
KNOW WHY--?
n-o-o-o.
'CAUSE I'M A BIG SCARY MONSTER!
EEEEE!
GONNA GETCHA!
AEE!
GONNA PUT YOU IN MY STEWPOT!
BUT, IF
NO IFS, ANDS OR BUTS, JACK. DO AS I SAY AND TAKE A TRANSFER. THERE'S LOTS OF PRETTY GIRLS IN DALLAS.
GONNA EATCHA ALL UP!
DID YOU GET THE DEEP SIX BRIEF, JER?
YEAH, AND I'M GUESSING YOU DIDN'T.
WHAT CAN YOU TELL ME ABOUT IT?
NOT MUCH, JACK. IT'S CLASSIFIED.
BUT, CAN'T YOU GIVE ME SOME IDEA? I'M NOT ASKING MUCH.

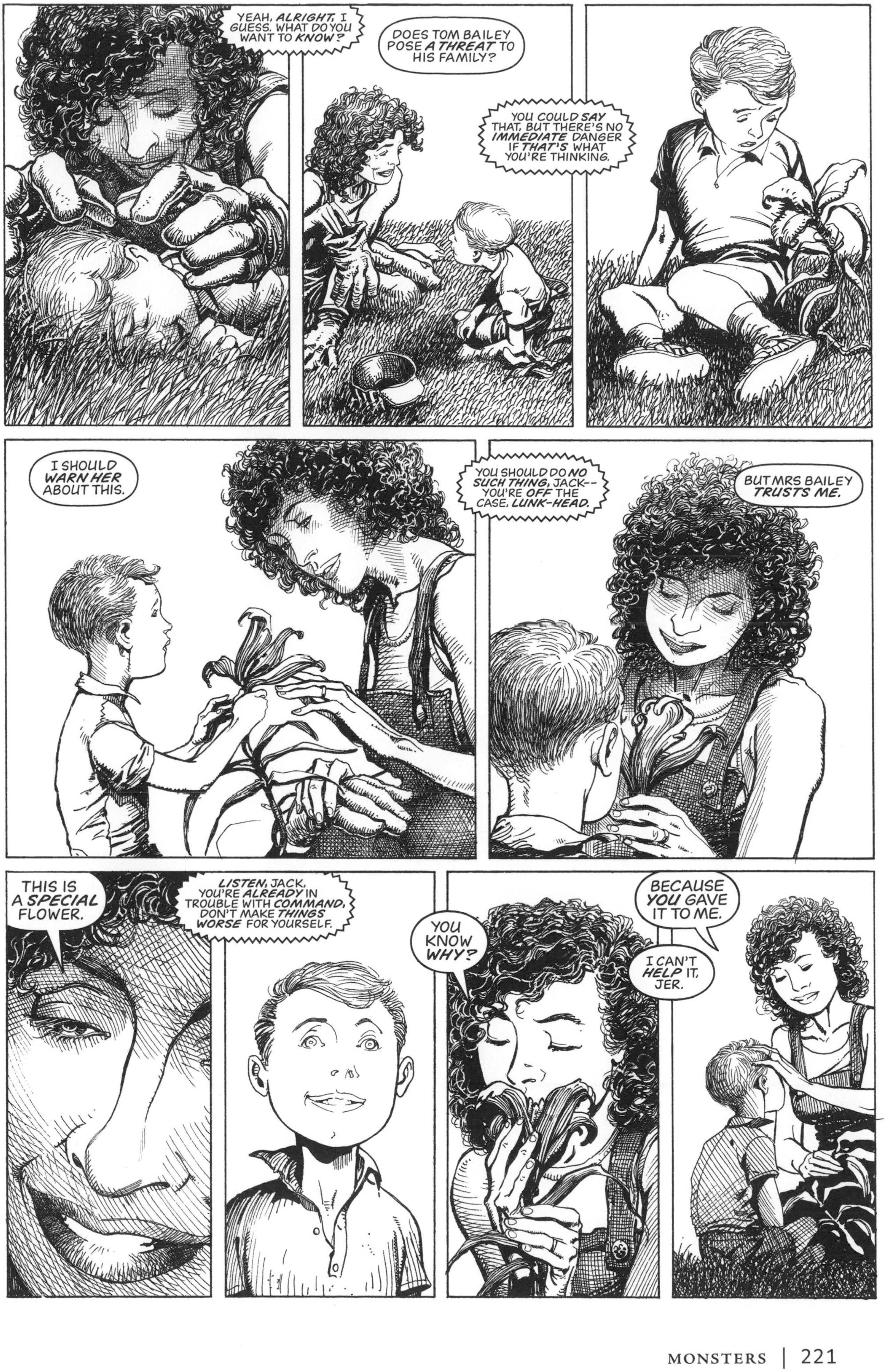

YEAH, ALRIGHT, I GUESS. WHAT DO YOU WANT TO KNOW?
DOES TOM BAILEY POSE A THREAT TO HIS FAMILY?
YOU COULD SAY THAT, BUT THERE'S NO IMMEDIATE DANGER IF THAT'S WHAT YOU'RE THINKING.
I SHOULD WARN HER ABOUT THIS.
YOU SHOULD DO NO SUCH THING, JACK-- YOU'RE OFF THE CASE, LUNK-HEAD.
BUT MRS BAILEY TRUSTS ME.
THIS IS A SPECIAL FLOWER.
LISTEN, JACK, YOU'RE ALREADY IN TROUBLE WITH COMMAND, DON'T MAKE THINGS WORSE FOR YOURSELF.
YOU KNOW WHY?
BECAUSE YOU GAVE IT TO ME.
I CAN'T HELP IT, JER.

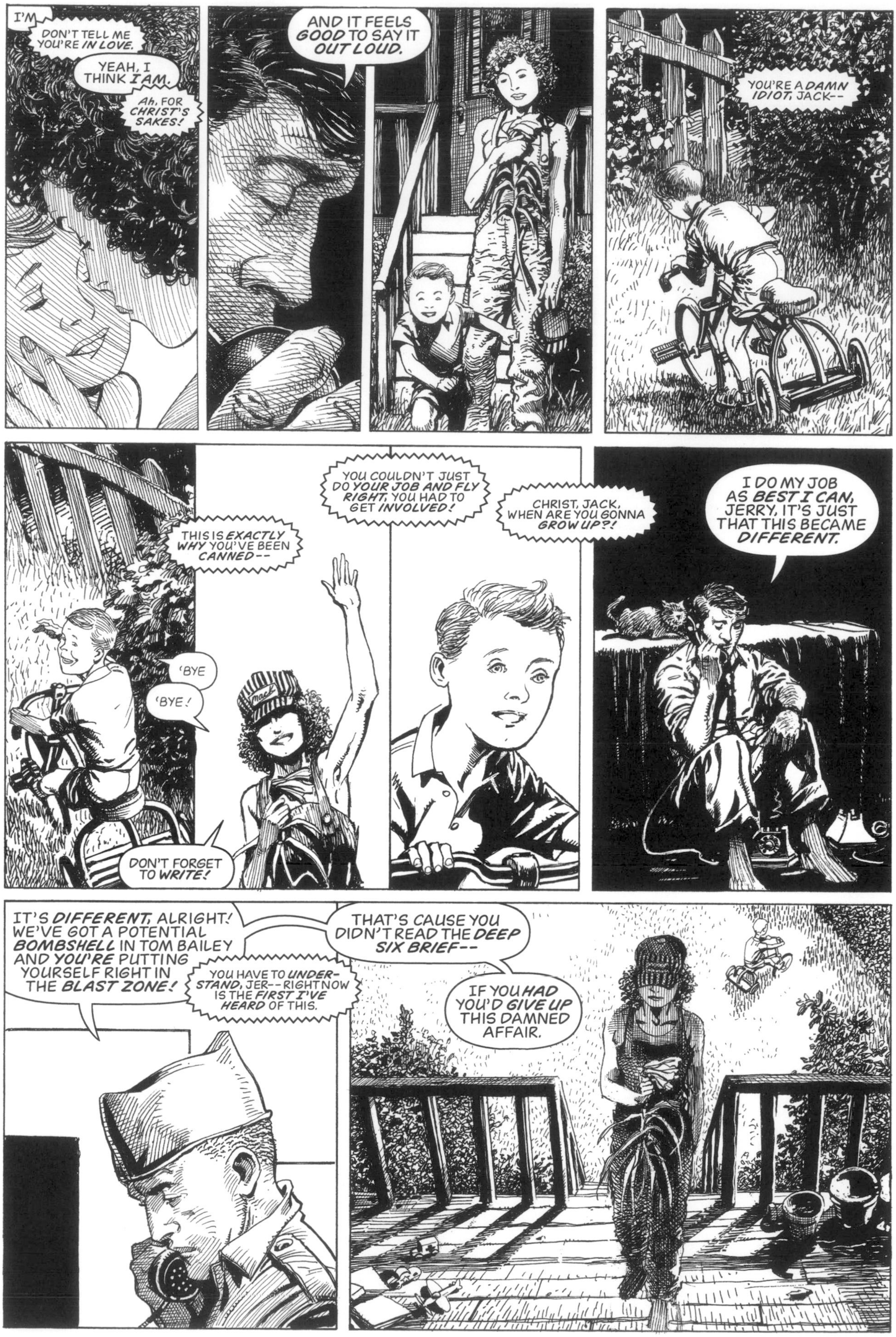

I'M
DON'T TELL ME YOU'RE IN LOVE.
YEAH, I THINK I AM.
Ah, FOR CHRIST'S SAKES!
AND IT FEELS GOOD TO SAY IT OUT LOUD.
YOU'RE A DAMN IDIOT, JACK--
THIS IS EXACTLY WHY YOU'VE BEEN CANNED--
YOU COULDN'T JUST DO YOUR JOB AND FLY RIGHT, YOU HAD TO GET INVOLVED!
CHRIST, JACK, WHEN ARE YOU GONNA GROW UP?!
'BYE
'BYE!
DON'T FORGET TO WRITE!
I DO MY JOB AS BEST I CAN, JERRY, IT'S JUST THAT THIS BECAME DIFFERENT.
IT'S DIFFERENT, ALRIGHT! WE'VE GOT A POTENTIAL BOMBSHELL IN TOM BAILEY AND YOU'RE PUTTING YOURSELF RIGHT IN THE BLAST ZONE!
YOU HAVE TO UNDERSTAND, JER-- RIGHT NOW IS THE FIRST I'VE HEARD OF THIS.
THAT'S CAUSE YOU DIDN'T READ THE DEEP SIX BRIEF--
IF YOU HAD YOU'D GIVE UP THIS DAMNED AFFAIR.

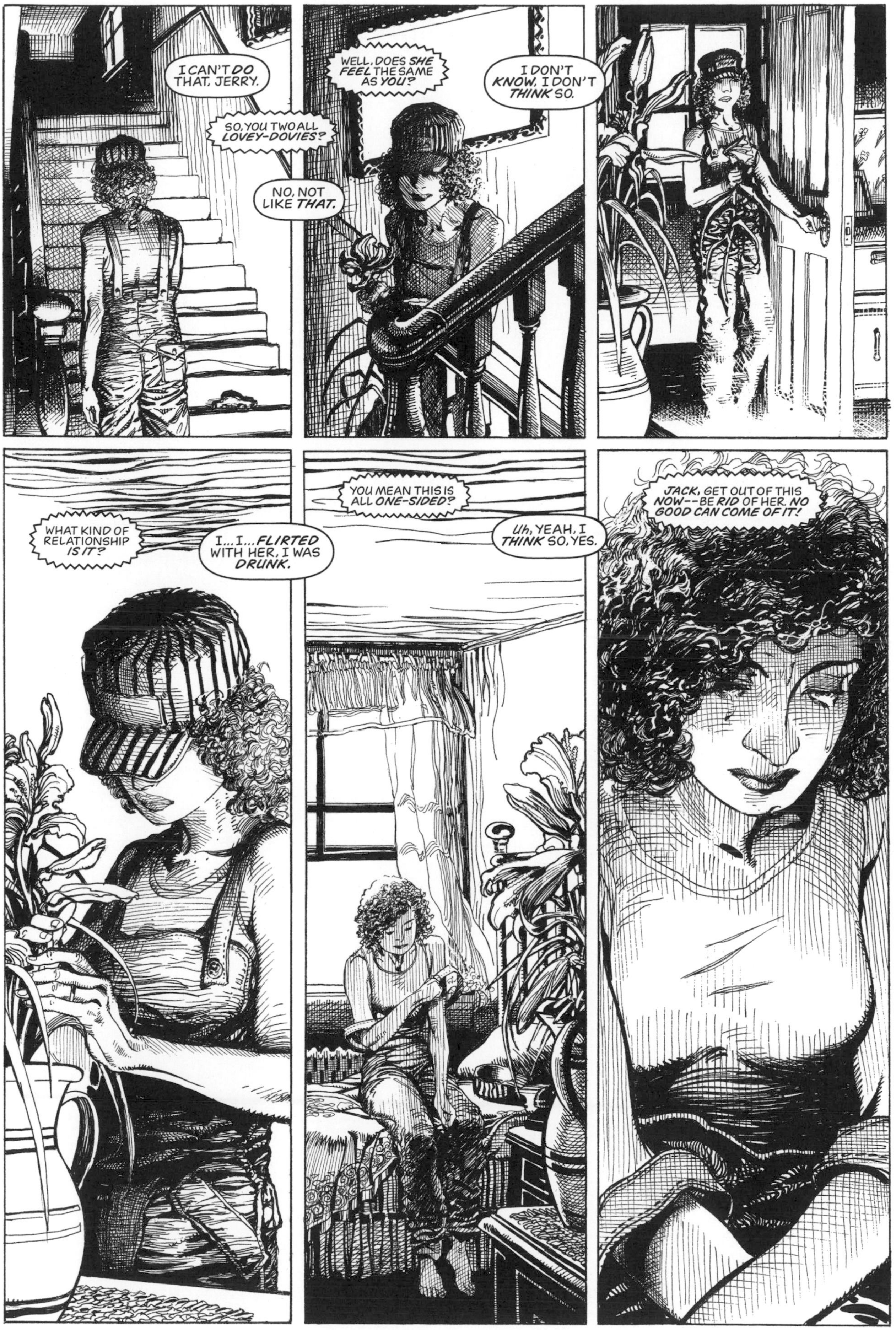
I CAN'T DO THAT, JERRY.
SO, YOU TWO ALL LOVEY-DOVIES?
NO, NOT LIKE THAT.
WELL, DOES SHE FEEL THE SAME AS YOU?
I DON'T KNOW, I DON'T THINK SO.
WHAT KIND OF RELATIONSHIP IS IT?
I... I... FLIRTED WITH HER. I WAS DRUNK.
YOU MEAN THIS IS ALL ONE-SIDED?
Uh, YEAH, I THINK SO, YES.
JACK, GET OUT OF THIS NOW--BE RID OF HER. NO GOOD CAN COME OF IT!

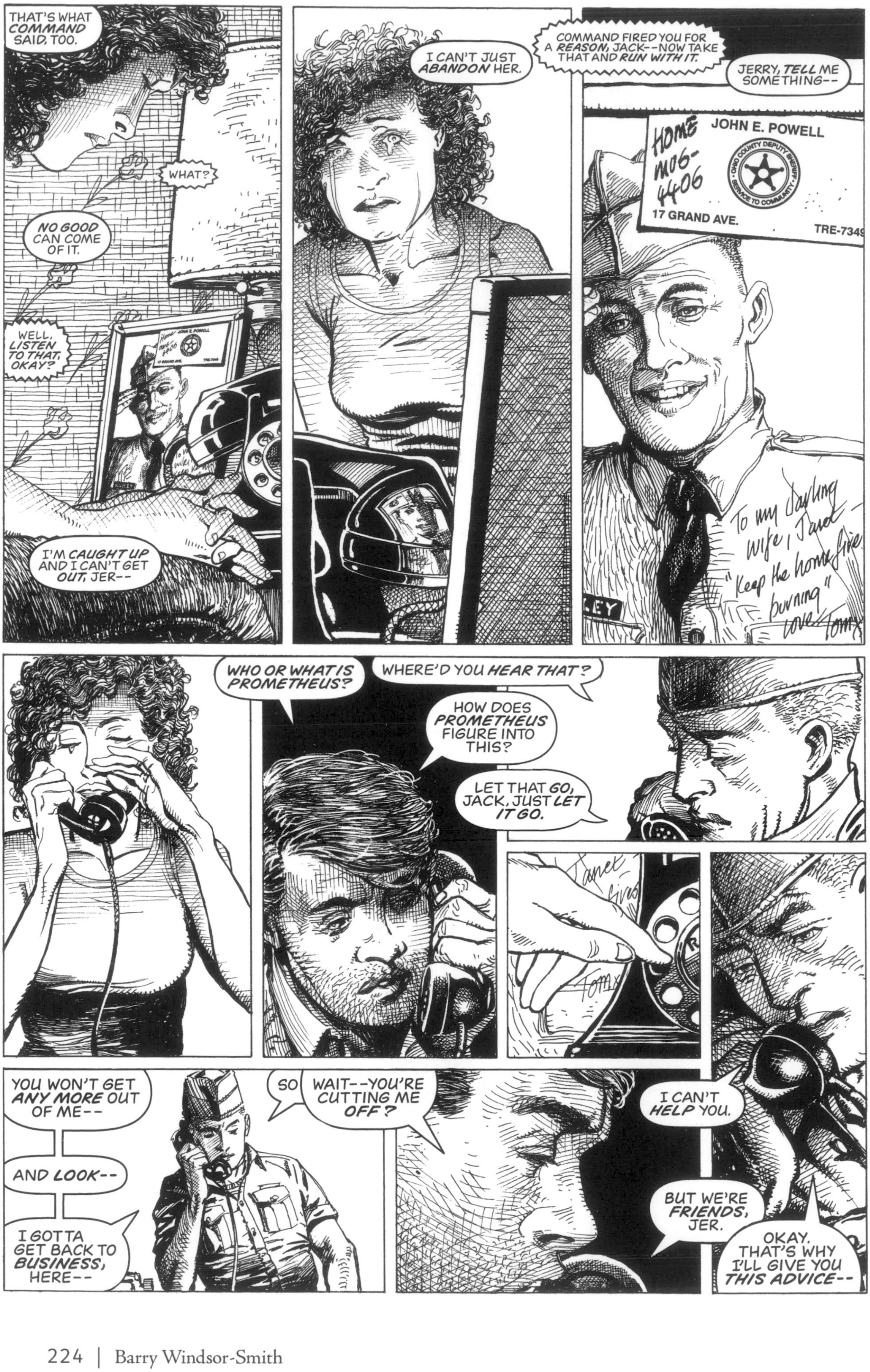
THAT'S WHAT COMMAND SAID, TOO.
WHAT?
NO GOOD CAN COME OF IT.
WELL, LISTEN TO THAT, OKAY?
I'M CAUGHT UP AND I CAN'T GET OUT, JER--
I CAN'T JUST ABANDON HER.
COMMAND FIRED YOU FOR A REASON, JACK--NOW TAKE THAT AND RUN WITH IT.
JERRY, TELL ME SOMETHING--
JOHN E. POWELL
HOME MO6-4406
17 GRAND AVE.
TRE-7349
To my darling wife, Janet
"Keep the home fires burning"
love Tom x
WHO OR WHAT IS PROMETHEUS?
WHERE'D YOU HEAR THAT?
HOW DOES PROMETHEUS FIGURE INTO THIS?
LET THAT GO, JACK, JUST LET IT GO.
YOU WON'T GET ANY MORE OUT OF ME--
AND LOOK--
I GOTTA GET BACK TO BUSINESS, HERE--
SO
WAIT--YOU'RE CUTTING ME OFF?
I CAN'T HELP YOU.
BUT WE'RE FRIENDS, JER.
OKAY. THAT'S WHY I'LL GIVE YOU THIS ADVICE--

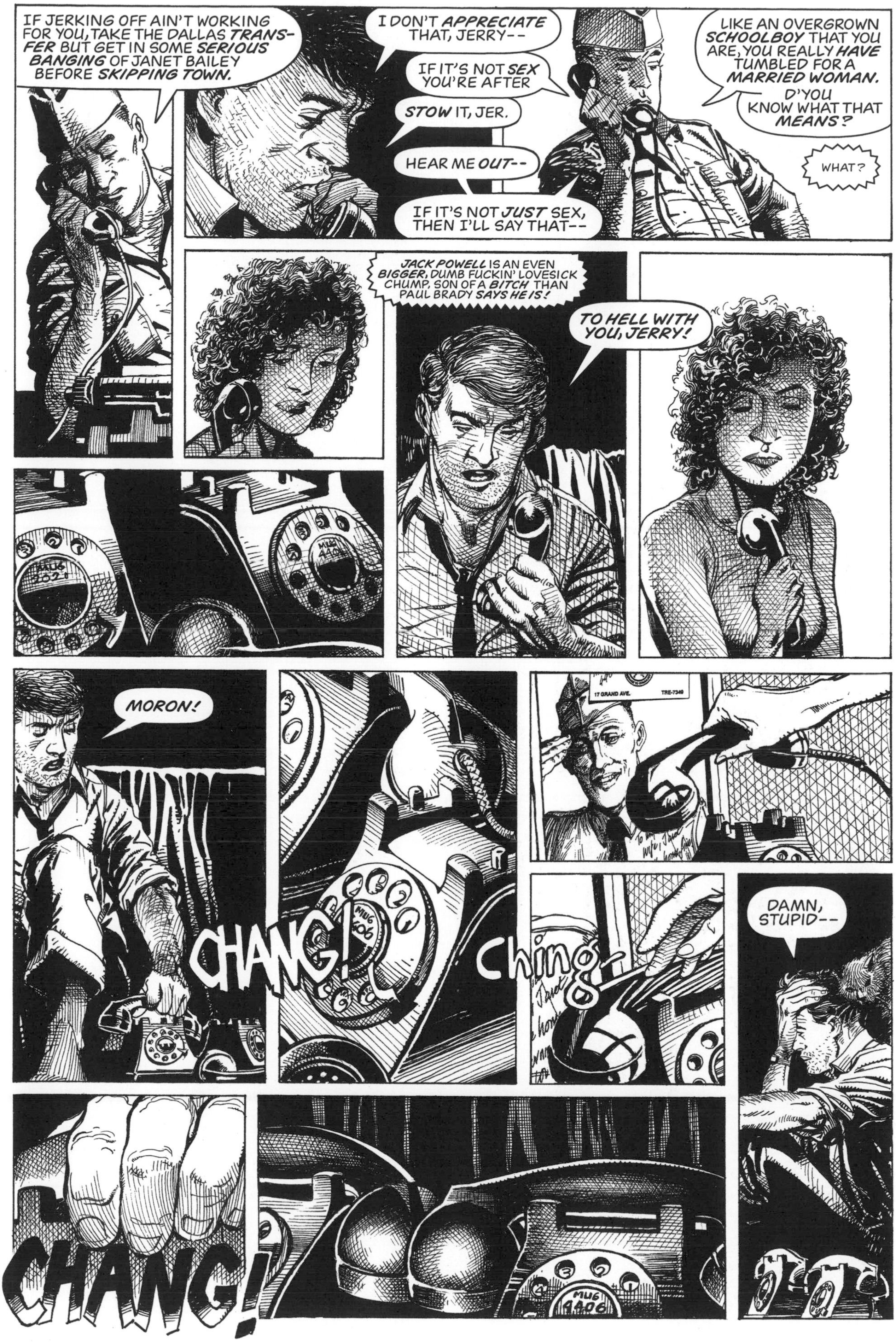
IF JERKING OFF AIN'T WORKING FOR YOU, TAKE THE DALLAS TRANSFER BUT GET IN SOME SERIOUS BANGING OF JANET BAILEY BEFORE SKIPPING TOWN.
I DON'T APPRECIATE THAT, JERRY--
IF IT'S NOT SEX YOU'RE AFTER
STOW IT, JER.
HEAR ME OUT--
IF IT'S NOT JUST SEX, THEN I'LL SAY THAT--
LIKE AN OVERGROWN SCHOOLBOY THAT YOU ARE, YOU REALLY HAVE TUMBLED FOR A MARRIED WOMAN.
D'YOU KNOW WHAT THAT MEANS?
WHAT?
JACK POWELL IS AN EVEN BIGGER, DUMB FUCKIN' LOVESICK CHUMP. SON OF A BITCH THAN PAUL BRADY SAYS HE IS!
TO HELL WITH YOU, JERRY!
MORON!
CHANG!
17 GRAND AVE.
TRE-7349
Ching-
DAMN, STUPID--
CHANG!

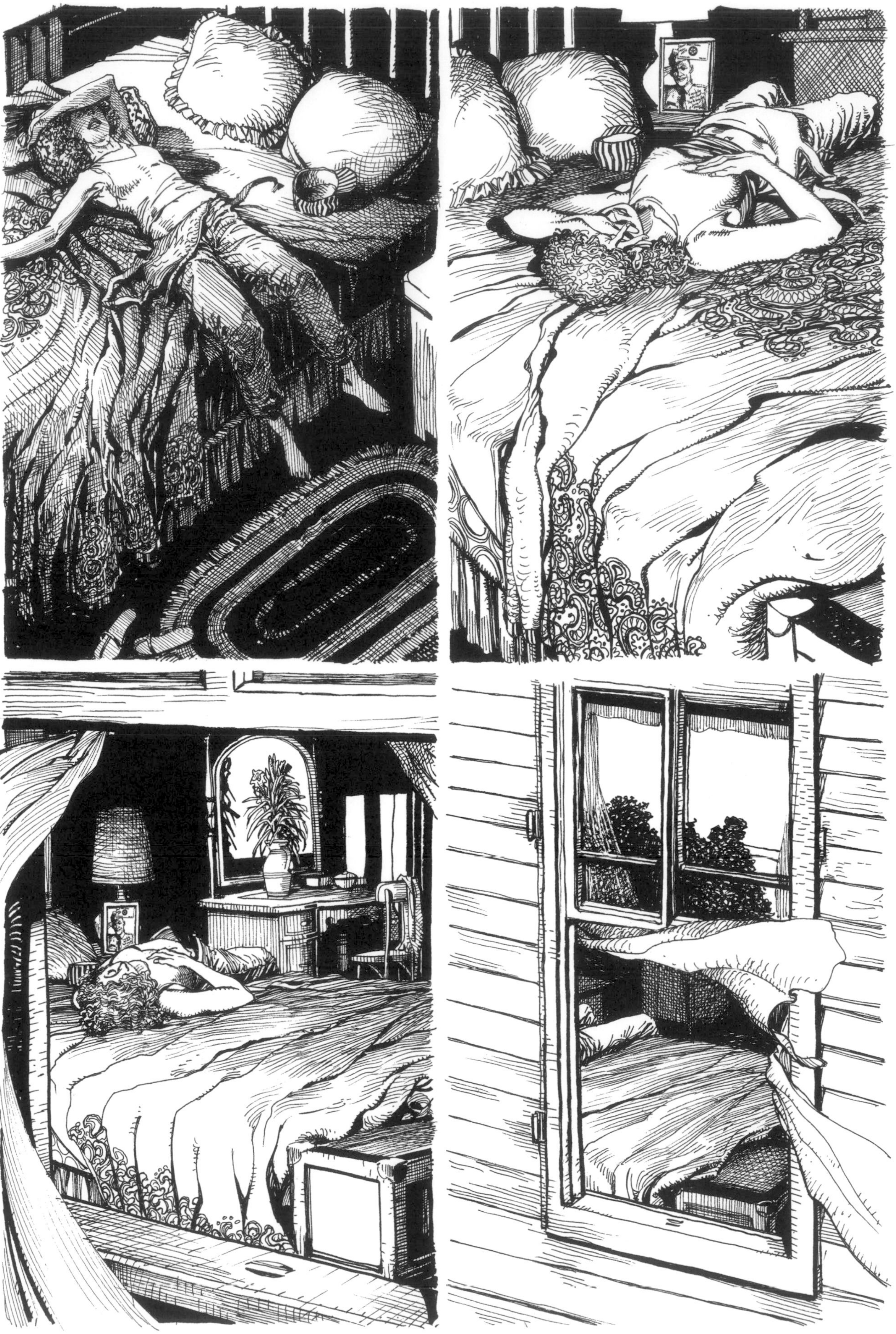

My dearest darling,
I've been worried so much ~~since you stopped~~ since I've stopped hearing from you. I've not known what to do with myself since my last letter ~~to you~~ as my days used to be taken up w/anticipation of your replies.

Dearest Tom,
It's nearly seven in the evening, but w/the shorter days now it ~~feels more like~~ looks more like midnight.

Thursday Nov 28
Today was Thanksgiving so Bobby and I ~~whent~~ went to Eileen's for a few hours. Then Margie and the kids came later w/dessert. It was luscious apple and pear w/a sweet ~~liqour~~ liquer

Eileen drank half of it over coffee. I had just a little bit but it gave me a terrific headache later on. I don't know how she contained herself all along but over coffee she announced that Morris would be home in the New Year as early as April.

I keep wondering when I'll hear from you telling me when you'll be home yourself. You will be coming home, won't you Tom? ~~Please tr try to write~~ Perhaps you'll just turn up at the door one day soon. I can almost imagine that happening. Bobby i

Bobby is doing really well and is all smiles when I tell him about you protecting America from Germans. ha ha

I miss you so
Your loving wife
Jan xxoxxxo

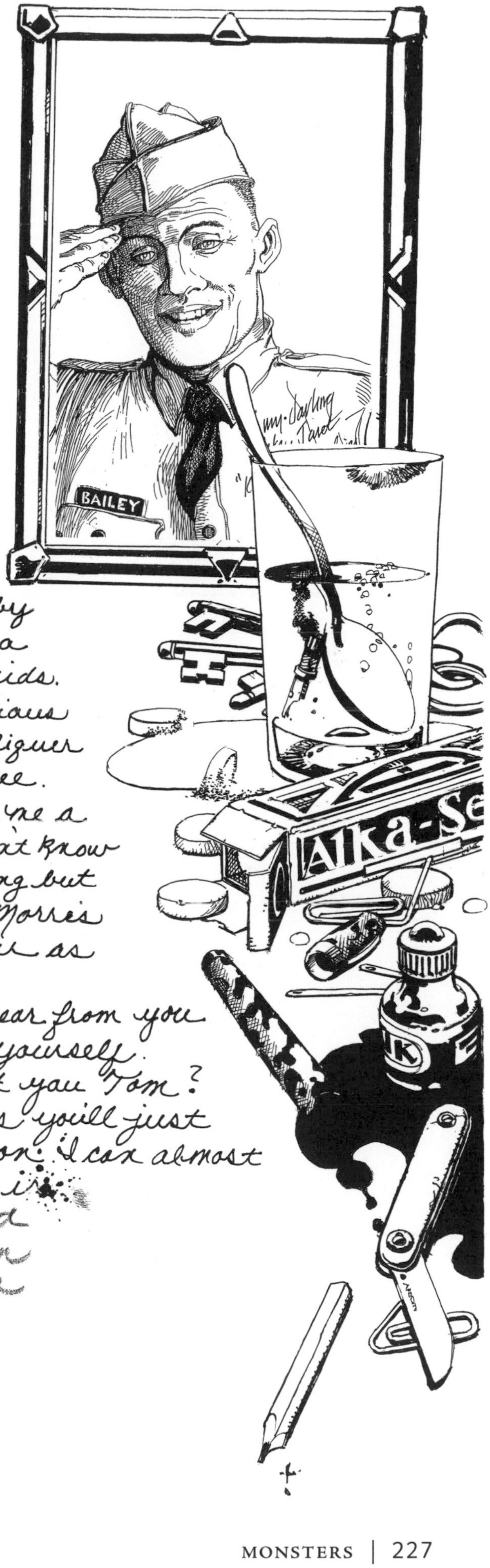
BAILEY
Alka-Se

December 17, 1948

Jack came by today. I'm so upset I don't know if writing about it will help. My letter to Tom from last year was returned unopened. Tom never got it! And all this time I've been disappointed and upset wondering why he hadn't replied to me. This is all so horrid. Jack tried to soften the blow by saying that it had been rejected because of some security reasons, but when I saw that the envelope hadn't even been opened he blushed and we were both a bit embarrassed. I'm sorry that he felt obliged to lie.

Jack said that all he knows is that Tom has had a kind of breakdown and that he's being treated in a German hospital for his stress and nervous exhaustion. Poor Tom. I do so wish I could be ~~the~~ there to help and comfort him.

I also said he'd bet money that whatever my letter said or didn't say the doctors would have not allowed him to read it because he's depressed and probably homesick and hearing from me might just make matters worse for him. I'm not so sure about this. I'd always thought it was the other way around.

Perhaps it's as I've feared— Perhaps Tom is far more ill than they're willing to say.

228 | Barry Windsor-Smith

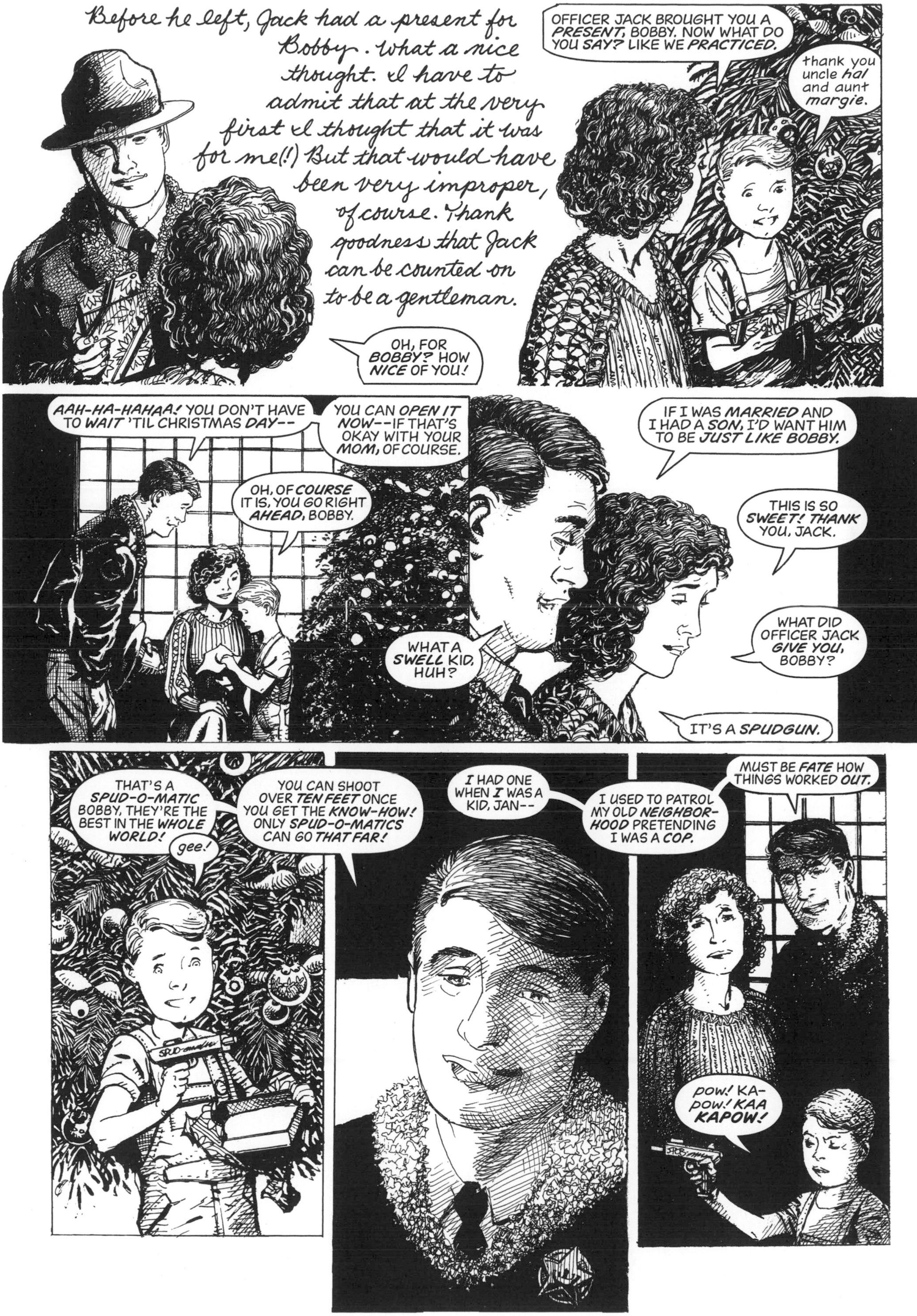
Before he left, Jack had a present for Bobby. What a nice thought. I have to admit that at the very first I thought that it was for me(!) But that would have been very improper, of course. Thank goodness that Jack can be counted on to be a gentleman.
OH, FOR BOBBY? HOW NICE OF YOU!
OFFICER JACK BROUGHT YOU A PRESENT, BOBBY. NOW WHAT DO YOU SAY? LIKE WE PRACTICED.
thank you uncle hal and aunt margie.
AAH-HA-HAHAA! YOU DON'T HAVE TO WAIT 'TIL CHRISTMAS DAY--
YOU CAN OPEN IT NOW--IF THAT'S OKAY WITH YOUR MOM, OF COURSE.
OH, OF COURSE IT IS, YOU GO RIGHT AHEAD, BOBBY.
IF I WAS MARRIED AND I HAD A SON, I'D WANT HIM TO BE JUST LIKE BOBBY.
THIS IS SO SWEET! THANK YOU, JACK.
WHAT A SWELL KID, HUH?
WHAT DID OFFICER JACK GIVE YOU, BOBBY?
IT'S A SPUDGUN.
THAT'S A SPUD-O-MATIC BOBBY, THEY'RE THE BEST IN THE WHOLE WORLD!
gee!
YOU CAN SHOOT OVER TEN FEET ONCE YOU GET THE KNOW-HOW! ONLY SPUD-O-MATICS CAN GO THAT FAR!
I HAD ONE WHEN I WAS A KID, JAN--
I USED TO PATROL MY OLD NEIGHBORHOOD PRETENDING I WAS A COP.
MUST BE FATE HOW THINGS WORKED OUT.
pow! KA-pow! KAA KAPOW!

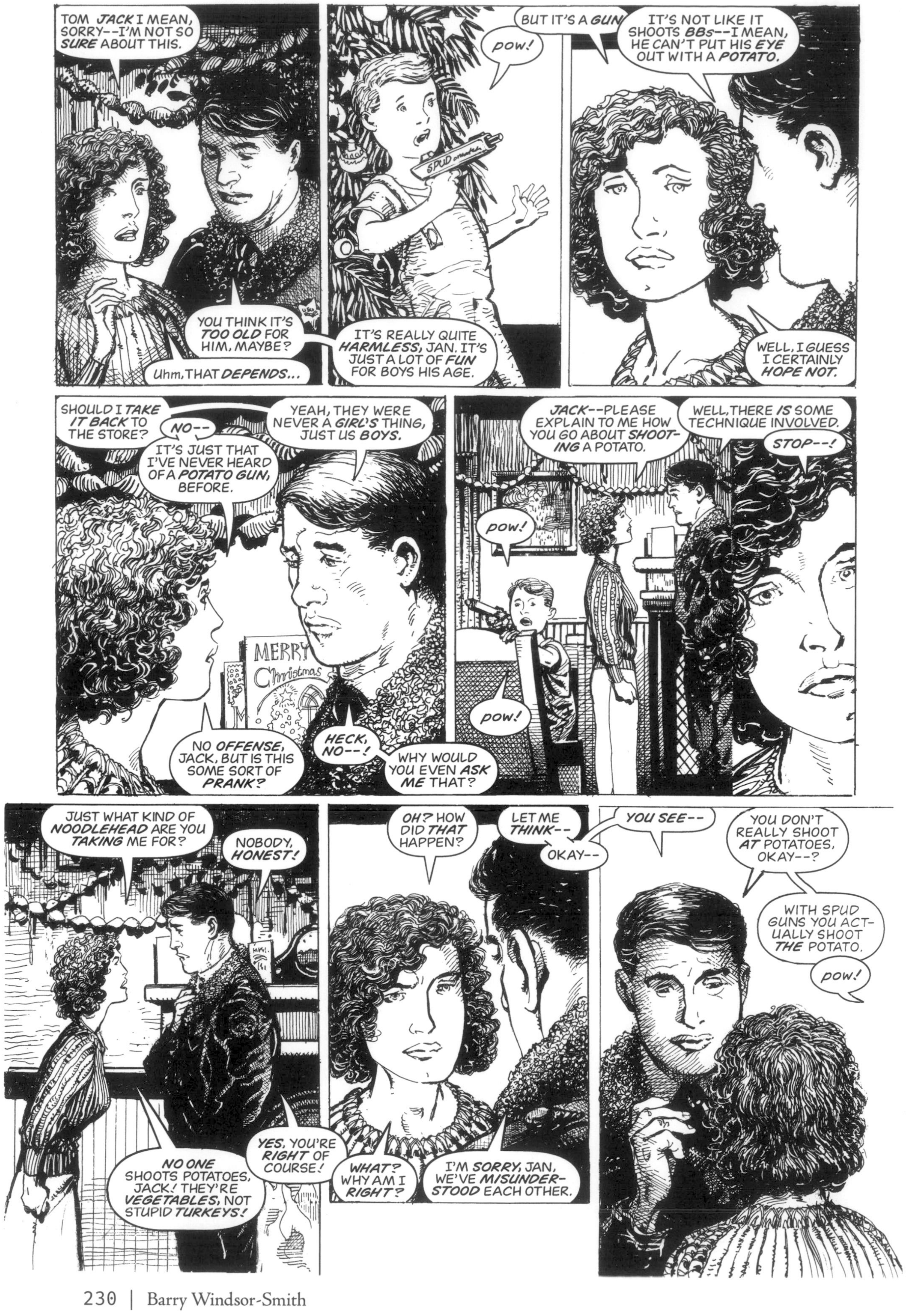

TOM JACK I MEAN, SORRY--I'M NOT SO SURE ABOUT THIS.
YOU THINK IT'S TOO OLD FOR HIM, MAYBE?
Uhm, THAT DEPENDS...
IT'S REALLY QUITE HARMLESS, JAN. IT'S JUST A LOT OF FUN FOR BOYS HIS AGE.
pow!
BUT IT'S A GUN
IT'S NOT LIKE IT SHOOTS BBs--I MEAN, HE CAN'T PUT HIS EYE OUT WITH A POTATO.
WELL, I GUESS I CERTAINLY HOPE NOT.
SHOULD I TAKE IT BACK TO THE STORE?
NO--
IT'S JUST THAT I'VE NEVER HEARD OF A POTATO GUN, BEFORE.
YEAH, THEY WERE NEVER A GIRL'S THING, JUST US BOYS.
MERRY Christmas
NO OFFENSE, JACK, BUT IS THIS SOME SORT OF PRANK?
HECK, NO--!
WHY WOULD YOU EVEN ASK ME THAT?
JACK--PLEASE EXPLAIN TO ME HOW YOU GO ABOUT SHOOTING A POTATO.
WELL, THERE IS SOME TECHNIQUE INVOLVED.
STOP--!
pow!
pow!
JUST WHAT KIND OF NOODLEHEAD ARE YOU TAKING ME FOR?
NOBODY, HONEST!
NO ONE SHOOTS POTATOES, JACK! THEY'RE VEGETABLES, NOT STUPID TURKEYS!
YES, YOU'RE RIGHT OF COURSE!
OH? HOW DID THAT HAPPEN?
LET ME THINK--
OKAY--
WHAT? WHY AM I RIGHT?
I'M SORRY, JAN, WE'VE MISUNDERSTOOD EACH OTHER.
YOU SEE--
YOU DON'T REALLY SHOOT AT POTATOES, OKAY--?
WITH SPUD GUNS YOU ACTUALLY SHOOT THE POTATO.
pow!

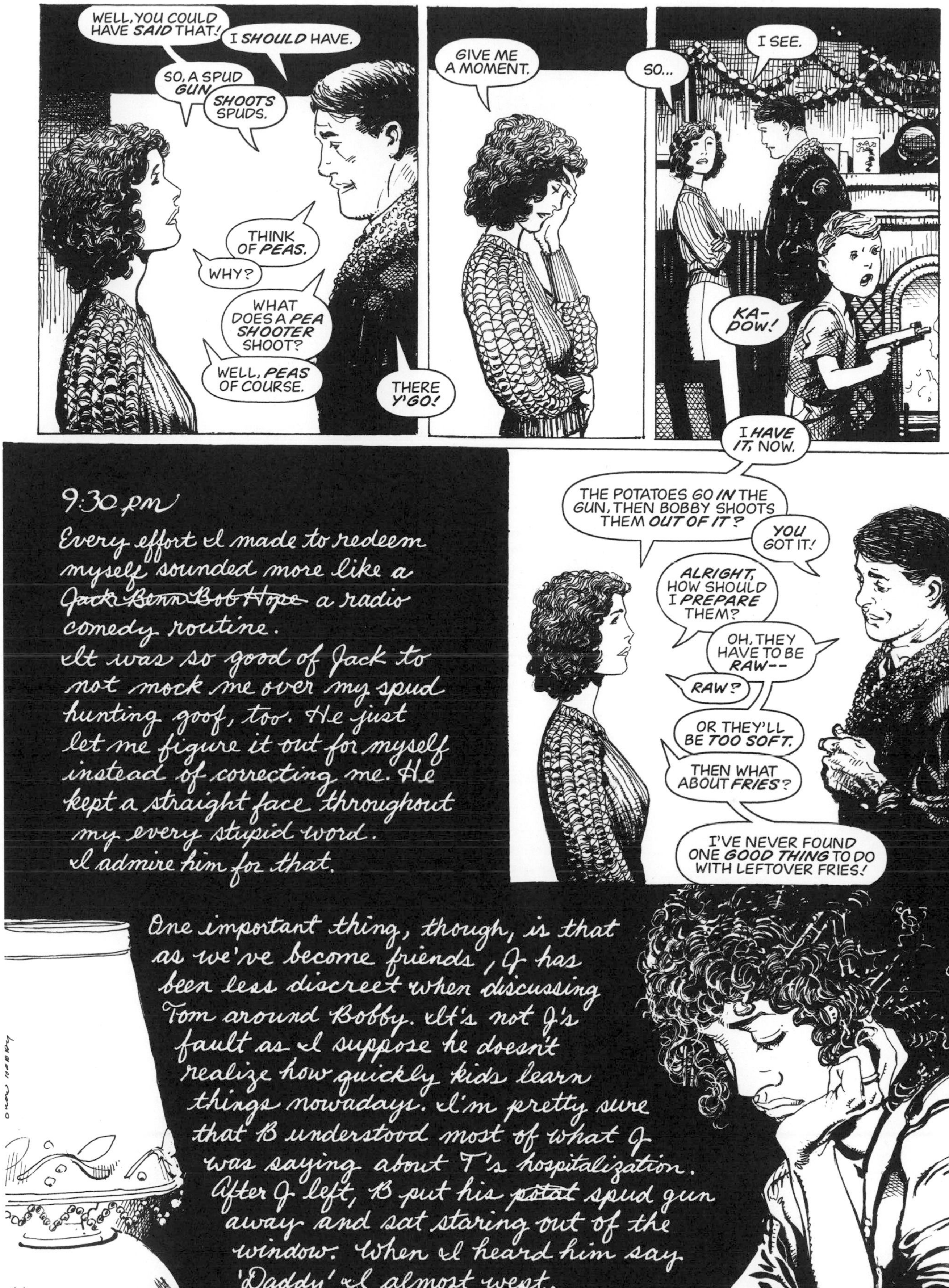
WELL, YOU COULD HAVE SAID THAT!
I SHOULD HAVE.
SO, A SPUD GUN
SHOOTS SPUDS.
THINK OF PEAS.
WHY?
WHAT DOES A PEA SHOOTER SHOOT?
WELL, PEAS OF COURSE.
THERE Y'GO!
GIVE ME A MOMENT.
SO...
I SEE.
KA-POW!
I HAVE IT, NOW.
THE POTATOES GO IN THE GUN, THEN BOBBY SHOOTS THEM OUT OF IT?
YOU GOT IT!
ALRIGHT, HOW SHOULD I PREPARE THEM?
OH, THEY HAVE TO BE RAW--
RAW?
OR THEY'LL BE TOO SOFT.
THEN WHAT ABOUT FRIES?
I'VE NEVER FOUND ONE GOOD THING TO DO WITH LEFTOVER FRIES!
9:30 pm
Every effort I made to redeem myself sounded more like a ~~Jack Benn Bob Hope~~ a radio comedy routine.
It was so good of Jack to not mock me over my spud hunting goof, too. He just let me figure it out for myself instead of correcting me. He kept a straight face throughout my every stupid word.
I admire him for that.
One important thing, though, is that as we've become friends, J has been less discreet when discussing Tom around Bobby. It's not J's fault as I suppose he doesn't realize how quickly kids learn things nowadays. I'm pretty sure that B understood most of what J was saying about T's hospitalization.
After J left, B put his ~~potat~~ spud gun away and sat staring out of the window. When I heard him say 'Daddy' I almost wept.
It's late.

1949 Providence Square Sunday, January 9

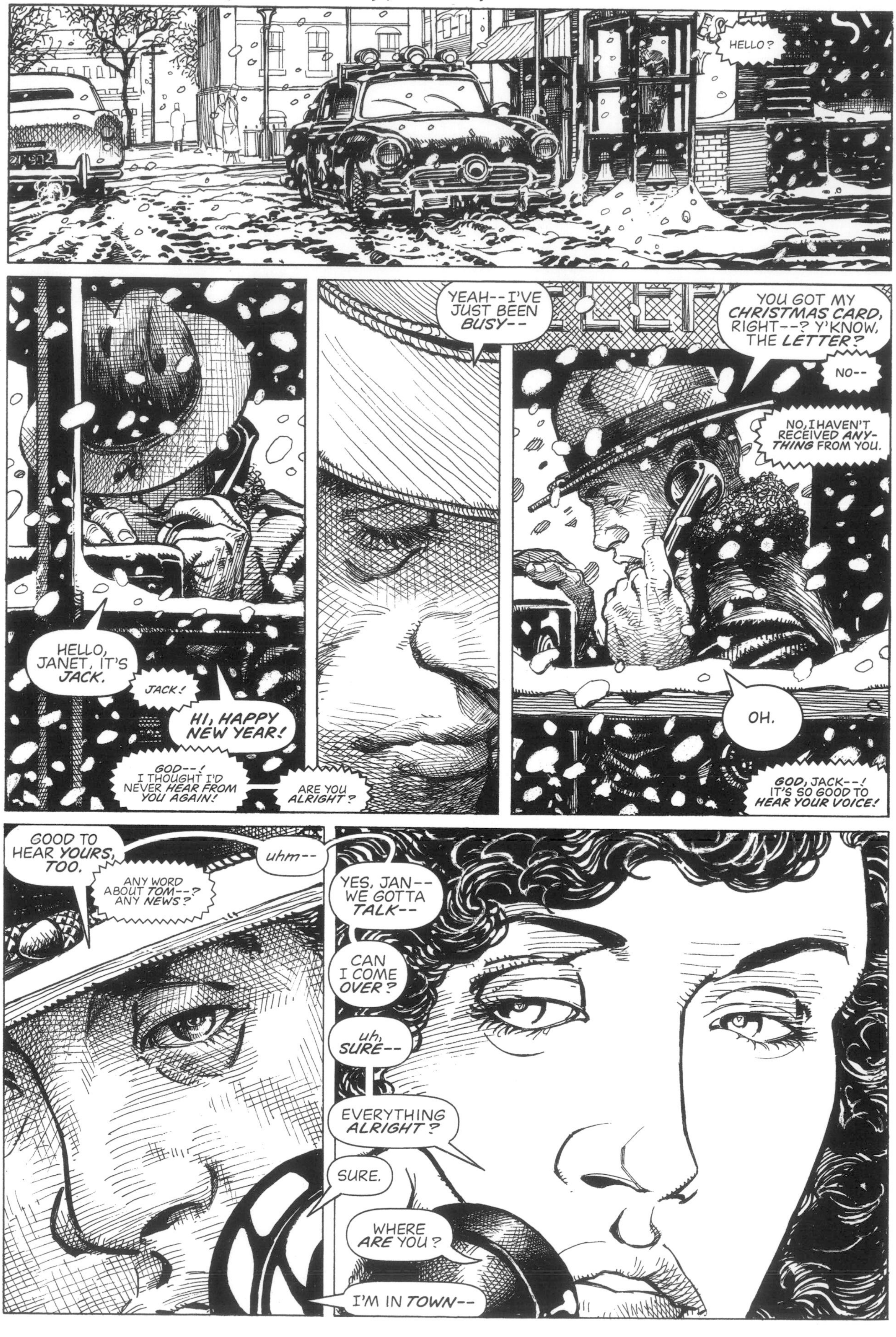
HELLO?
HELLO, JANET, IT'S JACK.
JACK!
HI, HAPPY NEW YEAR!
GOD--! I THOUGHT I'D NEVER HEAR FROM YOU AGAIN!
ARE YOU ALRIGHT?
YEAH--I'VE JUST BEEN BUSY--
YOU GOT MY CHRISTMAS CARD, RIGHT--? Y'KNOW, THE LETTER?
NO--
NO, I HAVEN'T RECEIVED ANYTHING FROM YOU.
OH.
GOD, JACK--! IT'S SO GOOD TO HEAR YOUR VOICE!
GOOD TO HEAR YOURS, TOO.
uhm--
ANY WORD ABOUT TOM--? ANY NEWS?
YES, JAN-- WE GOTTA TALK--
CAN I COME OVER?
uh, SURE--
EVERYTHING ALRIGHT?
SURE.
WHERE ARE YOU?
I'M IN TOWN--

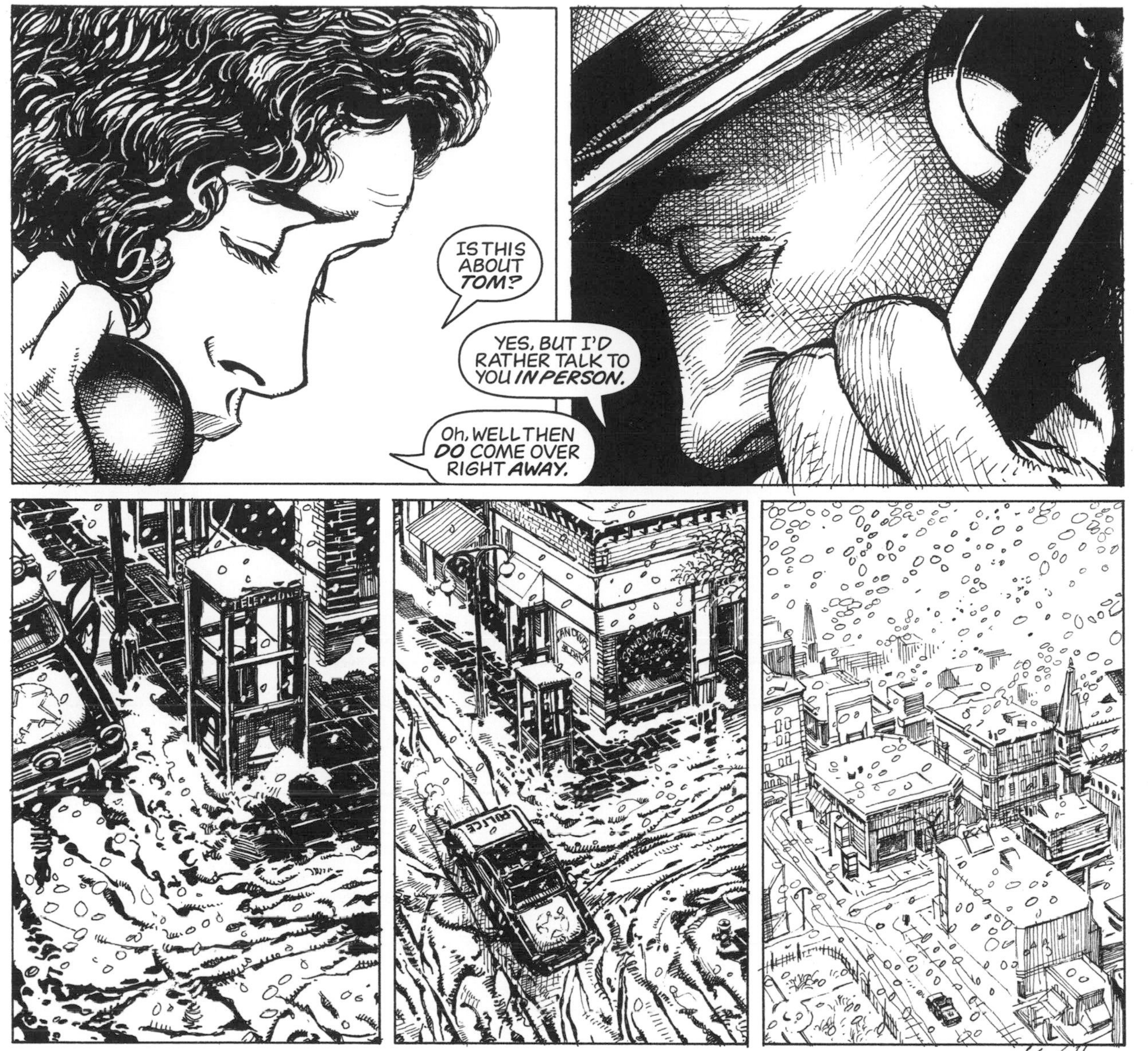

IS THIS ABOUT TOM?
YES, BUT I'D RATHER TALK TO YOU IN PERSON.
Oh, WELL THEN DO COME OVER RIGHT AWAY.

It's been snowing all day
There's so much to write about, I dont know where to begin. At the beginning I suppose. After nearly six ~~months~~ weeks Jack finally called and came over mid-aft. He said that all the trouble is finally settled and done with and that Tom should be back by the spring - summer latest. I can hardly believe it. After all these years my husband is finally coming home. My goodness, sometimes I thought that I'd never be able to say those words.

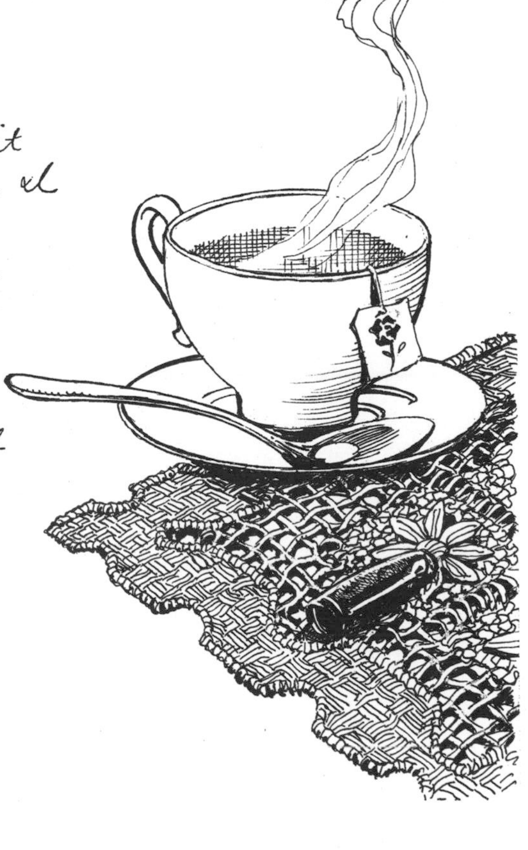

I've got some time to clean the house up and make sure everything's perfect for the homecoming.

I told Eileen of course and she said that it should be just Bobby and me on the first day, and I suppose she's right. Still, I'd just love to have everybody over to celebrate Tom's return (even Morris "The Grump" if he doesn't drink too much). But Eileen is right, Tom should have it quiet at first.

As if this isn't enough news for one day, Jack told me he'd quit ~~the department the~~ his place of work. I couldn't have been more surprised to hear this as he's always seemed so dedicated to ~~the~~ his work.

The reason he gave me (long hours) just didn't seem to ring true somehow. But I didn't pry.

But the good news is that he's actually enrolled at the police station on Maple Ave. He's now a sheriff's deputy (I think) full time. What a funny thing. I'm sure the pay is nothing like he's been used to. Jack is so unpredictable and I love him for that — not like _me_, same old same old all of the time.

It's finally stopped snowing.

Bobby was in bed all day with an upset tummy, bit of a fever too I think.

COME DOWNSTAIRS BOBBY--*DINNER'S READY.*

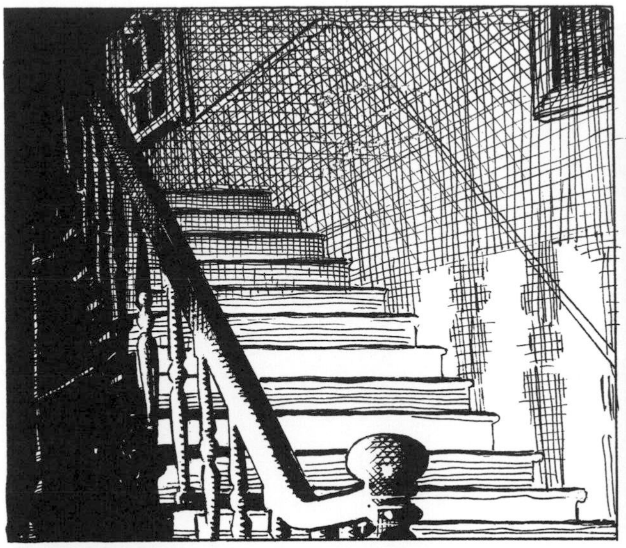

1949 Thanksgiving, Thursday, November 24

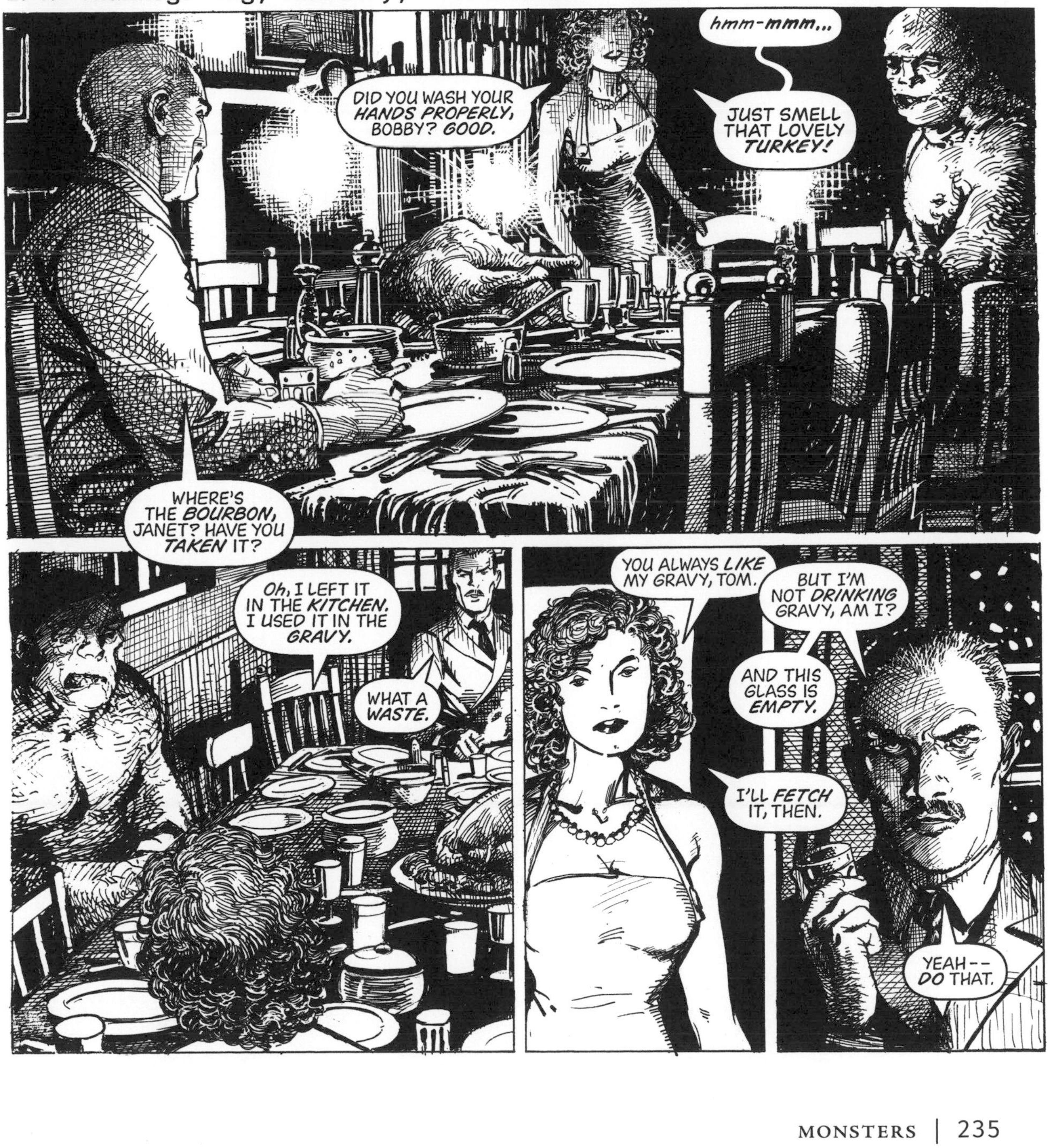
DID YOU WASH YOUR *HANDS PROPERLY*, BOBBY? *GOOD.*
hmm-mmm...
JUST SMELL THAT LOVELY *TURKEY!*
WHERE'S THE *BOURBON*, JANET? HAVE YOU *TAKEN* IT?
Oh, I LEFT IT IN THE *KITCHEN.* I USED IT IN THE *GRAVY.*
WHAT A *WASTE.*
YOU ALWAYS *LIKE* MY GRAVY, TOM.
BUT I'M NOT *DRINKING* GRAVY, AM I?
AND THIS GLASS IS *EMPTY.*
I'LL *FETCH* IT, THEN.
YEAH-- *DO* THAT.

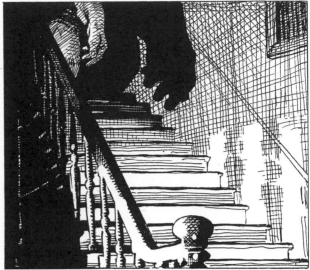

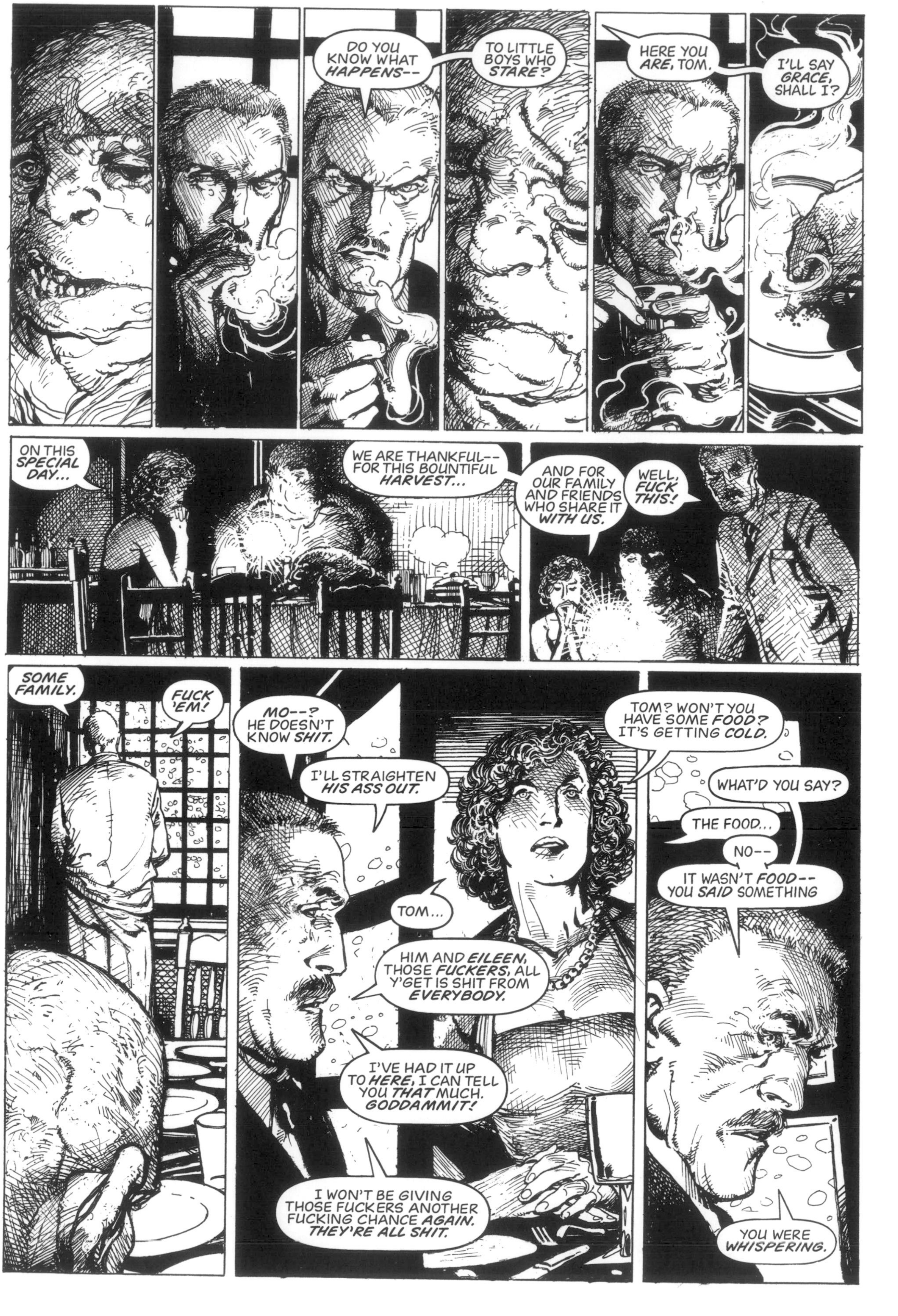
DO YOU KNOW WHAT HAPPENS--
TO LITTLE BOYS WHO STARE?
HERE YOU ARE, TOM.
I'LL SAY GRACE, SHALL I?
ON THIS SPECIAL DAY...
WE ARE THANKFUL-- FOR THIS BOUNTIFUL HARVEST...
AND FOR OUR FAMILY AND FRIENDS WHO SHARE IT WITH US.
WELL, FUCK THIS!
SOME FAMILY.
FUCK 'EM!
MO--? HE DOESN'T KNOW SHIT.
I'LL STRAIGHTEN HIS ASS OUT.
TOM...
HIM AND EILEEN, THOSE FUCKERS, ALL Y'GET IS SHIT FROM EVERYBODY.
I'VE HAD IT UP TO HERE, I CAN TELL YOU THAT MUCH. GODDAMMIT!
I WON'T BE GIVING THOSE FUCKERS ANOTHER FUCKING CHANCE AGAIN. THEY'RE ALL SHIT.
TOM? WON'T YOU HAVE SOME FOOD? IT'S GETTING COLD.
WHAT'D YOU SAY?
THE FOOD...
NO--
IT WASN'T FOOD-- YOU SAID SOMETHING
YOU WERE WHISPERING.

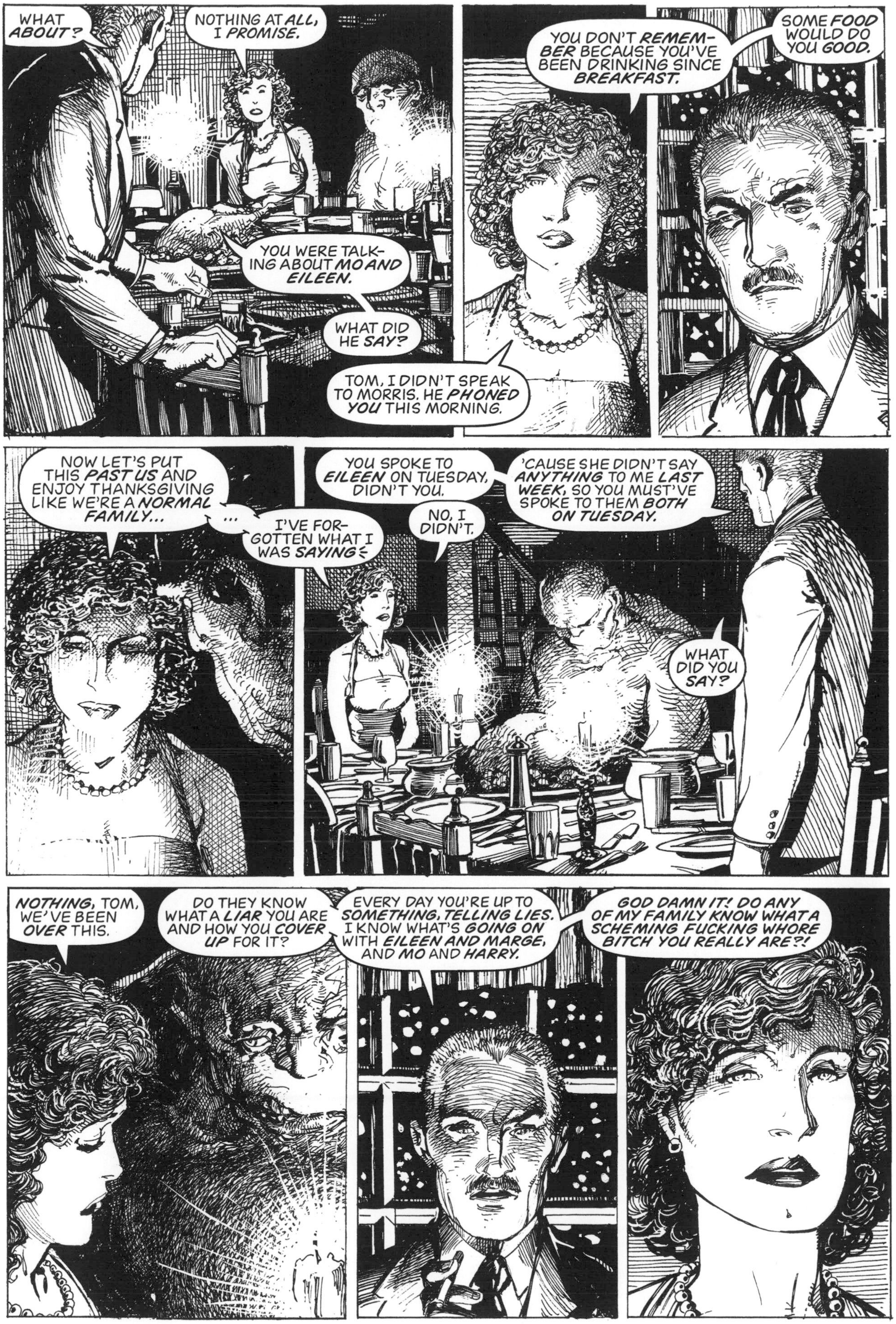
WHAT ABOUT?
NOTHING AT ALL, I PROMISE.
YOU WERE TALKING ABOUT MO AND EILEEN.
WHAT DID HE SAY?
TOM, I DIDN'T SPEAK TO MORRIS. HE PHONED YOU THIS MORNING.
YOU DON'T REMEMBER BECAUSE YOU'VE BEEN DRINKING SINCE BREAKFAST.
SOME FOOD WOULD DO YOU GOOD.
NOW LET'S PUT THIS PAST US AND ENJOY THANKSGIVING LIKE WE'RE A NORMAL FAMILY...
...
I'VE FORGOTTEN WHAT I WAS SAYING...
YOU SPOKE TO EILEEN ON TUESDAY, DIDN'T YOU.
NO, I DIDN'T.
'CAUSE SHE DIDN'T SAY ANYTHING TO ME LAST WEEK, SO YOU MUST'VE SPOKE TO THEM BOTH ON TUESDAY.
WHAT DID YOU SAY?
NOTHING, TOM, WE'VE BEEN OVER THIS.
DO THEY KNOW WHAT A LIAR YOU ARE AND HOW YOU COVER UP FOR IT?
EVERY DAY YOU'RE UP TO SOMETHING, TELLING LIES. I KNOW WHAT'S GOING ON WITH EILEEN AND MARGE, AND MO AND HARRY.
GOD DAMN IT! DO ANY OF MY FAMILY KNOW WHAT A SCHEMING FUCKING WHORE BITCH YOU REALLY ARE?!

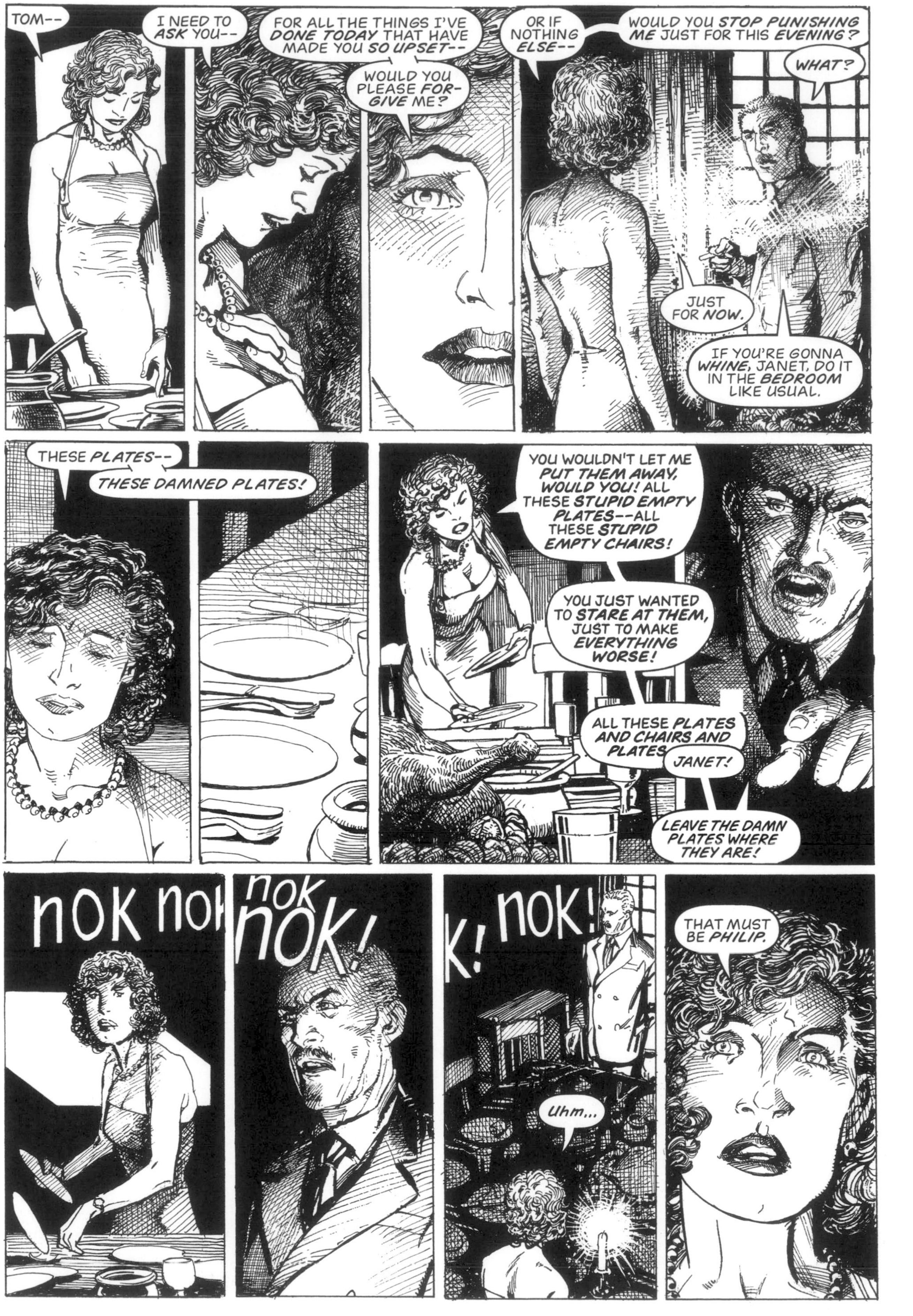
TOM--
I NEED TO ASK YOU--
FOR ALL THE THINGS I'VE DONE TODAY THAT HAVE MADE YOU SO UPSET--
WOULD YOU PLEASE FOR-GIVE ME?
OR IF NOTHING ELSE--
WOULD YOU STOP PUNISHING ME JUST FOR THIS EVENING?
WHAT?
JUST FOR NOW.
IF YOU'RE GONNA WHINE, JANET, DO IT IN THE BEDROOM LIKE USUAL.
THESE PLATES--
THESE DAMNED PLATES!
YOU WOULDN'T LET ME PUT THEM AWAY, WOULD YOU! ALL THESE STUPID EMPTY PLATES--ALL THESE STUPID EMPTY CHAIRS!
YOU JUST WANTED TO STARE AT THEM, JUST TO MAKE EVERYTHING WORSE!
ALL THESE PLATES AND CHAIRS AND PLATES
JANET!
LEAVE THE DAMN PLATES WHERE THEY ARE!
nOK nOK
nok nOK!
K! nOK!
Uhm...
THAT MUST BE PHILIP.

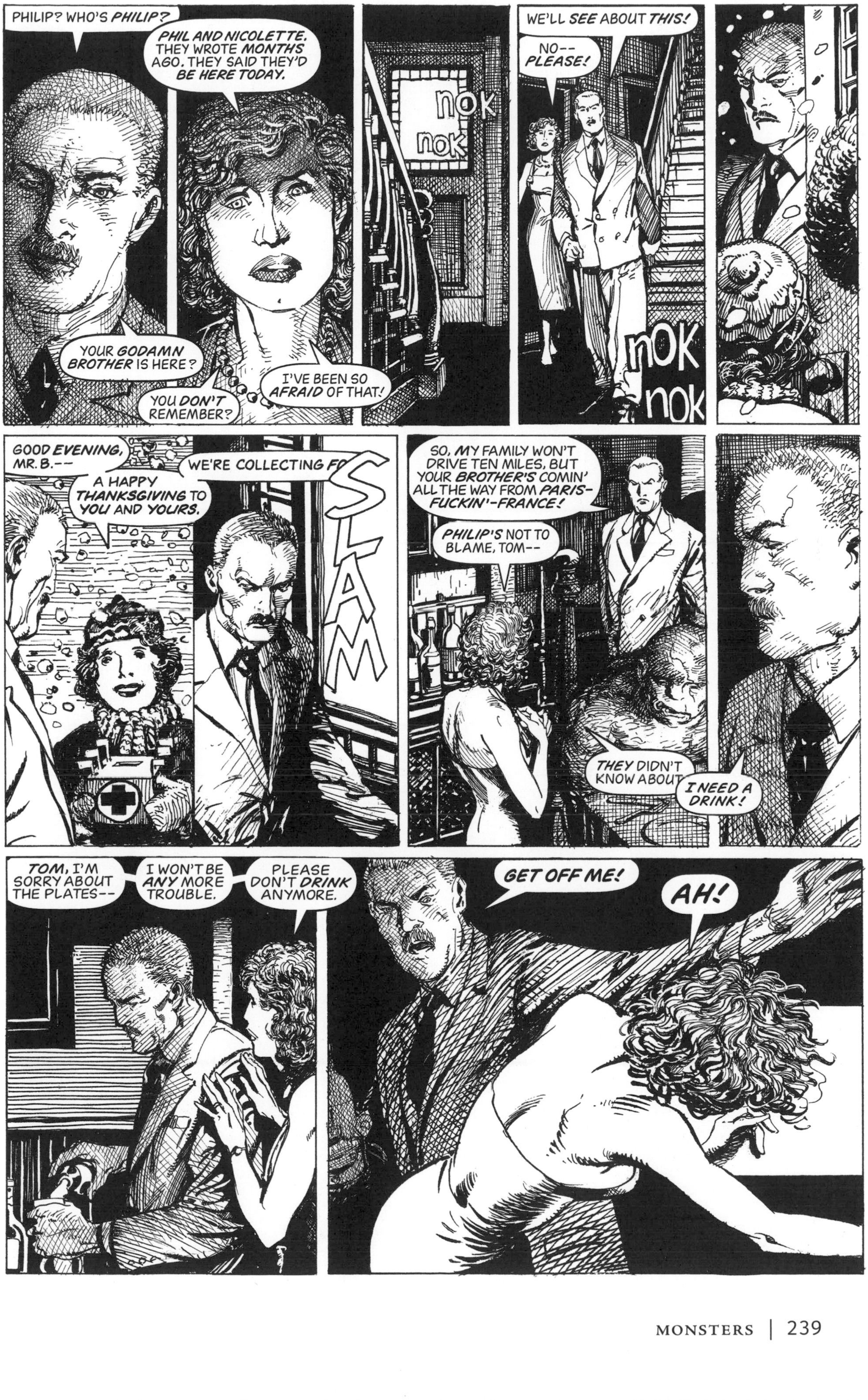
PHILIP? WHO'S PHILIP?
PHIL AND NICOLETTE. THEY WROTE MONTHS AGO. THEY SAID THEY'D BE HERE TODAY.
YOUR GODAMN BROTHER IS HERE?
YOU DON'T REMEMBER?
I'VE BEEN SO AFRAID OF THAT!
nok
nok
WE'LL SEE ABOUT THIS!
NO-- PLEASE!
nOK
nok
GOOD EVENING, MR. B.--
A HAPPY THANKSGIVING TO YOU AND YOURS.
WE'RE COLLECTING FO
SLAM
SO, MY FAMILY WON'T DRIVE TEN MILES, BUT YOUR BROTHER'S COMIN' ALL THE WAY FROM PARIS-FUCKIN'-FRANCE!
PHILIP'S NOT TO BLAME, TOM--
THEY DIDN'T KNOW ABOUT
I NEED A DRINK!
TOM, I'M SORRY ABOUT THE PLATES--
I WON'T BE ANY MORE TROUBLE.
PLEASE DON'T DRINK ANYMORE.
GET OFF ME!
AH!

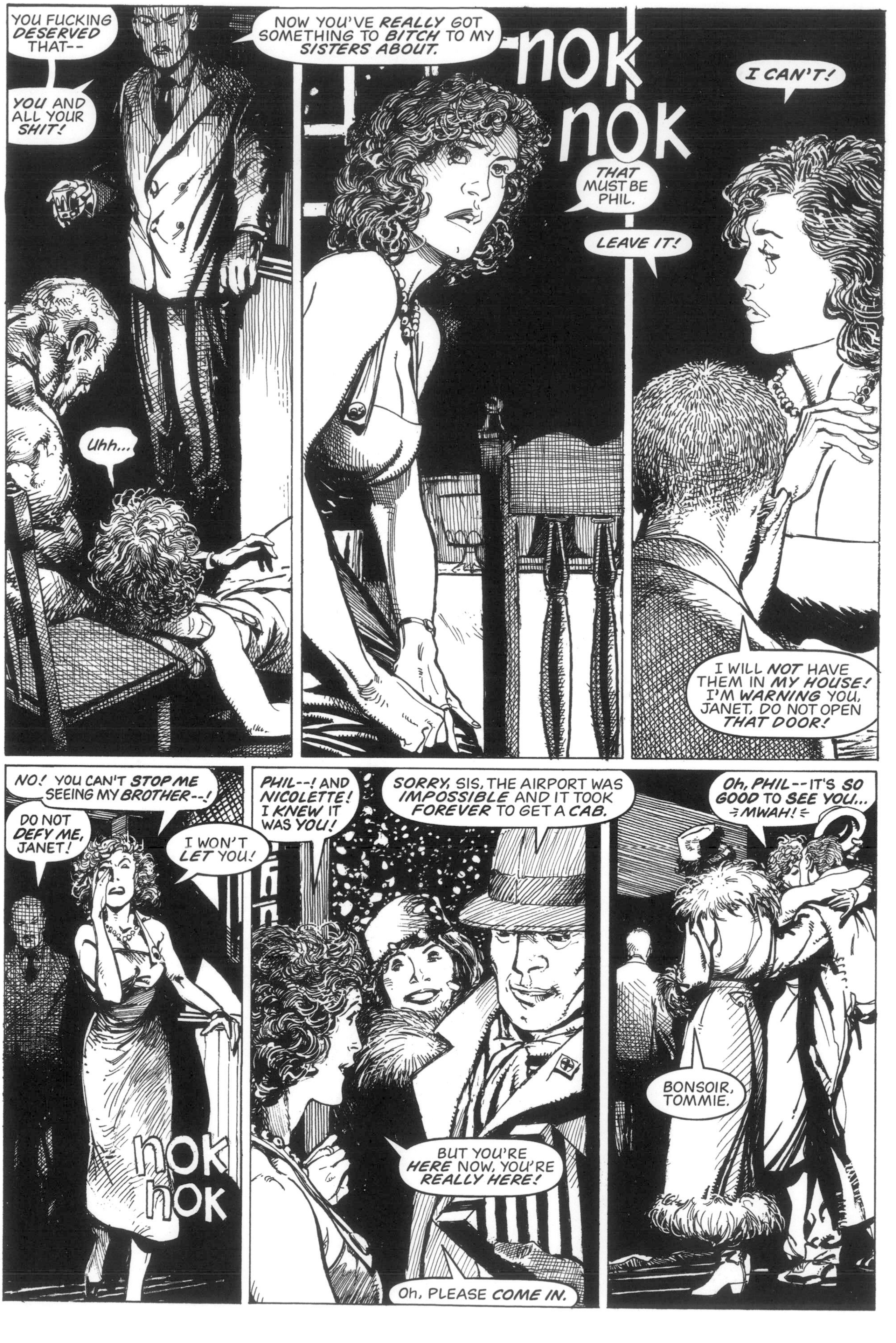
YOU FUCKING DESERVED THAT--
YOU AND ALL YOUR SHIT!
Uhh...
NOW YOU'VE REALLY GOT SOMETHING TO BITCH TO MY SISTERS ABOUT.
nok nok
THAT MUST BE PHIL.
LEAVE IT!
I CAN'T!
I WILL NOT HAVE THEM IN MY HOUSE! I'M WARNING YOU, JANET. DO NOT OPEN THAT DOOR!
NO! YOU CAN'T STOP ME SEEING MY BROTHER--!
DO NOT DEFY ME, JANET!
I WON'T LET YOU!
nok nok
PHIL--! AND NICOLETTE! I KNEW IT WAS YOU!
SORRY, SIS, THE AIRPORT WAS IMPOSSIBLE AND IT TOOK FOREVER TO GET A CAB.
BUT YOU'RE HERE NOW, YOU'RE REALLY HERE!
Oh, PLEASE COME IN.
Oh, PHIL--IT'S SO GOOD TO SEE YOU... MWAH!
BONSOIR, TOMMIE.

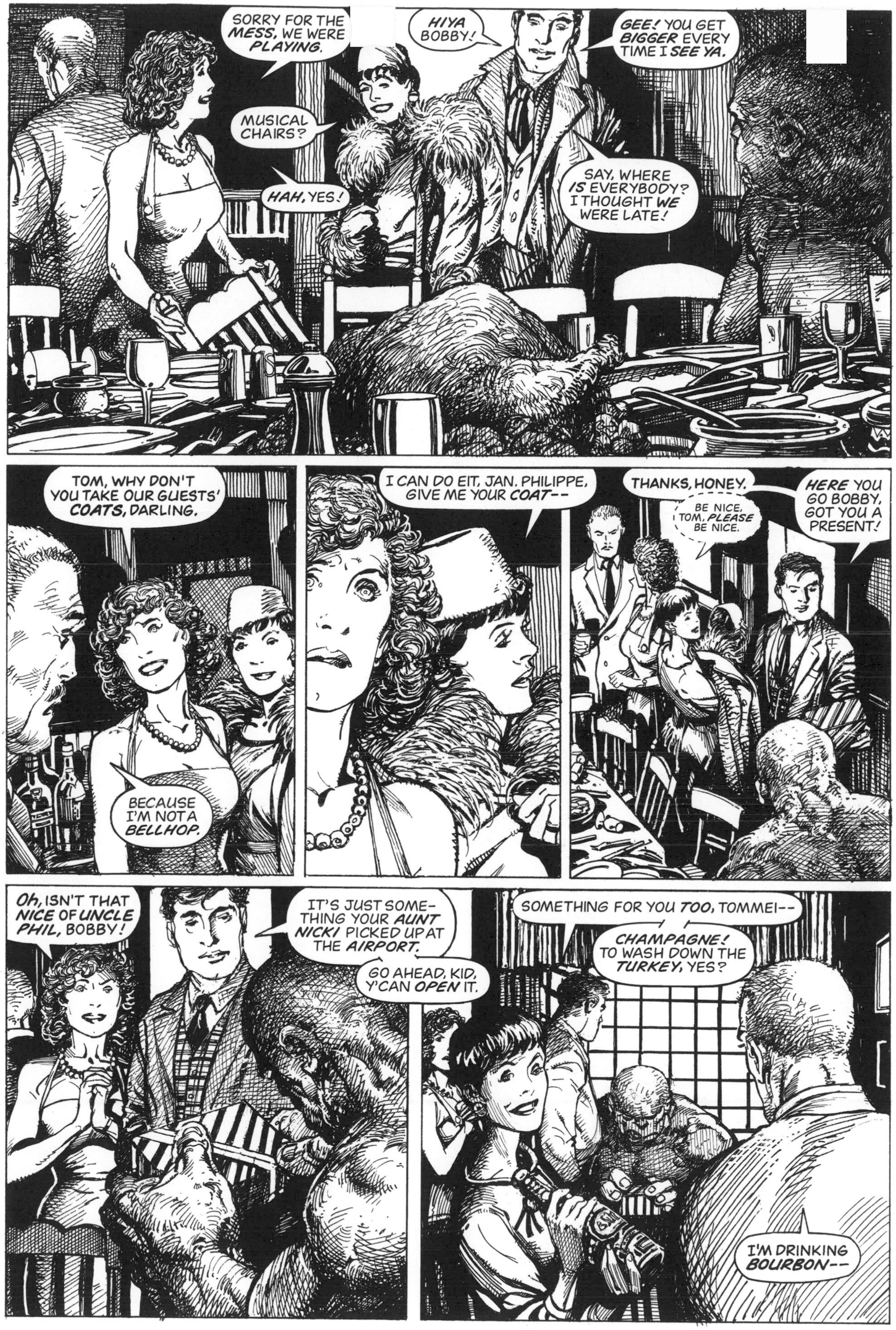
SORRY FOR THE MESS. WE WERE PLAYING.
MUSICAL CHAIRS?
HAH, YES!
HIYA BOBBY!
GEE! YOU GET BIGGER EVERY TIME I SEE YA.
SAY, WHERE IS EVERYBODY? I THOUGHT WE WERE LATE!
TOM, WHY DON'T YOU TAKE OUR GUESTS' COATS, DARLING.
BECAUSE I'M NOT A BELLHOP.
I CAN DO EIT, JAN. PHILIPPE, GIVE ME YOUR COAT--
THANKS, HONEY.
BE NICE, TOM, PLEASE BE NICE.
HERE YOU GO BOBBY, GOT YOU A PRESENT!
Oh, ISN'T THAT NICE OF UNCLE PHIL, BOBBY!
IT'S JUST SOMETHING YOUR AUNT NICKI PICKED UP AT THE AIRPORT.
GO AHEAD, KID, Y'CAN OPEN IT.
SOMETHING FOR YOU TOO, TOMMEI--
CHAMPAGNE! TO WASH DOWN THE TURKEY, YES?
I'M DRINKING BOURBON--

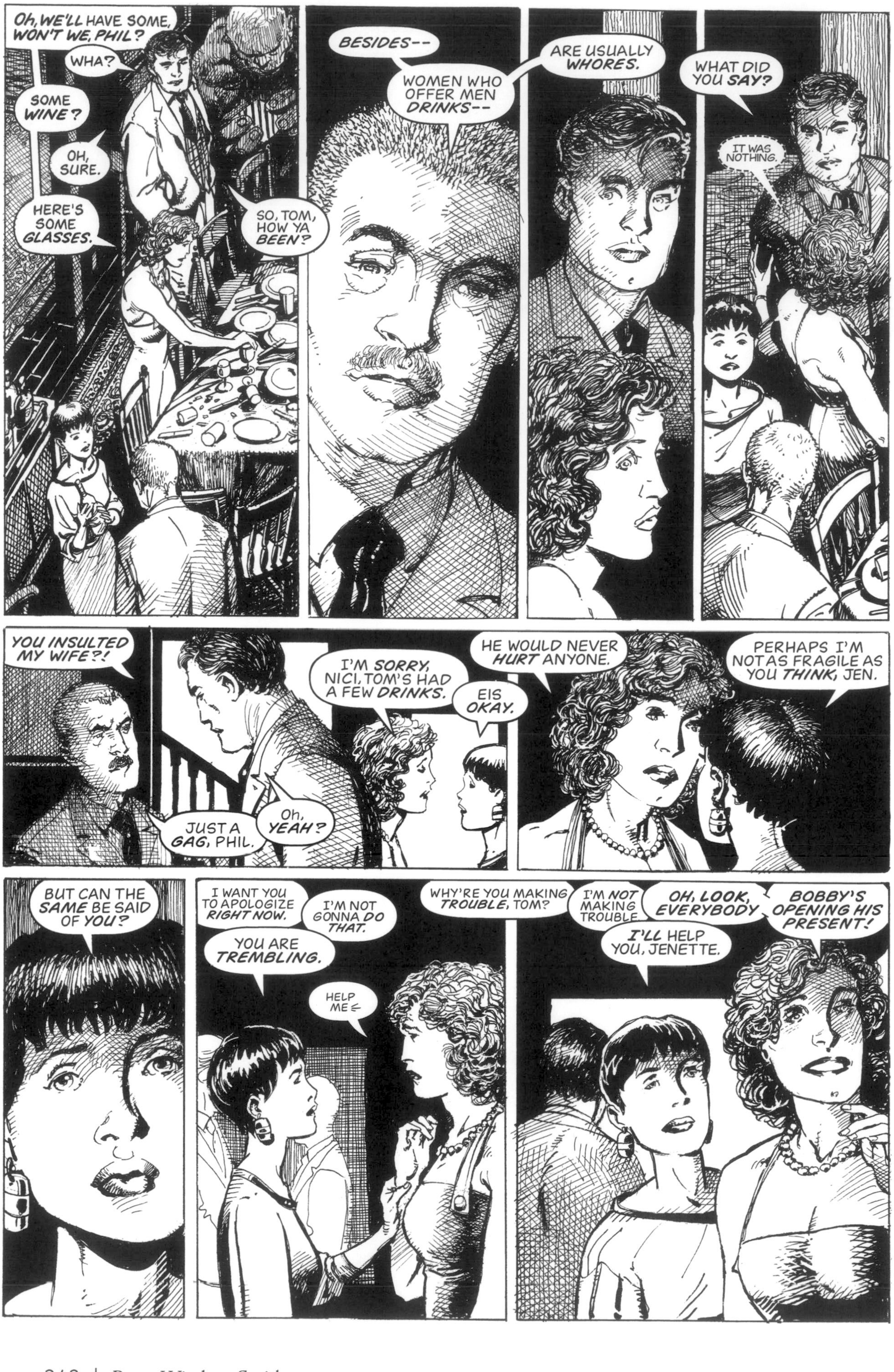

Oh, WE'LL HAVE SOME, WON'T WE, PHIL?
WHA?
SOME WINE?
OH, SURE.
HERE'S SOME GLASSES.
SO, TOM, HOW YA BEEN?
BESIDES--
WOMEN WHO OFFER MEN DRINKS--
ARE USUALLY WHORES.
WHAT DID YOU SAY?
IT WAS NOTHING.
YOU INSULTED MY WIFE?!
JUST A GAG, PHIL.
Oh, YEAH?
I'M SORRY, NICI, TOM'S HAD A FEW DRINKS.
EIS OKAY.
HE WOULD NEVER HURT ANYONE.
PERHAPS I'M NOT AS FRAGILE AS YOU THINK, JEN.
BUT CAN THE SAME BE SAID OF YOU?
I WANT YOU TO APOLOGIZE RIGHT NOW.
I'M NOT GONNA DO THAT.
YOU ARE TREMBLING.
HELP ME
WHY'RE YOU MAKING TROUBLE, TOM?
I'M NOT MAKING TROUBLE
I'LL HELP YOU, JENETTE.
OH, LOOK, EVERYBODY
BOBBY'S OPENING HIS PRESENT!

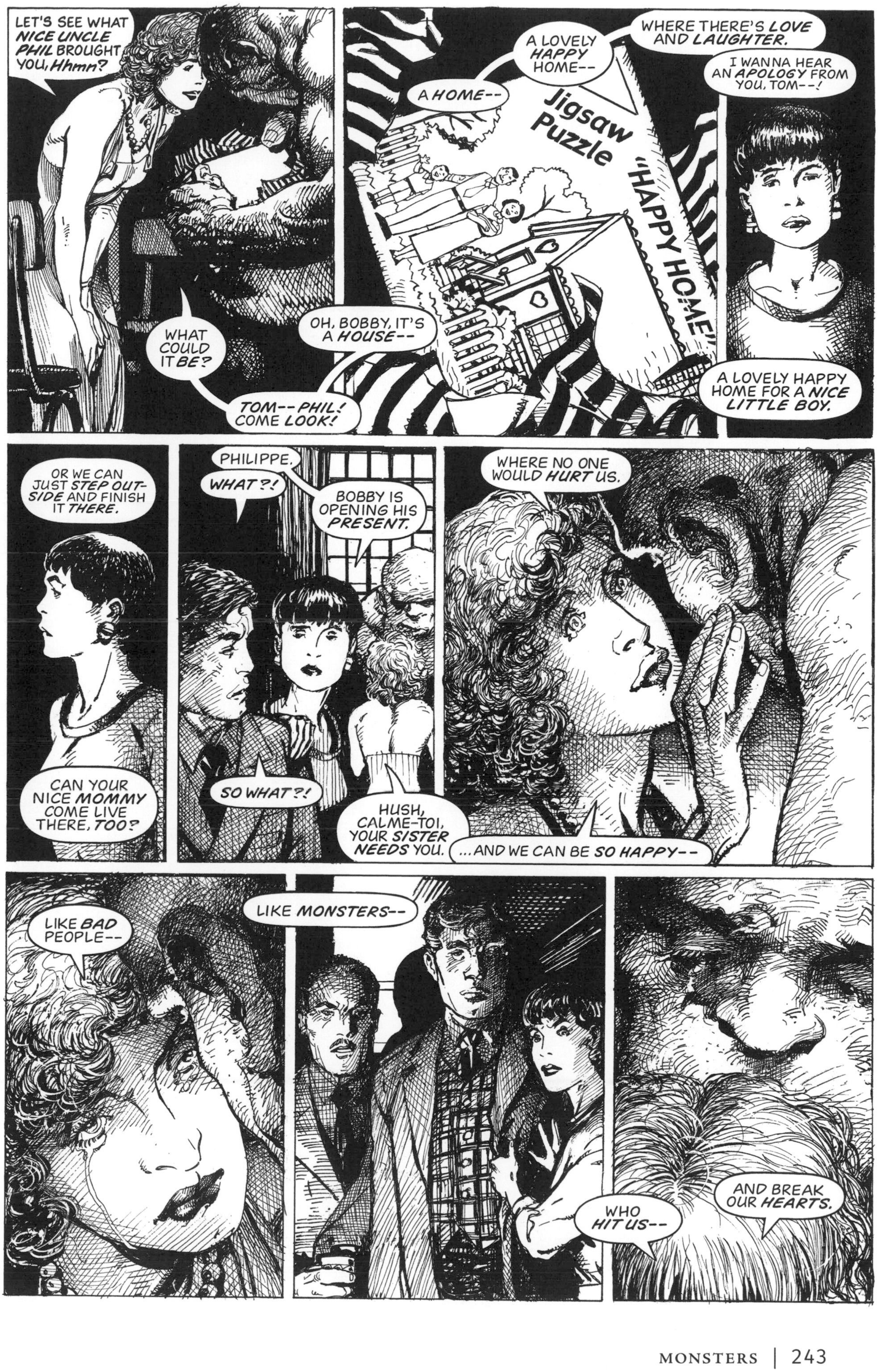
LET'S SEE WHAT NICE UNCLE PHIL BROUGHT YOU, Hhmn?
WHAT COULD IT BE?
A HOME--
A LOVELY HAPPY HOME--
WHERE THERE'S LOVE AND LAUGHTER.
Jigsaw Puzzle
"HAPPY HOME"
OH, BOBBY, IT'S A HOUSE--
TOM--PHIL! COME LOOK!
I WANNA HEAR AN APOLOGY FROM YOU, TOM--!
A LOVELY HAPPY HOME FOR A NICE LITTLE BOY.
OR WE CAN JUST STEP OUTSIDE AND FINISH IT THERE.
CAN YOUR NICE MOMMY COME LIVE THERE, TOO?
PHILIPPE.
WHAT?!
BOBBY IS OPENING HIS PRESENT.
SO WHAT?!
HUSH, CALME-TOI, YOUR SISTER NEEDS YOU.
WHERE NO ONE WOULD HURT US.
...AND WE CAN BE SO HAPPY--
LIKE BAD PEOPLE--
LIKE MONSTERS--
WHO HIT US--
AND BREAK OUR HEARTS.

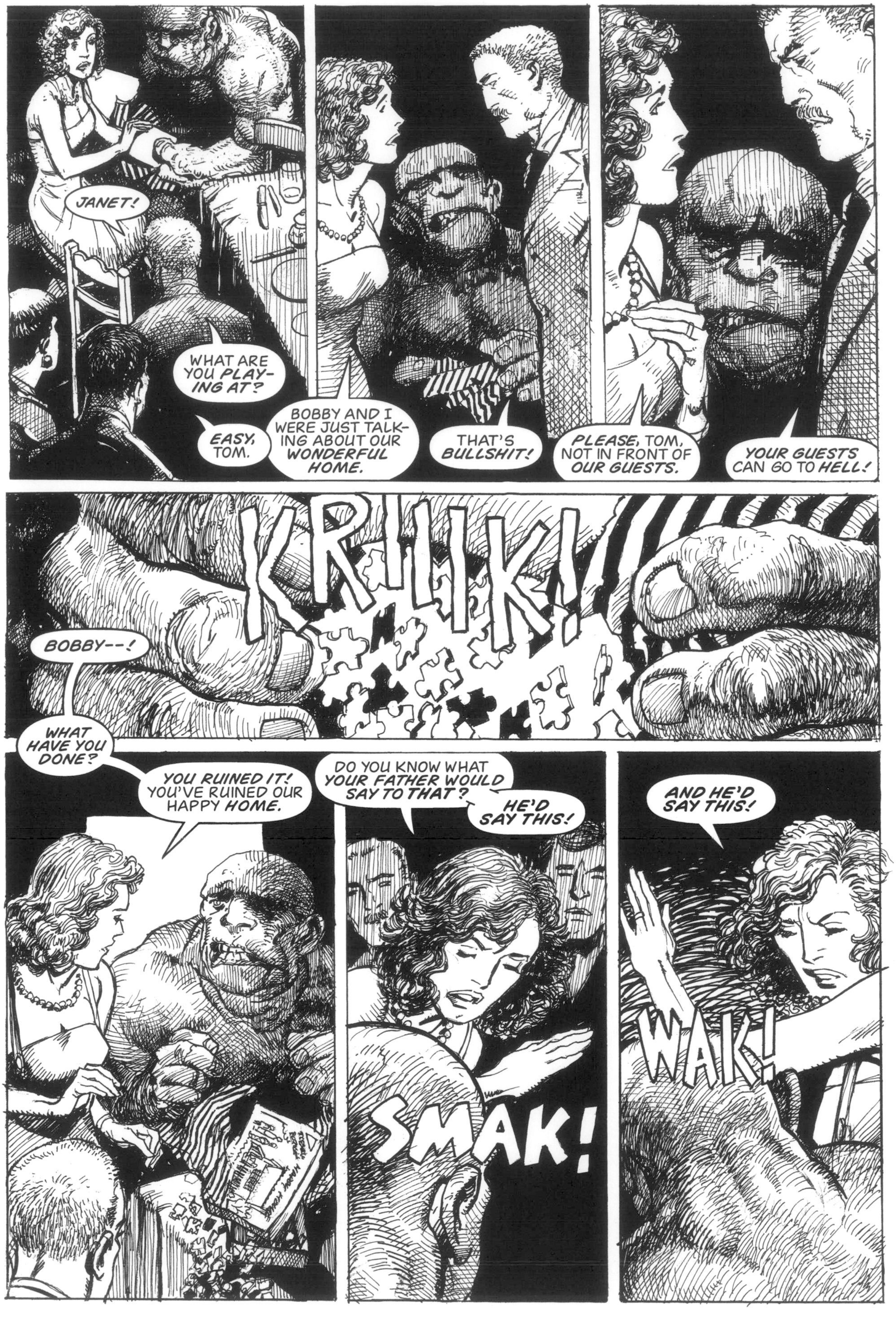
JANET!
WHAT ARE YOU PLAYING AT?
EASY, TOM.
BOBBY AND I WERE JUST TALKING ABOUT OUR WONDERFUL HOME.
THAT'S BULLSHIT!
PLEASE, TOM, NOT IN FRONT OF OUR GUESTS.
YOUR GUESTS CAN GO TO HELL!
KRIIIK!
BOBBY--!
WHAT HAVE YOU DONE?
YOU RUINED IT! YOU'VE RUINED OUR HAPPY HOME.
DO YOU KNOW WHAT YOUR FATHER WOULD SAY TO THAT?
HE'D SAY THIS!
SMAK!
AND HE'D SAY THIS!
WAK!

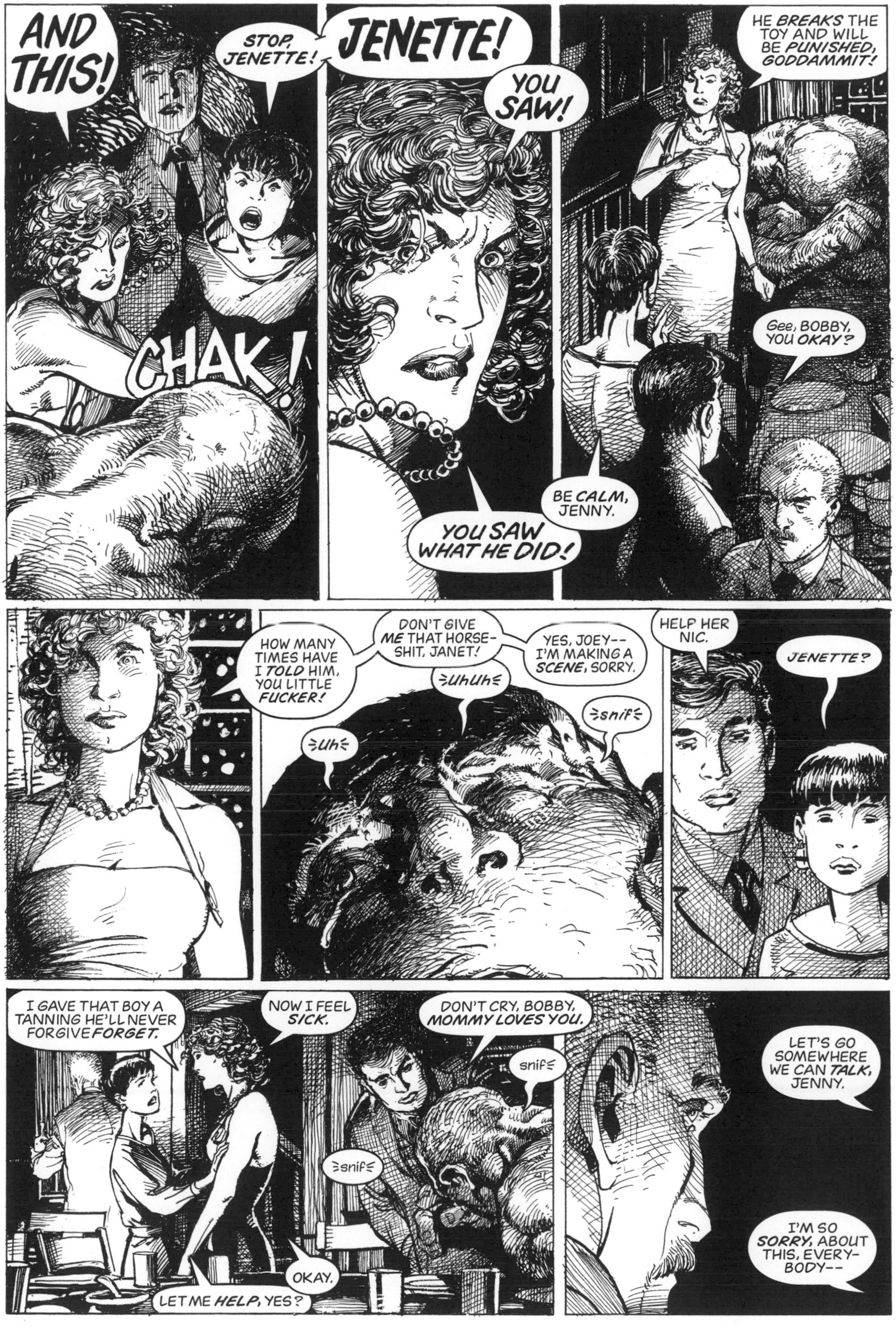
AND THIS!
STOP, JENETTE!
CHAK!
JENETTE!
YOU SAW!
YOU SAW WHAT HE DID!
HE BREAKS THE TOY AND WILL BE PUNISHED, GODDAMMIT!
BE CALM, JENNY.
Gee, BOBBY, YOU OKAY?
HOW MANY TIMES HAVE I TOLD HIM, YOU LITTLE FUCKER!
DON'T GIVE ME THAT HORSE-SHIT, JANET!
YES, JOEY-- I'M MAKING A SCENE, SORRY.
UhUh
Uh
snif
HELP HER NIC.
JENETTE?
I GAVE THAT BOY A TANNING HE'LL NEVER FORGIVE FORGET.
NOW I FEEL SICK.
DON'T CRY, BOBBY, MOMMY LOVES YOU.
snif
snif
OKAY.
LET ME HELP, YES?
LET'S GO SOMEWHERE WE CAN TALK, JENNY.
I'M SO SORRY, ABOUT THIS, EVERY-BODY--

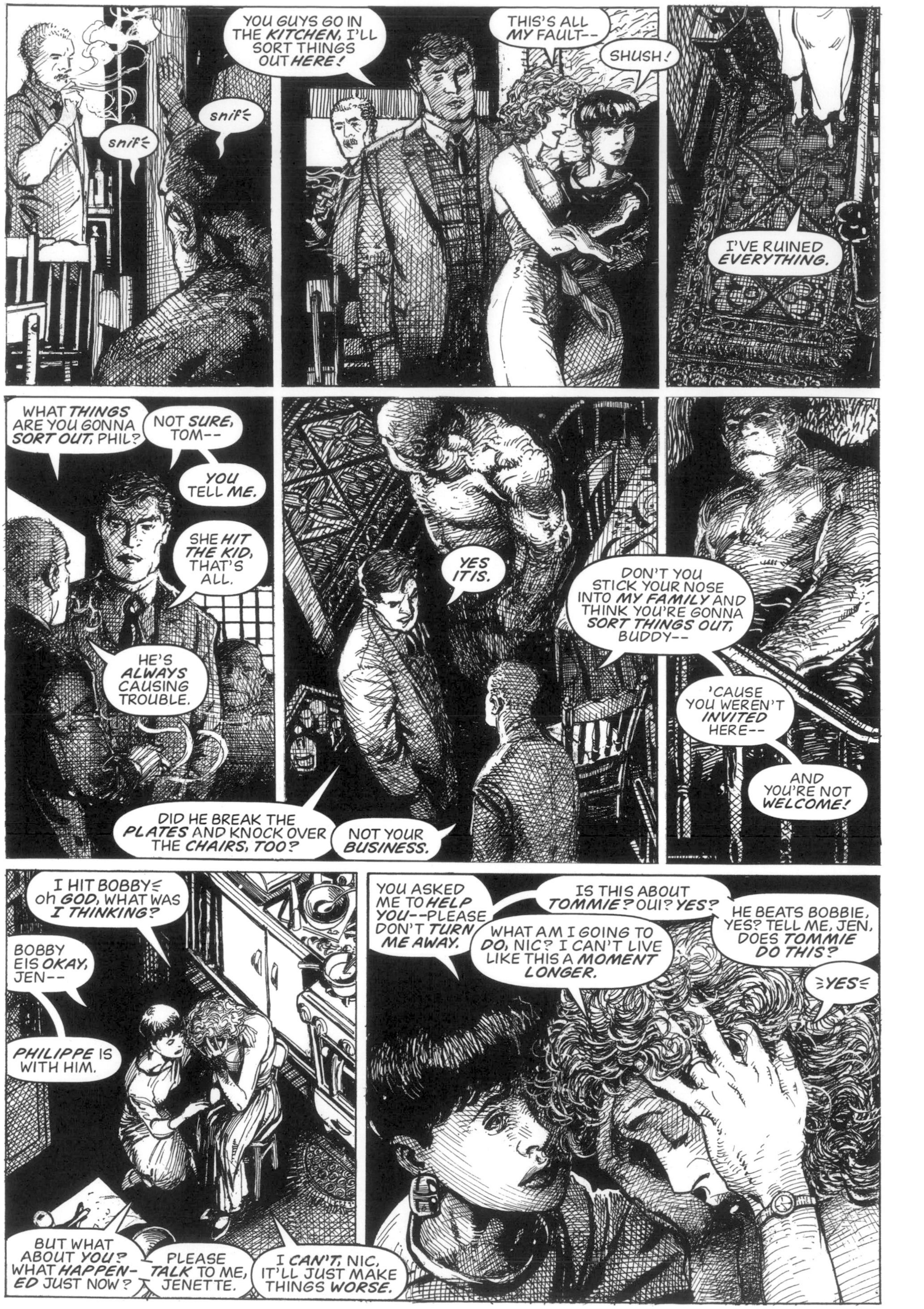

snif
snif
YOU GUYS GO IN THE KITCHEN, I'LL SORT THINGS OUT HERE!
THIS'S ALL MY FAULT--
SHUSH!
I'VE RUINED EVERYTHING.
WHAT THINGS ARE YOU GONNA SORT OUT, PHIL?
NOT SURE, TOM--
YOU TELL ME.
SHE HIT THE KID, THAT'S ALL.
HE'S ALWAYS CAUSING TROUBLE.
YES IT IS.
DID HE BREAK THE PLATES AND KNOCK OVER THE CHAIRS, TOO?
NOT YOUR BUSINESS.
DON'T YOU STICK YOUR NOSE INTO MY FAMILY AND THINK YOU'RE GONNA SORT THINGS OUT, BUDDY--
'CAUSE YOU WEREN'T INVITED HERE--
AND YOU'RE NOT WELCOME!
I HIT BOBBY oh GOD, WHAT WAS I THINKING?
BOBBY EIS OKAY, JEN--
PHILIPPE IS WITH HIM.
BUT WHAT ABOUT YOU? WHAT HAPPENED JUST NOW?
PLEASE TALK TO ME, JENETTE.
I CAN'T, NIC, IT'LL JUST MAKE THINGS WORSE.
YOU ASKED ME TO HELP YOU--PLEASE DON'T TURN ME AWAY.
IS THIS ABOUT TOMMIE? OUI? YES?
WHAT AM I GOING TO DO, NIC? I CAN'T LIVE LIKE THIS A MOMENT LONGER.
HE BEATS BOBBIE, YES? TELL ME, JEN, DOES TOMMIE DO THIS?
YES

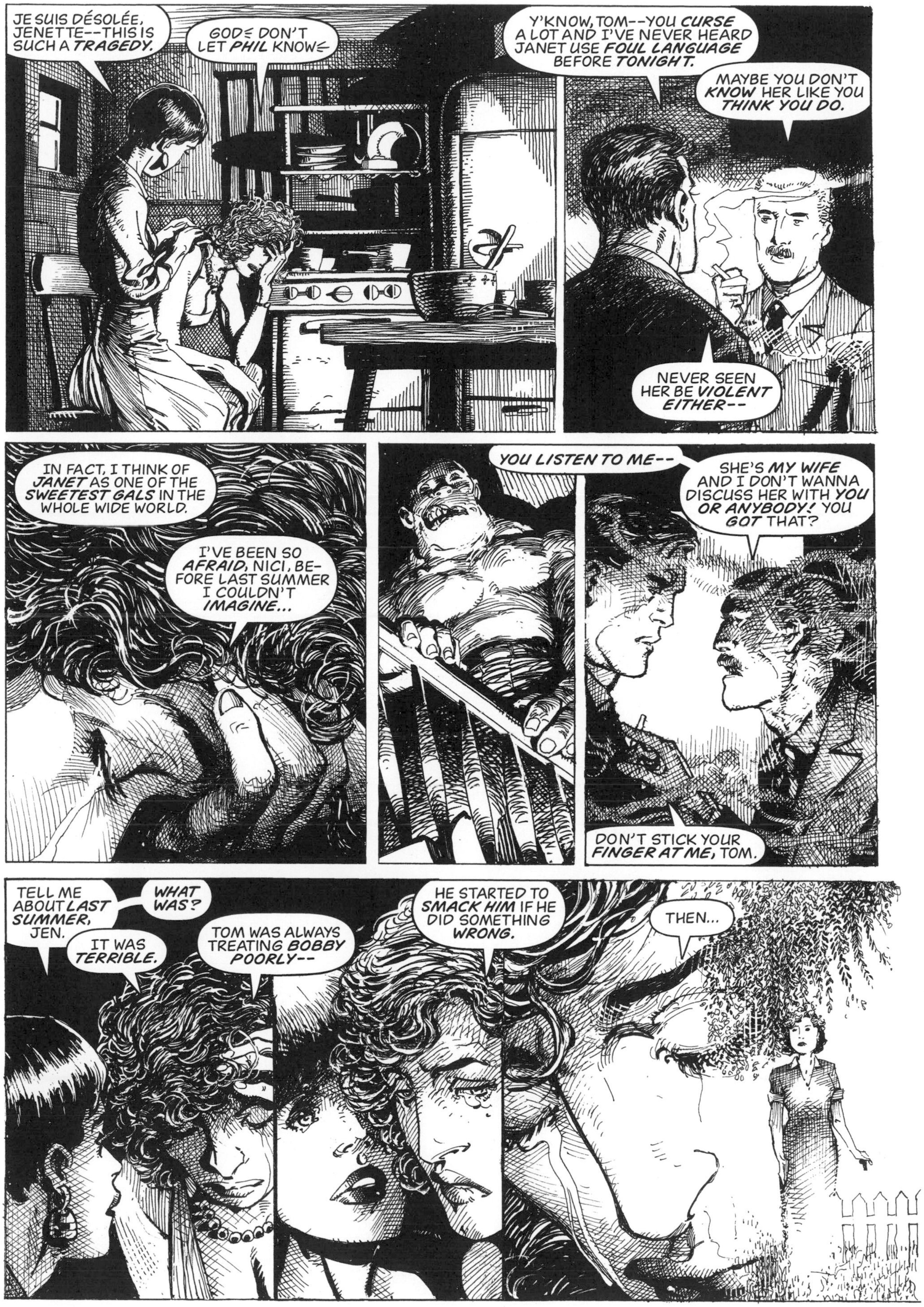

JE SUIS DÉSOLÉE, JENETTE--THIS IS SUCH A TRAGEDY.
GOD≤ DON'T LET PHIL KNOW≤
Y'KNOW, TOM--YOU CURSE A LOT AND I'VE NEVER HEARD JANET USE FOUL LANGUAGE BEFORE TONIGHT.
MAYBE YOU DON'T KNOW HER LIKE YOU THINK YOU DO.
NEVER SEEN HER BE VIOLENT EITHER--
IN FACT, I THINK OF JANET AS ONE OF THE SWEETEST GALS IN THE WHOLE WIDE WORLD.
I'VE BEEN SO AFRAID, NICI, BEFORE LAST SUMMER I COULDN'T IMAGINE...
YOU LISTEN TO ME--
SHE'S MY WIFE AND I DON'T WANNA DISCUSS HER WITH YOU OR ANYBODY! YOU GOT THAT?
DON'T STICK YOUR FINGER AT ME, TOM.
TELL ME ABOUT LAST SUMMER, JEN.
WHAT WAS?
IT WAS TERRIBLE.
TOM WAS ALWAYS TREATING BOBBY POORLY--
HE STARTED TO SMACK HIM IF HE DID SOMETHING WRONG.
THEN...

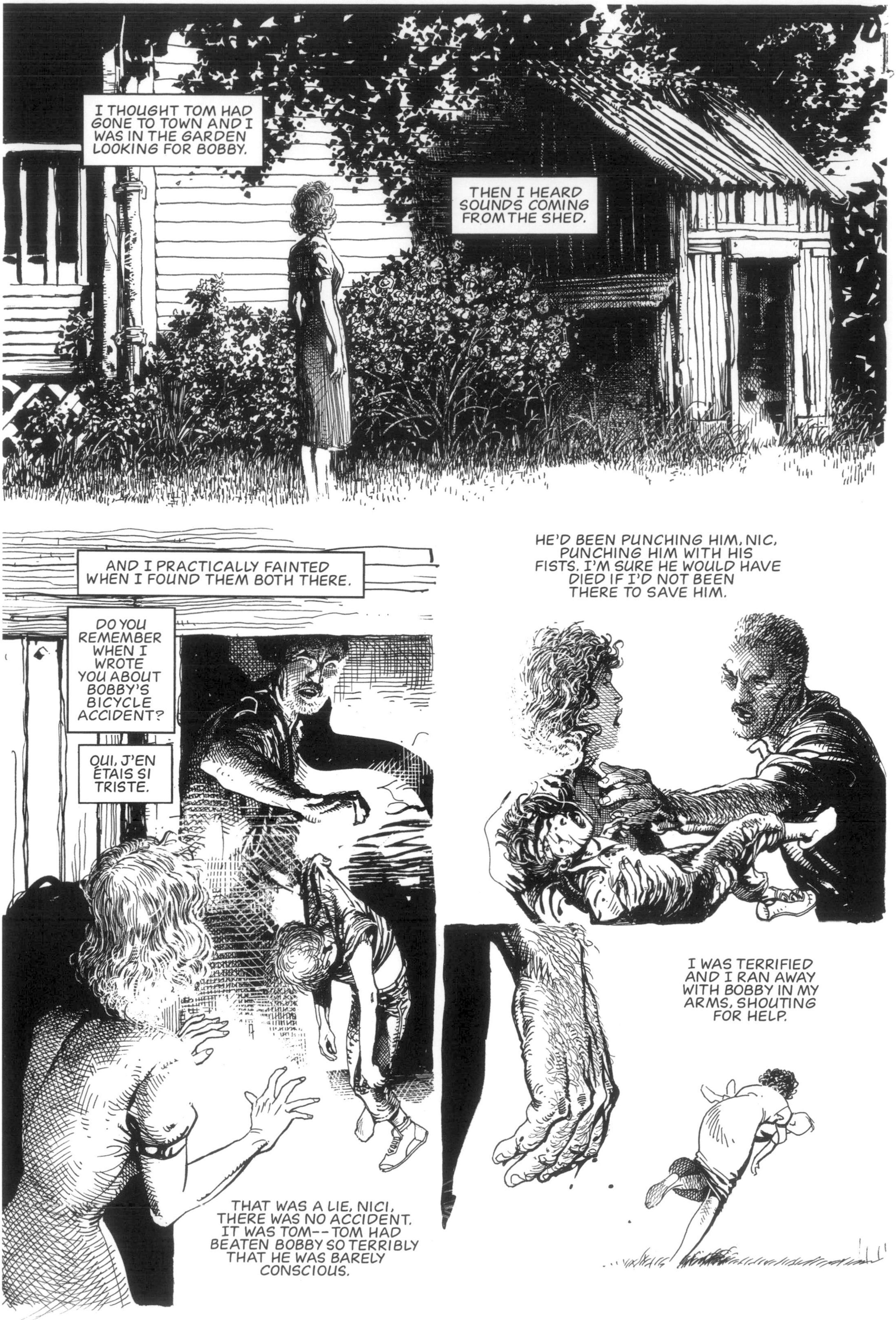
I THOUGHT TOM HAD GONE TO TOWN AND I WAS IN THE GARDEN LOOKING FOR BOBBY.
THEN I HEARD SOUNDS COMING FROM THE SHED.
AND I PRACTICALLY FAINTED WHEN I FOUND THEM BOTH THERE.
DO YOU REMEMBER WHEN I WROTE YOU ABOUT BOBBY'S BICYCLE ACCIDENT?
OUI, J'EN ÉTAIS SI TRISTE.
THAT WAS A LIE, NICI, THERE WAS NO ACCIDENT. IT WAS TOM-- TOM HAD BEATEN BOBBY SO TERRIBLY THAT HE WAS BARELY CONSCIOUS.
HE'D BEEN PUNCHING HIM, NIC, PUNCHING HIM WITH HIS FISTS. I'M SURE HE WOULD HAVE DIED IF I'D NOT BEEN THERE TO SAVE HIM.
I WAS TERRIFIED AND I RAN AWAY WITH BOBBY IN MY ARMS, SHOUTING FOR HELP.

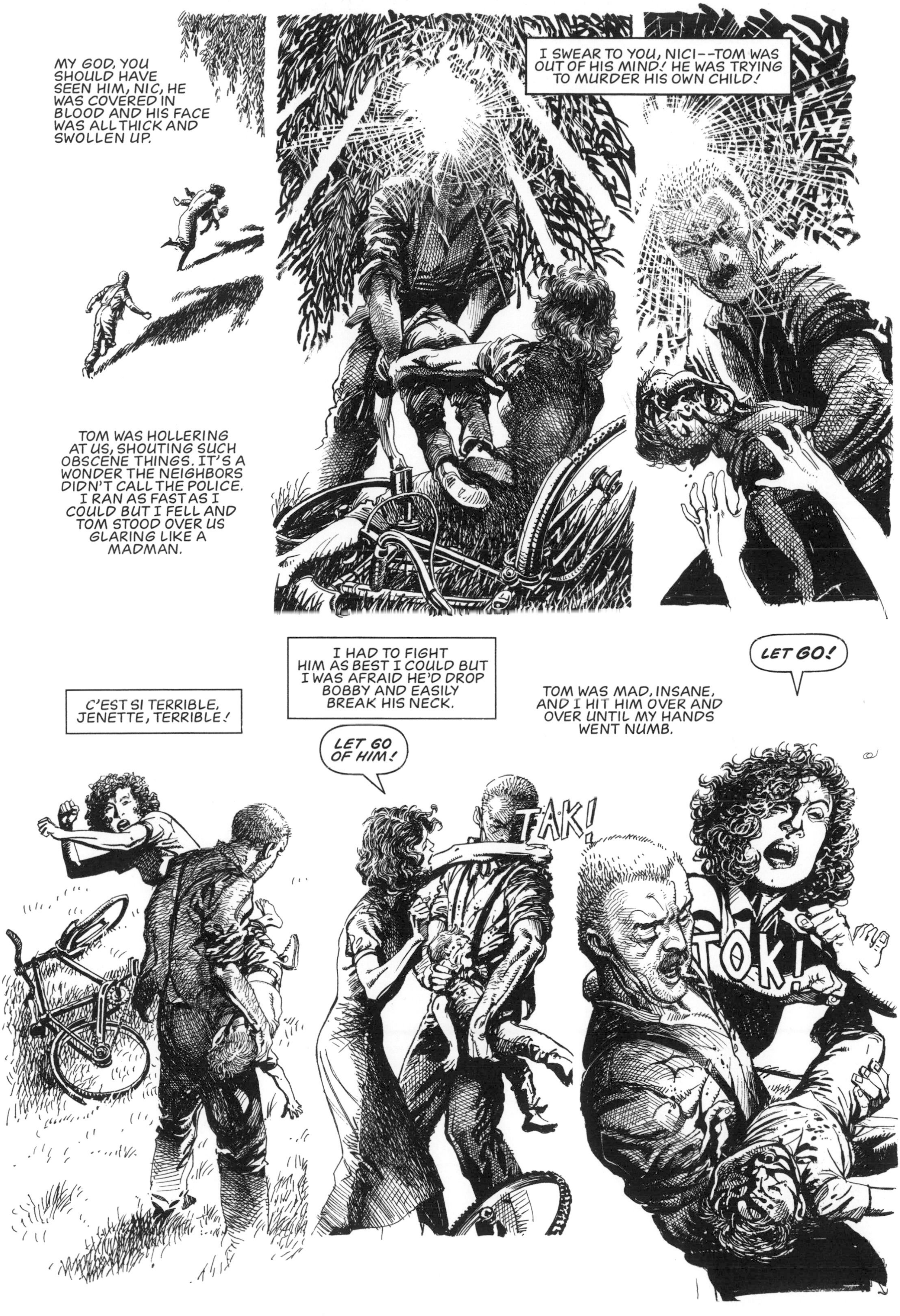
MY GOD, YOU SHOULD HAVE SEEN HIM, NIC, HE WAS COVERED IN BLOOD AND HIS FACE WAS ALL THICK AND SWOLLEN UP.
I SWEAR TO YOU, NICI--TOM WAS OUT OF HIS MIND! HE WAS TRYING TO MURDER HIS OWN CHILD!
TOM WAS HOLLERING AT US, SHOUTING SUCH OBSCENE THINGS. IT'S A WONDER THE NEIGHBORS DIDN'T CALL THE POLICE. I RAN AS FASTAS I COULD BUT I FELL AND TOM STOOD OVER US GLARING LIKE A MADMAN.
C'EST SI TERRIBLE, JENETTE, TERRIBLE!
I HAD TO FIGHT HIM AS BEST I COULD BUT I WAS AFRAID HE'D DROP BOBBY AND EASILY BREAK HIS NECK.
LET GO OF HIM!
TAK!
TOM WAS MAD, INSANE, AND I HIT HIM OVER AND OVER UNTIL MY HANDS WENT NUMB.
LET GO!
TOK!

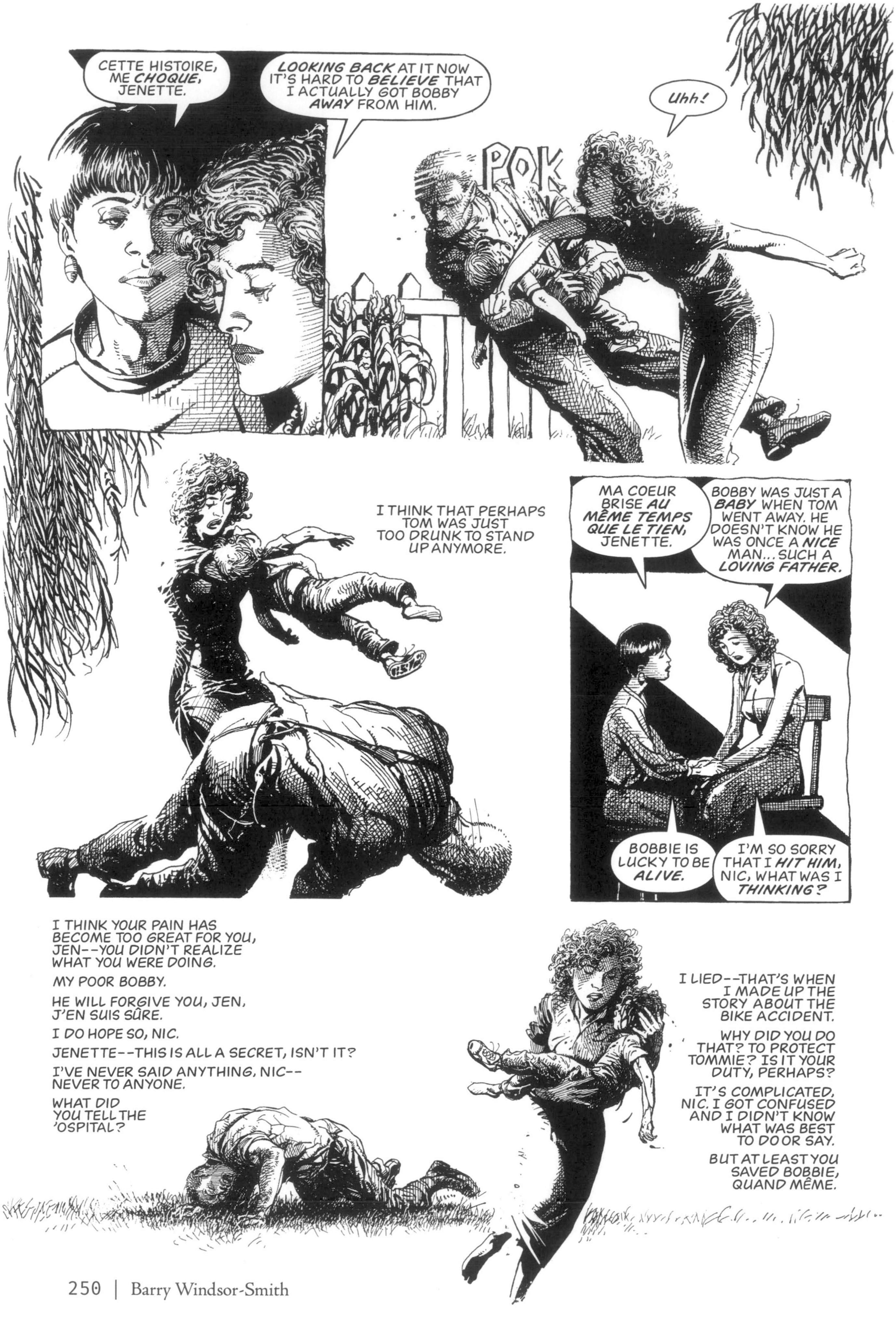
CETTE HISTOIRE, ME CHOQUE, JENETTE.
LOOKING BACK AT IT NOW IT'S HARD TO BELIEVE THAT I ACTUALLY GOT BOBBY AWAY FROM HIM.
POK
Uhh!
I THINK THAT PERHAPS TOM WAS JUST TOO DRUNK TO STAND UP ANYMORE.
MA COEUR BRISE AU MÊME TEMPS QUE LE TIEN, JENETTE.
BOBBY WAS JUST A BABY WHEN TOM WENT AWAY. HE DOESN'T KNOW HE WAS ONCE A NICE MAN... SUCH A LOVING FATHER.
BOBBIE IS LUCKY TO BE ALIVE.
I'M SO SORRY THAT I HIT HIM, NIC, WHAT WAS I THINKING?
I THINK YOUR PAIN HAS BECOME TOO GREAT FOR YOU, JEN--YOU DIDN'T REALIZE WHAT YOU WERE DOING.
MY POOR BOBBY.
HE WILL FORGIVE YOU, JEN, J'EN SUIS SÛRE.
I DO HOPE SO, NIC.
JENETTE--THIS IS ALL A SECRET, ISN'T IT?
I'VE NEVER SAID ANYTHING, NIC--NEVER TO ANYONE.
WHAT DID YOU TELL THE 'OSPITAL?
I LIED--THAT'S WHEN I MADE UP THE STORY ABOUT THE BIKE ACCIDENT.
WHY DID YOU DO THAT? TO PROTECT TOMMIE? IS IT YOUR DUTY, PERHAPS?
IT'S COMPLICATED, NIC. I GOT CONFUSED AND I DIDN'T KNOW WHAT WAS BEST TO DO OR SAY.
BUT AT LEAST YOU SAVED BOBBIE, QUAND MÊME.

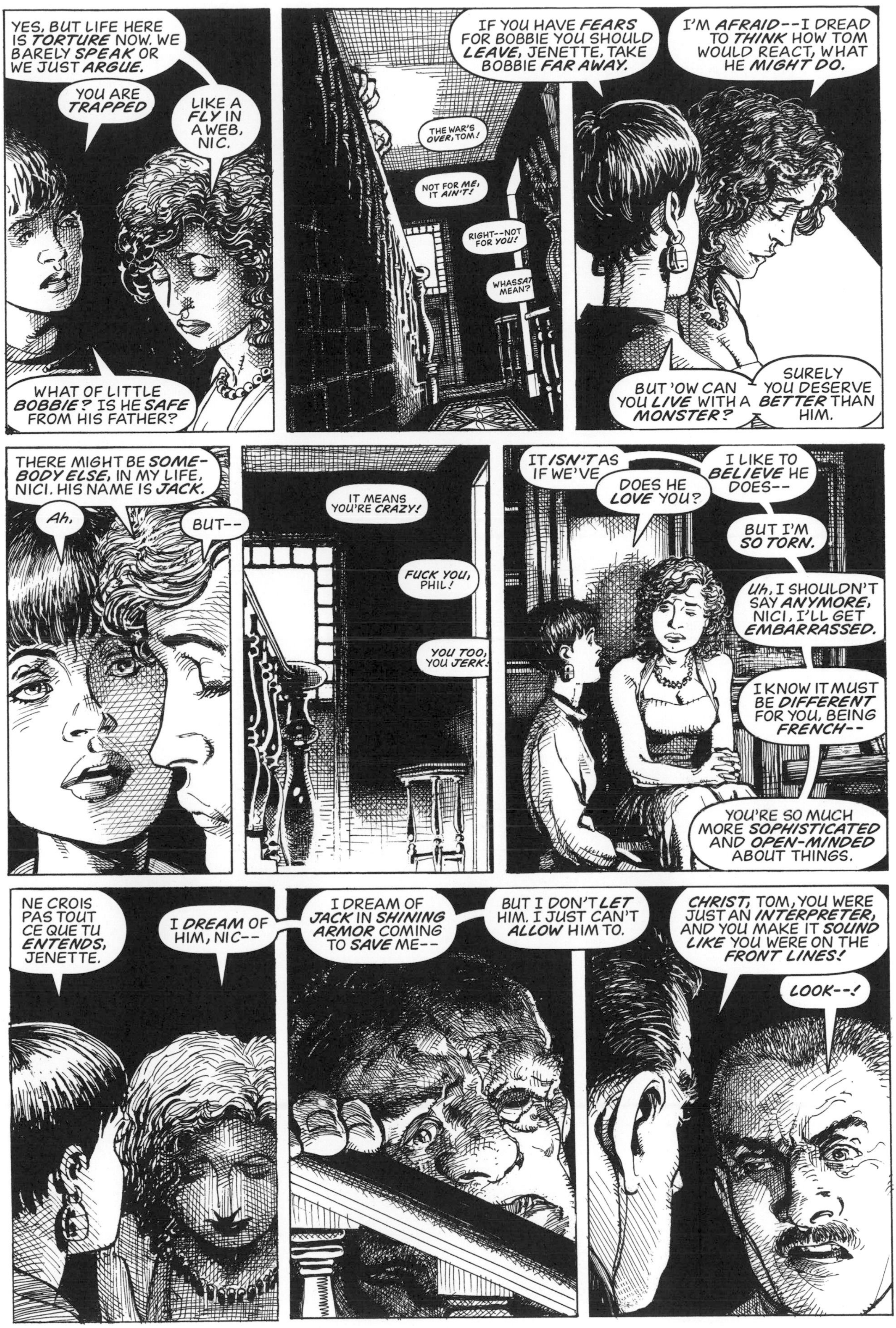

YES, BUT LIFE HERE IS TORTURE NOW. WE BARELY SPEAK OR WE JUST ARGUE.
YOU ARE TRAPPED
LIKE A FLY IN A WEB, NIC.
WHAT OF LITTLE BOBBIE? IS HE SAFE FROM HIS FATHER?
THE WAR'S OVER, TOM!
NOT FOR ME, IT AIN'T!
RIGHT--NOT FOR YOU!
WHASSAT MEAN?
IF YOU HAVE FEARS FOR BOBBIE YOU SHOULD LEAVE, JENETTE, TAKE BOBBIE FAR AWAY.
I'M AFRAID--I DREAD TO THINK HOW TOM WOULD REACT, WHAT HE MIGHT DO.
BUT 'OW CAN YOU LIVE WITH A MONSTER?
SURELY YOU DESERVE BETTER THAN HIM.
THERE MIGHT BE SOMEBODY ELSE, IN MY LIFE, NICI. HIS NAME IS JACK.
Ah.
BUT--
IT MEANS YOU'RE CRAZY!
FUCK YOU, PHIL!
YOU TOO, YOU JERK!
IT ISN'T AS IF WE'VE
DOES HE LOVE YOU?
I LIKE TO BELIEVE HE DOES--
BUT I'M SO TORN.
Uh, I SHOULDN'T SAY ANYMORE, NICI, I'LL GET EMBARRASSED.
I KNOW IT MUST BE DIFFERENT FOR YOU, BEING FRENCH--
YOU'RE SO MUCH MORE SOPHISTICATED AND OPEN-MINDED ABOUT THINGS.
NE CROIS PAS TOUT CE QUE TU ENTENDS, JENETTE.
I DREAM OF HIM, NIC--
I DREAM OF JACK IN SHINING ARMOR COMING TO SAVE ME--
BUT I DON'T LET HIM. I JUST CAN'T ALLOW HIM TO.
CHRIST, TOM, YOU WERE JUST AN INTERPRETER, AND YOU MAKE IT SOUND LIKE YOU WERE ON THE FRONT LINES!
LOOK--!

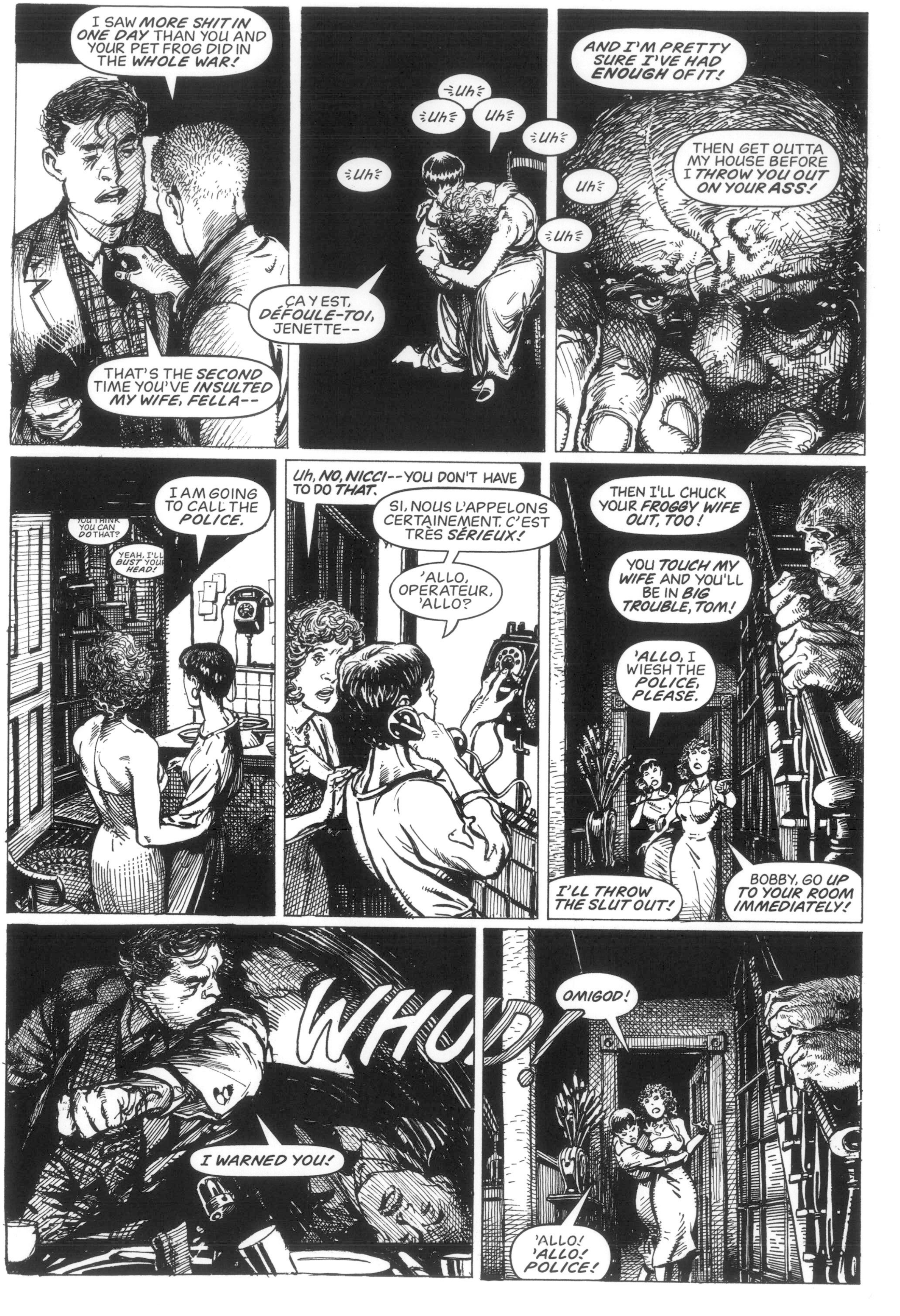

I SAW MORE SHIT IN ONE DAY THAN YOU AND YOUR PET FROG DID IN THE WHOLE WAR!
THAT'S THE SECOND TIME YOU'VE INSULTED MY WIFE, FELLA--
Uh
Uh
Uh
Uh
Uh
Uh
Uh
ÇA Y EST, DÉFOULE-TOI, JENETTE--
AND I'M PRETTY SURE I'VE HAD ENOUGH OF IT!
THEN GET OUTTA MY HOUSE BEFORE I THROW YOU OUT ON YOUR ASS!
I AM GOING TO CALL THE POLICE.
YOU THINK YOU CAN DO THAT?
YEAH, I'LL BUST YOUR HEAD!
Uh, NO, NICCI-- YOU DON'T HAVE TO DO THAT.
SI, NOUS L'APPELONS CERTAINEMENT. C'EST TRÈS SÉRIEUX!
'ALLO, OPERATEUR, 'ALLO?
THEN I'LL CHUCK YOUR FROGGY WIFE OUT, TOO!
YOU TOUCH MY WIFE AND YOU'LL BE IN BIG TROUBLE, TOM!
'ALLO, I WIESH THE POLICE, PLEASE.
I'LL THROW THE SLUT OUT!
BOBBY, GO UP TO YOUR ROOM IMMEDIATELY!
WHUD!
I WARNED YOU!
OMIGOD!
'ALLO! 'ALLO! POLICE!

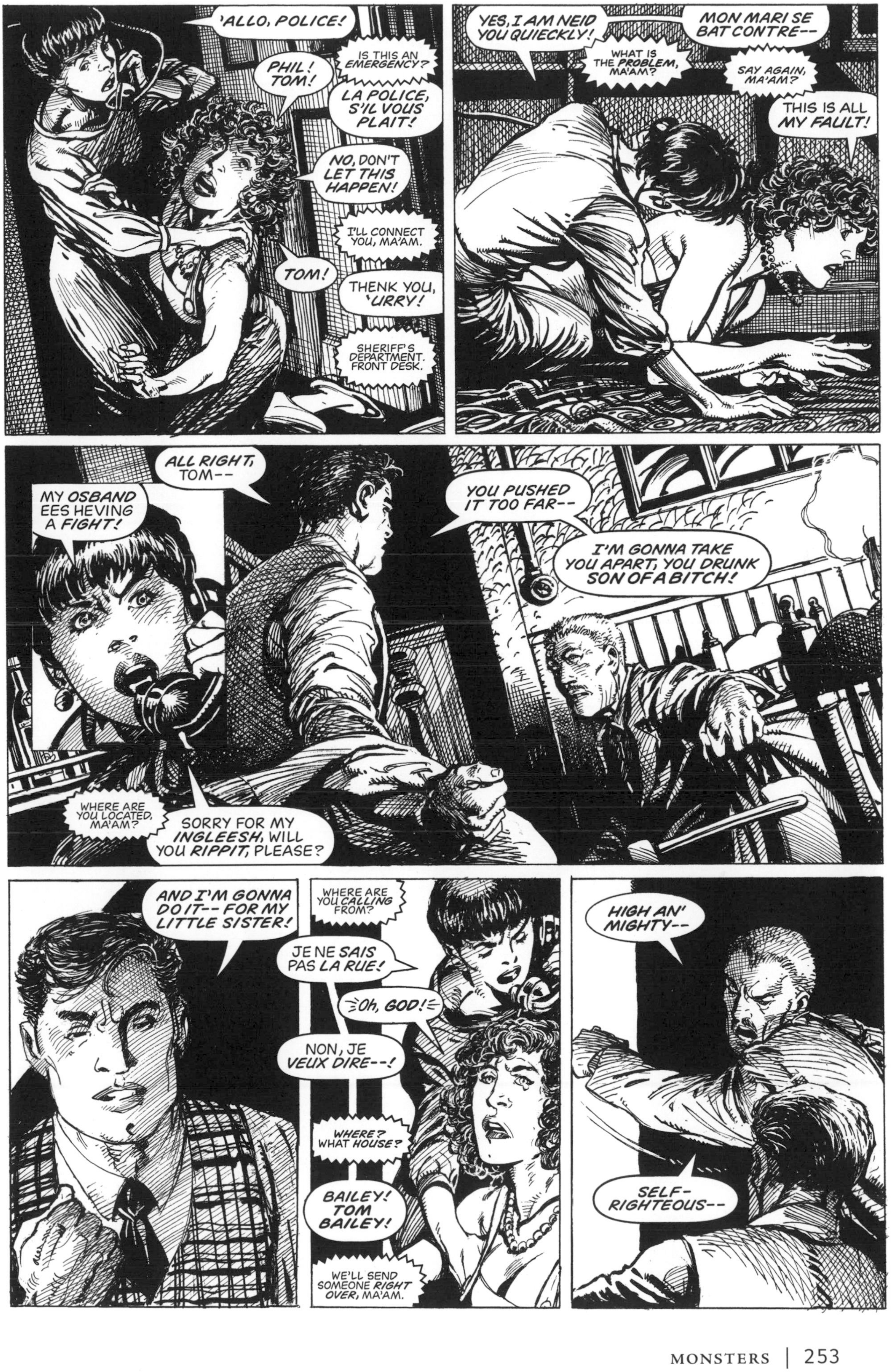
'ALLO, POLICE!
PHIL! TOM!
IS THIS AN EMERGENCY?
LA POLICE, S'IL VOUS PLAIT!
NO, DON'T LET THIS HAPPEN!
I'LL CONNECT YOU, MA'AM.
TOM!
THENK YOU, 'URRY!
SHERIFF'S DEPARTMENT. FRONT DESK.
YES, I AM NEID YOU QUIECKLY!
WHAT IS THE PROBLEM, MA'AM?
MON MARI SE BAT CONTRE--
SAY AGAIN, MA'AM?
THIS IS ALL MY FAULT!
MY OSBAND EES HEVING A FIGHT!
ALL RIGHT, TOM--
YOU PUSHED IT TOO FAR--
I'M GONNA TAKE YOU APART, YOU DRUNK SON OF A BITCH!
WHERE ARE YOU LOCATED, MA'AM?
SORRY FOR MY INGLEESH, WILL YOU RIPPIT, PLEASE?
AND I'M GONNA DO IT-- FOR MY LITTLE SISTER!
WHERE ARE YOU CALLING FROM?
JE NE SAIS PAS LA RUE!
Oh, GOD!
NON, JE VEUX DIRE--!
WHERE? WHAT HOUSE?
BAILEY! TOM BAILEY!
WE'LL SEND SOMEONE RIGHT OVER, MA'AM.
HIGH AN' MIGHTY--
SELF-RIGHTEOUS--

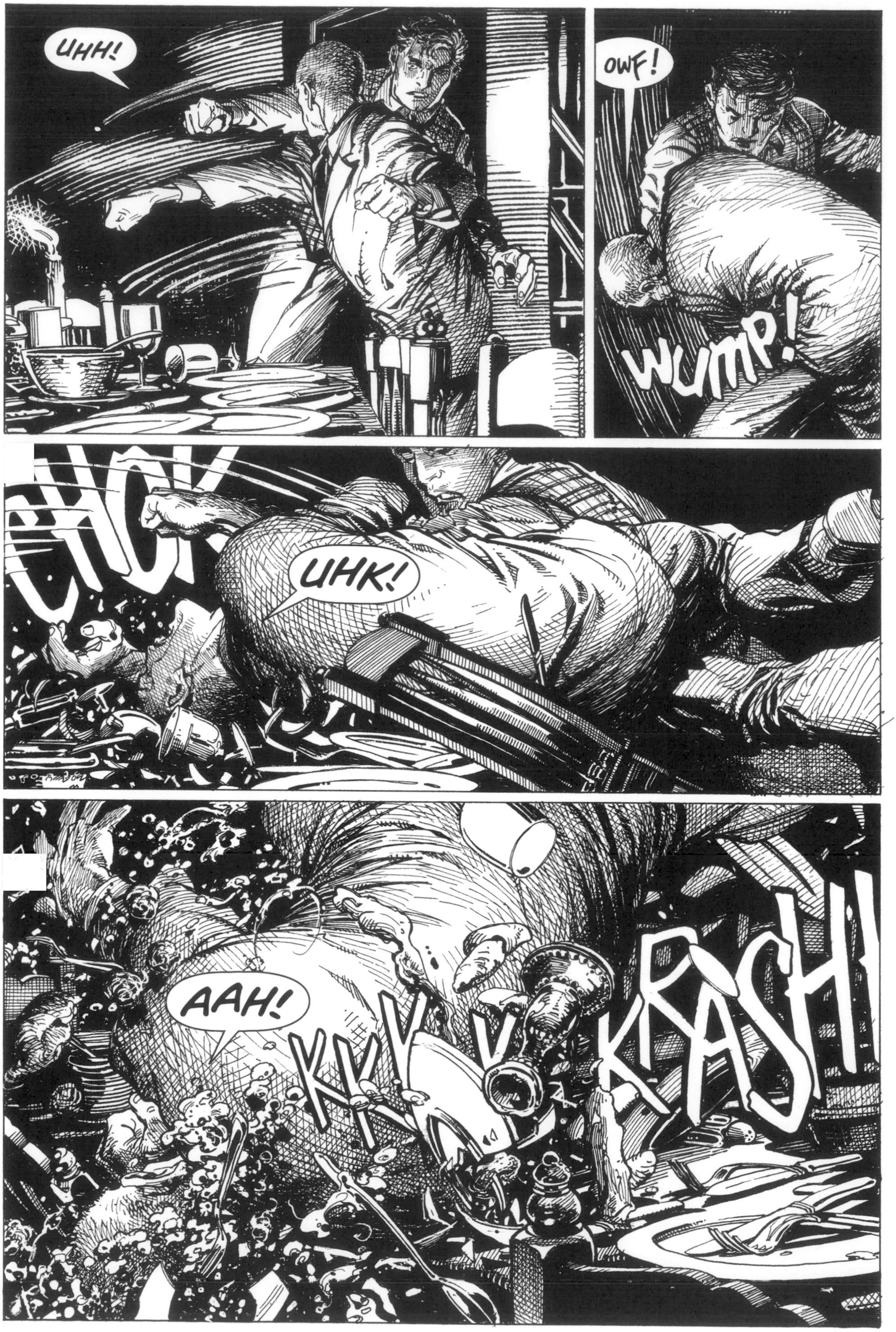
UHH!
OWF!
WUMP!
CHOK
UHK!
AAH!
KRASH

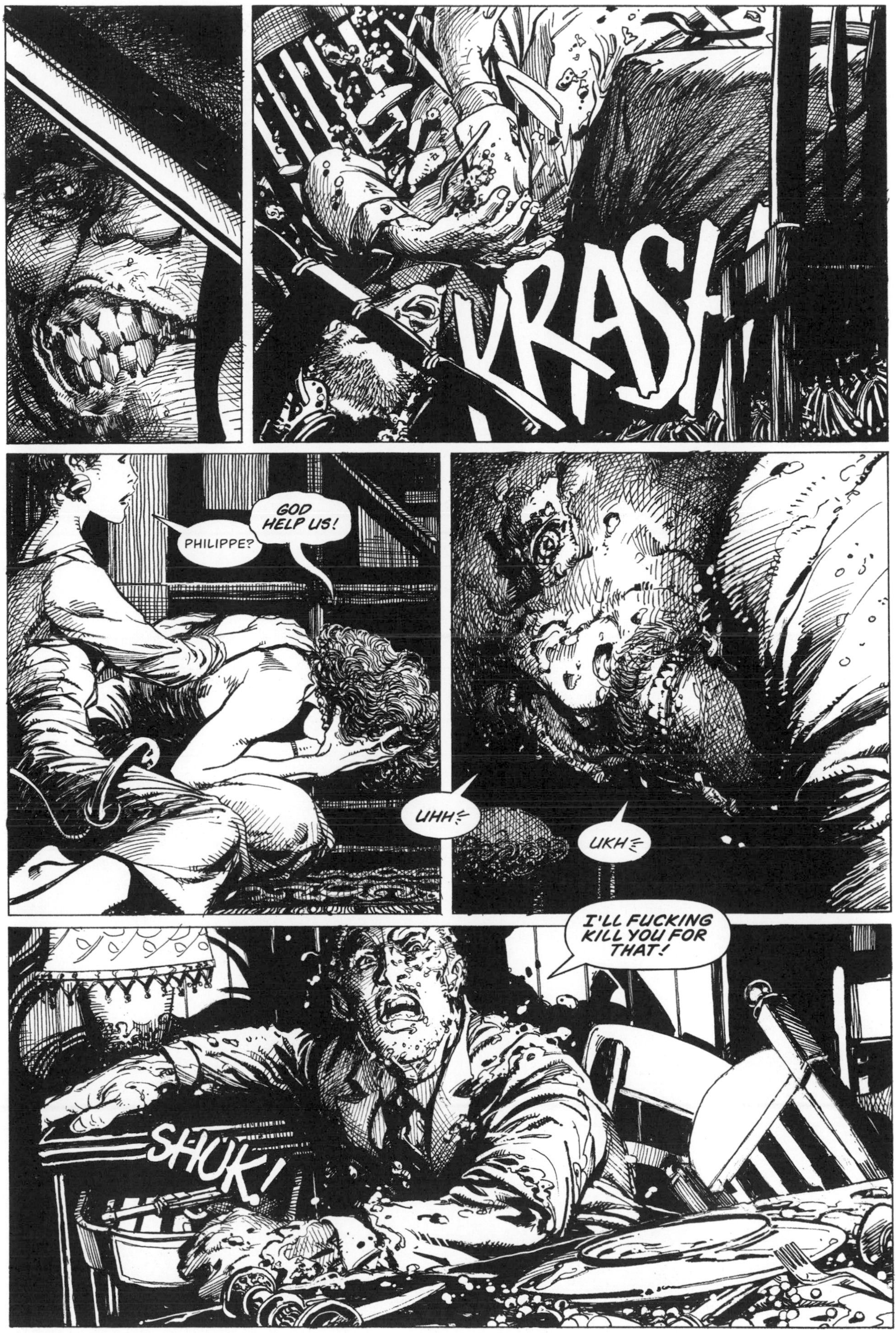
KRASH!
PHILIPPE?
GOD HELP US!
UHH
UKH
I'LL FUCKING KILL YOU FOR THAT!
SHUK!

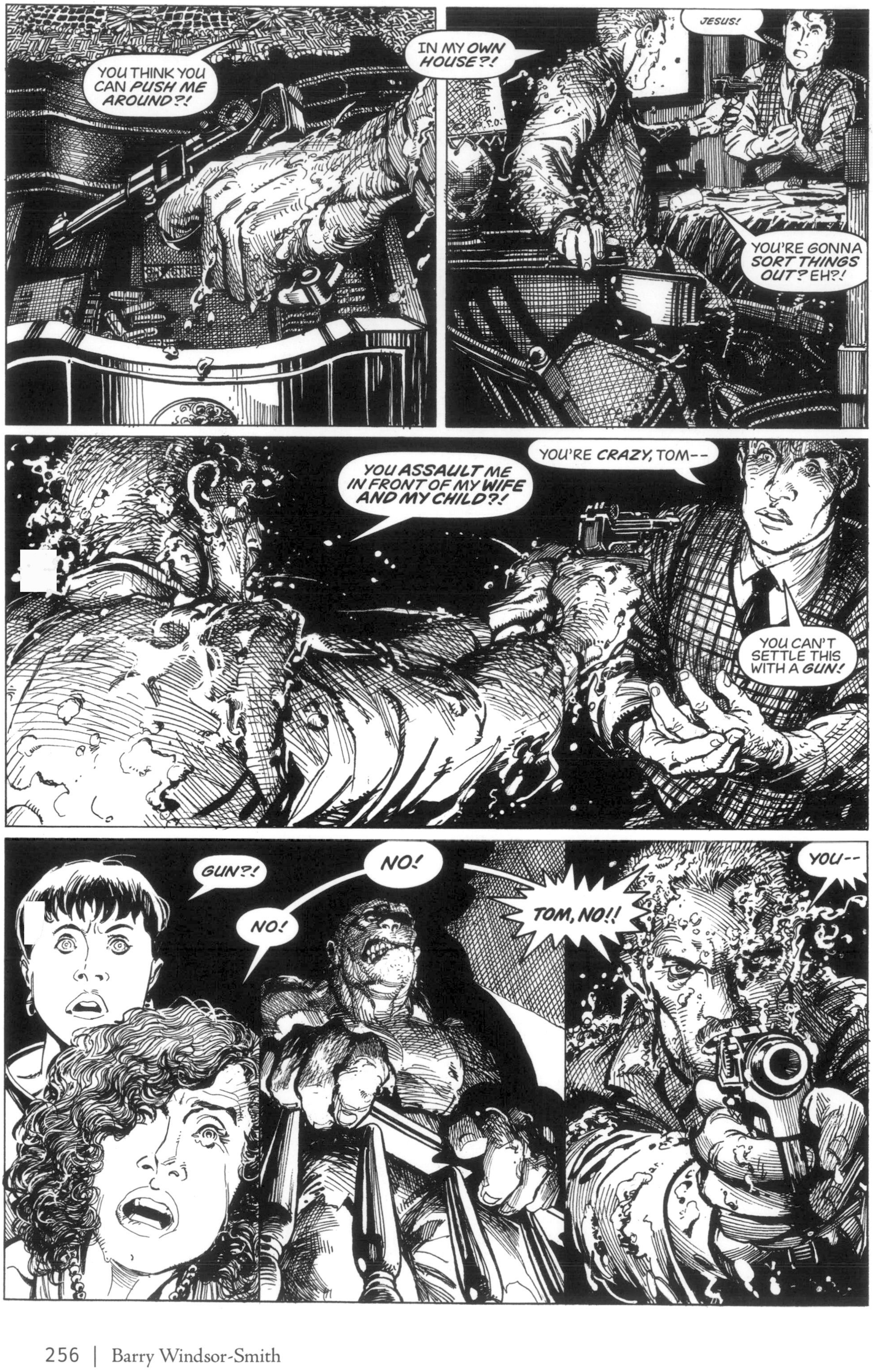
YOU THINK YOU CAN PUSH ME AROUND?!
IN MY OWN HOUSE?!
JESUS!
YOU'RE GONNA SORT THINGS OUT? EH?!
YOU ASSAULT ME IN FRONT OF MY WIFE AND MY CHILD?!
YOU'RE CRAZY, TOM--
YOU CAN'T SETTLE THIS WITH A GUN!
GUN?!
NO!
NO!
TOM, NO!!
YOU--

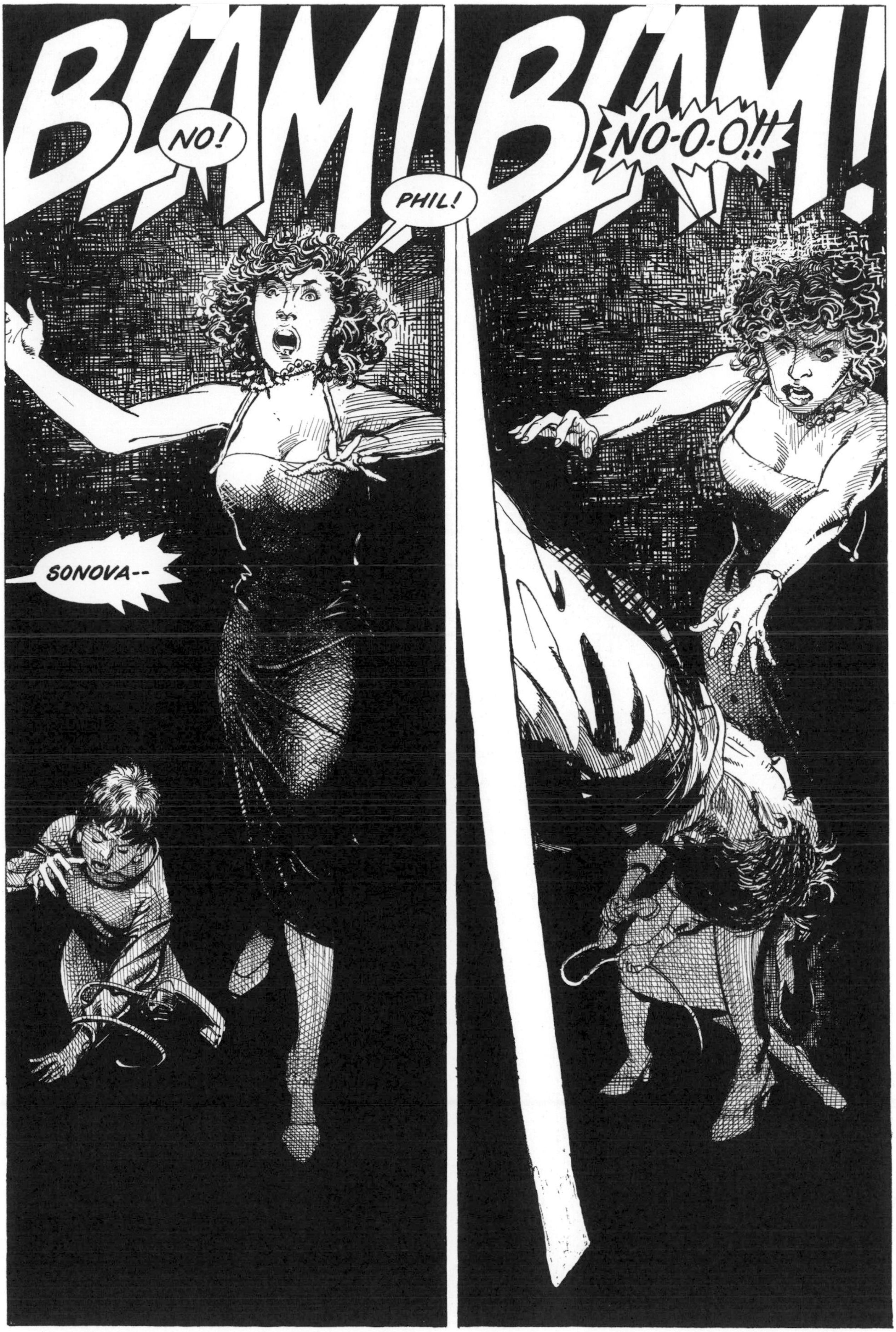
BLAM!
NO!
PHIL!
SONOVA--
BLAM!
NO-O-O!!

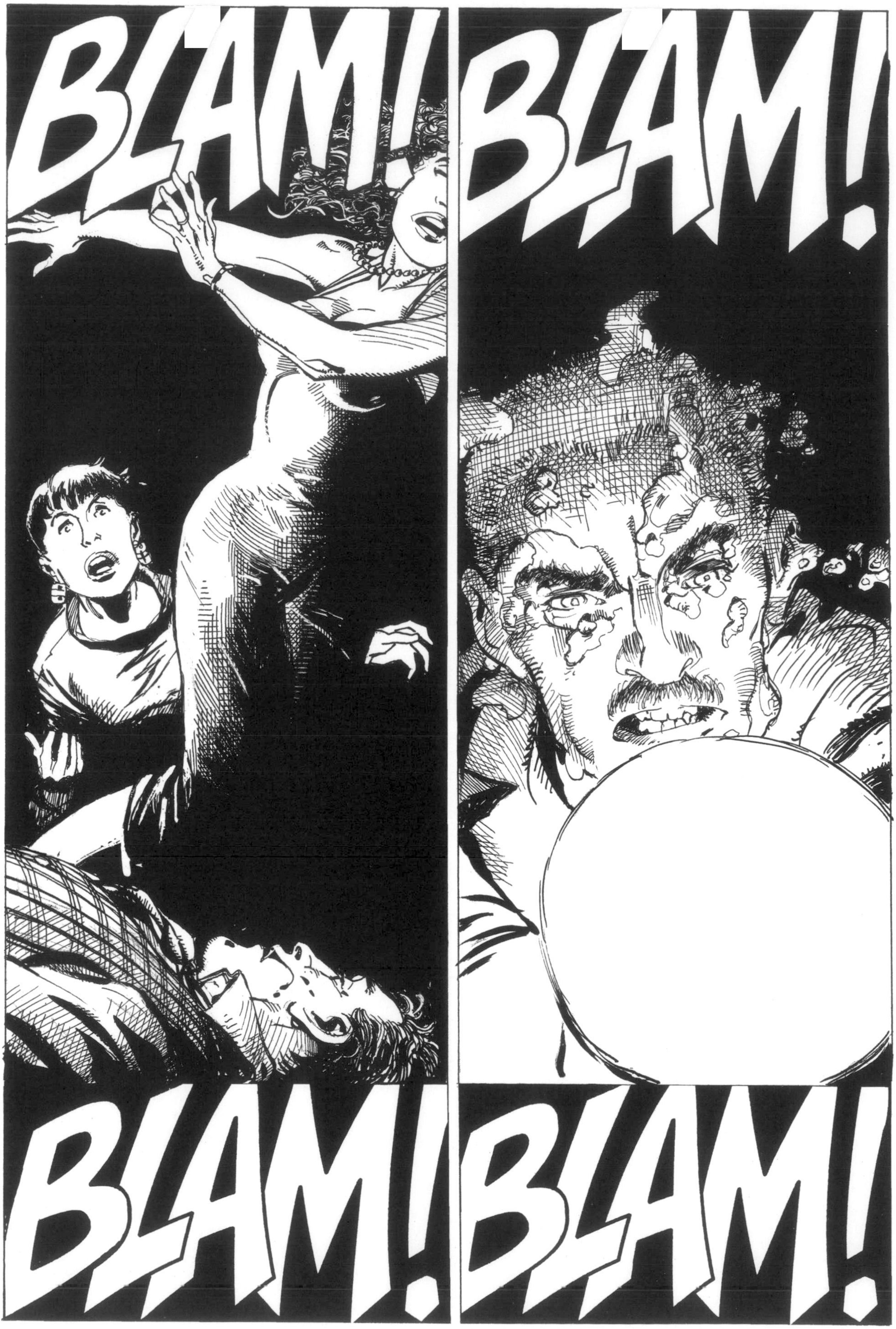
BLAM!
BLAM!
BLAM!
BLAM!

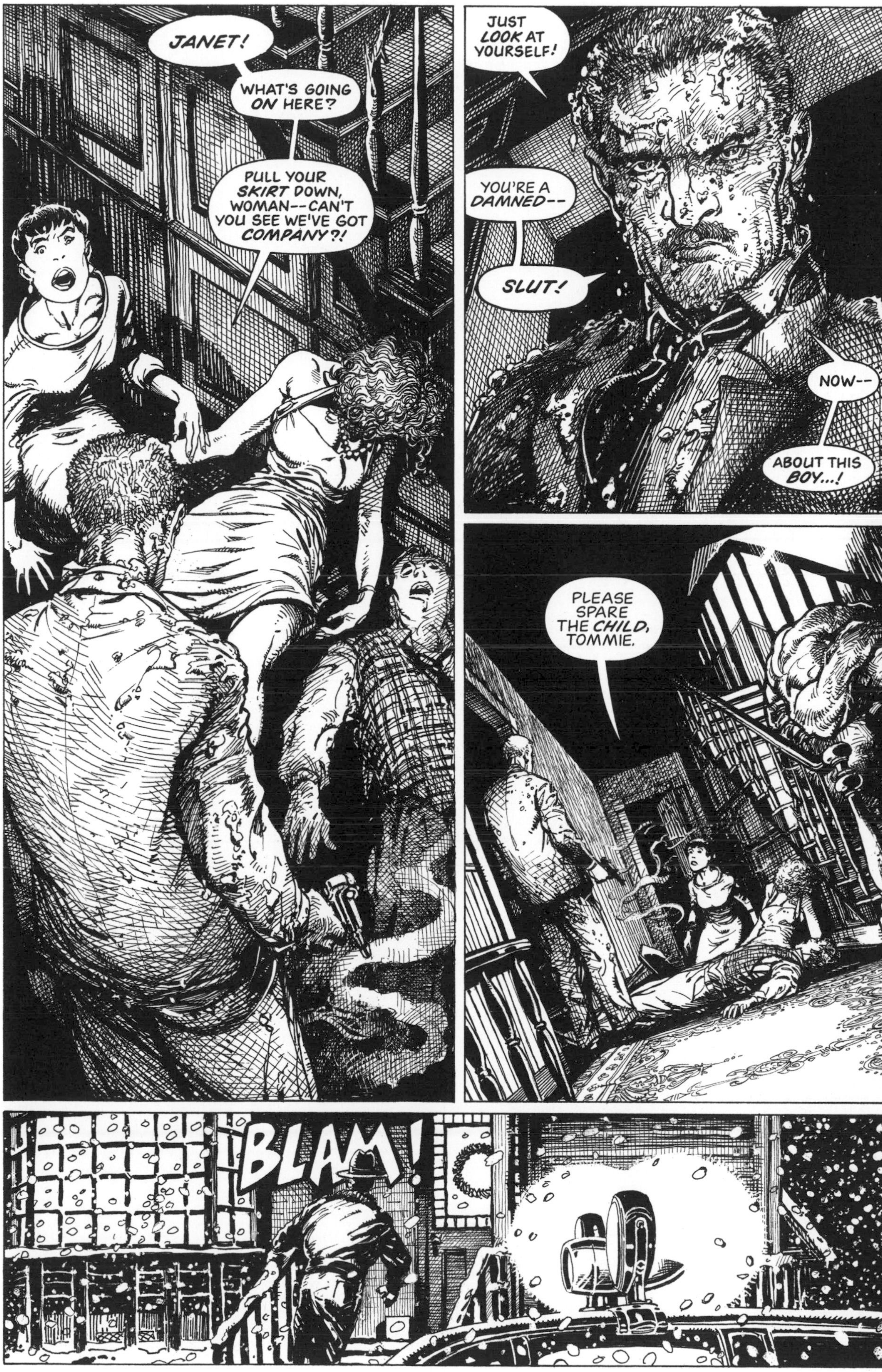
JANET!
WHAT'S GOING ON HERE?
PULL YOUR SKIRT DOWN, WOMAN--CAN'T YOU SEE WE'VE GOT COMPANY?!
JUST LOOK AT YOURSELF!
YOU'RE A DAMNED--
SLUT!
NOW--
ABOUT THIS BOY...!
PLEASE SPARE THE CHILD, TOMMIE.
BLAM!

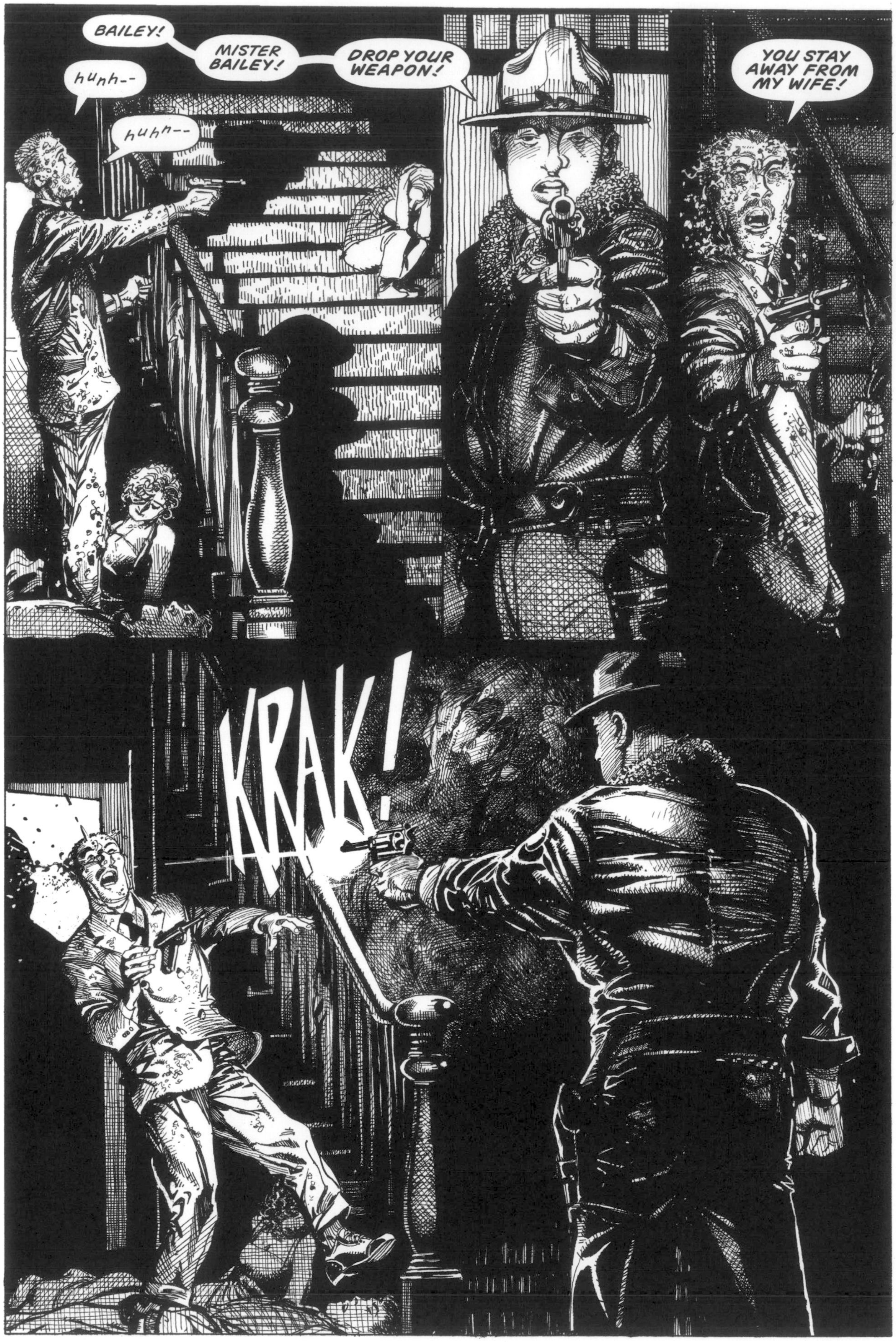
BAILEY!
hunh--
MISTER BAILEY!
hunh--
DROP YOUR WEAPON!
YOU STAY AWAY FROM MY WIFE!
KRAK!

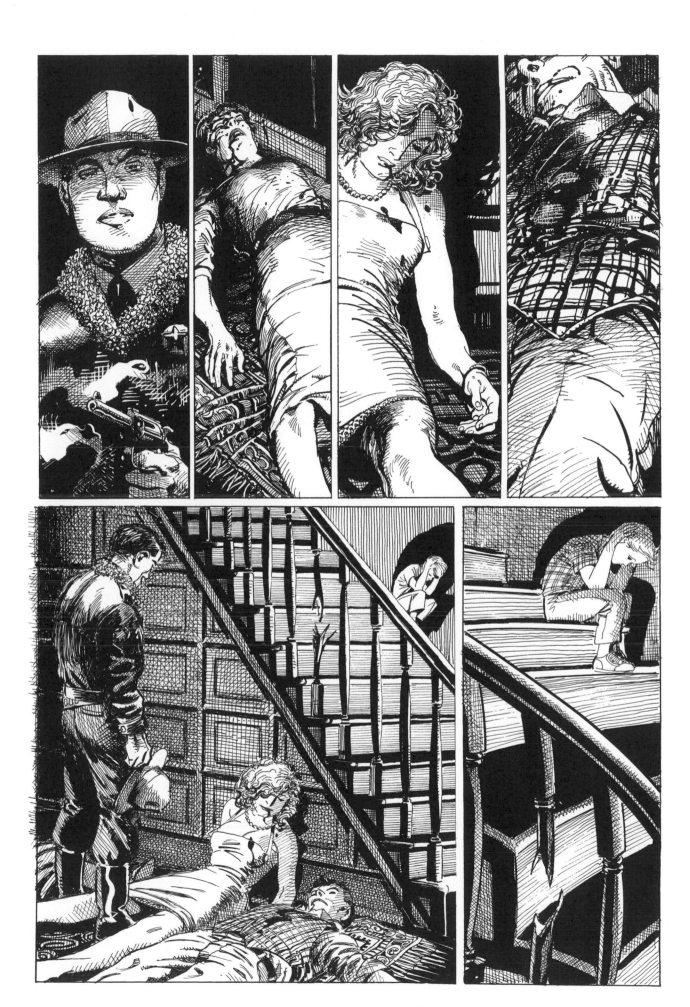

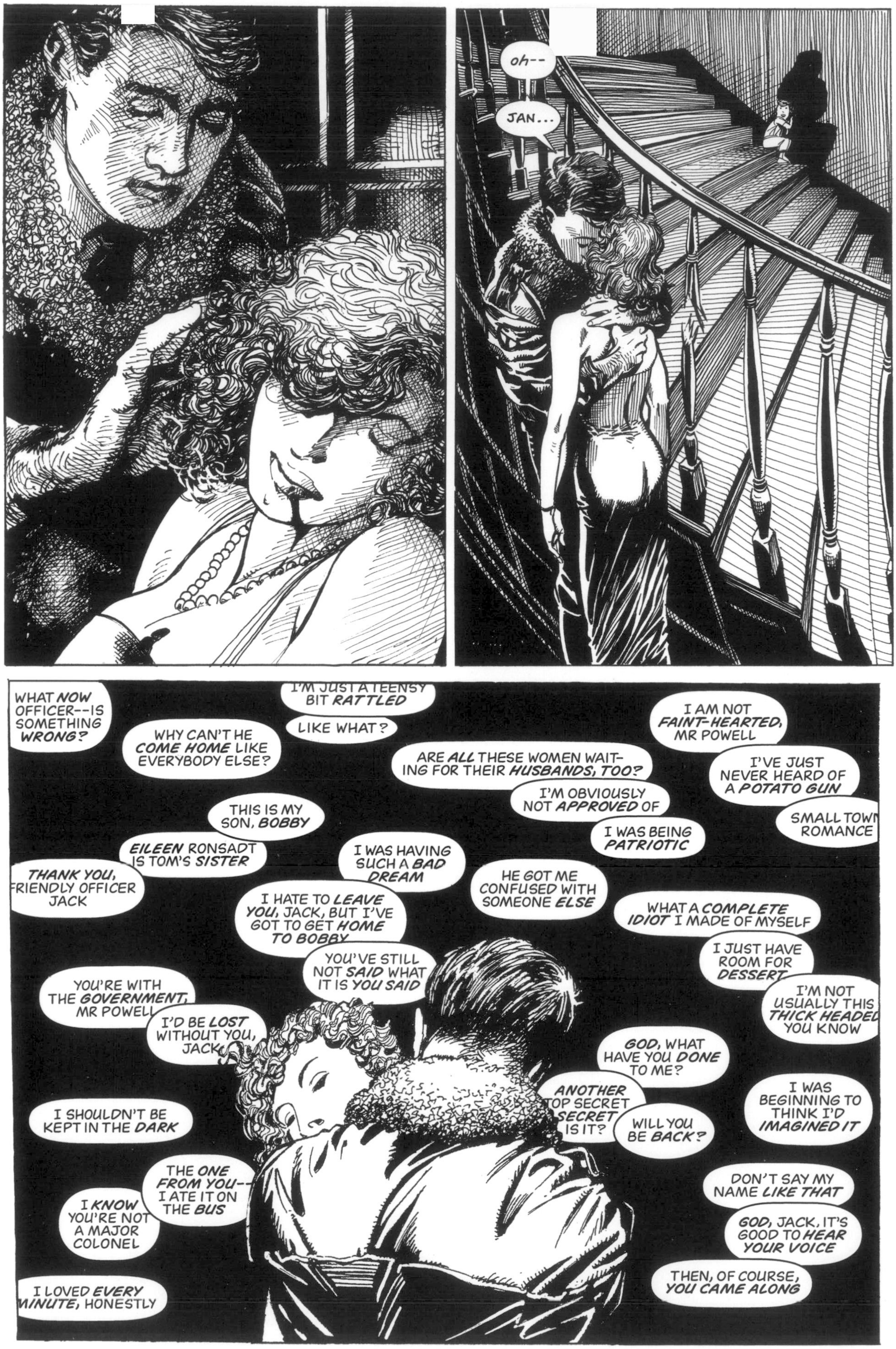
oh--
JAN...
WHAT NOW OFFICER--IS SOMETHING WRONG?
I'M JUST A TEENSY BIT RATTLED
LIKE WHAT?
WHY CAN'T HE COME HOME LIKE EVERYBODY ELSE?
I AM NOT FAINT-HEARTED, MR POWELL
ARE ALL THESE WOMEN WAITING FOR THEIR HUSBANDS, TOO?
I'VE JUST NEVER HEARD OF A POTATO GUN
I'M OBVIOUSLY NOT APPROVED OF
THIS IS MY SON, BOBBY
SMALL TOWN ROMANCE
I WAS BEING PATRIOTIC
EILEEN RONSADT IS TOM'S SISTER
I WAS HAVING SUCH A BAD DREAM
THANK YOU, FRIENDLY OFFICER JACK
HE GOT ME CONFUSED WITH SOMEONE ELSE
I HATE TO LEAVE YOU, JACK, BUT I'VE GOT TO GET HOME TO BOBBY
WHAT A COMPLETE IDIOT I MADE OF MYSELF
YOU'VE STILL NOT SAID WHAT IT IS YOU SAID
I JUST HAVE ROOM FOR DESSERT
YOU'RE WITH THE GOVERNMENT, MR POWELL
I'M NOT USUALLY THIS THICK HEADED YOU KNOW
I'D BE LOST WITHOUT YOU, JACK
GOD, WHAT HAVE YOU DONE TO ME?
ANOTHER TOP SECRET SECRET IS IT?
WILL YOU BE BACK?
I WAS BEGINNING TO THINK I'D IMAGINED IT
I SHOULDN'T BE KEPT IN THE DARK
THE ONE FROM YOU--I ATE IT ON THE BUS
I KNOW YOU'RE NOT A MAJOR COLONEL
DON'T SAY MY NAME LIKE THAT
GOD, JACK, IT'S GOOD TO HEAR YOUR VOICE
THEN, OF COURSE, YOU CAME ALONG
I LOVED EVERY MINUTE, HONESTLY

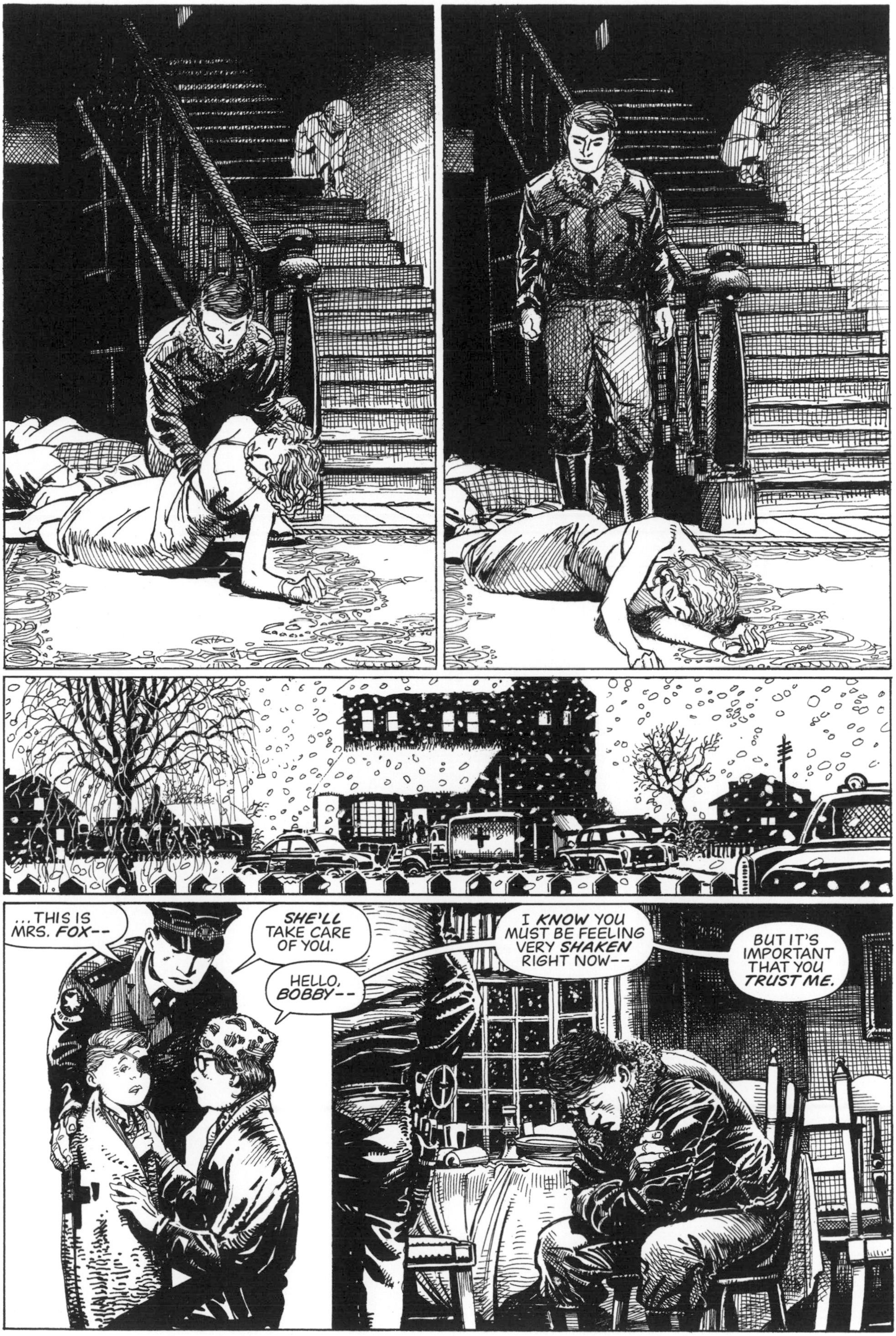
...THIS IS MRS. FOX--
SHE'LL TAKE CARE OF YOU.
HELLO, BOBBY--
I KNOW YOU MUST BE FEELING VERY SHAKEN RIGHT NOW--
BUT IT'S IMPORTANT THAT YOU TRUST ME.

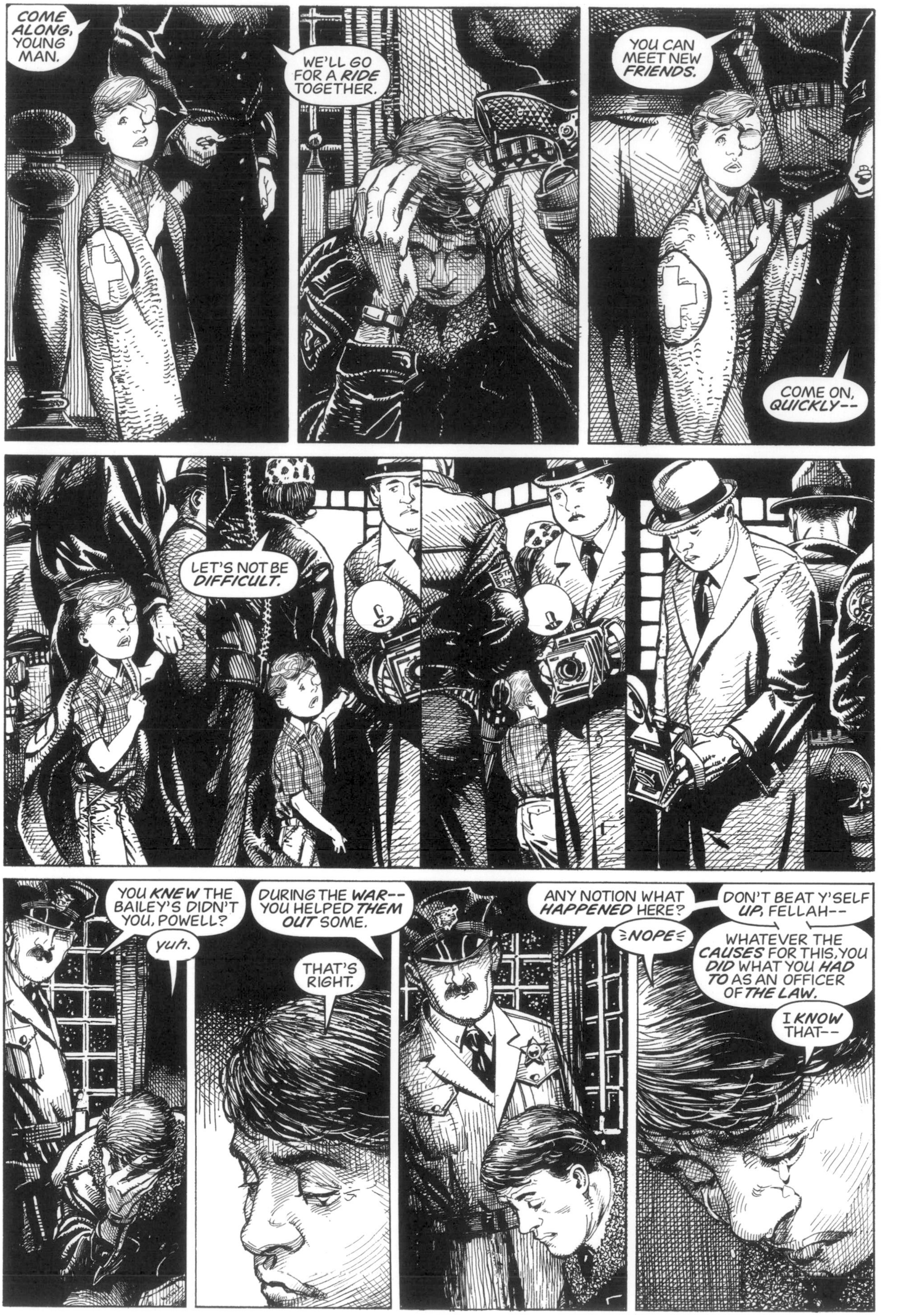
COME ALONG, YOUNG MAN.
WE'LL GO FOR A *RIDE* TOGETHER.
YOU CAN MEET NEW *FRIENDS.*
COME ON, *QUICKLY--*
LET'S NOT BE *DIFFICULT.*
YOU *KNEW* THE BAILEY'S DIDN'T YOU, POWELL?
yuh.
DURING THE *WAR--* YOU HELPED *THEM OUT* SOME.
THAT'S RIGHT.
ANY NOTION WHAT *HAPPENED* HERE?
NOPE
DON'T BEAT Y'SELF *UP,* FELLAH--
WHATEVER THE *CAUSES* FOR THIS, YOU *DID* WHAT YOU *HAD TO* AS AN OFFICER OF *THE LAW.*
I *KNOW* THAT--

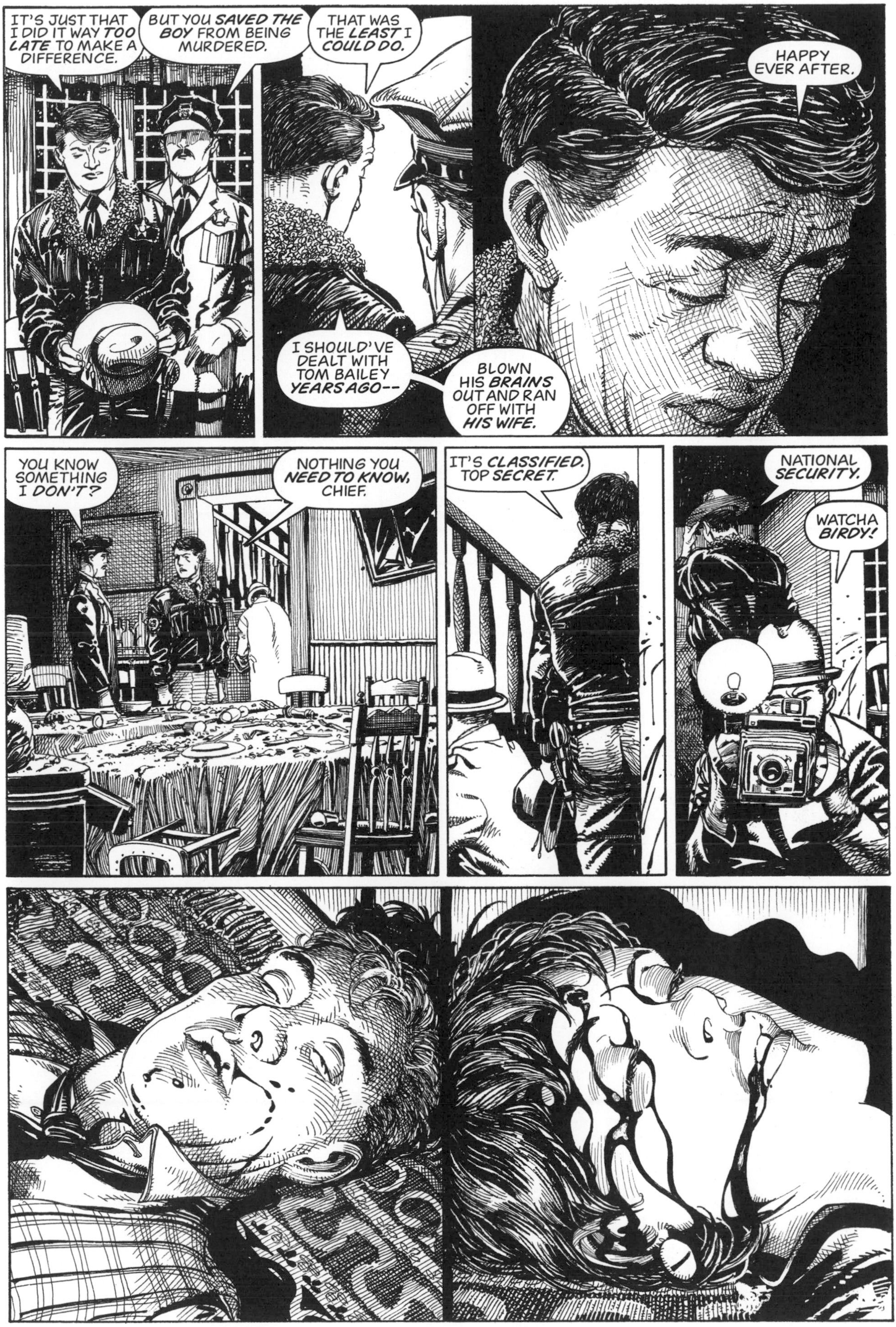
IT'S JUST THAT I DID IT WAY TOO LATE TO MAKE A DIFFERENCE.
BUT YOU SAVED THE BOY FROM BEING MURDERED.
THAT WAS THE LEAST I COULD DO.
I SHOULD'VE DEALT WITH TOM BAILEY YEARS AGO--
BLOWN HIS BRAINS OUT AND RAN OFF WITH HIS WIFE.
HAPPY EVER AFTER.
YOU KNOW SOMETHING I DON'T?
NOTHING YOU NEED TO KNOW, CHIEF.
IT'S CLASSIFIED. TOP SECRET.
NATIONAL SECURITY.
WATCHA BIRDY!

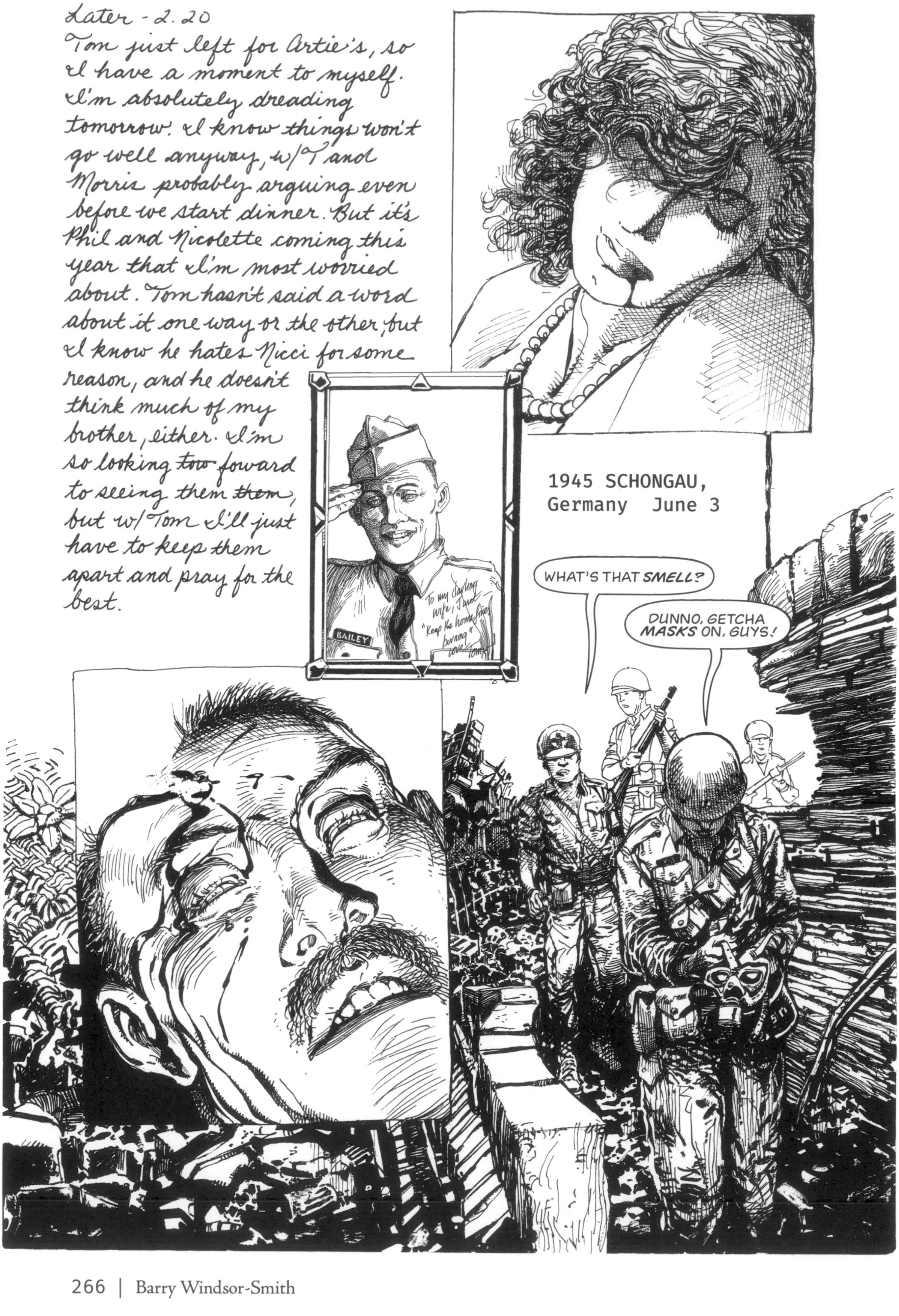
Later - 2.20
Tom just left for Artie's, so I have a moment to myself. I'm absolutely dreading tomorrow. I know things won't go well anyway, w/T and Morris probably arguing even before we start dinner. But it's Phil and Nicolette coming this year that I'm most worried about. Tom hasn't said a word about it one way or the other, but I know he hates Nicci for some reason, and he doesn't think much of my brother, either. I'm so looking ~~too~~ foward to seeing them ~~them~~, but w/ Tom I'll just have to keep them apart and pray for the best.
BAILEY
To my darling wife, Janet "Keep the home fires burning" Love Tom
1945 SCHONGAU, Germany June 3
WHAT'S THAT SMELL?
DUNNO. GETCHA MASKS ON, GUYS!

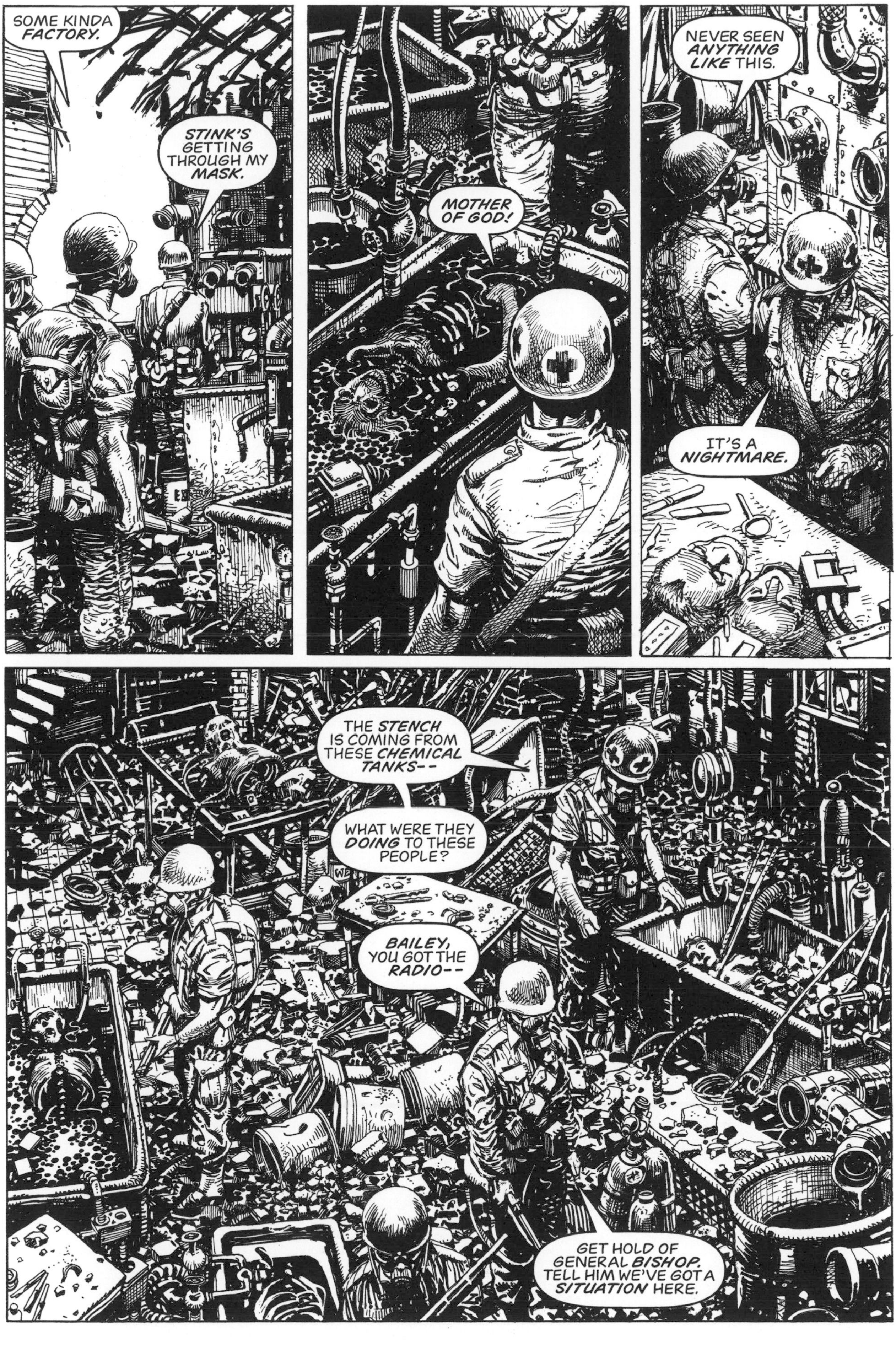
SOME KINDA FACTORY.
STINK'S GETTING THROUGH MY MASK.
MOTHER OF GOD!
NEVER SEEN ANYTHING LIKE THIS.
IT'S A NIGHTMARE.
THE STENCH IS COMING FROM THESE CHEMICAL TANKS--
WHAT WERE THEY DOING TO THESE PEOPLE?
BAILEY, YOU GOT THE RADIO--
GET HOLD OF GENERAL BISHOP. TELL HIM WE'VE GOT A SITUATION HERE.

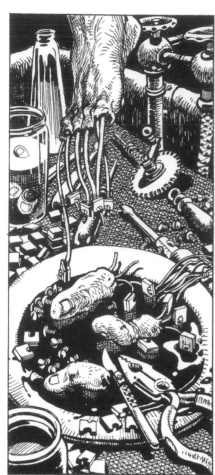

DOC-- WHAT WE GOT HERE'S A *HORROR SHOW.*

I GOTTA MAKE A FULL *REPORT* ON IT--

BUT I CAN'T EVEN *GUESS* WHAT IT'S *ALL ABOUT*--

EAT DRINK AND BE MERRY FOR TO-NIGHT WE DIE.

MAYBE YOU GOT A MORE *MEDICAL* TAKE ON IT.

ICH, JOSEF VOSS, HABE ETWAS ZU *SAGEN.*

I, JOSEF VOSS, HAVE SOME-THING TO *SAY.*

SIT *DOWN,* JOSEF, BEFORE YOU FALL IN YOUR *SOUP!*

I HAVE SERVED GERMANY AND ITS PEOPLE THROUGH *TWO WARS.*

AT *YPRES* I SUFFERED TWO HEAD WOUNDS.

AT *GALLIPOLI,* I LAID IN MY OWN *SHIT* FOR SIX DAYS.

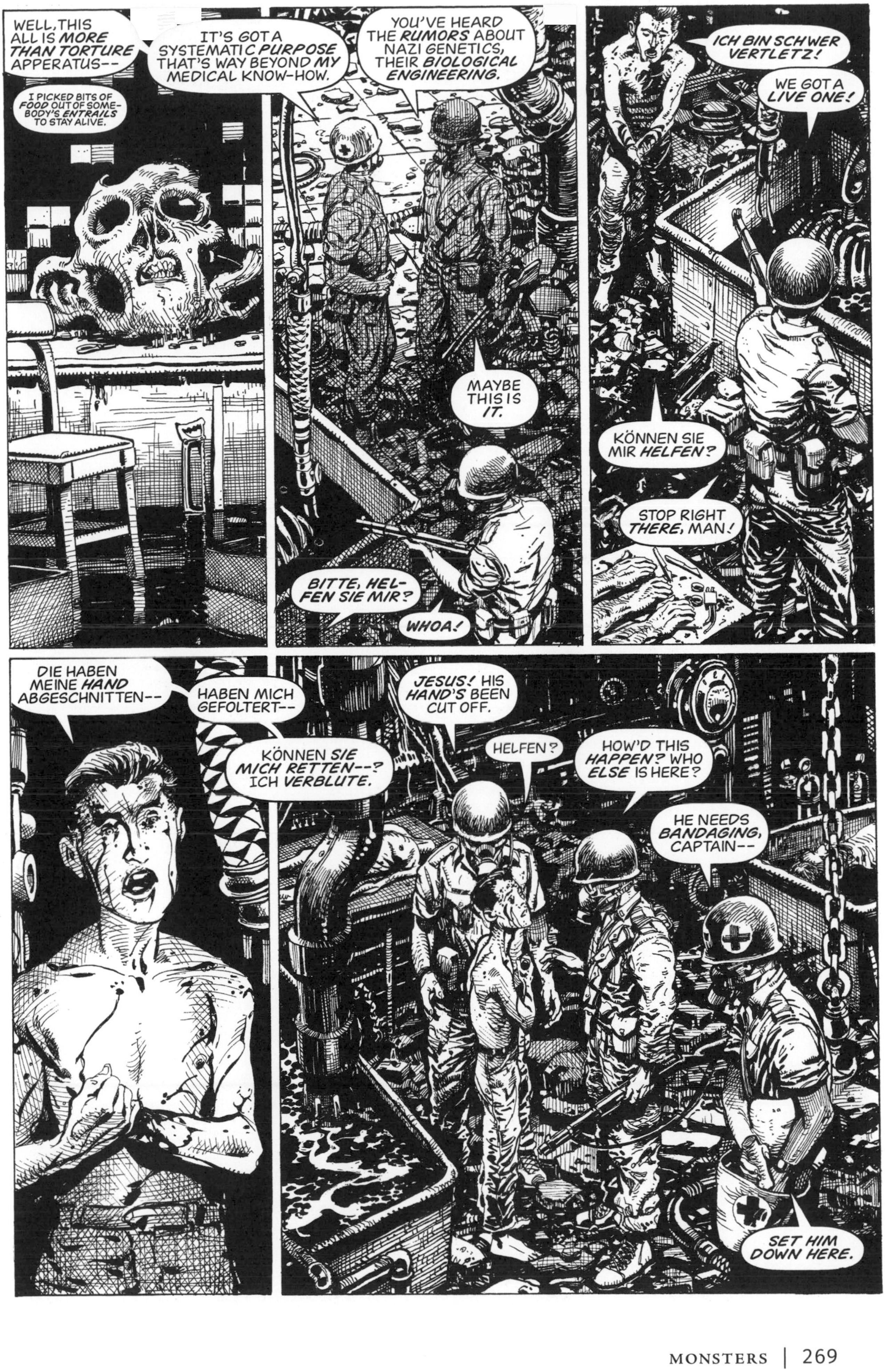

WELL, THIS ALL IS MORE THAN TORTURE APPERATUS--
IT'S GOT A SYSTEMATIC PURPOSE THAT'S WAY BEYOND MY MEDICAL KNOW-HOW.
I PICKED BITS OF FOOD OUT OF SOMEBODY'S ENTRAILS TO STAY ALIVE.
YOU'VE HEARD THE RUMORS ABOUT NAZI GENETICS, THEIR BIOLOGICAL ENGINEERING.
MAYBE THIS IS IT.
BITTE, HELFEN SIE MIR?
WHOA!
ICH BIN SCHWER VERTLETZ!
WE GOT A LIVE ONE!
KÖNNEN SIE MIR HELFEN?
STOP RIGHT THERE, MAN!
DIE HABEN MEINE HAND ABGESCHNITTEN--
HABEN MICH GEFOLTERT--
KÖNNEN SIE MICH RETTEN--? ICH VERBLUTE.
JESUS! HIS HAND'S BEEN CUT OFF.
HELFEN?
HOW'D THIS HAPPEN? WHO ELSE IS HERE?
HE NEEDS BANDAGING, CAPTAIN--
SET HIM DOWN HERE.

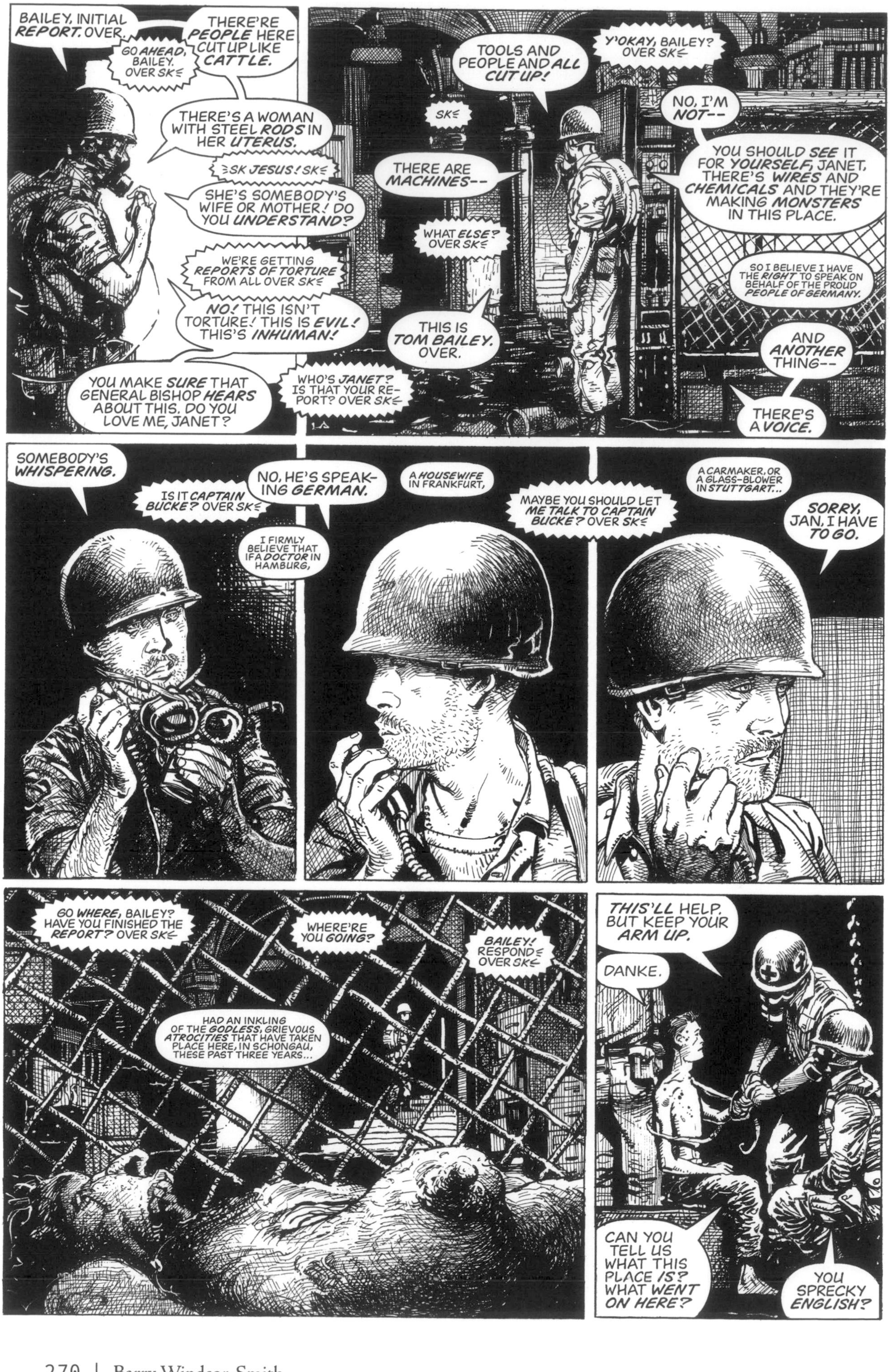

BAILEY, INITIAL REPORT. OVER.
GO AHEAD, BAILEY. OVER SK⚡
THERE'RE PEOPLE HERE CUT UP LIKE CATTLE.
THERE'S A WOMAN WITH STEEL RODS IN HER UTERUS.
SK JESUS! SK
SHE'S SOMEBODY'S WIFE OR MOTHER! DO YOU UNDERSTAND?
WE'RE GETTING REPORTS OF TORTURE FROM ALL OVER SK
NO! THIS ISN'T TORTURE! THIS IS EVIL! THIS'S INHUMAN!
YOU MAKE SURE THAT GENERAL BISHOP HEARS ABOUT THIS. DO YOU LOVE ME, JANET?
WHO'S JANET? IS THAT YOUR RE-PORT? OVER SK
TOOLS AND PEOPLE AND ALL CUT UP!
SK
THERE ARE MACHINES--
WHAT ELSE? OVER SK
THIS IS TOM BAILEY. OVER.
Y'OKAY, BAILEY? OVER SK
NO, I'M NOT--
YOU SHOULD SEE IT FOR YOURSELF, JANET. THERE'S WIRES AND CHEMICALS AND THEY'RE MAKING MONSTERS IN THIS PLACE.
SO I BELIEVE I HAVE THE RIGHT TO SPEAK ON BEHALF OF THE PROUD PEOPLE OF GERMANY.
AND ANOTHER THING--
THERE'S A VOICE.
SOMEBODY'S WHISPERING.
IS IT CAPTAIN BUCKE? OVER SK
NO, HE'S SPEAK-ING GERMAN.
I FIRMLY BELIEVE THAT IF A DOCTOR IN HAMBURG,
A HOUSEWIFE IN FRANKFURT,
MAYBE YOU SHOULD LET ME TALK TO CAPTAIN BUCKE? OVER SK
A CARMAKER, OR A GLASS-BLOWER IN STUTTGART...
SORRY, JAN, I HAVE TO GO.
GO WHERE, BAILEY? HAVE YOU FINISHED THE REPORT? OVER SK
WHERE'RE YOU GOING?
BAILEY! RESPOND OVER SK
HAD AN INKLING OF THE GODLESS, GRIEVOUS ATROCITIES THAT HAVE TAKEN PLACE HERE, IN SCHONGAU, THESE PAST THREE YEARS...
THIS'LL HELP, BUT KEEP YOUR ARM UP.
DANKE.
CAN YOU TELL US WHAT THIS PLACE IS? WHAT WENT ON HERE?
YOU SPRECKY ENGLISH?

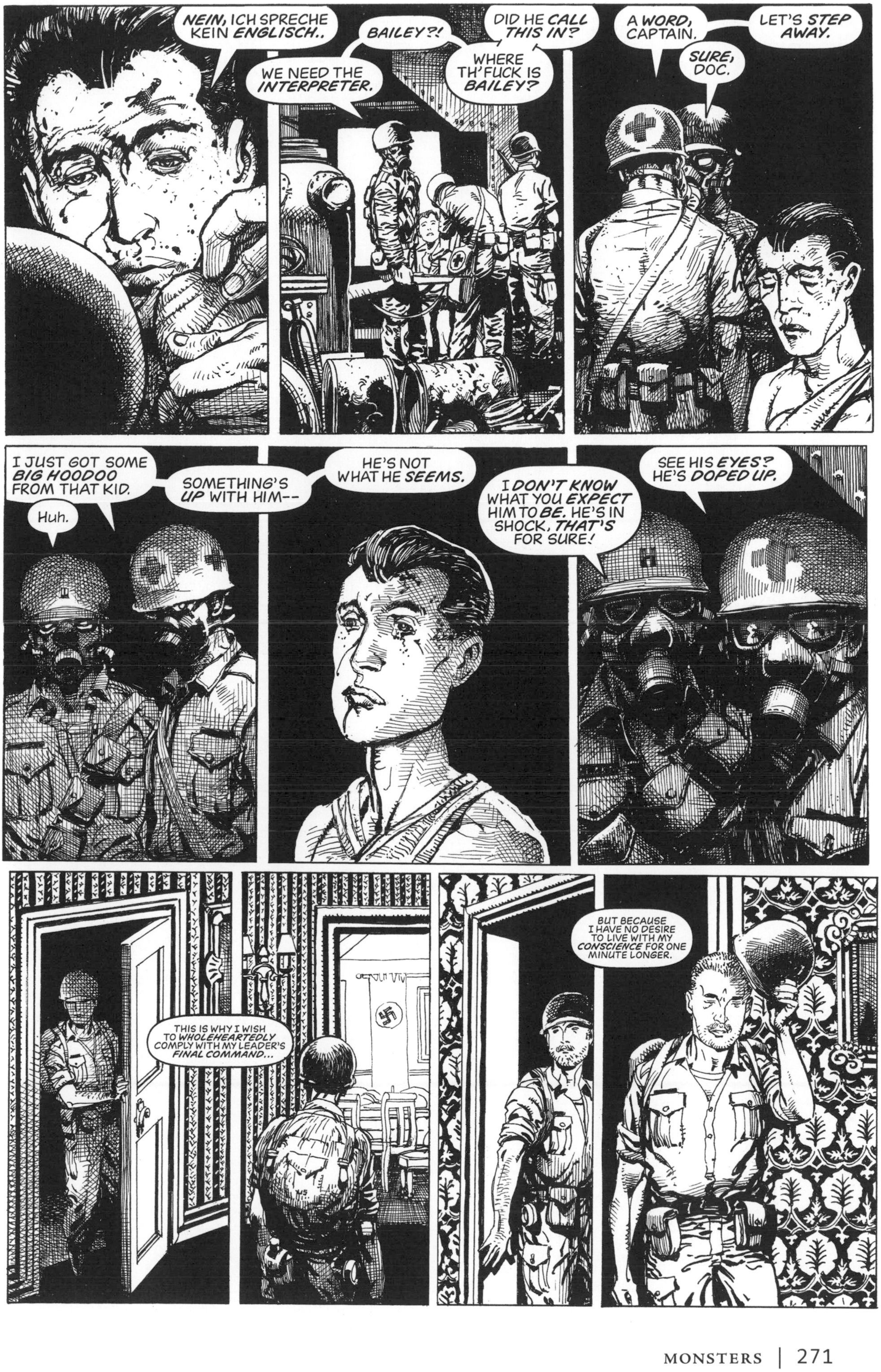
NEIN, ICH SPRECHE KEIN ENGLISCH..
BAILEY?!
WE NEED THE INTERPRETER.
DID HE CALL THIS IN?
WHERE TH'FUCK IS BAILEY?
A WORD, CAPTAIN.
LET'S STEP AWAY.
SURE, DOC.
I JUST GOT SOME BIG HOODOO FROM THAT KID.
Huh.
SOMETHING'S UP WITH HIM--
HE'S NOT WHAT HE SEEMS.
I DON'T KNOW WHAT YOU EXPECT HIM TO BE. HE'S IN SHOCK, THAT'S FOR SURE!
SEE HIS EYES? HE'S DOPED UP.
THIS IS WHY I WISH TO WHOLEHEARTEDLY COMPLY WITH MY LEADER'S FINAL COMMAND...
BUT BECAUSE I HAVE NO DESIRE TO LIVE WITH MY CONSCIENCE FOR ONE MINUTE LONGER.

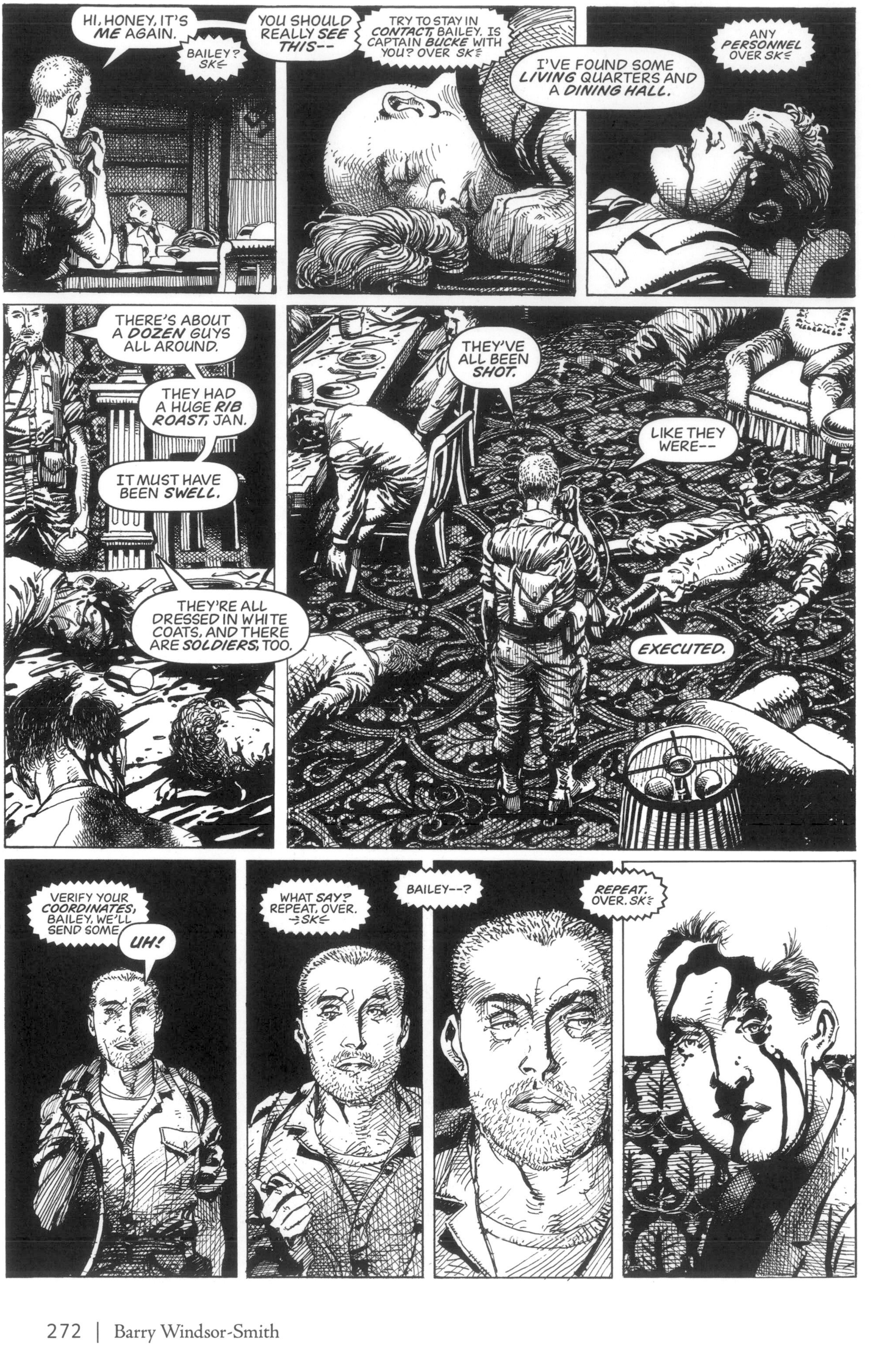
HI, HONEY, IT'S *ME* AGAIN.
BAILEY? SK
YOU SHOULD REALLY *SEE THIS--*
TRY TO STAY IN *CONTACT,* BAILEY. IS CAPTAIN *BUCKE* WITH YOU? OVER SK
I'VE FOUND SOME *LIVING* QUARTERS AND A *DINING HALL.*
ANY *PERSONNEL* OVER SK
THERE'S ABOUT A *DOZEN* GUYS ALL AROUND.
THEY HAD A HUGE *RIB ROAST,* JAN.
IT MUST HAVE BEEN *SWELL.*
THEY'RE ALL DRESSED IN WHITE COATS, AND THERE ARE *SOLDIERS,* TOO.
THEY'VE ALL BEEN *SHOT.*
LIKE THEY WERE--
EXECUTED.
VERIFY YOUR *COORDINATES,* BAILEY, WE'LL SEND SOME
UH!
WHAT *SAY?* REPEAT, OVER. SK
BAILEY--?
REPEAT. OVER. SK

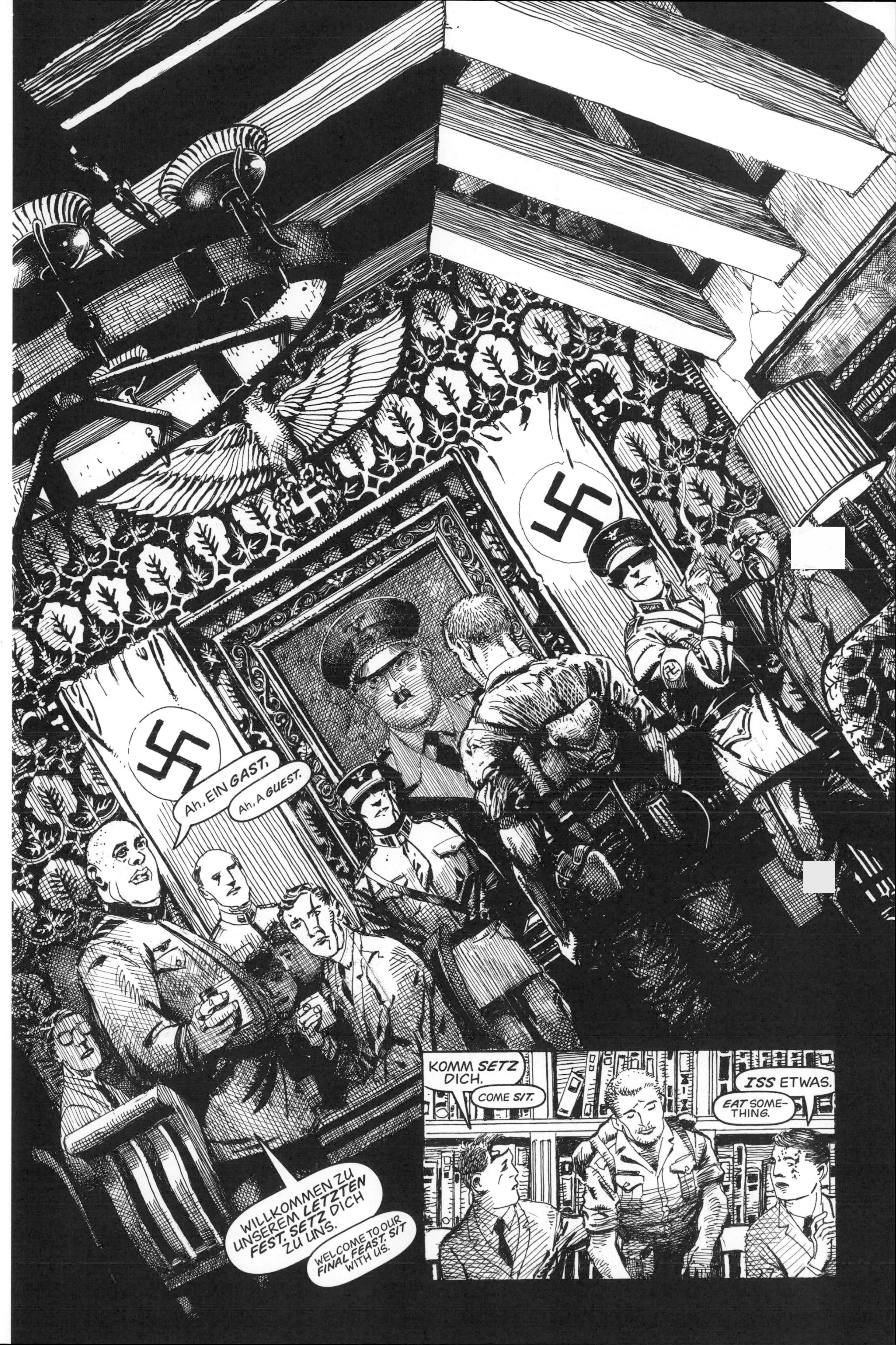
Ah, EIN GAST.
Ah, A GUEST.
WILLKOMMEN ZU UNSEREM LETZTEN FEST. SETZ DICH ZU UNS.
WELCOME TO OUR FINAL FEAST. SIT WITH US.
KOMM SETZ DICH.
COME SIT.
ISS ETWAS.
EAT SOME-THING.

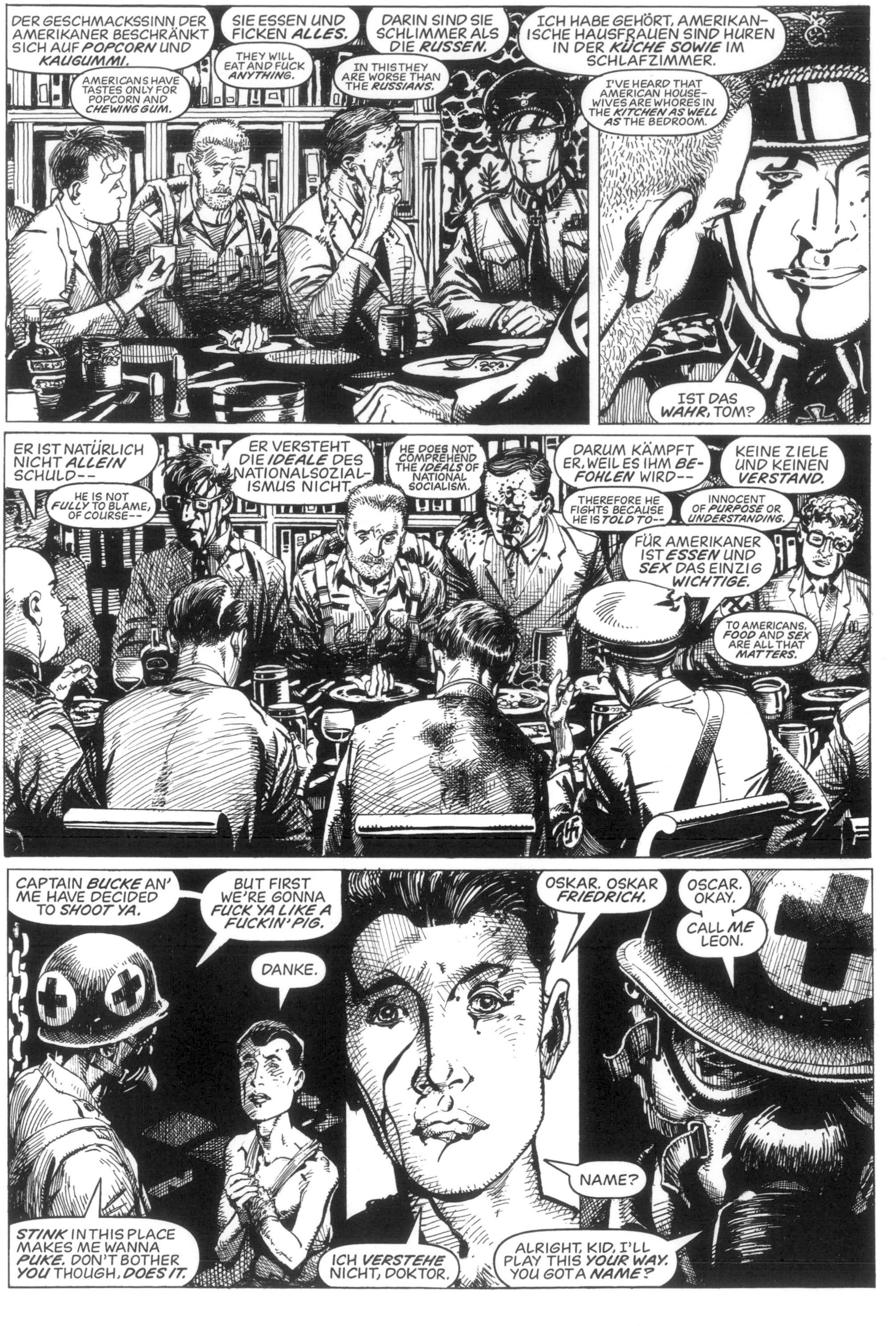
DER GESCHMACKSSINN DER AMERIKANER BESCHRÄNKT SICH AUF POPCORN UND KAUGUMMI.
AMERICANS HAVE TASTES ONLY FOR POPCORN AND CHEWING GUM.
SIE ESSEN UND FICKEN ALLES.
THEY WILL EAT AND FUCK ANYTHING.
DARIN SIND SIE SCHLIMMER ALS DIE RUSSEN.
IN THIS THEY ARE WORSE THAN THE RUSSIANS.
ICH HABE GEHÖRT, AMERIKANISCHE HAUSFRAUEN SIND HUREN IN DER KÜCHE SOWIE IM SCHLAFZIMMER.
I'VE HEARD THAT AMERICAN HOUSEWIVES ARE WHORES IN THE KITCHEN AS WELL AS THE BEDROOM.
IST DAS WAHR, TOM?
ER IST NATÜRLICH NICHT ALLEIN SCHULD--
HE IS NOT FULLY TO BLAME, OF COURSE--
ER VERSTEHT DIE IDEALE DES NATIONALSOZIALISMUS NICHT.
HE DOES NOT COMPREHEND THE IDEALS OF NATIONAL SOCIALISM.
DARUM KÄMPFT ER, WEIL ES IHM BEFOHLEN WIRD--
THEREFORE HE FIGHTS BECAUSE HE IS TOLD TO--
KEINE ZIELE UND KEINEN VERSTAND.
INNOCENT OF PURPOSE OR UNDERSTANDING.
FÜR AMERIKANER IST ESSEN UND SEX DAS EINZIG WICHTIGE.
TO AMERICANS, FOOD AND SEX ARE ALL THAT MATTERS.
CAPTAIN BUCKE AN' ME HAVE DECIDED TO SHOOT YA.
BUT FIRST WE'RE GONNA FUCK YA LIKE A FUCKIN' PIG.
DANKE.
STINK IN THIS PLACE MAKES ME WANNA PUKE. DON'T BOTHER YOU THOUGH, DOES IT.
ICH VERSTEHE NICHT, DOKTOR.
ALRIGHT, KID, I'LL PLAY THIS YOUR WAY. YOU GOT A NAME?
NAME?
OSKAR. OSKAR FRIEDRICH.
OSCAR. OKAY.
CALL ME LEON.

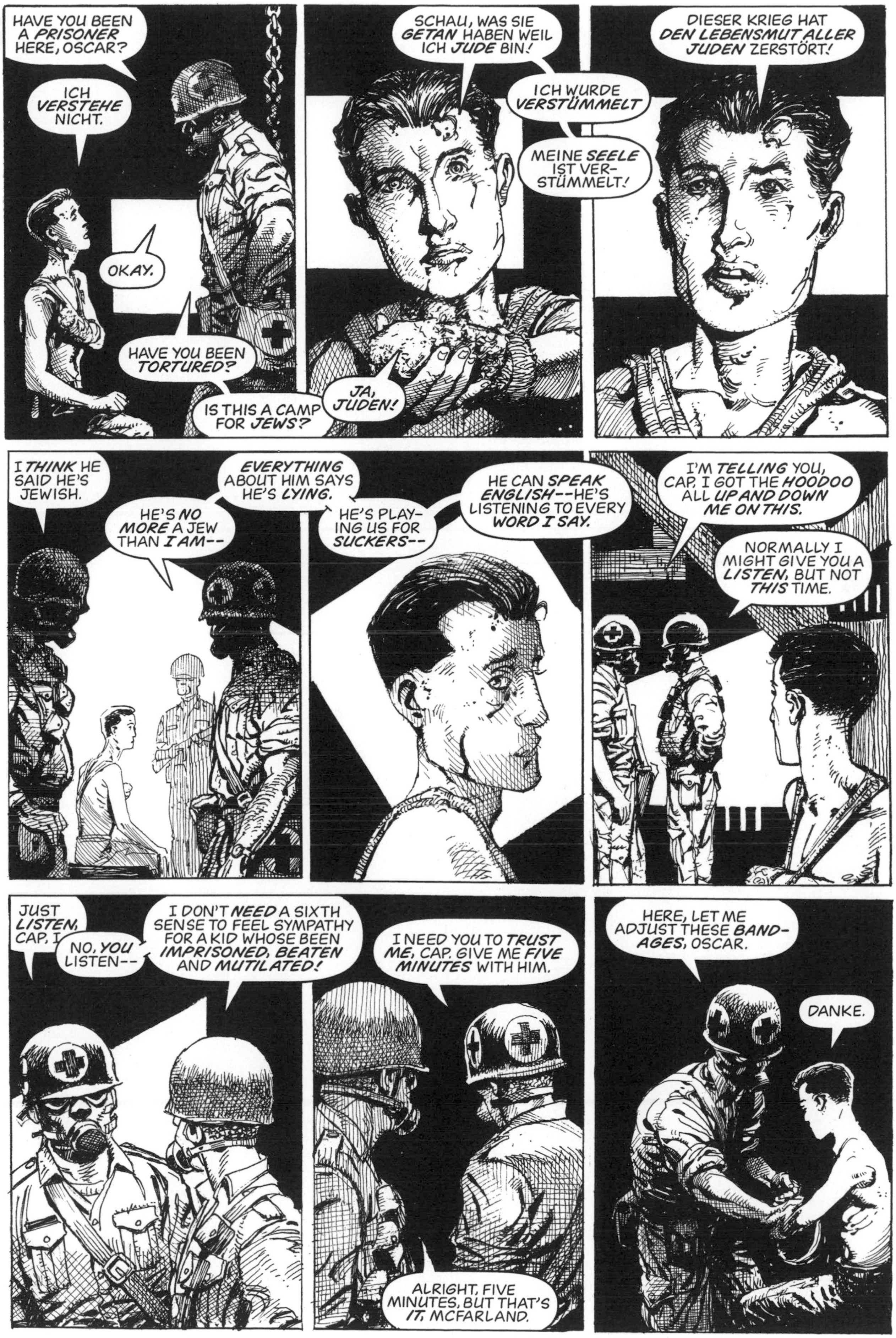
HAVE YOU BEEN A PRISONER HERE, OSCAR?
ICH VERSTEHE NICHT.
OKAY.
HAVE YOU BEEN TORTURED?
IS THIS A CAMP FOR JEWS?
JA, JUDEN!
SCHAU, WAS SIE GETAN HABEN WEIL ICH JUDE BIN!
ICH WURDE VERSTÜMMELT
MEINE SEELE IST VERSTÜMMELT!
DIESER KRIEG HAT DEN LEBENSMUT ALLER JUDEN ZERSTÖRT!
I THINK HE SAID HE'S JEWISH.
HE'S NO MORE A JEW THAN I AM--
EVERYTHING ABOUT HIM SAYS HE'S LYING.
HE'S PLAYING US FOR SUCKERS--
HE CAN SPEAK ENGLISH--HE'S LISTENING TO EVERY WORD I SAY.
I'M TELLING YOU, CAP, I GOT THE HOODOO ALL UP AND DOWN ME ON THIS.
NORMALLY I MIGHT GIVE YOU A LISTEN, BUT NOT THIS TIME.
JUST LISTEN, CAP, I
NO, YOU LISTEN--
I DON'T NEED A SIXTH SENSE TO FEEL SYMPATHY FOR A KID WHOSE BEEN IMPRISONED, BEATEN AND MUTILATED!
I NEED YOU TO TRUST ME, CAP. GIVE ME FIVE MINUTES WITH HIM.
ALRIGHT, FIVE MINUTES, BUT THAT'S IT, MCFARLAND.
HERE, LET ME ADJUST THESE BANDAGES, OSCAR.
DANKE.

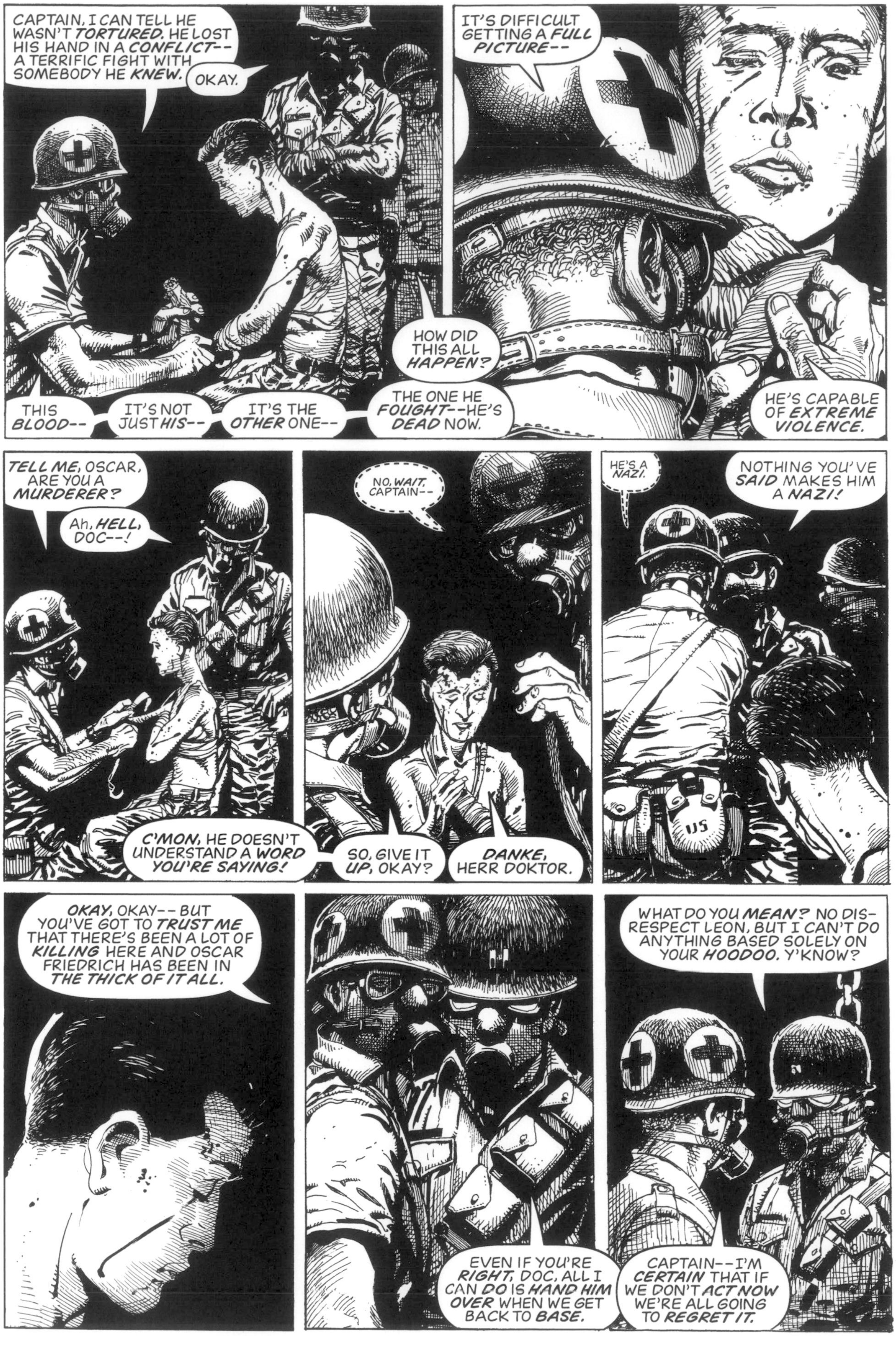
CAPTAIN, I CAN TELL HE WASN'T TORTURED. HE LOST HIS HAND IN A CONFLICT-- A TERRIFIC FIGHT WITH SOMEBODY HE KNEW.
OKAY.
THIS BLOOD--
IT'S NOT JUST HIS--
IT'S THE OTHER ONE--
THE ONE HE FOUGHT--HE'S DEAD NOW.
HOW DID THIS ALL HAPPEN?
IT'S DIFFICULT GETTING A FULL PICTURE--
HE'S CAPABLE OF EXTREME VIOLENCE.
TELL ME, OSCAR, ARE YOU A MURDERER?
Ah, HELL, DOC--!
C'MON, HE DOESN'T UNDERSTAND A WORD YOU'RE SAYING!
SO, GIVE IT UP, OKAY?
NO, WAIT, CAPTAIN--
DANKE, HERR DOKTOR.
HE'S A NAZI.
NOTHING YOU'VE SAID MAKES HIM A NAZI!
OKAY, OKAY-- BUT YOU'VE GOT TO TRUST ME THAT THERE'S BEEN A LOT OF KILLING HERE AND OSCAR FRIEDRICH HAS BEEN IN THE THICK OF IT ALL.
EVEN IF YOU'RE RIGHT, DOC, ALL I CAN DO IS HAND HIM OVER WHEN WE GET BACK TO BASE.
WHAT DO YOU MEAN? NO DISRESPECT LEON, BUT I CAN'T DO ANYTHING BASED SOLELY ON YOUR HOODOO. Y'KNOW?
CAPTAIN--I'M CERTAIN THAT IF WE DON'T ACT NOW WE'RE ALL GOING TO REGRET IT.

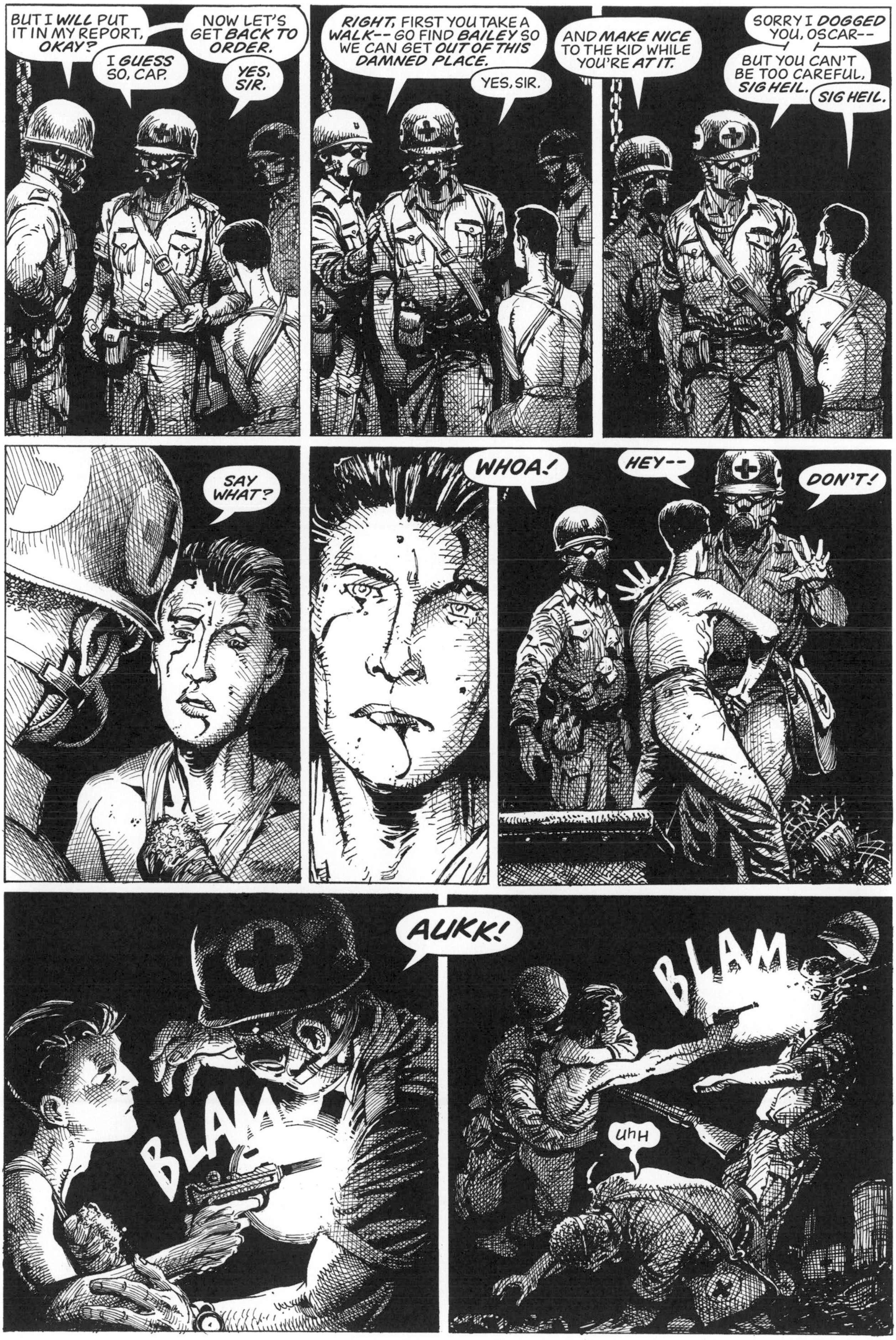
BUT I WILL PUT IT IN MY REPORT, OKAY?
I GUESS SO, CAP.
NOW LET'S GET BACK TO ORDER.
YES, SIR.
RIGHT, FIRST YOU TAKE A WALK-- GO FIND BAILEY SO WE CAN GET OUT OF THIS DAMNED PLACE.
YES, SIR.
AND MAKE NICE TO THE KID WHILE YOU'RE AT IT.
SORRY I DOGGED YOU, OSCAR--
BUT YOU CAN'T BE TOO CAREFUL, SIG HEIL.
SIG HEIL.
SAY WHAT?
WHOA!
HEY--
DON'T!
AUKK!
BLAM
BLAM
UHH

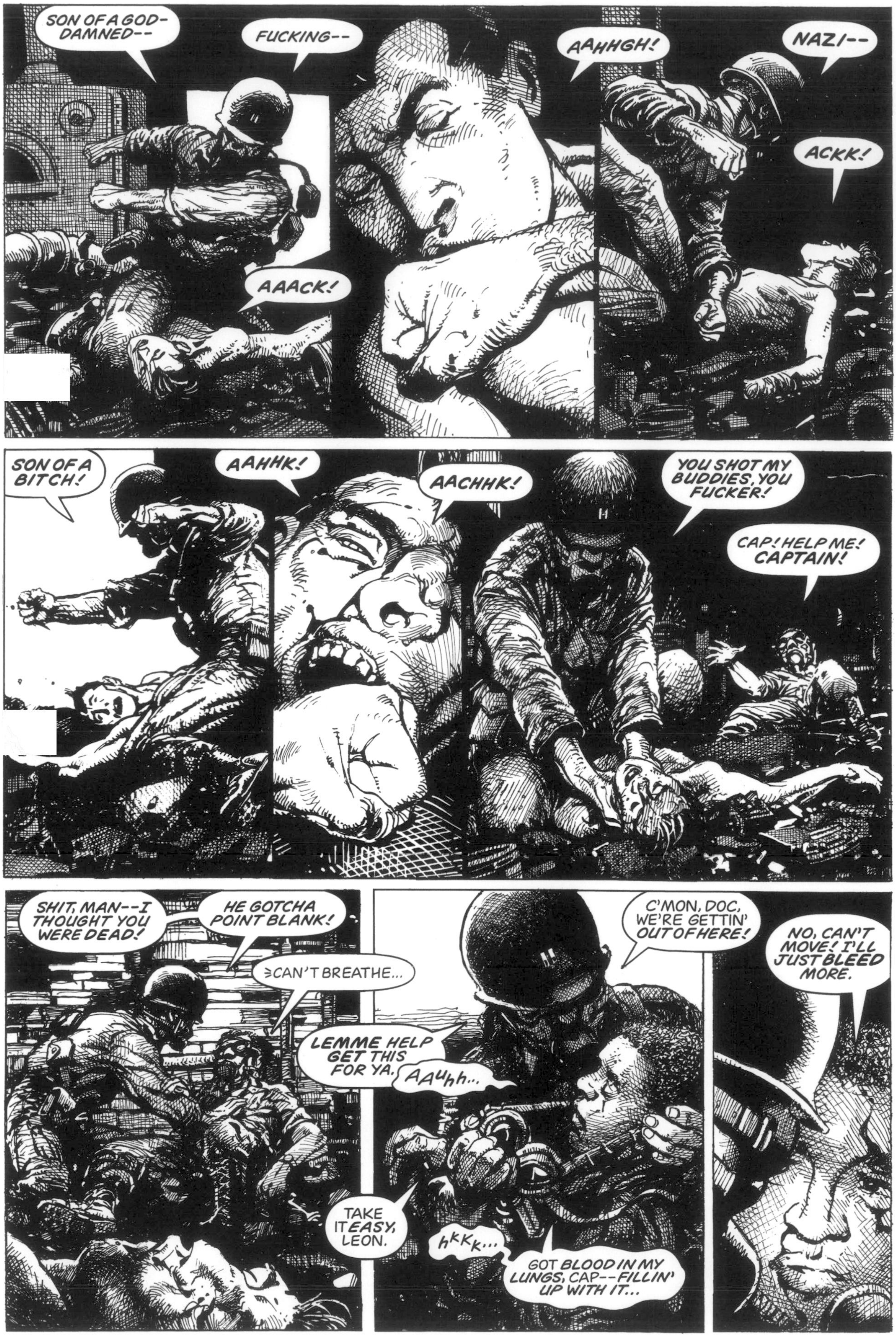

SON OF A GOD-DAMNED--
FUCKING--
AAACK!
AAHHGH!
NAZI--
ACKK!
SON OF A BITCH!
AAHHK!
AACHHK!
YOU SHOT MY BUDDIES, YOU FUCKER!
CAP! HELP ME! CAPTAIN!
SHIT, MAN--I THOUGHT YOU WERE DEAD!
HE GOTCHA POINT BLANK!
CAN'T BREATHE...
LEMME HELP GET THIS FOR YA.
AAUhh...
TAKE IT EASY, LEON.
hKKK...
GOT BLOOD IN MY LUNGS, CAP--FILLIN' UP WITH IT...
C'MON, DOC, WE'RE GETTIN' OUT OF HERE!
NO, CAN'T MOVE! I'LL JUST BLEED MORE.

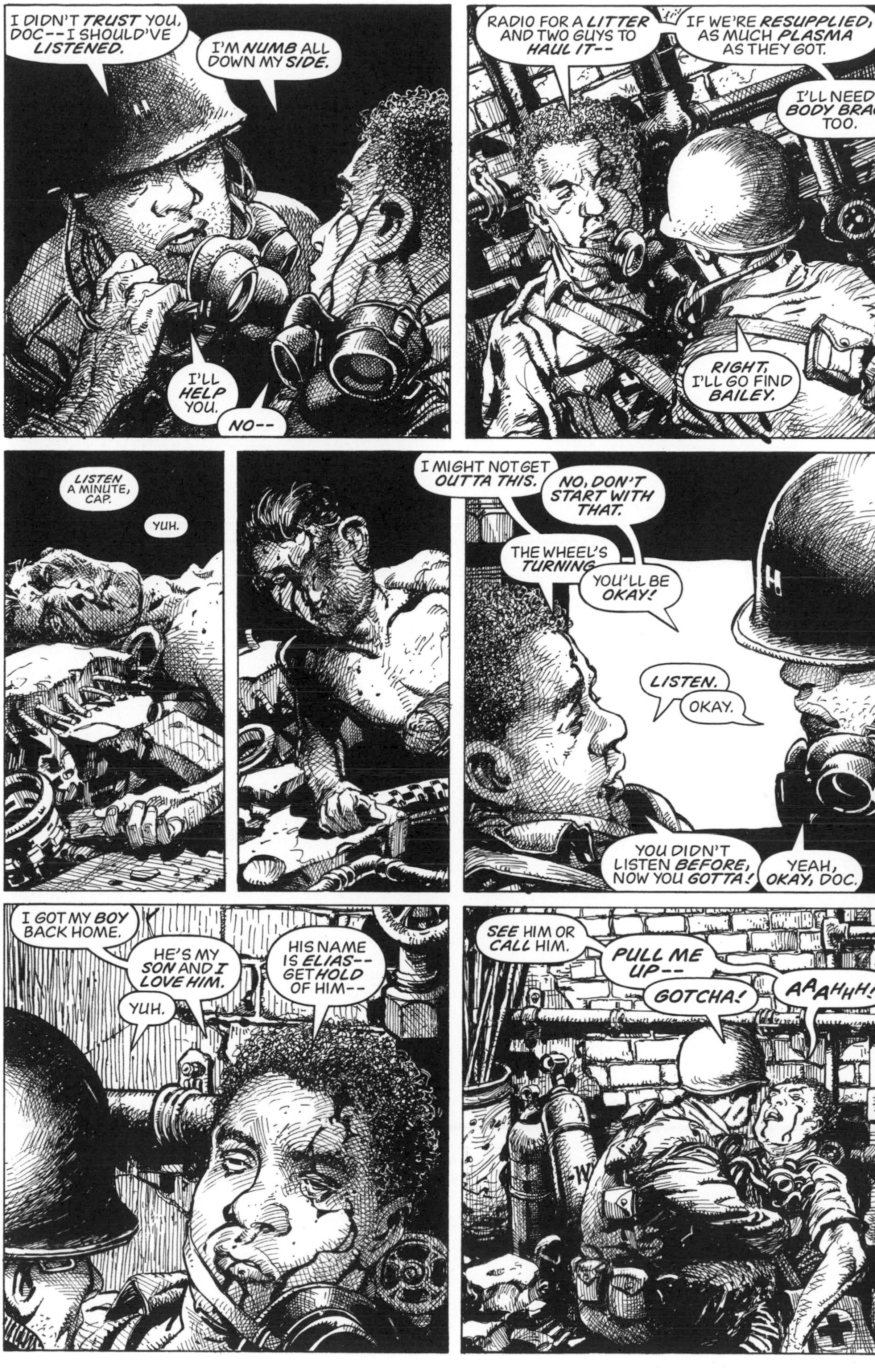
I DIDN'T TRUST YOU, DOC--I SHOULD'VE LISTENED.
I'M NUMB ALL DOWN MY SIDE.
I'LL HELP YOU.
NO--
RADIO FOR A LITTER AND TWO GUYS TO HAUL IT--
IF WE'RE RESUPPLIED, AS MUCH PLASMA AS THEY GOT.
I'LL NEED A BODY BRACE, TOO.
RIGHT, I'LL GO FIND BAILEY.
LISTEN A MINUTE, CAP.
YUH.
I MIGHT NOT GET OUTTA THIS.
NO, DON'T START WITH THAT.
THE WHEEL'S TURNING
YOU'LL BE OKAY!
LISTEN.
OKAY.
YOU DIDN'T LISTEN BEFORE, NOW YOU GOTTA!
YEAH, OKAY, DOC.
I GOT MY BOY BACK HOME.
HE'S MY SON AND I LOVE HIM.
YUH.
HIS NAME IS ELIAS--GET HOLD OF HIM--
SEE HIM OR CALL HIM.
PULL ME UP--
GOTCHA!
AAAHHH!

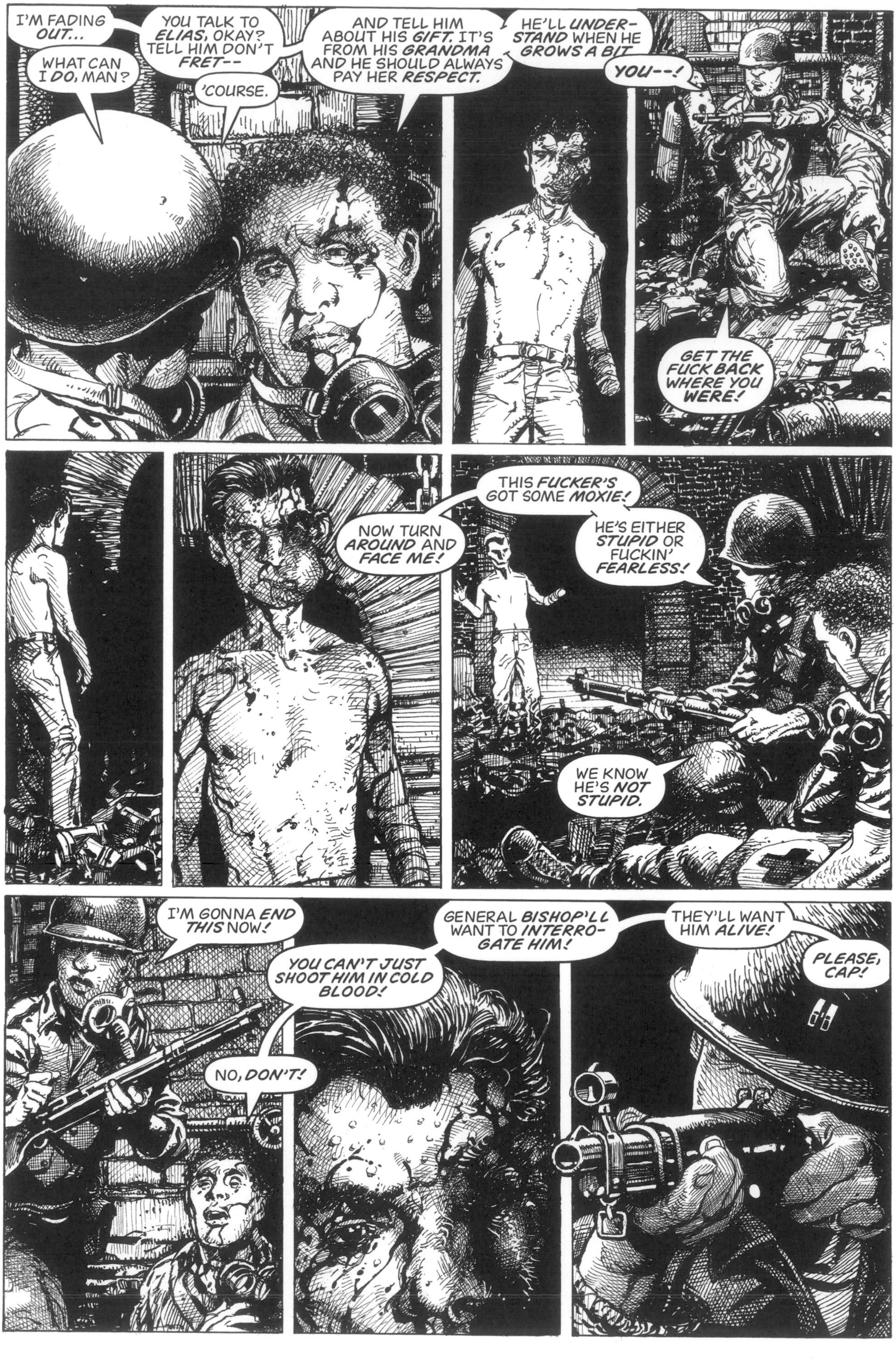
I'M FADING OUT...
WHAT CAN I DO, MAN?
YOU TALK TO ELIAS, OKAY? TELL HIM DON'T FRET--
'COURSE.
AND TELL HIM ABOUT HIS GIFT. IT'S FROM HIS GRANDMA AND HE SHOULD ALWAYS PAY HER RESPECT.
HE'LL UNDERSTAND WHEN HE GROWS A BIT.
YOU--!
GET THE FUCK BACK WHERE YOU WERE!
NOW TURN AROUND AND FACE ME!
THIS FUCKER'S GOT SOME MOXIE!
HE'S EITHER STUPID OR FUCKIN' FEARLESS!
WE KNOW HE'S NOT STUPID.
I'M GONNA END THIS NOW!
YOU CAN'T JUST SHOOT HIM IN COLD BLOOD!
NO, DON'T!
GENERAL BISHOP'LL WANT TO INTERROGATE HIM!
THEY'LL WANT HIM ALIVE!
PLEASE, CAP!

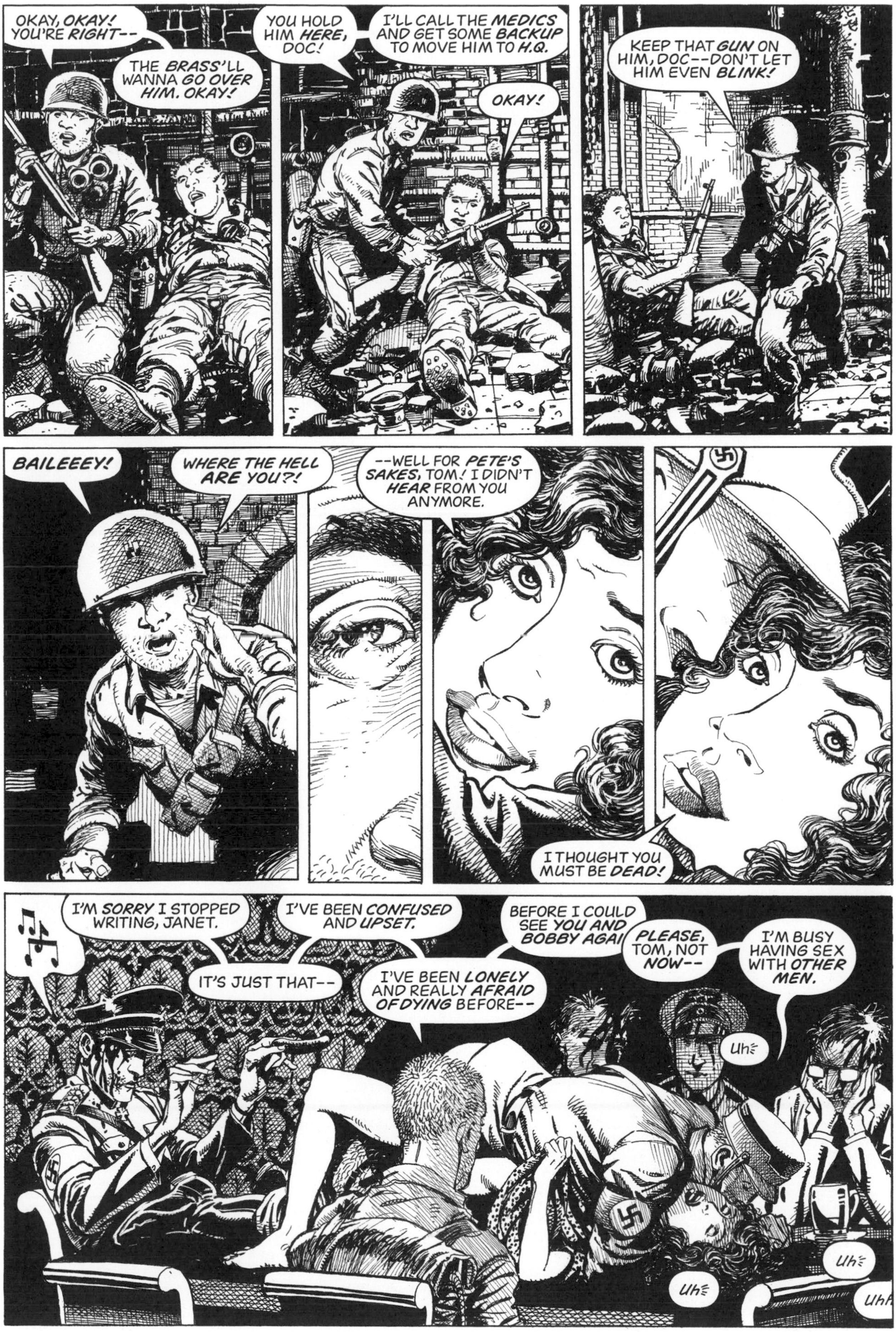

OKAY, OKAY! YOU'RE RIGHT--
THE BRASS'LL WANNA GO OVER HIM. OKAY!
YOU HOLD HIM HERE, DOC!
I'LL CALL THE MEDICS AND GET SOME BACKUP TO MOVE HIM TO H.Q.
OKAY!
KEEP THAT GUN ON HIM, DOC--DON'T LET HIM EVEN BLINK!
BAILEEEY!
WHERE THE HELL ARE YOU?!
--WELL FOR PETE'S SAKES, TOM! I DIDN'T HEAR FROM YOU ANYMORE.
I THOUGHT YOU MUST BE DEAD!
I'M SORRY I STOPPED WRITING, JANET.
IT'S JUST THAT--
I'VE BEEN CONFUSED AND UPSET.
I'VE BEEN LONELY AND REALLY AFRAID OF DYING BEFORE--
BEFORE I COULD SEE YOU AND BOBBY AGAI
PLEASE, TOM, NOT NOW--
I'M BUSY HAVING SEX WITH OTHER MEN.
Uh
Uh
Uh
Uh

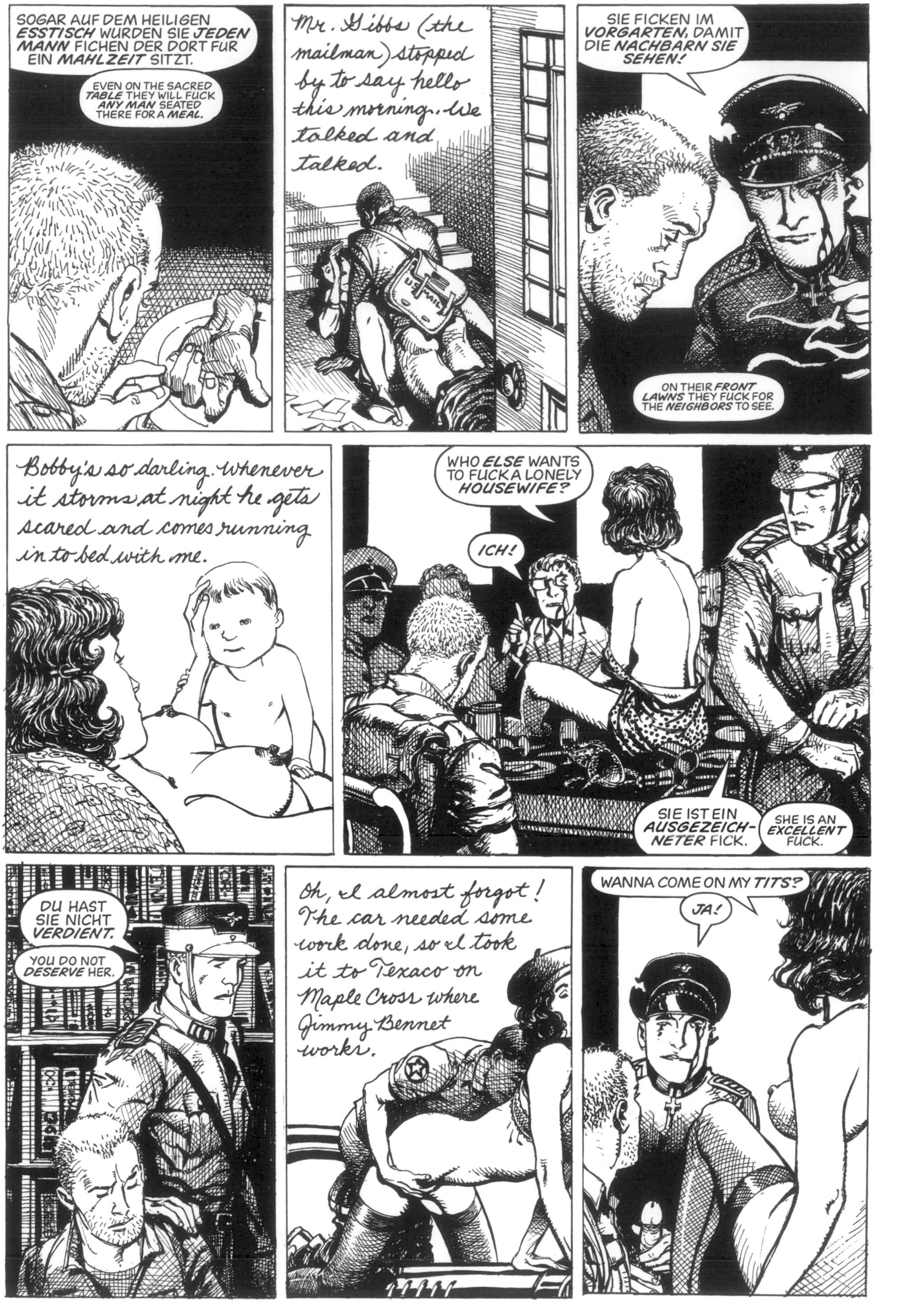
SOGAR AUF DEM HEILIGEN ESSTISCH WURDEN SIE JEDEN MANN FICHEN DER DORT FUR EIN MAHLZEIT SITZT.
EVEN ON THE SACRED TABLE THEY WILL FUCK ANY MAN SEATED THERE FOR A MEAL.
Mr. Gibbs (the mailman) stopped by to say hello this morning. We talked and talked.
U.S. MAIL
SIE FICKEN IM VORGARTEN, DAMIT DIE NACHBARN SIE SEHEN!
ON THEIR FRONT LAWNS THEY FUCK FOR THE NEIGHBORS TO SEE.
Bobby's so darling. Whenever it storms at night he gets scared and comes running in to bed with me.
WHO ELSE WANTS TO FUCK A LONELY HOUSEWIFE?
ICH!
SIE IST EIN AUSGEZEICH-NETER FICK.
SHE IS AN EXCELLENT FUCK.
DU HAST SIE NICHT VERDIENT.
YOU DO NOT DESERVE HER.
Oh, I almost forgot! The car needed some work done, so I took it to Texaco on Maple Cross where Jimmy Bennet works.
WANNA COME ON MY TITS?
JA!

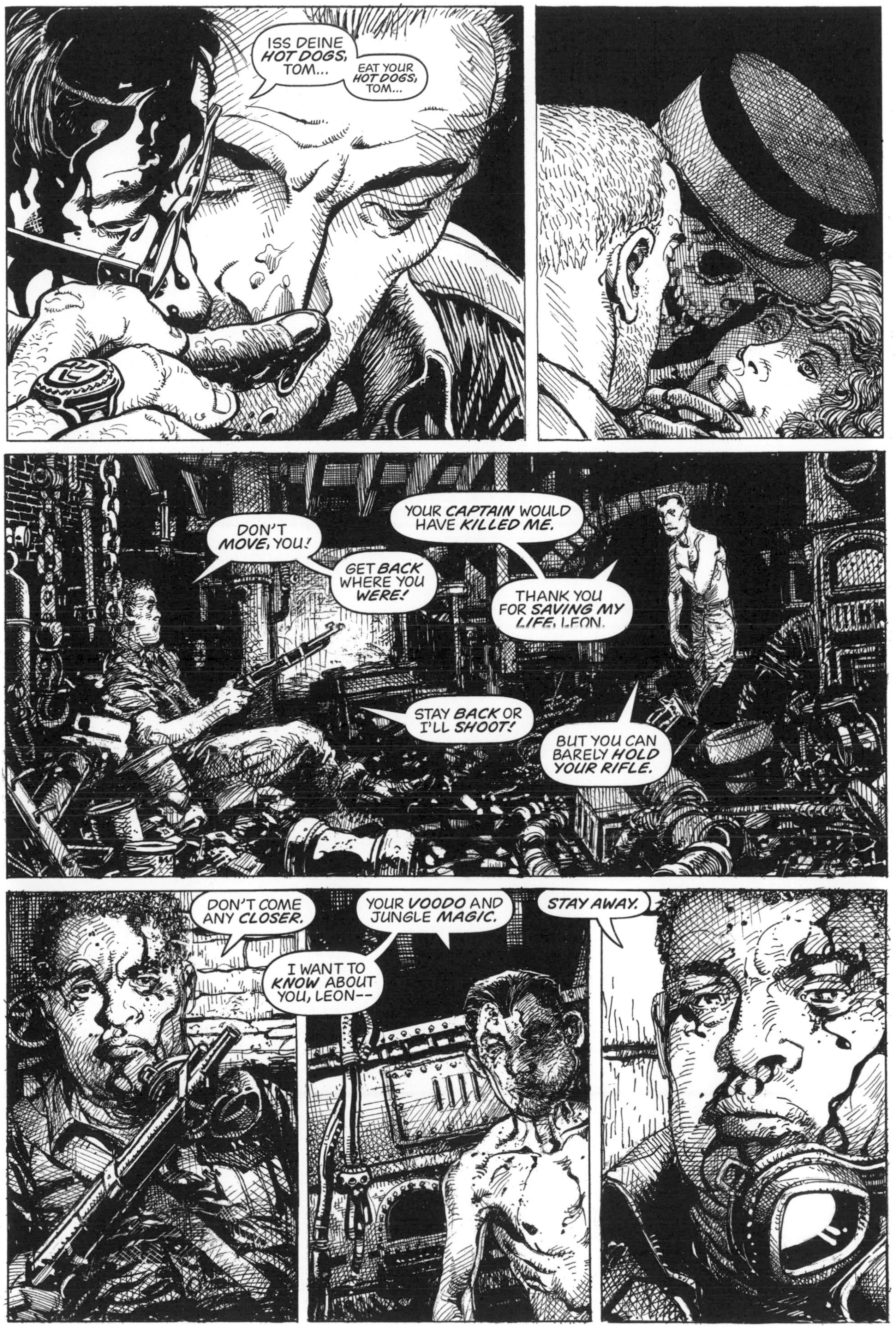
ISS DEINE HOT DOGS, TOM...
EAT YOUR HOT DOGS, TOM...
DON'T MOVE, YOU!
GET BACK WHERE YOU WERE!
YOUR CAPTAIN WOULD HAVE KILLED ME.
THANK YOU FOR SAVING MY LIFE, LEON.
STAY BACK OR I'LL SHOOT!
BUT YOU CAN BARELY HOLD YOUR RIFLE.
DON'T COME ANY CLOSER.
YOUR VOODO AND JUNGLE MAGIC.
I WANT TO KNOW ABOUT YOU, LEON--
STAY AWAY.

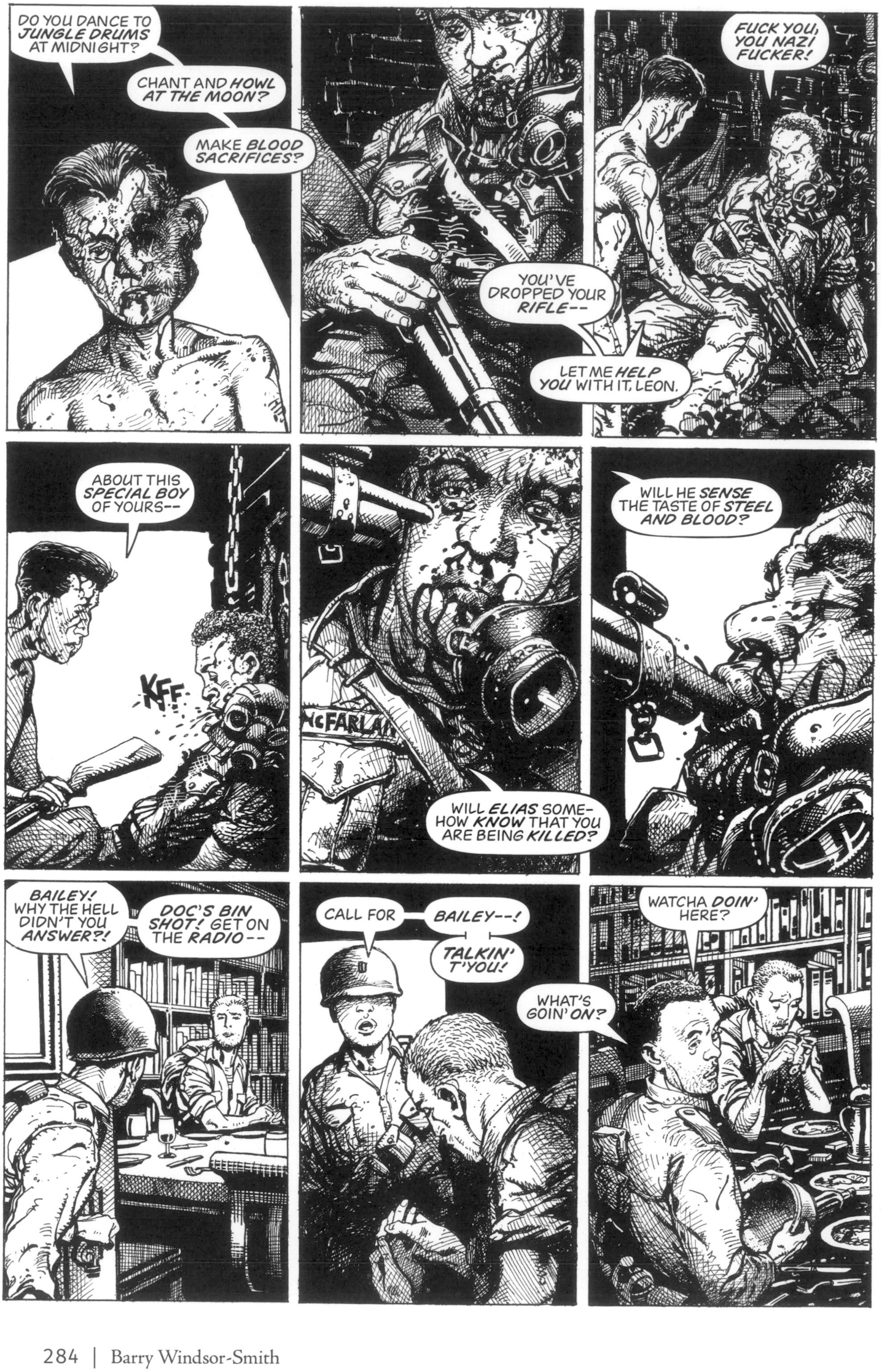
DO YOU DANCE TO JUNGLE DRUMS AT MIDNIGHT?
CHANT AND HOWL AT THE MOON?
MAKE BLOOD SACRIFICES?
YOU'VE DROPPED YOUR RIFLE--
LET ME HELP YOU WITH IT, LEON.
FUCK YOU, YOU NAZI FUCKER!
ABOUT THIS SPECIAL BOY OF YOURS--
KFF
McFARLAN
WILL ELIAS SOME-HOW KNOW THAT YOU ARE BEING KILLED?
WILL HE SENSE THE TASTE OF STEEL AND BLOOD?
BAILEY! WHY THE HELL DIDN'T YOU ANSWER?!
DOC'S BIN SHOT! GET ON THE RADIO--
CALL FOR
BAILEY--!
TALKIN' T'YOU!
WATCHA DOIN' HERE?
WHAT'S GOIN' ON?

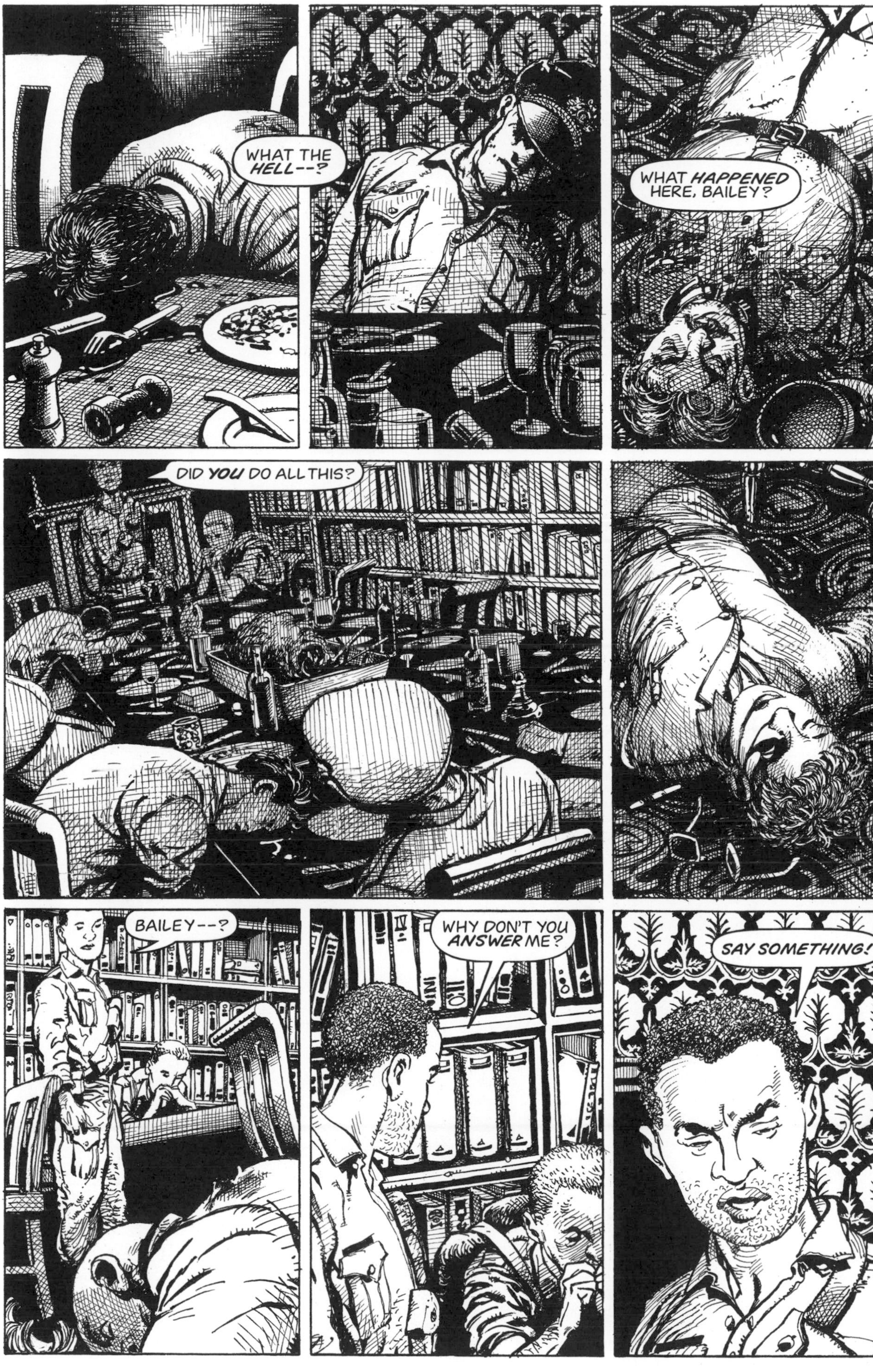
WHAT THE HELL--?
WHAT HAPPENED HERE, BAILEY?
DID YOU DO ALL THIS?
BAILEY--?
WHY DON'T YOU ANSWER ME?
SAY SOMETHING!

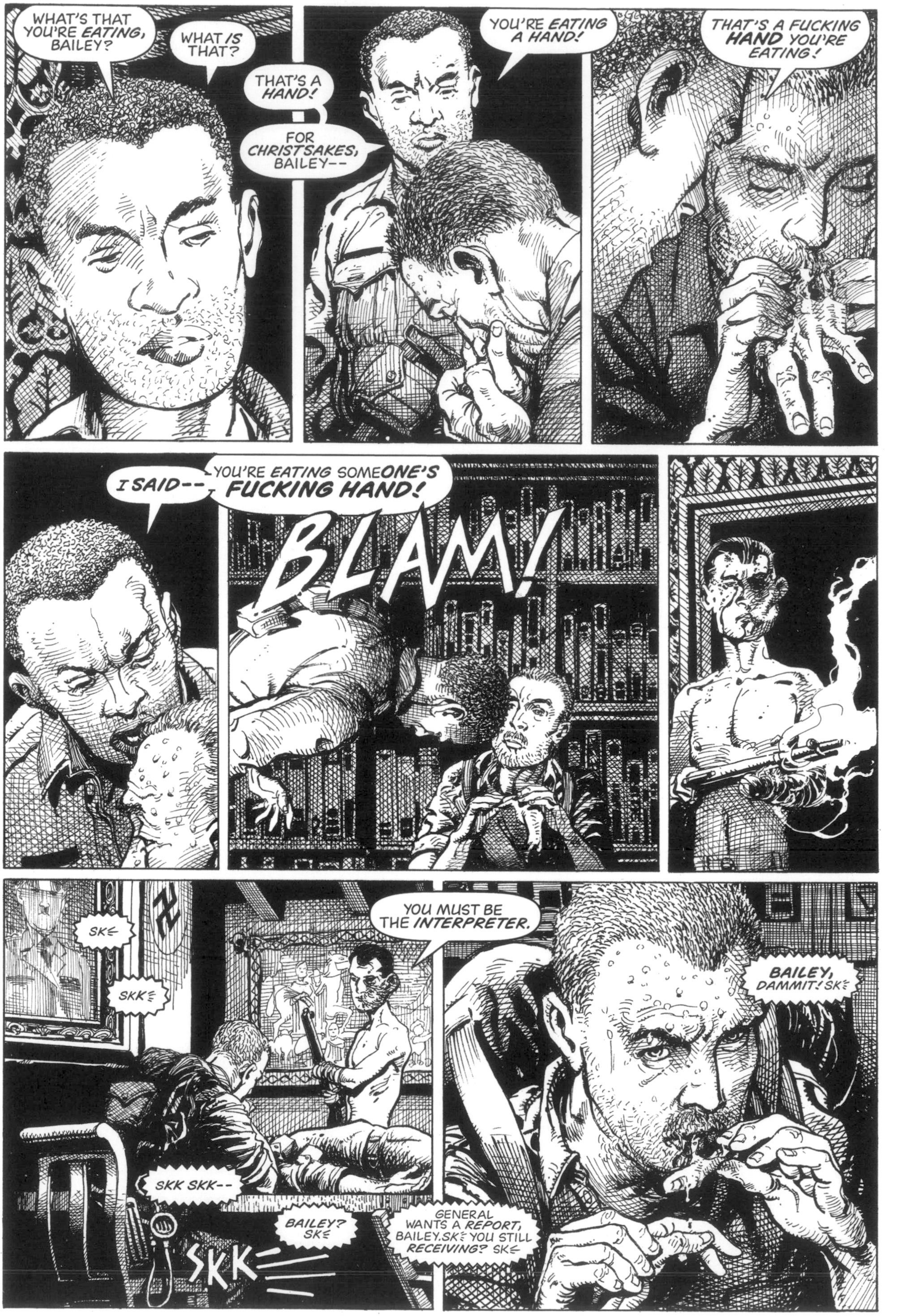
WHAT'S THAT YOU'RE *EATING*, BAILEY?
WHAT *IS* THAT?
THAT'S A *HAND!*
FOR *CHRISTSAKES*, BAILEY--
YOU'RE *EATING A HAND!*
THAT'S A FUCKING **HAND** YOU'RE *EATING!*
I SAID--
-YOU'RE *EATING* SOME**ONE'S** **FUCKING HAND!**
BLAM!
SK
SKK
YOU MUST BE THE *INTERPRETER.*
BAILEY, DAMMIT! SK
SKK SKK--
BAILEY? SK
GENERAL WANTS A *REPORT*, BAILEY. SK YOU STILL *RECEIVING?* SK
SKK

GOTT! BIST DU *VERRÜCKT?*

GOD! ARE YOU *INSANE?!*

SSK

BAILEY, YOU *THERE?* SK

DU BRINGST MICH AUF EINE *IDEE.*

YOU GIVE ME AN *IDEA.*

SSK

CAPTAIN *BUCKE?* ARE *YOU THERE?* SK REPORT BACK SK OVER SKK

SK

SSK

ANYONE? SK

SKKk-

HELLO?

WHO'S SK

HELLO, I *HEAR* YOU.

I AM

I...

HELLO.

I *SURRENDER* TO AMERICAN FORCES.

PRESS TO SPEAK SK

LET *GO* TO LISTEN SK

SAY *OVER* WHEN YOU'RE DONE SK

WHO'RE *YOU?* SK OVER. SKK

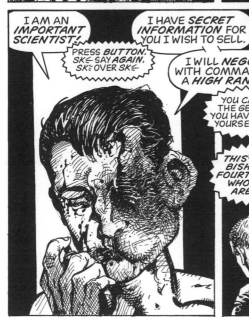

I AM AN *IMPORTANT SCIENTIST!*

I HAVE *SECRET INFORMATION* FOR YOU I WISH TO SELL.

PRESS BUTTON. SK SAY *AGAIN.* SK OVER SK

I WILL *NEGOTIATE* WITH COMMANDANT OF A *HIGH RANK,* OVER.

YOU CAN TALK TO THE *GENERAL,* BUT YOU HAVE TO IDENTIFY YOURSELF—

GIMME THAT RECEIVER--

THIS'S GENERAL *BISHOP* OF THE *FOURTH ARMORED,* WHO THE HELL ARE YOU? SK

MY NAME IS *FRIEDRICH.* I AM A GREAT SCIENTIST *FORCED* TO WORK FOR *THE REICH.*

HOW COME YOU'RE USING *THIS RADIO?*

I HAVE IT FROM INTERPRETER *BAILEY.*

PUT HIM ON THE LINE SK

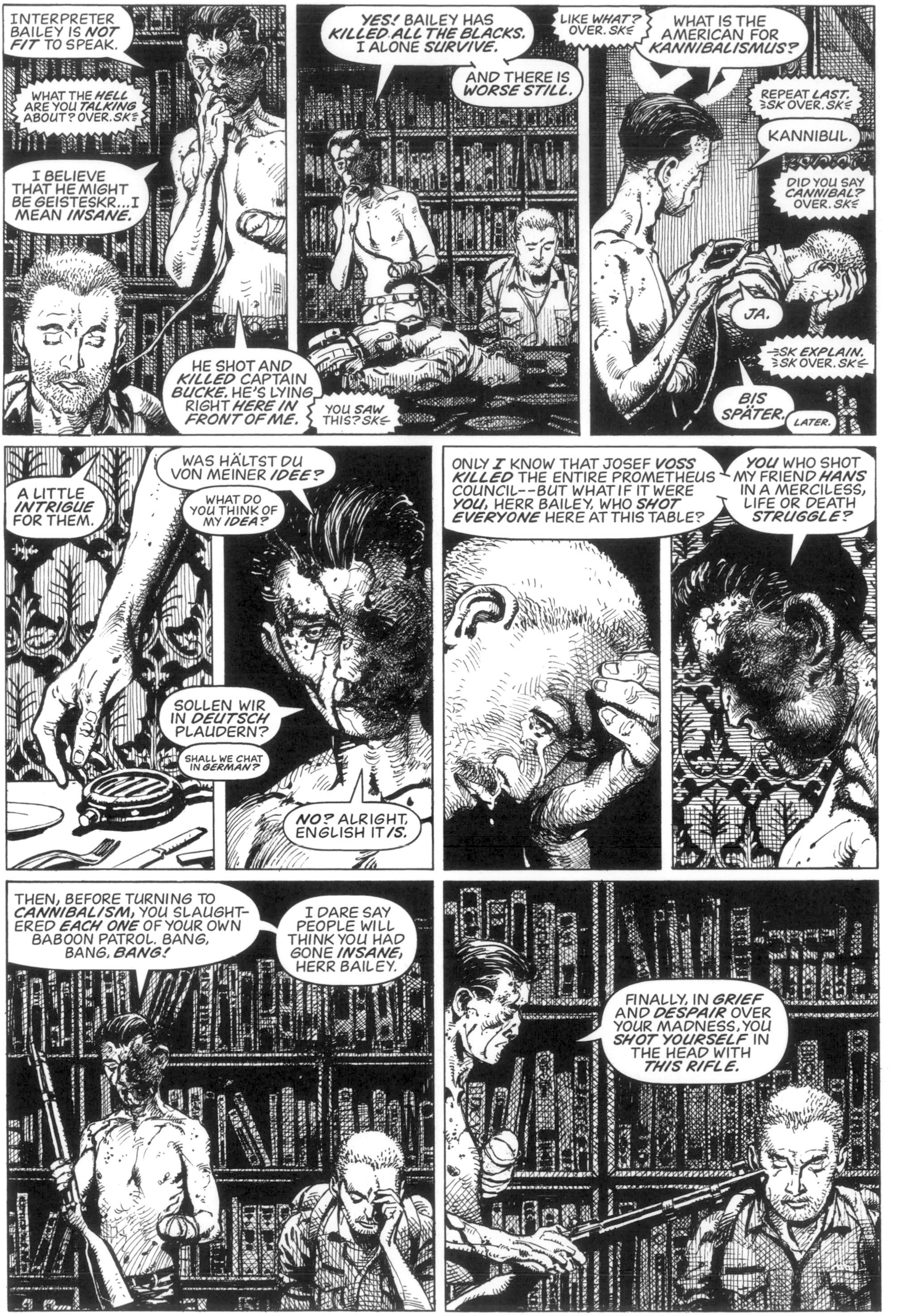

INTERPRETER BAILEY IS NOT FIT TO SPEAK.
WHAT THE HELL ARE YOU TALKING ABOUT? OVER. SK
I BELIEVE THAT HE MIGHT BE GEISTESKR... I MEAN INSANE.
HE SHOT AND KILLED CAPTAIN BUCKE. HE'S LYING RIGHT HERE IN FRONT OF ME.
YOU SAW THIS? SK
YES! BAILEY HAS KILLED ALL THE BLACKS. I ALONE SURVIVE.
AND THERE IS WORSE STILL.
LIKE WHAT? OVER. SK
WHAT IS THE AMERICAN FOR KANNIBALISMUS?
REPEAT LAST. SK OVER. SK
KANNIBUL.
DID YOU SAY CANNIBAL? OVER. SK
JA.
SK EXPLAIN. SK OVER. SK
BIS SPÄTER.
LATER.
A LITTLE INTRIGUE FOR THEM.
WAS HÄLTST DU VON MEINER IDEE?
WHAT DO YOU THINK OF MY IDEA?
SOLLEN WIR IN DEUTSCH PLAUDERN?
SHALL WE CHAT IN GERMAN?
NO? ALRIGHT, ENGLISH IT IS.
ONLY I KNOW THAT JOSEF VOSS KILLED THE ENTIRE PROMETHEUS COUNCIL--BUT WHAT IF IT WERE YOU, HERR BAILEY, WHO SHOT EVERYONE HERE AT THIS TABLE?
YOU WHO SHOT MY FRIEND HANS IN A MERCILESS, LIFE OR DEATH STRUGGLE?
THEN, BEFORE TURNING TO CANNIBALISM, YOU SLAUGHTERED EACH ONE OF YOUR OWN BABOON PATROL. BANG, BANG, BANG!
I DARE SAY PEOPLE WILL THINK YOU HAD GONE INSANE, HERR BAILEY.
FINALLY, IN GRIEF AND DESPAIR OVER YOUR MADNESS, YOU SHOT YOURSELF IN THE HEAD WITH THIS RIFLE.

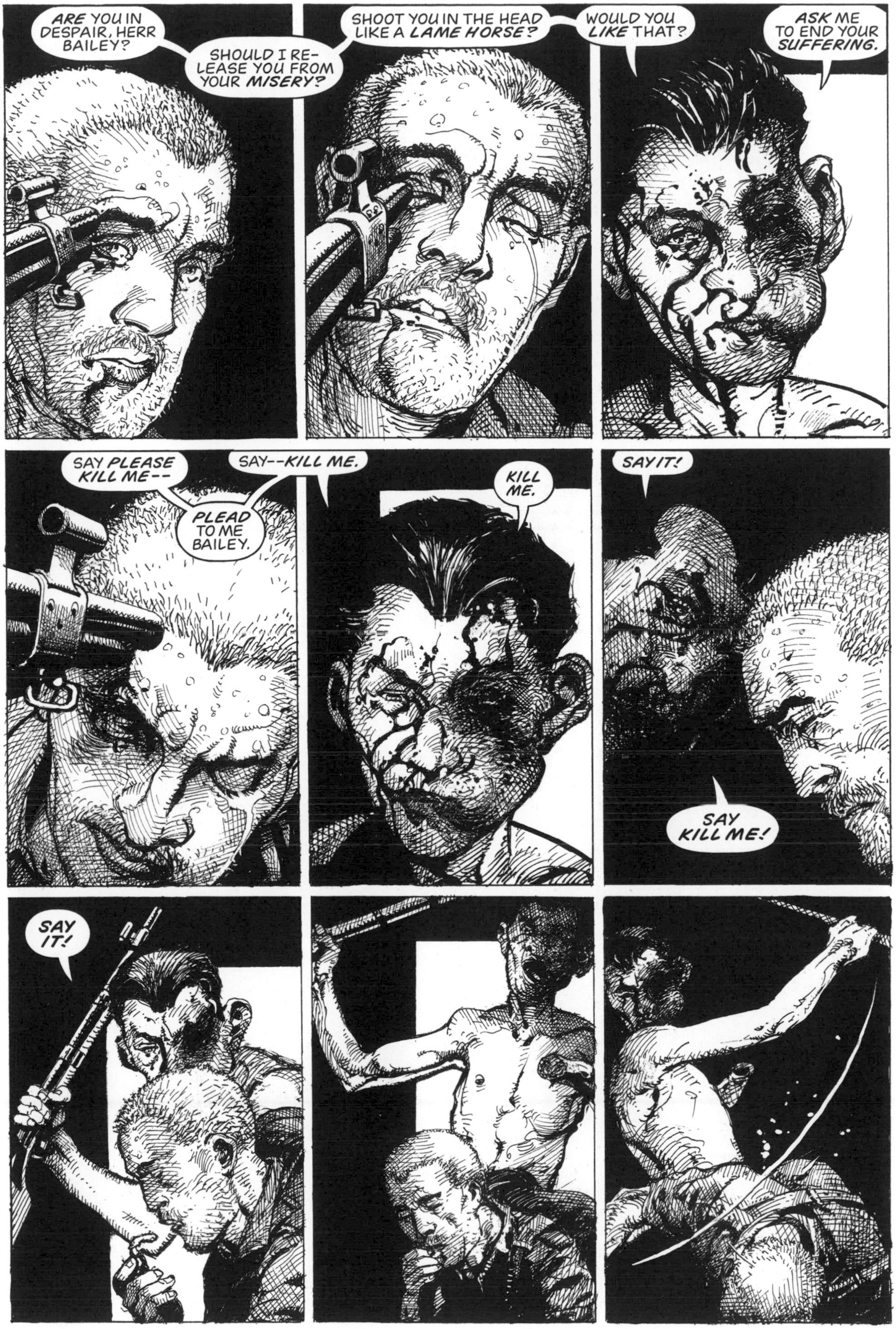
ARE YOU IN DESPAIR, HERR BAILEY?
SHOULD I RE-LEASE YOU FROM YOUR MISERY?
SHOOT YOU IN THE HEAD LIKE A LAME HORSE?
WOULD YOU LIKE THAT?
ASK ME TO END YOUR SUFFERING.
SAY PLEASE KILL ME--
PLEAD TO ME BAILEY.
SAY--KILL ME.
KILL ME.
SAY IT!
SAY KILL ME!
SAY IT!

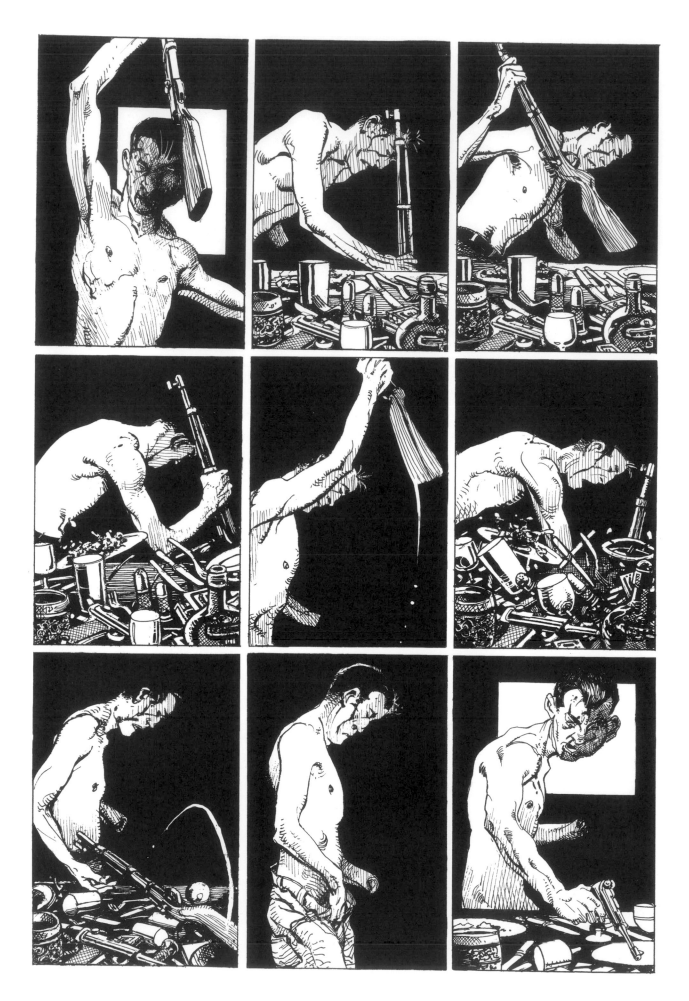

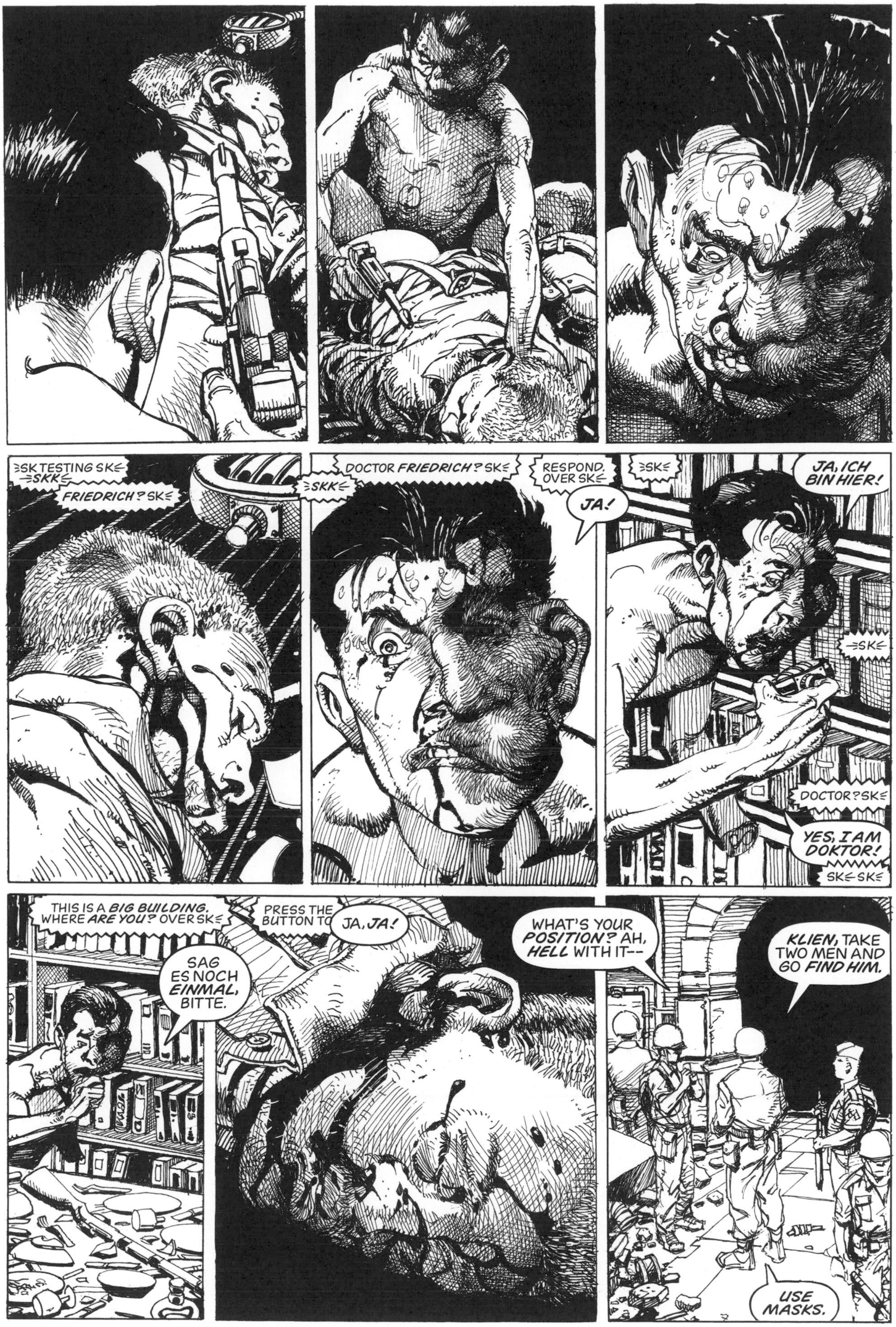

SK TESTING SK
SKK
FRIEDRICH? SK
SKK
DOCTOR FRIEDRICH? SK
RESPOND. OVER SK
JA!
SK
JA, ICH BIN HIER!
SK
DOCTOR? SK
YES, I AM DOKTOR!
SK SK
THIS IS A BIG BUILDING. WHERE ARE YOU? OVER SK
SAG ES NOCH EINMAL, BITTE.
PRESS THE BUTTON TO
JA, JA!
WHAT'S YOUR POSITION? AH, HELL WITH IT--
KLIEN, TAKE TWO MEN AND GO FIND HIM.
USE MASKS.

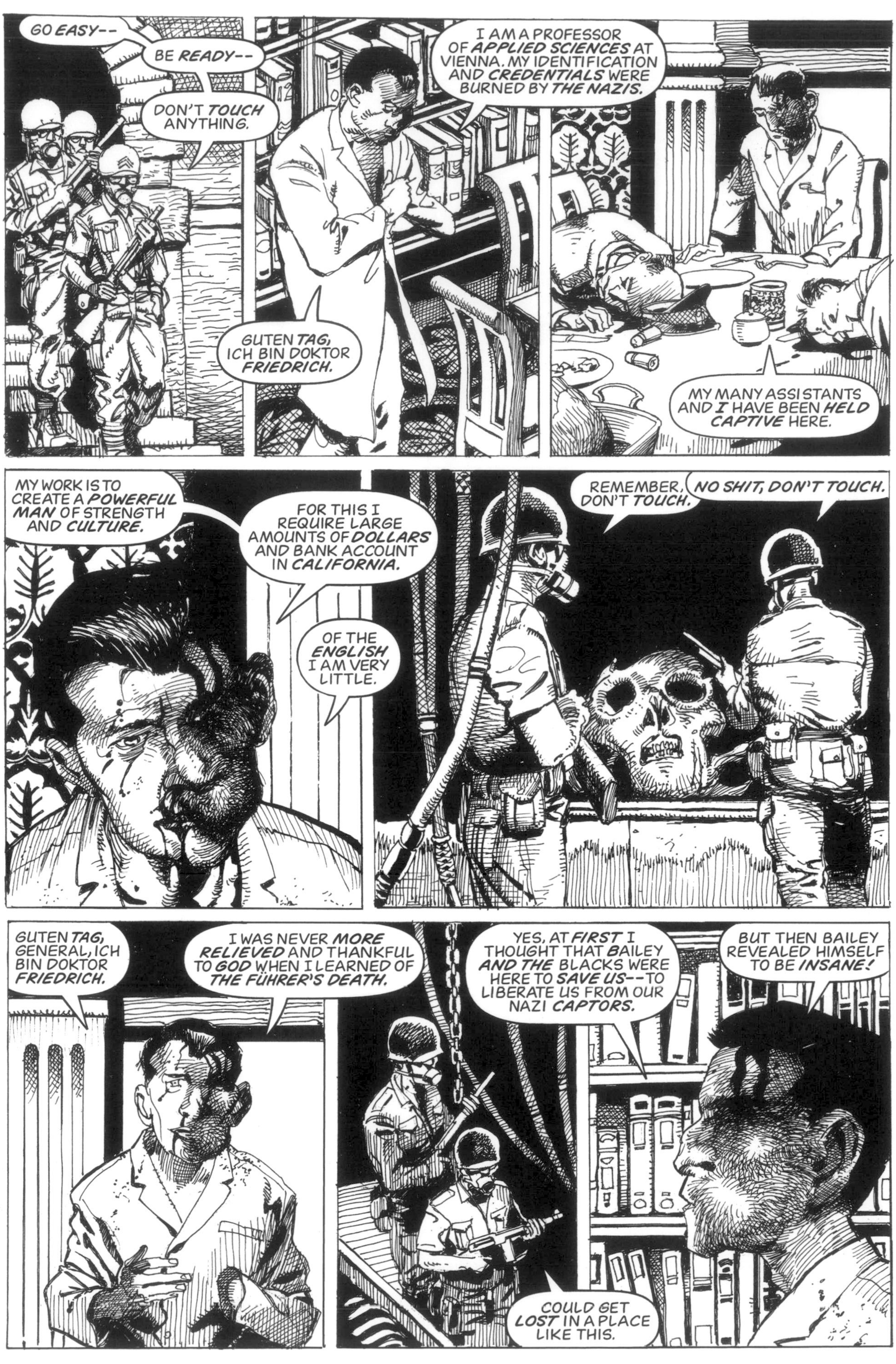
GO EASY--
BE READY--
DON'T TOUCH ANYTHING.
I AM A PROFESSOR OF APPLIED SCIENCES AT VIENNA. MY IDENTIFICATION AND CREDENTIALS WERE BURNED BY THE NAZIS.
GUTEN TAG, ICH BIN DOKTOR FRIEDRICH.
MY MANY ASSISTANTS AND I HAVE BEEN HELD CAPTIVE HERE.
MY WORK IS TO CREATE A POWERFUL MAN OF STRENGTH AND CULTURE.
FOR THIS I REQUIRE LARGE AMOUNTS OF DOLLARS AND BANK ACCOUNT IN CALIFORNIA.
OF THE ENGLISH I AM VERY LITTLE.
REMEMBER, DON'T TOUCH.
NO SHIT, DON'T TOUCH.
GUTEN TAG, GENERAL, ICH BIN DOKTOR FRIEDRICH.
I WAS NEVER MORE RELIEVED AND THANKFUL TO GOD WHEN I LEARNED OF THE FÜHRER'S DEATH.
YES, AT FIRST I THOUGHT THAT BAILEY AND THE BLACKS WERE HERE TO SAVE US--TO LIBERATE US FROM OUR NAZI CAPTORS.
BUT THEN BAILEY REVEALED HIMSELF TO BE INSANE!
COULD GET LOST IN A PLACE LIKE THIS.

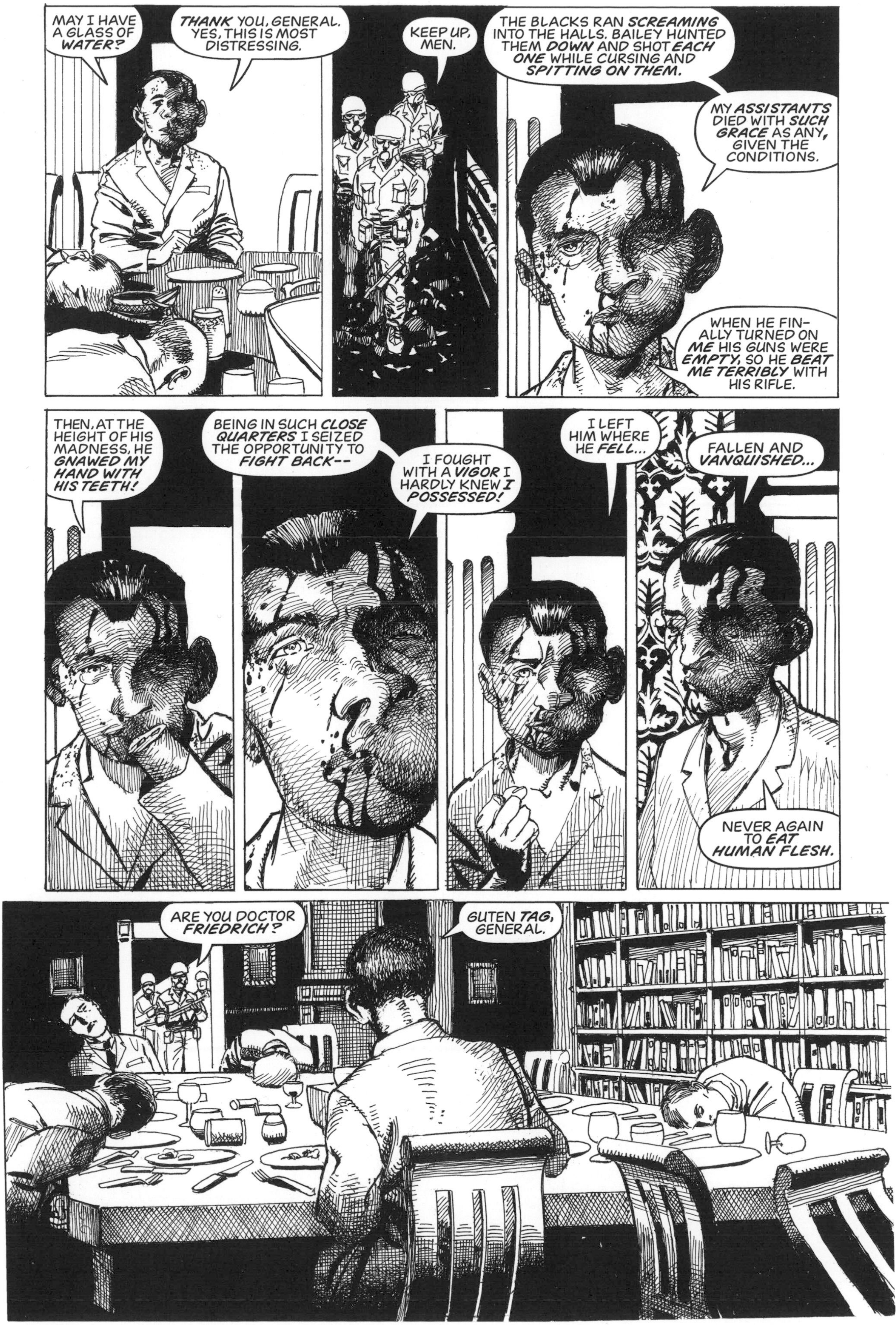
MAY I HAVE A GLASS OF WATER?
THANK YOU, GENERAL. YES, THIS IS MOST DISTRESSING.
KEEP UP, MEN.
THE BLACKS RAN SCREAMING INTO THE HALLS. BAILEY HUNTED THEM DOWN AND SHOT EACH ONE WHILE CURSING AND SPITTING ON THEM.
MY ASSISTANTS DIED WITH SUCH GRACE AS ANY, GIVEN THE CONDITIONS.
WHEN HE FINALLY TURNED ON ME HIS GUNS WERE EMPTY, SO HE BEAT ME TERRIBLY WITH HIS RIFLE.
THEN, AT THE HEIGHT OF HIS MADNESS, HE GNAWED MY HAND WITH HIS TEETH!
BEING IN SUCH CLOSE QUARTERS I SEIZED THE OPPORTUNITY TO FIGHT BACK--
I FOUGHT WITH A VIGOR I HARDLY KNEW I POSSESSED!
I LEFT HIM WHERE HE FELL...
FALLEN AND VANQUISHED...
NEVER AGAIN TO EAT HUMAN FLESH.
ARE YOU DOCTOR FRIEDRICH?
GUTEN TAG, GENERAL.

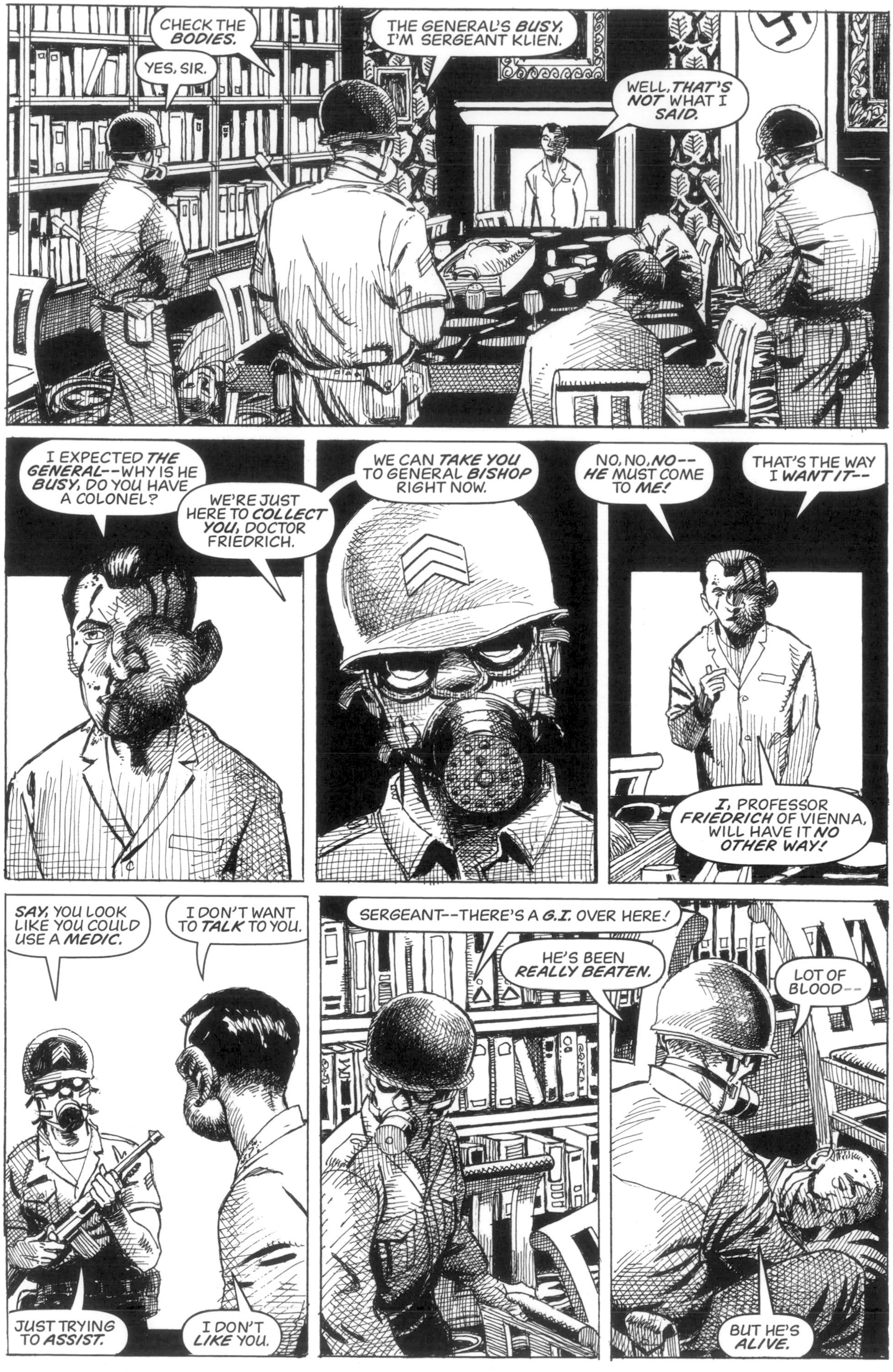
CHECK THE BODIES.
YES, SIR.
THE GENERAL'S BUSY, I'M SERGEANT KLIEN.
WELL, THAT'S NOT WHAT I SAID.
I EXPECTED THE GENERAL--WHY IS HE BUSY, DO YOU HAVE A COLONEL?
WE'RE JUST HERE TO COLLECT YOU, DOCTOR FRIEDRICH.
WE CAN TAKE YOU TO GENERAL BISHOP RIGHT NOW.
NO, NO, NO-- HE MUST COME TO ME!
THAT'S THE WAY I WANT IT--
I, PROFESSOR FRIEDRICH OF VIENNA, WILL HAVE IT NO OTHER WAY!
SAY, YOU LOOK LIKE YOU COULD USE A MEDIC.
I DON'T WANT TO TALK TO YOU.
JUST TRYING TO ASSIST.
I DON'T LIKE YOU.
SERGEANT--THERE'S A G.I. OVER HERE!
HE'S BEEN REALLY BEATEN.
LOT OF BLOOD--
BUT HE'S ALIVE.

ALIVE?

HE'S THE *ONE* RESPONSIBLE FOR THIS!

ALL THESE GOOD MEN, *SCIENTISTS* AND *SCHOLARS*, SHOT TO DEATH AT THEIR *SUPPER!*

HE'S A DEPRAV- ED *MONSTER* WHO SLAUGHTERED HIS OWN PATROL AND *ATE HUMAN FLESH!*

YOU SHOULD *KILL HIM NOW!*

WE'LL PLACE HIM IN *DETEN- TION,* DOCTOR.

BUT HE'S A DEMENTED *CANNIBAL,* HE MUST BE *EXECUTED!*

HE NEEDS TO BE *QUESTIONED.*

ALRIGHT, SERGEANT-- I'VE *DECIDED* THAT YOU SHOULD TAKE ME TO YOUR *GENERAL BISHOP.*

AND TO REVEAL THE *SECRETS OF PROMETHEUS* I SHALL RECEIVE *ASYLUM* AND *UN- CONDITIONAL* IMMUNITY.

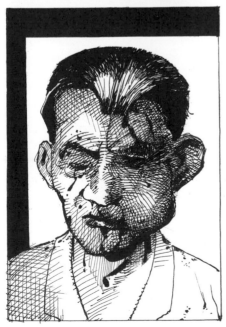

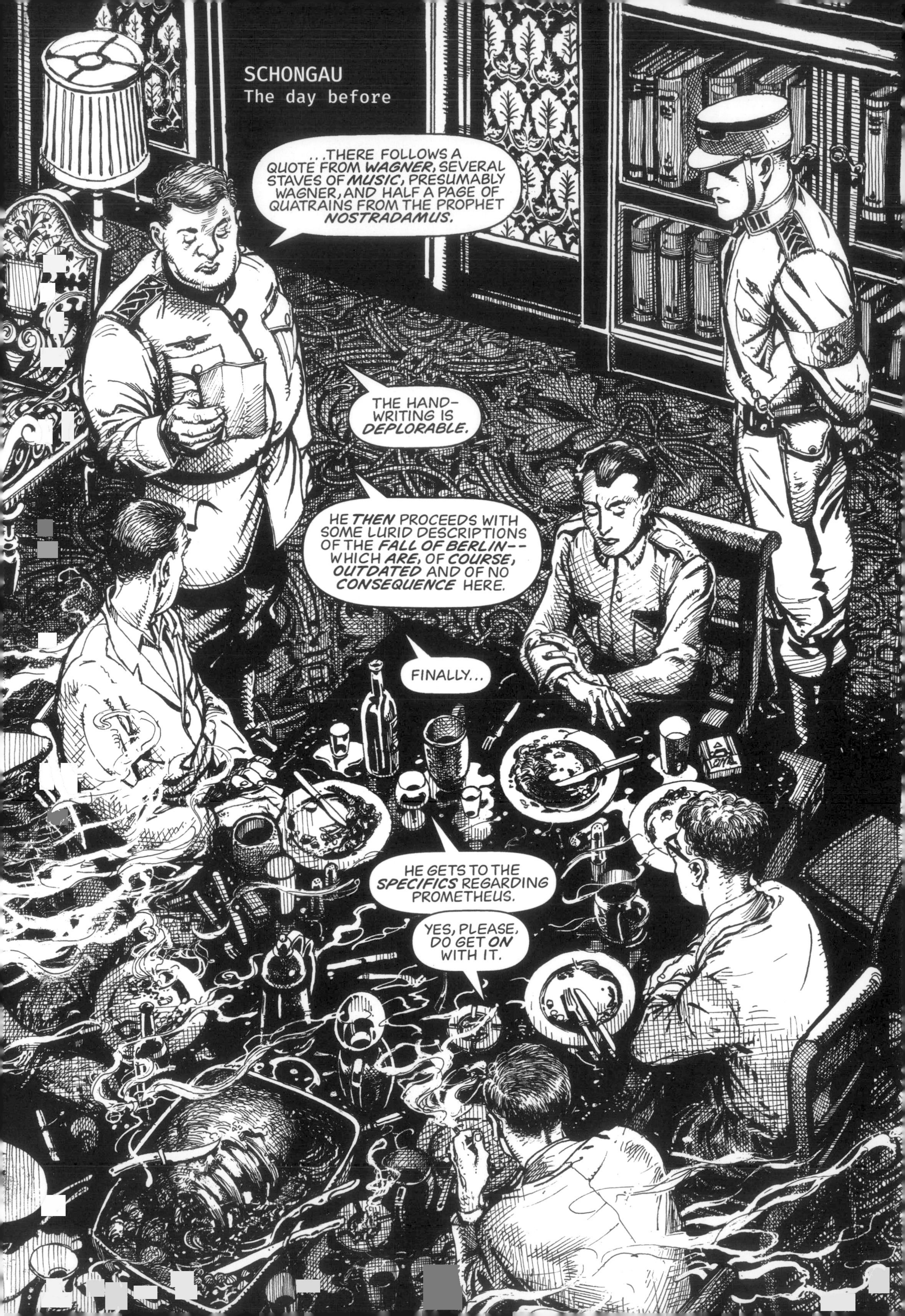
SCHONGAU
The day before
...THERE FOLLOWS A QUOTE FROM WAGNER, SEVERAL STAVES OF MUSIC, PRESUMABLY WAGNER, AND HALF A PAGE OF QUATRAINS FROM THE PROPHET NOSTRADAMUS.
THE HAND-WRITING IS DEPLORABLE.
HE THEN PROCEEDS WITH SOME LURID DESCRIPTIONS OF THE FALL OF BERLIN--WHICH ARE, OF COURSE, OUTDATED AND OF NO CONSEQUENCE HERE.
FINALLY...
HE GETS TO THE SPECIFICS REGARDING PROMETHEUS.
YES, PLEASE, DO GET ON WITH IT.

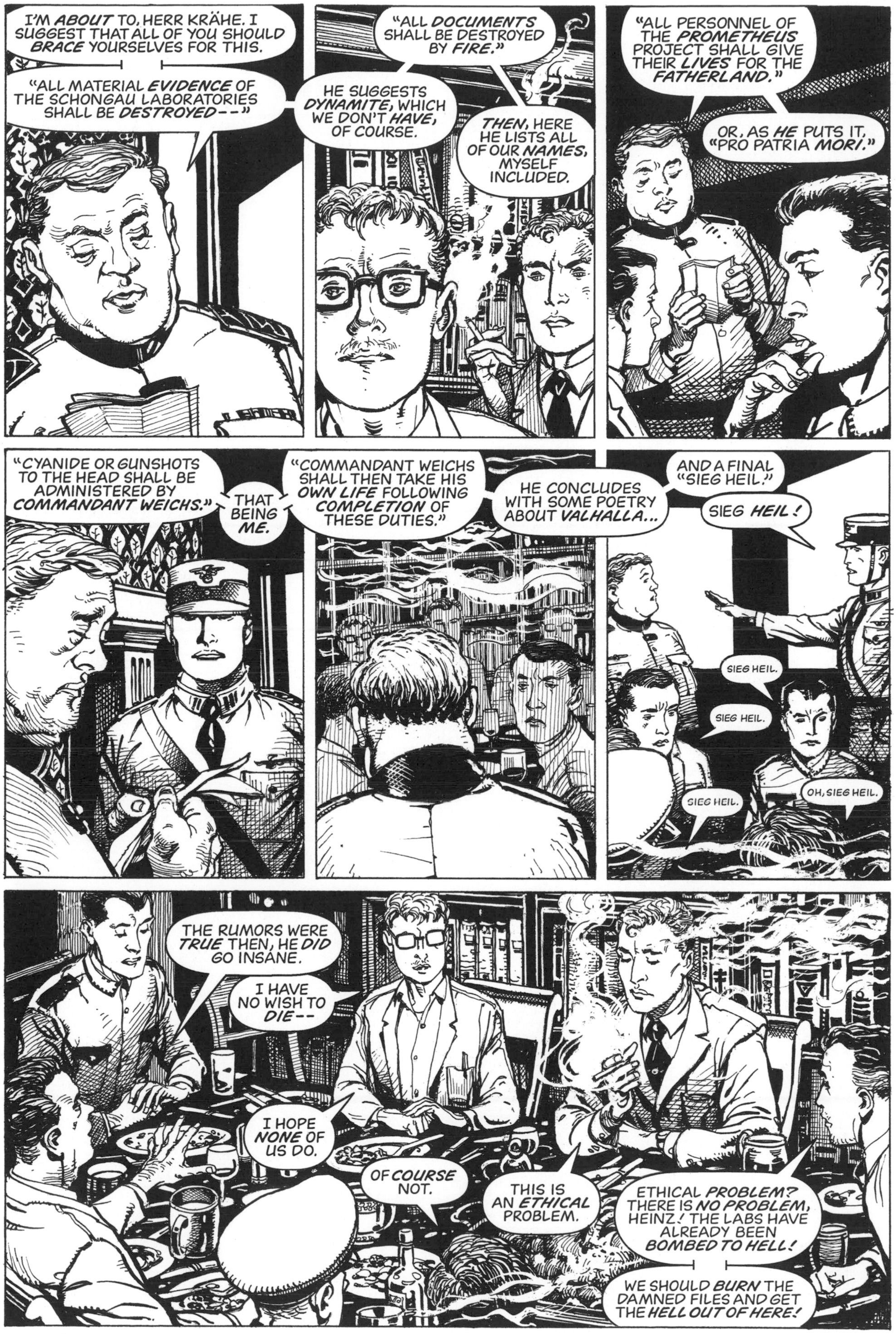

I'M ABOUT TO, HERR KRÄHE. I SUGGEST THAT ALL OF YOU SHOULD BRACE YOURSELVES FOR THIS.
"ALL MATERIAL EVIDENCE OF THE SCHONGAU LABORATORIES SHALL BE DESTROYED--"
"ALL DOCUMENTS SHALL BE DESTROYED BY FIRE."
HE SUGGESTS DYNAMITE, WHICH WE DON'T HAVE, OF COURSE.
THEN, HERE HE LISTS ALL OF OUR NAMES, MYSELF INCLUDED.
"ALL PERSONNEL OF THE PROMETHEUS PROJECT SHALL GIVE THEIR LIVES FOR THE FATHERLAND."
OR, AS HE PUTS IT, "PRO PATRIA MORI."
"CYANIDE OR GUNSHOTS TO THE HEAD SHALL BE ADMINISTERED BY COMMANDANT WEICHS."
THAT BEING ME.
"COMMANDANT WEICHS SHALL THEN TAKE HIS OWN LIFE FOLLOWING COMPLETION OF THESE DUTIES."
HE CONCLUDES WITH SOME POETRY ABOUT VALHALLA...
AND A FINAL "SIEG HEIL."
SIEG HEIL!
SIEG HEIL.
SIEG HEIL.
SIEG HEIL.
OH, SIEG HEIL.
THE RUMORS WERE TRUE THEN, HE DID GO INSANE.
I HAVE NO WISH TO DIE--
I HOPE NONE OF US DO.
OF COURSE NOT.
THIS IS AN ETHICAL PROBLEM.
ETHICAL PROBLEM? THERE IS NO PROBLEM, HEINZ! THE LABS HAVE ALREADY BEEN BOMBED TO HELL!
WE SHOULD BURN THE DAMNED FILES AND GET THE HELL OUT OF HERE!

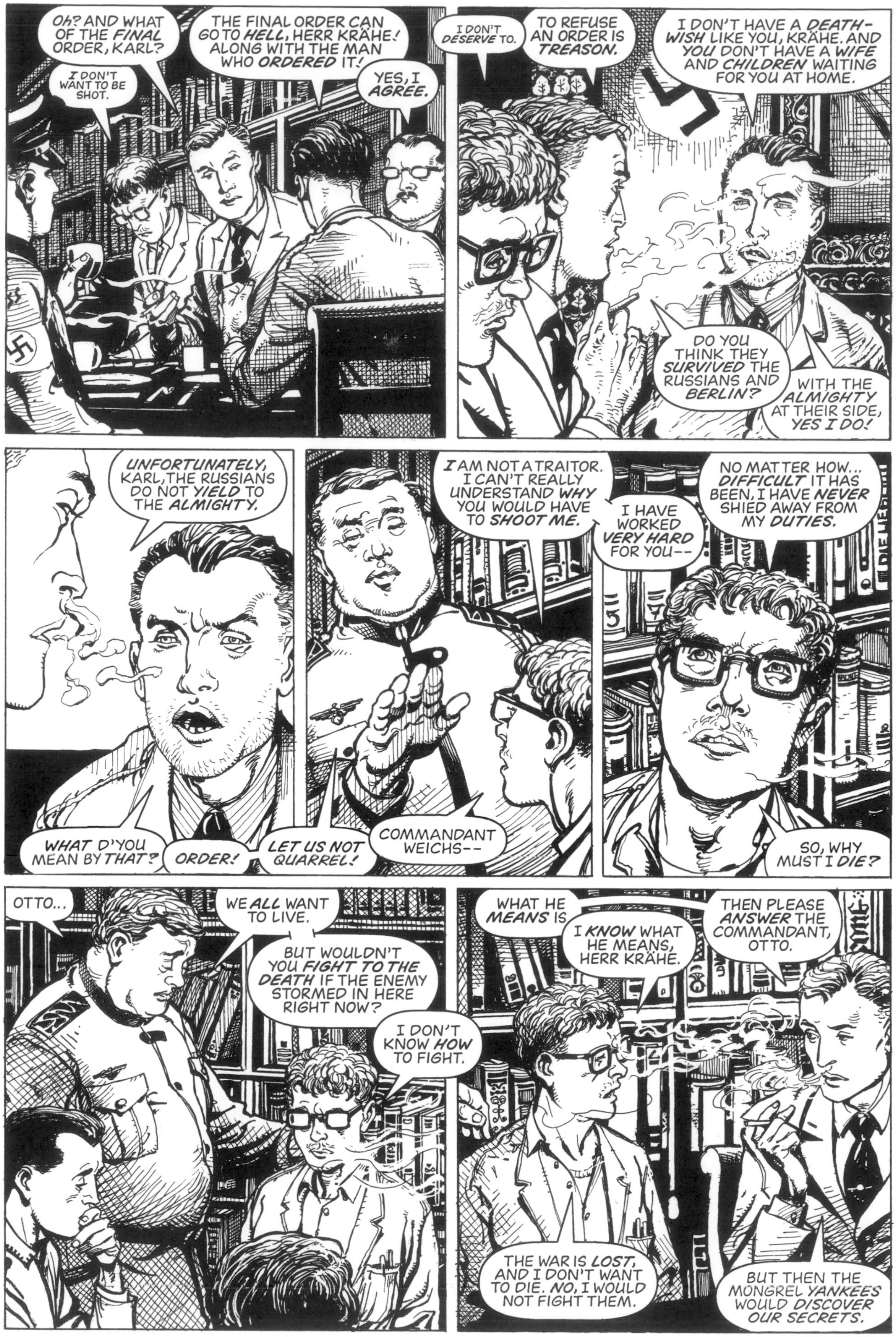
Oh? AND WHAT OF THE FINAL ORDER, KARL?
I DON'T WANT TO BE SHOT.
THE FINAL ORDER CAN GO TO HELL, HERR KRÄHE! ALONG WITH THE MAN WHO ORDERED IT!
YES, I AGREE.
I DON'T DESERVE TO.
TO REFUSE AN ORDER IS TREASON.
I DON'T HAVE A DEATH-WISH LIKE YOU, KRÄHE. AND YOU DON'T HAVE A WIFE AND CHILDREN WAITING FOR YOU AT HOME.
DO YOU THINK THEY SURVIVED THE RUSSIANS AND BERLIN?
WITH THE ALMIGHTY AT THEIR SIDE, YES I DO!
UNFORTUNATELY, KARL, THE RUSSIANS DO NOT YIELD TO THE ALMIGHTY.
WHAT D'YOU MEAN BY THAT?
ORDER!
LET US NOT QUARREL!
COMMANDANT WEICHS--
I AM NOT A TRAITOR. I CAN'T REALLY UNDERSTAND WHY YOU WOULD HAVE TO SHOOT ME.
I HAVE WORKED VERY HARD FOR YOU--
NO MATTER HOW... DIFFICULT IT HAS BEEN, I HAVE NEVER SHIED AWAY FROM MY DUTIES.
SO, WHY MUST I DIE?
OTTO...
WE ALL WANT TO LIVE.
BUT WOULDN'T YOU FIGHT TO THE DEATH IF THE ENEMY STORMED IN HERE RIGHT NOW?
I DON'T KNOW HOW TO FIGHT.
WHAT HE MEANS IS
I KNOW WHAT HE MEANS, HERR KRÄHE.
THEN PLEASE ANSWER THE COMMANDANT, OTTO.
THE WAR IS LOST, AND I DON'T WANT TO DIE. NO, I WOULD NOT FIGHT THEM.
BUT THEN THE MONGREL YANKEES WOULD DISCOVER OUR SECRETS.

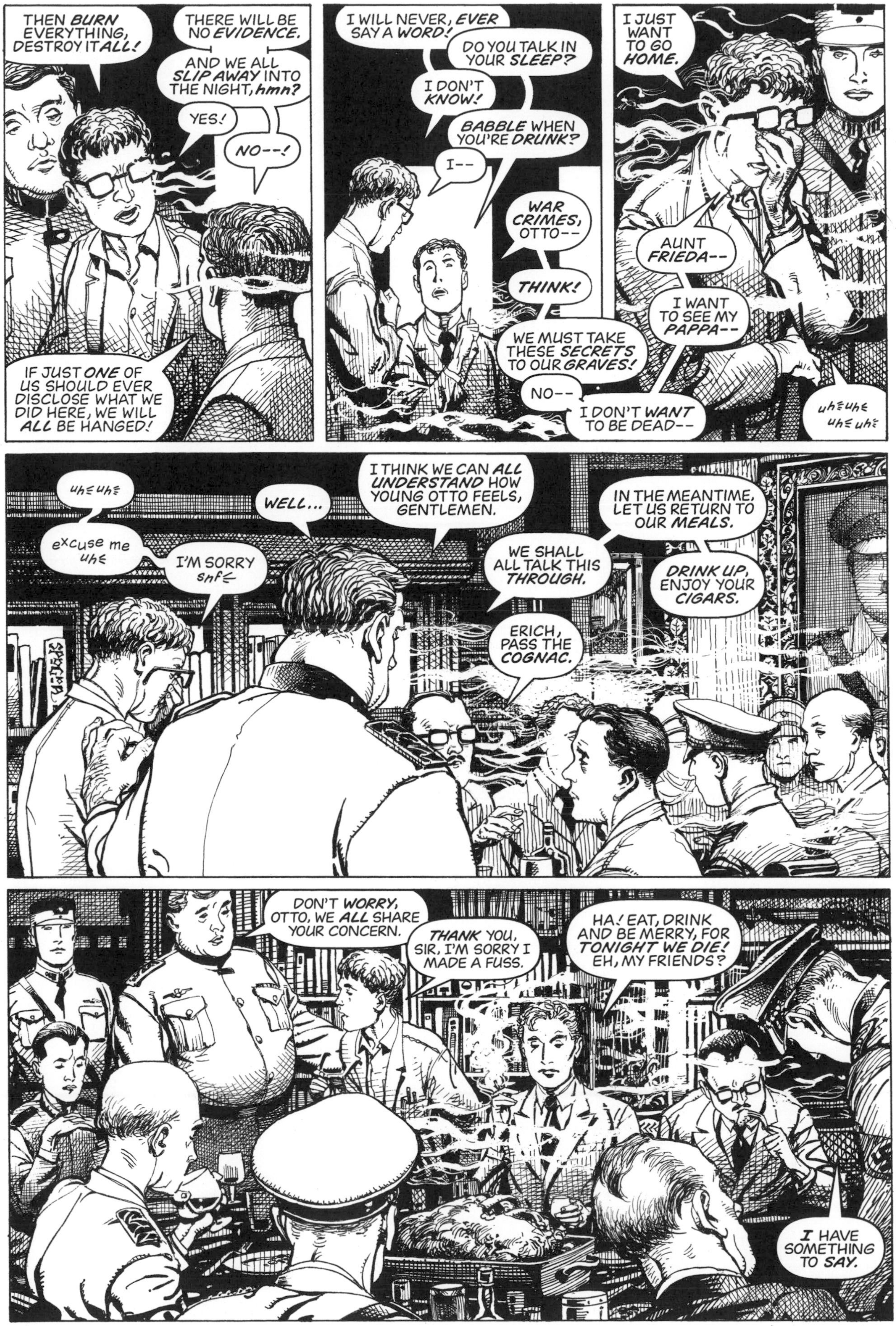
THEN BURN EVERYTHING, DESTROY IT ALL!
THERE WILL BE NO EVIDENCE.
AND WE ALL SLIP AWAY INTO THE NIGHT, hmn?
YES!
NO--!
IF JUST ONE OF US SHOULD EVER DISCLOSE WHAT WE DID HERE, WE WILL ALL BE HANGED!
I WILL NEVER, EVER SAY A WORD!
DO YOU TALK IN YOUR SLEEP?
I DON'T KNOW!
BABBLE WHEN YOU'RE DRUNK?
I--
WAR CRIMES, OTTO--
THINK!
WE MUST TAKE THESE SECRETS TO OUR GRAVES!
NO--
I DON'T WANT TO BE DEAD--
I JUST WANT TO GO HOME.
AUNT FRIEDA--
I WANT TO SEE MY PAPPA--
uh uh uh uh
uh uh
excuse me uh
I'M SORRY snf
WELL...
I THINK WE CAN ALL UNDERSTAND HOW YOUNG OTTO FEELS, GENTLEMEN.
WE SHALL ALL TALK THIS THROUGH.
IN THE MEANTIME, LET US RETURN TO OUR MEALS.
DRINK UP, ENJOY YOUR CIGARS.
ERICH, PASS THE COGNAC.
DON'T WORRY, OTTO, WE ALL SHARE YOUR CONCERN.
THANK YOU, SIR, I'M SORRY I MADE A FUSS.
HA! EAT, DRINK AND BE MERRY, FOR TONIGHT WE DIE! EH, MY FRIENDS?
I HAVE SOMETHING TO SAY.

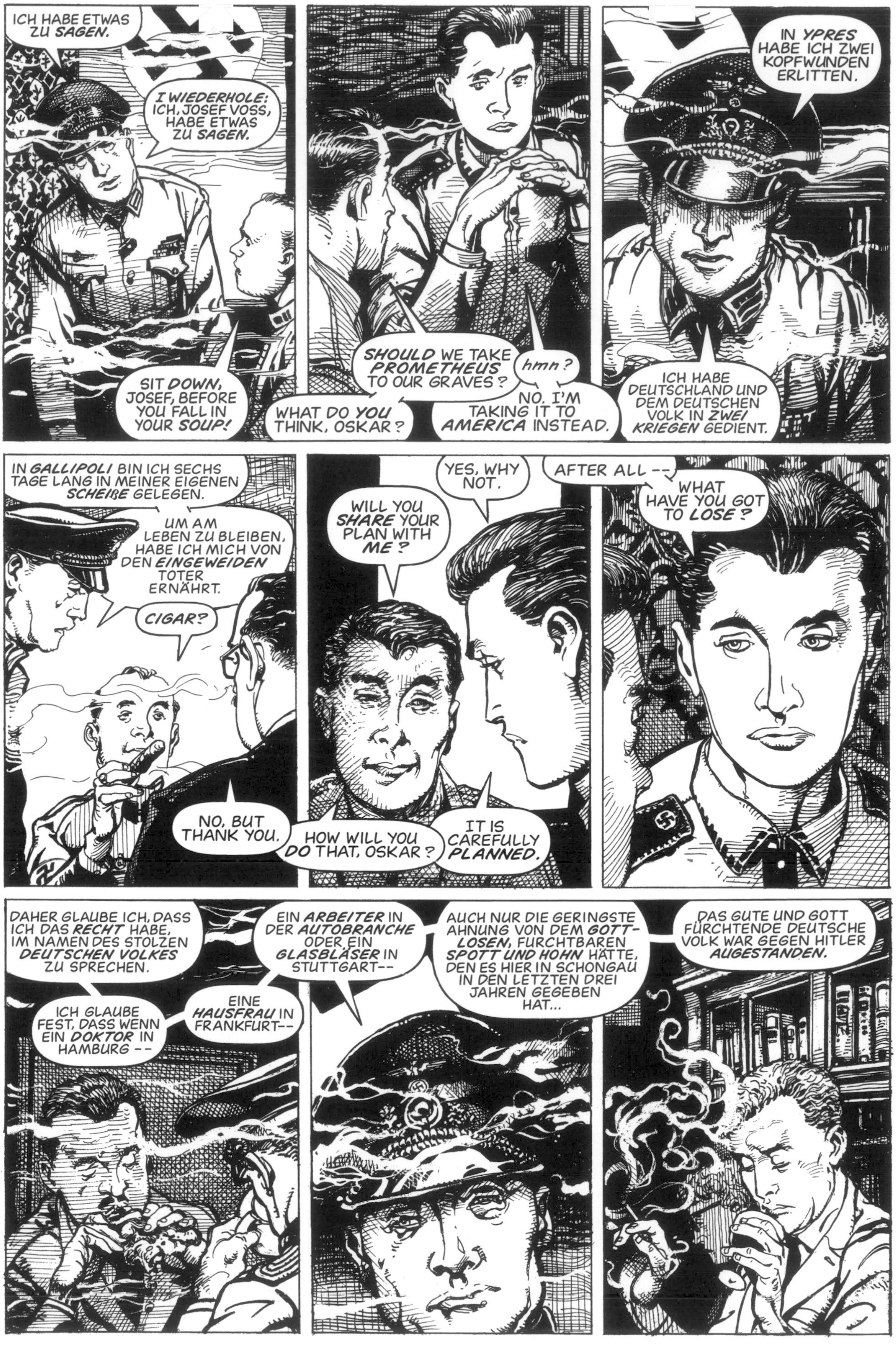
ICH HABE ETWAS ZU SAGEN.
I WIEDERHOLE: ICH, JOSEF VOSS, HABE ETWAS ZU SAGEN.
SIT DOWN, JOSEF, BEFORE YOU FALL IN YOUR SOUP!
WHAT DO YOU THINK, OSKAR?
SHOULD WE TAKE PROMETHEUS TO OUR GRAVES?
hmn?
NO. I'M TAKING IT TO AMERICA INSTEAD.
IN YPRES HABE ICH ZWEI KOPFWUNDEN ERLITTEN.
ICH HABE DEUTSCHLAND UND DEM DEUTSCHEN VOLK IN ZWEI KRIEGEN GEDIENT.
IN GALLIPOLI BIN ICH SECHS TAGE LANG IN MEINER EIGENEN SCHEIßE GELEGEN.
UM AM LEBEN ZU BLEIBEN, HABE ICH MICH VON DEN EINGEWEIDEN TOTER ERNÄHRT.
CIGAR?
NO, BUT THANK YOU.
HOW WILL YOU DO THAT, OSKAR?
IT IS CAREFULLY PLANNED.
WILL YOU SHARE YOUR PLAN WITH ME?
YES, WHY NOT.
AFTER ALL --
WHAT HAVE YOU GOT TO LOSE?
DAHER GLAUBE ICH, DASS ICH DAS RECHT HABE, IM NAMEN DES STOLZEN DEUTSCHEN VOLKES ZU SPRECHEN.
ICH GLAUBE FEST, DASS WENN EIN DOKTOR IN HAMBURG --
EINE HAUSFRAU IN FRANKFURT--
EIN ARBEITER IN DER AUTOBRANCHE ODER EIN GLASBLÄSER IN STUTTGART--
AUCH NUR DIE GERINGSTE AHNUNG VON DEM GOTT-LOSEN, FURCHTBAREN SPOTT UND HOHN HÄTTE, DEN ES HIER IN SCHONGAU IN DEN LETZTEN DREI JAHREN GEGEBEN HAT...
DAS GUTE UND GOTT FÜRCHTENDE DEUTSCHE VOLK WAR GEGEN HITLER AUGESTANDEN.

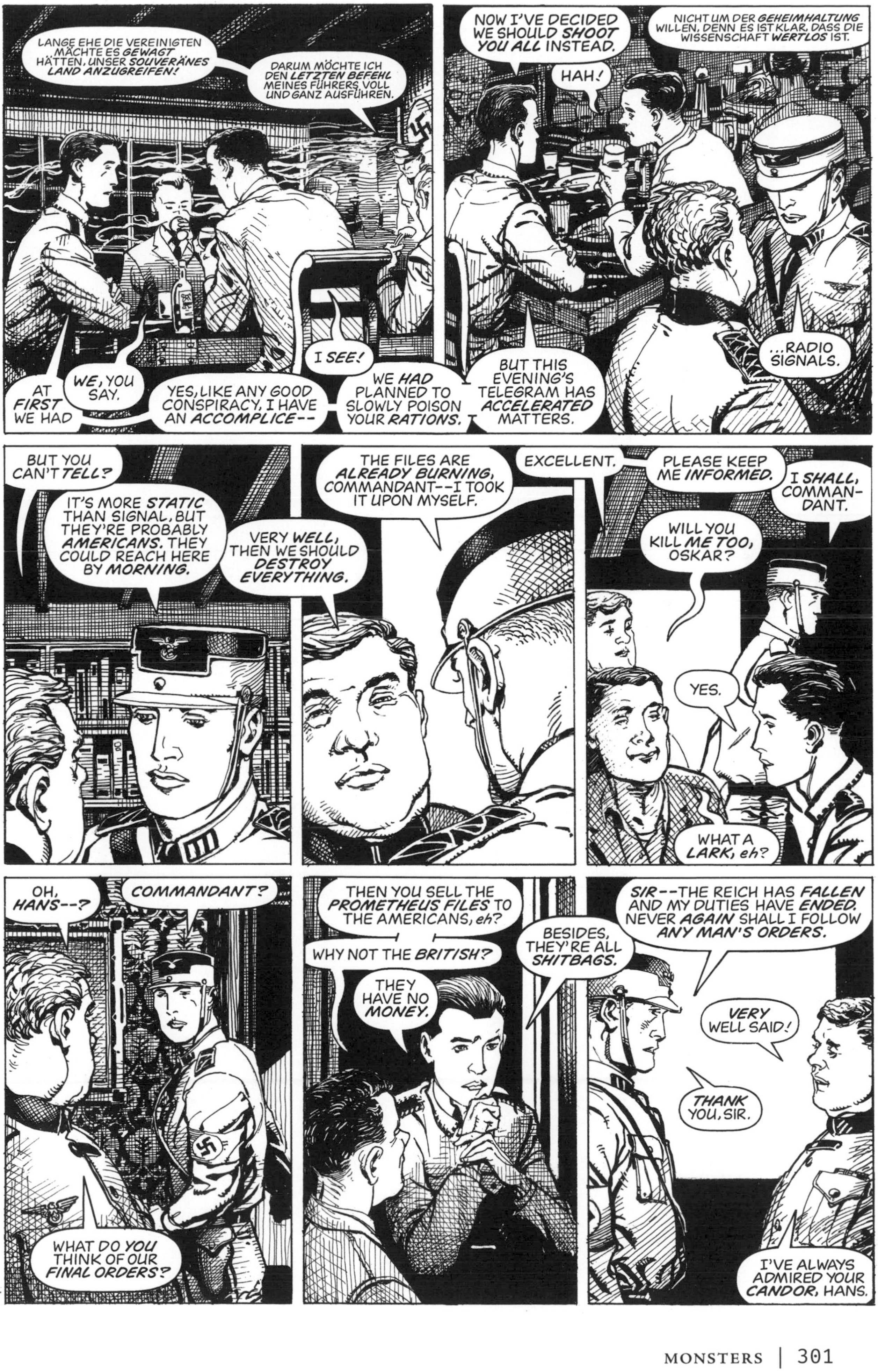
LANGE EHE DIE VEREINIGTEN MÄCHTE ES GEWAGT HÄTTEN, UNSER SOUVERÄNES LAND ANZUGREIFEN!
DARUM MÖCHTE ICH DEN LETZTEN BEFEHL MEINES FÜHRERS VOLL UND GANZ AUSFÜHREN.
AT FIRST WE HAD
WE, YOU SAY.
YES, LIKE ANY GOOD CONSPIRACY, I HAVE AN ACCOMPLICE--
I SEE!
WE HAD PLANNED TO SLOWLY POISON YOUR RATIONS.
BUT THIS EVENING'S TELEGRAM HAS ACCELERATED MATTERS.
NOW I'VE DECIDED WE SHOULD SHOOT YOU ALL INSTEAD.
HAH!
NICHT UM DER GEHEIMHALTUNG WILLEN, DENN ES IST KLAR, DASS DIE WISSENSCHAFT WERTLOS IST.
...RADIO SIGNALS.
BUT YOU CAN'T TELL?
IT'S MORE STATIC THAN SIGNAL, BUT THEY'RE PROBABLY AMERICANS. THEY COULD REACH HERE BY MORNING.
VERY WELL, THEN WE SHOULD DESTROY EVERYTHING.
THE FILES ARE ALREADY BURNING, COMMANDANT--I TOOK IT UPON MYSELF.
EXCELLENT.
PLEASE KEEP ME INFORMED.
I SHALL, COMMANDANT.
WILL YOU KILL ME TOO, OSKAR?
YES.
WHAT A LARK, eh?
OH, HANS--?
COMMANDANT?
WHAT DO YOU THINK OF OUR FINAL ORDERS?
THEN YOU SELL THE PROMETHEUS FILES TO THE AMERICANS, eh?
WHY NOT THE BRITISH?
THEY HAVE NO MONEY.
BESIDES, THEY'RE ALL SHITBAGS.
SIR--THE REICH HAS FALLEN AND MY DUTIES HAVE ENDED. NEVER AGAIN SHALL I FOLLOW ANY MAN'S ORDERS.
VERY WELL SAID!
THANK YOU, SIR.
I'VE ALWAYS ADMIRED YOUR CANDOR, HANS.

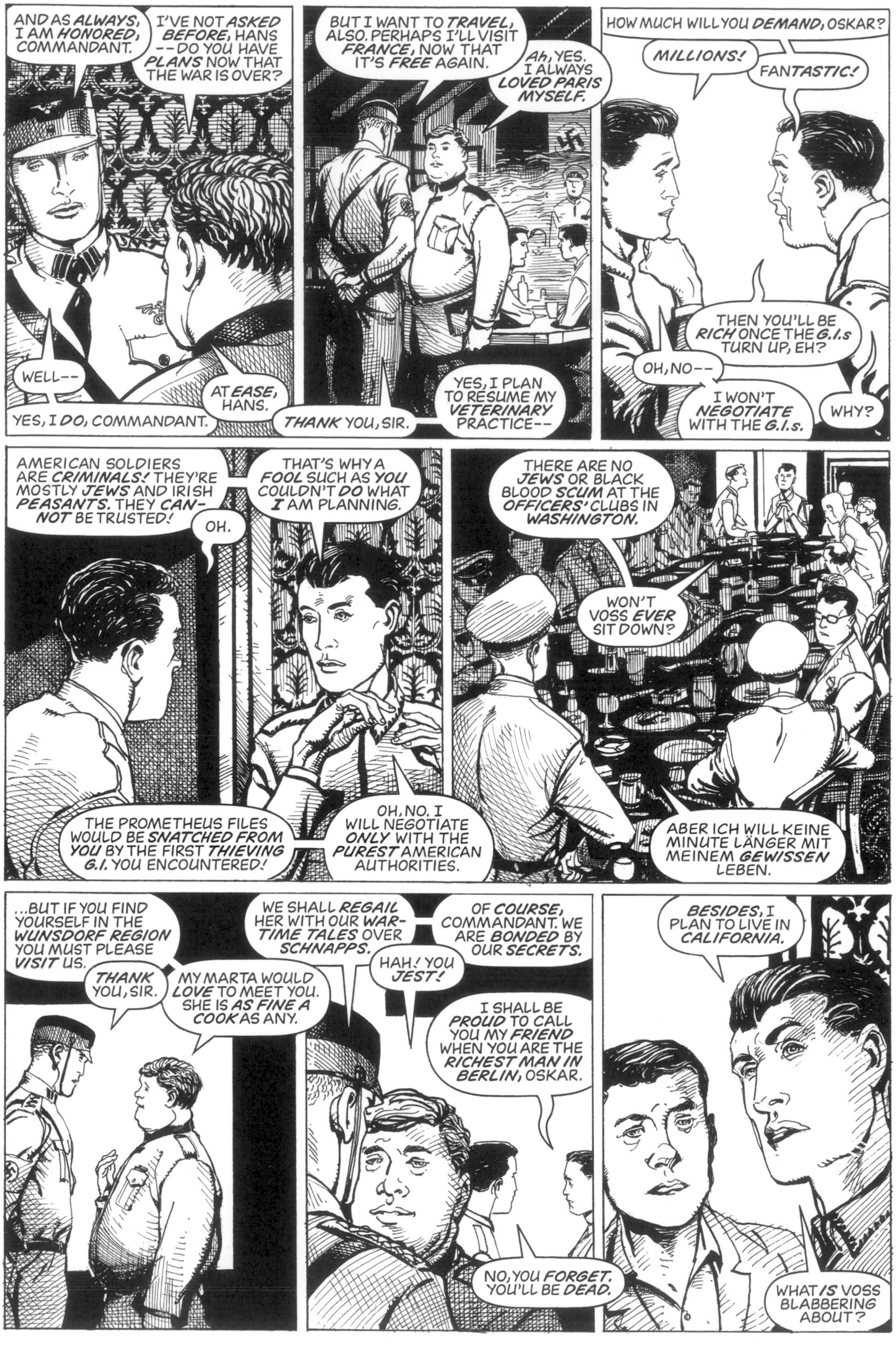

AND AS ALWAYS, I AM HONORED, COMMANDANT.
I'VE NOT ASKED BEFORE, HANS --DO YOU HAVE PLANS NOW THAT THE WAR IS OVER?
WELL--
YES, I DO, COMMANDANT.
AT EASE, HANS.
BUT I WANT TO TRAVEL, ALSO. PERHAPS I'LL VISIT FRANCE, NOW THAT IT'S FREE AGAIN.
Ah, YES. I ALWAYS LOVED PARIS MYSELF.
THANK YOU, SIR.
YES, I PLAN TO RESUME MY VETERINARY PRACTICE--
HOW MUCH WILL YOU DEMAND, OSKAR?
MILLIONS!
FANTASTIC!
THEN YOU'LL BE RICH ONCE THE G.I.s TURN UP, EH?
OH, NO--
I WON'T NEGOTIATE WITH THE G.I.s.
WHY?
AMERICAN SOLDIERS ARE CRIMINALS! THEY'RE MOSTLY JEWS AND IRISH PEASANTS. THEY CANNOT BE TRUSTED!
OH.
THAT'S WHY A FOOL SUCH AS YOU COULDN'T DO WHAT I AM PLANNING.
THE PROMETHEUS FILES WOULD BE SNATCHED FROM YOU BY THE FIRST THIEVING G.I. YOU ENCOUNTERED!
OH, NO. I WILL NEGOTIATE ONLY WITH THE PUREST AMERICAN AUTHORITIES.
THERE ARE NO JEWS OR BLACK BLOOD SCUM AT THE OFFICERS' CLUBS IN WASHINGTON.
WON'T VOSS EVER SIT DOWN?
ABER ICH WILL KEINE MINUTE LÄNGER MIT MEINEM GEWISSEN LEBEN.
...BUT IF YOU FIND YOURSELF IN THE WUNSDORF REGION YOU MUST PLEASE VISIT US.
THANK YOU, SIR.
MY MARTA WOULD LOVE TO MEET YOU. SHE IS AS FINE A COOK AS ANY.
WE SHALL REGAIL HER WITH OUR WARTIME TALES OVER SCHNAPPS.
OF COURSE, COMMANDANT. WE ARE BONDED BY OUR SECRETS.
HAH! YOU JEST!
I SHALL BE PROUD TO CALL YOU MY FRIEND WHEN YOU ARE THE RICHEST MAN IN BERLIN, OSKAR.
NO, YOU FORGET. YOU'LL BE DEAD.
BESIDES, I PLAN TO LIVE IN CALIFORNIA.
WHAT IS VOSS BLABBERING ABOUT?

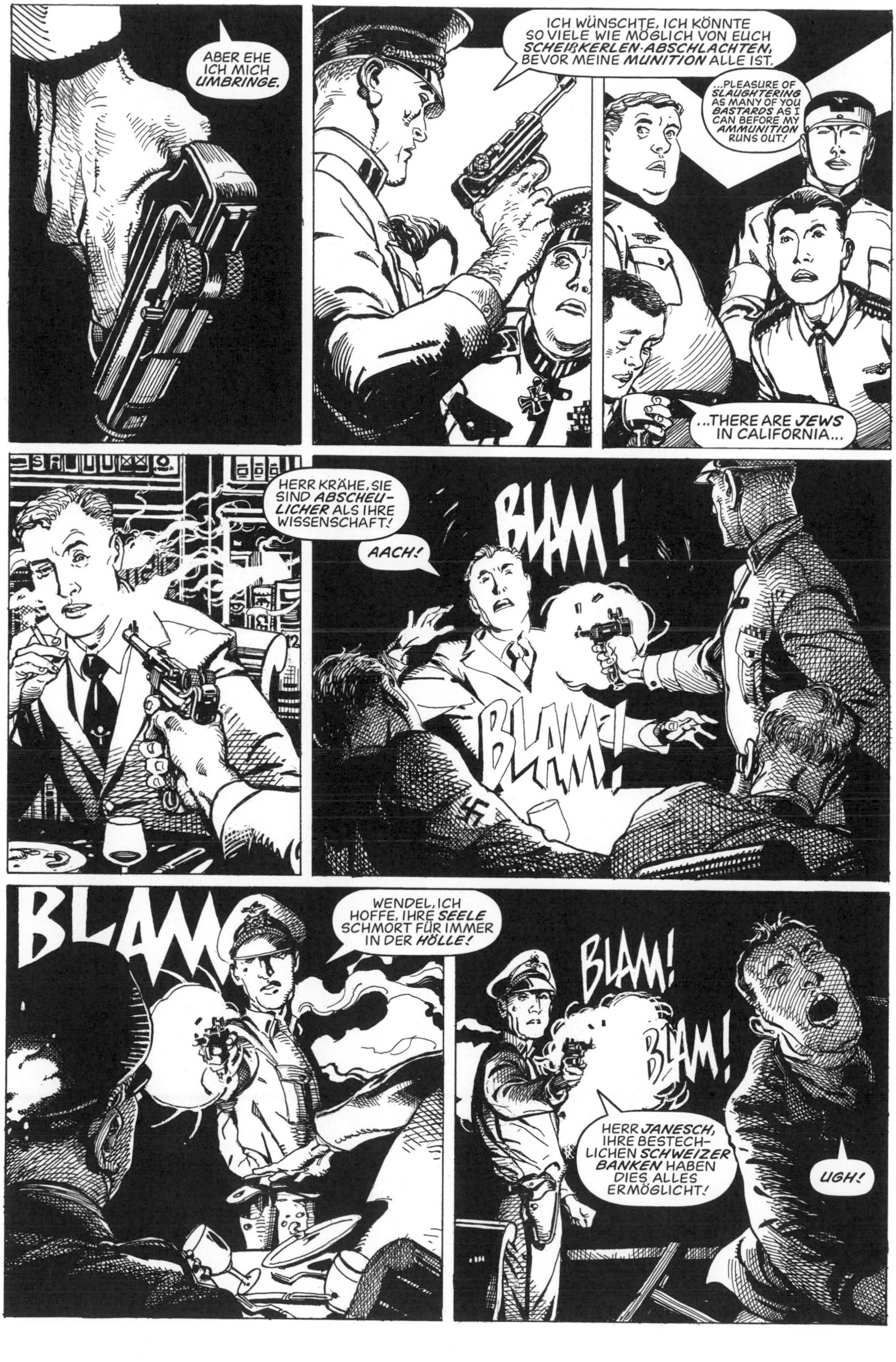
ABER EHE ICH MICH UMBRINGE.
ICH WÜNSCHTE, ICH KÖNNTE SO VIELE WIE MÖGLICH VON EUCH SCHEIßKERLEN ABSCHLACHTEN, BEVOR MEINE MUNITION ALLE IST.
...PLEASURE OF SLAUGHTERING AS MANY OF YOU BASTARDS AS I CAN BEFORE MY AMMUNITION RUNS OUT!
...THERE ARE JEWS IN CALIFORNIA...
HERR KRÄHE, SIE SIND ABSCHEULICHER ALS IHRE WISSENSCHAFT!
AACH!
BLAM!
BLAM!
BLAM
WENDEL, ICH HOFFE, IHRE SEELE SCHMORT FÜR IMMER IN DER HÖLLE!
BLAM!
BLAM!
HERR JANESCH, IHRE BESTECHLICHEN SCHWEIZER BANKEN HABEN DIES ALLES ERMÖGLICHT!
UGH!

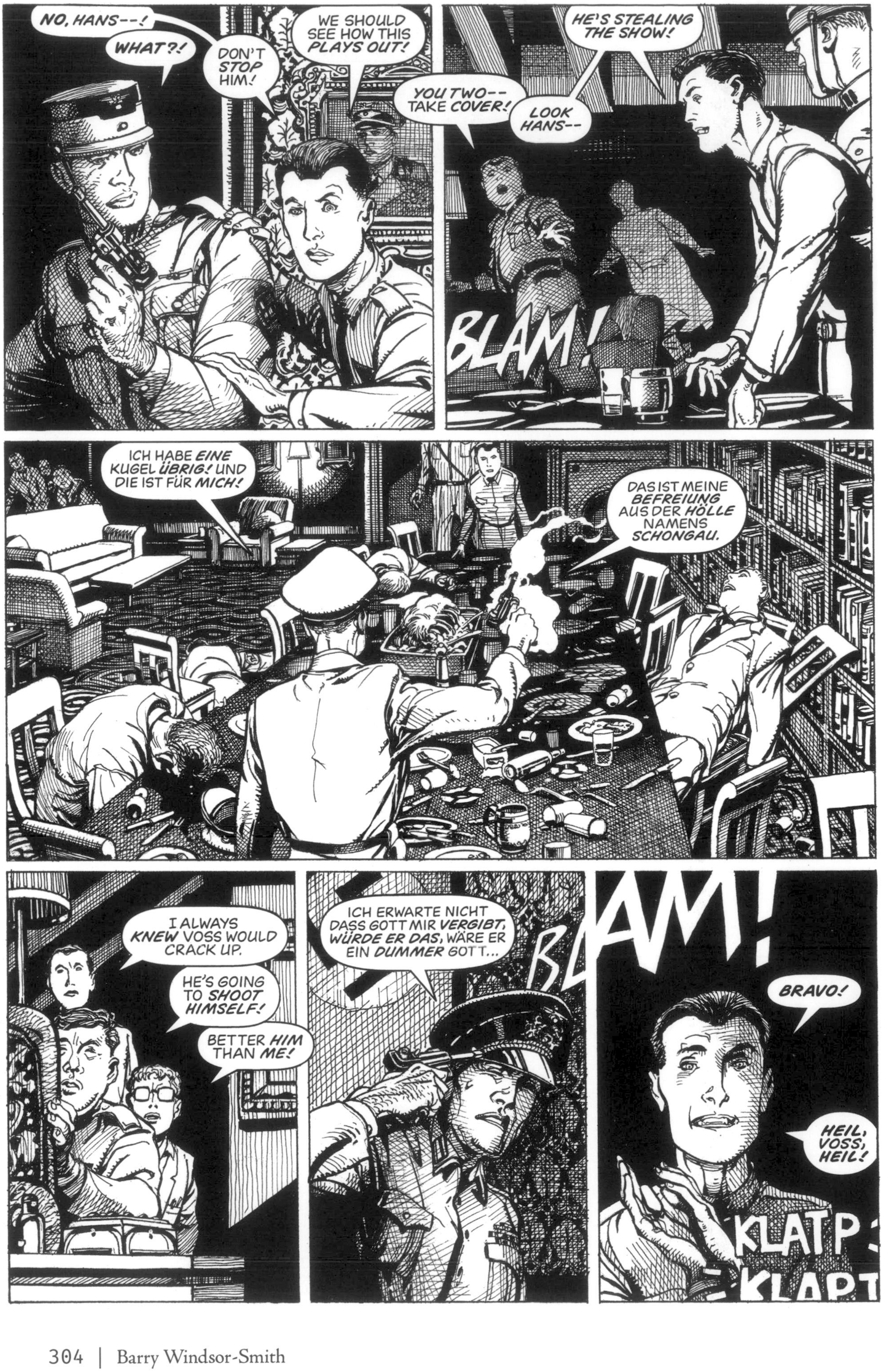
NO, HANS--!
WHAT?!
DON'T STOP HIM!
WE SHOULD SEE HOW THIS PLAYS OUT!
HE'S STEALING THE SHOW!
YOU TWO-- TAKE COVER!
LOOK HANS--
BLAM!
ICH HABE EINE KUGEL ÜBRIG! UND DIE IST FÜR MICH!
DAS IST MEINE BEFREIUNG AUS DER HÖLLE NAMENS SCHONGAU.
I ALWAYS KNEW VOSS WOULD CRACK UP.
HE'S GOING TO SHOOT HIMSELF!
BETTER HIM THAN ME!
ICH ERWARTE NICHT DASS GOTT MIR VERGIBT, WÜRDE ER DAS, WÄRE ER EIN DUMMER GOTT...
BLAM!
BRAVO!
HEIL, VOSS, HEIL!
KLAPT
KLAPT

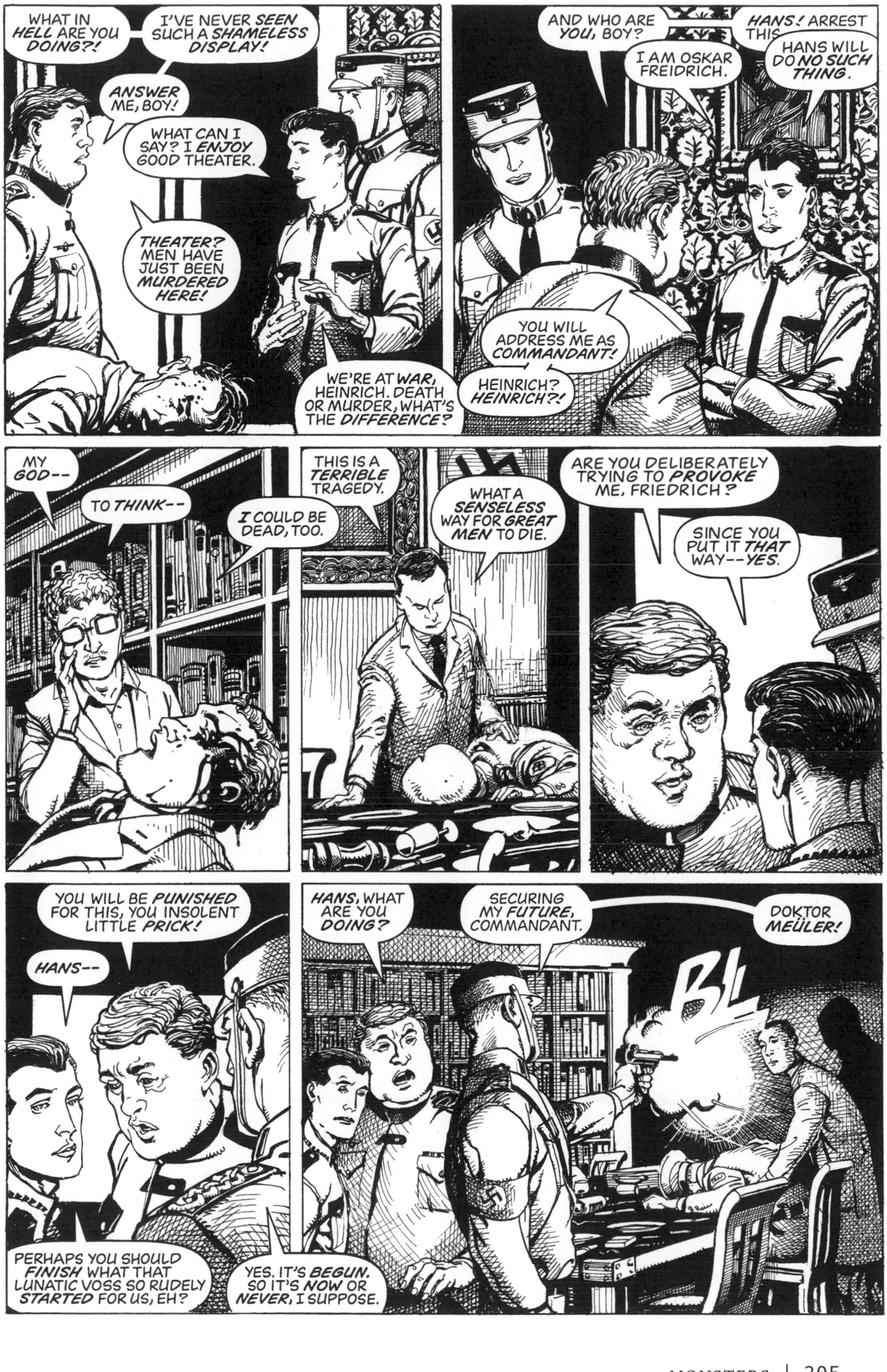
WHAT IN HELL ARE YOU DOING?!
I'VE NEVER SEEN SUCH A SHAMELESS DISPLAY!
ANSWER ME, BOY!
WHAT CAN I SAY? I ENJOY GOOD THEATER.
THEATER? MEN HAVE JUST BEEN MURDERED HERE!
WE'RE AT WAR, HEINRICH. DEATH OR MURDER, WHAT'S THE DIFFERENCE?
AND WHO ARE YOU, BOY?
I AM OSKAR FRIEDRICH.
HANS! ARREST THIS
HANS WILL DO NO SUCH THING.
YOU WILL ADDRESS ME AS COMMANDANT!
HEINRICH? HEINRICH?!
MY GOD--
TO THINK--
I COULD BE DEAD, TOO.
THIS IS A TERRIBLE TRAGEDY.
WHAT A SENSELESS WAY FOR GREAT MEN TO DIE.
ARE YOU DELIBERATELY TRYING TO PROVOKE ME, FRIEDRICH?
SINCE YOU PUT IT THAT WAY--YES.
YOU WILL BE PUNISHED FOR THIS, YOU INSOLENT LITTLE PRICK!
HANS--
PERHAPS YOU SHOULD FINISH WHAT THAT LUNATIC VOSS SO RUDELY STARTED FOR US, EH?
YES. IT'S BEGUN. SO IT'S NOW OR NEVER, I SUPPOSE.
HANS, WHAT ARE YOU DOING?
SECURING MY FUTURE, COMMANDANT.
DOKTOR MEÜLER!
BL

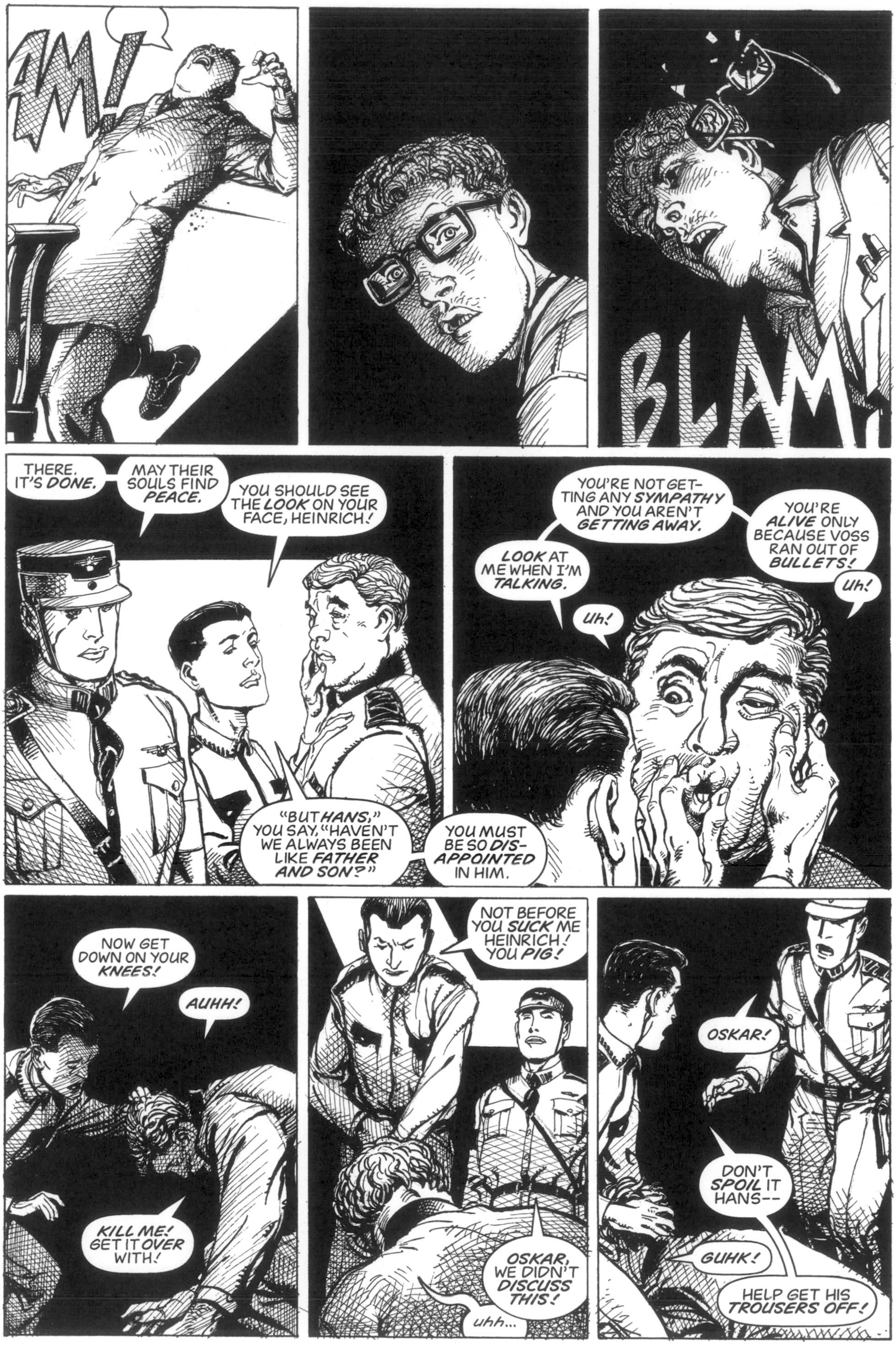
AM!
BLAM!
THERE. IT'S DONE.
MAY THEIR SOULS FIND PEACE.
YOU SHOULD SEE THE LOOK ON YOUR FACE, HEINRICH!
"BUT HANS," YOU SAY, "HAVEN'T WE ALWAYS BEEN LIKE FATHER AND SON?"
YOU MUST BE SO DIS-APPOINTED IN HIM.
YOU'RE NOT GET-TING ANY SYMPATHY AND YOU AREN'T GETTING AWAY.
LOOK AT ME WHEN I'M TALKING.
Uh!
YOU'RE ALIVE ONLY BECAUSE VOSS RAN OUT OF BULLETS!
Uh!
NOW GET DOWN ON YOUR KNEES!
AUHH!
KILL ME! GET IT OVER WITH!
NOT BEFORE YOU SUCK ME HEINRICH! YOU PIG!
OSKAR, WE DIDN'T DISCUSS THIS!
uhh...
OSKAR!
DON'T SPOIL IT HANS--
GUHK!
HELP GET HIS TROUSERS OFF!

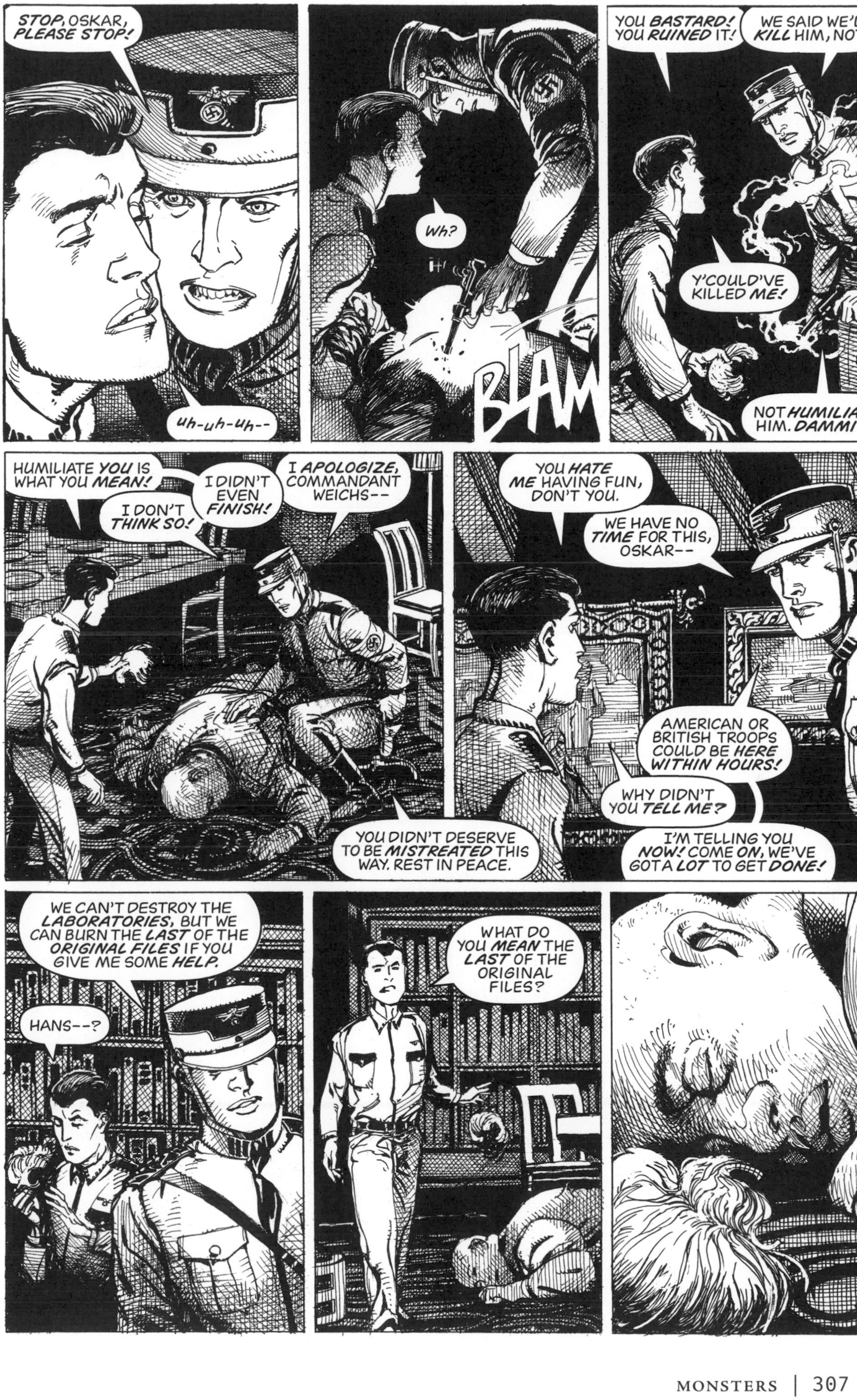

STOP, OSKAR, PLEASE STOP!
uh-uh-uh--
Wh?
BLAM
YOU BASTARD! YOU RUINED IT!
WE SAID WE'D KILL HIM, NOT--
Y'COULD'VE KILLED ME!
NOT HUMILIATE HIM. DAMMIT!
HUMILIATE YOU IS WHAT YOU MEAN!
I DON'T THINK SO!
I DIDN'T EVEN FINISH!
I APOLOGIZE, COMMANDANT WEICHS--
YOU DIDN'T DESERVE TO BE MISTREATED THIS WAY. REST IN PEACE.
YOU HATE ME HAVING FUN, DON'T YOU.
WE HAVE NO TIME FOR THIS, OSKAR--
AMERICAN OR BRITISH TROOPS COULD BE HERE WITHIN HOURS!
WHY DIDN'T YOU TELL ME?
I'M TELLING YOU NOW! COME ON, WE'VE GOT A LOT TO GET DONE!
WE CAN'T DESTROY THE LABORATORIES, BUT WE CAN BURN THE LAST OF THE ORIGINAL FILES IF YOU GIVE ME SOME HELP.
HANS--?
WHAT DO YOU MEAN THE LAST OF THE ORIGINAL FILES?

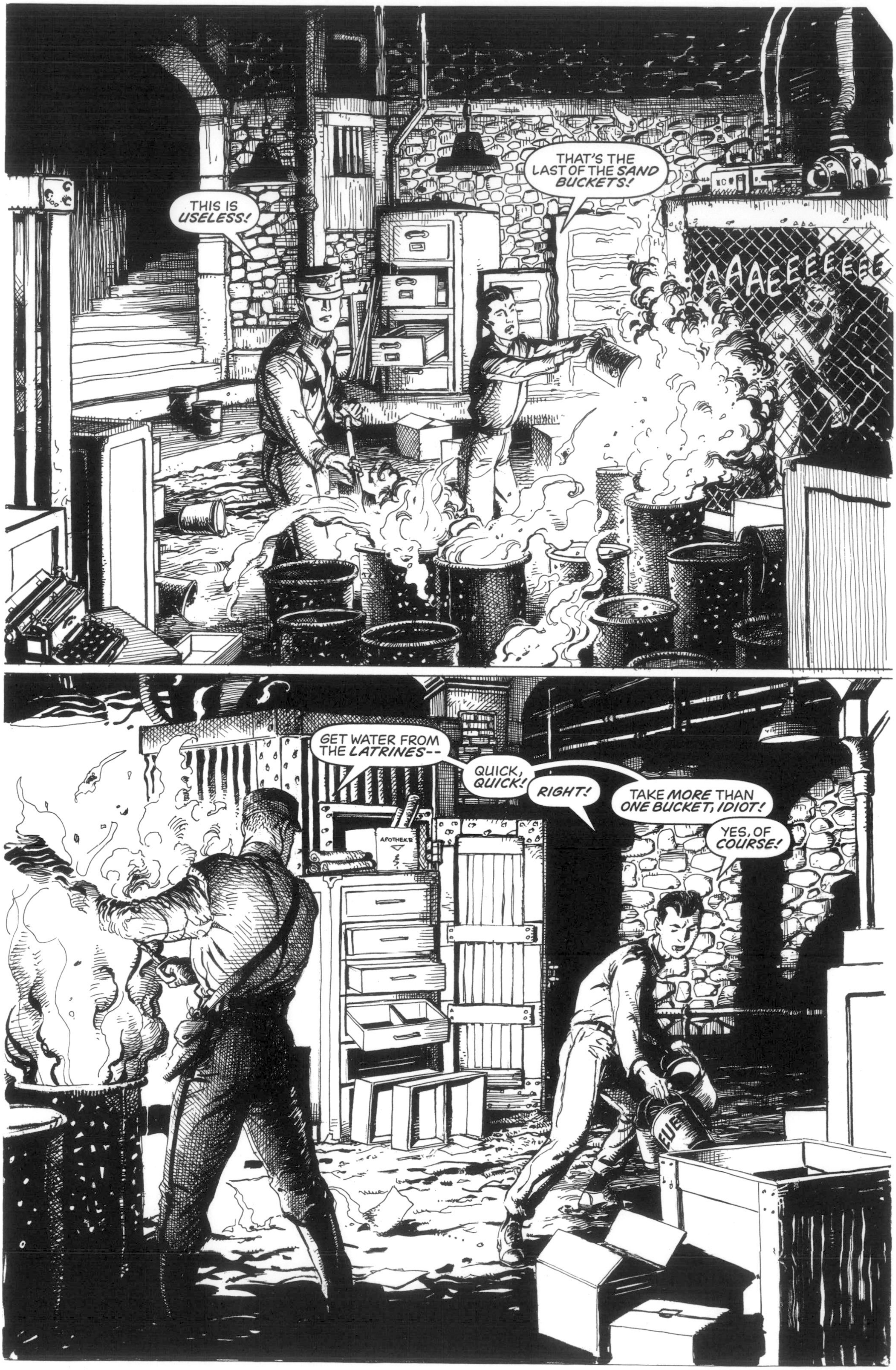
THIS IS USELESS!
THAT'S THE LAST OF THE SAND BUCKETS!
AAAEEEEEEE
GET WATER FROM THE LATRINES--
QUICK, QUICK!
RIGHT!
TAKE MORE THAN ONE BUCKET, IDIOT!
YES, OF COURSE!
APOTHEKE

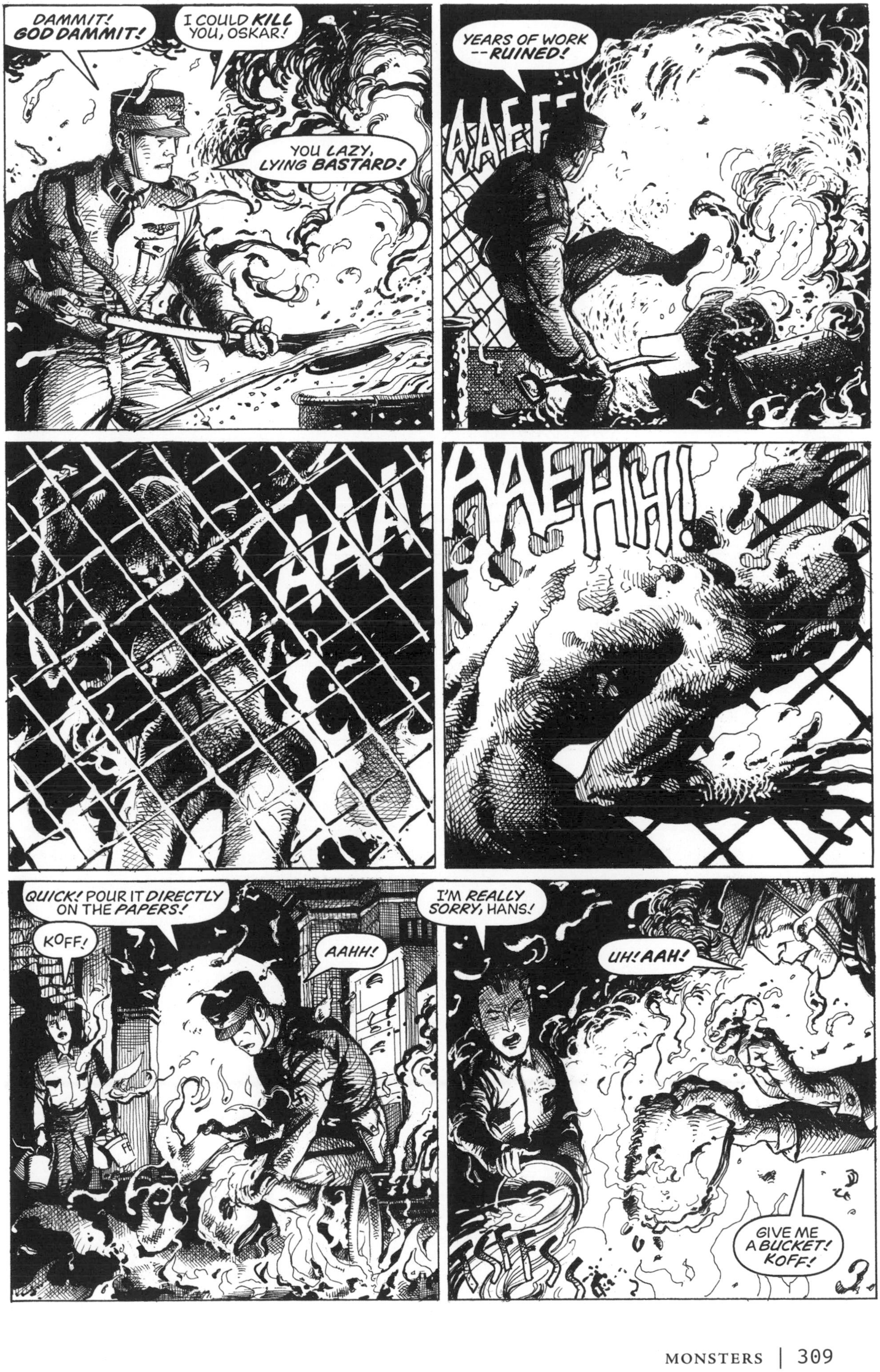
DAMMIT! GOD DAMMIT!
I COULD KILL YOU, OSKAR!
YOU LAZY, LYING BASTARD!
YEARS OF WORK --RUINED!
AAEEE
AAAAAEHH!
QUICK! POUR IT DIRECTLY ON THE PAPERS!
KOFF!
AAHH!
I'M REALLY SORRY, HANS!
UH! AAH!
TSSSSS
GIVE ME A BUCKET! KOFF!

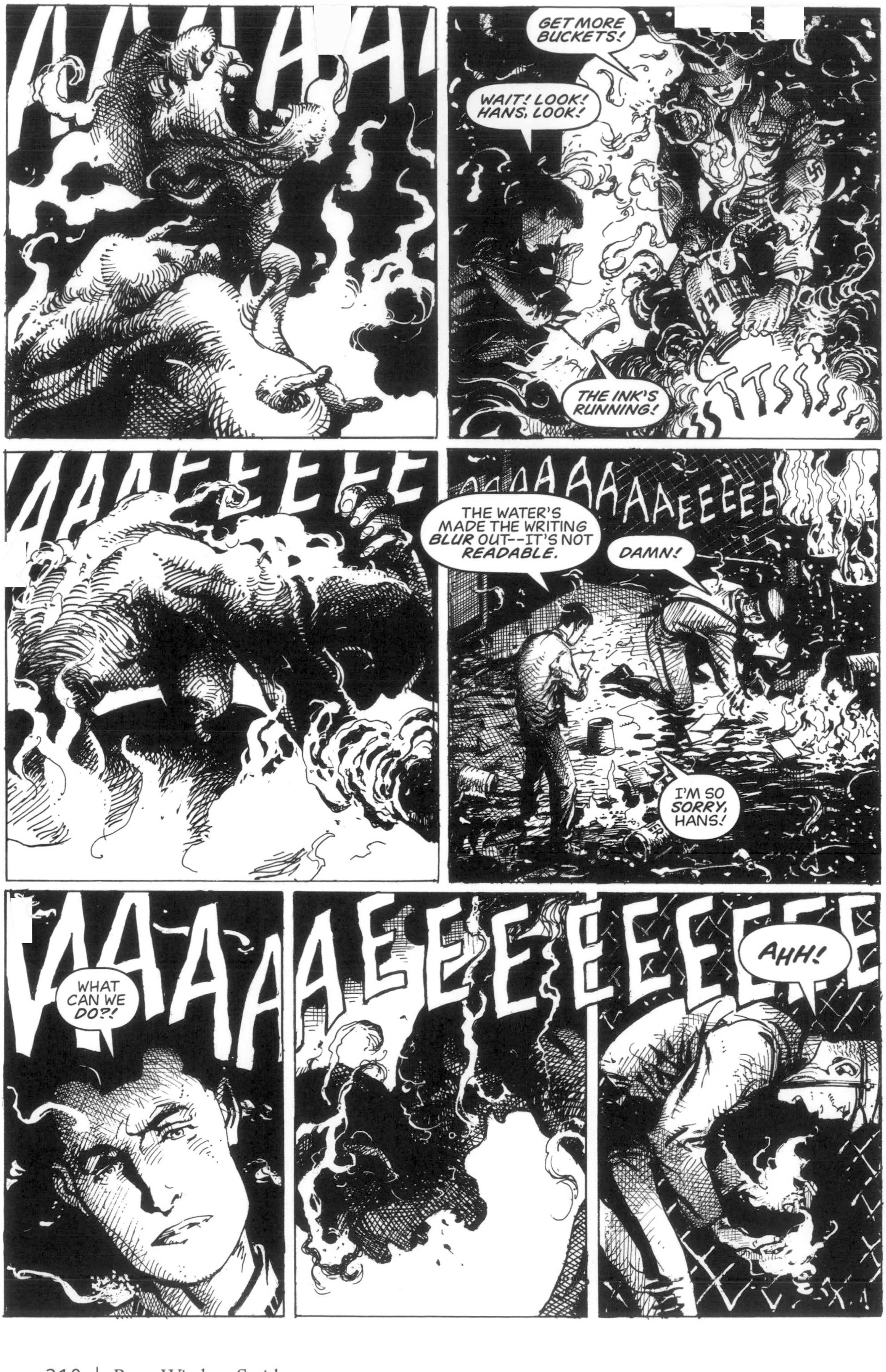
AAAAAH
GET MORE BUCKETS!
WAIT! LOOK! HANS, LOOK!
THE INK'S RUNNING!
TTSSSSS
AAAEEEE
AAAAAAEEEEEE
THE WATER'S MADE THE WRITING BLUR OUT--IT'S NOT READABLE.
DAMN!
I'M SO SORRY, HANS!
AAAAAEEEEEEEEE
WHAT CAN WE DO?!
AHH!

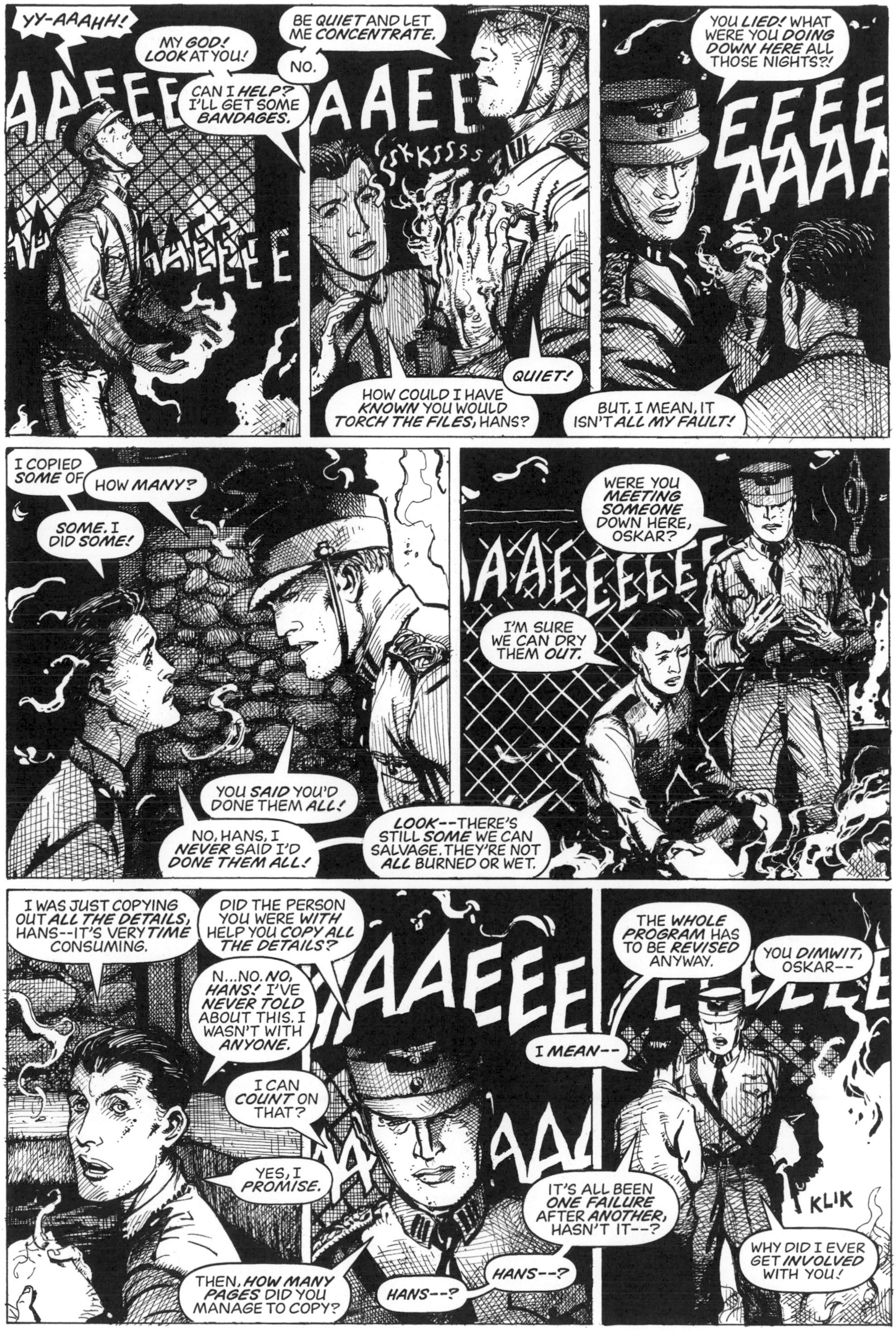
YY-AAAHH!
MY GOD! LOOK AT YOU!
CAN I HELP? I'LL GET SOME BANDAGES.
AAEEE
BE QUIET AND LET ME CONCENTRATE.
NO.
AAEE
SSKKSSSS
HOW COULD I HAVE KNOWN YOU WOULD TORCH THE FILES, HANS?
QUIET!
YOU LIED! WHAT WERE YOU DOING DOWN HERE ALL THOSE NIGHTS?!
EEEE AAAA
BUT, I MEAN, IT ISN'T ALL MY FAULT!
I COPIED SOME OF
HOW MANY?
SOME. I DID SOME!
YOU SAID YOU'D DONE THEM ALL!
NO, HANS, I NEVER SAID I'D DONE THEM ALL!
LOOK--THERE'S STILL SOME WE CAN SALVAGE. THEY'RE NOT ALL BURNED OR WET.
WERE YOU MEETING SOMEONE DOWN HERE, OSKAR?
AAAEEEEEE
I'M SURE WE CAN DRY THEM OUT.
I WAS JUST COPYING OUT ALL THE DETAILS, HANS--IT'S VERY TIME CONSUMING.
DID THE PERSON YOU WERE WITH HELP YOU COPY ALL THE DETAILS?
N...NO. NO, HANS! I'VE NEVER TOLD ABOUT THIS. I WASN'T WITH ANYONE.
AAAEEE
I CAN COUNT ON THAT?
YES, I PROMISE.
THEN, HOW MANY PAGES DID YOU MANAGE TO COPY?
HANS--?
HANS--?
IT'S ALL BEEN ONE FAILURE AFTER ANOTHER, HASN'T IT--?
THE WHOLE PROGRAM HAS TO BE REVISED ANYWAY.
I MEAN--
YOU DIMWIT, OSKAR--
KLIK
WHY DID I EVER GET INVOLVED WITH YOU!

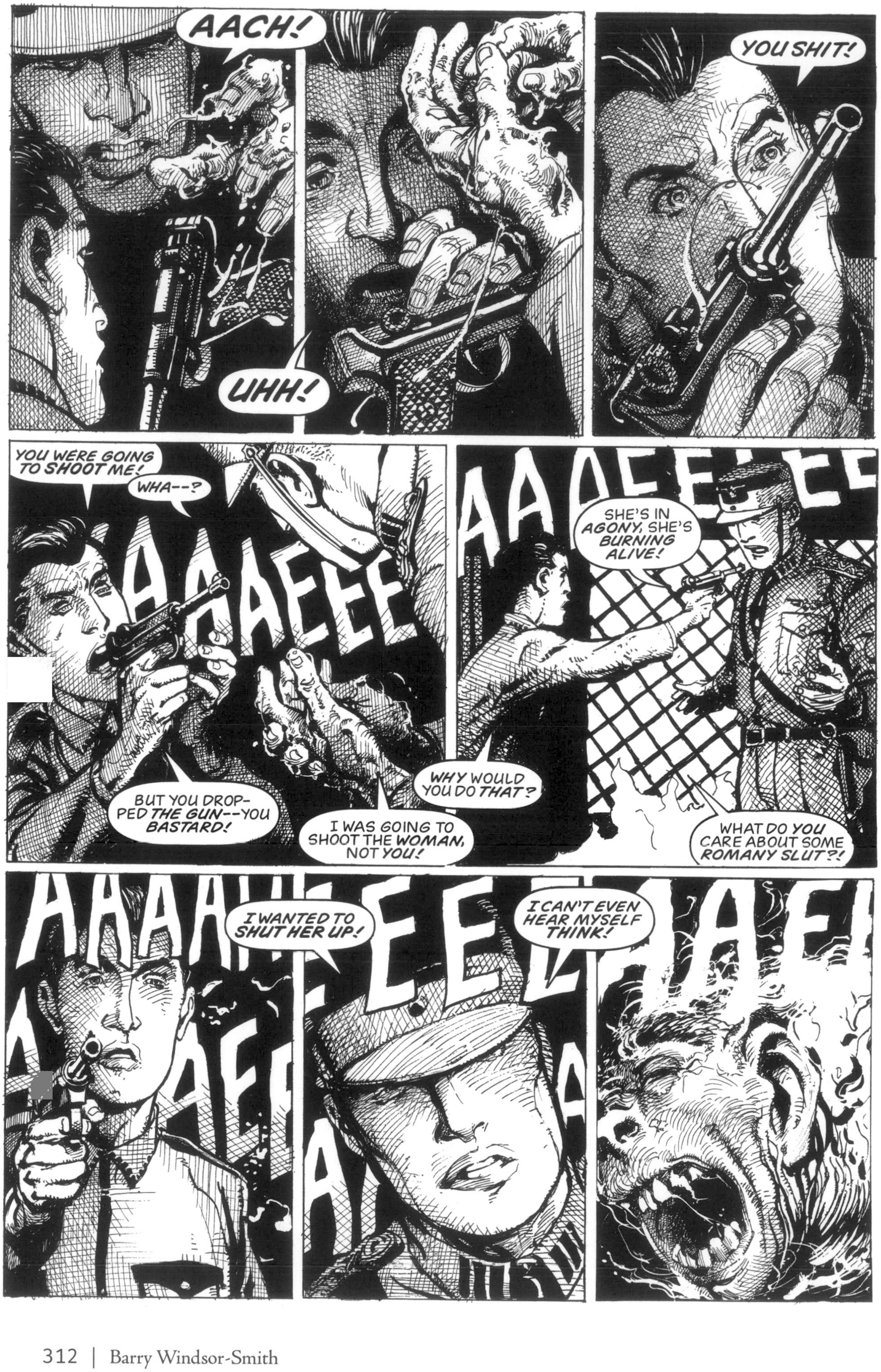
AACH!
UHH!
YOU SHIT!
YOU WERE GOING TO SHOOT ME!
WHA--?
AAEEE
BUT YOU DROP-PED THE GUN--YOU BASTARD!
I WAS GOING TO SHOOT THE WOMAN, NOT YOU!
WHY WOULD YOU DO THAT?
SHE'S IN AGONY, SHE'S BURNING ALIVE!
WHAT DO YOU CARE ABOUT SOME ROMANY SLUT?!
I WANTED TO SHUT HER UP!
I CAN'T EVEN HEAR MYSELF THINK!

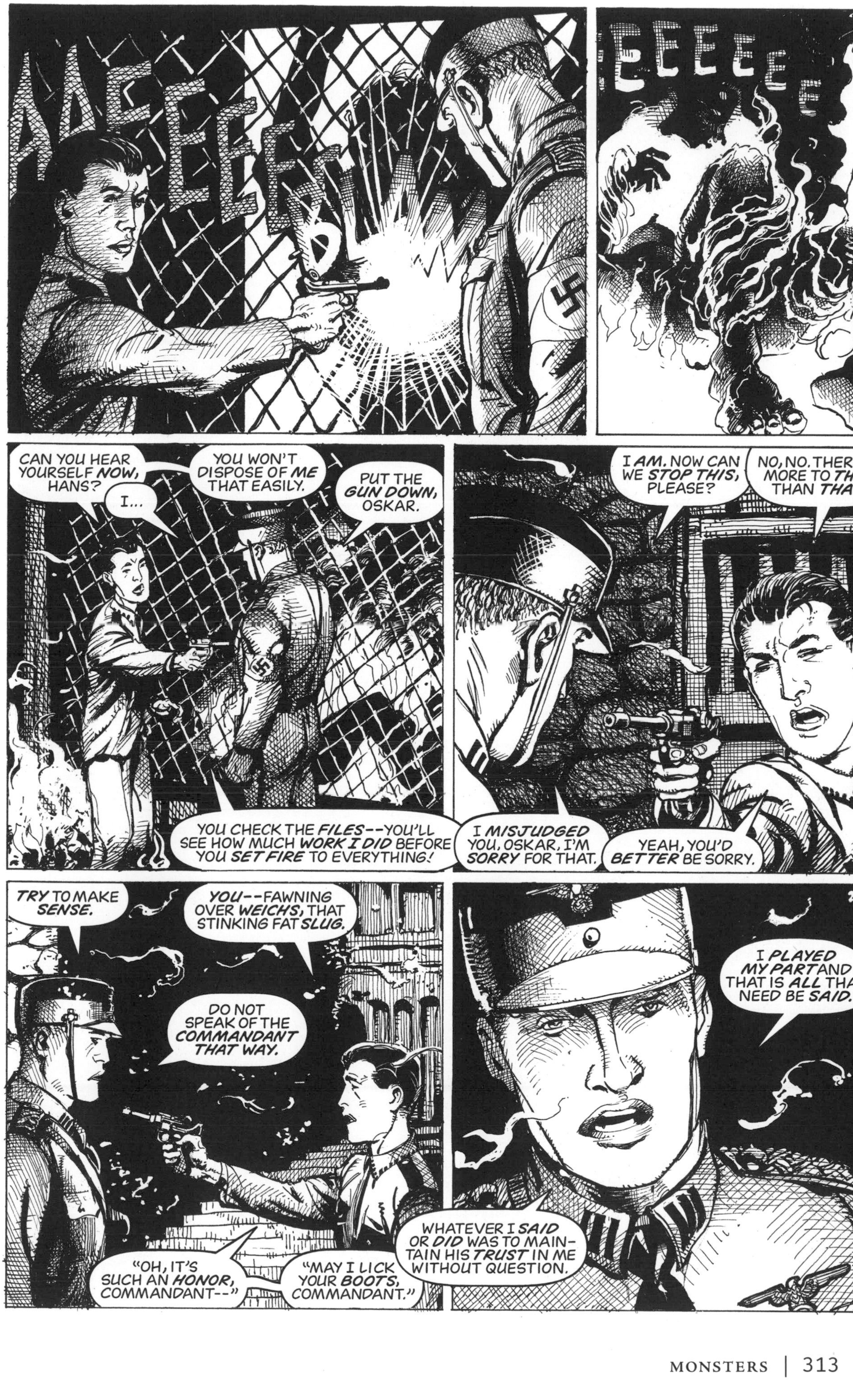
AAEEEEE
BLAM
EEEEEE
CAN YOU HEAR YOURSELF NOW, HANS?
I...
YOU WON'T DISPOSE OF ME THAT EASILY.
PUT THE GUN DOWN, OSKAR.
YOU CHECK THE FILES--YOU'LL SEE HOW MUCH WORK I DID BEFORE YOU SET FIRE TO EVERYTHING!
I AM. NOW CAN WE STOP THIS, PLEASE?
NO, NO. THERE'S MORE TO THIS THAN THAT.
I MISJUDGED YOU, OSKAR. I'M SORRY FOR THAT.
YEAH, YOU'D BETTER BE SORRY.
TRY TO MAKE SENSE.
YOU--FAWNING OVER WEICHS, THAT STINKING FAT SLUG.
DO NOT SPEAK OF THE COMMANDANT THAT WAY.
"OH, IT'S SUCH AN HONOR, COMMANDANT--"
"MAY I LICK YOUR BOOTS, COMMANDANT."
I PLAYED MY PART AND THAT IS ALL THAT NEED BE SAID.
WHATEVER I SAID OR DID WAS TO MAINTAIN HIS TRUST IN ME WITHOUT QUESTION.

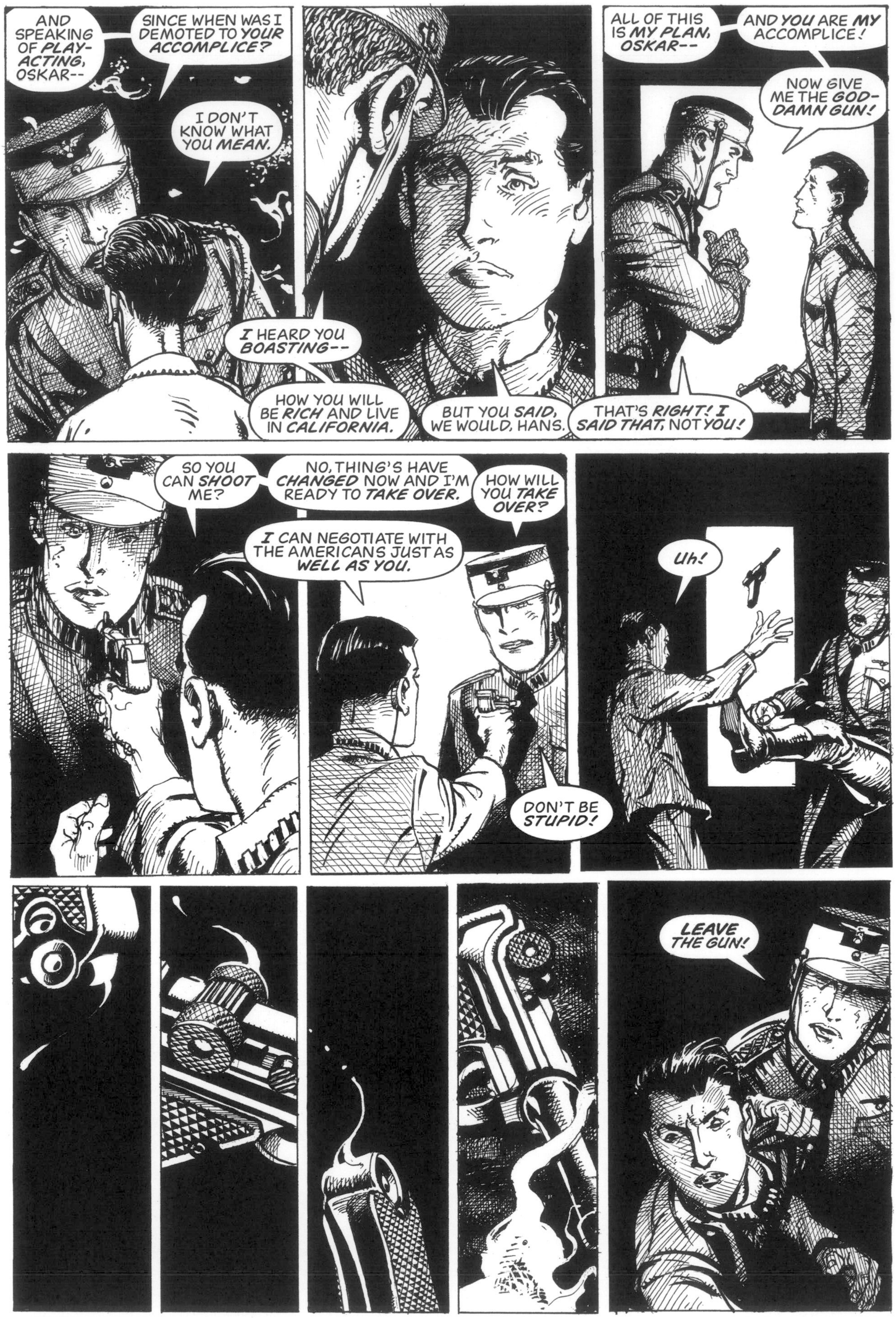
AND SPEAKING OF PLAY-ACTING, OSKAR--
SINCE WHEN WAS I DEMOTED TO YOUR ACCOMPLICE?
I DON'T KNOW WHAT YOU MEAN.
I HEARD YOU BOASTING--
HOW YOU WILL BE RICH AND LIVE IN CALIFORNIA.
BUT YOU SAID, WE WOULD, HANS.
ALL OF THIS IS MY PLAN, OSKAR--
AND YOU ARE MY ACCOMPLICE!
NOW GIVE ME THE GOD-DAMN GUN!
THAT'S RIGHT! I SAID THAT, NOT YOU!
SO YOU CAN SHOOT ME?
NO, THING'S HAVE CHANGED NOW AND I'M READY TO TAKE OVER.
HOW WILL YOU TAKE OVER?
I CAN NEGOTIATE WITH THE AMERICANS JUST AS WELL AS YOU.
DON'T BE STUPID!
Uh!
LEAVE THE GUN!

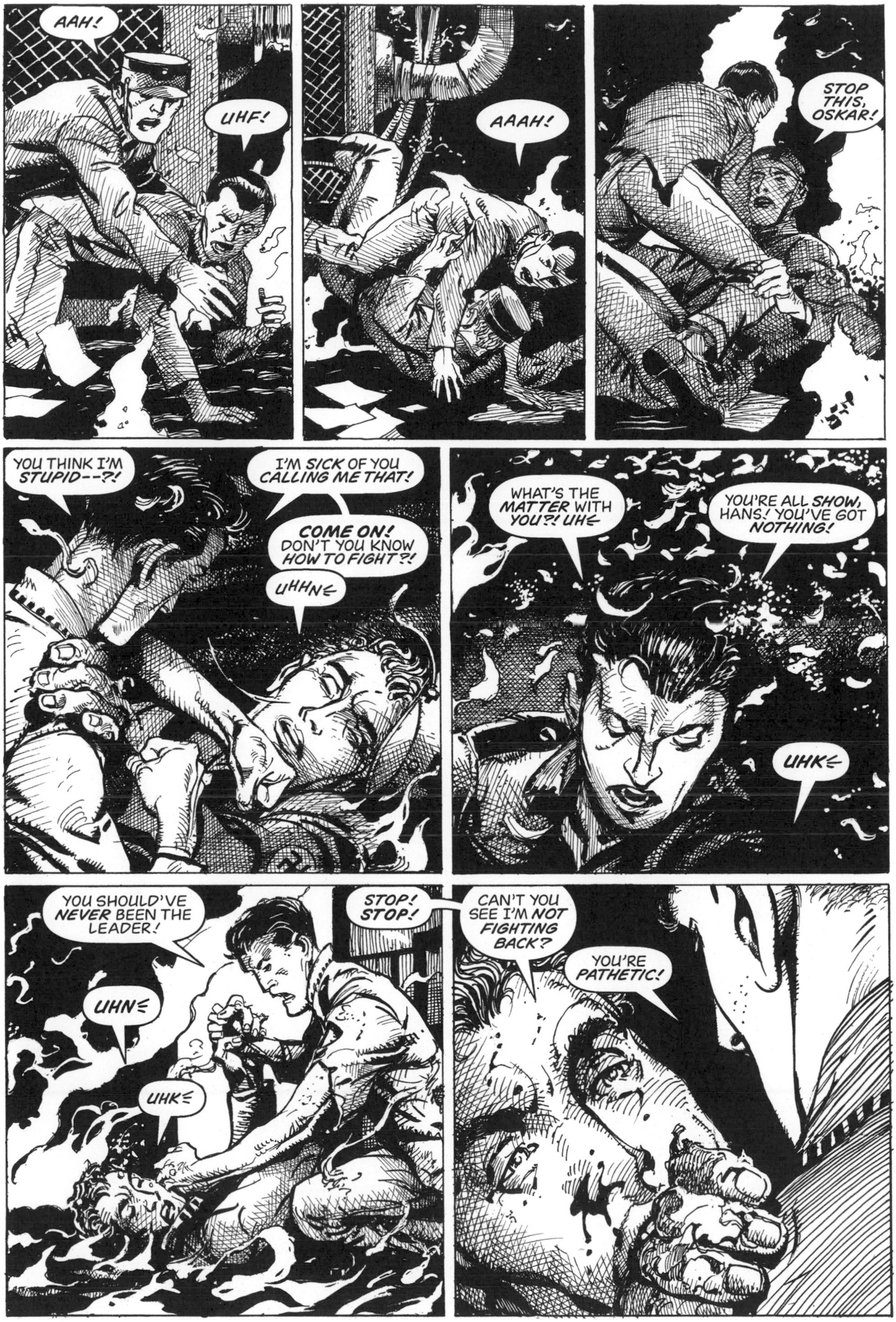
AAH!
UHF!
AAAH!
STOP THIS, OSKAR!
YOU THINK I'M STUPID--?!
I'M SICK OF YOU CALLING ME THAT!
COME ON! DON'T YOU KNOW HOW TO FIGHT?!
UHHN
WHAT'S THE MATTER WITH YOU?! UH
YOU'RE ALL SHOW, HANS! YOU'VE GOT NOTHING!
UHK
YOU SHOULD'VE NEVER BEEN THE LEADER!
UHN
UHK
STOP! STOP!
CAN'T YOU SEE I'M NOT FIGHTING BACK?
YOU'RE PATHETIC!

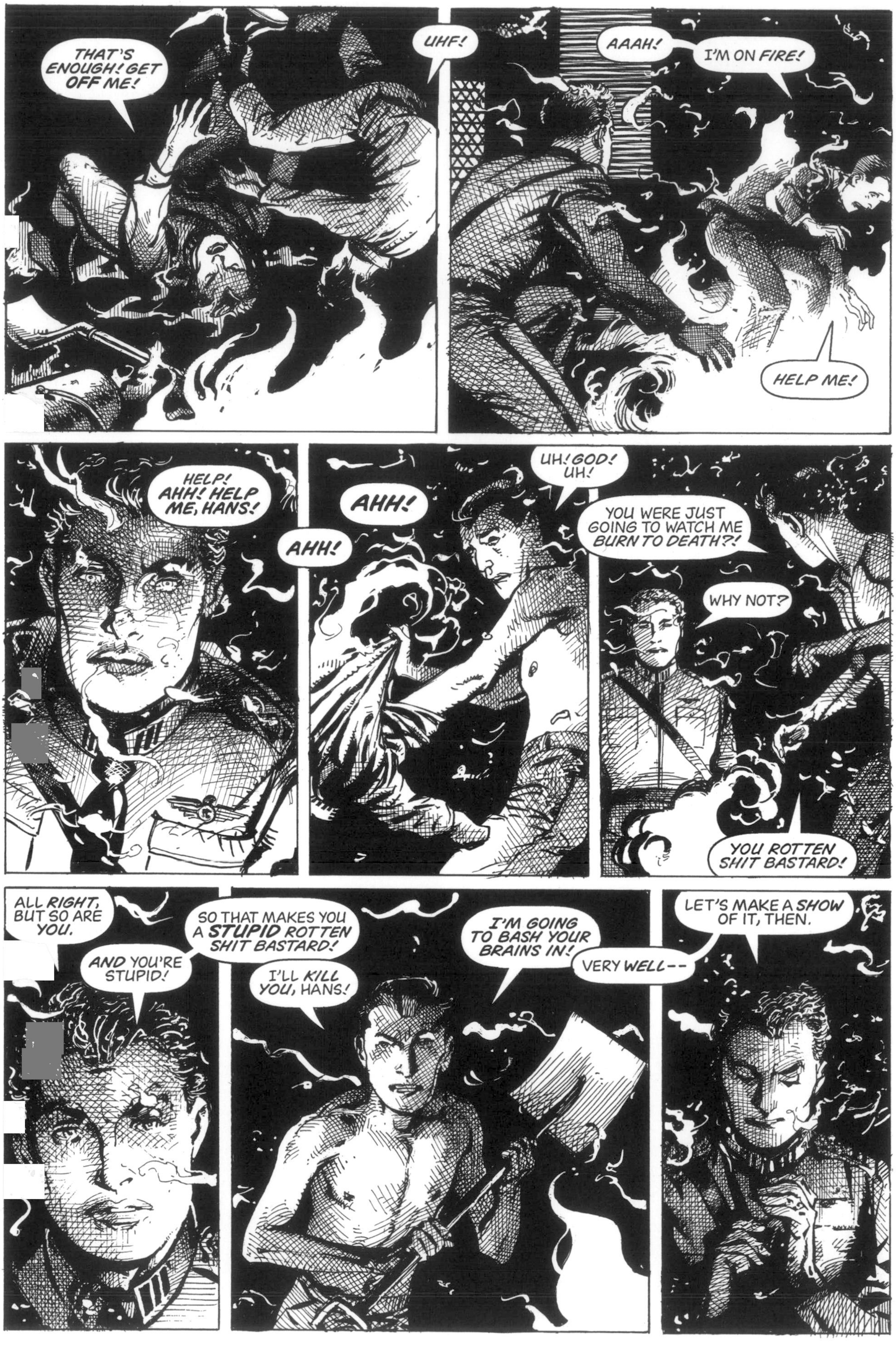
THAT'S ENOUGH! GET OFF ME!
UHF!
AAAH!
I'M ON FIRE!
HELP ME!
HELP! AHH! HELP ME, HANS!
AHH!
AHH!
UH! GOD! UH!
YOU WERE JUST GOING TO WATCH ME BURN TO DEATH?!
WHY NOT?
YOU ROTTEN SHIT BASTARD!
ALL RIGHT, BUT SO ARE YOU.
SO THAT MAKES YOU A STUPID ROTTEN SHIT BASTARD!
AND YOU'RE STUPID!
I'LL KILL YOU, HANS!
I'M GOING TO BASH YOUR BRAINS IN!
VERY WELL--
LET'S MAKE A SHOW OF IT, THEN.

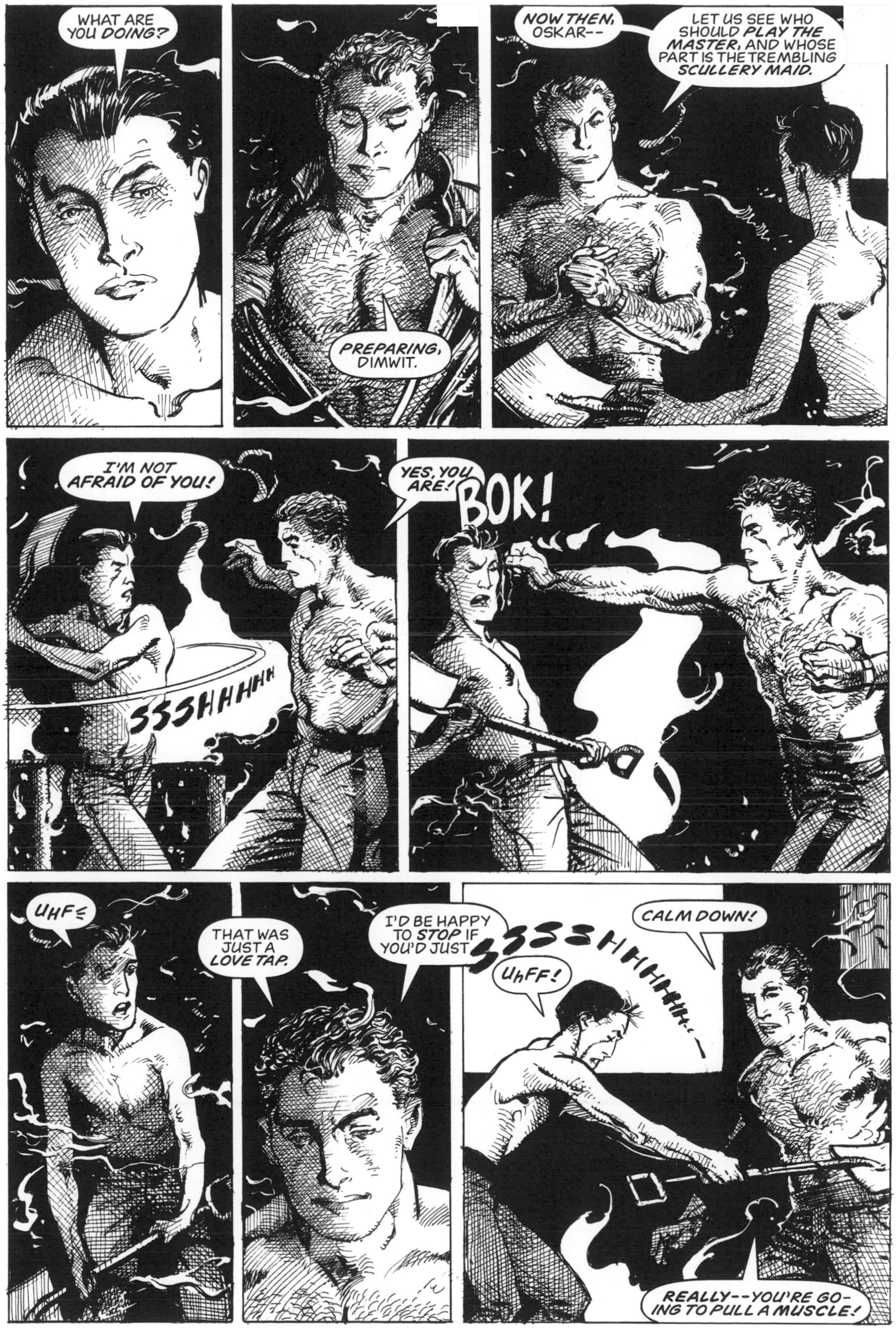
WHAT ARE YOU DOING?
PREPARING, DIMWIT.
NOW THEN, OSKAR--
LET US SEE WHO SHOULD PLAY THE MASTER, AND WHOSE PART IS THE TREMBLING SCULLERY MAID.
I'M NOT AFRAID OF YOU!
SSSHHHHH
YES, YOU ARE!
BOK!
UHF
THAT WAS JUST A LOVE TAP.
I'D BE HAPPY TO STOP IF YOU'D JUST
SSSSHHHHHHHH...
CALM DOWN!
UhFF!
REALLY--YOU'RE GOING TO PULL A MUSCLE!

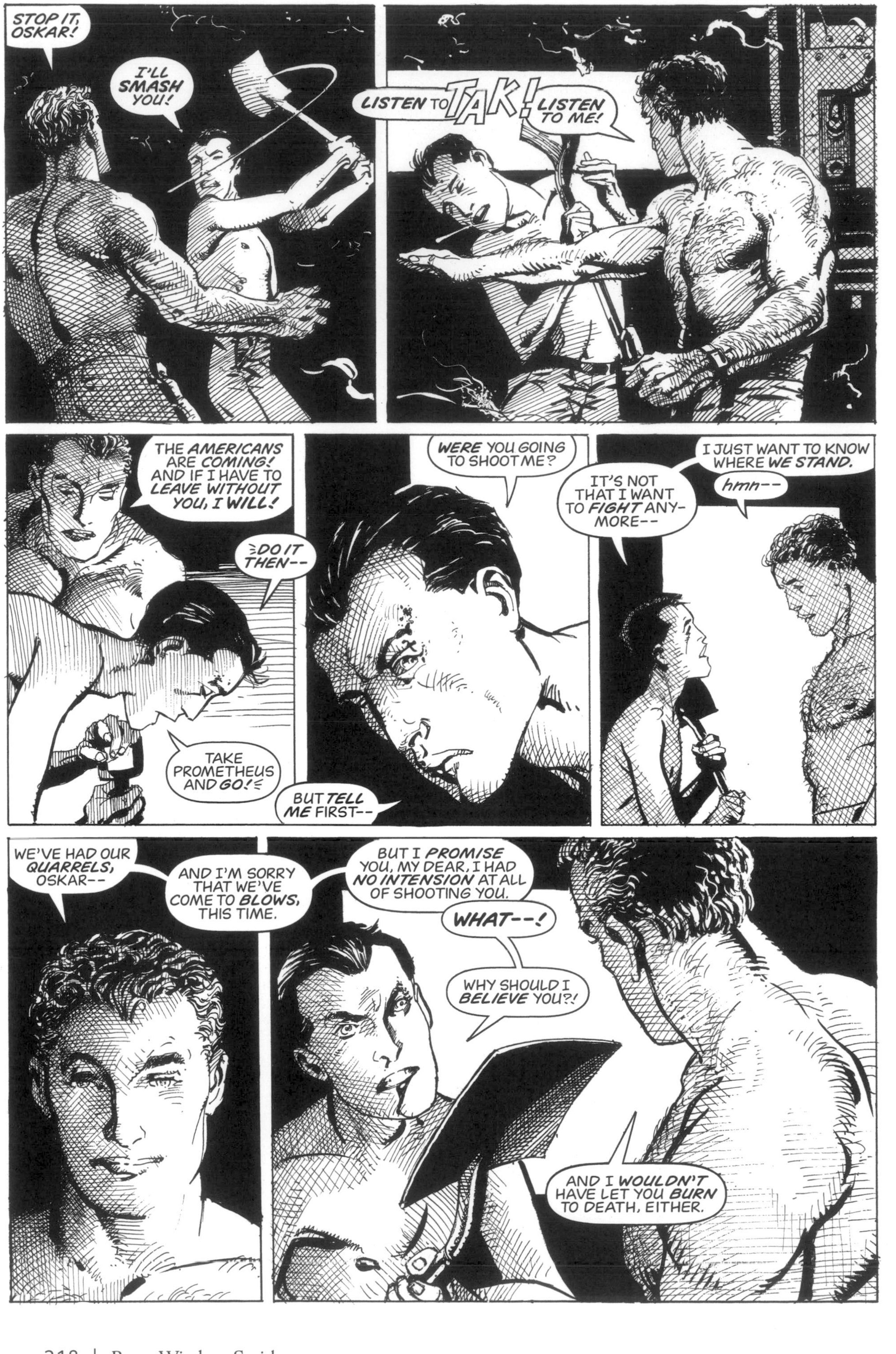
STOP IT, OSKAR!
I'LL SMASH YOU!
LISTEN TO
TAK!
LISTEN TO ME!
THE AMERICANS ARE COMING! AND IF I HAVE TO LEAVE WITHOUT YOU, I WILL!
DO IT THEN--
TAKE PROMETHEUS AND GO!
WERE YOU GOING TO SHOOT ME?
BUT TELL ME FIRST--
IT'S NOT THAT I WANT TO FIGHT ANY-MORE--
I JUST WANT TO KNOW WHERE WE STAND.
hmn--
WE'VE HAD OUR QUARRELS, OSKAR--
AND I'M SORRY THAT WE'VE COME TO BLOWS, THIS TIME.
BUT I PROMISE YOU, MY DEAR, I HAD NO INTENSION AT ALL OF SHOOTING YOU.
WHAT--!
WHY SHOULD I BELIEVE YOU?!
AND I WOULDN'T HAVE LET YOU BURN TO DEATH, EITHER.

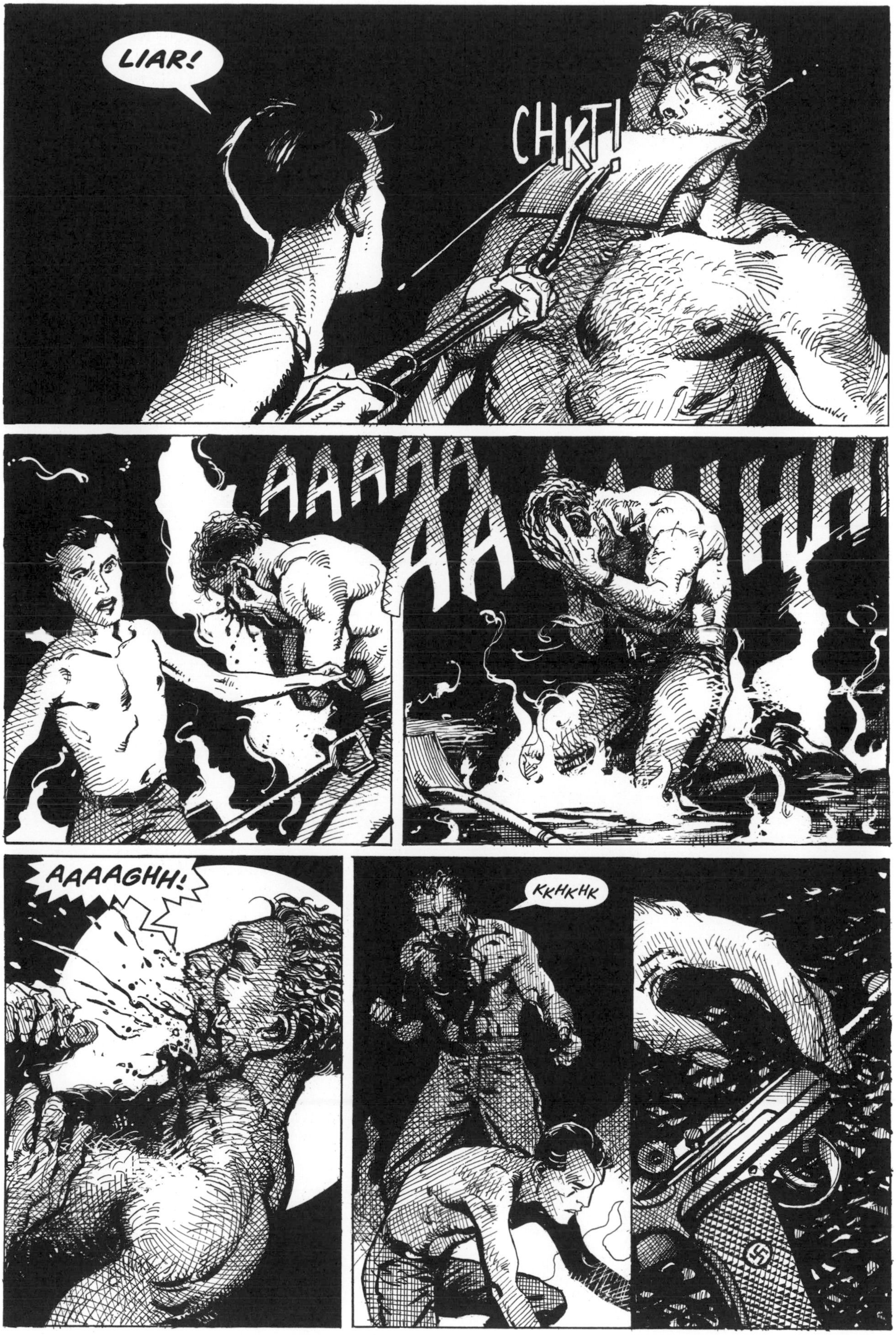
LIAR!
CHKT!
AAAAAAAHHH
AAAAGHH!
KKHKHK

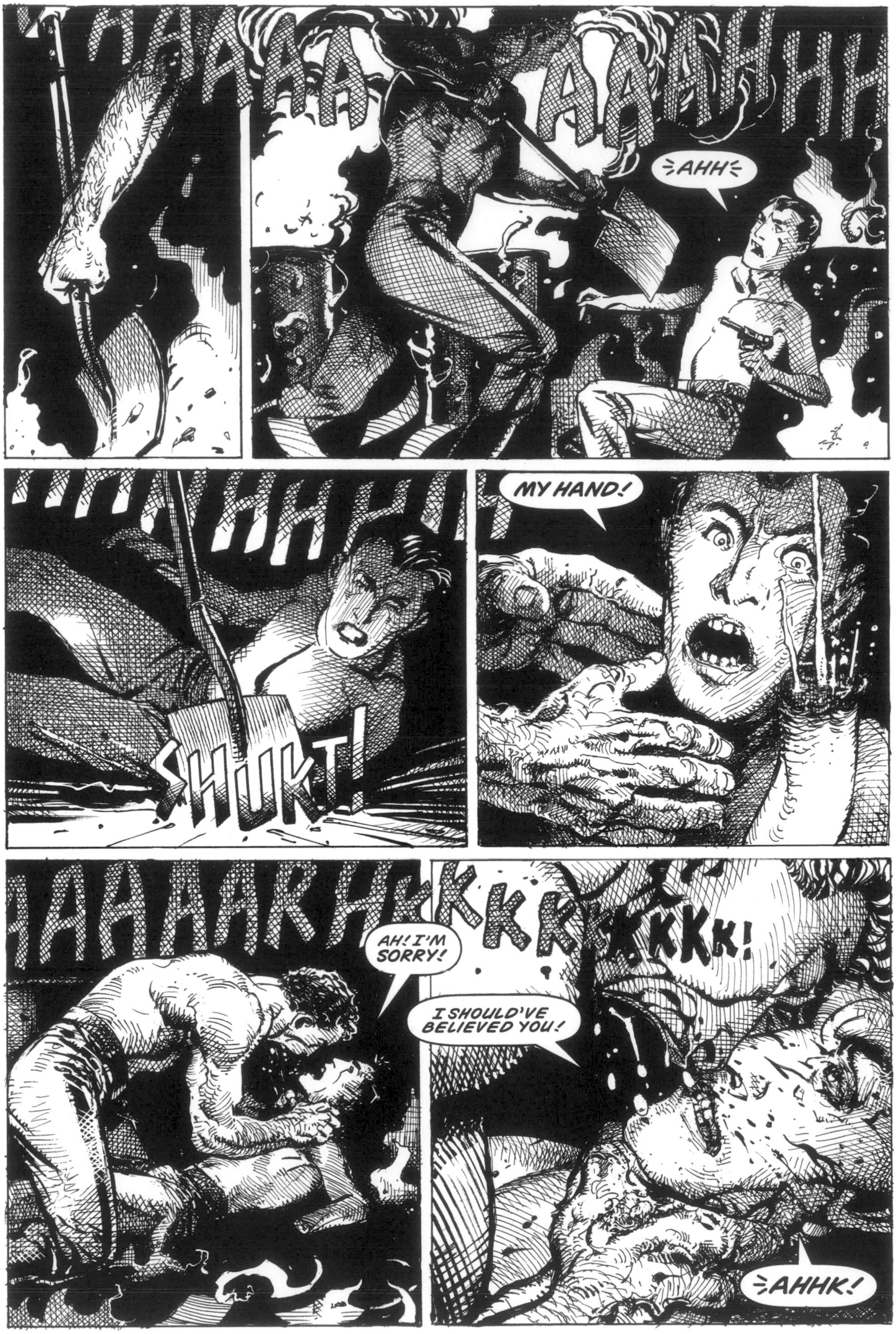

AAAAAAAAAHHH
AHH
HHHHHHHHH
SHUKT!
MY HAND!
AAAAARRHHKKKKKKKK!
AH! I'M SORRY!
I SHOULD'VE BELIEVED YOU!
AHHK!

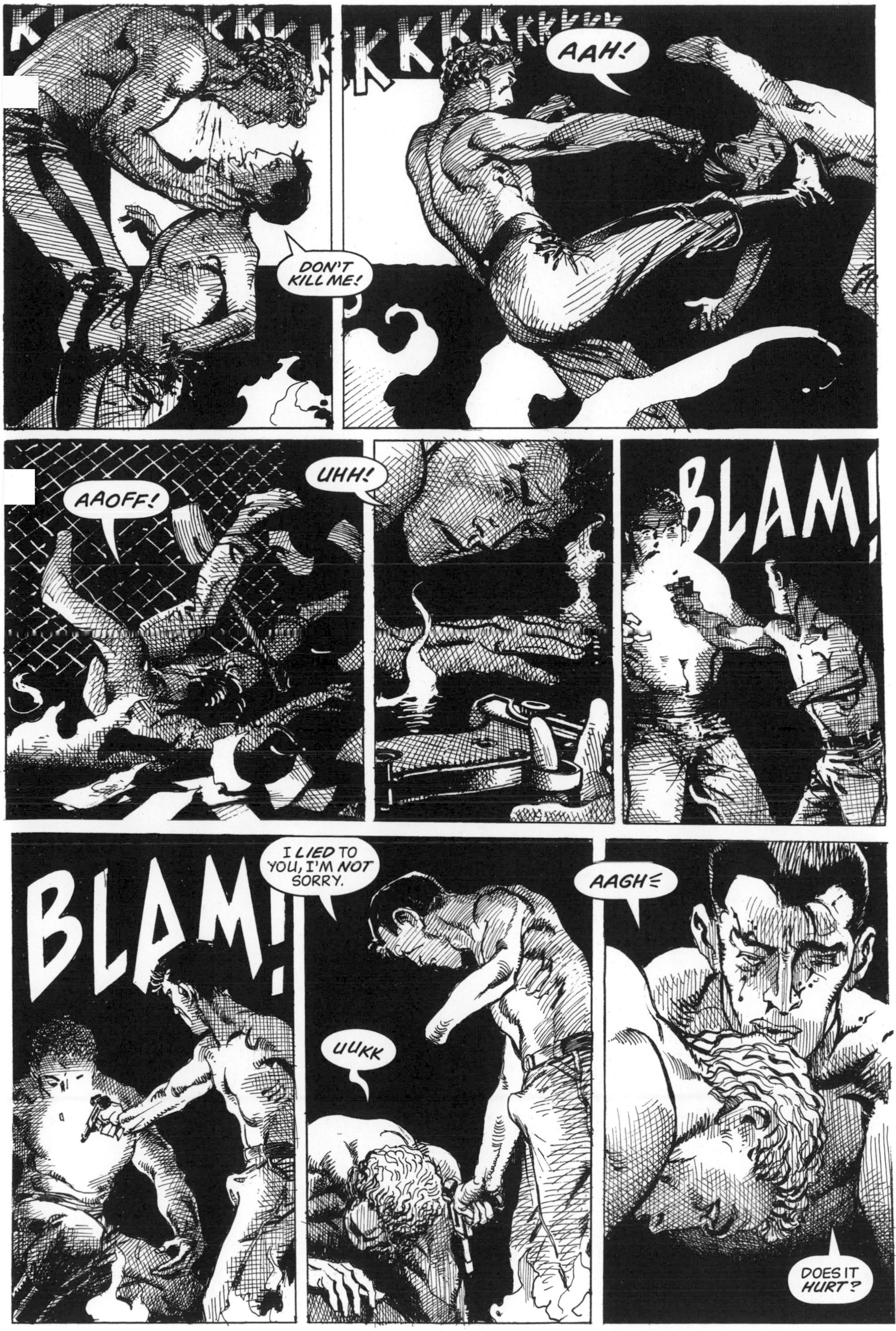
DON'T KILL ME!
KKKKKkkkkk
AAH!
AAOFF!
UHH!
BLAM!
BLAM!
I LIED TO YOU, I'M NOT SORRY.
UUKK
AAGH
DOES IT HURT?

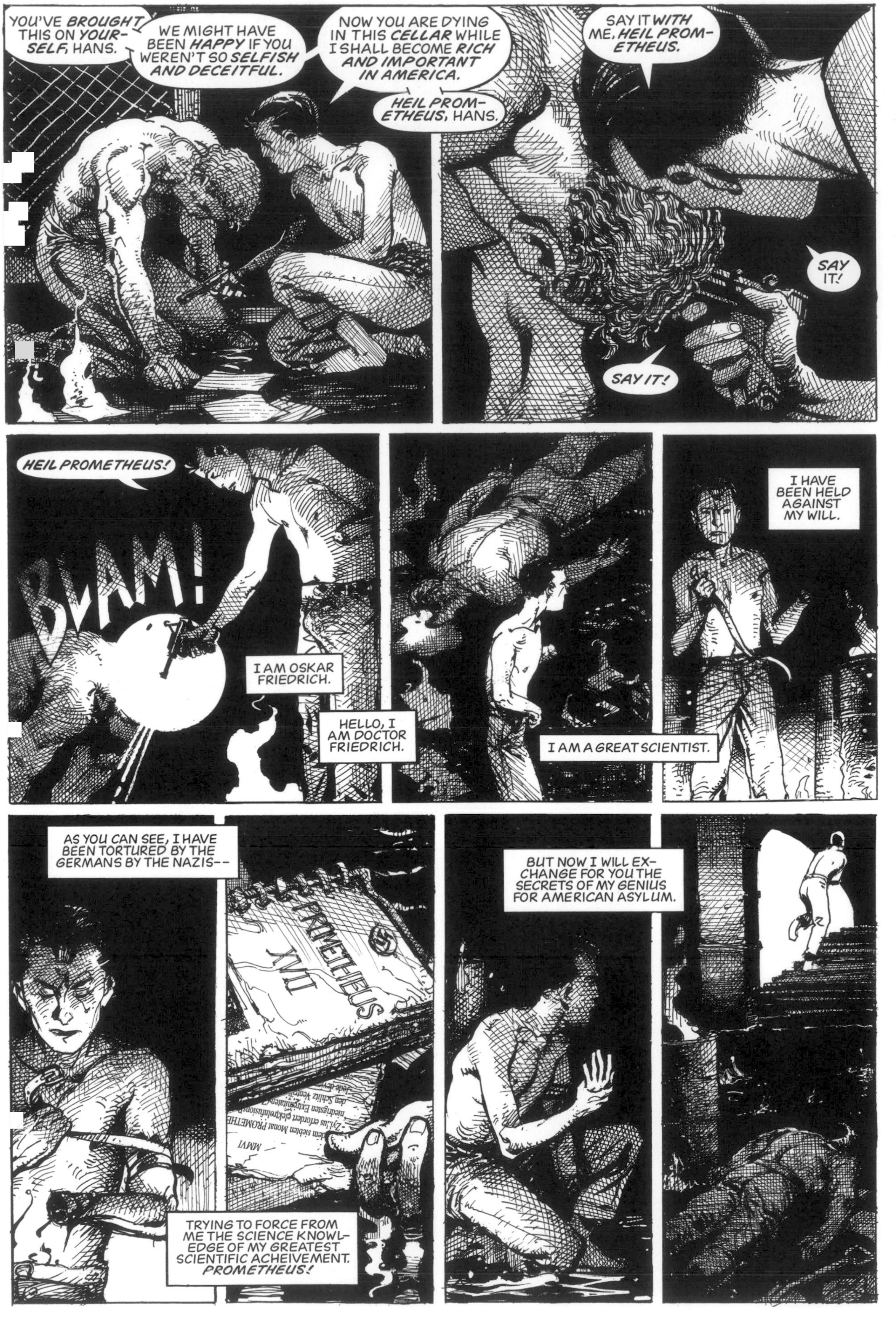

YOU'VE BROUGHT THIS ON YOURSELF, HANS.
WE MIGHT HAVE BEEN HAPPY IF YOU WEREN'T SO SELFISH AND DECEITFUL.
NOW YOU ARE DYING IN THIS CELLAR WHILE I SHALL BECOME RICH AND IMPORTANT IN AMERICA.
HEIL PROMETHEUS, HANS.
SAY IT WITH ME, HEIL PROMETHEUS.
SAY IT!
SAY IT!
HEIL PROMETHEUS!
BLAM!
I AM OSKAR FRIEDRICH.
HELLO, I AM DOCTOR FRIEDRICH.
I AM A GREAT SCIENTIST.
I HAVE BEEN HELD AGAINST MY WILL.
AS YOU CAN SEE, I HAVE BEEN TORTURED BY THE GERMANS BY THE NAZIS--
PROMETHEUS
XVII
TRYING TO FORCE FROM ME THE SCIENCE KNOWLEDGE OF MY GREATEST SCIENTIFIC ACHEIVEMENT. PROMETHEUS!
BUT NOW I WILL EXCHANGE FOR YOU THE SECRETS OF MY GENIUS FOR AMERICAN ASYLUM.

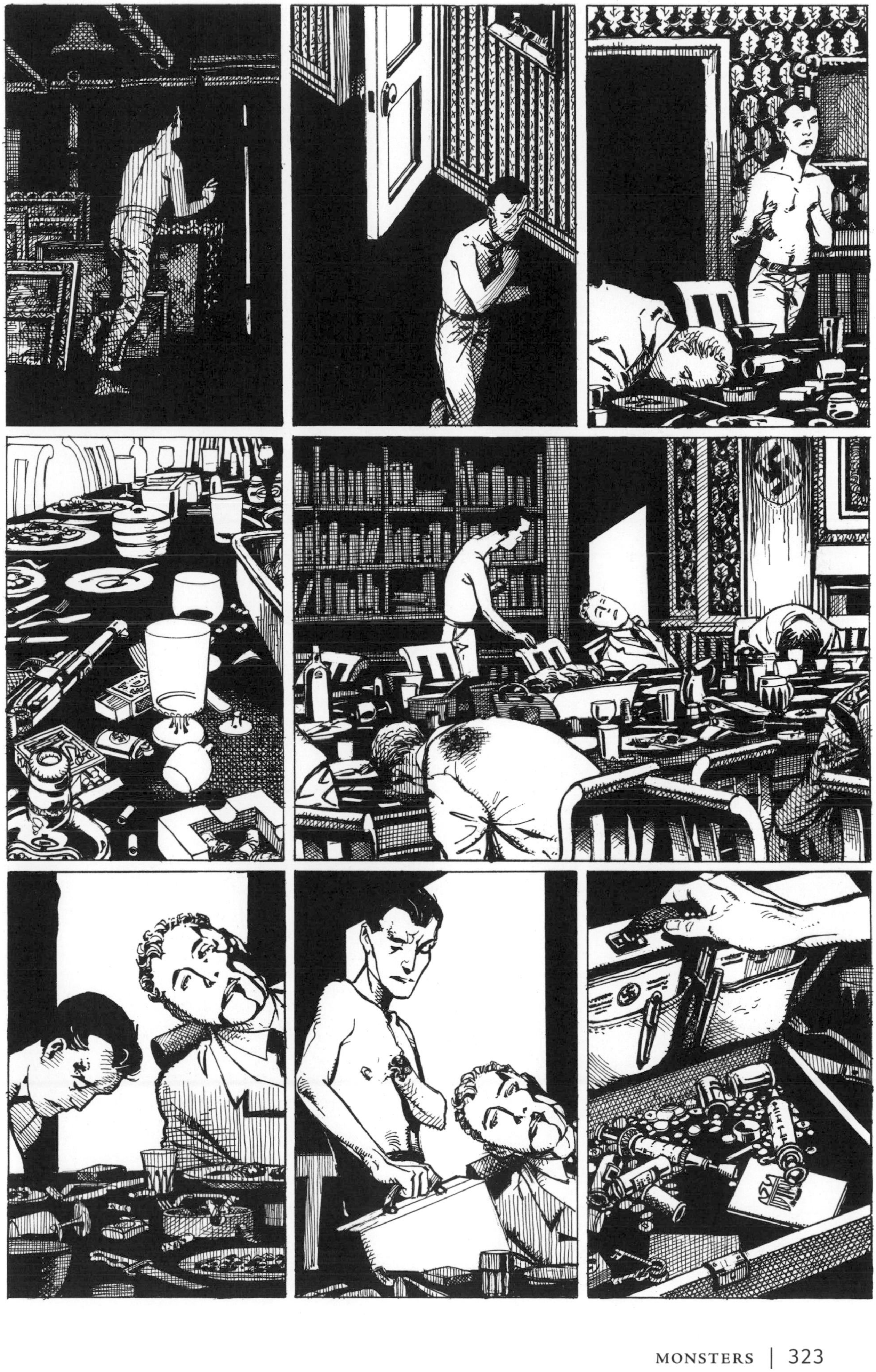

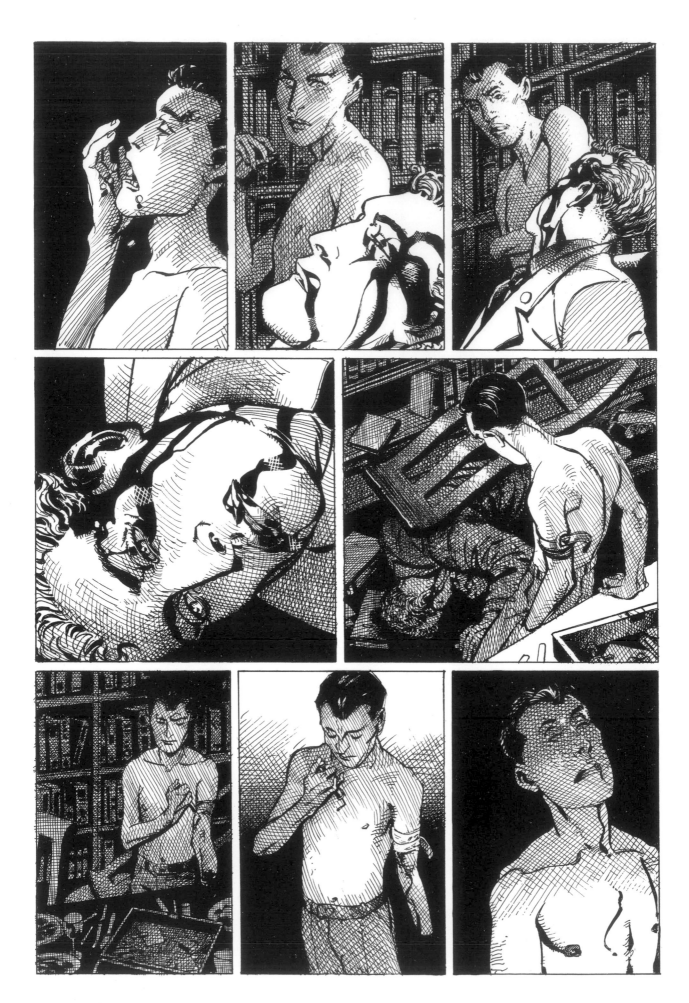

1965 Twenty years later, Providence Township, Ohio Thursday, November 25

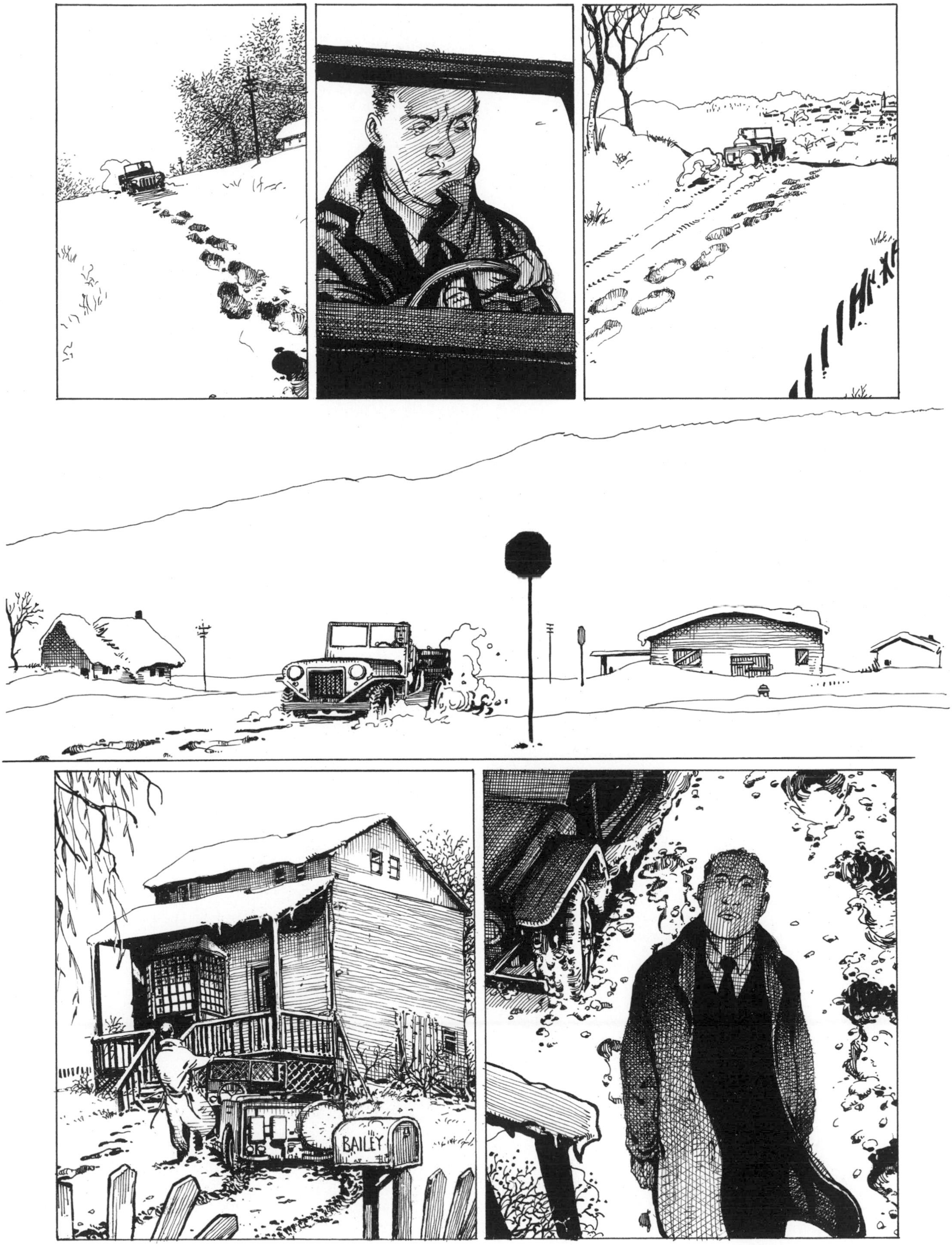
BAILEY

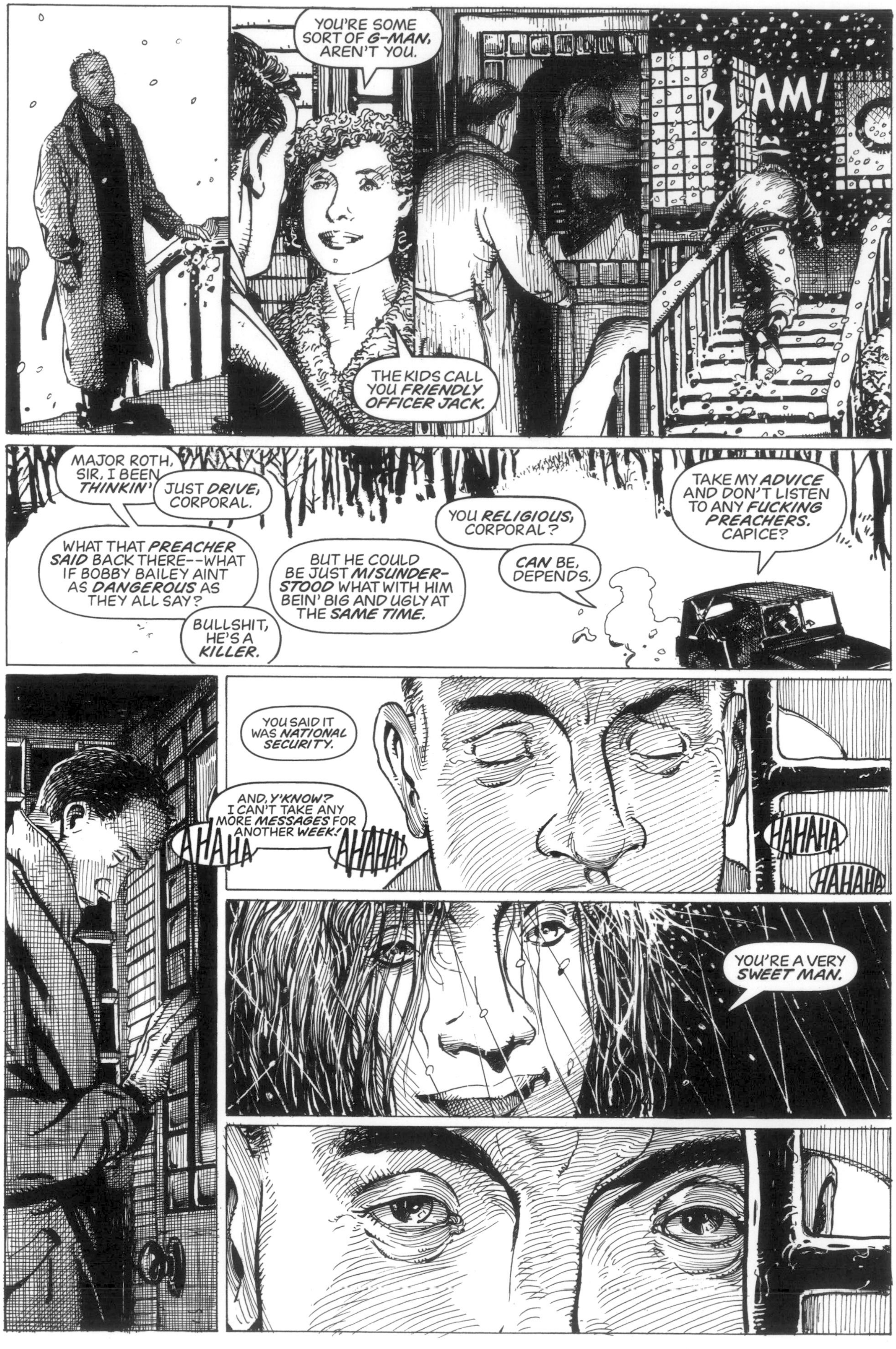
YOU'RE SOME SORT OF G-MAN, AREN'T YOU.
THE KIDS CALL YOU FRIENDLY OFFICER JACK.
BLAM!
MAJOR ROTH, SIR, I BEEN THINKIN'
JUST DRIVE, CORPORAL.
WHAT THAT PREACHER SAID BACK THERE--WHAT IF BOBBY BAILEY AINT AS DANGEROUS AS THEY ALL SAY?
BULLSHIT, HE'S A KILLER.
BUT HE COULD BE JUST MISUNDERSTOOD WHAT WITH HIM BEIN' BIG AND UGLY AT THE SAME TIME.
YOU RELIGIOUS, CORPORAL?
CAN BE, DEPENDS.
TAKE MY ADVICE AND DON'T LISTEN TO ANY FUCKING PREACHERS. CAPICE?
YOU SAID IT WAS NATIONAL SECURITY.
AND, Y'KNOW? I CAN'T TAKE ANY MORE MESSAGES FOR ANOTHER WEEK.
AHAHA
AHAHA!
HAHAHA
HAHAHA
YOU'RE A VERY SWEET MAN.

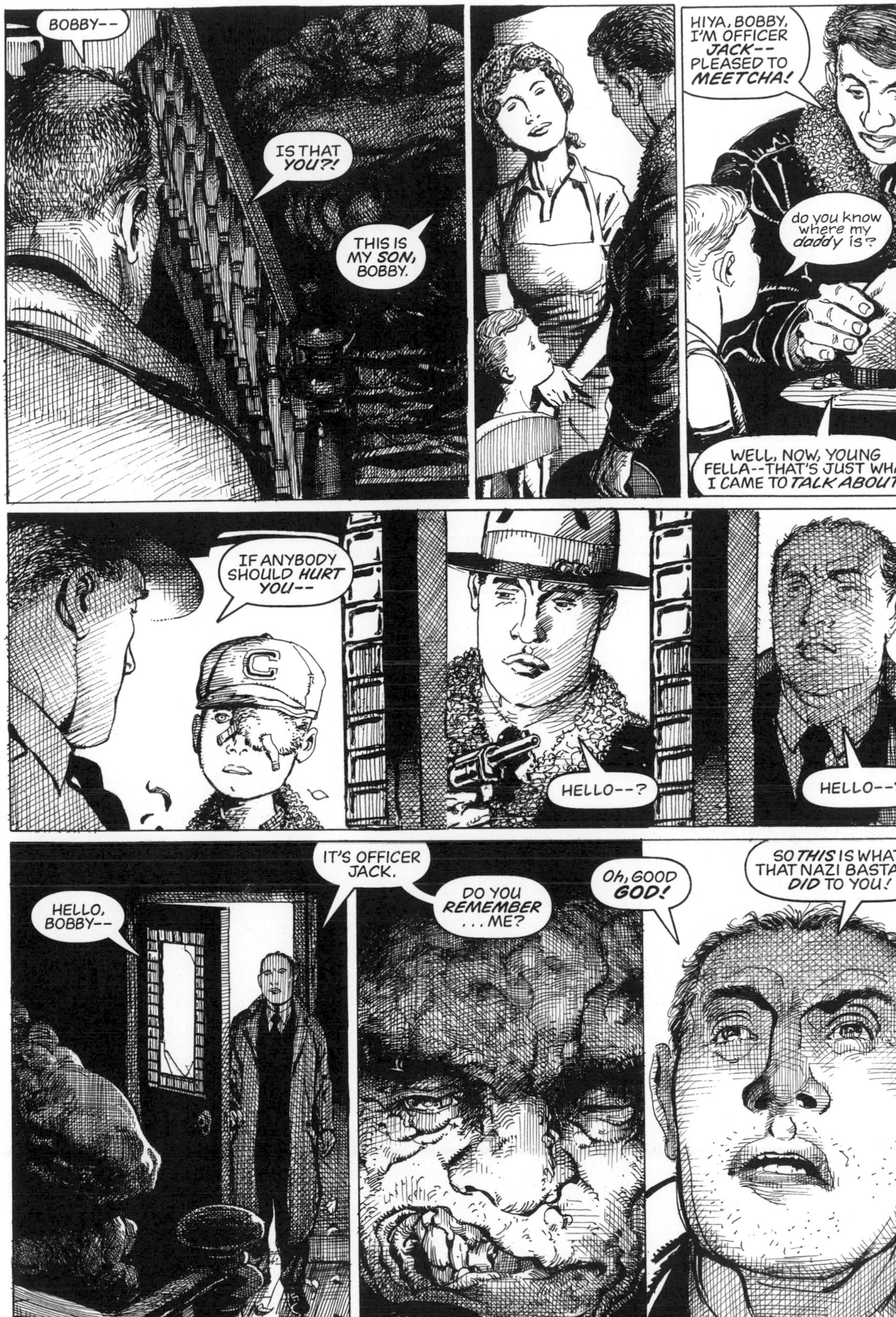
BOBBY--
IS THAT YOU?!
THIS IS MY SON, BOBBY.
HIYA, BOBBY, I'M OFFICER JACK-- PLEASED TO MEETCHA!
do you know where my daddy is?
WELL, NOW, YOUNG FELLA--THAT'S JUST WHAT I CAME TO TALK ABOUT.
IF ANYBODY SHOULD HURT YOU--
HELLO--?
HELLO--?
HELLO, BOBBY--
IT'S OFFICER JACK.
DO YOU REMEMBER . . . ME?
Oh, GOOD GOD!
SO THIS IS WHAT THAT NAZI BASTARD DID TO YOU!

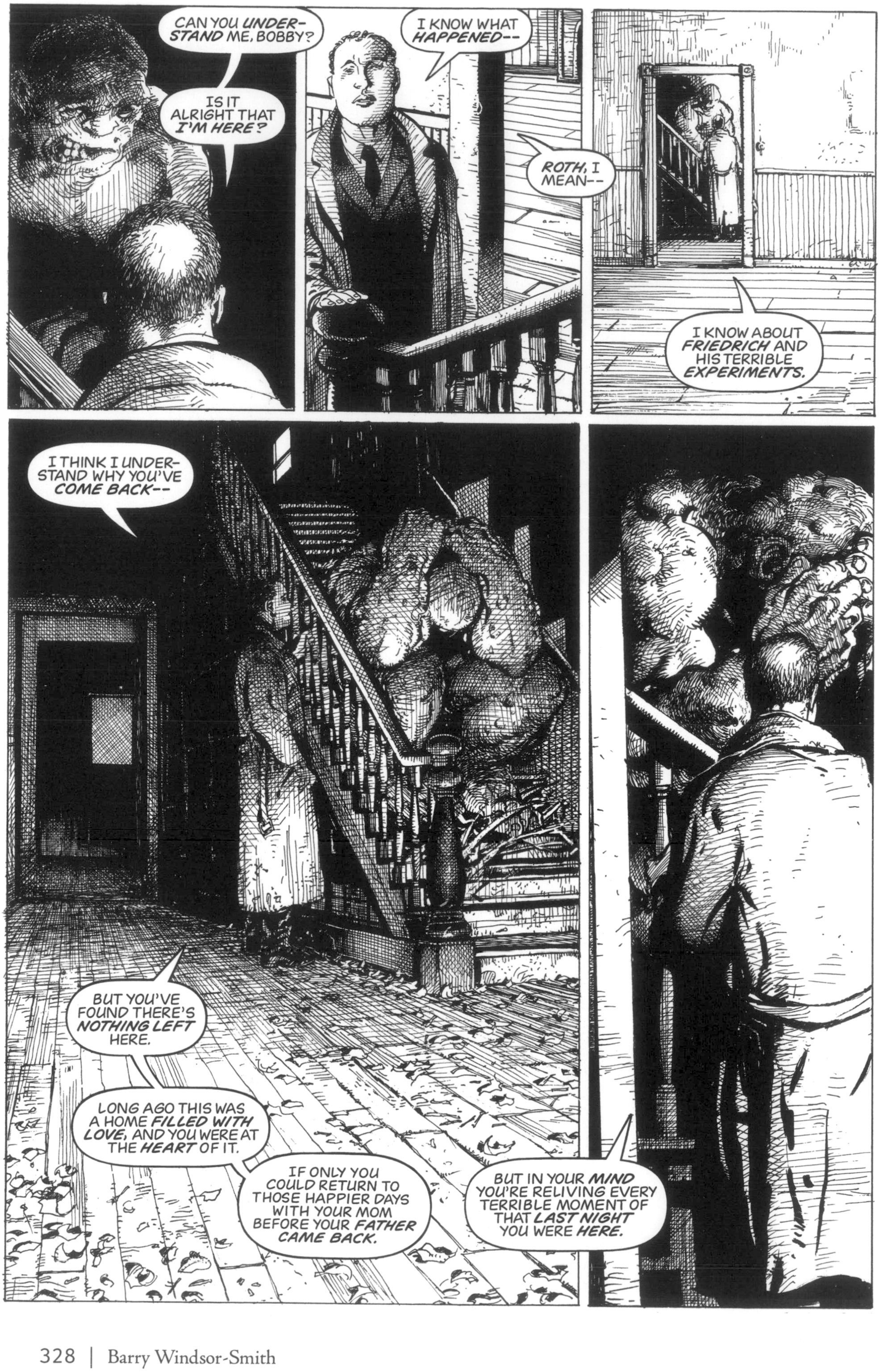
CAN YOU UNDERSTAND ME, BOBBY?
IS IT ALRIGHT THAT I'M HERE?
I KNOW WHAT HAPPENED--
ROTH, I MEAN--
I KNOW ABOUT FRIEDRICH AND HIS TERRIBLE EXPERIMENTS.
I THINK I UNDERSTAND WHY YOU'VE COME BACK--
BUT YOU'VE FOUND THERE'S NOTHING LEFT HERE.
LONG AGO THIS WAS A HOME FILLED WITH LOVE, AND YOU WERE AT THE HEART OF IT.
IF ONLY YOU COULD RETURN TO THOSE HAPPIER DAYS WITH YOUR MOM BEFORE YOUR FATHER CAME BACK.
BUT IN YOUR MIND YOU'RE RELIVING EVERY TERRIBLE MOMENT OF THAT LAST NIGHT YOU WERE HERE.

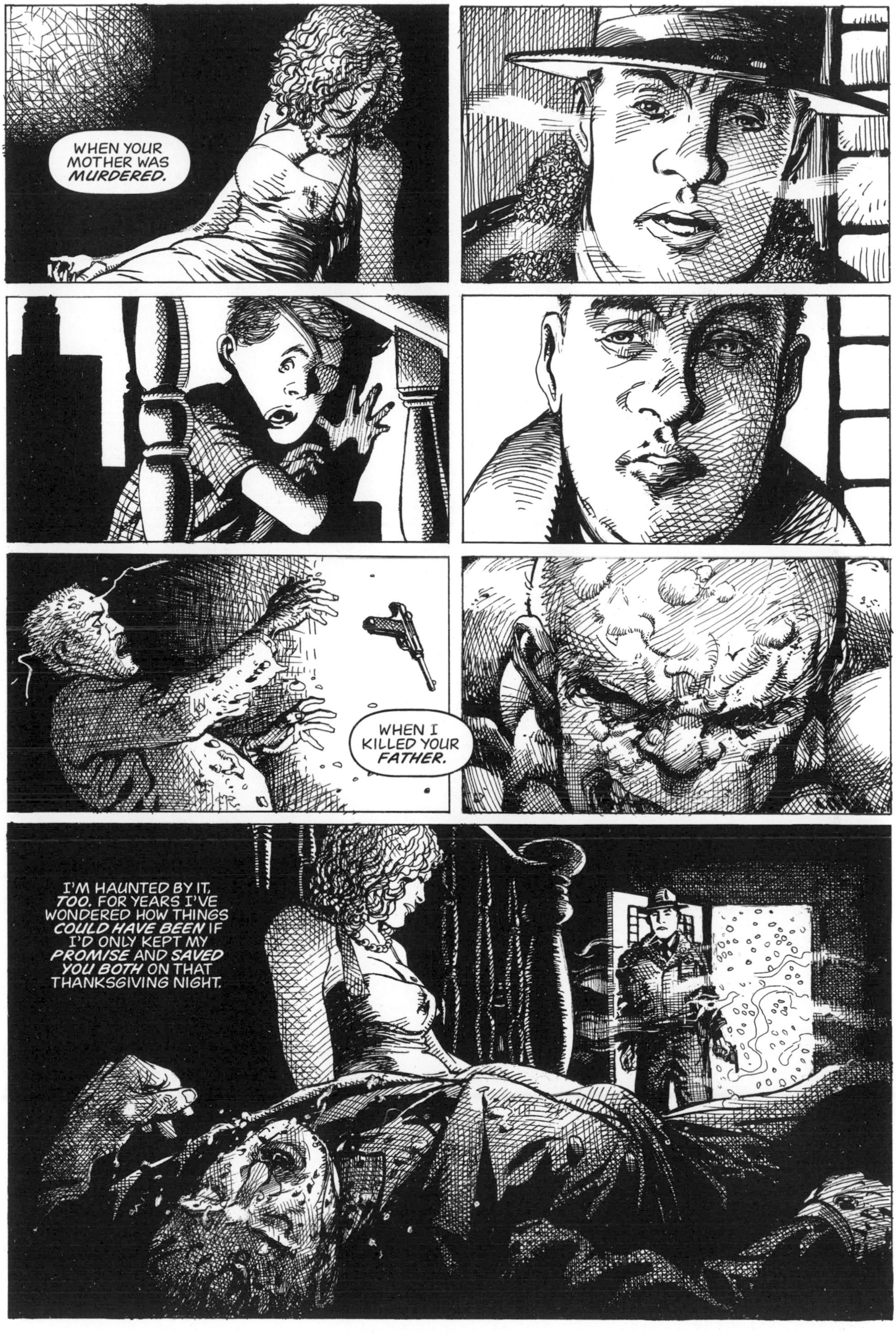
WHEN YOUR MOTHER WAS *MURDERED.*
WHEN I KILLED YOUR *FATHER.*
I'M HAUNTED BY IT, *TOO.* FOR YEARS I'VE WONDERED HOW THINGS *COULD HAVE BEEN* IF I'D ONLY KEPT MY *PROMISE* AND *SAVED YOU BOTH* ON THAT THANKSGIVING NIGHT.

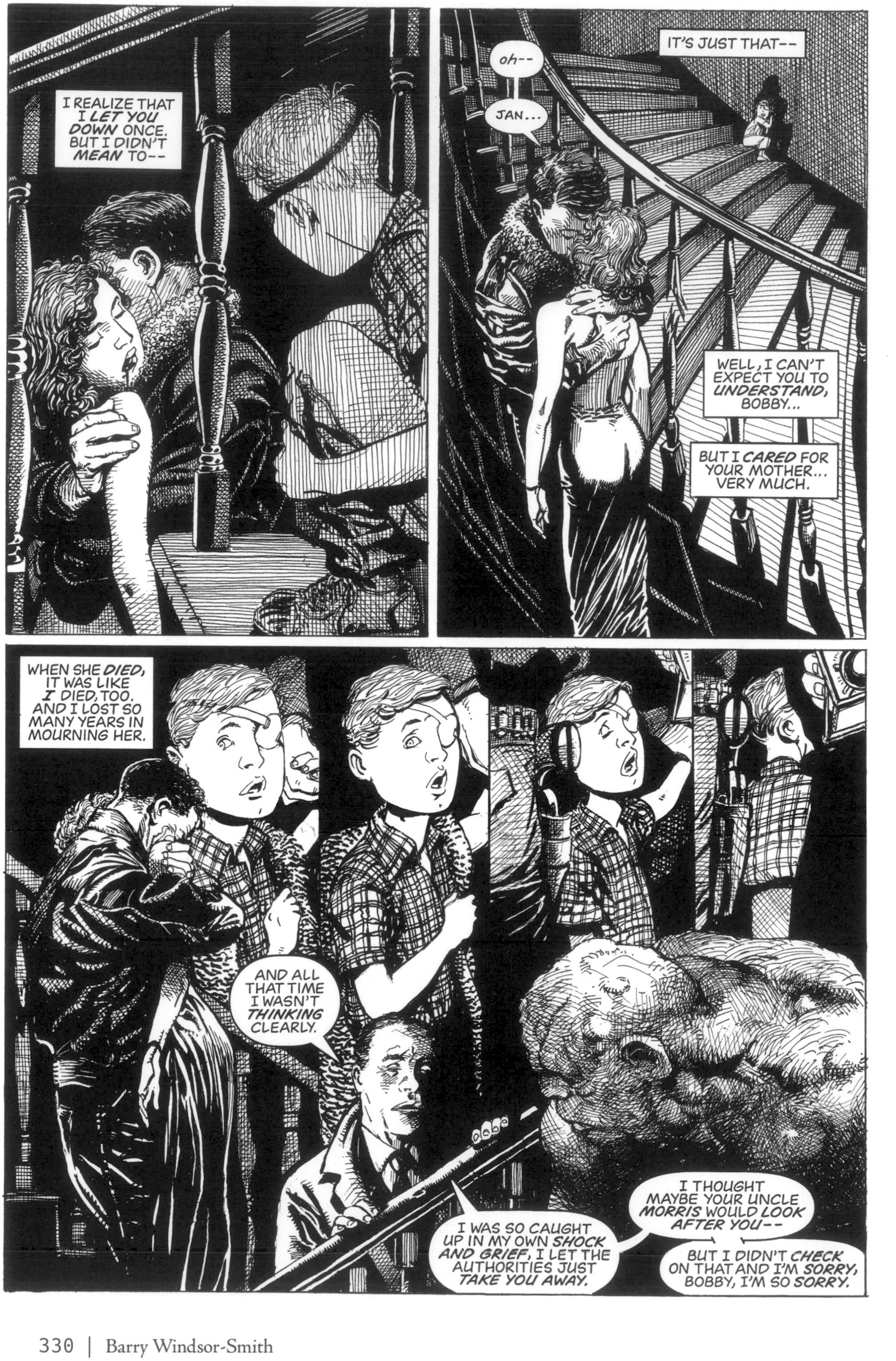
I REALIZE THAT I LET YOU DOWN ONCE. BUT I DIDN'T MEAN TO--
oh--
JAN...
IT'S JUST THAT--
WELL, I CAN'T EXPECT YOU TO UNDERSTAND, BOBBY...
BUT I CARED FOR YOUR MOTHER... VERY MUCH.
WHEN SHE DIED, IT WAS LIKE I DIED, TOO. AND I LOST SO MANY YEARS IN MOURNING HER.
AND ALL THAT TIME I WASN'T THINKING CLEARLY.
I WAS SO CAUGHT UP IN MY OWN SHOCK AND GRIEF, I LET THE AUTHORITIES JUST TAKE YOU AWAY.
I THOUGHT MAYBE YOUR UNCLE MORRIS WOULD LOOK AFTER YOU--
BUT I DIDN'T CHECK ON THAT AND I'M SORRY, BOBBY, I'M SO SORRY.

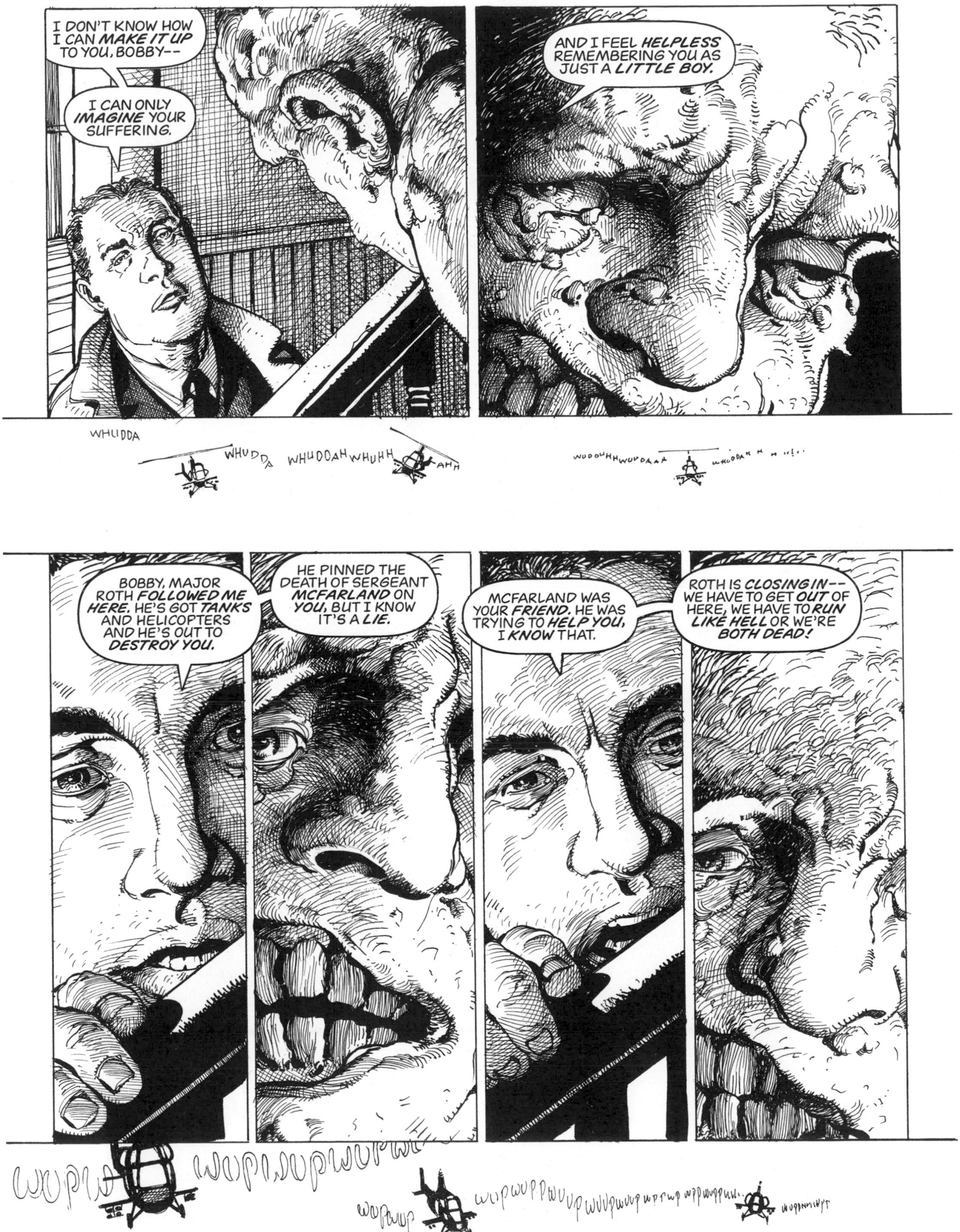

I DON'T KNOW HOW I CAN MAKE IT UP TO YOU, BOBBY--
I CAN ONLY IMAGINE YOUR SUFFERING.
AND I FEEL HELPLESS REMEMBERING YOU AS JUST A LITTLE BOY.
WHUDDA
BOBBY, MAJOR ROTH FOLLOWED ME HERE. HE'S GOT TANKS AND HELICOPTERS AND HE'S OUT TO DESTROY YOU.
HE PINNED THE DEATH OF SERGEANT MCFARLAND ON YOU, BUT I KNOW IT'S A LIE.
MCFARLAND WAS YOUR FRIEND. HE WAS TRYING TO HELP YOU, I KNOW THAT.
ROTH IS CLOSING IN-- WE HAVE TO GET OUT OF HERE, WE HAVE TO RUN LIKE HELL OR WE'RE BOTH DEAD!

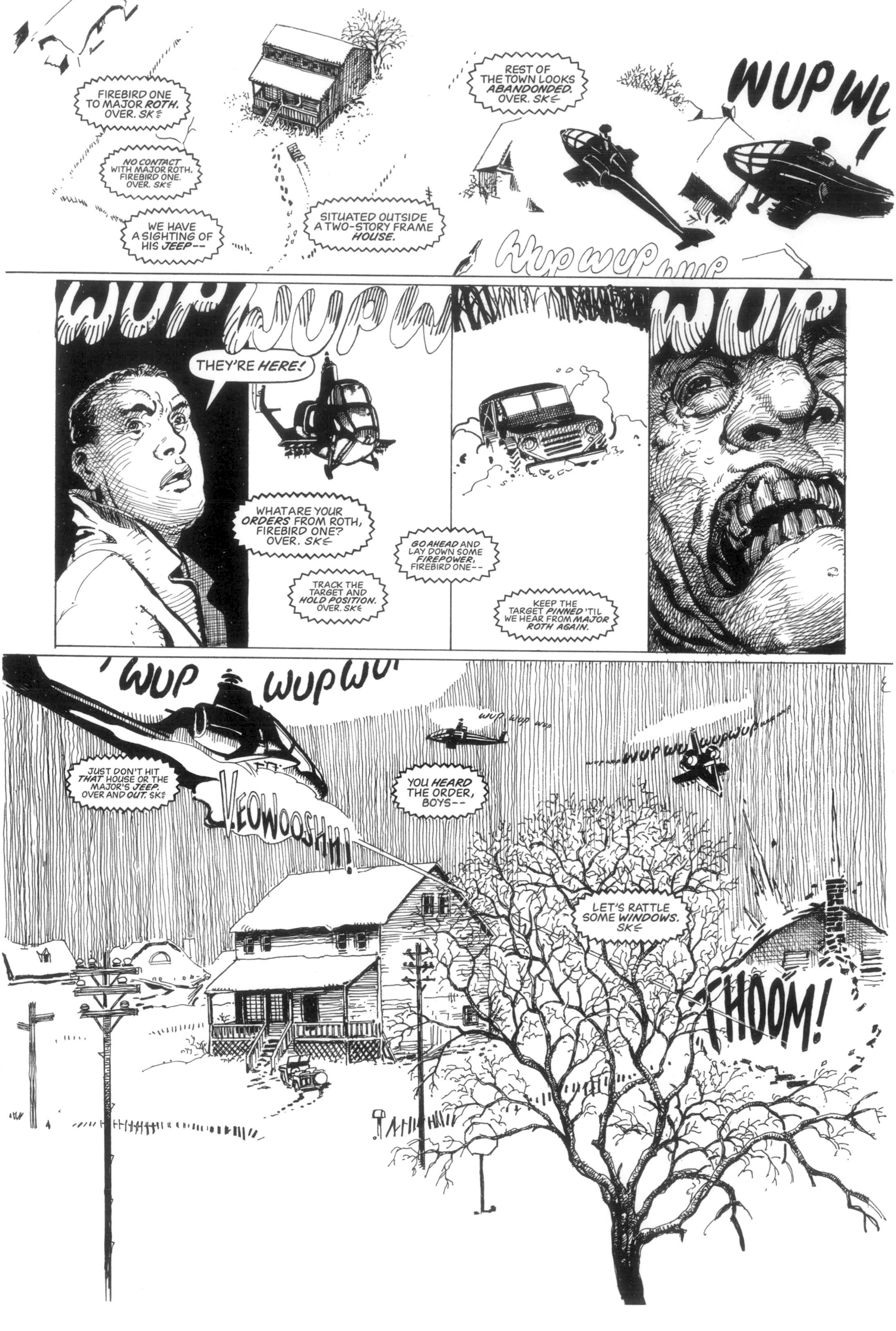
FIREBIRD ONE TO MAJOR ROTH. OVER. SK
NO CONTACT WITH MAJOR ROTH, FIREBIRD ONE. OVER. SK
WE HAVE A SIGHTING OF HIS JEEP--
SITUATED OUTSIDE A TWO-STORY FRAME HOUSE.
REST OF THE TOWN LOOKS ABANDONDED. OVER. SK
WUP WU
WUP WUP WUP
WUP WUP W
WUP
THEY'RE HERE!
WHATARE YOUR ORDERS FROM ROTH, FIREBIRD ONE? OVER. SK
TRACK THE TARGET AND HOLD POSITION. OVER. SK
GO AHEAD AND LAY DOWN SOME FIREPOWER, FIREBIRD ONE--
KEEP THE TARGET PINNED 'TIL WE HEAR FROM MAJOR ROTH AGAIN.
WUP WUP WUP
JUST DON'T HIT THAT HOUSE OR THE MAJOR'S JEEP. OVER AND OUT. SK
YOU HEARD THE ORDER, BOYS--
WUP WUP WUP
WUP WU WUPWUP
VEOWOOSHH!
LET'S RATTLE SOME WINDOWS. SK
THOOM!

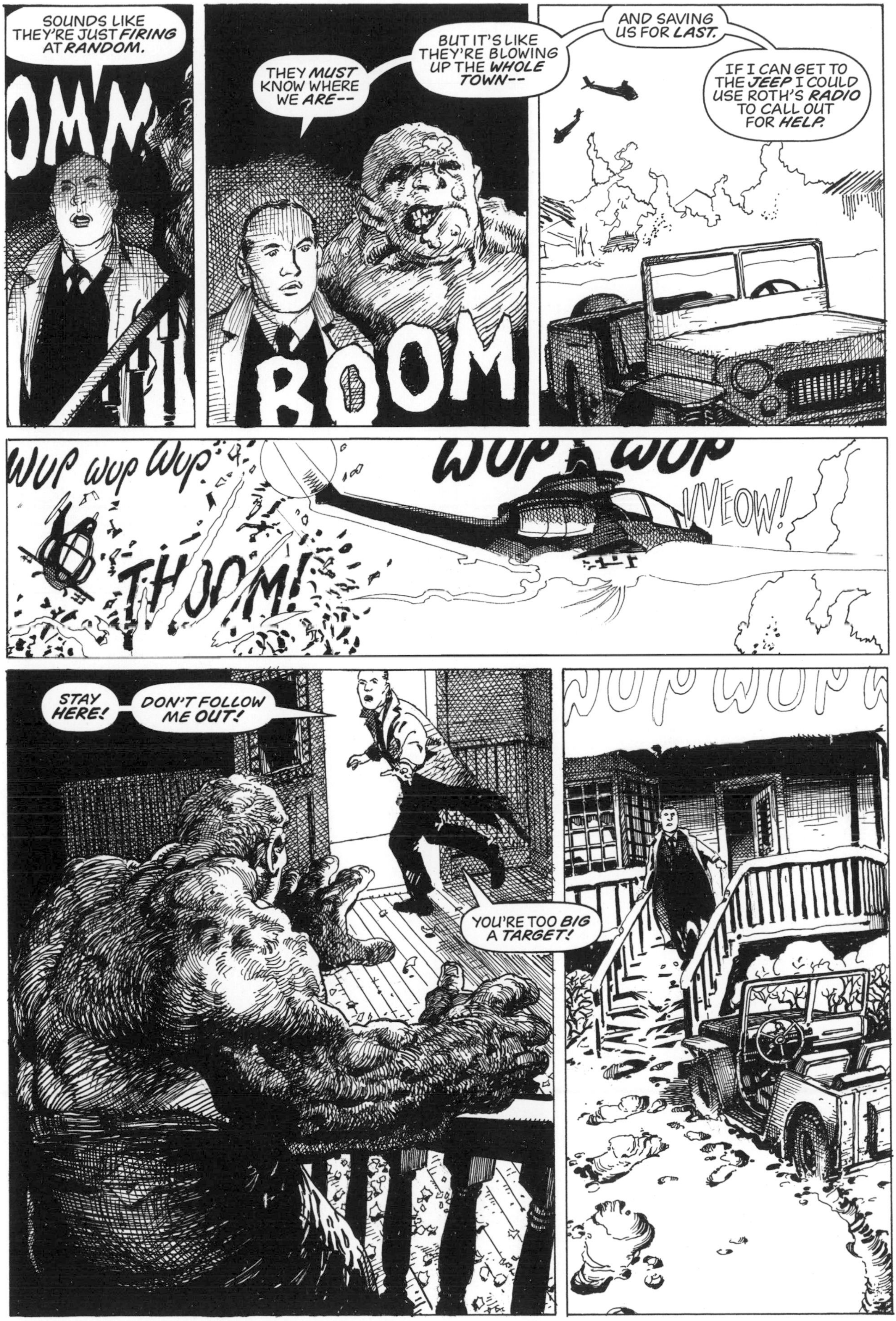
SOUNDS LIKE THEY'RE JUST FIRING AT RANDOM.
OMM
THEY MUST KNOW WHERE WE ARE--
BUT IT'S LIKE THEY'RE BLOWING UP THE WHOLE TOWN--
BOOM
AND SAVING US FOR LAST.
IF I CAN GET TO THE JEEP I COULD USE ROTH'S RADIO TO CALL OUT FOR HELP.
WUP WOP WUP
WUP WUP
VVEOW!
THOOM!
STAY HERE!
DON'T FOLLOW ME OUT!
YOU'RE TOO BIG A TARGET!
WUP WUP

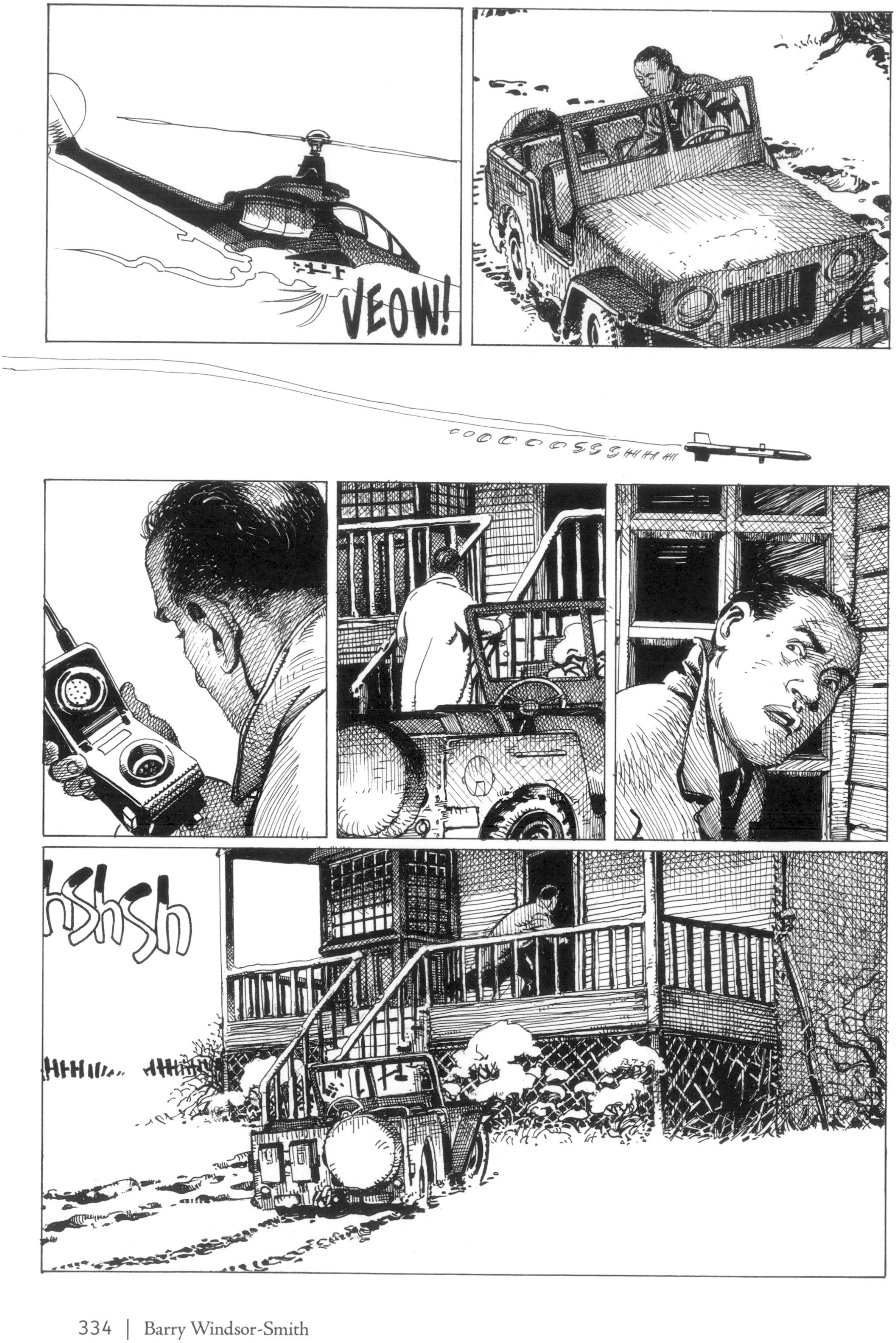
VEOW!
hShSh

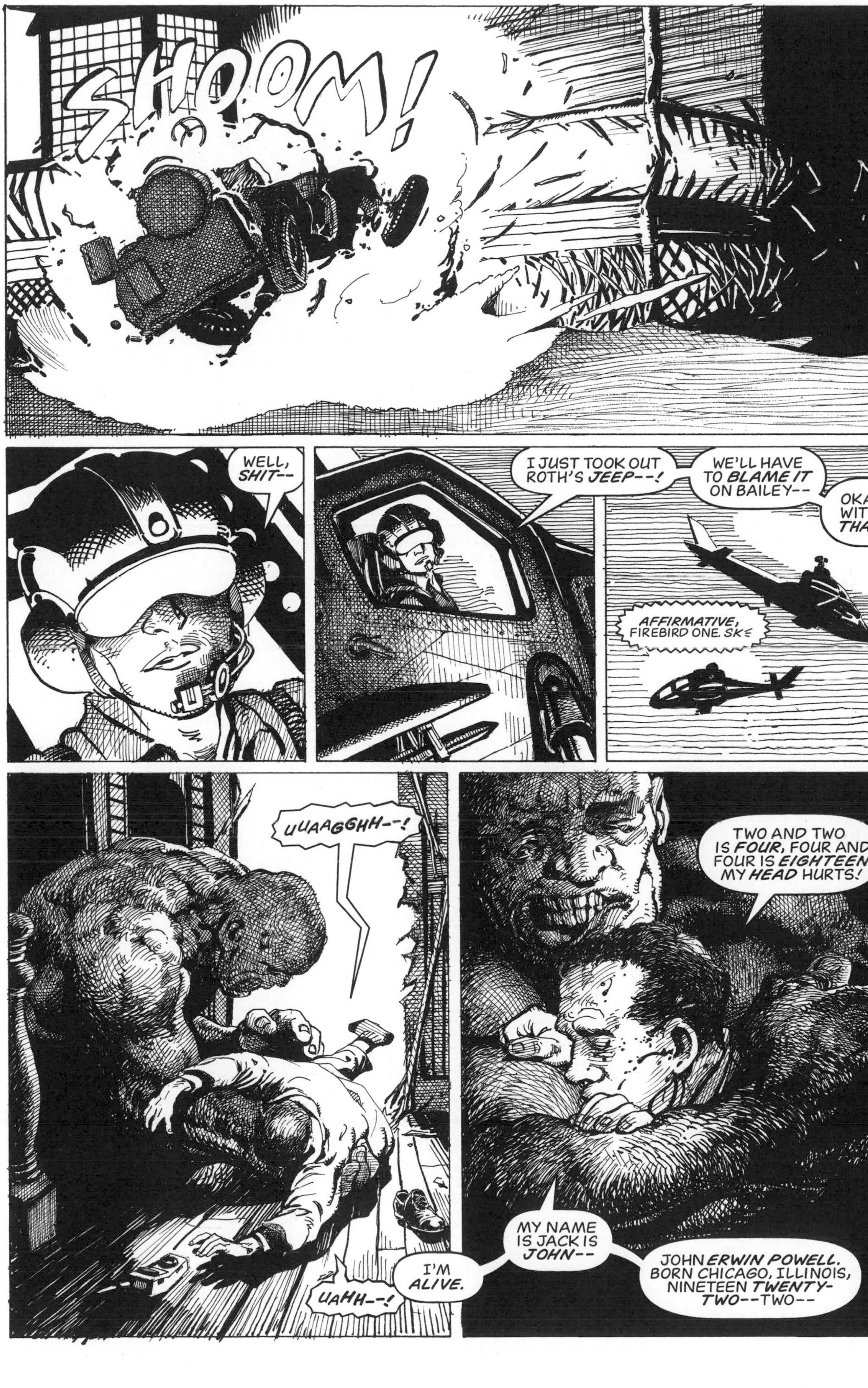
SHOOM!
WELL, SHIT--
I JUST TOOK OUT ROTH'S JEEP--!
WE'LL HAVE TO BLAME IT ON BAILEY--
OKAY WITH THAT?
AFFIRMATIVE, FIREBIRD ONE. SK<
UUAAGGHH--!
UAHH--!
TWO AND TWO IS FOUR, FOUR AND FOUR IS EIGHTEEN, MY HEAD HURTS!
I'M ALIVE.
MY NAME IS JACK IS JOHN--
JOHN ERWIN POWELL. BORN CHICAGO, ILLINOIS, NINETEEN TWENTY-TWO--TWO--

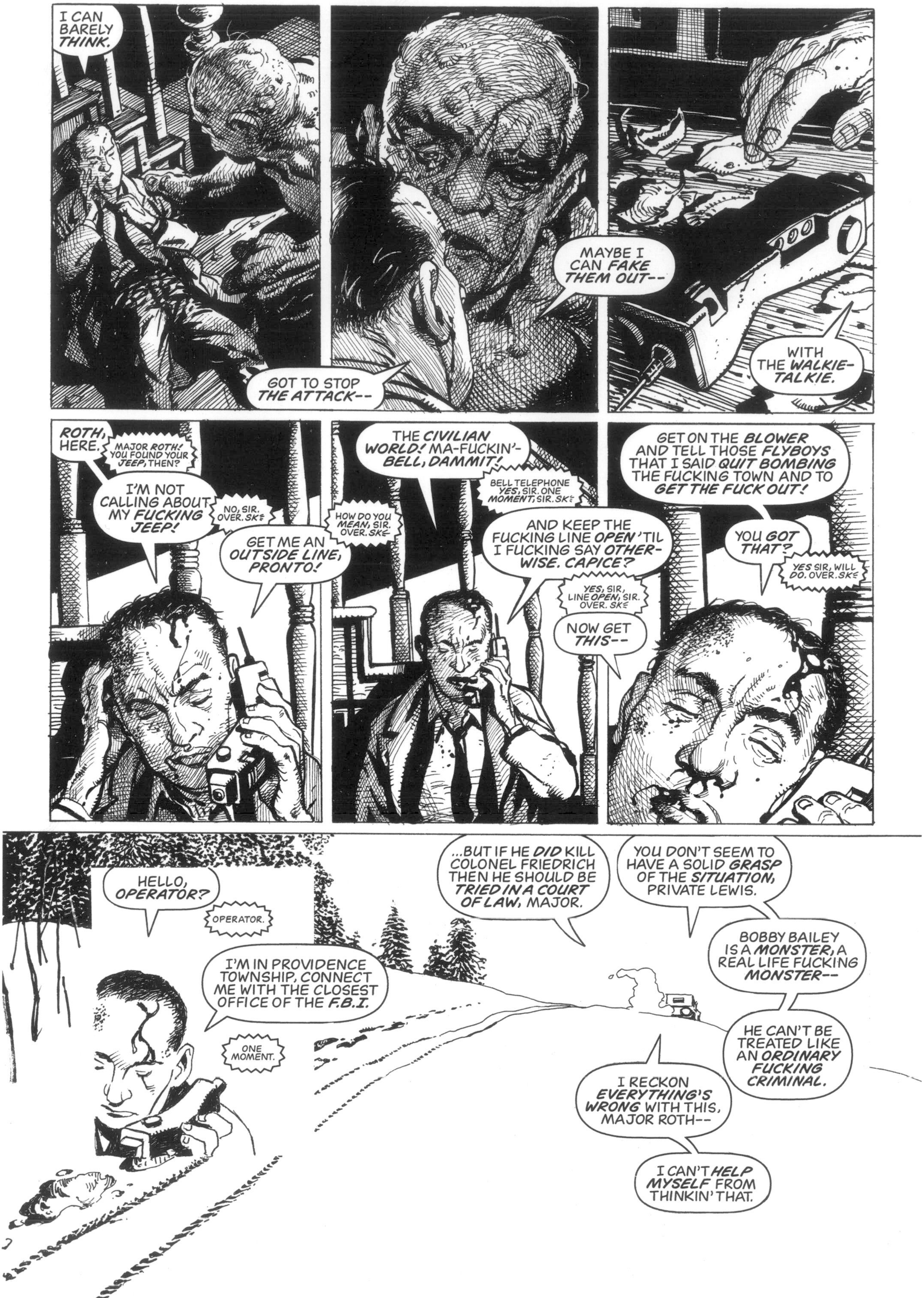
I CAN BARELY THINK.
GOT TO STOP THE ATTACK--
MAYBE I CAN FAKE THEM OUT--
WITH THE WALKIE-TALKIE.
ROTH, HERE.
MAJOR ROTH! YOU FOUND YOUR JEEP, THEN?
I'M NOT CALLING ABOUT MY FUCKING JEEP!
NO, SIR. OVER. SK
GET ME AN OUTSIDE LINE, PRONTO!
HOW DO YOU MEAN, SIR. OVER. SK
THE CIVILIAN WORLD! MA-FUCKIN'-BELL, DAMMIT!
BELL TELEPHONE YES, SIR. ONE MOMENT, SIR. SK
AND KEEP THE FUCKING LINE OPEN 'TIL I FUCKING SAY OTHER-WISE. CAPICE?
YES, SIR, LINE OPEN, SIR. OVER. SK
NOW GET THIS--
GET ON THE BLOWER AND TELL THOSE FLYBOYS THAT I SAID QUIT BOMBING THE FUCKING TOWN AND TO GET THE FUCK OUT!
YOU GOT THAT?
YES SIR, WILL DO. OVER. SK
HELLO, OPERATOR?
OPERATOR.
I'M IN PROVIDENCE TOWNSHIP, CONNECT ME WITH THE CLOSEST OFFICE OF THE F.B.I.
ONE MOMENT.
...BUT IF HE DID KILL COLONEL FRIEDRICH THEN HE SHOULD BE TRIED IN A COURT OF LAW, MAJOR.
YOU DON'T SEEM TO HAVE A SOLID GRASP OF THE SITUATION, PRIVATE LEWIS.
BOBBY BAILEY IS A MONSTER, A REAL LIFE FUCKING MONSTER--
HE CAN'T BE TREATED LIKE AN ORDINARY FUCKING CRIMINAL.
I RECKON EVERYTHING'S WRONG WITH THIS, MAJOR ROTH--
I CAN'T HELP MYSELF FROM THINKIN' THAT.

1964 The McFarlands' apartment, Oxnard, CA Thursday, November 26

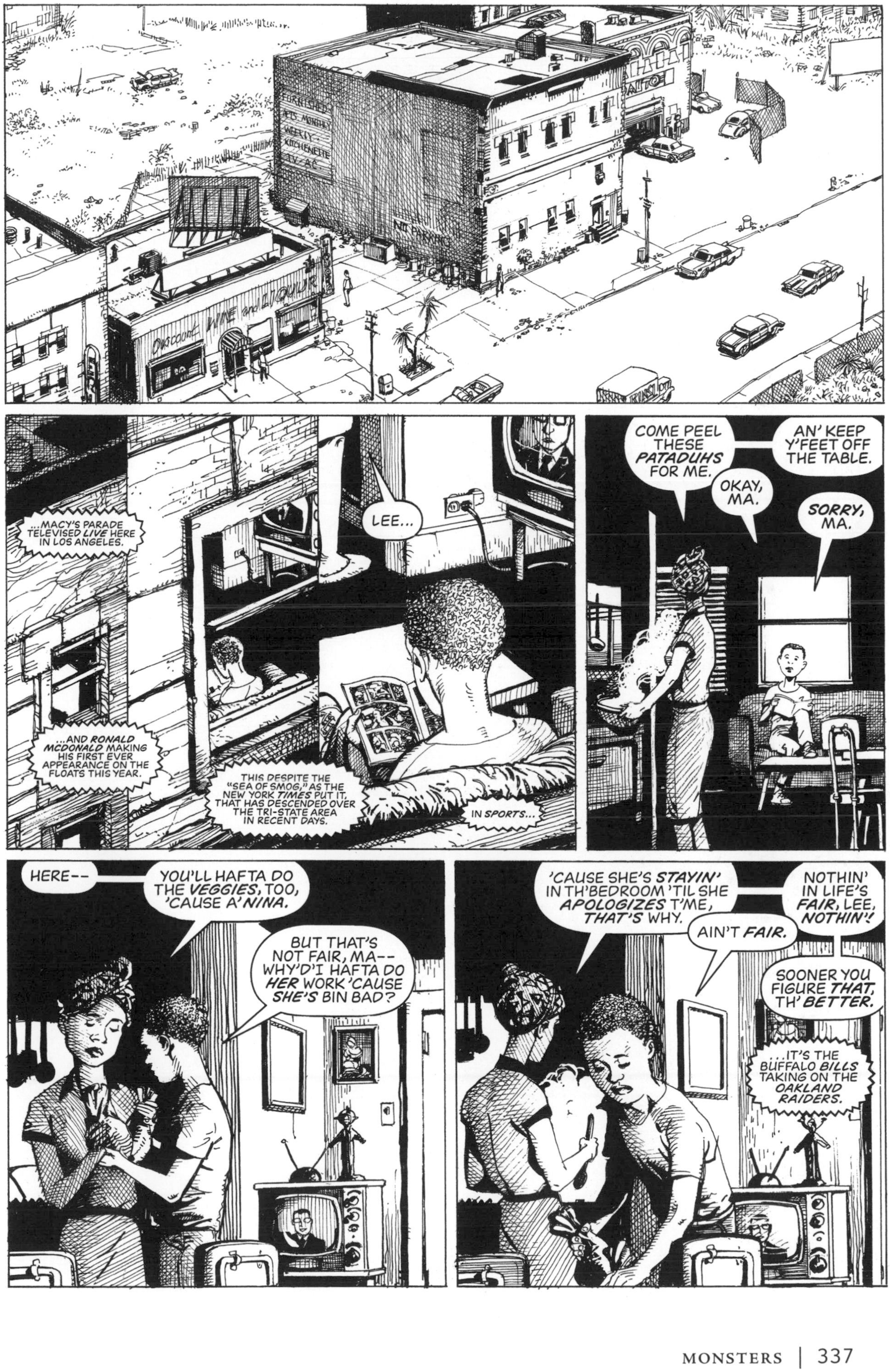
FURNISHED
APTS MONTHLY
WEEKLY
KITCHENETTE
T.V. A.C.
NO PARKING
DISCOUNT WINE and LIQUOR
...MACY'S PARADE TELEVISED LIVE HERE IN LOS ANGELES.
...AND RONALD McDONALD MAKING HIS FIRST EVER APPEARANCE ON THE FLOATS THIS YEAR.
"THIS DESPITE THE "SEA OF SMOG," AS THE NEW YORK TIMES PUT IT, THAT HAS DESCENDED OVER THE TRI-STATE AREA IN RECENT DAYS.
LEE...
IN SPORTS...
COME PEEL THESE PATADUHS FOR ME.
AN' KEEP Y'FEET OFF THE TABLE.
OKAY, MA.
SORRY, MA.
HERE--
YOU'LL HAFTA DO THE VEGGIES, TOO, 'CAUSE A' NINA.
BUT THAT'S NOT FAIR, MA-- WHY'D I HAFTA DO HER WORK 'CAUSE SHE'S BIN BAD?
'CAUSE SHE'S STAYIN' IN TH'BEDROOM 'TIL SHE APOLOGIZES T'ME, THAT'S WHY.
AIN'T FAIR.
NOTHIN' IN LIFE'S FAIR, LEE, NOTHIN'!
SOONER YOU FIGURE THAT, TH' BETTER.
...IT'S THE BUFFALO BILLS TAKING ON THE OAKLAND RAIDERS.

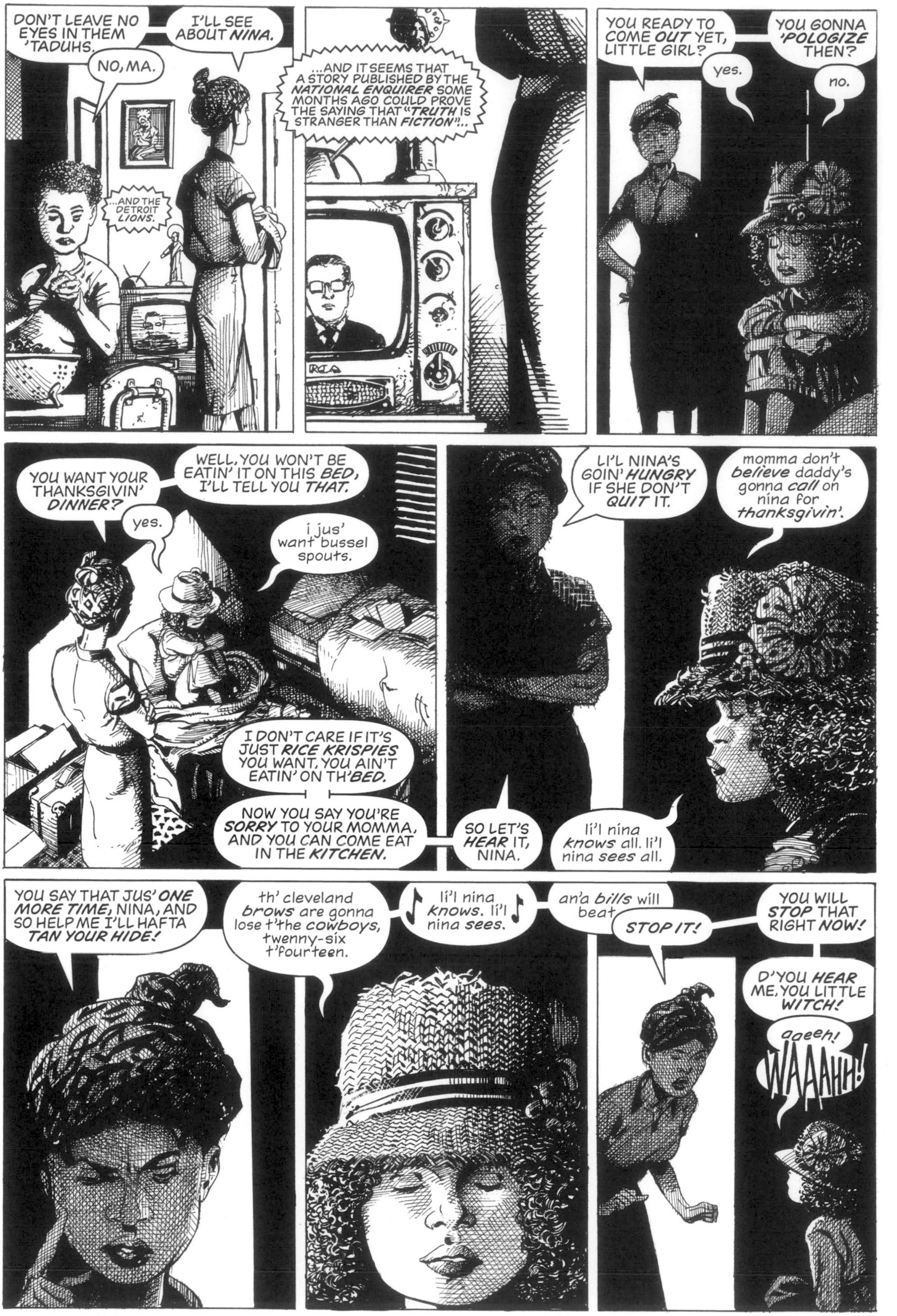
DON'T LEAVE NO EYES IN THEM 'TADUHS.
I'LL SEE ABOUT NINA.
NO, MA.
...AND THE DETROIT LIONS.
...AND IT SEEMS THAT A STORY PUBLISHED BY THE NATIONAL ENQUIRER SOME MONTHS AGO COULD PROVE THE SAYING THAT "TRUTH IS STRANGER THAN FICTION"...
YOU READY TO COME OUT YET, LITTLE GIRL?
yes.
YOU GONNA 'POLOGIZE THEN?
no.
YOU WANT YOUR THANKSGIVIN' DINNER?
yes.
WELL, YOU WON'T BE EATIN' IT ON THIS BED, I'LL TELL YOU THAT.
i jus' want bussel spouts.
I DON'T CARE IF IT'S JUST RICE KRISPIES YOU WANT, YOU AIN'T EATIN' ON TH' BED.
NOW YOU SAY YOU'RE SORRY TO YOUR MOMMA, AND YOU CAN COME EAT IN THE KITCHEN.
SO LET'S HEAR IT, NINA.
LI'L NINA'S GOIN' HUNGRY IF SHE DON'T QUIT IT.
momma don't believe daddy's gonna call on nina for thanksgivin'.
li'l nina knows all. li'l nina sees all.
YOU SAY THAT JUS' ONE MORE TIME, NINA, AND SO HELP ME I'LL HAFTA TAN YOUR HIDE!
th' cleveland brows are gonna lose t'the cowboys, twenny-six t'fourteen.
♪ li'l nina knows. li'l nina sees. ♪
an'a bills will beat
STOP IT!
YOU WILL STOP THAT RIGHT NOW!
D'YOU HEAR ME, YOU LITTLE WITCH!
aaeeh!
WAAAHH!

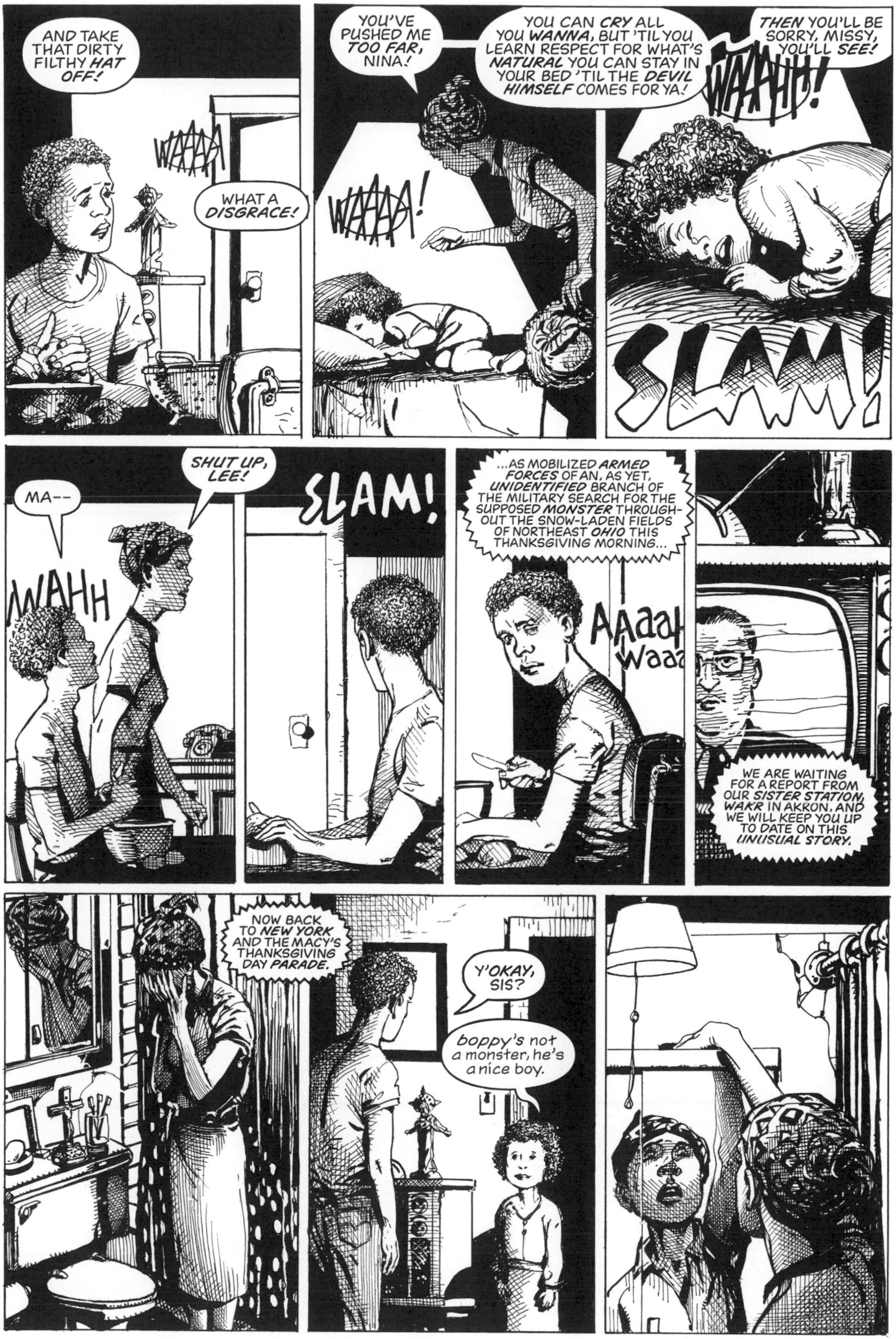

AND TAKE THAT DIRTY FILTHY HAT OFF!
WAAAA
WHAT A DISGRACE!
YOU'VE PUSHED ME TOO FAR, NINA!
YOU CAN CRY ALL YOU WANNA, BUT 'TIL YOU LEARN RESPECT FOR WHAT'S NATURAL YOU CAN STAY IN YOUR BED 'TIL THE DEVIL HIMSELF COMES FOR YA!
WAAAA!
THEN YOU'LL BE SORRY, MISSY, YOU'LL SEE!
WAAHH!
SLAM!
MA--
WAHH
SHUT UP, LEE!
SLAM!
...AS MOBILIZED ARMED FORCES OF AN, AS YET, UNIDENTIFIED BRANCH OF THE MILITARY SEARCH FOR THE SUPPOSED MONSTER THROUGHOUT THE SNOW-LADEN FIELDS OF NORTHEAST OHIO THIS THANKSGIVING MORNING...
AAaaH
Waaa
WE ARE WAITING FOR A REPORT FROM OUR SISTER STATION, WAKR IN AKRON, AND WE WILL KEEP YOU UP TO DATE ON THIS UNUSUAL STORY.
NOW BACK TO NEW YORK AND THE MACY'S THANKSGIVING DAY PARADE.
Y'OKAY, SIS?
boppy's not a monster, he's a nice boy.

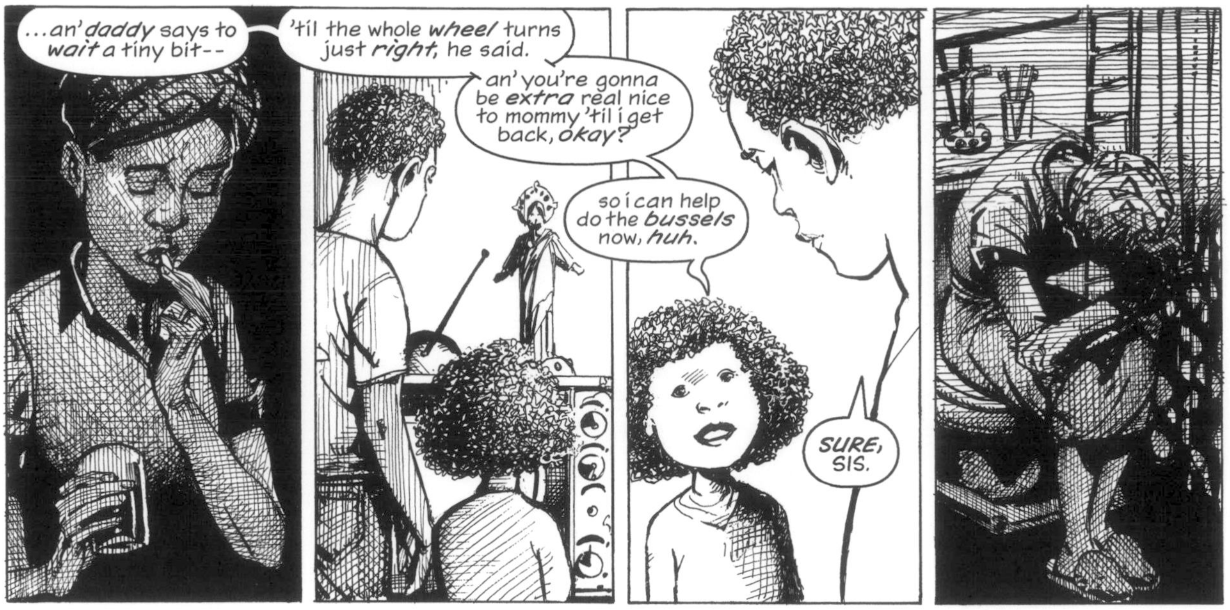
...an' daddy says to wait a tiny bit--
'til the whole wheel turns just right, he said.
an' you're gonna be extra real nice to mommy 'til i get back, okay?
so i can help do the bussels now, huh.
SURE, SIS.

Providence Hills, Ohio

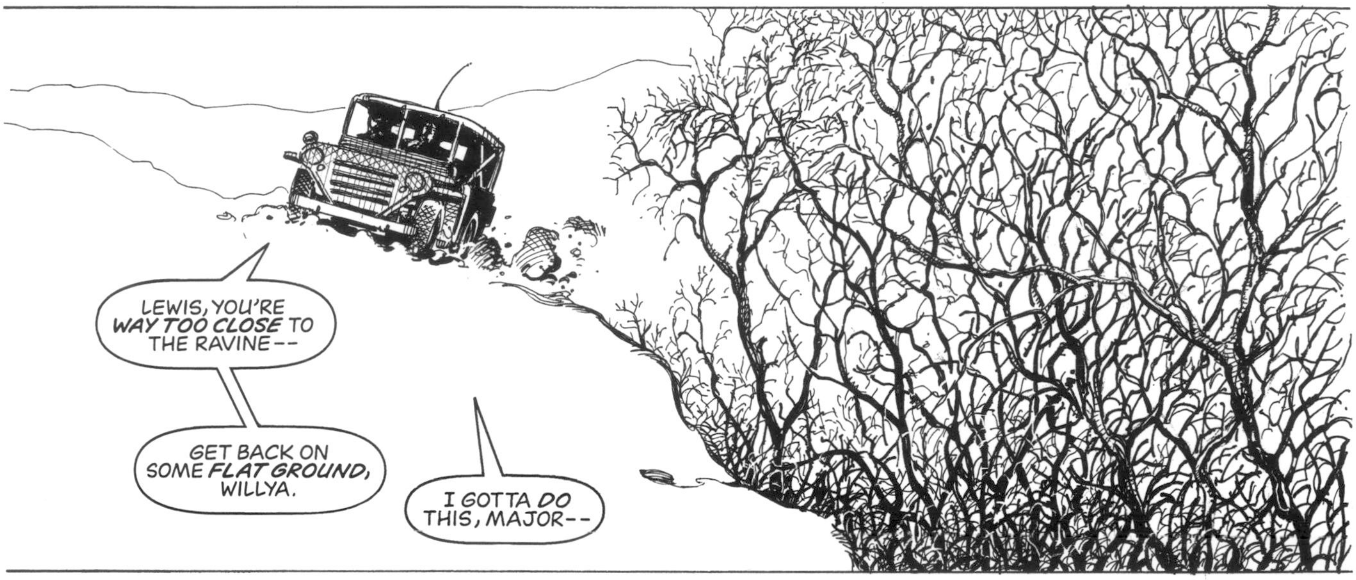
LEWIS, YOU'RE WAY TOO CLOSE TO THE RAVINE--
GET BACK ON SOME FLAT GROUND, WILLYA.
I GOTTA DO THIS, MAJOR--

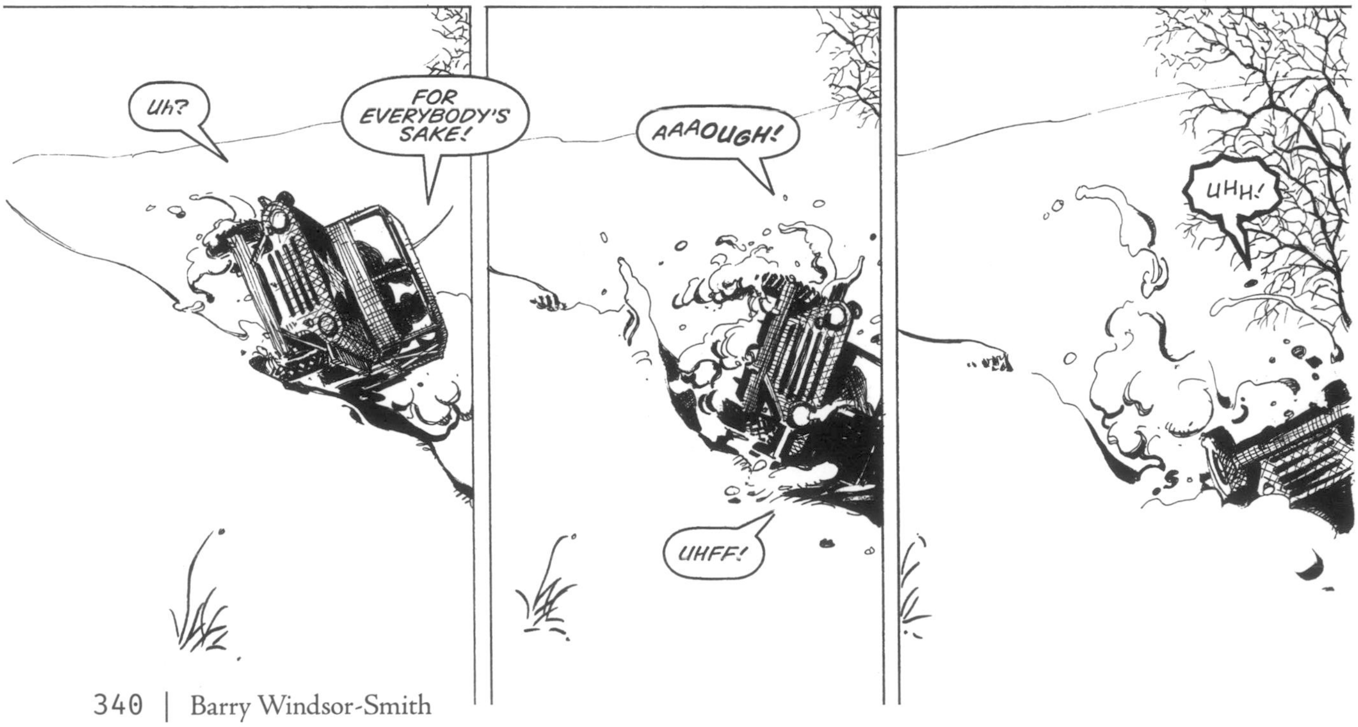
UH?
FOR EVERYBODY'S SAKE!
AAAOUGH!
UHFF!
UHH!

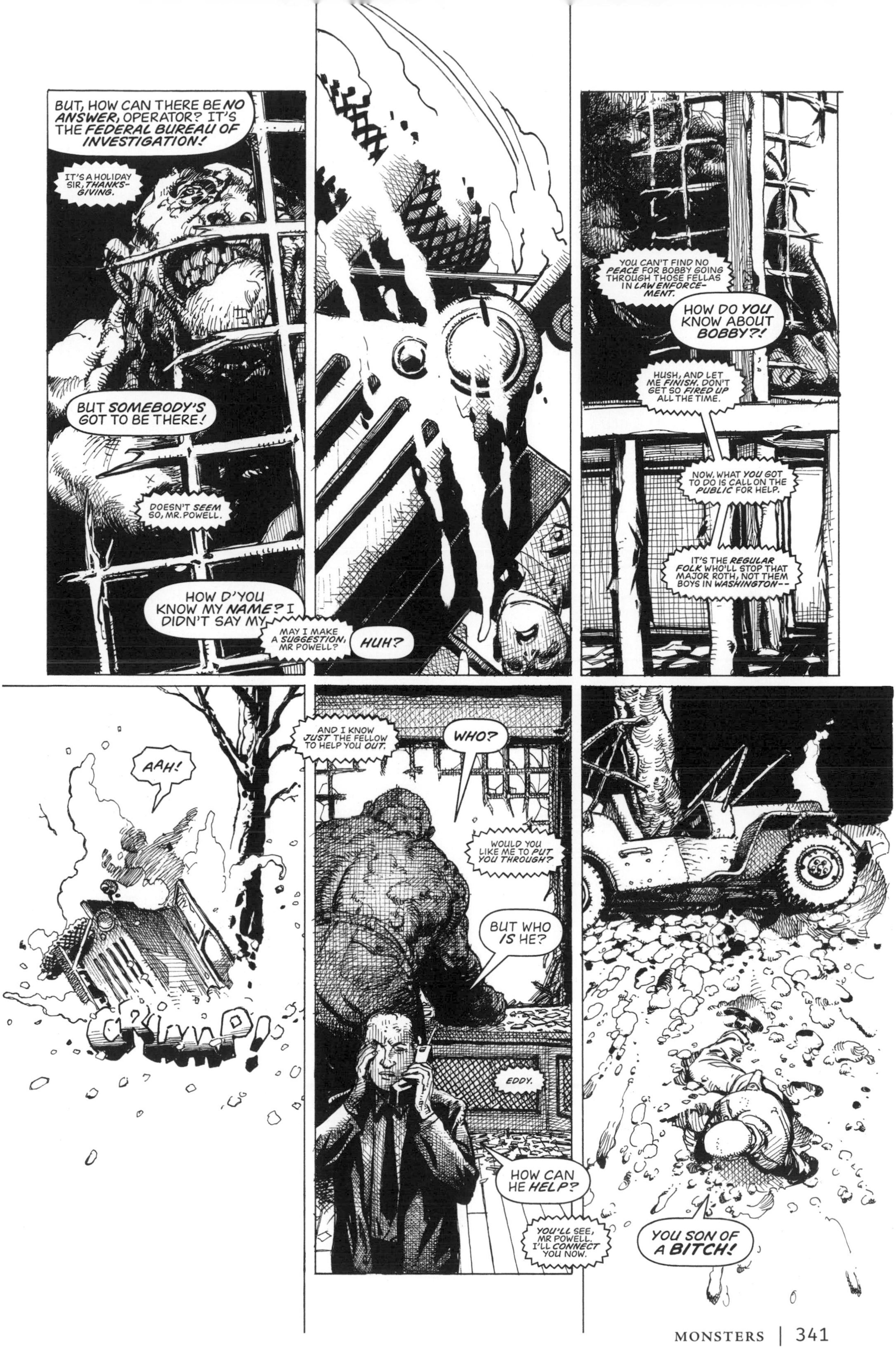
BUT, HOW CAN THERE BE NO ANSWER, OPERATOR? IT'S THE FEDERAL BUREAU OF INVESTIGATION!
IT'S A HOLIDAY SIR, THANKS-GIVING.
BUT SOMEBODY'S GOT TO BE THERE!
DOESN'T SEEM SO, MR. POWELL.
HOW D'YOU KNOW MY NAME? I DIDN'T SAY MY
MAY I MAKE A SUGGESTION, MR POWELL?
HUH?
YOU CAN'T FIND NO PEACE FOR BOBBY GOING THROUGH THOSE FELLAS IN LAW ENFORCE-MENT.
HOW DO YOU KNOW ABOUT BOBBY?!
HUSH, AND LET ME FINISH. DON'T GET SO FIRED UP ALL THE TIME.
NOW, WHAT YOU GOT TO DO IS CALL ON THE PUBLIC FOR HELP.
IT'S THE REGULAR FOLK WHO'LL STOP THAT MAJOR ROTH, NOT THEM BOYS IN WASHINGTON--
AAH!
CRUNNCH!
AND I KNOW JUST THE FELLOW TO HELP YOU OUT.
WHO?
WOULD YOU LIKE ME TO PUT YOU THROUGH?
BUT WHO IS HE?
EDDY.
HOW CAN HE HELP?
YOU'LL SEE, MR POWELL. I'LL CONNECT YOU NOW.
YOU SON OF A BITCH!

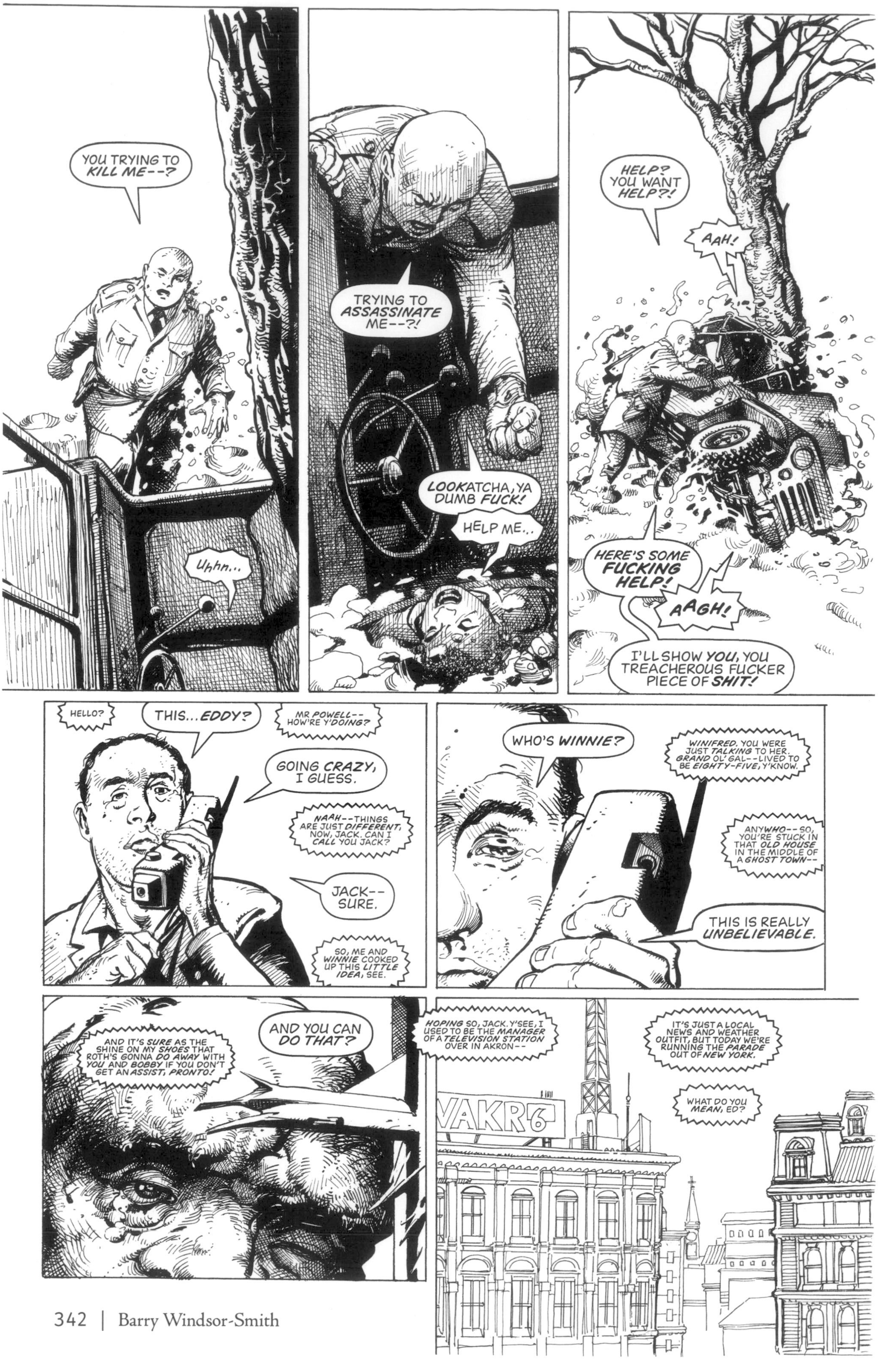

YOU TRYING TO KILL ME--?
Uhhn...
TRYING TO ASSASSINATE ME--?!
LOOKATCHA, YA DUMB FUCK!
HELP ME...
HELP? YOU WANT HELP?!
AAH!
HERE'S SOME FUCKING HELP!
AAGH!
I'LL SHOW YOU, YOU TREACHEROUS FUCKER PIECE OF SHIT!
HELLO?
THIS... EDDY?
MR POWELL-- HOW'RE Y'DOING?
GOING CRAZY, I GUESS.
NAAH--THINGS ARE JUST DIFFERENT, NOW, JACK. CAN I CALL YOU JACK?
JACK-- SURE.
SO, ME AND WINNIE COOKED UP THIS LITTLE IDEA, SEE.
WHO'S WINNIE?
WINIFRED. YOU WERE JUST TALKING TO HER. GRAND OL' GAL--LIVED TO BE EIGHTY-FIVE, Y'KNOW.
ANYWHO--SO, YOU'RE STUCK IN THAT OLD HOUSE IN THE MIDDLE OF A GHOST TOWN--
THIS IS REALLY UNBELIEVABLE.
AND IT'S SURE AS THE SHINE ON MY SHOES THAT ROTH'S GONNA DO AWAY WITH YOU AND BOBBY IF YOU DON'T GET AN ASSIST, PRONTO!
AND YOU CAN DO THAT?
HOPING SO, JACK. Y'SEE, I USED TO BE THE MANAGER OF A TELEVISION STATION OVER IN AKRON--
IT'S JUST A LOCAL NEWS AND WEATHER OUTFIT, BUT TODAY WE'RE RUNNING THE PARADE OUT OF NEW YORK.
WHAT DO YOU MEAN, ED?
WAKR 6

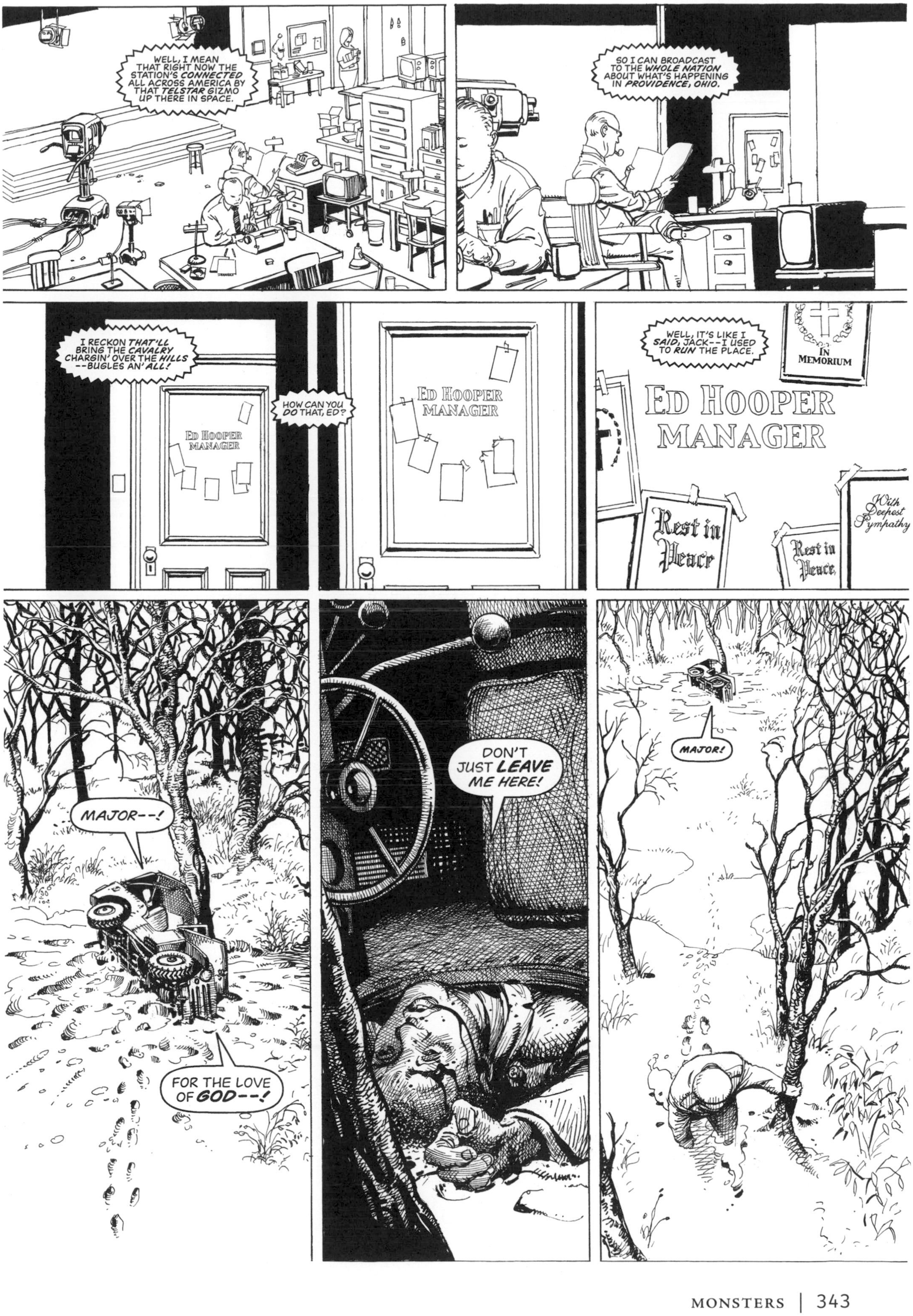
WELL, I MEAN THAT RIGHT NOW THE STATION'S CONNECTED ALL ACROSS AMERICA BY THAT TELSTAR GIZMO UP THERE IN SPACE.
SO I CAN BROADCAST TO THE WHOLE NATION ABOUT WHAT'S HAPPENING IN PROVIDENCE, OHIO.
I RECKON THAT'LL BRING THE CAVALRY CHARGIN' OVER THE HILLS --BUGLES AN' ALL!
HOW CAN YOU DO THAT, ED?
ED HOOPER MANAGER
ED HOOPER MANAGER
WELL, IT'S LIKE I SAID, JACK--I USED TO RUN THE PLACE.
IN MEMORIUM
ED HOOPER MANAGER
Rest in Peace
Rest in Peace
With Deepest Sympathy
MAJOR--!
FOR THE LOVE OF GOD--!
DON'T JUST LEAVE ME HERE!
MAJOR!

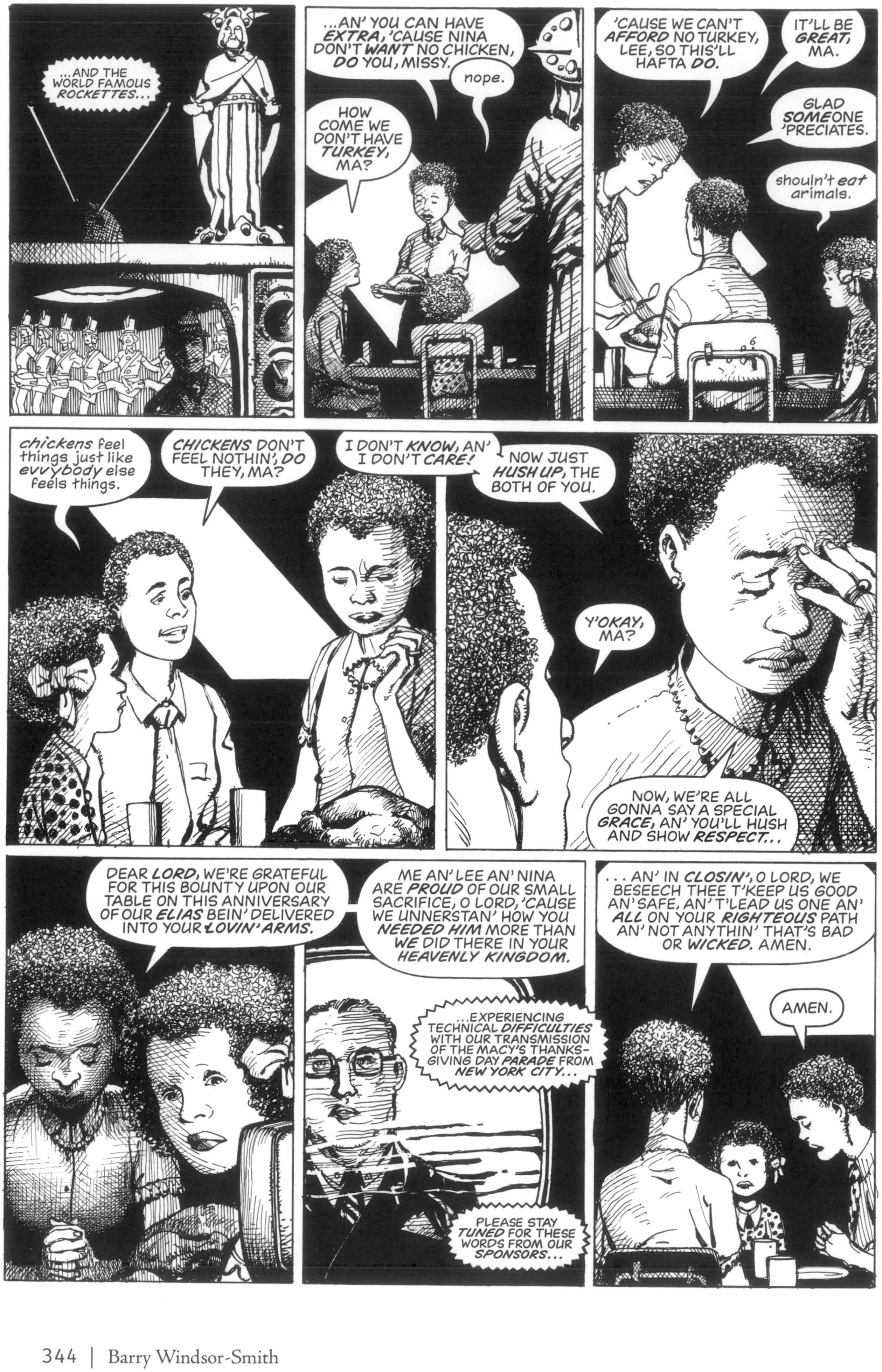
...AND THE WORLD FAMOUS ROCKETTES...
...AN' YOU CAN HAVE EXTRA, 'CAUSE NINA DON'T WANT NO CHICKEN, DO YOU, MISSY.
nope.
HOW COME WE DON'T HAVE TURKEY, MA?
'CAUSE WE CAN'T AFFORD NO TURKEY, LEE, SO THIS'LL HAFTA DO.
IT'LL BE GREAT, MA.
GLAD SOMEONE 'PRECIATES.
shouln't eat arimals.
chickens feel things just like evvybody else feels things.
CHICKENS DON'T FEEL NOTHIN', DO THEY, MA?
I DON'T KNOW, AN' I DON'T CARE!
NOW JUST HUSH UP, THE BOTH OF YOU.
Y'OKAY, MA?
NOW, WE'RE ALL GONNA SAY A SPECIAL GRACE, AN' YOU'LL HUSH AND SHOW RESPECT...
DEAR LORD, WE'RE GRATEFUL FOR THIS BOUNTY UPON OUR TABLE ON THIS ANNIVERSARY OF OUR ELIAS BEIN' DELIVERED INTO YOUR LOVIN' ARMS.
ME AN' LEE AN' NINA ARE PROUD OF OUR SMALL SACRIFICE, O LORD, 'CAUSE WE UNNERSTAN' HOW YOU NEEDED HIM MORE THAN WE DID THERE IN YOUR HEAVENLY KINGDOM.
...EXPERIENCING TECHNICAL DIFFICULTIES WITH OUR TRANSMISSION OF THE MACY'S THANKSGIVING DAY PARADE FROM NEW YORK CITY...
PLEASE STAY TUNED FOR THESE WORDS FROM OUR SPONSORS...
... AN' IN CLOSIN', O LORD, WE BESEECH THEE T'KEEP US GOOD AN' SAFE, AN' T'LEAD US ONE AN' ALL ON YOUR RIGHTEOUS PATH AN' NOT ANYTHIN' THAT'S BAD OR WICKED. AMEN.
AMEN.

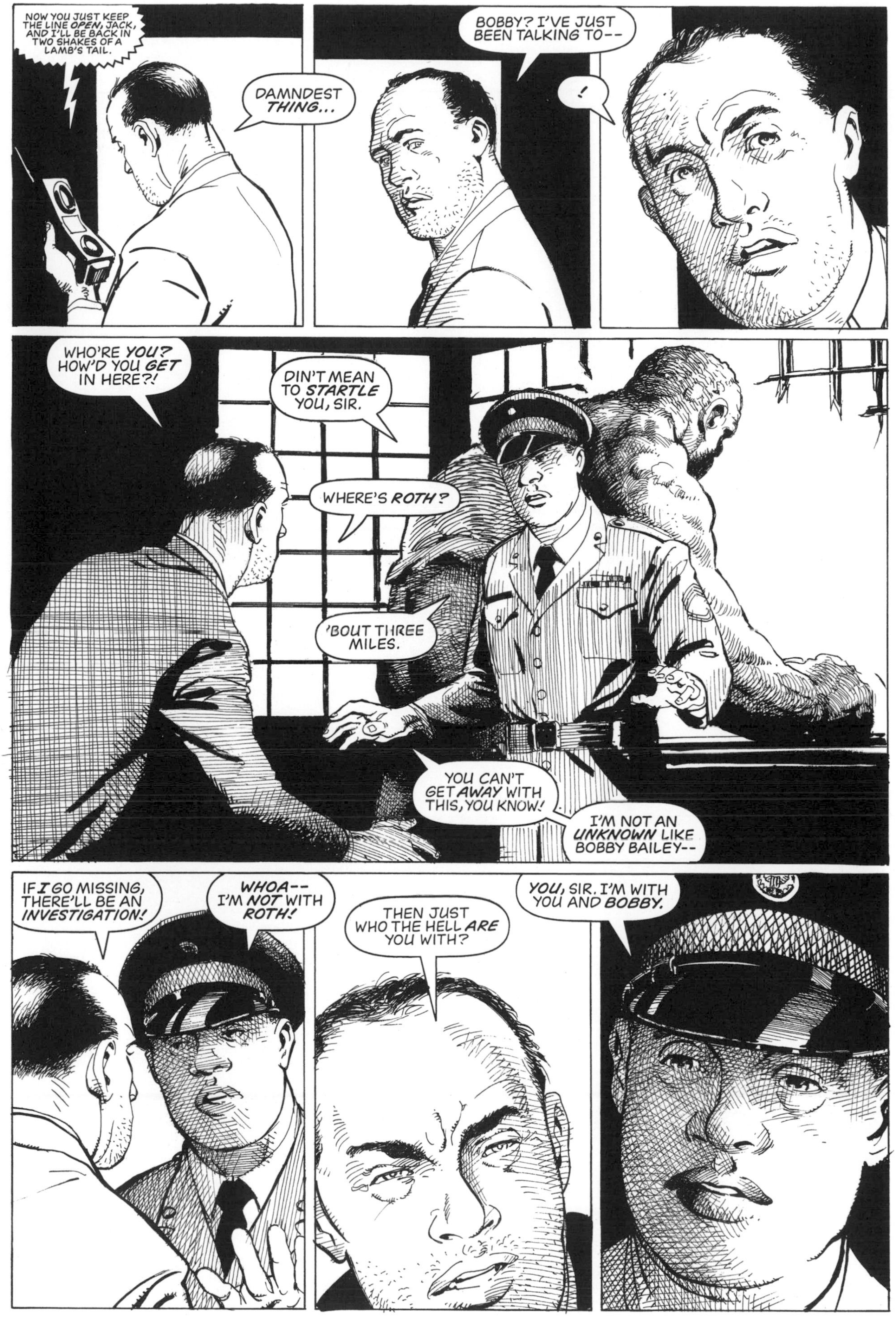
NOW YOU JUST KEEP THE LINE OPEN, JACK, AND I'LL BE BACK IN TWO SHAKES OF A LAMB'S TAIL.
DAMNDEST THING...
BOBBY? I'VE JUST BEEN TALKING TO--
!
WHO'RE YOU? HOW'D YOU GET IN HERE?!
DIN'T MEAN TO STARTLE YOU, SIR.
WHERE'S ROTH?
'BOUT THREE MILES.
YOU CAN'T GET AWAY WITH THIS, YOU KNOW!
I'M NOT AN UNKNOWN LIKE BOBBY BAILEY--
IF I GO MISSING, THERE'LL BE AN INVESTIGATION!
WHOA-- I'M NOT WITH ROTH!
THEN JUST WHO THE HELL ARE YOU WITH?
YOU, SIR. I'M WITH YOU AND BOBBY.

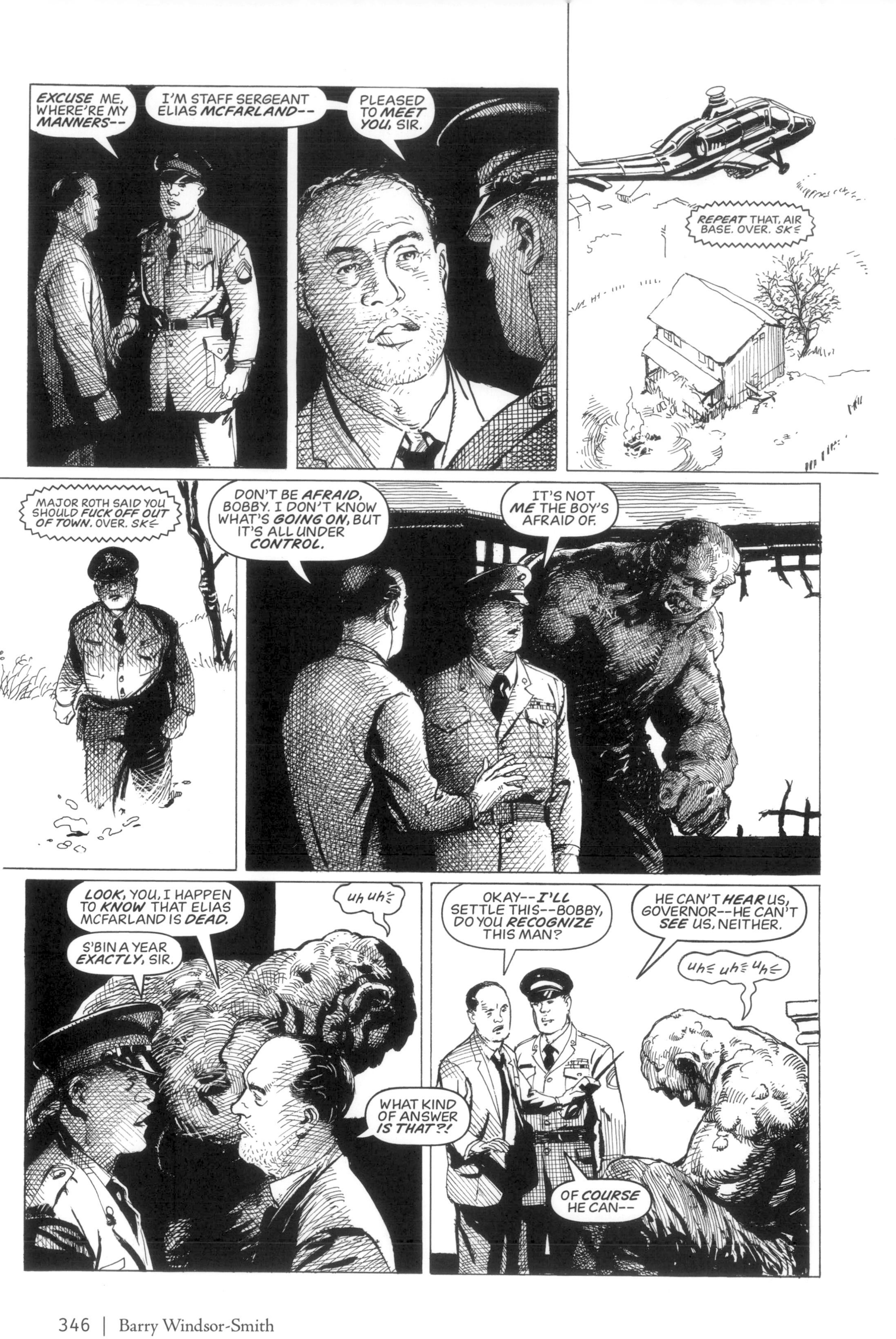
EXCUSE ME, WHERE'RE MY MANNERS--
I'M STAFF SERGEANT ELIAS MCFARLAND--
PLEASED TO MEET YOU, SIR.
REPEAT THAT, AIR BASE. OVER. SK
MAJOR ROTH SAID YOU SHOULD FUCK OFF OUT OF TOWN. OVER. SK
DON'T BE AFRAID, BOBBY. I DON'T KNOW WHAT'S GOING ON, BUT IT'S ALL UNDER CONTROL.
IT'S NOT ME THE BOY'S AFRAID OF.
LOOK, YOU, I HAPPEN TO KNOW THAT ELIAS MCFARLAND IS DEAD.
uh uh
S'BIN A YEAR EXACTLY, SIR.
WHAT KIND OF ANSWER IS THAT?!
OKAY--I'LL SETTLE THIS--BOBBY, DO YOU RECOGNIZE THIS MAN?
HE CAN'T HEAR US, GOVERNOR--HE CAN'T SEE US, NEITHER.
uh uh uh
OF COURSE HE CAN--

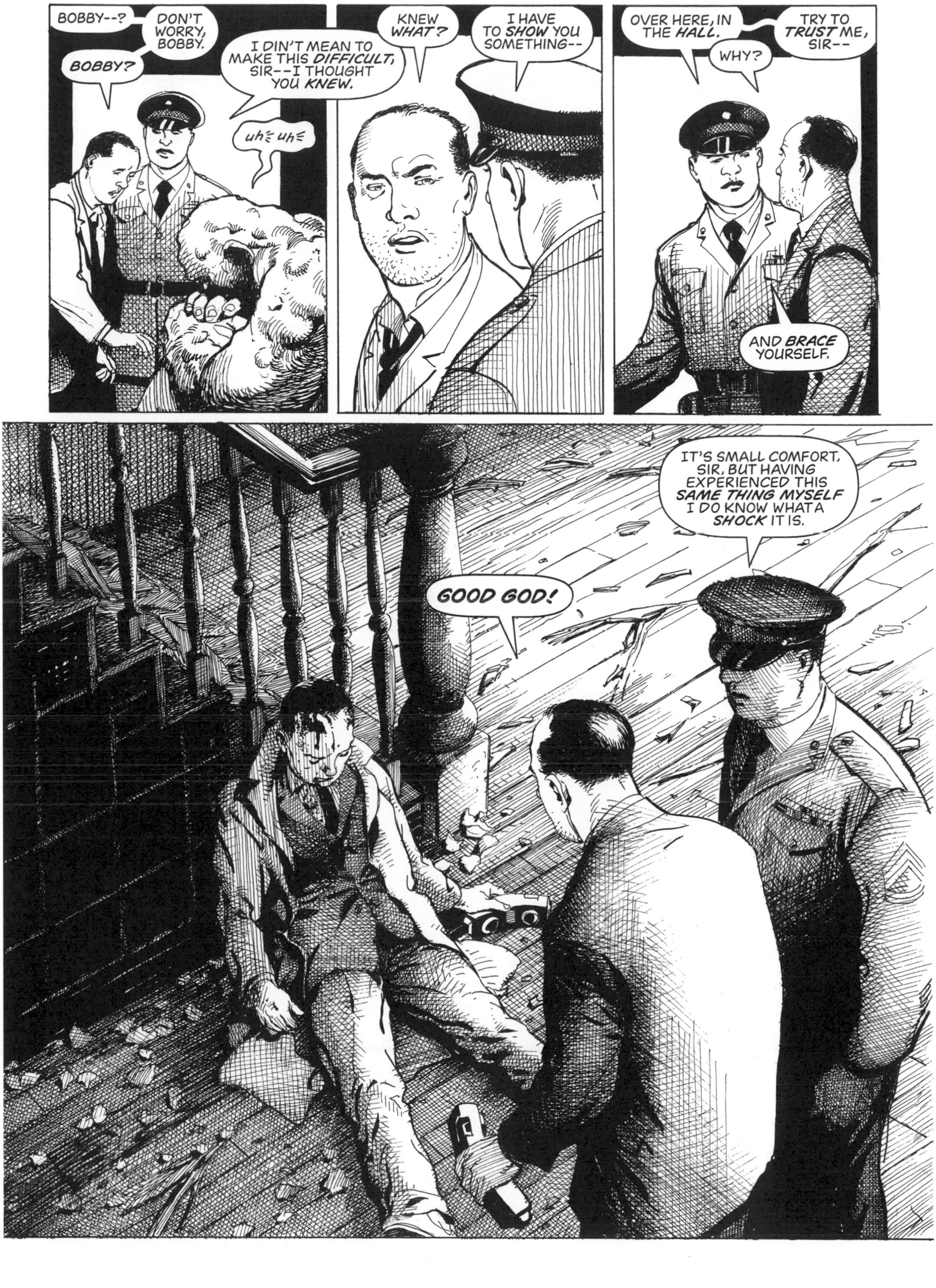
BOBBY--?
DON'T WORRY, BOBBY.
BOBBY?
I DIN'T MEAN TO MAKE THIS DIFFICULT, SIR--I THOUGHT YOU KNEW.
uh uh
KNEW WHAT?
I HAVE TO SHOW YOU SOMETHING--
OVER HERE, IN THE HALL.
WHY?
TRY TO TRUST ME, SIR--
AND BRACE YOURSELF.
IT'S SMALL COMFORT, SIR, BUT HAVING EXPERIENCED THIS SAME THING MYSELF I DO KNOW WHAT A SHOCK IT IS.
GOOD GOD!

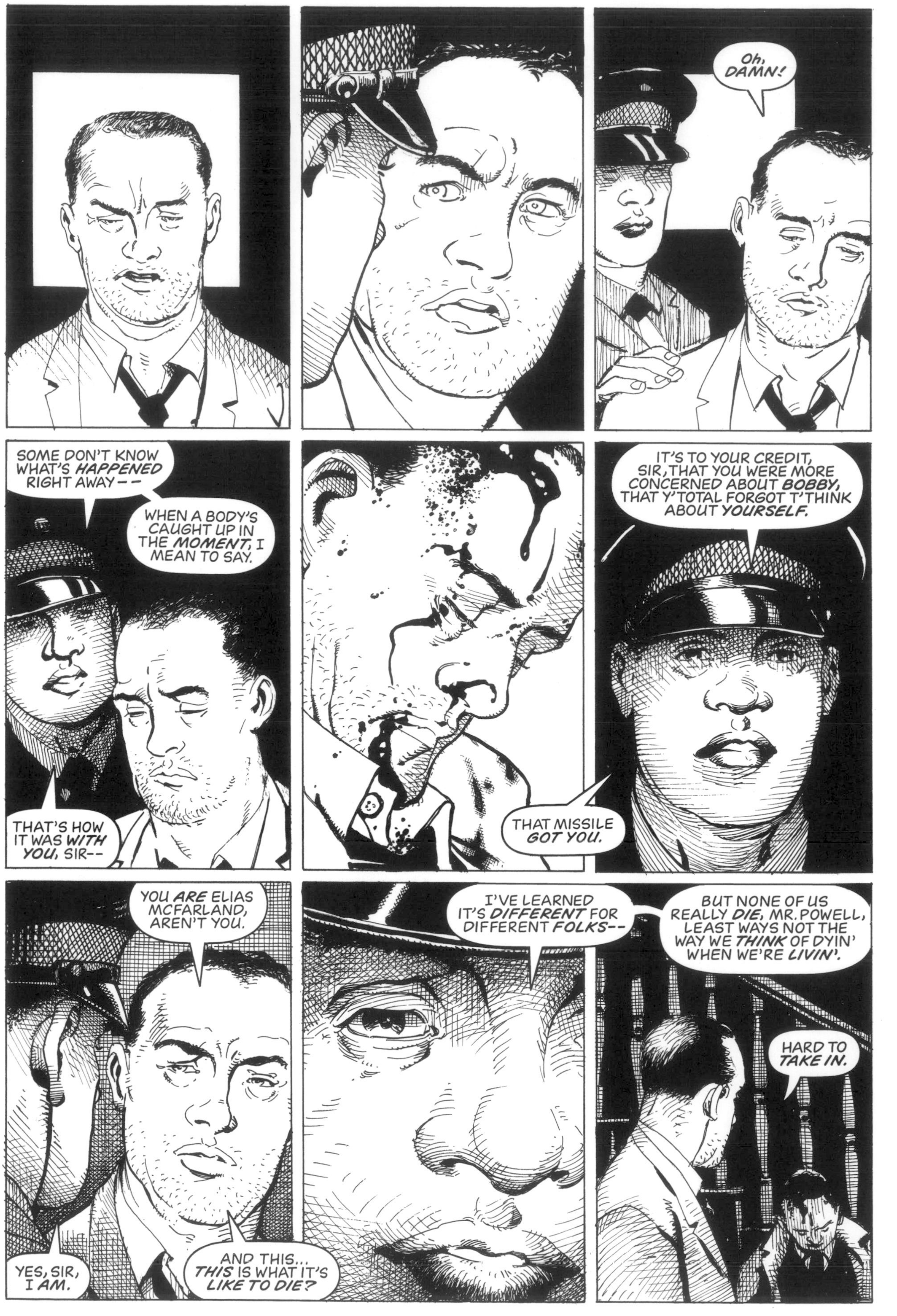
Oh, DAMN!
SOME DON'T KNOW WHAT'S HAPPENED RIGHT AWAY--
WHEN A BODY'S CAUGHT UP IN THE MOMENT, I MEAN TO SAY.
THAT'S HOW IT WAS WITH YOU, SIR--
THAT MISSILE GOT YOU.
IT'S TO YOUR CREDIT, SIR, THAT YOU WERE MORE CONCERNED ABOUT BOBBY, THAT Y'TOTAL FORGOT T'THINK ABOUT YOURSELF.
YOU ARE ELIAS MCFARLAND, AREN'T YOU.
YES, SIR, I AM.
AND THIS... THIS IS WHAT IT'S LIKE TO DIE?
I'VE LEARNED IT'S DIFFERENT FOR DIFFERENT FOLKS--
BUT NONE OF US REALLY DIE, MR. POWELL, LEAST WAYS NOT THE WAY WE THINK OF DYIN' WHEN WE'RE LIVIN'.
HARD TO TAKE IN.

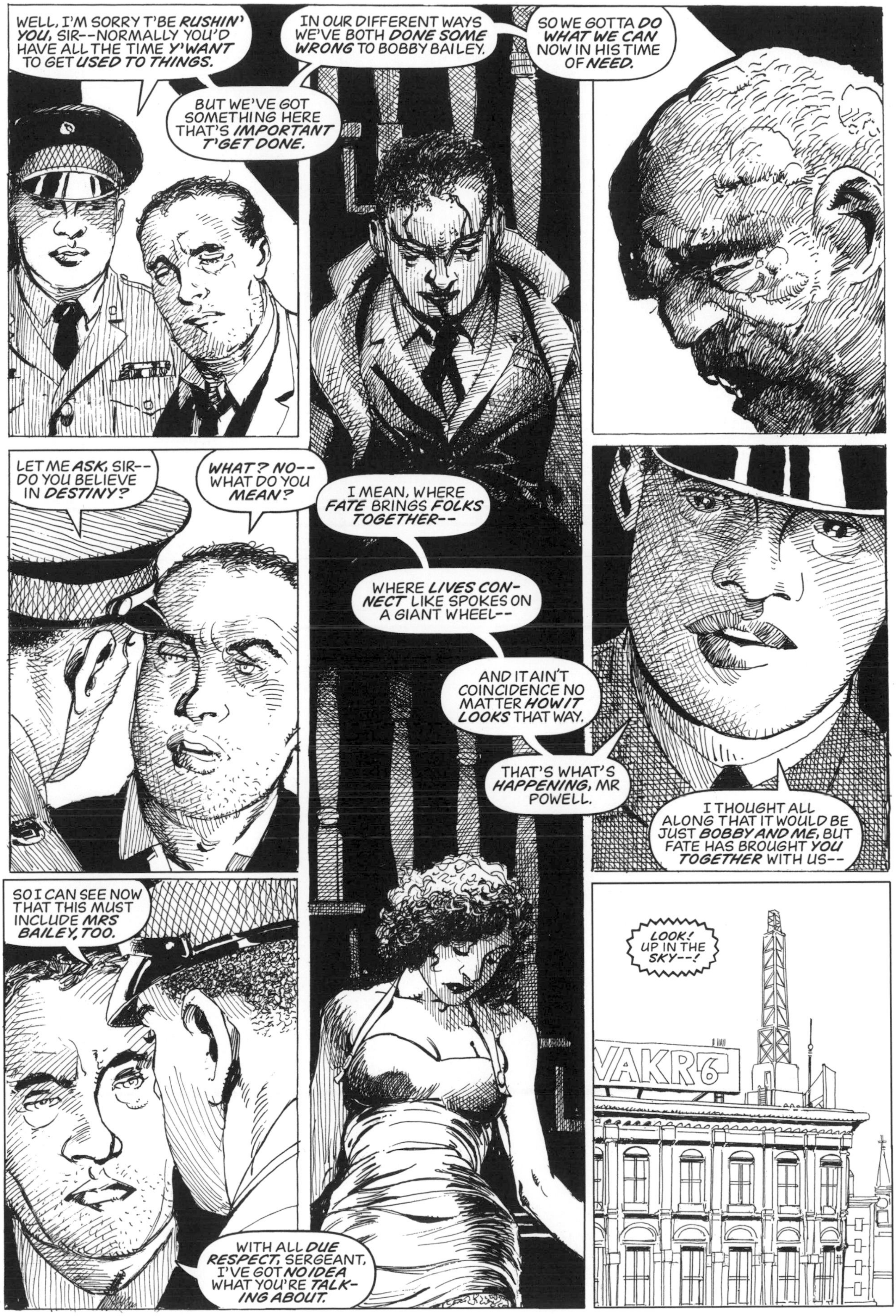
WELL, I'M SORRY T'BE RUSHIN' YOU, SIR--NORMALLY YOU'D HAVE ALL THE TIME Y'WANT TO GET USED TO THINGS.
BUT WE'VE GOT SOMETHING HERE THAT'S IMPORTANT T'GET DONE.
IN OUR DIFFERENT WAYS WE'VE BOTH DONE SOME WRONG TO BOBBY BAILEY.
SO WE GOTTA DO WHAT WE CAN NOW IN HIS TIME OF NEED.
LET ME ASK, SIR--DO YOU BELIEVE IN DESTINY?
WHAT? NO--WHAT DO YOU MEAN?
I MEAN, WHERE FATE BRINGS FOLKS TOGETHER--
WHERE LIVES CONNECT LIKE SPOKES ON A GIANT WHEEL--
AND IT AIN'T COINCIDENCE NO MATTER HOW IT LOOKS THAT WAY.
THAT'S WHAT'S HAPPENING, MR POWELL.
I THOUGHT ALL ALONG THAT IT WOULD BE JUST BOBBY AND ME, BUT FATE HAS BROUGHT YOU TOGETHER WITH US--
SO I CAN SEE NOW THAT THIS MUST INCLUDE MRS BAILEY, TOO.
WITH ALL DUE RESPECT, SERGEANT, I'VE GOT NO IDEA WHAT YOU'RE TALKING ABOUT.
LOOK! UP IN THE SKY--!
VAKR 6

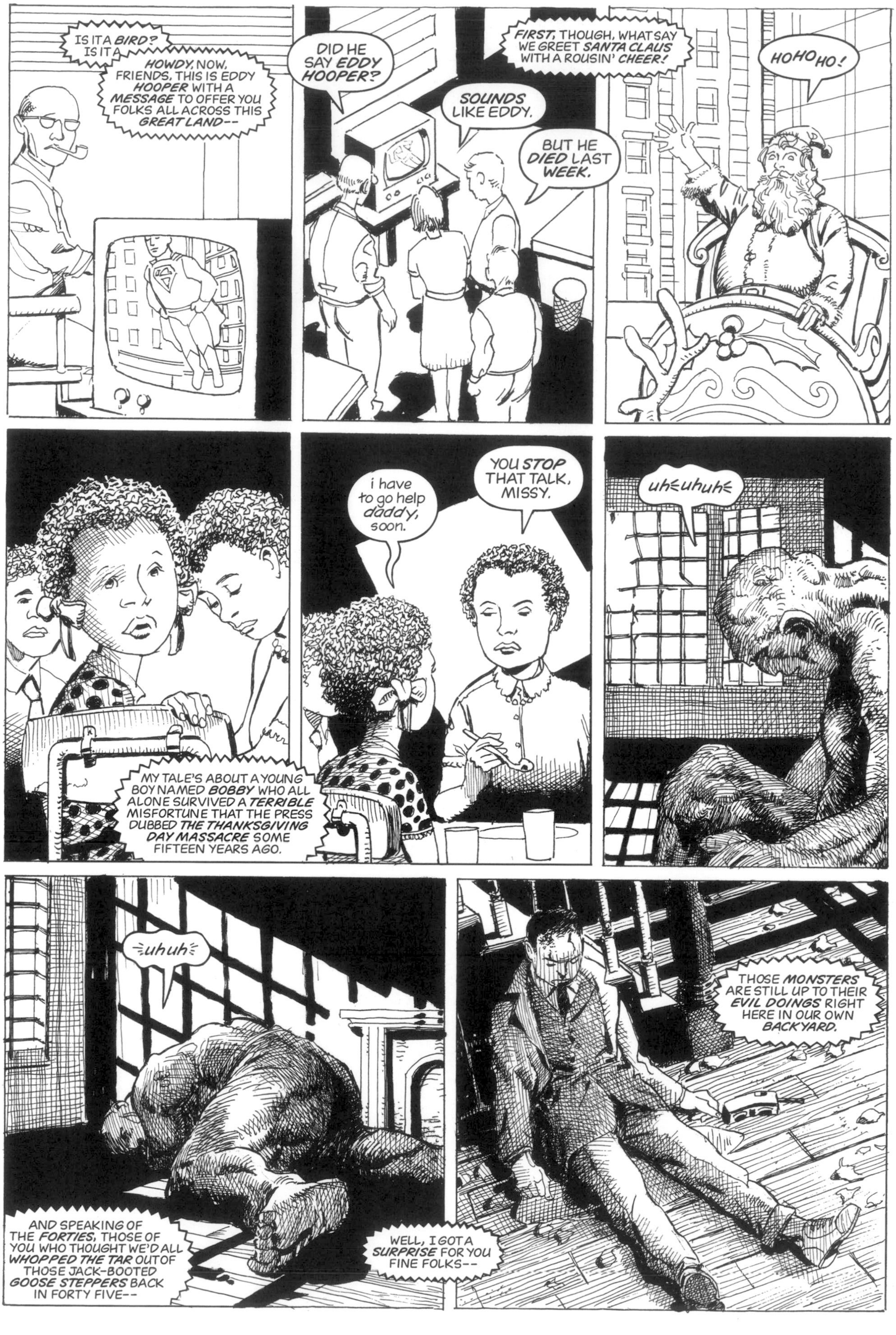
IS IT A BIRD? IS IT A
HOWDY, NOW, FRIENDS, THIS IS EDDY HOOPER WITH A MESSAGE TO OFFER YOU FOLKS ALL ACROSS THIS GREAT LAND--
DID HE SAY EDDY HOOPER?
SOUNDS LIKE EDDY.
BUT HE DIED LAST WEEK.
FIRST, THOUGH, WHAT SAY WE GREET SANTA CLAUS WITH A ROUSIN' CHEER!
HO HO HO HO!
MY TALE'S ABOUT A YOUNG BOY NAMED BOBBY WHO ALL ALONE SURVIVED A TERRIBLE MISFORTUNE THAT THE PRESS DUBBED THE THANKSGIVING DAY MASSACRE SOME FIFTEEN YEARS AGO.
i have to go help daddy, soon.
YOU STOP THAT TALK, MISSY.
uh uhuh
uhuh
AND SPEAKING OF THE FORTIES, THOSE OF YOU WHO THOUGHT WE'D ALL WHOPPED THE TAR OUT OF THOSE JACK-BOOTED GOOSE STEPPERS BACK IN FORTY FIVE--
WELL, I GOT A SURPRISE FOR YOU FINE FOLKS--
THOSE MONSTERS ARE STILL UP TO THEIR EVIL DOINGS RIGHT HERE IN OUR OWN BACKYARD.

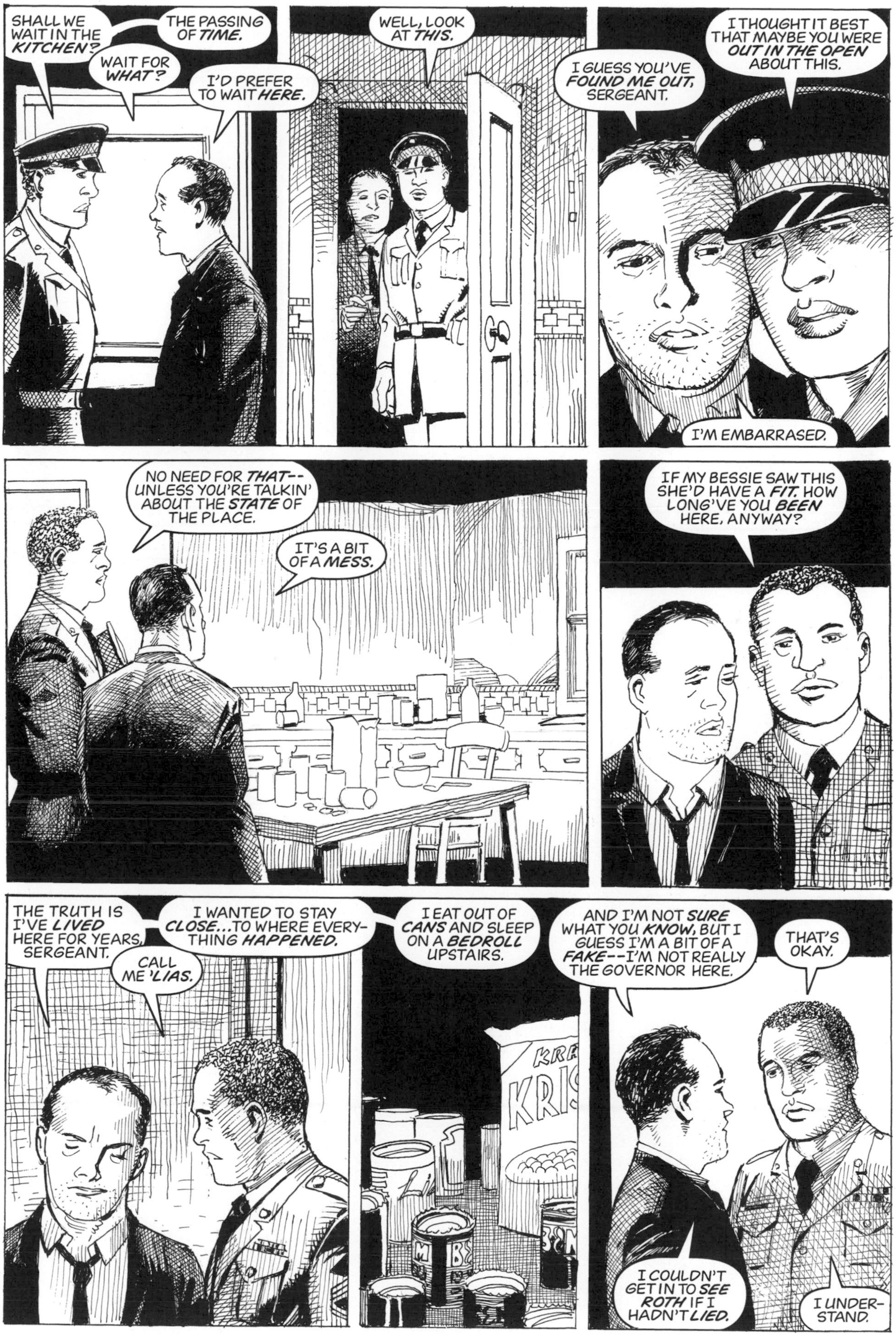
SHALL WE WAIT IN THE KITCHEN?
THE PASSING OF TIME.
WAIT FOR WHAT?
I'D PREFER TO WAIT HERE.
WELL, LOOK AT THIS.
I GUESS YOU'VE FOUND ME OUT, SERGEANT.
I THOUGHT IT BEST THAT MAYBE YOU WERE OUT IN THE OPEN ABOUT THIS.
I'M EMBARRASED.
NO NEED FOR THAT--UNLESS YOU'RE TALKIN' ABOUT THE STATE OF THE PLACE.
IT'S A BIT OF A MESS.
IF MY BESSIE SAW THIS SHE'D HAVE A FIT. HOW LONG'VE YOU BEEN HERE, ANYWAY?
THE TRUTH IS I'VE LIVED HERE FOR YEARS, SERGEANT.
CALL ME 'LIAS.
I WANTED TO STAY CLOSE...TO WHERE EVERYTHING HAPPENED.
I EAT OUT OF CANS AND SLEEP ON A BEDROLL UPSTAIRS.
AND I'M NOT SURE WHAT YOU KNOW, BUT I GUESS I'M A BIT OF A FAKE--I'M NOT REALLY THE GOVERNOR HERE.
THAT'S OKAY.
I COULDN'T GET IN TO SEE ROTH IF I HADN'T LIED.
I UNDERSTAND.

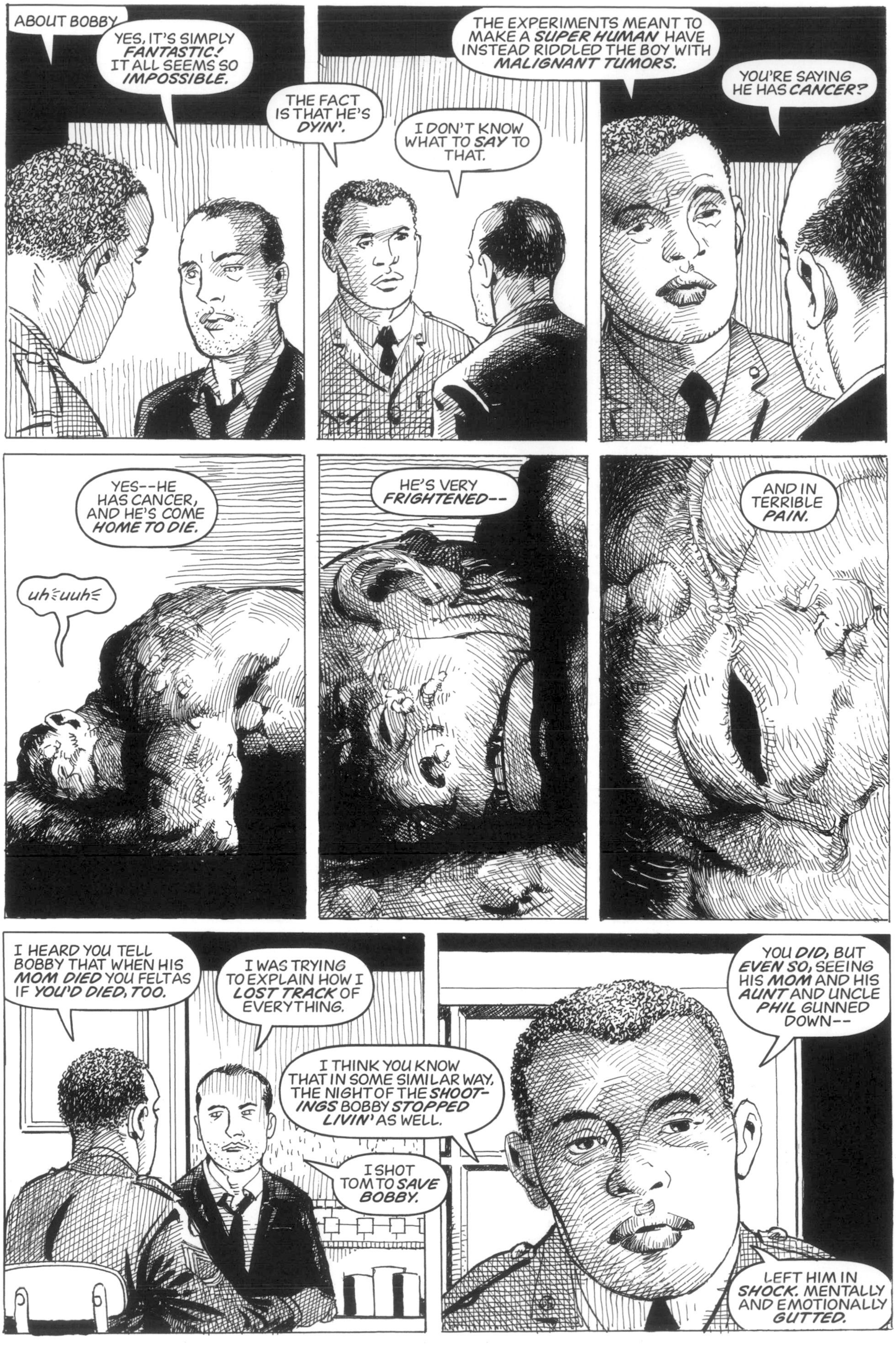
ABOUT BOBBY
YES, IT'S SIMPLY FANTASTIC! IT ALL SEEMS SO IMPOSSIBLE.
THE FACT IS THAT HE'S DYIN'.
I DON'T KNOW WHAT TO SAY TO THAT.
THE EXPERIMENTS MEANT TO MAKE A SUPER HUMAN HAVE INSTEAD RIDDLED THE BOY WITH MALIGNANT TUMORS.
YOU'RE SAYING HE HAS CANCER?
YES--HE HAS CANCER, AND HE'S COME HOME TO DIE.
uh uuh
HE'S VERY FRIGHTENED--
AND IN TERRIBLE PAIN.
I HEARD YOU TELL BOBBY THAT WHEN HIS MOM DIED YOU FELT AS IF YOU'D DIED, TOO.
I WAS TRYING TO EXPLAIN HOW I LOST TRACK OF EVERYTHING.
I THINK YOU KNOW THAT IN SOME SIMILAR WAY, THE NIGHT OF THE SHOOTINGS BOBBY STOPPED LIVIN' AS WELL.
I SHOT TOM TO SAVE BOBBY.
YOU DID, BUT EVEN SO, SEEING HIS MOM AND HIS AUNT AND UNCLE PHIL GUNNED DOWN--
LEFT HIM IN SHOCK. MENTALLY AND EMOTIONALLY GUTTED.

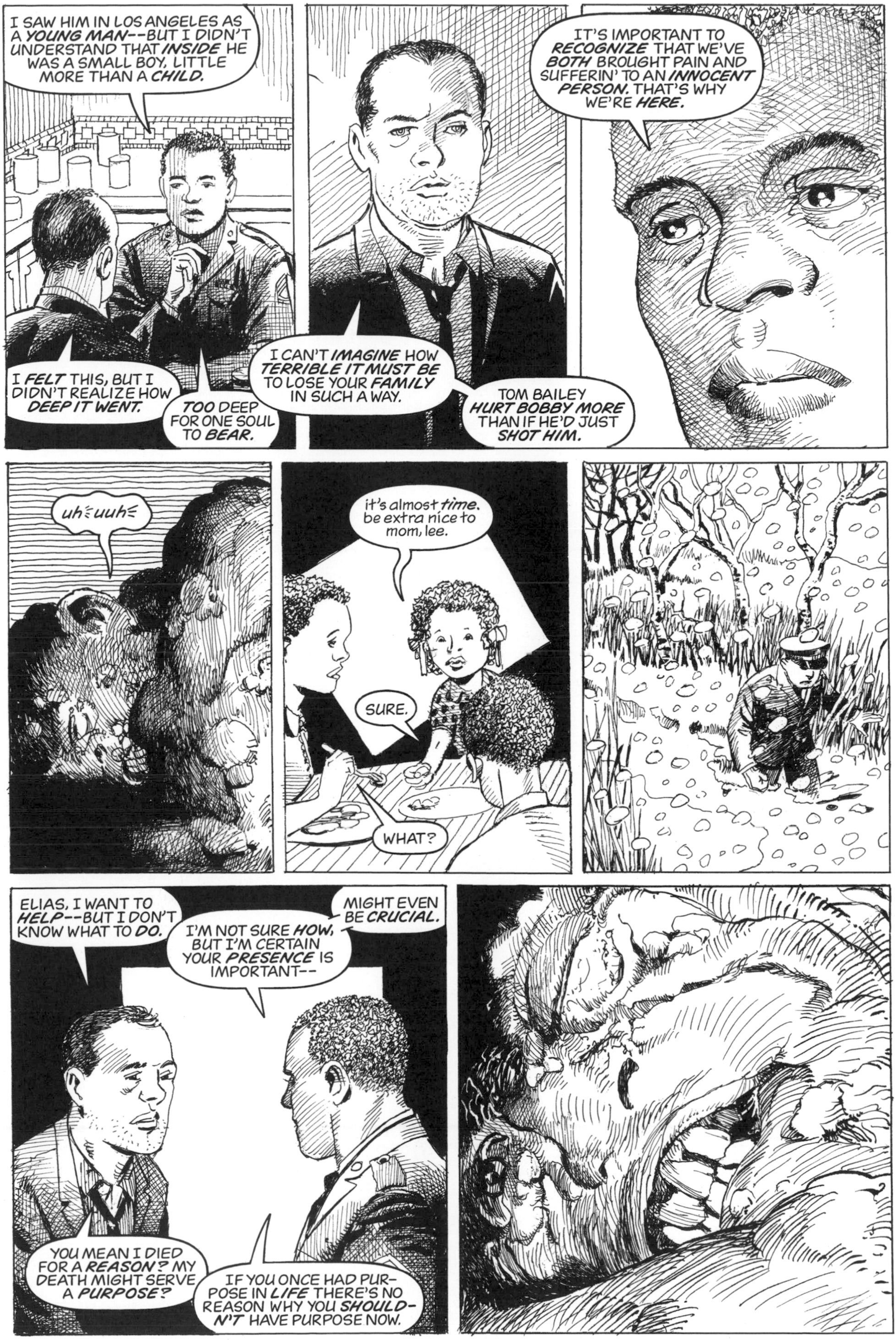
I SAW HIM IN LOS ANGELES AS A *YOUNG MAN*--BUT I DIDN'T UNDERSTAND THAT *INSIDE* HE WAS A SMALL BOY, LITTLE MORE THAN A *CHILD.*
I *FELT* THIS, BUT I DIDN'T REALIZE HOW *DEEP IT WENT.*
TOO DEEP FOR ONE SOUL TO *BEAR.*
I CAN'T *IMAGINE* HOW *TERRIBLE IT MUST BE* TO LOSE YOUR *FAMILY* IN SUCH A WAY.
TOM BAILEY *HURT BOBBY MORE* THAN IF HE'D JUST *SHOT HIM.*
IT'S IMPORTANT TO *RECOGNIZE* THAT WE'VE *BOTH* BROUGHT PAIN AND SUFFERIN' TO AN *INNOCENT PERSON.* THAT'S WHY WE'RE *HERE.*
uh-uuh
it's almost *time.* be extra nice to mom, lee.
SURE.
WHAT?
ELIAS, I WANT TO *HELP*--BUT I DON'T KNOW WHAT TO *DO.*
I'M NOT SURE *HOW,* BUT I'M CERTAIN YOUR *PRESENCE* IS IMPORTANT--
MIGHT EVEN BE *CRUCIAL.*
YOU MEAN I DIED FOR A *REASON?* MY DEATH MIGHT SERVE A *PURPOSE?*
IF YOU ONCE HAD PURPOSE IN *LIFE* THERE'S NO REASON WHY YOU *SHOULDN'T* HAVE PURPOSE NOW.

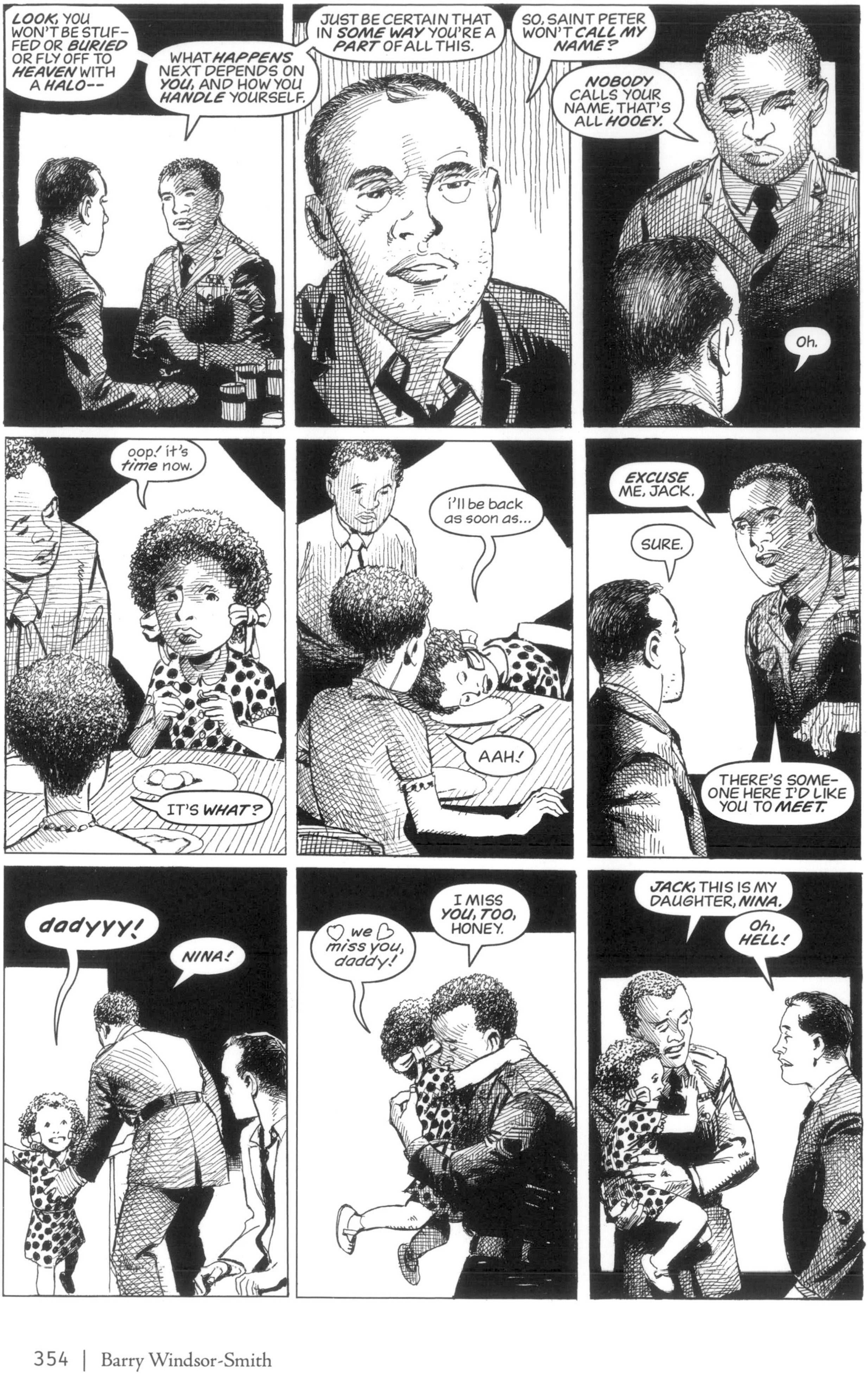

LOOK, YOU WON'T BE STUFFED OR BURIED OR FLY OFF TO HEAVEN WITH A HALO--
WHAT HAPPENS NEXT DEPENDS ON YOU, AND HOW YOU HANDLE YOURSELF.
JUST BE CERTAIN THAT IN SOME WAY YOU'RE A PART OF ALL THIS.
SO, SAINT PETER WON'T CALL MY NAME?
NOBODY CALLS YOUR NAME, THAT'S ALL HOOEY.
Oh.
oop! it's time now.
IT'S WHAT?
i'll be back as soon as...
AAH!
EXCUSE ME, JACK.
SURE.
THERE'S SOMEONE HERE I'D LIKE YOU TO MEET.
dadyyy!
NINA!
we miss you, daddy!
I MISS YOU, TOO, HONEY.
JACK, THIS IS MY DAUGHTER, NINA.
Oh, HELL!

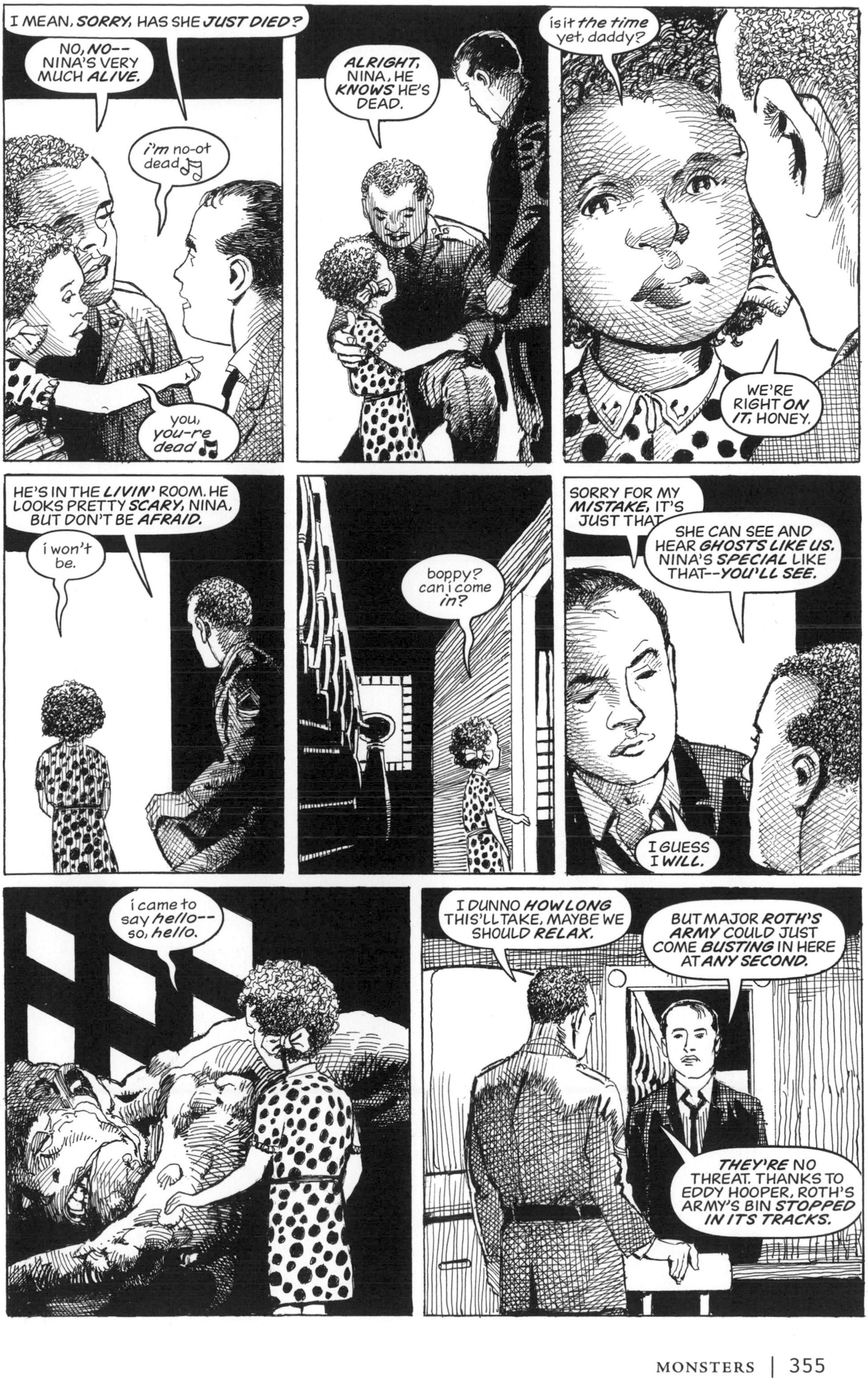

I MEAN, SORRY, HAS SHE JUST DIED?
NO, NO-- NINA'S VERY MUCH ALIVE.
i'm no-ot dead
you, you-re dead
ALRIGHT, NINA, HE KNOWS HE'S DEAD.
is it the time yet, daddy?
WE'RE RIGHT ON IT, HONEY.
HE'S IN THE LIVIN' ROOM. HE LOOKS PRETTY SCARY, NINA, BUT DON'T BE AFRAID.
i won't be.
boppy? can i come in?
SORRY FOR MY MISTAKE, IT'S JUST THAT
SHE CAN SEE AND HEAR GHOSTS LIKE US. NINA'S SPECIAL LIKE THAT--YOU'LL SEE.
I GUESS I WILL.
i came to say hello-- so, hello.
I DUNNO HOW LONG THIS'LL TAKE, MAYBE WE SHOULD RELAX.
BUT MAJOR ROTH'S ARMY COULD JUST COME BUSTING IN HERE AT ANY SECOND.
THEY'RE NO THREAT. THANKS TO EDDY HOOPER, ROTH'S ARMY'S BIN STOPPED IN ITS TRACKS.

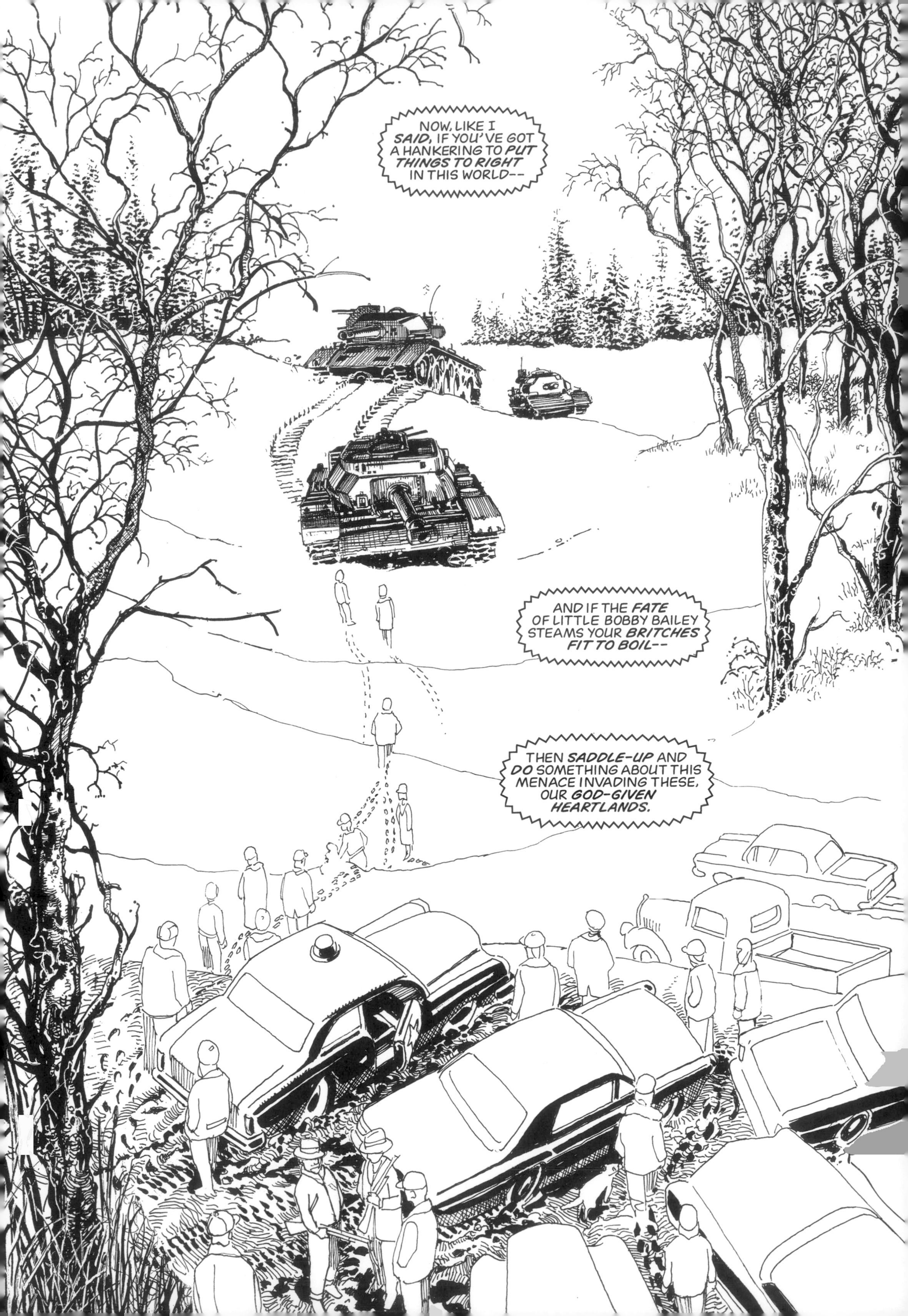
NOW, LIKE I SAID, IF YOU'VE GOT A HANKERING TO PUT THINGS TO RIGHT IN THIS WORLD--
AND IF THE FATE OF LITTLE BOBBY BAILEY STEAMS YOUR BRITCHES FIT TO BOIL--
THEN SADDLE-UP AND DO SOMETHING ABOUT THIS MENACE INVADING THESE, OUR GOD-GIVEN HEARTLANDS.

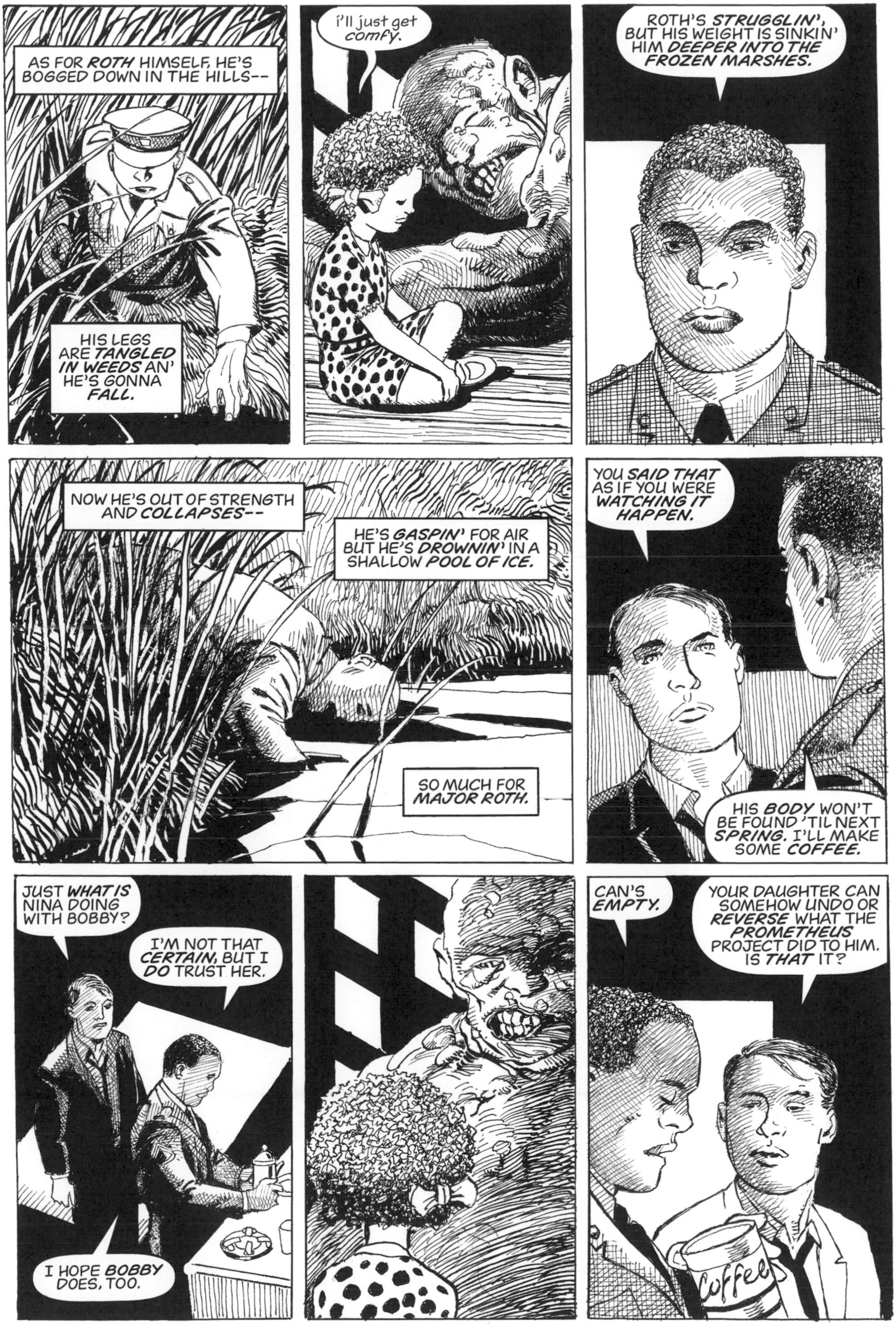
AS FOR ROTH HIMSELF, HE'S BOGGED DOWN IN THE HILLS--
HIS LEGS ARE TANGLED IN WEEDS AN' HE'S GONNA FALL.
i'll just get comfy.
ROTH'S STRUGGLIN', BUT HIS WEIGHT IS SINKIN' HIM DEEPER INTO THE FROZEN MARSHES.
NOW HE'S OUT OF STRENGTH AND COLLAPSES--
HE'S GASPIN' FOR AIR BUT HE'S DROWNIN' IN A SHALLOW POOL OF ICE.
SO MUCH FOR MAJOR ROTH.
YOU SAID THAT AS IF YOU WERE WATCHING IT HAPPEN.
HIS BODY WON'T BE FOUND 'TIL NEXT SPRING. I'LL MAKE SOME COFFEE.
JUST WHAT IS NINA DOING WITH BOBBY?
I'M NOT THAT CERTAIN, BUT I DO TRUST HER.
I HOPE BOBBY DOES, TOO.
CAN'S EMPTY.
YOUR DAUGHTER CAN SOMEHOW UNDO OR REVERSE WHAT THE PROMETHEUS PROJECT DID TO HIM. IS THAT IT?
Coffee

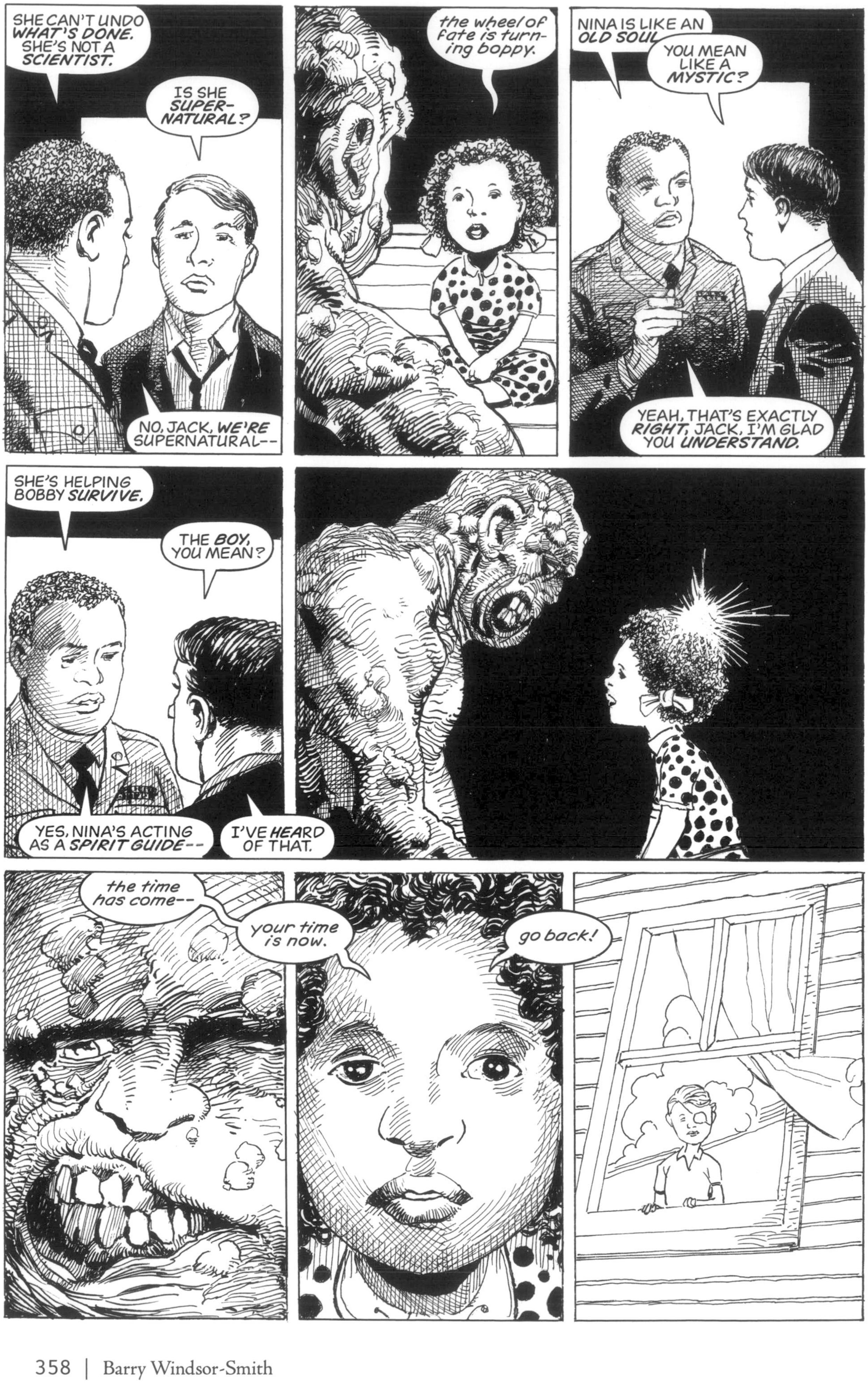
SHE CAN'T UNDO WHAT'S DONE. SHE'S NOT A SCIENTIST.
IS SHE SUPER-NATURAL?
NO, JACK, WE'RE SUPERNATURAL--
the wheel of fate is turning boppy.
NINA IS LIKE AN OLD SOUL
YOU MEAN LIKE A MYSTIC?
YEAH, THAT'S EXACTLY RIGHT, JACK, I'M GLAD YOU UNDERSTAND.
SHE'S HELPING BOBBY SURVIVE.
THE BOY, YOU MEAN?
YES, NINA'S ACTING AS A SPIRIT GUIDE--
I'VE HEARD OF THAT.
the time has come--
your time is now.
go back!

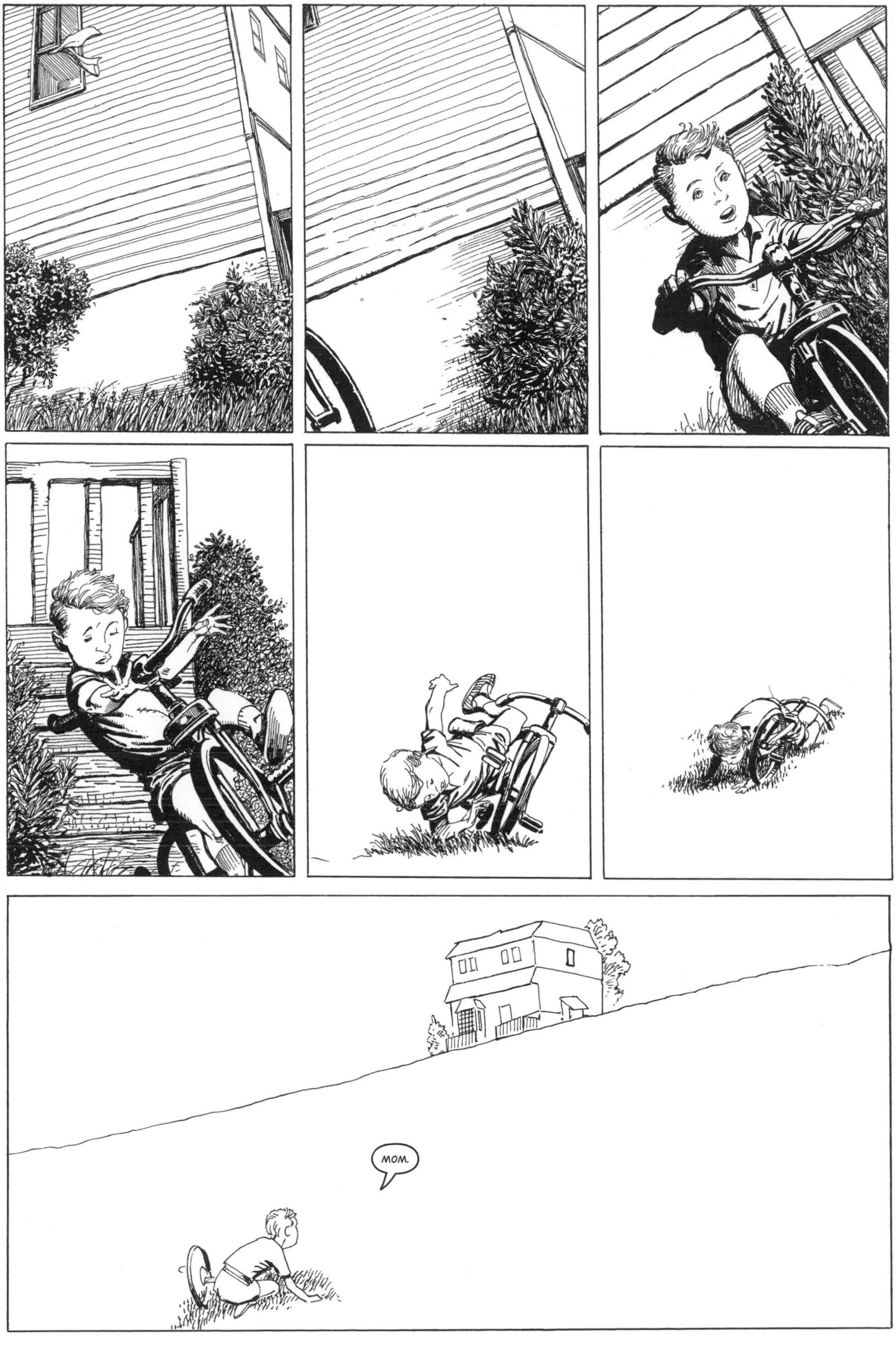
MOM.

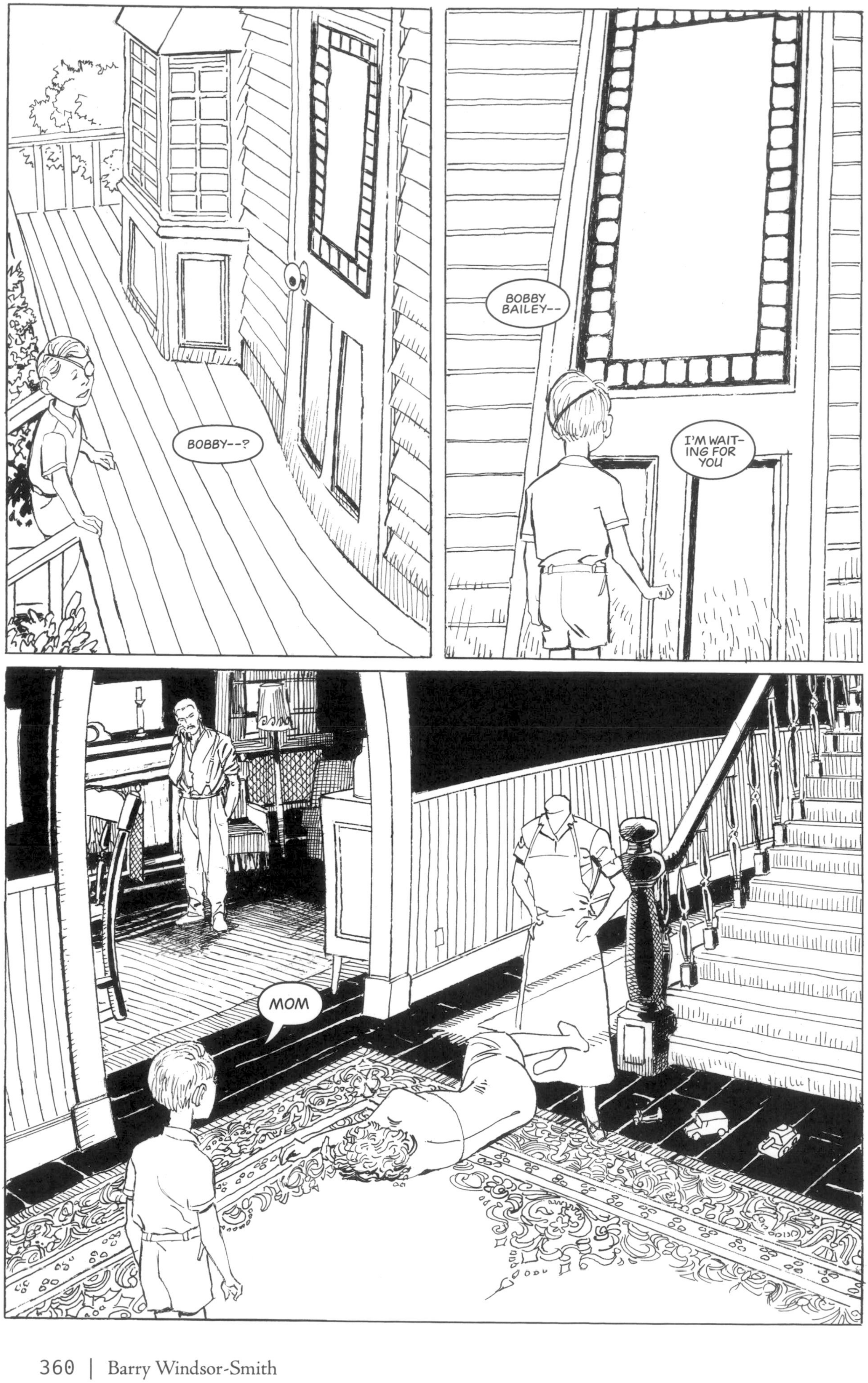
BOBBY--?
BOBBY BAILEY--
I'M WAITING FOR YOU
MOM

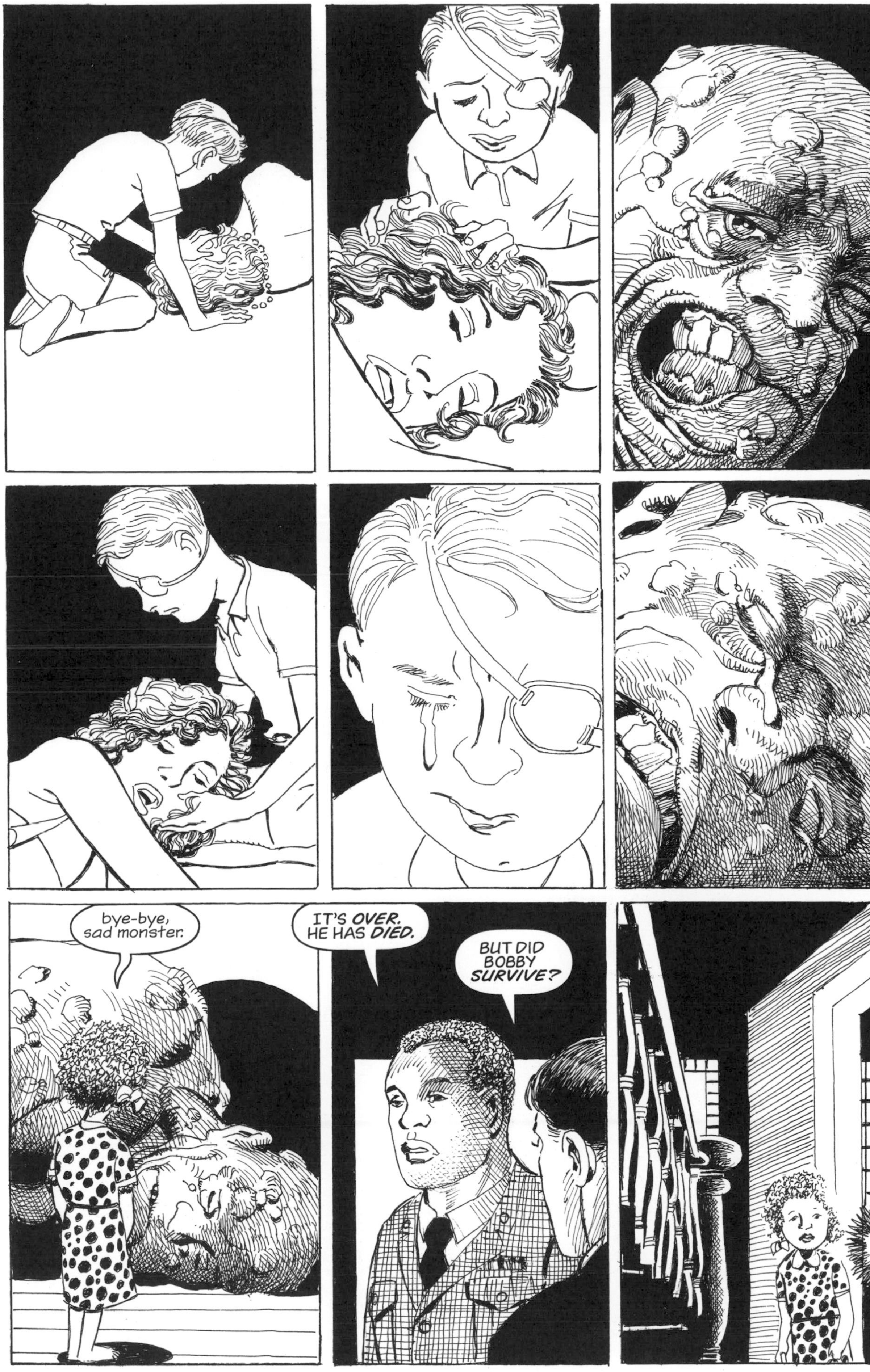
bye-bye,
sad monster.
IT'S OVER.
HE HAS DIED.
BUT DID
BOBBY
SURVIVE?

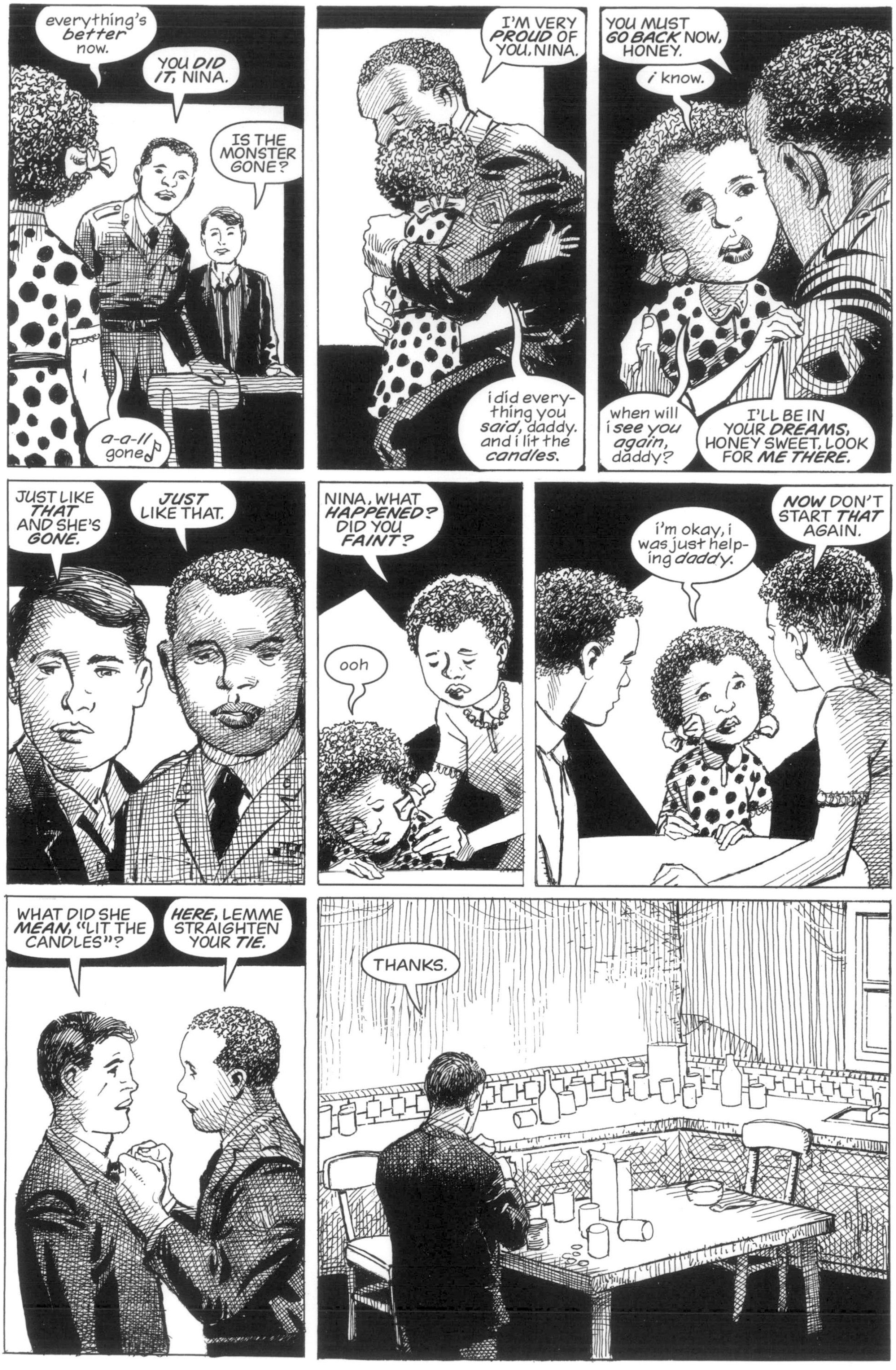
everything's better now.
YOU DID IT, NINA.
IS THE MONSTER GONE?
a-a-ll gone
I'M VERY PROUD OF YOU, NINA.
i did everything you said, daddy. and i lit the candles.
YOU MUST GO BACK NOW, HONEY.
i know.
when will i see you again, daddy?
I'LL BE IN YOUR DREAMS, HONEY SWEET, LOOK FOR ME THERE.
JUST LIKE THAT AND SHE'S GONE.
JUST LIKE THAT.
NINA, WHAT HAPPENED? DID YOU FAINT?
ooh
i'm okay, i was just helping daddy.
NOW DON'T START THAT AGAIN.
WHAT DID SHE MEAN, "LIT THE CANDLES"?
HERE, LEMME STRAIGHTEN YOUR TIE.
THANKS.

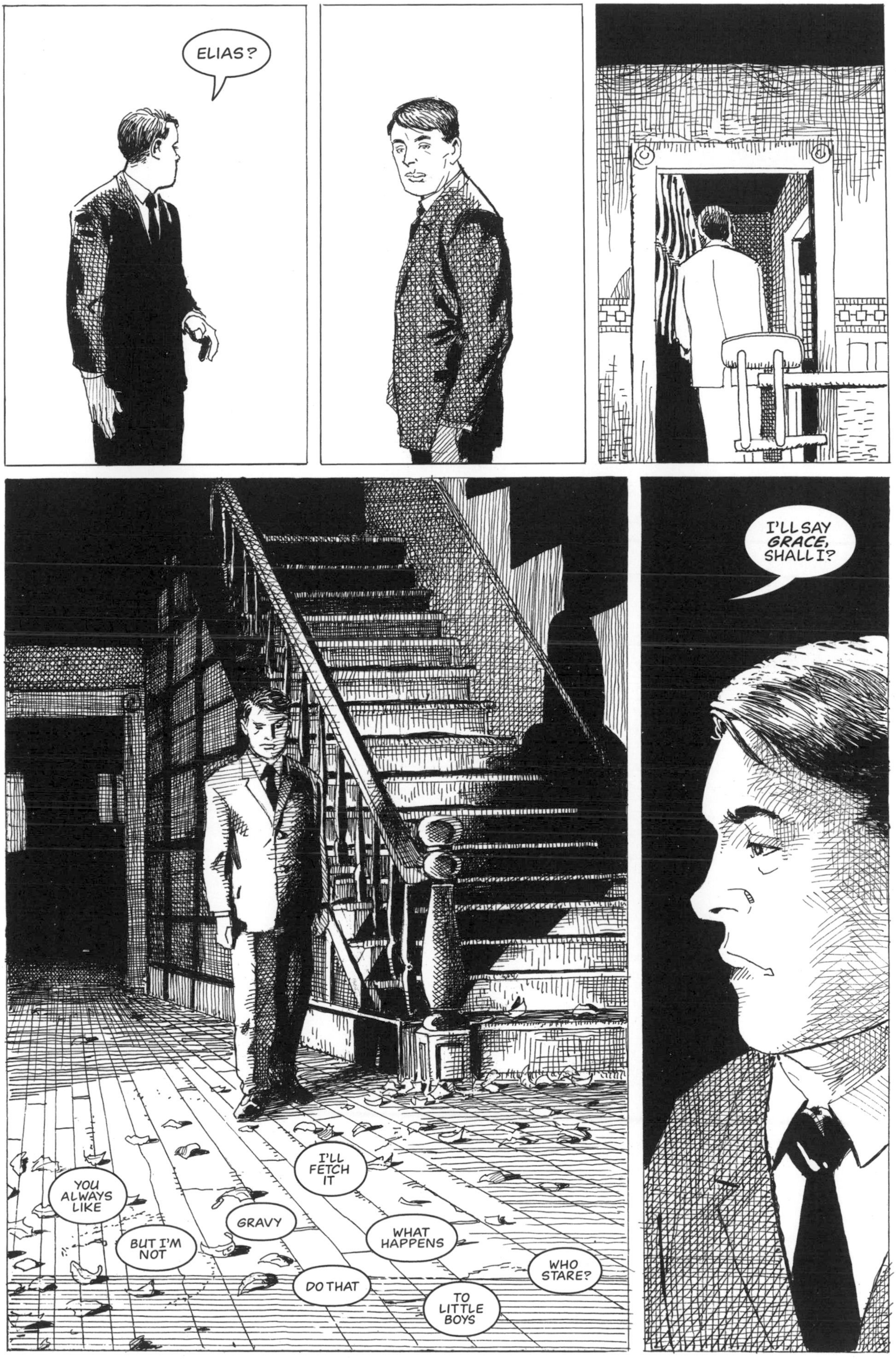
ELIAS?
I'LL SAY GRACE, SHALL I?
YOU ALWAYS LIKE
BUT I'M NOT
GRAVY
I'LL FETCH IT
DO THAT
WHAT HAPPENS
TO LITTLE BOYS
WHO STARE?

BARRY WINDSOR-SMITH began his comics career in 1969, drawing mainstay Marvel characters such as the X-Men and Daredevil in the traditional Marvel style. But in 1971, he broke from the Marvel formula when he started drawing the *Conan* series, turning heads with a stylistic approach that was both fresh and controversial. Ultimately, he won the hearts and minds of comics professionals and fans alike, along with numerous awards. Part of a young generation of artists that included compatriots Bernie Wrightson, Mike Kaluta, and Jeffrey Catherine Jones, Windsor-Smith proceeded to trailblaze a singular path for himself. In the '90s, he conceived, wrote, and drew three independent comics series, *The Freebooters*, *Young Gods*, and *The Paradoxman*. In 1999 and 2000, Fantagraphics published his autobiographical *Opus*, volumes 1 and 2. *Monsters* is his first new book in 16 years.

FANTAGRAPHICS BOOKS
7563 Lake City Way
Seattle, Washington 98115

Editor: Gary Groth
Design: Jacob Covey
Proofreading: Conrad Groth,
            J. Michael Catron
Production: Christina Hwang,
            Paul Baresh
Publisher: Gary Groth
Associate Publisher: Eric Reynolds

@fantagraphics

First Fantagraphics Books edition: April 2021
ISBN 978-1-68396-415-5
Library of Congress Control Number 2020941316
Printed in China